18—

THE MAN WHO MADE

IRELAND

THE MAN WHO MADE
IRELAND

The Life and Death
of Michael Collins

TIM PAT COOGAN

ROBERTS RINEHART PUBLISHERS

International Standard Book Number 1-879373-71-8
Library of Congress Catalog Card Number 92-60268

Published in the United States of America by
Roberts Rinehart Publishers, Post Office Box 666
Niwot, Colorado 80544

Published in Canada by Key Porter Books, 70 The Esplanade,
Toronto, Ontario M5E 1R2

Originally published under the title *Michael Collins* by Hutchinson,
The Random Century Group, London

First U.S. edition

*For Barbara, her mother Mabel, my father Eamon Coogan, who worked
for Collins, and my mother Beatrice*

Contents

	List of Illustrations	vi
	Acknowledgements	vii
	Preface	xi
	Prologue	1
1	The Little Fella	3
2	Easter 1916	32
3	Kicking Down a Rotten Door	58
4	The Twelve Apostles	94
5	The Year of Terror	121
6	The Sky Darkens	157
7	Peace Comes Dropping Slow	185
8	Settling This Old Strife	236
9	Fighting the Waves	277
10	Wading Through Blood	308
11	Setting up the Six	333
12	The Mouth of Flowers	386
13	Honouring the Dead?	416
	Notes	433
	Appendix	451
	Bibliography and Sources	461
	Index	469

List of Illustrations

FIRST SECTION
Page 1: Marianne Collins, Mary Collins and baby, Mrs O'Brien; Michael Collins, aged six; Hannie; Sr Celestine.
Page 2: Mrs Erskine Childers and Mary Spring-Rice; Edward Carson; John Redmond.
Page 3: (The Easter Rising, 1916): Talbot St barricade; ruins of Liberty Hall; Sean MacDiarmada; James Connolly.
Page 4: Collins in Stafford Jail; Eamon de Valera; Collins 1916.

SECOND SECTION
Page 1: Nancy O'Brien; Kitty Kiernan; Lady Londonderry; Lady Lavery.
Page 2: Collins on his bicycle; Captain Hardy; Dave Neligan; Volunteers Robinson, Treacy, Breen and Brennan.
Page 3: Joe Leonard, Joe Slattery, Joe Dolan, Gearoid O'Sullivan, William Stapleton and Charlie Dalton; the Cairo Gang.
Page 4: Thomas Ashe, Kevin Barry; Terence MacSwiney; woman awaiting husband's hanging, 1921.

THIRD SECTION
Page 1: Tom Barry's wedding photograph, 1921.
Page 2: The sack of Balbriggan; Sinn Feiners and Auxiliaries; the British Tommy in Dublin.
Page 3: Collins and Harry Boland; Cathal Brugha; Richard Mulcahy; the 'Long Fellow' with Griffith.
Page 4: Bodies of the MacMahon family; Field Marshal Sir Henry Wilson.

FOURTH SECTION
Page 1: Dail Eireann, 17 August 1921; Irish Delegates.
Page 2: Austin Chamberlain; Collins leaves Downing St; David Lloyd George and Winston Churchill; Lord Birkenhead; Collins at pro-Treaty rally.
Page 3: Collins at Griffith's funeral; Mass card of Sonny O'Neill; Collins in Cork, 22 August 1922.
Page 4: Collins' body; Joe O'Reilly; Liam Tobin and Tom Cullen; Johnny Collins at memorial service, 1939.

MAPS
Dublin 1916 (p. 80); County Cork (p. 413).

Acknowledgements

It is a measure of Michael Collins' standing in the eyes of his countrymen, not a race noticeable for an excess of charity towards the reputations of their fellow men, that I can truly say that of all the books and research projects I have undertaken, this was the one for which I received the most unstinted and widespread assistance with material and information.

One great tragedy darkened this bright landscape of friendship and helpfulness. Before this American edition appeared, a motor accident had claimed the life of the person who was my greatest single source of encouragement, editorial and psychological support from the time I first began researching to the moment the last proof went to the printers: Barbara Hayley, Professor of English at St. Patrick's College, Maynooth. A wonderful human being, an inspired teacher, her contribution to this work was an illustration of the meaning of the latin word "educare", from which "education" is derived: to draw out. Barbara was the one who drew out this book.

The Collins family were unfailingly courteous and co-operative. I must particularly thank Mr Michael Collins, Mr Liam Collins, Col Pat Collins, Gen Sean Collins-Powell, Ms Nancy Hurley and Ms Mary-Clare O'Malley, for all the information and material they provided. The Collins' family friend and historian, the late Mr Liam O'Donnadcha, also provided invaluable notes and guidance. The historian, the late Leon O'Broin, was a tower of strength and inspiration before his health failed. The first-hand reminiscences of Vinnie Bryne, Sr Margaret Mary and Ms Eileen O'Donovan were not only valuable but fascinating. Mr Eamonn de Barra provided me with both reminiscences and some extremely valuable documents. Lord Longford placed his unrivalled knowledge of the Treaty negotiations and of Irish affairs generally at my disposal. Heavy debts of gratitude are also owed to Ms Maire Molloy, for allowing me to reproduce the letters of Michael Collins to her mother and to Liam Tobin's daughters, Ms Ann Thornton and Ms Marie Tobin, for entrusting me with their father's papers and those of his close comrade, Frank Thornton; to Mr Felix Cronin for giving me unpublished letters of Collins to his mother (Kitty Kiernan), also to Professor Edith Sagarra for the file on exchanges between Churchill and Collins.

I cannot say enough about the kindness and assistance rendered by the staffs and directors of the various libraries and archives which I consulted. Though I single out a number of names for especial mention, I can truly say that I met with an almost universally helpful response. My thanks go to Mr Donal MacCartney and to Mr Seamus Helferty at University College Dublin, and Ms Kerry Holland of the Archives Department for making available to me the invaluable Mulcahy and O'Malley collections and other papers; at Dublin University, Dr Bernard Meehan, Keeper of Manuscripts, and Ms Felicity O'Mahony were unfailingly helpful; as were the staff of the National Library of Ireland, in particular Mr Gerry Lyne. My thanks too to the Director of National Archives, Dr David Craig, and his courteous and knowledgeable staffs in The State Paper Office and the Public Records Office; to Mr John Toolin and Mr Patrick Long at the Kilmainham Museum; Former Minister for Defence, Mr Brian Lenihan, Minister for Justice, for providing me with Department of Defence material; Mr Gregoir O'Duill for his assistance with Department of Finance Archives; Mr John Teehan of the National Museum of Ireland for facilitating my inspection of Collins memorabilia at a time when the museum was undergoing renovation; Mr David C. Sheehy, Diocesan Archivist to the Archdioces of Dublin, for his help with the immensely valuable Archbishops' Byrne and Walsh Collections; Mr Trevor Parkhill for his assistance at the Public Record Office of Northern Ireland; Ms Hilary Jones, her colleagues at the Public Records Office, London, and John and Angela Heuston, who all combined to make my sojourn at Kew both enjoyable and enlightening; Mr Nicholas B. Scheetz for his helpfulness in guiding me through the Shane Leslie papers at Georgetown University; Lady Leslie for granting me permission to consult the collection; Dr Margaret O'Donoghue for allowing me to make use of the Florrie O'Donoghue collection in the National Library of Ireland; to Mr Paddy Cooney, BL TD, for granting me permission to inspect the MacEoin papers in the Franciscan Archives, Killiney; Cannon John Brennan for giving me the unpublished memoirs of Kathleen Napoli McKenna; Archbishop Ryan of Perth for assistance with the history of the Dr Clune peace mission; to Faber & Faber for allowing me to quote from Louis MacNeice's poem 'Dublin'.

For their kind permission to reproduce the illustrations in this book, I must also thank Joe Cashman; the Collins family; Felix Cronin, the Hulton-Deutsch Collection; Kilmainham Jail Historical Museum; George Morrison; the National Library of Ireland; the National Museum of Ireland; Ms Eileen O'Donovan; Ms Essie Driscoll; Dr C. O'Reilly; Popperfoto; and the State Paper Office, Dublin. I am especially grateful to Kenneth Griffith for his expert help in the compilation of the pictures.

For overall guidance as to source material and assistance with proof-reading I am more indebted than I can say to Dr Michael Hopkinson, Mr John O'Mahony, and to Brid and Michael O'Siadhail, who rendered most useful assistance in these spheres. Mr Uinseann MacEoin, Mr Harold O'Sullivan, Dr Maurice O'Connell, Dr Dermot Keogh and Fr F. X. Martin also contributed invaluable guidance and material. Help came also from Professor J.B. Lyons; Mrs Sinead Derrig (née Mason), Dr Martin Gilbert, Dr Eamonn Phoenix, Dr John Dalat, Mr Liam MacAndrews, Mr Liam Flynn and Mr Liam Moher. The warmest of thanks to Lord Longford, the author of the classic study of the Treaty negotiations, *Peace By Ordeal*, for his advice and encouragement. Mr Rory Brady B.L. was kind enough to provide the invaluable service of reading the book from a legal standpoint and Ms Carmel Frawley came to my assistance with typing at a critical juncture. I should also like to record with pride and gratitude the research assistance rendered by those two fine journalists, my daughter Jackie and my son Tom.

I wish to express my sincere thanks to Frank Delaney for helping to get this book started and, in particular, to Richard Cohen of Hutchinson for his tactful and enlightened encouragement through first the writing, and then the editing stage—and here I speak as one who was himself an editor for twenty years—before handing over to Annelise Evans who proved herself a model of everything a good editor should be.

Last, but far from least, I wish to express my appreciation for the very Irish solution which presented itself to the even more Irish problem of dealing with the fact that de Valera's papers, in the Franciscan Archives, Killiney, are closed to researchers until cataloguing is completed in some years' time. Until the eleventh hour it appeared that this ban might prevent me gaining access to the Sean MacEoin papers held there also, but at the eleventh hour, while this book was going through the printers, thanks to the good offices of Fr Benignus Millet OFM, Mr Liam O'Lonargain and Mr Brendan MacGiolla Choille and his wife Eilis, I was given access to the MacEoin collection. Mr MacGiolla Choille, a former Keeper of the Public Records, also gave me the benefit of his unrivalled personal insights into matters concerning de Valera. I had earlier had the benefit of two major sources of assistance, one mysterious, but welcome, the anonymous gift of photostats of some interesting de Valera letters, 'from an admirer', after I had appeared on a television documentary about Collins; the other more substantial, and even more welcome—the continued provision of advice, documents and original manuscripts of his own writings on de Valera from Dr T.P. O'Neill, de Valera's official biographer. Dr O'Neill manfully contributed valuable help all through the writing of this book although we disagree profoundly about de Valera's role in the events described. His continuing supportive friendship, and that of his wife, Marie, is an indication that though ideas may contend, men need not. Would that his example was followed in other parts of our country.

Preface to The American edition

America's loss was to be Ireland's gain. For if Michael Collins had taken his brother Pat's advice, the Republic of Ireland might not exist today. Watching the storm clouds of World War I gather over Europe, Pat had written to Michael from Chicago urging his young brother to leave his job in a London stockbroker's office and come to join him in America. Had they teamed up, one is tempted to speculate that one of the all-time great Pat-and-Mike success stories might have resulted. But twenty-six-year-old Michael agonized over the decision while walking the docks of London, seeing the ships leave for the New World. War was imminent; a call up would surely follow, bringing with it an unthinkable choice: either become a conscientious objector or don a British uniform and fight for the Crown.

Eventually Collins solved the problem in his own inimitable way. He put on an Irish uniform and went to fight for Ireland, in the 1916 Easter Rebellion in Dublin. That searing week of flame and folly claimed the lives of some of the people he most admired: Tom Clarke, James Connolly, Sean Hurley, Sean MacDiarmida, Joseph Plunkett. Their names, and the parts they played in his career, will figure in subsequent pages. With their deaths, there also died his faith in conventional methods of fighting for Ireland's freedom. He still believed in fighting. But in the parliamentary game as played at Westminster the rules were so arranged that the outnumbered Irish nationalists always lost. Now he understood that static warfare—seizing a stronghold, be it a building such as Dublin's General Post Office, in which he fought during the rebellion, or a mountain top, and then slugging it out with rifles and shot guns against an adversary who possessed heavy artillery—would continue to provide the Irish with heroes and martyrs, and the British with victories.

Instead Collins evolved a new concept of guerilla warfare that in time would be copied by guerilla leaders all over the globe from Mao to Shamir. The Collins philosophy was based not on the capture of enemy bricks and mortar, but of its information. Traditionally Dublin Castle, the seat of British administration in Ireland, had used a network of spies and informers to infiltrate and then snuff out movements directed at securing Irish independence.

Collins perfected a system of spying on the spies. Every important branch of the Castle system, whether it was banking, policing, the railways, shipping, the postal service—whatever—was infiltrated by his agents. These were not highly-trained, CIA-style operatives, but ordinary men and women, little people whom nobody had ever taken notice of before. Collins gave them a belief in themselves, a courage they did not know they possessed, and they in return gave him a complete picture of how their masters operated.

A secretary in Military Intelligence saw to it that Collins had a copy of the Colonel's orders to the Captain before he received the originals. A railway porter carried dispatches, the docker smuggled in revolvers, the detective told him who the informers were—and the Squad used the revolvers to deal with those informers. For the first time in their history the Irish had a team of assassins trained to eliminate informers. Collins demoralized the hitherto invincible Royal Irish Constabulary, the armed police force that operated from fortified barracks and held Ireland for the Crown. Inevitably more generalized warfare broke out all over the country as the British introduced new men and new methods in a vain effort to counter the guerilla tactics of Collins's Active Service Units and the Flying Columns of Volunteers, which lived on the run, eating and sleeping where they could.

Held back from making a full scale use of their Army by the force of world opinion—largely Irish-American opinion—the British tried to fight a "police war" carried on by hastily-formed forces of ex-service men and officers troubled by little discipline and less conscience. The Black and Tans and the Auxiliaries wrote new chapters of horror in the bloodstained story of the Anglo-Irish relationship. Reprisals for the activities of Collins and his colleagues included the burning of homes and creameries, random murder and the widespread use of torture. Through it all Collins lived a "life on the bicycle." The most-wanted man in Europe, he smiled his way through a hundred hold-ups never wearing a disguise, never missing an appointment, never certain where he would spend the night.

In addition to his campaign of warfare, he ran a national loan, which was banned by the British so that either its advertisement or sale became illegal. Yet the loan was fully subscribed, and every subscriber got a receipt. He was president of the omnipresent secret society, the Irish Republican Brotherhood, which regarded him as the real president of the Irish Republic, and he was Minister for Finance in the *Sinn Fein* cabinet. In addition he was Director of Intelligence of the Irish Republican Army. Any one of those jobs would have consumed the energy of an ordinary man, but Collins combined them all efficiently and effectively.

He had little formal education (that part of his development ceased when he passed his junior-grade civil service examinations at the age of sixteen), but he was an omnivorous reader and combined a mind like a laser beam with a hawk-like eye for detail. Nothing escaped his attention. Everything attracted his interest: Shaw's latest play, the way the Swiss organized a Citizen Army, Benjamin Franklin's proposals for dealing with loyalists, or the latest edition of Popular Mechanics. An article in that journal in November of 1920 led to the first use in warfare of the Thomson gun. Collins saw the article on the recently-invented weapon and had enquiries made about this "splendid thing,"* which led to the Irish-American leader Joseph McGarrity of Philadelphia buying five hundred of the weapons. Two Irish-American ex-officers were sent to Ireland to train the I.R.A. in the use of the weapons. Only a handful got through the American customs, but these were duly used in a number of Dublin ambushes.

Tough and abrasive with his male, and sometimes female, colleagues, Collins was gentle and playful with children and old people. Throughout the eighteen months that Eamon de Valera was in America on a propaganda and fund-raising mission, Collins risked his life to call each week to his absent chief's family, bringing them money and companionship. Eventually the war effort Collins had spearheaded drove the British to a conference table and a settlement as foreseeable as it was unpalatable to many Irishmen and women; a partitioned Irish Free State that would owe allegiance to the Crown. It was a deal that had been foreshadowed to de Valera in four days of talks between himself and Lloyd George, the British Prime Minister, in London during July 1921. De Valera did not want to be the man who faced up to the implications of that deal. Instead he repaid the kindness Collins had shown his family in Machiavellian fashion. He stayed away himself from the opprobrious negotiations but manipulated Collins into going to London as part of the delegation that signed the Anglo-Irish Treaty of December 6th, 1921, the constitutional foundation document of modern Ireland. Collins took the leading part in the Treaty's negotiation. Subsequently, he became Chairman of the Executive Council (in effect, the Government) of the Irish Free State that emerged, and later Commander-in-Chief of the Army.

The Treaty did not yield the Republic he had hoped for but it provided what Collins prophetically termed a "stepping stone" to today's Irish Republic. All the other stepping stones to the tragedy of today's Northern Ireland situation were part of that negotiation too. In a very real sense Collins' premature death was caused by the forces that still rage about the Northeastern corner of the land

and people for whom he fought. The story of his life explains tomorrow's news from Belfast. Would he have brought fire or prosperity to his country had he lived? Or would he have died of drink or disillusionment at the effects of the civil war that broke out over the terms of the Treaty?

We don't know. What we can be sure of is that this Irish Sigfried kept his Appointment in Samarra a couple of months short of his thirty-second birthday in a remote Cork valley known as *Beal na mBlath,* The Mouth of Flowers. He died, not far from where he was born, in an ambush laid by a former comrade in arms, a man who had undergone sadistic tortures at the hands of British Intelligence Officers rather than betray his boyhood friend, Michael Collins. Collins' career is a paradigm of the tragedy of modern Ireland: the suffering, the waste of talent, the hope, the bedeviling effect of history and nomenclature whereby one man's terrorist is another man's freedom fighter. Like Prometheus, Collins stole fire. Like Prometheus, he paid for his feat and much of what he set about doing remains undone. But his name burns brightly wherever the Irish meet. Michael Collins was the man who made Ireland possible.

*Described by Sean Cronin in *The McGarrity Papers,* Anvil Books, Tralee, Co. Kerry, 1978, p.98.

Prologue

Dublin, May 1916. A line of prisoners marches along the quays towards a boat that is going to take them to jail somewhere in England. Not the most pleasant of prospects, but at least they've come safely out of the fighting that has left the centre of the city in ruins and none of them was picked out to face a firing squad. Some of their friends were not so lucky. In fact quite a number of the people they pass on the street think they have got off too lightly. Here and there a man calls out a jeer or an oath. He might have a brother or a son at the front. Generally it is the women who are most vituperative. These are 'separation women'. Their only income is the separation allowance they are paid by the British Government while their husbands are away fighting for the rights of small nations. Their comments express both their disgust at the destruction and killing caused by the week-long rebellion and their fears that the Government may react by cutting off their livelihood.

'Bleedin' bastards, my husband's out in the war fightin' for you bowsies and yiz go and yiz stab them in the back.' 'Yiz are too cowardly to fight, and too lazy to work.' One lady with a shawl yells something about her two fine sons and runs along the line of soldiers guarding the prisoners to call out, 'Everyone of yiz should get a dose of capital punishment, and a bloody good kick up the arse after.'

But here and there the prisoners get an occasional word of encouragement too. From the top of the tram a respectable looking man in a bowler hat calls out, 'God save ye, lads – up the Republic.' Another man wearing an apron and covered in flour, obviously a baker, breaks through the soldiers to thrust fistfuls of chocolate and cigarettes into the hands of a prisoner who is so surprised that he can only think to shout his thanks a few seconds after the stranger has dropped back into the crowd. As the column passes the ruins of Liberty Hall shelled into rubble by the gunboat *Helga* during the fighting, a good-looking, well-dressed young woman, Nancy O'Brien, at last catches up with the prisoner she's been searching for, her cousin.

A few weeks ago, he and his friend Sean MacDiarmada had taken part in the Easter Rising, and her cousin had marched out of Liberty Hall in his new Volunteer's uniform, to fight. For a week she had gone to the top of Howth Head to listen to the shelling and watch the flames rise from the Post Office. At least part of her prayer had been answered. Although MacDiarmada had been condemned to death her cousin Michael had emerged safely from the conflagration, even if he was going off into captivity.

Slightly breathless from having to jog to keep up, she called over a soldier's head, 'What will you do now?' 'Do?' asked the tall, mocking young man with a West Cork accent nearly as broad as his shoulders. 'Do? Sure I'll get ready for the next round, of course. I've got some of the names taken down already,' he said, waving a diary, 'the besht of min.' Nancy was flabbergasted. 'But . . . what? . . . How are you going to train them?' she called out finally, just as the column neared the cattle-boat waiting for the prisoners. 'Sure won't His Majesty's Government train them for me?'

1

The Little Fella

'One day he'll be a great man. He'll do great work for Ireland.'

Michael Collins Senior, on his deathbed

Dear Sirr,
Lord Edward Fitzgerald will be this evening in Watling St. Place a watch in Watling St two houses up from Usher's Island and another towards Queen's Bridge, a third in Island St, the rear of the stables near Watling St which leads up to Thomas St and Dirty Lane at one of three places Lord Edward will be found – he wears a wig and will have one or two more with him – they may be armed.

Dublin Castle, 18 May 1798.[1]

Anyone who might have seen the young Michael Collins in a loft on a sunny summer day on the family farm at Woodfield in West Cork a hundred years after the foregoing letter was written would have found it very hard to credit that he would ever survive to march into captivity – or live to smash the system of informers and intelligence-gathering that enabled Major Sirr to be in the right place at the right time to capture Lord Edward Fitzgerald. For, as he crawled across the loft which his sister had covered in blooms, the little boy was very obviously in the wrong place at the wrong time. In creating the floral carpeting his sisters had inadvertently left the trap door unbolted and the child suddenly disappeared through the treacherous blooms.[2] Terrified at what they might see sprawled beneath them the two girls rushed to the opening to discover their youngest brother unhurt, his fall broken by a pile of hay. On this occasion Michael Collins had escaped the jaws of *bael na mblath*, the mouth of flowers. Ironically, however, when death did come for him nearly thirty years later it would find him in a little Cork valley called – Bael na mBlath. Before that he would have become a legend in his lifetime and would have had a variety of escapes which made his safe emergence from the 1916 Rebellion seem like child's play.

Much of Collins' life's work was directed at destroying not only Dublin Castle's intelligence system, but the legislative Union of Great Britain and Ireland which it maintained. This Union came into being as a result of the 1798 Rebellion which was broken by the capture of Lord Edward Fitzgerald and by that of Theobald Wolfe Tone, the daring Republican theoretician who had succeeded in prising a French fleet from the Directory in the unfulfilled hope of driving the British out of Ireland. The Union meant that Ireland's parliament in Dublin was subsumed into the British parliament at Westminister. Dublin, Ireland's capital, had declined after the legislative shot-gun marriage and with the decay of Dublin there followed a parallel decline in the Irish economy leading to heavy emigration, famine, sporadic rebellion and the creation of a Protestant landlord class which increasingly absented itself from Ireland. Irish estates, viewed too often merely as sources of rent, not responsibility, were inefficiently managed, and uneconomically divided amongst tenants who if they fell behind in their rents could be evicted at will, or if they improved their holdings have their rents increased. The Clonakilty district of West Cork in which Michael Collins grew up[3] had more than its share of the land agitations which convulsed Ireland in the late nineteenth century. Two of the great onslaughts against landlordism took place on the Bence Jones and Smith-Barry estates near Clonakilty, under what was known as the Plan of Campaign. This combined the withholding of rent with boycotting, a refusal to have any dealings whatsoever with the object of the boycott. A landlord placed under this interdiction could not be traded with, worked for, or even spoken to. Both landlordism and the reaction of boycotting which it provoked were to leave their marks on the Collins family.

Two of Michael's uncles had once come to blows with two members of the landlord class who came roistering through the Woodfield crops on horseback. The Collinses used the trespassers' own riding whips to drive them off and spent a year in Cork jail for their pains. Michael's father made a day-long journey on horseback each month to visit them. Within the ranks of landlordism there was of course a responsible minority who cared for their estates and their tenantry. But that could give rise to problems too. One local landlord, a Protestant clergyman, was kind to one of Michael's sisters, treating her for burns she sustained at Woodfield through the carelessness of a servant girl. However when Michael senior sought to repay his goodness in a small way, by obliging the cleric with the loan of a winnowing machine, he was beaten up by another member of the Collins clan, a cousin.[4] The clergyman might have been kindly, but he was one of 'them', a landlord who at the time was being boycotted. He bravely lent the winnowing machine to the clergyman the day after he was beaten but escaped further embarrassment by building a new barn and concreting the contentious machine into the floor so that no one could borrow it again! Michael Senior was equally hard to shift when a local merchant dunned him for the bill which he claimed to have paid he allowed the man to take him to law so that he could publicly get the better of him, triumphantly producing his receipt in open court.[5] The Plan of Campaign was actually ruined by the opposition of a group of Unionist landlords under the resolute leadership of Arthur Smith-Barry. The Plan leaders, including William Smith O'Brien and John Dillon, who were also two of the leaders of the Irish Parliamentary Party, were summoned to court but failed to turn up, and disappeared for several weeks into a cloud of national gossip and excitement. It was afterwards noted[6] that the first time they were seen again in public was in Paris on the day that Michael Collins was born, 16 October 1890.

The case against the fleeing Irish leaders had been gathered efficiently by the principal force on the side of landlordism and the British connection, the Royal Irish Constabulary, a force built on a lengthy tradition of spies and informers, radiating out from Dublin Castle. The RIC's Register of Informants[7] describes the nature of these sources whose identities were carefully guarded, being entered only under 'Cognomen of Informant'. Around the time Collins was born, in the years 1889-90, the Register, which covered the whole country, contained many references to people and movements that would affect his life such as The Gaelic Athletic Association, The Gaelic League, The Irish Republican Brotherhood, the Labour movement, and to specific agitations such as the Smith-Barry affair.

Even in far-away County Armagh there was 'Easer', described as an 'old IRB man, friend of O'Donovan Rossa, gives information about IRB'. 'Steam' of Cork was 'well in with the boys', and a member of the IRB. 'Jennings', a recognised synonym for treachery, was 'one of our oldest and most reliable men' in Cork City. 'Charon' was 'most useful, with regard to Trades and Labour Unions'. 'H' was trustworthy as to 'state of district. Plots to assassinate and contemporary outrages as to infernal machines'. Many of the payments recorded were quite small, a pound or two over a year, so one can only speculate as to the place in society and the services rendered to the crown by 'Nero' who was described as being 'worth any money' and was paid £205. The standard of morality engendered by the 'Informant' system may be gauged by the fact that many of the entries stressed that the spies were 'sworn IRB men'.

The greatest 'sworn IRB man' of them all, Michael Collins, was born into the O'Coileain clan, formerly the lords of Ui Chonaill, known today as Upper and Lower Connelloe in County Limerick. The O'Coileains have their roots in both the bardic and warrior traditions of Ireland. Sean O'Coileain was a celebrated eighteenth-

century poet and the O'Coileains' prowess in warfare is recalled in the
ancient topographical poem by Giolla na Naomh O hUidhrin:

> The Ui Chonaill of the battalion of Munster
> Ample is the gathering
> A great family with whom it is not fitting
> to contend
> Is the battle-trooped host of the O'Coileains.

The Collinses were people of some consequence in the district and
Collins' childhood was exceptionally happy, but the spores of
memory, an interweaving of dispossession, of the consciousness of
being a member of the *Duainaire* (the Dispossessed), of landlordism,
of the famine, hung in his folk-consciousness with all the virulence of
the potato blight. For example one of the local ballads which the
Collins children learned to sing was a 'come-all-ye' ballad on the
Bence Jones affair.[8] It was poor stuff, but potent:

> Come all ye noble Land Leaguers
> I hope you will draw near
> And drop a tear of sympathy around Billy
> Jones' bier
> He died last night in Brighton
> From land-leaguing and boycotting and all
> such landlord woe.

The Collinses did not suffer unduly from 'landlord woes'. Life was
hard but by the standards of the Catholic farmers of the time the
family was comfortably off, living on a holding of 90 acres with eight
children to help with the work. These were Margaret, John, Johanna
(or Hannie as she was always called), Mary, Helena, Patrick and Kate.
Michael, the youngest, was pampered and spoiled by everyone.

One of the most significant factors in Collins' background was the
age of his parents. His father, Michael senior, was seventy-five years
old when Michael was born. He died at eighty-one when Michael was
six, leaving the boy with a reverence for old people which he never
lost. But his father's death also had the result of leaving an
impressionable boy without fatherly control and susceptible to
outside influences, in particular those of a nationalist-minded teacher,
Denis Lyons, and an equally nationalist-inclined blacksmith, James
Santry, both of whom as we shall see may be said to have guided his
feet along the road to rebellion.

Michael John Collins was in his sixtieth year when he married
Marianne O'Brien, a local girl of twenty-three. The seventh son of a
seventh son, he had a reputation as a healer of animals, with in addition
a knowledge of French, Latin and Greek. He was apparently also a
gifted mathematician, was widely read and had a phenomenal

memory. He received the basis of his unusual education from a cousin on his mother's side, Diarmuid O'Suillibhain, a hedge schoolmaster, one of the itinerant schoolteachers who defied the penal laws in the era before Catholic Emancipation (1829) to teach their pupils, sometimes literally under hedges. O'Suilleabhain was said to have studied at a Belgian university and to have been a friend of Wolfe Tone's. His father had also joined the Irish Republican Brotherhood, popularly named the Fenians, though he does not seem to have taken part in the aborted Fenian rising of 1865. Thus in the person of his father, Michael Collins in his childhood had a not insignificant link with the founder of Irish Republicanism.

That a man of such ability should wait so long before taking a wife speaks volumes for the uncertainties and conservatism created by the conditions of the Irish rural economy. When weighing up the normal pros and cons of marriage one had to add to the cons the thought of having to leave with one's offspring for the insecurity of America or, worse, see them die of famine or its infections. Some of course saw the situation differently, as an Irish toast of those years shows: '*Sláinte go saol agat, páiste gach bliadhan agat agus bás in Eirin.*' It means 'Health and life to you, a child every year to you, and death in Ireland.' The child every year was the parents' insurance against accident or old age, and death in Ireland meant one would be spared the pangs of emigration.

Marianne O'Brien's life was a demonstration of the last two wishes coming true. She had had to care for her many brothers and sisters from her middle teens when her father was killed and her mother injured after their horse shied, throwing them out of their trap as they returned one evening from a funeral. Obviously she regarded the courtship of Michael John Collins and his ninety acres as being preferable to her situation at home. But at Woodfield, she soon had a very large household to cope with again. When she moved there, apart from Michael John she had to care for his three brothers, Maurice, Tom and Paddy. Children duly arrived with the rapidity demanded by the Catholic church of the time.

Woodfield was almost completely self-supporting. And it was principally Marianne who supported the farmstead.[9] Carding the wool from their own sheep. Milking the twelve cows, curing the bacon from their own pigs. Baking, cleaning, sewing, ironing, making butter, making clothes, making babies. So good with money that she built a new house on the farm after Michael John died, despite the fact that a thief began the work by stealing the workmen's wages. So hospitable, that in an area noted for hospitality she was described as 'a hostess in ten thousand'.[10] Certainly on a perceived, obvious level, Marianne Collins left a powerful force of example behind her.

Though her busy life did not leave her with much time for any revolutionary branch of nationalism, she nevertheless had a sturdy sense of Irishness that manifested itself at an extraordinarily early age. There is a well-attested story in the Collins family[11] of how she took part when she was seven in a ceremony organised by the school at Lisavaird, then run by a Miss Collins, no relation, in honour of the local Big House family, the Freakes. The children had to recite a verse containing the line 'Thank God I am a happy English child'. But Marianne suddenly piped up, in front of the dignitaries, 'Thank God I am a happy *Irish* child!' She was badly beaten and sent to Coventry as a result. In later life Marianne also learned Latin and Greek from a hedge schoolmaster, an alcoholic priest.

Her daughter Mary recalled the night before Michael was born:

My mother carried the heaviest burden (of work) and at this time suffered greatly from pain in a broken ankle which I suppose was never properly set. I remember the night before Michael was born – I was then nine – I held the strainer while she poured the milk, fresh from the cow, from very heavy pails into the pans for setting the cream. She moaned occasionally and when I asked her was she sick she said she had a toothache and would go to bed when the cakes were made for tomorrow. I said nothing as in those days children were to be seen but not heard. The next morning there was the miracle of the baby. No doctor. No trained nurse and mother and baby well and comfortable! To say that we loved this baby would be an understatement – we simply adored him. Old Uncle Paddy said as soon as he saw him, 'Be careful of this child for he will be a great and mighty man when we are all forgotten.'[12]

One is entitled to wonder how 'comfortable' in reality was Marianne O'Brien. What tumult of the blood and of the intellect did that vibrant, loving young woman quench within herself as she was turned on the Woodfield lathe into that archetypical figure of self-sacrificial Irish motherhood? All contemporary records stress the happiness of the marriage despite the disparity in ages. The father was so vigorous that his children did not think of him as old. 'My father never had an old age', wrote Mary, and this seems to have been a generally accepted verdict.

But '*uisce fĕ talamh*' (literally: water under the ground) is an old Irish saying to describe secret currents, hidden matters. If 'beauty born of murmuring sound' was held to infuse the personality of Lucy in the Wordsworth poem one wonders what deep, unspoken discordancies and intimations did the discrepancies of age and the strain of Marianne's labours cause her to pass on to her son along with her love of reading and of flowers? The buoyant personality that swung so easily from elation to despair and back again? The cloud-burst temper? The demanding energy that achieved impossible tasks and still had strength left over for exuberant wrestling matches? The bluff, the courage, the love of children and of old people. And somewhere inside, hidden, *uisce fé talamh*, stone in the peach of West Cork charm and personality, the relentless mind that tore down the RIC's Judas tapestry. Where did these qualities come from?

Katie told a curiously prophetic anecdote of those days concerning his choice of reading. Starting with Lamb's tales, the young Michael worked his way through Shakespeare and, in the fashion of literary minded young patriots of the day, through a combination of English classics and sentimental historical Irish novels and ballads. Out of this medley it emerged that his favourite work was *The Mill on the Floss*. He told Katie, who was closest to him at the time, 'We're like Tom and Maggie Tulliver.' Katie replied that he could never be cruel like Tom. After a moment's silence Collins said, 'I could be worse. . . .'[13]

From his earliest days Michael seems to have wanted to be the leader in everything that went on around him. His cousin Michael O'Brien wrote of him[14] in their childhood days that Collins would always 'insist on running the show at Woodfield when we were kids, even to holding the pike (fork) when we endeavoured to spear salmon'. (There were only small trout in the river.) The family history abounds with doting anecdotes of the young Collins. Celestine, going away to be a nun in England, recalls the little boy waving goodbye until the pony and trap took her around a bend and out of sight. Mary tells of being left to look after the household for a day of drudgery during which she forgot to dig the potatoes until evening. Wearily forcing herself to the kitchen garden she was met by her three-year-old brother dragging behind him a bucket of potatoes that he had somehow managed to dig up by himself. Johnny remembers his prowess with horses, in particular, being found one day while still a baby curled up fast asleep in a stable between the hoofs of a notoriously vicious animal. His father on his deathbed told his grieving family to mind Michael because, 'One day he'll be a great man. He'll do great work for Ireland.'[15] Michael was six years old at the time.

Such are the stories told about him. But many of the stories told *to* him were products of hatred, not love. These grew out of the history of his race and place and they had a powerful, formative influence on his imagination. For pikes of a sort other than those used in efforts to spear fish had traditionally been fashioned at what in Collins' childhood was the neighbourhood place of enchantment, the forge at nearby Lisavaird, run by the blacksmith, James Santry. Santry's grandfather had fought in 1798 and his grandfather had made pikes for two of the revolutions which Tone's teachings had helped to inspire in the subsequent century, 1848 and 1865. In a very literal sense the sparks of revolution were fanned into life for Michael Collins in James Santry's old forge. Close by in Lisavaird National School what was begun by Santry was continued by the local schoolmaster, Denis Lyons, an active member of the Irish Republican Brotherhood, the

IRB, which had set off the Fenian revolt of 1865. Lyons' rule was harsh. He could never be accused of spoiling any child through sparing the rod, but his excellent results made the community overlook both his methods and his dangerous politics.

Collins never seems to have held any grudge about Lyons' severity and he revelled in the doctrines of Wolfe Tone's physical force republicanism which the teacher imparted along with the three Rs:

To subvert the tyranny of our execrable Government, to break the connection with England, the never failing source of all our political evils, and to assert the independence of my country – these were my objects. To unite the whole people of Ireland, to abolish the memory of all past dissensions, and to substitute the common name of Irishman in place of the denomination of Protestant, Catholic and Dissenter – these were my means.[16]

Later in life, during a period of self-analysis[17], Collins gave a friend an assessment of the importance of Santry and Lyons to the development of his political thinking which shows how highly he rated their influence:

In Denis Lyons and James Santry I had my first tutors capable of – because of their personalities alone – infusing into me a pride of the Irish as a race. Other men may have helped me along the searching path to a political goal. I may have worked hard myself in the long search, nevertheless Denis Lyons and James Santry remain to me my first stalwarts. In Denis Lyons especially his manner, although seemingly hiding what meant most to him, had this pride of Irishness that has always meant most to me.

Woodfield is a lightly wooded hill, overlooking a fertile, picturesque valley with a river that the Collins children fished and played in. Although naturally athletic, Michael, like most Irish boys of his and many subsequent generations, never learned to swim, a commentary on the education and attitudes of a sea-girt society whose once valuable fishing trade had been wiped out and which viewed the sea as a phenomenon that either created employment in the British Navy or was one's means of emigration. Only a small percentage of the population had a tradition of earning a dangerous living, usually in small open boats, from the fertile but furious coastline. 'What the sea gives it takes back' is an old Irish saying. And part of Collins' life's work would be to try to get his countrymen to take back from the sea the harvest they once reaped. The sea is only a few miles away from his birthplace, the beaches, cliffs and fjords of West Cork being punctuated to the east by the thriving town of Clonakilty four miles away and three miles to the west by the cliff-crowned village of Rosscarbery where one of Collins' heroes was born: O'Donovan Rossa, the Fenian leader, who actually visited Lisavaird School while the Collins children were there. At Rosscarbery the children heard stories of Cliodhna, the queen of the Munster fairies. A favourite Sunday trip

was to the cliffs above Cliodhna's rock. Here, Collins' friend Piaras
Beaslai tells us, 'Michael heard many a wonderful tale of Cliodhna's
enchantments, of wrecks and perils, and drownings and treasure
trove.'[18]

The tales were not all of enchantment. The sufferings of
O'Donovan Rossa in English prisons were recounted. Of Skibbereen
a few miles west of Rosscarbery where at that time all the principal
shops were still owned by Protestants and the history of eviction and
emigration is commemorated by the ballad 'Old Skibbereen', in
which a father tells his orphaned son how they came to be in America:

> Oh, well do I remember the bleak December day,
> The landlord and the sheriff came to drive us all away;
> They set my roof on fire with their cursed English spleen.
> And that's another reason that I left old Skibbereen.

Collins himself would live to experience his own roof set on fire,
and during his childhood a familiar sight to him, off the coast near
Skibbereen, was the awesome Fastnet Rock lighthouse. It owes its
existence to a disaster which occurred at the height of the famine. In
November 1847 the US–registered *Stephen Whitney* laden with men,
women and children escaping to the new world was wrecked on the
Fastnet during a gale.

His early years were crisscrossed by such contrasting strands of joy
and horror, myth and reality, love and hate, in a way that seems to
foreshadow his later life. Sam's Cross, his native hamlet near
Woodfield, is named after Sam Wallace, a highwayman, who is said to
have robbed the rich to feed the poor. The major attraction of the
crossroads is The Four Alls, a pub owned by a member of the Collins
clan. It doesn't display photographs of its most famous patron: 'Some
of our customers mightn't like them.' And even today the signpost on
the main road from Clonakilty pointing to Collins' birthplace is
sometimes vandalised: 'Ah sure you wouldn't know who'd do these
things', is the customary explanation of locals, delivered in a tone that
suggests the speaker knows exactly who does such things.

At home Collins received a gentler, more complex, but nevertheless complementary vision of history and politics, from that taught
by Santry and Lyons. Unlike his family and neighbours his father
never sang rebel songs. Yet he had lived through the famine and joined
the Fenians and told his children that he thought the land should be
owned by the people, in other words their people, the Catholics. The
last eviction in the district had occurred while the owner of the farm
lay on his deathbed. An enraged son had reacted by driving a fork into
the agent's eye. That stopped the eviction, it was said locally. 'The
only thing they understand is violence', was the corollary. It was a
corollary Michael Collins agreed with. He told his cousin Sean

Hurley, as they passed the home of a once notorious evicting landlord: 'When I'm a man we'll have him and his kind out of Ireland.'[19]

The talk around the Collins fireside frequently turned as it did at the firesides of their neighbours to landlords and their methods, 'hanging gales', rack-renting, and the occasional exercise of the *droit de seigneur*, for Wolfe Tone's vision had not been fulfilled. Protestant and Catholic had not united in the common name of Irishmen and the big estates and big businesses, what there were of them, were generally held by Protestants. Any time the Collinses wished to go to Cork they had to pass through the town of Bandon. This solidly Protestant oasis in the ever-encroaching desert of Catholicism at the time of Collins' boyhood was still infused with the spirit of its builder, Richard Boyle, Earl of Cork, who thanked Almighty God that there was not an Irishman nor a Papist in the place.[20] But this fact never created any anti- Protestant feeling at Woodfield. Marianne died attended by Protestant neighbours and there was a large concourse of Protestants at her funeral.

There is no evidence at any stage in his life, even when he was at the height of his disagreements with Northern Ireland's Protestant leadership, that Michael Collins ever uttered a sectarian sentiment. A celebrated liberal Presbyterian, the Rev. J. B. Armour, came from Northern Ireland to study in Cork University not long before Collins was born, and wrote: 'There seems to be none of that bigotry with regard to religious principle which is all too evident in Belfast.'[21] But though Armour was correct in his observation that Catholics and Protestants were closer together in Cork than they were in Belfast, where the holders of the land were concerned it was the closeness of apartness, never more savagely described than by a Protestant poet from Northern Ireland, Louis MacNeice:

> The mist on the Wicklow Hills
> Is close, as close
> As the peasantry were to the landlord
> As the Irish to the Anglo-Irish,
> As the killer is close one moment
> To the man he kills.[22]

What the Protestant-Catholic divide did mean in practice was that when the Anglo-Irish war started it was to Protestants, as Loyalists, that the British automatically turned for their sources of intelligence whereas Collins drew his mainly, though not exclusively, from Catholics, and the IRA would be largely a Catholic force.

Two other influences which Michael John and Marianne also passed on to their children were a strongly held Catholic faith and a love of Nationalist literature and songs. Helena, the innocent cause of the winnowing-machine controversy, walked for the first time after the burning when she was five, following a pilgrimage made by Marianne to the shrine of St Fachtna, a local saint, an event which was probably a contributory factor in Helena's becoming a nun. Michael always had a deeply felt religious sensibility, though he did pass through the usual Republican anti-clerical period when he lived in London.

His sister, Mary Collins, played her part in helping to heighten her young brother's interest in the Nationalist struggle and in guerrilla warfare. While at school in Edinburgh she developed a sympathy with the Boers and on her return for holidays to Woodfield would tell Michael of her fights at school with 'pro-jingoists'. It was from Mary that Michael heard 'how the gallant Boer farmers used to leave their work, take part in an ambush and return perhaps to milk the cows the next morning.'[23] De Wet became one of Collins' heroes.[24] Mary Collins Powell quotes a ballad of the time, 'which, no doubt, left a lasting impression on Michael's young mind':

> Great faith I have in moral force
> Great trust in thought and pen
> I know the value of discourse
> To sway the minds of men
> But why should words my frenzy whet
> Unless we are to strike
> Our despot lords who fear no threat
> But reverence the pike
> Oh, do be wise, leave moral force
> The strength of thought and pen
> And all the value of discourse
> To lily-livered men
> But if you covet not to die
> Of hunger in a dyke
> If life we prize is liberty
> A Pike – A Pike – A Pike.

In its own unsophisticated way that ballad may be said to have done more than leave a 'lasting impression' on Collins' mind. It summed up the Santry and Lyons arguments and policy he advocated throughout his short, turbulent life. The condition of Ireland could only be improved by the use of force.

The young Michael devoured the writings of Thomas Davis, the nationalist philosopher and propagandist of the Young Ireland movement which led to the revolt of 1848, the songs and Fenian tales of A. M. and T. D. Sullivan, the songs and poetry of Thomas Moore. The novels of Banim and Kickham, set against a background of tenant strife, landlordism, oppression and emigration, stirred him deeply. He was found weeping one day over the sufferings of the peasantry in Kickham's *Knocknagow*.

His contemporary and biographer, Frank O'Connor says: 'If I had recorded all the occasions when he wept I should have given the impression that he was hysterical. He wasn't; he laughed and wept as a child does (and indeed as people in earlier centuries seem to have done) quite without self-consciousness.'[25]

One force which moved him early on in life, though not to tears, was Arthur Griffith's *United Irishman*, whose editorials he began studying when he was twelve years of age. He wrote at this time: 'In Arthur Griffith there is a mighty force afoot in Ireland. He has none of the wildness of some I could name. Instead there is an abundance of wisdom and an awareness of things that ARE Ireland.'[26] By contrast he was totally dismissive of the Irish Parliamentary Party: those 'slaves of England' were nothing but 'chains around Irish necks'.[27]

Denis Lyons, for whom he wrote the foregoing in an essay, and who probably introduced him to Griffith, must have been pleased with his pupil. Along with Griffith's separatism, illustrations of how England had systematically suppressed Irish trade, and doctrines of Irish national self-development, he took aboard the preachings of another editor, D. P. Moran of *The Leader*, which advocated an 'Irish Ireland'. Both writers sought to promote a heightened consciousness of being Irish across a broad spectrum, encouraging support for Irish goods, games, art, literature, music and language. Collins' parents spoke Irish, but only when they didn't want their children to understand them. For like many patriotic Irish parents of the time they feared that the Irish language would be a barrier to their children's prospects of advancement in the English-speaking world.

As a boy Michael was popular, but regarded as somewhat 'wild'. Galloping about on the Collinses' white mare, Gypsy. Playing football and hurling, and the popular Cork sport of 'bowling', throwing an iron ball along the country roads, with more enthusiasm than skill but with plentiful explosions of temperament. Skylarking with his close companion, Sean Hurley, a cousin of the same age who shared his interest in sport and, increasingly, in the political situation. Marianne was worried that if he stayed at home he might fall into bad company. 'He is head of his class and I am afraid he will get into mischief', she told his sisters[28]. By now the only man at Woodfield was his eldest brother Johnny, twelve years older than Michael. Employment opportunities in the district were limited. The RIC and the Services were unattractive to someone of his outlook. Watching her youngest in his teens as her health began to fail, Marianne decided that his future lay in London.

There was a tradition in the area that when a male child was born in Clonakilty the neighbours would say, 'Musha, God bless him. It's the fine sorter he'll make'.[29] His sister Johanna, 'Hannie', was already in London working for the post office, and Michael was sent to

Clonakilty to study for the post office examinations and live with his sister Margaret, whose husband P. J. O'Driscoll owned the *West Cork People*, a local newspaper which was founded through the 'kindly aid' of Marianne. Here Collins developed an interest in newspapers which never left him. He learnt to type, acted as a copyboy, and wrote up sporting events.

After a year and a half in Clonakilty, he passed the Post Office examination and was given a job in the Post Office Savings Bank in West Kensington. In July 1906, Collins moved to London at the age of fifteen to live with Hannie at 5 Netherwood Road, West Kensington, which, his family believes, was his home for the next nine years, though the plaque on the house, erected by the Hammersmith authorities, only records his last year there, 1914–15, the period for which evidence of his occupancy appears on the voters' lists.[30]

Marianne died of cancer the following year, showing 'Christian fortitude' after a 'lingering and torturing illness . . . cold water . . . her food and drink for seven weeks previous to her happy release'. On her death, 'one who knew her' wrote a poem which was reproduced in the *West Cork People*.[31] It contained the following:

> Friend and stranger at her smiling board
> Found a welcome ever warmly stored;
> In her pulse the quickening rush
> Spoke the bosom's generous flush.
> An honest pleasure beamed in her eye;
> At her home 'twas ever so –
> Those who came were loath to go;
> Hers was Irish hospitality.

Collins preserved it in an envelope which also contained Marianne's mass card.[32] It gives her age as '54 years'. Underneath the figure, Collins, ever sentimental, ever meticulous, simply wrote, in tiny script, '52'. He did not cross out the wrong age, nor is it likely that in either his memory or his character, very much of Marianne was ever crossed out. One's seventeenth year is an impressionable age at which to see your mother follow the father you hardly knew into the grave.

Given the ideological baggage which he took with him to London, it is not surprising that Collins threw himself into the Irish rather than the English world of that city. Though Collins was taken out of West Cork, West Cork was never taken out of him. His closest friend in London was his closest friend in Clonakilty, his cousin Sean Hurley. He joined the Gaelic Athletic Association, playing football and hurling and, as he grew physically, developed into a fine athlete, particularly in hurling and the long jump. Though he played fair, his hair-trigger temperament meant that if a row developed on the field he was generally either its cause or a participant. Off the field when Collins was about eighteen there was a major row over GAA members playing soccer, one of the four games proscribed by the Association. (The others were rugby, hockey and cricket.) Collins was one of those who objected vigorously to 'garrison games'[33] which he saw as aiding 'the peaceful penetration of Ireland'. There should be 'no soccer for gaels'.

The London GAA split over the issue, several clubs breaking up so that only three remained, one of them Collins', the Geraldines, of which he became treasurer. Collins' report for the second half of 1909 reads:

An eventful half year has followed a somewhat riotous general meeting. Great hopes instead of being fulfilled have been rudely shattered. . . . Our internal troubles were saddening but our efforts in football and hurling were perfectly heartbreaking. In no single contest have our colours been crowned with success. . . . In hurling . . . we were drawn to play five matches but disgraceful to say in only one case did we field a full team. If members are not prepared to act more harmoniously together and more self-sacrificingly generally . . . the club will soon have faded into inglorious and well-deserved oblivion.[34]

The Collins approach worked and the Geraldines grew and prospered. His career in London's Irish world[35] was a combination of logical progression from the ideas and attitudes imparted at the Woodfield fireside, in forge and school at Lisavaird, by his reading of Irish history and by his own determination, in Michael O'Brien's words, 'to insist on running the show', whatever that show might be. He was involved in further controversy during 1909 because of his then pronounced anti-clericalism. The year before he had come to London, 1905, Arthur Griffith had founded a political party, Sinn Fein ('We Ourselves'), as a vehicle for his *United Irishman* ideas.

Invited by a Sinn Fein club to read a paper on 'The Catholic Church in Ireland', Collins delivered a broadside against the church's attitude to Irish nationalism, concluding with the recommendation that the way to deal with the Irish hierarchy was 'to exterminate them'. The most significant step Collins took that year was attended not by controversy, but by total secrecy, which paradoxically is commemorated annually today by unwitting but enthusiastic crowds at Ireland's premier sporting event, the All-Ireland Gaelic Football Final. In November 1909, at Barnsbury Hall, Michael Collins was sworn in as a member of the Irish Republican Brotherhood by his fellow post office worker, Sam Maguire. Maguire, who died in obscurity, is commemorated by the trophy awarded to the winning All-Ireland team, the Sam Maguire Cup. In the Irish world Collins went on to become both treasurer of the IRB for London and the South of England and treasurer of the London GAA.

In the outer, commercial world he moved to positions of less authority, though he was building up a knowledge of financial dealings and of organisation that blossomed when he needed it, in a way that suggests that he may have deliberately set out to acquire such skills. This would certainly have been in accordance with the IRB's policy of infiltrating every possible branch of activity likely to be of use to the Brotherhood. For, though an understanding of financial affairs came easily to him, and it appears obvious that he could have become a wealthy man with comparative ease, he seems to have had an inner dissatisfaction, an 'other' directed sense, where ordinary career values were concerned. He once wrote:

However happy I happen to be in a particular job, the thought is always with me that my future is otherwise than among the facts and figures of money. Yet I do not really dream of greater things . . . only the thought is always there.[36]

He afterwards wrote of himself:

The trade I know best is the financial trade, but from study and observation I have acquired a wide knowledge of social and economic conditions and have specially studied the building trade and unskilled labour. Proficient in typewriting, but have never tested speed. Thorough knowledge of double-entry system and well used to making trial balances and balance sheets.[37]

He also seems to have known enough about agriculture to win an agricultural scholarship in 1913 which, had he had the financial backing, would have brought him a training course in Athlone. His sister Mary regarded this as one of his most extraordinary achievements as he had no agricultural science textbooks apart from a national school handbook.

He remained at the Savings Bank until 1910 when he moved to a firm of stockbrokers, Horne and Co., 23 Moorgate St, where he was put in charge of messengers.

He had taken evening classes at the King's College to prepare for civil service examinations and left Horne's to join the Board of Trade as a clerk on 1 September 1914. The pay scale may have something to do with his brief stay there. It was £70–£150. There was also a pressure from the family to get him away from the approaching war and over to his brother Pat in Chicago. This is usually cited by his family and biographers as the cause of his moving to the Guaranty Trust Company of New York's London branch in Lombard St in May 1915. As we shall see later, however, there may have been other reasons connected with his inner, IRB world.

Insofar as his outer, cultural and social worlds were concerned, Hannie encouraged him to broaden his nationalist readings. An omnivorous reader, he developed an appetite for a wide variety of authors – Hardy, Meredith, H. G. Wells, Arnold Bennett, Conrad and Swinburne, as well as Wilde, Yeats, Padraig Colum and James

Stephens. He was a keen theatre-goer, Shaw being his first favourite in the London theatre, Barrie second. He took pride in being able to declaim tracts of Synge, Wilde and Yeats. In a judgement which underlines the tragedy of his early death Frank O'Connor says: 'Collins' studiousness was the mental activity of a highly gifted country lad to whom culture remained a mysterious and all powerful magic. Though not one for everyday use.'[38]

Perhaps not 'everyday use'. In the theatre of Michael Collins' life what stage performance could hold his attention against the dramas that filled many of his ordinary days? But in a moment of reflection, quarried out of the hurly-burly of a prison camp he would write to a friend in a natural way that showed that he found theatre neither remote from him nor mysterious:

Glad you liked Widower's Houses: Does this mean that you approved of all the unpleasant things as well, if my memory doesn't trick me that episode about the Duke of W and the letters is in it, the my Dear Jenny – publish and be damned thing. Somehow that has always struck me as being particularly tickling. I think you'll like Candida too, but Marie O'Neill doesn't strike me as being the correct thing for the name part, all the Abbey taught players were and are very narrow, excluding Fay or the much admired Sara who are the men? By the way Shaw himself has written a most excellent skit on Candida – perhaps you've read it. 'How she lied to her husband.' Oh lovely! It's in the volume containing John Bull and Major Barbara.[39]

Who knows to what 'everyday use' he might have devoted his powers had he lived or what his breadth of culture might have been.

Hannie increasingly disapproved of his political activities. She shared their mother's fears that these might 'get him into mischief' and, in effect, both by advice and the provision of alternative reading material, provided a counterbalancing influence to her sister Mary's nationalist promptings. She also introduced him to her wide circle of English friends, though obviously, before he ever left Cork, Collins' mind had been firmly cast in the Fenian tradition and no sisterly urgings would break that mould.

All Collins' family admired and respected him. But the difference between Hannie and Mary, for example, lay in the fact that Hannie, who never married, lived in London and made a successful, lifelong, career in the British postal service. Mary lived in Ireland, in Cork, and actively helped Collins in his work in any way she could. Her son, Sean Collins-Powell, ultimately became Chief of Staff of the National Army founded by his famous uncle. Why two people from the same family and background so often go in such different directions is a question which frequently puzzles observers of Ireland. A chief of the Irish Special Branch told me once that after he had arrested certain young IRA men, and established their identity, he could immediately tell what teacher had influenced them into joining the movement. But what influenced the teacher? And why did the IRA men's older or younger brothers not join? These are questions which will continue to be asked as long as the Anglo-Irish difficulty is unresolved and British uniforms remain in Ireland.

Collins had a tendency to rise to the bait of any anti-Irish slur, real or inferred. After his death, his Guaranty Trust supervisor wrote that 'the staff, who were privileged to know him, will never believe that he could do an unworthy act'.[40] But he also noted that: 'Only on very rare occasions did his sunny smile disappear, and this was usually the result of one of his fellow clerks making some disparaging and, probably unthinking, remark about his beloved Ireland. Then he would look as though he might prove a dangerous enemy.'

The fact that Collins, who prevented an unfortunate Irish soldier in British uniform from watching a hurling match, and who, in later life, would frequently have cause to write in despatches of the English as the Enemy, never developed any knee-jerk anti-British sentiment was probably helped by entrée to Hannie's social circle. She certainly helped him financially. His wages when he came first to Netherwood Road were fifteen shillings a week. And she added to her role of friend and elder sister by attempting to exercise a maternal influence where drink and sex were concerned. He certainly drank, but not to excess like many of his contemporaries in the Irish community, and Frank O'Connor solemnly assures us that he was 'shrewd enough'[41] to know about the evils of prostitution 'only at second hand through the works of Tolstoy and Shaw'. But P. S. O'Hegarty, one of his greatest admirers, gives a more believable picture of a strong-willed adolescent boy, with normal healthy urges, who had been reared without a father and was now living in a big city with no surveillance save that of his eldest sister:

Everybody in Sinn Fein circles knew him, and everybody liked him, but he was not a leader. He had strong individuality, clearly-held opinions, and noticeable maturity even as a boy of seventeen when he made his appearance in Irish circles in London. But his place was rather as the raw material of a leader than as a leader. When he came to London as a mere boy, he fell into spasmodic association with a hard-drinking, hard-living crowd from his own place, and their influence on him was not good. During most of his years in London he was in the 'blast and bloody' stage of adolescent evolution, and was regarded as a wild youth with plenty of ability, who was spoiled by his wildness. Not that his wildness was any deeper than the surface. Behind it his mind grew and his ideas enlarged.[42]

His second cousin Nancy O'Brien who also worked in the post office said of him at this time: 'All the girls were mad about him. He'd turn up at the ceilidhe with Padraic O'Conaire and would not give them a "reck".' He was the sort of man that women either empathise with or seek to pull down. Generally in his London years women of his own class found him 'cheeky', his 'Big Fellow' sobriquet indicating swollen- headedness as much as height, just under six feet. They were attracted to his energy, his athletic build, the dark brown hair, the square-jawed truculent look that could change so suddenly to a boyish grin. But in the battle of the sexes, the strong-minded Irish Catholic women have always displayed to a high degree the sexual combativeness of the peer group. They can be generous with love but niggardly with understanding. The women that Collins was to find generous in both respects as his hero–reputation grew had no impulse towards competitiveness, being of a different class and out of his range through marriage and circumstances: Moya Llewelyn Davies and Lady Lavery. These we will meet later, at the point where they exerted an influence on the Collins story. In their positions they could be helpful and supportive without being competitive.

Another who was apparently helpful, though hardly supportive, would be Lady Londonderry. Collins was not being condescending to the type of girl he met at the ceilidhes but he had a shyness that took refuge in a pose of indifference in public and could come out as an awkward stiltedness when he was corresponding with someone he cared for.

In the 1914–18 period of his life that 'someone' was Susan Killeen, from County Clare, who later, curiously enough, went to live in Granard, County Longford, where the girl he later became engaged to, Kitty Kiernan, came from. Even in the midst of other pre-occupations revolutionaries have traditionally found time for women, and Collins was far from being an exception. Women were strongly attracted to him and he appears to have had several girlfriends. Susan, who for some reason appears to have escaped the notice of other biographers, was a highly intelligent girl, who secured her education through scholarships. She also worked in the London Post Office and was active in the same Irish-Ireland social circles in which Collins moved and in which they met. From Collins' correspondence with her it is obvious that they had a number of close friends in common. Nancy O'Brien shared digs with her in Dublin, for instance, and she worked in P. S. O'Hegarty's bookshop in Dawson St after she had returned to Ireland at the outbreak of the First World War rather than give her allegiance to England. She and Collins remained friendly, though their correspondence had tapered off, until after his engage-ment to Kiernan was announced in 1922. By then she was becoming politically as well as romantically estranged from him. Yet she preserved his letters. Or rather, most of them, because not long before she died, she spent a day in the attic going through the correspond-ence, and her family feel that she may have destroyed some on that occasion. Those that survive provide an insight into less complicated days, before the Anglo–Irish relationship had descended to its bloodier depths or civil war was even thought of.

The following letter[43] from Collins was written as his time in London was drawing to a close and it is illuminating as an indication of how he felt as the strands of his private and public lives began to draw together, as well as of his relationship with Susan:

5, Netherwood Rd
West Kensington.
19–10–15

A cara dilis,

Beleive [sic] me I don't remember ever being more disappointed in my life than I was on Saturday week, when I found on calling at the A.D. that you were on leave and would not be back before I left Dublin although indeed I had feared that some such ill-luck was coming my way as I didn't hear from you before leaving London. It appears I must regard it as a punishment for not writing – but I really do hate letter-writing, and I'm not good at it and can't write down the things I want to say – however don't think that because I don't write I forget.

Well how did you enjoy your holiday? Do you think it worth the after feeling? And of course the keener the enjoyment of a holiday the more miserable the after-feeling. I'm trying to make myself beleive [sic] that if one was in Dublin it wouldn't be so bad but I suppose that's because I'm selfish and want to think I'm the only one in the world's [sic] who's lonely and despondent. But London is a terrible place, worse than ever now – I'll never be happy until I'm out of it and then mightn't either.

Will you please tell Dolly Brennan that I'm very sorry I wasn't able to call at the office on Saturday morning but something else turned up and I was taken out to Lucan.

When you write, as I'm sure you will, I hope you will tell me about all the interesting things you did on the 'Hills of Clare'. Have you that poem off by heart yet?

With fondest rememberances,
do cara go deo
Miceal O'Coileain

The poem Collins was referring to was 'The Hills of Clare' by Thomas Hayes, a typically sentimental exile's lament. He had copied out its seven verses and sent it to Susan. It includes the following:

Ah yes I've been to many lands
I've climbed the Himalay . . .

I've been to where La Plata flows,
By Argentina's plains,
To western isles where beauty grows,
To India's mosques and fanes,
But still I hoped 'twould be my lot
One day the hearth to share
With those I loved and ne'er forgot
Upon the hills of Clare.

Michael Collins was never destined to see either the Himalay or Argentine plains. His world would be bounded by London and Liverpool, Dublin and West Cork. Other cities and places he would know only by correspondence. But one thing he did know and share with Irishmen scattered across the world in such places: what it was to have a burning sense of race and place but through exile to be denied contact with it except for occasions such as language classes, which by now had at least given him the proficiency to write his name in Irish. Once near the end of his life he told his friend P. S. O'Hegarty what it was he fought for. Struggling for words to express his feelings properly, he said, with many pauses and hesitations:

I stand for an Irish civilisation based on the people and embodying and maintaining the things – their habits, ways of thought, customs – that make them different – the sort of life I was brought up in . . . Once, years ago, a crowd of us were going along the Shepherd's Bush Road when out of a lane came a chap with a donkey – just the sort of donkey and just the sort of cart they have at home. He came out quite suddenly and abruptly and we all cheered him. Nobody who has not been an exile will understand me, but I stand for that.[44]

When he wrote to Susan Killeen, Collins' term of exile was drawing to a close. Part of his feeling that 'London was a terrible place – worse than ever now' was to do with his dislike of the threat facing him of having either to fight for England or to become a conscientious objector, both courses being abhorrent to his way of thinking. But part was due to the tension and uncertainty caused by the fact that he knew that the Nationalist tradition which had formed him was about to break out in rebellion once more against the British and Unionist alliance. The Irish Republican Brotherhood was planning another uprising. This time the issue was not about land, but about freedom.

By 1915 the land question in Ireland had largely been settled through a series of ameliorative Acts which, culminating in the Wyndham Act of 1903, created a system of tenant purchase. Collins' angst was caused by the fact that though landlordism and 'hanging gales' were passing away, the other great dream of Irish Nationalists, Home Rule, still hung in the balance. It was on the Statute Book, at last, but postponed until after the end of the war.

The demand had been first formulated by the parliamentary strain of Irish self-assertion beginning with Daniel O'Connell, the nineteenth-century inventor of today's mass, peaceful civil rights demonstrations. It continued with Isaac Butt who founded the Irish Home Rule League in 1870 and led an Irish Home Rule party at Westminster. His attempts at ameliorating conditions in Ireland by normal parliamentary methods were systematically frustrated.

Twenty-eight Bills aimed at improving the lot of the Irish peasantry, in other words staving off famine, were blocked between 1870 and 1880.[45] As a result he adopted the tactic of obstructionism: 'They block our bills, we'll block theirs.' His tactics were developed and amplified by Charles Stewart Parnell (1846–1891), the 'uncrowned king of Ireland', who used the Irish MPs to make and unmake British governments so as to force them to concede a parliament of their own to the Irish. Parnell and his party were destroyed by the O'Shea divorce case, but as the First World War approached the Irish political leadership of William O'Brien, John Dillon and John Redmond had managed, devotedly and painfully, to put the parliamentary pieces together. Hampered at Westminster by a lack of finance and, at best, a lack of understanding of the Irish situation on the part of their hearers, at worst by a positive anti-Irish prejudice, they had nevertheless manoeuvred so successfully that the House of Lords veto had been smashed and their efforts, combined with changes in British electoral outlook, had for the first time forced a Home Rule measure through both the Commons and the Lords. Compared to the mountainous opposition it had aroused, it was a fairly mouse-like proposal. There was to be a two-chambered parliament in Dublin, but Westminster was to retain both wide legislative powers and an Irish representation; hardly Wolfe Tone's 'breaking of the link', yet sufficient nevertheless to give rise to three traditions that continue to bedevil Anglo-Irish relationships and the peace of Ireland itself, even today.

The first was of course the resistance of the Anglo-Irish and, particularly potent in the north-east, their Scots-Irish Presbyterian supporters, to any attempt either to dilute their cherished union with Great Britain, or to thrust them under an All-Ireland parliament, which they saw as threatening to drown them in Popery. More particularly they saw an end to the union as giving flesh and blood, the latter being more likely, to the proposition that behind every Protestant land-holder there loomed the brooding spectre of a vengeful dispossessed Catholic.

The second was the calculated decision by a succession of Tory leaders, beginning with Randolph Churchill, to use Ulster sentiment on the Home Rule issue for political gain in England. It was a dangerous and a discreditable ploy. By the time Gladstone moved the first Home Rule Bill in 1886 there was already a long and bloody history of sectarian bloodletting in Northern Ireland stemming from the widespread 'plantation' of Protestants in the area begun under James I at the beginning of the seventeenth century. Insurrection by dispossessed Catholics had provoked Protestant backlashes under both Cromwell and William of Orange, whose victory at the Battle of the Boyne in 1690 continues to be one of the more significant dates in contemporary Irish history. It left Ulster with most of the land securely in Protestant hands, many of them specially imported Scots Presbyterian 'planters', and a desire on the part of Protestants to commemorate and continue with that scheme of things, symbolised by the para-military Orange Order formed a hundred years later.

The parts of the province where the Protestants failed to triumph were left with an equally blood-drenched Catholic tradition of withstanding the Orangemen. Here is what a prominent IRA man of Collins' day, John McCoy, wrote of an area that is still a no-go area to British troops as this is being written:

The natives killed and, in some cases mutilated, the new settlers, their wives and families. One family in the centre of the valley were overpowered and their tongues cut out. The husband was a school teacher and the fear that he would be able to write the names of his attackers prompted the cutting off of his hands. This man lived to write the names of the men he knew . . . with a pen between his toes and several of them were hanged from the shafts of a cart. Such methods broke the efforts to plant the area and in my day the mountain districts stretching in Southern Armagh from Newry to Cross-maglen near the Monaghan border contained a concentrated area composed of the old Gaelic people unmixed with foreign blood.[46]

Orangism, combined with the industrial revolution, meant that the province emerged into the Home Rule era with a red-bricked, Mancunian capital, Belfast, and a surrounding countryside that looked like the Scottish lowlands, peopled by a hard-working, hard-fighting breed who took their Presbyterianism from the narrower versions of the covenanting tradition and kept their powder as dry as their pawky sense of humour. In the cities the landscape of the mind had been equally blood-drenched. In Derry by the hardship of the defenders before the eventual triumph of the Williamites in the siege. In Belfast by the several outbreaks of ferocious communal rioting that marked the scramble of Catholic and Protestant workers for the crumbs, the jobs, which fell from the tables of the rich millowners and shipbuilders. The fortunes of the latter grew as their workers combined against each other rather than their employers in outbursts of sectarian passion that restricted growth in either trade unions or wages, but not in profits.

Thus it was against a lowering orange-hued background of bigotry, pogrom and privilege that Gladstone set about introducing the first Home Rule Bill. He was moved by a combination of genuine conviction that the Irish question should be settled and by the fact that he was dependent on the Irish vote at Westminster to remain in power. Churchill shared neither compulsion. He told a friend, 'I had decided some time ago that if the GOM went for home rule, the Orange Card would be the one to play. Please God it may turn out the ace of trumps and not the two.'[47] It was an ace, for the Tories. Churchill played his hand with duplicitous finesse, winning over a great audience of

Unionists at the Ulster Hall in Belfast where he began his campaign by revealing to them that he had had an ancestor who had been a General on the side of William of Orange – but not that he had also served under James II. He coined the slogan 'Ulster will fight and Ulster will be right.'[48] As another Randolph Churchill, his grandson, observed many years later, 'that pithy phrase contains the reason Ulster is part of the United Kingdom today.' More immediately it also contained the reason why Gladstone was driven from office on the Home Rule issue.

The second Home Rule attempt also went down before the same combination of Ulster Unionist obduracy and high placed Tory incitement to extra-parliamentary resistance. In 1893 as the Unionists prepared for fresh battle with Gladstone, once more in office and espousing Home Rule as the price for Irish nationalist parliamentary support, the exhortations came from the Prime Minister himself, Lord Salisbury.[49]

A third significant delivery of highly charged, highly placed, Tory rhetoric took place in 1912 at an event described as 'the wedding of Protestant Ulster with the Conservative and Unionist party'. It was to prove a blood wedding, though the occasion itself passed off peacefully, impressively. More than 100,000 people, including a platform party that included some seventy English, Scottish and Welsh MPs, gathered at Belfast's Balmoral show grounds under 'the largest Union Jack ever woven' to hear Bonar Law, the Conservative leader, warn them, in imagery drawn from the siege of Derry, against Asquith's Home Rule proposals:

Once more you hold the pass, the pass for the Empire. You are a besieged city. The timid have left you; your Lundys have betrayed you; but you have closed your gates. The Government have erected by their Parliamentary Act a boom against you to shut you off from the help of the British people. You will burst that boom. That help will come, and when the crisis is over men will say to you in words not unlike those used by Pitt – you have saved yourselves by your exertions, and you will save the Empire by your example.[50]

Bonar Law's Balmoral speech brings us to the third factor in the triad of misfortunes that continue to disrupt Anglo-Irish relationships in our day. For the unionist 'marriage' oratory with its evocation of a combination of what we know in our time as the 'Falklands spirit', references such as 'the pass for the Empire', and the menacing exhortation to Unionists to prepare for 'exertions' confirmed the belief of Michael Collins and those who thought like him that democracy as practised from Westminster was a sham. No matter what the ballot box said in Ireland, in London its findings would always be ignored by the politicians. Certainly he had historical precedent for this belief. Apart from the Home Rule controversies mentioned above, nationalist and Catholic Ireland had been trying unsuccessfully since the days of O'Connell to undo the Union by parliamentary methods. But the particular tragedy of the Home Rule controversies for constitutional nationalists was that they provided conclusive proof that although in successive elections Ireland as a whole voted for Home Rule, and sent sufficient MPs to London to get it for them, such democratic majorities did not count at Westminster where the Irish were submerged, as the Act of Union intended them to be, into a one-to-five minority of the total membership. Even though over the period of Home Rule agitation the percentage of pro-Home Rule Irish MPs did not materially change from the first result in 1886, of eighty-six for to seventeen opposed, in the end the rule of law would always come down to Bonar Law, or someone like him.

Sterner methods were called for. These would result in the destruction of the Irish Parliamentary Party, destruction most ungratefully hailed by Frank O'Connor in words which Collins nevertheless would certainly have applauded: 'The Parliamentary Party, heavy with sleep and sin, simply disappeared; rarely has any democratic country known such a sweeping up of reactionaries.'[51] A harsh, unjust judgement, but as George III once observed, 'If you want to baste an Irishman you can easily get an Irishman to turn the spit.'[52] The hand that turned the third Home Rule Bill on the spit, even more fervently than did Law, was that of an Irishman, the Dublin-born lawyer Edward Carson. It was he who first read the terms of the Ulster Covenant, based on the old Scottish Covenant, to the world on the steps of Craigavon, the mansion on the outskirts of Belfast owned by James Craig, the millionaire inheritor of a whiskey fortune who would one day lead Ulster in Carson's stead. The Covenant contained the following:

Being convinced in our consciences that home rule would be disastrous to the material well-being of Ulster as well as the whole of Ireland, subversive of our civil and religious freedom, destructive of our citzenship, and perilous to the unity of the empire, we . . . loyal subjects of His Gracious Majesty King George V . . . do hereby pledge ourselves in solemn covenant . . . to stand by one another in defending for ourselves and our children our cherished position of equal citzenship in the United Kingdom, and in using all means which may be found necessary to defeat the present conspiracy to set up a home rule parliament in Ireland . . . and mutually pledge ourselves to refuse to recognise its authority.[53]

By now, on their third assault against Home Rule, the Unionists were so well organised that they were eventually able to collect 471,414 signatures to this document in and outside Ulster, chiefly in. And behind the signatures there stood various groupings of some 90,000 men, soon to be reorganised and formed into the Ulster Volunteer Force (UVF). Carson was the leader of a formidable movement. He had come to prominence as part of the process known as 'killing Home Rule by kindness'. A carrot-and-stick method of attempting to pacify the country by resolving the land crisis – by a benign approach that ultimately resulted in the Wyndham Land Act – and at the same time employing coercion to damp down extremism in the pursuit of either land or political objectives. The stick was never more assiduously wielded than in the combination of Arthur Balfour as Chief Secretary of Ireland and Edward Carson as his crown prosecutor. As Balfour told his niece afterwards:

I made Carson and he made me. I've told you how no one had courage. Everyone right up to the top was trembling. Some of the RMs were splendid, but on the whole it was an impossible state of affairs. Carson had nerve, however. I sent him all over the place, getting convictions, we worked together.[54]

Not everyone thought so highly of Carson. When he prosecuted William O'Brien for Plan of Campaign activities in 1887, three years before Collins was born, in Mitchelstown, County Cork, police shot and killed a number of stone-throwers in an episode often recalled around the Collins fireside. At the hearing O'Brien's defence counsel told Carson: 'You are low, mean and contemptible, venal and corrupt. You think by this display you will get some position from the Tory Government, for whom you are doing this job.'[55] Carson certainly did attain 'some position', becoming one of the top earners at the English Bar, a Unionist MP for Trinity, and a member of the British wartime Coalition Cabinet. More importantly, where Ireland was concerned, he also became leader of the Unionists in their coalition with the Tories in pre-war resistance to Home Rule. Fears that that resistance might get to the point of civil war were heightened by what Asquith termed 'reckless rodomontade' at a huge demonstration at Blenheim Palace on 24 July 1912 where Bonar Law spelled out where he and his party stood in relation to opposition to Home Rule and the Liberals and support for the Unionists:

We regard the government as a revolutionary committee which has seized upon despotic power by fraud. In our opposition to them we shall not be guided by the considerations or bound by the restraints which would influence us in an ordinary constitutional struggle . . . I can imagine no length of resistance to which Ulster can go in which I should not be prepared to support them, and in which, in my belief, they would not be supported by the overwhelming majority of the British people.[56]

Law was moved by a number of considerations such as the fact that his party had been out of office for several years, and that Ulster seemed to offer a means of getting back in again. There was also his Scots-Canadian, Presbyterian ancestry and his own experience of Ulster, based on his memories of his father's time there as a minister, and the hospitality bestowed on him by his political hostess Lady

Londonderry. After his Blenheim 'rhodomontade', Irish nationalists were further embittered, but not surprised, when the 'Curragh Incident' of March 1914 seemed to indicate that that 'overwhelming majority' included the British Army. A group of officers stationed at the Curragh in County Kildare, the Army's major centre in Ireland, made known their reluctance to proceed against their fellow Conservatives, the Ulster anti-Home Rulers. The 'mutiny' ended not with courts martial but with the return in triumph to Ireland from the War Office of the officers' spokesman, Brigadier-General H. P. Gough, with a document drafted by a man whom Michael Collins later had shot, the Director of Military Operations, General (later Field Marshal) Sir Henry Wilson. It ended, in Gough's own handwriting: 'I understand the reading of the last paragraph to be that that the troops under our command will not be called upon to enforce the present Home Rule Bill on Ulster, and that we can so assure our officers.'[57] The usefulness of this document to the Unionists was underscored a month later when under the eyes of police and customs officials the Ulstermen, in flagrant defiance of the law, ran in three hundred tons of rifles to the province from Germany.[58] The Ulster Unionists now had a strong Ulster Volunteer Force (UVF), guns to put in their hands, and the support or more probably the acquiescence, of every property-owning or decision-taking Protestant of consequence in the province. In England, apart from Law and his party rank and file, they drew aid and comfort from figures of the eminence of Lord Milner, Waldorf Astor, Lord Rothschild, Lord Iveagh and the Duke of Bedford, Sir Edward Elgar and Rudyard Kipling.

War brought down the curtain on this particular phase of the Home Rule saga. Asquith was able to introduce Home Rule to law on 18 September 1914 and to accompany this step with an Amending Bill to suspend its operation until after the war. By this time partition had been added to the nomenclature of the debate, Law having suggested exclusion of the six north-eastern counties of Antrim, Armagh, Tyrone, Down, Fermanagh and Tyrone at an all-party conference convened by the King at Buckingham Palace on 21 July.[59] John Redmond was bitterly opposed to this and would only advocate the county option in which the wishes of the nationalists could be considered. Knowing the Liberals, and some Tories, favoured the county option, Carson adroitly avoided criticism on grounds of obduracy by arguing that the greater the number of Catholics included, the greater would be the pressure for ultimate unification – and he held out for all nine counties of Ulster.

Watching the drama unfold from Dublin the prophet of Irish nationalism, Padraig Pearse 1879–1916 had once declared, 'Personally I think the Orangeman with the rifle is a much less ridiculous figure than the Nationalist without a rifle.'[60] Pearse was a distinguished educationalist, who had founded his own school, St Enda's, to impart a distinctively Irish system of education. He wrote with equal facility in both Irish and English. The son of an Irish mother and an English father, he qualified as a barrister but, unlike Carson, devoted his oratorical gifts to the IRB rather than the Bar and the Unionist cause. There were many who agreed with him, particularly in the ranks of the [Irish] Volunteers formed by a professor of Gaelic, Eoin MacNeill, at a meeting in the Rotunda in Parnell Square, Dublin, on 25 November 1913, with the intention of defending Home Rule should force be used against it.

Five months later to the day, 25 April 1914, Michael Collins was enrolled[61] into the No. 1 Company of the London Volunteers by his cousin, Sean Hurley. Thereafter the pair, with another friend, Padraic O'Conaire, the Gaelic writer, would drill each week in the German gymnasium at King's Cross, using hired, sawn-off Martini-Henry rifles, while they put aside weekly contributions against the day when rifles of their own would become available.

Unknown to MacNeill, the Volunteers were infiltrated[62] and largely controlled by the IRB from the time of their inception. They were intent not on defence, but offence, and were in touch with the American wing of the Brotherhood, Clan na nGael, from whom money was sent, through the Clan leader, John Devoy, an associate of O'Donovan Rossa's, to help fund an uprising.[63] At the same time the Wolfe Tone/J. B. Armour/Parnell strain of Irish Protestantism that had traditionally allied itself to Catholic claims for independence and civil rights began to assert itself. The month before the Volunteers' formation at the Rotunda a meeting of Protestants opposed to Carson's activities was held, appropriately enough, in J. B. Armour's town of Ballymoney. Those present included a hero of the relief of Ladysmith, Captain Jack White, who had already helped the workers of Dublin to drill in the Irish Citizen Army.

Another celebrated figure was Roger Casement, who as a member of the British Consular Service had earned a knighthood and world-wide fame for his courage and humanity in exposing the Belgians' ill-treatment of their colonial subjects in the Belgian Congo and Putumayo. By 1914 he had increasingingly espoused the Irish cause and was well-known as a writer and publicist in the Nationalist interest. The attendance included the historian Alice Stopford Greene and Mary Spring-Rice, a daughter of Lord Monteagle. Following the Ballymoney meeting, a Committee, which included the three last-named, was set up in London to arrange for the purchase and shipment of arms to the Irish Volunteers.

In Washington, Devoy was heavily involved with Count Von Bernstorff, the German Ambassador who, like most foreign observers, regarded the Home Rule crisis as a potentially priceless sapping of Great Britain's strength in the event of war. And so, in July 1914, a week before the Great War did break out, Erskine Childers, an Englishman, with Mary Spring-Rice amongst his crew, sailed his yacht, the *Asgard*, into Howth Harbour and history with a cargo of German rifles aboard. The difference in the authorities' view of those who ran 35,000 rifles into Ulster to oppose Home Rule and those who smuggled 1,500 into Dublin in support of it was underscored on the evening of the landing when troops fired on a Dublin crowd and killed three people. Three more arguments in favour of the revolutionaries and against those who favoured 'due process'.

Was Collins present at the gun-running? That question helped to start me thinking of writing this book. I was prevented from attending the State funeral for Childers' son, also called Erskine, who had become President of Ireland, by the need to attend the funeral of a colleague of my own which took place near Howth, and afterwards went for a walk around the harbour. Here I met two old men who had spent the morning watching the planes fly overhead bringing in foreign dignitaries for the President's funeral. 'You know,' said one of them, 'I was here the day his father sailed in the guns. Michael Collins put me up on his shoulder so as I could see.' I had never heard that Collins had taken part in the gun-running and was disposed to argue with him. It must have been someone else. 'No. I knew him well,' the old man said. 'He used to stay up there sometimes with some of the lads. There was a house up there,' he said, gesticulating, 'and there was good-looking girls living in it. The lads used to be after them. He was a fine-looking fellow himself, God rest him.'

Subsequently I read all the accounts of the gun-running I could find, but came across no mention of Collins. I realised that this in itself proved nothing one way or the other, as despite his 'Big Fellow', swash-buckling, side Collins could shun publicity when he wanted to, and working in England, involved with the IRB, this might have been such an occasion. At all events my interest in Collins eventually led to this book and during my research I came across Susan Killeen. She lived around this time at 1 Island View, Howth, lodging with a Mrs Quick along with a number of other girls whom Collins frequently enquired after in his letters to Susan. The letters also contain references to Howth and his yearnings to be there.

He may have also had yearnings to be somewhere else. It is established that Collins was in direct contact with John Devoy after the 1916 Rising. But there could have been either direct or indirect contact before that. Biographers speak of Collins after the outbreak of war, and before returning to Ireland, walking the docklands of London, looking at the ships and wondering if he should go to America and make a new life away from the calls of Ireland and possibly conscription. At this stage Devoy and the German Embassy in Washington had arranged that Sir Roger Casement should go to Germany, both to get arms and to try to enlist Irish prisoners of war in an Irish Brigade which would fight the British in Ireland. It is a matter of speculation as to how different subsequent Irish history might have been had Casement succeeded in his mission. In the event the arms didn't get in, the Brigade idea failed also and Casement was captured and hanged in 1916. The following telegram was sent from the German Embassy in Washington to the Foreign Office, Berlin. It is dated 1 September 1914 and reads: 'An Irish priest (sic) named Michael Collins and Sir Roger Casement are going to Germany in order to visit the Irish prisoners.'[64]

That '(sic)' is revealing. Whoever that 'priest' was intended to be it is not unreasonable to assume that (a) he did not take holy orders and (b) may have spoken with a rich West Cork accent. In fact Casement took with him a Norwegian sailor called Christiansen, and Collins never got to Germany. He gave in his notice to the Guaranty Trust Company, saying that he was going 'to join up', for which he received an extra week's pay which he donated to the Brotherhood, and on the following day, 15 January 1916, he crossed to Ireland. The IRB had put an end to his uncertainties by telling him that a rising was definitely planned.

When he told Hannie that he was going back to Dublin to join his friends in the coming fray she was aghast. 'They'll let you down Michael. They'll let you down',[65] she told him prophetically. But Collins was impervious to entreaty. The gospel of historical continuity had ruled that it was time for a pike, a pike . . . and so, with a toss of his head and a jut to his jaw, to Dublin he went.

2

Easter 1916

'No man has a right to fix the boundary
to the march of a nation.'

Charles Stewart Parnell

Collins was now twenty-six. Such reputation as he had was largely based amongst the London Irish. His enemies saw a bossy, hot-tempered character given to outbursts of fury and intolerance, his friends, a generous, outgoing man capable of great kindness, interested in the affairs of the day, particularly anything to do with Ireland.

A good athlete, of lithe movement and sudden gesture, he was an attractive but not remarkable figure. Of his life and struggles in London, P. S. O'Hegarty wrote: '. . . there was very little of the Mick Collins of those days to give promise of the man who was to come'. Yet O'Hegarty noted:

he was always on the right side in the many battles, on the many platforms, in which Sinn Fein fought. In its own organisation, in the Gaelic League, in the Gaelic Athletic Association, and finally in the Irish Volunteers . . . He was well-read in modern literature and drama and keen to talk about them, and in the great years of the Court Theatre, and in the weeks when the Manchester Repertory Company came to the Coronet, you would find him constantly in the gallery. He was growing and deepening in those years in body and mind, reaching out . . . towards every quickening and ennobling thing in life.[1]

Collins was well enough thought of within the IRB to be kept fairly near to the centre of the action. His first job in Dublin was, as he described it, 'financial advisor' to Count Plunkett for three days a week. The job brought him £1 a week and his lunch at the Plunkett home at Larkfield, Kimmage. It also brought him into touch with 'the refugees', the group of Irish camping at Larkfield, who like himself had come over to Dublin to get away from conscription and to take part in the rumoured uprising. At least one member of the Plunkett family obviously had more in mind for Collins than the family book-keeping. This was Joseph Plunkett, the tubercular poet and an organiser of the 1916 Rising, who was literally to lean on Collins' shoulder when the fighting started. It was he who lent Collins the book that was to colour his whole approach to the subsequent Anglo-Irish War, Chesterton's *The Man Who Was Thursday*, in which the head anarchist makes the point, 'If you don't seem to be hiding, nobody hunts you out.' Collins also found another job to augment his income from the Plunketts, with the accountancy firm of Craig Gardiner and Co., Dawson St, and after an interlude staying with relatives got himself lodgings at 16 Rathdown Road.

During this short spell in Dublin Collins became a member of the Keating Branch of the Gaelic League. It would be difficult to overstress the importance of the Irish language to Collins. It was bound up in his mind with the necessity of shaking off the colonial shackles and of creating a distinctively Irish mode of thought and self-development. He deemed the formation of the Gaelic League to revive the Irish language and culture, in 1893, as the most important event of 'not only the nineteenth century, but in the whole history of our nation'. He later studied the language intensively and began signing his name, in its Irish form, Miceal O'Coileain, expecting others, including his fiancée, to address him that way. The heritage of the Clan O'Coileain he descended from was a very real thing to him.

Cultural and economic well-being had a correlation, in a distinctively Sinn Fein, 'we ourselves' context which he would sum up as follows:

Millionaires can spend their surplus wealth bestowing libraries broadcast upon the world. But who will say that the benefits accruing could be compared with those arising from a condition of things in which the people themselves . . . were prosperous enough to buy their own books and to put together their own local libraries in which they could take a personal interest and acquire knowledge in proportion to that interest?[2]

In the Gaelic League, he associated with men who, apart from becoming leaders in the struggles that lay ahead, were to become his closest allies and bitterest enemies. These included Richard Mulcahy, Gearoid O'Sullivan, Cathal Brugha and Rory O'Connor. Mulcahy, known as 'the tic tac man' from his habit of tracing invisible patterns in the air with his fingers as he spoke, was a slim, blue-eyed aesthetic figure, who gave up his medical studies at University College Dublin to become a full-time revolutionary. He would eventually became Chief of Staff of the IRA, working closely with Collins and succeeding him as Commander-in-Chief of the Irish Army. O'Sullivan, a cousin of Collins', was a fellow Corkman. In a very real sense he hoisted the flag of rebellion over Dublin, because, being the youngest officer in the General Post Office which became the rebels' HQ in the Rising, he was given the honour of raising the tricolour over the GPO. He would later be one of Collins' closest allies in his role of Adjutant General of the IRA. Cathal Brugha, whom Mulcahy described as being 'as brave and as brainless as a bull', grew to hate Collins in a feud that was to be a causal factor in creating civil war.[3] The director of a firm of church candle-makers, he was also President of the Keating Branch.

His enthusiasm for the Irish language led him to change his name to Cathal Brugha from its English form, Charles Burgess. O'Connor, who had been working as engineer in Canada had, like Collins, returned to Dublin to take part in the Rising. He and Collins were close friends during the Anglo-Irish war, in which O'Connor became Director of Engineering and for a time Director of Operations in England, but were destined to die on opposite sides in the subsequent civil war.

Rory O'Connor said of Collins at this period: 'There was no one at Kimmage to equal him.' O'Connor at that stage was assisting the refugees' chief instructor in bomb-making, Dr Thomas Dillon. Collins is remembered as getting materials for the devices but, characteristically, along with iron washers and such-like, he is also recalled for supplying secondhand clothes to the more impoverished Volunteers.[4] Two other figures with whom Collins would not have time to establish a lasting relationship, but whom he admired greatly, were Sean MacDiarmada and Tom Clarke. MacDiarmada, a man with a light, pleasing personality, had travelled all over the country, sometimes on foot or on bicycle despite the fact that an attack of polio had left him practically a cripple. Clarke was the movement's link with the Fenians, an old dynamiter who had somehow kept his sanity through penal servitude in England, made his way to America, and then returned to Dublin to set up a little shop in the ironically named Great Britain St, which dispensed tobacco and revolutionary doctrines that struck more deadly sparks than any of his matches. Collins, with his equal regard for age and for Fenianism, revered Clarke in particular.

The economic conditions of the Dublin of the day mirrored the indifference of London to political initiative. Appalling slums, high infant mortality and unemployment[5] had driven workers to militant, but unsuccessful, trade union activity in what became known as the great Dublin lock-out of 1913. The workers were defeated and one of their two principal leaders, James Larkin, left for America. The other, James Connolly, remained at the head of the tiny Citizen Army formed to protect the workers from police brutality during 1913. Connolly had come to believe that social amelioration could only come in the wake of political independence. The IRB shared this view but feared that his war-like manoeuvrings would bring the British down on them before they were ready to strike.[6] Accordingly he was co-opted into the Brotherhood's inner circle and took part in the planning of the proposed rebellion. Thus separatism and socialism forged a hard cutting edge to their grievances. But it was still only a very small blade.

John E. Redmond had forced a measure of control on the original Volunteer force formed at the Rotunda in response to the Carsonites. However, on 20 September 1914, after the outbreak of war, he made a recruiting speech at Woodenbridge in County Wicklow and the Volunteers split, leaving Redmond with the larger section, under the name of National Volunteers, and the IRB with the re-christened smaller, but more militant, Irish Volunteers, which Collins supported. At a Volunteer meeting in the St George's Hall in Southwark, a speaker proposed a Redmondite Man of Prudence for office with the recommendation, 'I'd go to hell and back with him.' Collins called out from the back of the hall, 'Don't mind about the return half of the ticket.'[7]

Redmond spoke both believing in the cause Britain said it was fighting the war for, the rights of small nations, and hoping that his own particular small nation would benefit at war's end through having shown loyalty to the Empire. But as Easter 1916 approached Redmond was coming to acknowledge, as the physical force school had traditionally claimed, that in Anglo-Irish affairs altruism on the part of an Irish nationalist leader was the sword of self-immolation.[8] The Orangemen, 'the Kaiser's Irish friends', who had but lately been threatening to take up arms against the British, had been rewarded by being allowed to form their own regiments but Nationalists, including Redmond's son, were refused commissions. Kitchener personally vetoed a scheme which envisaged using the Volunteers for coastal defence.[9] He had a particular animus against Irish nationalists, and ordered that a green banner emblazoned with a harp, designed by patriotic ladies for an Irish regiment that never materialised, be taken away, but that a similar banner adorned by the Red Hand of Ulster be proudly displayed. Lloyd George reckoned that this 'sinister order constituted the first word in a new chapter of Irish history'.[10] The relationship of Redmond to the Irish Parliamentary Party is symbolised today by the positioning of his bust at Westminster: he is recognised in bronze – but stands outside the Members' Bar.

A threat of enforced conscription hung over Ireland with Carson and Bonar Law in the Cabinet and Redmond out of it. Redmond and his long-term colleague, John Dillon, became estranged and the drift in his influence was such that the Chief Secretary for Ireland, Augustine Birrell[11], feared that Home Rule had been finished by the elevation of Carson to the Cabinet. 'Ireland', said the Chief Secretary, 'is in a rotten state – ripe for a row, without leadership'.

Though he lacked details Birrell was completely correct in the substance of his judgement. Ireland was 'ripe for a row'. The minority within the IRB had been in contact with the Germans through John Devoy in New York. Joseph Plunkett was received at the Foreign Office by Von Bethmann Holweig early in 1915 and it was arranged that a shipload of arms and ammunition would be sent to Ireland the following spring. An Irish uprising timed to coincide with a German offensive on the Western Front would benefit the Germans. The Devoy–Plunkett faction within the IRB then formed a Military Council some time in June 1915 to further these plans. The Council came to consist of Pearse, Plunkett, Eamonn Ceannt, a Gaelic Leaguer and traditional musician, Tom Clarke and Sean MacDiarmada. Connolly was added in January 1916 and Thomas MacDonagh in April of that year, only a few days before the date planned for the Rising, Easter Sunday. He too had seemingly been kept in ignorance of the Council's aims and existence until that time even though he was a close friend of Pearse's and taught with him in St Enda's, the Irish-Ireland school founded and run by Pearse at Rathfarnham, County Dublin. The secrecy paid off almost to the end insofar as the two major sources of expected opposition were concerned. One was Dublin Castle, the centre and symbol of British rule in Ireland, the other Eoin MacNeill and those who thought like him in the Volunteers. The MacNeillites believed that the corps should remain in being only to help prevent any attempt to frustrate Home Rule's introduction at the end of the war.

These included ironically enough a man without whom there would have been no IRB, Bulmer Hobson, who with Dinny McCullough had founded the Dungannon Clubs in Belfast and used the Clubs to revive the Brotherhood which was at the time practically moribund. It was Hobson and McCullough[12] who with P. S. O'Hegarty had co-opted Tom Clarke onto the Supreme Council of the IRB and appointed Sean MacDiarmada as full-time organiser, on a salary of thirty shillings a week. Now Clarke and MacDiarmada arranged that Hobson should be kidnapped lest he get word of their plans to MacNeill. A third source however dealt their plans a near fatal blow. Captain Hall's celebrated cypher centre, Room 40 at the Admiralty in London, had both intercepted and decoded the transmissions between Devoy/Bernsdorff and Berlin. As a result the German ship bringing the arms was intercepted off the Kerry coast on Good Friday and subsequently scuttled by her captain. Roger Casement got ashore from a U-boat in a half-drowned condition and was captured. The arms seizure clearly signalled that the Rising had lost whatever chance of success it might have had. In addition MacNeill learned of the Council's plans and, horror-struck at the duplicity and projected loss of life, sent officers round the country countermanding all Volunteer activities for the weekend, placing an advertisement to this effect in the *Sunday Independent* also. But the plotters decided to go ahead nevertheless. They had two reasons for proceeding. First, they reckoned that if they did not strike now it would soon be impossible because the Castle had to be on the verge of a round-up. Secondly, they believed a protest in arms was necessary because the general sense of nationality had sunk so low as to require a blood sacrifice to revive it. They expected to fail, and to pay for the failure with their lives, but they felt it was their historical duty to continue in the footsteps of Wolfe Tone and the tradition of a rising in every generation. And so on Easter Monday, 24 April 1916, the hopeless uprising began.

Nancy O'Brien must have been extraordinarily well-trusted by Michael, because he met her with MacDiarmada during Holy Week[13] and both he and MacDiarmada openly discussed the prospects of the coming rising with her in a Dublin cafe. They also met on Holy Saturday and shook hands on O'Connell Bridge. Nancy would normally have gone home to Sam's Cross for the Easter break, but made an excuse to Collins for not going, claiming that she was supposed to be at the Post Office the following Tuesday. With his usual instinct for trying to joke his way out of a serious moment Collins replied laughingly, 'Ah you'll have longer than that.' Nancy did have longer, an agonised week longer, much of which she spent on Howth Head watching the flames grow over Dublin. But Collins was afterwards remembered by friends who met him that day as being 'jocular and fooling about as usual'.[14]

But on the Monday morning he was sombre and tense. The accountancy side of his nature that dealt in practicalities was at war with the high heroic side that gloried in following in the footsteps of Rossa. On Good Friday he had dispatched Colm O'Lochlainn to Kerry as part of the German arms plot. Apart from its miscarrying, three of the five members of O'Lochlainn's party were drowned and Collins had a shrewd suspicion that these would be far from being the last of the casualties involved in the course he was following. At the Metropole Hotel he found he could well have been amongst the first of them.

Plunkett's throat had been operated on for tuberculosis in Switzerland and during Good Friday Collins had to transfer him to the Metropole so that he would be within easy reach of the GPO on the morning of the insurrection. In his room Plunkett warned Collins and another aide-de-camp, Commandant Brennan Whitmore, that they might be stopped on their way out of the hotel by a small dark-haired man. He gave Collins the key to a trunk in which there were three automatics which were to be used in the event of this happening. At the foot of the stairs they found the dark-haired man waiting. The lobby of the hotel was full of British officers preparing to depart for Fairyhouse Races. Hands closed on the pocketed automatics. But the dark-haired one offered them nothing beyond a greeting: 'Good-day to you gentlemen'.[15] Perhaps he belonged to that not inconsiderable body of British opinion which believed that insurrections do not happen after midday.

Collins was present at the final colloquy which had guaranteed that this one would. It took place in a shabby room at Liberty Hall, headquarters of the Irish Transport and General Workers' Union, between Connolly, Pearse and Plunkett. After it these three lined up at the head of their men outside Liberty Hall. Just before twelve o'clock, with Collins, one of the few to possess one, resplendent in his Volunteer's uniform, a couple of paces behind his leader, the thin, ragged column marched towards destiny. Much of their weaponry accompanied them in a handcart – obsolete German rifles (landed at Howth), shotguns, revolvers. The original plans for the rebellion, drawn up mainly by Connolly and Plunkett, called for risings at various centres throughout the country. But apart from some sieges and ambushes in north County Dublin, and Counties Galway, Wexford, Meath and Cork, fighting was confined to Dublin city around the centres which the divided and weakened rebels could hold. These formed a ring around the heart of Dublin.

Despite the splits and the setbacks they might have captured Dublin Castle because the citadel was practically undefended, though the spirit of Major Sirr had not entirely departed. The Permanant Under Secretary, Sir Matthew Nathan, and the Military Intelligence Officer, Major Ivor Price, were inside planning a widespread round-up of rebels, assisted in arranging the commandeering of telephone and telegraph facilities by the Secretary of the Post Office, Sir Arthur Hamilton Norway. But apart from some messengers and a few unarmed police that was all. The insurgents overcame the military guard at the gate and then withdrew, believing themselves too weak to do otherwise. One of the few places the Volunteers were to be found in any strength was in Norway's place of work, the General Post Office, which they took over a few minutes after he had left the building to go to the Castle to help deal with the threatened insurrection. The GPO, one of the handful of strong points which the Volunteers seized throughout the city, would be an inferno before the week was out. It was the rebels' headquarters.

That was where Padraig Pearse read the proclamation of the Republic to a bemused and, initially, amused Dublin crowd. The previous year he had delivered the oration over the grave of Collins' boyhood hero, O'Donovan Rossa. He spoke for Collins when he described Rossa's vision of Ireland: 'not free merely, but Gaelic as well: not Gaelic merely but free as well.' And he articulated the self-sacrificial philosophy of their revolution of plotters and poets when he finished the oration by declaring:

Life springs from death: and from the graves of patriot men and women spring living nations. The Defenders of this Realm have worked well in secret and in the open. They think they have pacified Ireland. They think that they have purchased half of us and intimidated the other half. They think they have foreseen everything; but the fools, the fools, the fools! – they have left us our Fenian dead, and while Ireland holds these graves, Ireland unfree shall never be at peace.[16]

By signing the proclamation Pearse guaranteed that his own grave would shortly be added to those of the Fenian dead. So did James Connolly, whose weaponry had been delivered to the GPO on a handcart. So did the other signatories. Plunkett, MacDonagh, MacDiarmada, Ceannt and Tom Clarke, given the honour of heading the list of signatories. ·

Apart from the GPO the rebels seized St Stephen's Green, Jacob's biscuit factory, the College of Surgeons, The Four Courts, the North and South Dublin Unions, Marrowbone Lane Distillery, Boland's Mill and outposts on Lower Mount St. However it's not the size of the dog in the fight that counts so much as the size of the fight in the dog. There may have been as many as 1,200 insurgents, including the Fianna, the IRB's militant counter-version of Baden-Powell's Boy Scouts. Though initially taken off-balance, the British, between forces in Dublin barracks and near to hand at the Curragh, were immediately able to call on some 6,000 officers and men. Later in the week reinforcements poured in from England and from Belfast, a source from which one notable gesture of assistance was refused. Carson, whose activities had done so much to the propel the lethal handcart across the cobblestones of Dublin, was not taken up on his offer of 50,000 UVF volunteers. The British, having co-operated with him in delaying the passage of Home Rule, now intended to be prompt and single-handed in dealing with the crisis that co-operation had produced.

Collins made a mark for himself as soon as he entered the GPO. He poured two tierces of stout down the drain[17] while making an observation (sanitised), to the effect that the rebels of 1798 had been condemned for drinking but that wouldn't happen to these Volunteers! He then took part in trussing up an English officer who had blundered into their midst to buy a stamp and reassured the man that he needn't worry, 'we don't shoot prisoners'. Most of his duties lay in the operations room where the leaders laid out maps and plans, the unreality of which were heightened as the week progressed by the glow cast on them by the ever-encircling fires. He sorted out a row involving the London Irish and Desmond Fitzgerald, his future Chief of Propaganda, over Fitzgerald's refusal to issue rations to the men because they hadn't chits! Fitzgerald later recorded how

Michael Collins . . . strode in one morning with some of his men who were covered with dust and had been demolishing walls and building barricades, and announced that these men were to be fed if it took the last food in the place. I did not attempt to argue with him, and the men sat down openly rejoicing that I had been crushed . . . But while they were eating, those of our most regular and assiduous customers who appeared at the door of the room were told to disappear quickly or they would be dealt with.[18]

Fitzgerald described Collins as 'the most active and efficient officer in the place'. He made an attempt to note the names and addresses of the combatants and generally speaking, his spirit and sense of humour held up throughout the week. When someone remarked to him, 'Terrible destruction, Mick,' he looked out over Dublin's rubble-strewn main street and replied, 'Don't worry, you old cod, we'll rebuild it, and the whole city, in ten years – if necessary.' And after a particularly furious fusillade he and Gearoid O'Sullivan went up to Pearse and asked would he mind if they popped out for a bit – they had a date with two girls they didn't like disappointing.

Later he would describe his feelings during the week to a friend in a stiff-upper-lip near-propagandist style that doesn't do him justice:

Although I was never actually scared in the GPO I was – and others also – witless enough to do the most stupid things. As the flames and heat increased so apparently did the shelling. Machine-gun fire made escape more or less impossible. Not that we wished to escape. No man wished to budge. In that building, the defiance of our men, and the gallantry, reached unimaginable proportions.[19]

Collins was no simpleton. He possessed more courage than ten, but he also had the crucifying gift we know as imagination. With his extraordinary facility for not only being able to see but to do there came the unnerving ability to foresee, to know the dangers involved. From the crucible of Easter Week there emerge two vivid descriptions of Collins and the man with whom his name is ever linked in comradeship and contest, Eamon de Valera, that paint both our Irish Danton and his Robespierre not in poster colours but in more human tints. They too had their agony in the garden.

De Valera was eight years older than Collins. He was born in New York on 14 October 1882, of a Spanish father and an Irish mother. The difference in the two men's characters is summarised in their early upbringing. Collins was doted on by his mother and sisters, secure and confident in his surroundings – so secure that he became cocky and wanted to be 'the Big Fellow' in all that was done. De Valera's mother wanted to have as little to do with him as possible. She had been left by his father not long after her son was born and she had him reared from infancy with her people in Limerick, while she remained in America and married again. Even when she had a new home and family she did not take him back and he seems to have preferred life in boarding school to life with his mother's relations.

A teacher of mathematics by profession, de Valera's interest in the Irish language had led him to join the Volunteers at the force's inception. During the Rising he commanded Boland's Mill, on the Grand Canal Basin in the eastern part of the city where the Grand Canal links up with the Liffey. The post also commanded a stretch of railway line running back into Dublin to Westland Row station and its outposts in Mount St dominated the main Dublin–Dun Laoghaire road. He also knew very well going into the fight that with the collapse of the German shipment the thing was a foredoomed failure.

The Easter after the rising de Valera was safely in prison but writing to his wife Sinead he relived his feelings during Easter 1916:

It is Easter Saturday and my mind naturally reverts to this and tomorrow's festival a year ago. How I thank God that you have not the agonies before you this year which I foresaw at the corresponding time last year. I could not tell you then the feelings that were rending my heart on your account. But sweetheart I know you will believe me – I know you will not think it was selfishness or callous indifference or senseless optimism that made me so calm when I was about to offer up you and the children as a sacrifice. If you could have seen my heart on that terrible day of anxiety for you, Easter Sunday, you would have known – when I called to see you and found that the strain had been too much for you, I only found what I had anticipated all the day long. Could you have seen me that night when I stooped over you to give you that parting kiss you would know that though I gave it lightly as if we were to meet again in the morning it was simply to save you, to give you some sixteen hours' respite; for in my heart I believed it was the last kiss I would give you on earth.[20]

Not surprisingly, de Valera didn't sleep very much either in the nights before or after the Rising's commencement. Strained, a tall, gangling figure with red socks, he ran around the rail line at night, having trenches dug and forgetting the password so that he nearly got shot. One of his men went mad and shot a comrade, being cut down himself in retaliation. A Volunteer wrote afterwards, 'You had a feeling that your comrades might go mad – or, what was even worse, that you might go mad yourself.'[21]

When one of his subordinates, Lt Fitzgerald, tried to make him sleep de Valera replied, 'I can't trust the men – they'll leave their posts or fall asleep if I don't watch them.' Only when Fitzgerald promised to sit beside him and wake him if anything happened did he lie down. Sleep hit him immediately, but turned to nightmare. He started to sweat and toss about and suddenly, 'His eyes wild, he sat bolt upright and in an awful voice, bawled, "Set fire to the railway! Set fire to the railway!" '

He insisted that papers dipped in whiskey be used to set fire to waiting rooms and rolling stock but another officer, Captain John McMahon, 'eventually persuaded de Valera to listen to reason and the fires were put out. De Valera quickly recovered his composure.'[22]

One of the many remarkable examples of the loyalty extended to de Valera is the way his contemporaries consistently remained silent about his crack-up in 1916. Years later, when they were in Ballykinlar Internment Camp together, Captain Michael Cullen, one of those placed in charge of him at the time, approached a fellow prisoner, Dr Tom O'Higgins, and, warning him first that he would shoot him if he ever mentioned the story to anyone, told him what had happened and asked him for a medical opinion on de Valera's condition.[23] By then (1920) de Valera was publicly quarrelling with the Clan na nGael leader, John Devoy, in America, and Cullen was worried that he might again have lost his reason.

De Valera was responsible for one of the most talked-of episodes of the entire week. After the British had begun shelling his position he ordered that a green flag be placed at the top of an empty tower a few hundred yards from his command post. The ruse worked and fire concentrated on the old tower thereafter, not on the mill. Subsequently there was controversy as to who actually hoisted the flag. One authoritative account[24] says that de Valera ordered Captain Michael Cullen and three volunteers to carry out the hoisting. But his own official biography states that he tied the flag to a pike and placed it in a corner of the tower himself. Whatever is the truth about this and whoever tied the flag, after the Rising the episode burnished a reputation already glittering by virtue of another circumstance, the fact that it was at a position some distance from Boland's Mill but occupied by Volunteers under his command that the 'Irish Thermopylae' occurred: No. 25 Northumberland Rd.

Here Captain Michael Malone and his men inflicted the heaviest casualties of the week on the British troops whose officers continuously urged them up an open road under his Mauser. Malone was shot by a trigger-happy soldier after the ceasefire and his automatic eventually passed into de Valera's possession. He kept it all his life, as well he might. In a very real sense de Valera's power grew out of the barrel of that gun. The fact that de Valera's was an isolated post, the last to act on Pearse's order to call a ceasefire, meant that though condemned to death, he was not included with the first batch of prisoners to be executed. The respite gave his mother time to produce evidence of his American citizenship and so have his sentence commuted to imprisonment from which he emerged a hero, the last Commandant to surrender during Easter Week.

The gunboat *Helga* came up the Liffey and its shelling, combined with sustained machine-gun and rifle fire, had Sackville Street in flames by Friday, the GPO being the epicentre of the holocaust. It had to be evacuated, first by tunnelling through shops alongside and then by making a dash across the bullet-swept street into Moore St and the temporary shelter of more tunnelled shops. Revolver in hand, his britches singed by burning debris, Collins led his men across, shouting encouragement at them. They got as far as No. 16, a grocery shop, but could go no further. Troops had the area sealed off. The London Irish had decided not to surrender but rather than be conscripted, and probably killed, for England, to fight to the end in Dublin. Collins knew that whatever slim chance of survival the leaders now had, protracted hostilities would guarantee their deaths. He tried to talk the Londoners out of fighting, one of the few occasions in his life when he ever argued such a course. Failing to move them he then went for MacDiarmada who for the last time exercised his extraordinary power of leadership. All he said was, 'We'll die. You'll escape. No one will try to conscript you.'[25] But the desperate London Irish laid down their arms. Though Collins had begun the revolution by pouring away porter he ended it with whiskey. Somehow he had managed to lay hands on a bottle and it helped to ease the misery of the last hours before surrender for himself and two friends, Fionan Lynch, who would one day serve in an Irish Government with Collins, and Jim Ryan, a young doctor from Wexford who had acted as medical officer to the Volunteers in the GPO. Thoughts of forming a government were far from the minds of the three men as the last action in the fight neared. Collins presented a brooding figure. Desmond Ryan, Pearse's literary executor, who fought alongside both of them in the GPO, drew this picture of him:

Michael Collins sat in a corner, a look of horror in his eyes, a pallor spreading over his face. Disjointed words told Harding that O'Rahilly's eviscerated corpse and the riddled civilians on the blood-clogged cobbles had come to life in one man's imagination, straining his control to breaking point. Moans escaped him and he huddled into his corner at every far-away sound. Macken went swiftly to Michael Collins and spoke to him in cheerful undertones . . . Collins looked up, and back, stoical and impassive, with the rest of the doomed Volunteers, waiting for the end.[26]

Apart from the obvious reasons of defeat and surrender, there may have been another reason for Collins' depression in those last hours depicted by Ryan. One of those killed in the final, unsuccessful attempts to break through the encircling British barricades around the GPO was his best friend since boyhood days, Sean Hurley. Something of what the death of Hurley must have meant to Collins can be gleaned from an appraisal of his cousin which Collins gave in a letter to a friend:

He has the sharpness of wit to see my own particular mood. We think the same way in Irish matters. We have walked London's streets on many a night, silently, because our thinking was elsewhere . . . I appreciate him because his mind seems compact whereas mine fritters away hours in idle thought. At worst he is a boon companion, at best there is no one else I would have as a friend.[27]

Hurley would not be the last friend Collins was to lose along the path to freedom. Many more such deaths lay in the future.

At 4 pm on Saturday 9 April there was a ceasefire and Pearse issued an order declaring an unconditional surrender, 'in order to prevent the further slaughter of Dublin citizens, and in the hope of saving the lives of our followers now surrounded and hopelessly outnumbered.'

After the surrender took effect the Volunteers were marched down O'Connell St, between rows of troops with fixed bayonets to Parnell Square, Collins remarking as he marched off with a backwards look at the GPO, 'Well at least the flag's still flying.'[28] At that moment there wasn't much else to take comfort from. Parnell had tried to restore Home Rule. He had failed. His statue now stood at the bottom of the square, inscribed 'No man has the right to set a boundary to the onward march of a nation.' At that moment in 1916 it would have been hard to know which was the more appropriate piece of symbolism, the fact that Parnell was pointing towards the Rotunda maternity hospital, or the fact that he had his back turned on the prisoners. Part of the Rotunda complex had been the scene of the formation of the Volunteers Collins had fought with. They had failed. Tom Clarke's little shop fifty yards from where they now huddled in the open was being used as a British operations centre. Overlooking the Square was Vaughan's Hotel. One day Collins would use it as an operations centre. But such a thought was far from his mind at that point. He was more concerned with the treatment that some of the prisoners, in particular Tom Clarke, were receiving from the officer in charge, a Captain Lee-Wilson.[29]

There had been some atrocities on the part of the British troops during the fighting. Fifteen innocent civilians were deliberately killed around the King Street area, and one officer, Captain Bowen Colthurst,[30] shot six people in cold blood, including the pacifist, Sheehy-Skeffington. But in general the troops behaved decently after the surrender. Looking at the Howth rifles and their bullets in awe rather than in anger, they talked of the wounds these had made. And the cheery word, and even the cup of tea, was not unknown, particularly when an Australian unit relieved the Royal Irish Rifles from Belfast. But Lee-Wilson, in classical bad apple fashion, lowered the tone considerably, ill-treating Collins amongst others when he found him trying to slip some malted milk tablets to a comrade.

Liam Tobin, then a slim twenty-two-year-old from Cork, apprenticed to the hardware trade, who would later develop an uncanny skill in intelligence-gathering, has left this account of his activities:

He wore a smoking cap with a fancy tassel hanging out of it. He kept walking round and round, stopping now and again to speak to his soldiers, saying, 'Whom do you consider worst, the Boches or the Sinn Feiners?' and of course they always answered that we were the worst. With the number of us lying in the small area of grass we were cramped for space, and it was damp and uncomfortable so that I got a bad cramp in my legs. As Lee-Wilson was passing, Piaras Beaslai, said to him, 'There's a young fellow here who is not well', explaining what was wrong and asking if I could stand up. Lee-Wilson said, 'No, let the so and so stay where he is.' Those of us who wanted to relieve ourselves had to do it on the grass lying alongside our comrades; we had to use the place where we lay.[31]

But what really enraged the prisoners was Lee-Wilson's practice of taking some of the prisoners, among them Clarke, to the steps of the Rotunda Hospital where he stripped them naked, apparently for the benefit of nurses looking out of the windows. Clarke suffered a good deal from an old wound to his elbow which made it difficult for him to bend his arm. However Lee-Wilson disregarded this and ripped off his jacket so that the wound opened. Tobin writes: 'I looked up at him and I vowed that I would deal with him some time in the future.' He did.

Some years later, the Collins intelligence network, developed with the aid of Tobin and another 1916 man, Frank Thornton, discovered that Lee-Wilson was acting as a District Inspector of the RIC in County Wexford. He was shot dead.

As Thornton's lot of prisoners were being marched off to Richmond Barracks in Inchicore, in the western part of the city, for screening, he says, 'If it weren't for the fact that we were so strongly guarded by British troops, we would have been torn asunder by the soldiers' wives in the area.'[32] These 'separation women' simply gave more extreme expression to the anger felt by most Dubliners at the destruction of life and property, and the effects of a week of terror, food shortages and looting as the slum dwellers poured out of the back streets to take their one chance in a lifetime of sampling the wares of the city's best shops. More civilians were killed and wounded than the combined total of British and Irish military casualties. Civilian casualties were 256 killed and some two thousand wounded. Sixty-two of the rebels had been killed outright and sixteen were executed subsequently. Piaras Beaslai gives this account of how the retribution process began:

On Sunday morning the prisoners were brought to Richmond Barracks. They were placed sitting on the floor of the gymnasium, and the political detectives of the 'G' Division of the Dublin Police came like a flock of carrion crows to pick out 'suspects' for court martial. I was one of the first to be picked out, and for the rest of the day could watch the detectives passing to and fro among the two thousand prisoners studying their faces for victims for the firing squad. Anybody who had seen that sight may be pardoned if he felt little compunction at the subsequent shooting of these same 'G' men.[33]

Of the men picked out by the 'G' men for court martial, those who did not merit death sentences were condemned to penal servitude in British prisons like Dartmoor or Portland. Those who received death sentences, subsequently commuted to life imprisonment as a result of public opinion, were also sent to hard labour in England. It was in Richmond Barracks that Collins had one of the luckiest escapes of his life. The 'G' men initially selected him for inclusion amongst those severely dealt with, but after Collins had been some time with the selected batch of prisoners, he heard his name being called from the further end of the building. Looking, he could not see who was calling him. After two or three attempts to locate the caller he grew impatient and decided to risk a walk across the room. And once there, he stayed. It was for him probably the luckiest escape of his career.[34] And, it may be added, one of the worst blunders the police ever made. For, as Frank O'Connor observed, the detectives, 'left behind them the one really dangerous man, the man who in a few short years would kill off the craftiest of them and render the rest so impotent that he would be able to walk the streets of Dublin undisguised'.[35]

Sean MacDiarmada very nearly survived the screening process also, but at the last moment one of the detectives, Hoey, whom Collins would later have eliminated, spotted him and dragged him out of the line of lesser offenders which was forming up to march to the ship taking them to prison in England. He was court-martialled at Richmond Barracks and sentenced to be shot in Kilmainham Jail. Frank Thornton, who was court-martialled along with him, describes their last interlude together:

Sean . . . walked with difficulty with the aid of a stick . . . and one of the first acts of our escort when we were ordered to fall-in for our march to Kilmainham, was to take away that stick, and immediately Harry Boland came to his rescue, and put his arm around him, Gerald Crofts doing likewise for myself, as my right leg by this time had got very stiff and sore from congealed blood. We were marched along the road to Kilmainham Jail, and with every yard there were indications of the changed attitudes of the people.

The open trams passing by always brought a cheer from somebody, even though rifles were pointed at the offender on every occasion. Old men stood at the street corners and saluted, despite being pushed around. Finally, reaching Kilmainham, Sean MacDermott turned round to the three of us, shook hands and said: 'I'll be shot, and it will be a bad day for Ireland that I'm not. You fellows will get an opportunity, even if in years to come, to follow on where we left off.' Well poor Sean was shot, as he felt he would be.[36]

But Michael Collins was safe, and because of his uncanny luck, well-placed, in the principal 'Republican University', to give vent to his burning determination to follow on in MacDiarmada's footsteps.

The 'Republican University'[37] which Irish revolutionaries have traditionally attended has many constituent colleges, the jails and internment camps of Ireland and England. Felons do not 'graduate' from these in the accepted sense – they are hammered out on the anvils of circumstance. Apart from the deadening effect of confinement and prison routine (and the correspondingly unduly enlivening effect of sexual deprivation), they have to survive the abrasion of the relationship between the authorities and themselves, an amalgam of the results of mutual prejudice, and a desire on the one side to be regarded as political prisoners, on the other to consider them as ordinary criminals. There is also the attrition of being thrust into the company of a collection of men with sharply contrasting personalities, economic, social and cultural backgrounds. One can emerge from this process either broken and disillusioned, or deepened in one's convictions and knowledge by the time and opportunity to study books, men and movements in a continuously testing environment wherein one learns more about oneself than about others. Collins was destined to graduate at the head of the class from his particular course which began at Stafford Detention Barracks on 1 May 1916.

The course was short but intensive, lasting from the beginning of May until Christmas week, 1916. The first three weeks were spent in solitary confinement from which communication with the outside world was established with difficulty. But obviously word of the executions had seeped through; when letters were allowed, on 16 May, Collins wrote to Hannie:

Positively you have no idea of what it's like, the dreadful monotony, the heart-scalding eternal brooding on all sorts of things, thoughts of friends dead & living, especially those recently dead, but above all the time, the horror of the way in which it refuses to pass . . . it is only with the utmost effort that I can concentrate my thoughts or be at all rational – you see I seem to have lost acquaintance with myself and with the people I knew. Wilde's 'Reading Gaol' keeps coming up. You remember 'All that we know who be in gaol . . .'[38]

But even in that dark night of the soul he looked forward, asking Hannie for 'a few good (& long) novels in cheap editions, and if still at the flat, Heath's *Practical French Grammar* or some such text book . . .'

He perked up greatly as soon as prison conditions eased, being remembered at Stafford for revealing, if contradictory, facets of his personality: Collins the butt of horse-play jokes, Collins the reflective, Collins the outgoing personality who could get unlikely people to work for him. Under the first heading his temper got him baited unmercifully. The prisoners had a rough game, a version of leapfrog called 'weak horses' whose ostensible aim was for two teams to compete in leaping over each others' backs until someone broke and became the 'weak sister'. In reality most of the fun was derived from riling Collins. The teams were picked so that the heaviest men, Jim Ryan, who had been the doctor in the GPO, Mort O'Connell and Denis Daly, were always on the team opposing Collins' and would deliberately set out to break him so that he would fly into one of his rages. The writer Desmond Ryan[39], however, noted that of all the men in the camp it was Collins who was attracted to a book he was reading and commented on it intelligently and sensitively. The acute Hannie observed[40] when she visited him that he seemed to have gained such control over one of the warders that the man couldn't do enough for him. Warders were to figure large in Collins' subsequent planning.

As soon as letter-writing was allowed he wrote to Susan, Sioban or Sheevaun as he called her, probably because he was beginning to study Irish and was experimenting with its forms. His letters show his restrained awkwardness in expressing himself to members of the opposite sex, his kind-heartedness and his eye for detail, even detail he disliked. He was listed under his Rathdown Rd address as 'Irish Prisoner 48F', a form of depersonalisation which irked him. 'Is one expected to lose one's identity, one's humanity, to become instead a numbered nonentity?' he asked[41]; but when Susan managed to get a parcel through to him he wrote back underlining '48F not 46F' at the head of his letter:

My dear Sioban,
      Today I was called away to recieve [sic] a parcel, which on examination I found to contain many very delightful articles, and in the writing on the wrapper, I think I discerned 'the fine touch of your claw'. It was very kind and thoughtful of you and I am very grateful indeed, my friends altogether have been most kind – a greater deal kinder than I deserve or have any right to expect.
      As you were fortunate enough to be away from the scene of our little 'shemozzle', it is profoundly to be hoped that you didn't stare 'upon the hills of Clare', as did I understand other of our friends 'Upon the Hill of Howth'. If our performance will only teach the housekeepers of Dublin to have more grub in reserve for the future it will surely not have been in vain, but seriously I'm afraid there must have been a lot of hardship and misery which must continue for many a day and which all our sympathy cannot soften.
      Life here has not been so ghastly since communications from the outer world have been allowed, and since we've been allowed reading matter and to write letters (this last concession being used by myself solely for the purpose of begging things). Also we are allowed to smoke, but no amount of privileges could compensate for the one thing which any of us haven't got in this or similar places. And the thoughts – I saw poor Pearse's last letter in the *Daily News* this day and it didn't make me exactly prayerful. However I

suppose things might be worse which, no less than ever, is something to be thankful for itself into the eternal question of what fate is thine unhappy Isle?

Well goodbye, the circumstances absolve me from the necessity of apologising for being uninteresting. Give my kindest regards to the friends I have among your colleagues. Tell Dolly I'd like to hear from her. Also an account from Nancy of her Howth experience would be most enlivening, because I'm sure she didn't lose her sense of humour unless she was very badly off. May I be looking forward to a letter from you? Really I cannot say how grateful I am to you for your kindness to me and that you should remember me.

> Love
> Michael Collins

Four days later a letter from Susan evidently got through in the wake of her parcel, and his reply to her[42], while characteristically somewhat stilted, also shows his essential kindheartedness and concern for others:

My dear Sheevaun,
Indeed was glad to get your letter – in spite of the effort at disparagement. I have already written you and no doubt you've received that precious document ere this. What impels me to this fresh effort is the following chiefly. Could you get in touch with some of the CmBan people and ask them to look up Mrs Kirwan of Maynooth whose husband is here. They have five or six children who are not I am afraid being attended to at all. Also Mrs Little, 31, The rear of Upper Clanbrassil St, more or less similarly placed. If you could get hold of a Miss Kearney she might be able to help . . .

Conditions have improved wonderfully during the last week. We are now allowed to communicate freely with each other so that I know all the other fellows' troubles. As for myself – a good deal changed, but do my level best to keep up appearances. Ghastly still at times. Well goodbye. 'See you again before the resurrection.' With all the thanks in the world for your kind thoughtfulness.

> Love
> Michael

Between 1 May and 16 June the British deported to England a total of 2,519 prisoners, many of them totally unconnected with the Volunteers or the Rising. These were initially scattered around the British penal landscape: Aylesbury, Glasgow, Knutsford, Lewes, Perth, Reading, Stafford, Wakefield, Wandsworth, Woking. But a degree of centralisation was thought necessary and a German prisoner-of-war camp at Frongoch, a remote beauty spot three miles from the town of Bala in Merionethshire, North Wales, was given over to the Irish, receiving its first contingent on 9 June. By the end of June, Collins knew that he would be transferred there. Writing to Susan from Stafford on 27 June he expressed little enthusiasm for the move:

. . . regarding our transfers. Removal instructions have been served on about 120 or 130 men and they'll be off tomorrow. . . . You will see in my letter to Dolly what the place is likely to be like. I shan't like the one letter a week in the very least. You have no idea of the number of letters I've been writing, especially for the past few weeks. I'm afraid I've lost my keen sense of the ridiculous, as in ordinary life I'd have the knowledge that they weren't fit to send anybody. But I can see myself writing the first letter in the camp and choking it full of requests just as I did my first one here. And my poor sister the victim. In spite of concessions, etc. one gets plenty of time to think here and my thoughts are often self-accusing goodness knows. I can't tell you how small I feel sometimes. Tis all very fine for writers to talk about the sublime thoughts which enter into people when they are faced by death – once, when I was in a pretty tight corner, what struck me was, how much nicer I might have been to the people who had a regard for me. You were one of them although I had no right to suppose, etc. Well I'm in that sort of mood again today – don't know why.

Glad to hear that you are all enjoying Howth. Sorry though that the weather isn't more suitable. But think of the 80 degree or 90 degree or something of November and how we'll all enjoy it. You on Howth we on Bala. Beannact leat [in English: A blessing on you].
Fondest love.

Frongoch, which was divided into two camps, North and South, had been a distillery. Apart from the prison complex formed around the old buildings dominated by a high brick chimney and the nearby railway siding, there was no sign of habitation. Collins wrote to Susan:

. . . It's situated most picturesquely on rising ground amid pretty Welsh hills. Up to the present it hasn't presented any good points to me, for it rained all the time . . . so that all the ground around and between the huts is a mass of slippery, shifting mud. We sleep 30 in an 'ut (this is the regulation name) the dimensions being 60 long, 16 wide and 10 foot high in the middle. Not too much room to spare! Of course when we've made roads etc. the place will be much better. But the cold at present is – well not pleasant even now, but I cheer them all up by asking them – what'll they do when the winter comes?[43]

Nethertheless the place had some amenities. In addition to a jail and the censor's office, the distillery also housed a hospital, an artists' shed, a cookhouse, a barber's shop and facilities for tailoring and shoe-making, as well as a carpenters' and an engineers' workshop. Collins wrote in another letter:

Prating about home, friends and so on doesn't alter the fact that this is Frongoch, an internment camp. There is only one thing to do while the situation is as it is. . . . make what I can of it.[44]

One of the best ways of dissipating pent-up tensions in a prison camp is sport. Collins is remembered at Frongoch for excelling at a number of sports.[45] He won the 100 yards during the camp sports on 8 August, overtaking M. W. O'Reilly with the amiable observation,

Above Michael Collins' mother, Marianne (standing), with his sister Mary, her baby Nora, and his grandmother, Mrs O'Brien, circa 1905

Michael Collins, aged six; and his sisters Hannie (*above*), with whom he lived for nine years in London, and Helena (*left*), later Sister Mary Celestine

(*Top*) Gun-running: Mrs Erskine Childers and Mary Spring-Rice on board the *Asgard*, 1914
(*Right*) Irish Parliamentary Party leader John Redmond
(*Above*) Carson addressing an anti-Home Rule meeting, 1913

The Easter Rising, 1916: (*top*) a barricade in Talbot Street; (*above*) the shelled ruins of Liberty Hall – a few days earlier, Collins had marched out of the Hall to take part in the Rising; Collins' heroes, Sean MacDiarmada (*far left*) and James Connolly (*left*), who were executed for their part in the Rising

Collins in Stafford Jail (marked with an arrow)

(Above) Eamon de Valera under arrest before his court martial
(*Right*) Collins on release from Frongoch internment camp, December 1916 — his hand is on his knee to hide a hole in his trousers

'Ah, you whore, you can't run,' and was runner-up to his friend Sean Hales, the Munster champion, in the 56-lb weight-throwing competition. He was particularly fond of wrestling, but his opponents can't have been too fond of him. Apart from his custom of claiming a 'bit of ear', biting the ear of a victim after he had overpowered him, he tended to lose his temper during bouts:

He would go into a bout with a friendly determination. Grimness would begin to rise later, particularly if he were closely matched, and the contest would end in a heated and often bloody fracas.[46]

He generated a wide force field, impressing himself on the camp staff as much as on his companions. Robert J. Roberts, a sixteen-year-old canteen assistant at Frongoch wrote later:

Hut 32 was the noisiest in Camp North with ceaseless activity close to the Camp 2 canteen. Collins was always dressed in very good clothing, but rarely wore a collar or tie and his boots were army boots unpolished. The North Camp was far superior to the South as far as hygiene was concerned, but frightfully cold and wet even in June and no roads in the camp except very rough ones from the entrance and to the cookhouse. Mud everywhere, deep liquid mud. An effort to repair them by using boiler house clinkers manhandled and moved in an old waggon by the prisoners at threepence an hour, that is how I came in contact with Michael Collins, coming into the canteen covered in mud with the crowd, and we objected and told them to wash their boots at the water taps outside. He just laughed. He had a great sense of humour but was a very stern disciplinarian.[47]

The prisoners took advantage of Roberts' youth to steal cherry-wood pipes from a box which he placed on the counter, before allowing himself to be called away to the end of the counter. He says:

. . . when I returned there were only very few pipes in the box and no payments for other goods missing. I reported what was going on and we complained to the senior prisoner, who was Michael Collins. He arranged to assist us by locking the canteen door and searching each prisoner. If a prisoner had one pipe or box of matches he was given the benefit of the doubt. Otherwise stolen goods were returned.

Roberts was a classic example of the person in a seemingly lowly, but in fact highly useful position, whom Collins was later to win over in great numbers and use to such devastating effect. He decided that he wanted to study Welsh, and persuaded Roberts, on his day off from the camp, to get hold of some dictionaries and elementary alphabet cards, leaflets and some chalk. 'Michael Collins paid for all. He was never short of money,' Roberts recalls. 'Collins must have told his mother about me, because she sent me a small present of a tie-pin in the pattern of the shamrock inlaid with green Connemara stone for my kindness to her son.' Of course Collins' mother had died nine years earlier, but he obviously used her name to impress on Roberts how much he thought of him. This use of psychology by Collins was so successful that over half a century later Roberts would write:

Michael Collins was very highly respected, especially by the civilian canteen staff. The manager used to remark that whenever we took a problem to him he always listened logically. He used to be one of the first to the morning Mass and one of the first at the breakfast table, the best meal of the day . . . He was a heavy smoker but would go without, proving that he was more self-willed than the rest . . . wonderfully fit, he could out-walk everyone on the route marches into the Welsh hills and would arrive back in camp none the worse for wear while some of the guards fell by the wayside.[48]

Frongoch was infested with rodents: the prisoners rechristened the place in a pun on the Irish word for rat, 'frangach'. In one of his letters to Susan, Collins notes: 'Had a most exciting experience myself the other night – woke up to find a rat between my blankets – didn't catch the blighter either.'[49]

But Collins at this time was a more sombre person than the jocosity would indicate. For him the GPO had been the crucible of a great, dangerous experiment. Frongoch was the laboratory where the results were analysed, not without some pain to himself, although character-istically he sought to leaven his broodings with humour. Writing to Susan on 27 July 1916 he said:

Oh! Yes, I got those papers quite alright. And I'm very much obliged for them. 'Pon my word but I get a queer feeling often – in spite of my selfishness – when I think of the trouble I'm putting people to. I do hope to repay in some small way though. Just at present I'm in good form over the smashing of the H R proposals. Anything but a divided Ireland – you understand of course that I mean geographically divided. From the letters and accounts I get the country seems to be very sound – I imagine there will be better material than ever in Ireland for the next European war, that at any rate is something to be thankful for.

'The next European war' – the next round. Collins was thinking ahead, in one sense. But in terms of Republican theology, thinking back, to Wolfe Tone and his teaching that England's difficulty was Ireland's opportunity. But was it the correct approach? Within a few days of his writing to Susan, word reached the camp of Roger Casement's execution,[50] heightening Collins' depressions and his questionings. A brave man had died. For what? Casement had in fact become disillusioned by the Germans,[51] their lack of commitment to an Irish uprising, and his submarine return to Ireland had been for the purpose of calling off the Rising. In the camp with Collins was the one surviving member of the party that had been sent down to Kerry to pick him up, the driver of the car that had gone over the pier. More tragic bungling, added to by the failure to signal to the *Aud* as she cruised fruitlessly off the Kerry coast instead of being brought into

Fenit harbour where transport had been provided for her cargo. And the whole thing was compounded by the local Volunteer commander, Austin Stack, finally deciding to call at the RIC barracks where Casement was held to find out what was happening – and getting himself arrested!

Stack, who worked in a solicitor's office, and had some legal training, was a famous Kerry Gaelic All-Ireland footballer and Commandant of the Kerry Brigade of the Irish Volunteers. After his arrest he was sentenced to death. This was then commuted to twenty years' penal servitude. In jail he built up a national reputation for his leadership of revolts against attempts to impose criminal status on Volunteers. His courage was unquestionable, but his judgement left something to be desired.

No wonder MacNeill had sent the O'Rahilly around vetoing the plans. The wonder lay in O'Rahilly's fatal gallantry in joining the doomed uprising after expending himself in trying to spare others its horrors. Collins didn't blame the men or the movement which had brought him to Frongoch. But by now he had too many first-hand impressions and reports of the Rising and its aftermath to be able to accept what had happened uncritically – or unmoved. His particular leader, Joseph Plunkett, had married Grace Gifford on the morning of his execution, fifteen soldiers with fixed bayonets lining the cell as an officer ticked off the seconds of the ten minutes bride and bridegroom were given together before the groom was taken out to be shot.[52] He had heard how Connolly, in such pain that he had to be given morphine to make him sleep, had then been woken up to be told he would be shot at dawn: but that he had composed himself sufficiently to pat his sobbing wife on the head and say, 'Don't cry, Lillie, you'll unman me.'[53] How Pearse had told the court martial that sentenced him to death, 'When I was a child of ten I went down on my knees by my bedside and promised God that I should devote my life in an effort to free my country. I have kept that promise.' With his belief in historical continuity he would have found himself largely in agreement with Pearse's concluding remarks to the court martial: 'You cannot extinguish the Irish passion for freedom. If our deed has not been sufficient to win freedom, then our children will win it by a better deed.'[54] But he had no intention of leaving the 'better deed' to the next generation and he had no great opinion of the planning of the Rising as he made clear in a letter to Kevin O'Brien:

It is so easy to fault the actions of others when their particular actions have resulted in defeat. I want to be quite fair about this – the Easter Rising – and say how much I admired the men in the ranks and the womenfolk thus engaged. But at the same time – as it must appear to others also – the actions of the leaders should not pass without comment. They have died nobly at the hands of the firing squads. So much I grant. But I do not think the Rising week was an appropriate time for the issue of memoranda couched in poetic phrases, nor of actions worked out in a similar fashion. Looking at it from the inside (I was in the GPO) it had the air of a Greek tragedy about it, the illusion being more or less completed with the issue of the before-mentioned memoranda. Of Pearse and Connolly I admire the latter the most. Connolly was a realist, Pearse the direct opposite. There was an air of earthy directness about Connolly. It impressed me. I would have followed him through hell had such action been necessary. But I honestly doubt very much if I would have followed Pearse – not without some thought anyway.

I think chiefly of Tom Clarke and MacDiarmada. Both built on the best foundations. Ireland will not see another Sean MacDiarmada.

These are sharp reflections. On the whole I think the Rising was bungled terribly, costing many a good life. It seemed at first to be well-organised, but afterwards became subjected to panic decisions and a great lack of very essential organisation and co-operation.[55]

Collins resolved that the vehicle for that 'very essential organisation and co-operation' should be the IRB.

And it may have been in Frongoch that the first glimmering of another method of warfare, along the lines of de Wet's approach, may have presented itself. It is known that there was considerable debate within the camp about the merits or demerits of 'static warfare'. In fact, before surrendering, one of the executed leaders, Major John MacBride, who had fought for the Boers in South Africa, had addressed his men and warned them never again to allow themselves to be locked up in buildings confronting an enemy who could easily subdue them with the aid of superior man- and fire-power. Collins was to become the supreme architect of the 'hit-and-run' ambush technique which effectively countered this superiority.

In that noticeable pattern of his life in which he formed friends easily with either youth or age the counterpoint to the youthful Roberts in Frongoch was Henry Dixon, a seventy-year-old solicitor, disciple of Arthur Griffith and a member of the IRB, who served as camp librarian – a useful position for establishing contact throughout the camp.[56] Outside the camp, contact was established with Mrs Kathleen Clarke, Tom's widow, and sister of Edward Daly, who was also executed for his part in the Rising, and the threads were also picked up in the other prisons where 1916 men had been incarcerated throughout England and, chiefly in Reading and Lewes, where de Valera was beginning to make a name for himself as the prisoners' leader. The IRB was organised on a cell system[57] wherein only the cell or circle leader knew who all the members were or how to make contact with the circle above him. The President of the Supreme Council was the controller, the chief of the entire Brotherhood. Michael Collins was elected Head Centre of the Frongoch outfit. Thus when the Frongoch gates swung open he was in a position to ensure that the spores of revolutionary violence blasted into the air above the GPO in Easter Week would be wafted into every corner of Ireland.

Another scheme which Collins helped to originate in Frongoch was the formation of what later became one of Ireland's largest insurance businesses, the New Ireland Assurance Company. This was born out of a desire to keep in Irish hands a portion of the large amount of money being sent out of the country to English insurers. It also provided a useful cover later on for IRB activities. Some of its principal figures, including M. W. O'Reilly and Denis McCullough, were Frongoch men.

Within Frongoch itself the great fear hanging over the prisoners was that they would be conscripted, and to avoid this they gave false names and confused the authorities in any way they could. Collins played a leading part in this form of defiance. He refused to co-operate with the authorities, insisting on the prisoners drawing up their own lists of names and addresses, even when these were only needed to buy tickets for the prisoners' correct home destinations. But it was remarked that he carefully noted the prisoners' identities for his own purposes. He had a capacity for being able to weave details into a useful pattern. For instance Brennan-Whitmore one day laughingly told a comrade how, as a result of the authorities' black propaganda to the effect that the prisoners were rich with German gold, a guard had wistfully enquired whether he was 'one of the boys with all the money'[58] – and Whitmore found himself hauled before an IRB meeting as a result. Collins wanted to be told everything he could about the soldier. A short time later the man became one of the conduits through which letters and information were smuggled out of the camp.

Such channels became vitally necessary as tensions built up, against the back-drop of the prisoners' desire to maintain their prisoner-of-war status at all costs. The proposals that they should work in nearby quarries and should provide scavenging and cinder removal services for the soldiers were refused. As a result, relationships within the camp soured. The route marches were introduced and parcels and letters were stopped. After the 'ash-pit incident', as it became known, up to a hundred men were confined to cells with loss of all privileges. The food was another bone of contention. Collins does not seem to have been exaggerating when he wrote:

With the exception of Friday when we get uneatable herrings, the food never varies, frozen meat quite frequently and dried beans are the staple diets. The potato ration is so small that one hardly notices it.[59]

Collins concluded that letter by saying, 'Mind you I'm not grumbling in the strict sense!' However the prisoners grumbled in other senses, and a great deal of propaganda was generated as they fought for prisoner-of-war status. The authorities sought to counter the unrest by transfers, and courts martial aimed at removing the trouble-makers to more controllable and more overtly criminal surroundings such as Reading jail.

But criminalisation was something Collins loathed with every fibre of his being. After being taken from Stafford to Frongoch, Collins was one of those removed from the camp a few days later and brought to London for screening by the Advisory Committee on the Internment of Rebels set up after the Rising in a vain attempt to apportion blame and find out who the real leaders of the revolutionary movement were. Before being returned to Frongoch, Collins wrote to Susan Killeen expressing his detestation of the criminalisation process:

This morning I was able to see through the open pane of my window the convicts at exercise. It was the most revolting thing I have ever seen. Each convict seems to have cultivated a ghastly expression to match the colour of his turf-ash-grey garb. Broad arrows everywhere. As the man walked round and round the ring – those wretched arrows simply danced before the eyes. That awful convict dress is one horror we're saved at any rate.[60]

Imbued with this spirit he rejected all suggestions of compromise or moderation, writing a reasoned rationale for his stance: 'Sit down – refuse to budge – you have the British beaten. For a time they'll raise war – in the end they'll despair. Method, but unorthodox, has them beaten the whole time',[61] but articulating it in a most unreasoning hectoring way to anyone who showed what he considered faint heartedness: 'Coward', 'Bloody lousers', 'ould cods'.[62] This inability to show to his peers in speech the restraint he displayed to the young and the old, or when he took a pen in hand, was to make many a dangerous enemy for Collins. But his policy paid dividends. Certainly the ploy of concealing their identities kept prisoners from being conscripted. Probably the propaganda engendered by their protest, particularly in America, got them home for Christmas. But not without cost.

Two hundred of the prisoners went on a three-day hunger strike on 2 November, and the prison commandant, Col Heygate-Lambert, declared that he would have discipline in the camp even though it was filled with nothing but dead bodies.[63] One prisoner, Eamonn Tierney, who had a fear of conscription, went mad after this. Four others cracked up in the foetid, confined conditions and died the following year. Many others suffered from sickness of various kinds. The two camp doctors followed instructions in not attending to patients who refused to give their names. But one of them, Dr Peters, 'worried by statements concerning the treatment of prisoners', broke under the strain and drowned himself in the River Tryweryn, near Bala.[64]

Michael Collins' statements concerning the battle of wills in the camp found their mark in a celebrated exposé in William O'Brien's *Cork Free Press* on 11 November, and in a number of other papers, notably the *Manchester Guardian*, later in the month. They detonated in America and on the floor of the House of Commons to such good effect that an amnesty was finally declared on 21 December by the Chief Secretary for Ireland, Henry Duke.

Collins exploded into freedom and Dublin on Christmas morning with Gearoid O'Sullivan. They went to see Joe O'Reilly, another Stafford and Frongoch graduate who, like Collins, was a Corkman, but a far gentler one. The pair burst through the door of the room O'Reilly was sharing with a friend, extracted 'a piece of ear' that left both his ears bleeding, 'pinched and savaged him',[65] poured what they could of a bottle of port down his throat and left O'Reilly to explain to his traumatised room-mate that it was only Collins having a bit of fun. Collins continued to roister round Dublin all that day until the evening when 'he was lifted on to a sidecar and, drunk as a lord, bundled by his friends into the Cork train'.[66]

3

Kicking Down a Rotten Door

'Put him in to get him out.'

Slogan on prisoner's election poster, 1917

The first visit home after Frongoch was anti-climactic. To begin with Christmas affected transport arrangements so that Collins had to walk from Clonakilty to Woodfield through December's darkness and chills. The good cheer with which he had departed Dublin further evaporated on arrival at the news that his grandmother had just died. An innocent old lady, her life bounded by her family and the small hills of Sam's Cross, she had greeted the news that Michael was involved in the Easter rebellion with the observation, 'I suppose that Michael is fighting for William O'Brien and James O'Brien is fighting for Mr Redmond. [William O'Brien was the old opponent of Collins's childhood ogre, Smith-Barry; O'Brien had become estranged from Redmond on the Home Rule issue. James O'Brien was another grandson.]

During his holiday Collins was to find a good deal of that lack of comprehension – coupled with a degree of fear that he might be the cause of bringing grief to the area. He obviously sensed something of this after calling on Sean Hurley's mother and wrote to Hannie: 'I think poor Sean Hurley's mother felt his loss more keenly when I came home than at any other time.' But he wasn't prepared to extend the same sensitivity to the generality of those he met. The First World War had brought unwonted prosperity to the farmers of the district, as it had to other parts of the country, and their reception of the returned firebrand may be gauged from his comments to 'Shiobhain a Cushla' (Susan my sweetheart). He had earlier met a mutual friend and apologised for being able to spend 'only a minute with her'. He said:

I was quite unable to talk to anyone and I didn't feel at all well; some kind of reaction was setting in and I was rapidly giving way. Better now but not very much. Lots of trouble here. Poor old grandmother was dead when I came home, and then that brother of mine and his wife were both very unwell. However think they're improving so I probably will have a decent rest next week and then go back to Dublin to thank you for all the kindnesses which have been bestowed on me.

It seems that the spirit prevailing here anyway is very poor. The people are much, much too careful and I've sustained myself principally on rows since returning.[1]

Accordingly, after three dispiriting weeks spent 'drinking Clonakilty wrastler on a Frongoch stomach', as he put it himself in a letter to Hannie, Collins returned to Dublin one step ahead of the RIC who came to his family seeking him in connection with a brawl in Cork. His relations say that the police visit was only an attempt at intimidation and that he had nothing to do with the fight in Cork. But of course! Who could imagine Michael Collins mixed up in a brawl! At all events he gave the police the slip, not for the last time in his career, and returned to Dublin. Here he found the 'national spirit' a good deal better. As he had written to Susan with unintentional prescience, 'some kind of reaction' was indeed setting in. The reaction manifested itself in two ways. One was a tremendous outpouring of support and sympathy for the insurgent Aprilists, now mistakenly all lumped together in the public's mind as 'Sinn Feiners', through an unselective use of the term by the British media and military, after the Rising. The other was a corresponding outburst of prejudice. The sympathy was engendered by the effect of the executions of the leaders coming against a backdrop of the frustration of the green constitutional traditions' hopes of Home Rule, which they had democratically expressed, by the undemocratic action of the Orange and Tory conspiracy. The execution of Roger Casement, which came in August, long after it was abundantly clear that all threat to Britain from the Rising was well past, summed up the different treatment meted out to Orange and Green. The man who successfully sought the death penalty for Casement was F. E. Smith, who later became Lord Birkenhead. He had told an audience at Ballyclare, County Antrim[2] that in resisting Home Rule he would be prepared to 'risk the collapse of the entire body politic to prevent this monstrous crime.' During his trial Casement had said, 'the Unionists' champion had chosen a part they felt would lead to the Woolsack, while I went a road that I knew must lead to the dock. And the events proved both were right.' Listening to this oration as he lolled back on the prosecutor's bench, F. E. Smith smiled and commented, 'And quite right too!' It seemed unlikely at the time that of all men he and Michael Collins would ever become friendly, but incredibly enough the conflicting currents swirling through Ireland in that January of 1917 were destined to throw the two men together and, out of their encounter, friendship would emerge.

Irish-American reaction to the immediate post-Rising executions was intense. A huge relief fund was set up. Dr Thomas Addis Emmet, a descendant of Robert Emmet's brother, became its president and there were scores of bishops and archbishops amongst its patrons. Well over a hundred thousand dollars was sent to Ireland as a result. This at a time when President Woodrow Wilson was telling Washingtonians: '. . . every people has a right to choose the sovereignty under which they shall live . . . small states . . . have a right to enjoy the same respect for their territorial integrity that great and powerful nations expect and insist on . . .'[3]

This at a time when Britain was being exhausted by Jutland and Verdun and needed American aid to survive but was being told by her Washington Ambassador, Sir Cecil Spring Rice, that it was 'most unfortunate that it has been found necessary to execute the Rebels'. He said:

I do not think we can count on American help, perhaps not even on American sympathy . . . the attitude towards England has been changed by recent events in Ireland . . . If we are able in some measure to settle the Home Rule question at once, the announcement will have a beneficial effect here, although I do not think that anything we can do would conciliate the Irish here. They have blood in their eyes when they look our way . . . Our cause for the present among the Irish here is a lost one . . .'[4]

With an American presidential election looming in November the British Cabinet knew it had to find some way of addressing the Irish question, but the method it chose was not to heed the electoral call for Home Rule but to go instead for a Lloyd George manoeuvre which would ensure that Irish nationalists would acquire even more 'blood in their eyes'. The deal in effect took Partition from the realms of debate, as it had been during the pre-war Buckingham Palace conference, and inscribed it on the Irish political agenda, albeit in Janus-faced, Lloyd-Georgian fashion.

At the end of May 1916 both Redmond and Carson received Home Rule proposals whereby the postponed 1914 Home Rule Act was to be brought into operation immediately for twenty-six counties only, the six north-eastern counties (Antrim, Down, Armagh, Derry, Fermanagh and Tyrone) being excluded for an undeclared period which was described as follows:

The Bill to remain in force during the continuance of the war and a period of twelve months thereafter; but, if Parliament has not by that time made further and permanent provision for the Government of Ireland, the period for which the Bill is to remain in force is to be extended by Order in Council for such time as may be necessary in order to enable Parliament to make such provision.

Initially at least, John Redmond thought he was quite clear as to its interpretation. At a meeting of Six-County Nationalists in Belfast on 23 June when he dealt with a report in that day's *Irish Times* concerning a promise that Lloyd George was supposed to have given Carson to the effect that Partition would be permanent, a voice in the audience cried 'never'. Redmond said: 'I entirely re-echo that cry of "never". That statement is an absolute lie . . . The proposals are temporary and provisional. If they were not I would oppose them.'

Alas for Redmond's trust in Lloyd George. Unknown to the unfortunate Irish parliamentarian, the 'Welsh wizard' had sent with Carson's copy of the draft proposal this note:

Whitehall Place
May 29th, 1916.

My dear Carson,
   I enclose Greer's draft propositions.
   We must make it clear that at the end of the provisional period Ulster does not, whether she wills it or not, merge in the rest of Ireland.

Ever sincerely,
D. Lloyd George.

P.S. Will you show it to Craig?

In the circumstances that 'Ever sincerely' is a nice touch, though understandably the nicety was rather lost on a John Redmond who was rapidly going down in a tide of post-Rising sentiment. When he discovered what had happened, under outraged pressure from his increasingly disillusioned supporters, he withdrew his assent on 24 July and the Government temporarily abandoned the scheme. These were the Home Rule proposals the news of whose 'smashing' had left Collins exultant in Frongoch, as he told Susan Killeen. He had also written to Nancy O'Brien on the same day (27 July) saying: 'I'm glad to see that this particular business has been dropped. Surely John E. & Co must be discredited now, although there's a lot of damn fools knocking about.'

But his exultation was premature. For as William O'Brien realised afterwards, that Lloyd George draft, as *realpolitik*, was a Magna Carta of Sir Edward Carson's Six Counties, an 'unhappy instrument' to which 'must be traced the responsibility for all the years of disappointment, bloodshed, and devastation that were to follow'.[5] They still follow as this is being written.

So much for the temper of the post-Rising Irish nationalists and the proposals made by the Government in London to deal with their ardour. As Michael Collins returned to Ireland in January 1917, to continue from Woodfield the assault on the system which he had begun the previous Easter, the country was being run by an Irish Executive, or Government, as it was equally known. It consisted of a Lord Lieutenant, a Chief Secretary and an Under Secretary, the first two being politicians, the third a civil servant. The military and naval establishments were directed from London, though the Lord

Lieutenant was supposed to be in charge of both. However, as at the time of the Rising the Chief Secretary was in the Cabinet, often absent from Dublin, and the Lord Lieutenant was not, the day-to-day running of the administration devolved upon the Under Secretary. As John Redmond, the leader of the Irish Parliamentary Party, also had to be in London, near to the Chief Secretary, the House of Commons was the effective source of Irish decision-making. Britain's influence was exercised through Dublin Castle where the offices of the Chief Secretary and the Under Secretary were located, as were those of the law officers who formed part of the Executive or Government. It was from the Castle also that the two police forces, the Royal Irish Constabulary and the Dublin Metropolitan Police, were controlled. The influence of the Castle on Ireland was such that to this day Dublin's major banking, insurance and administrative centres, including the Central Bank and the City Hall buildings, are all within a stone's throw of the pile, the former nerve centre of a great, colonial, civil and military bureaucracy. But in January 1917 the nerves were bad, and destined to get even worse. Augustine Birrell, the witty and cultivated Chief Secretary at the time of the Rising, had been made its political scapegoat and reshufflings and demoralisation had followed his fall. This process was to continue as the political situation deteriorated, in part under hammer blows inflicted by Michael Collins, until a report by Sir Warren Fisher to the British Government three years later would state:

The Castle Administration does not administer. On the mechanical side it can never have been good Irish Govt in relation to policy . . . it simply has no existence. The prevailing conception of the post of Under Secretary, who should be the principal permanent advisor of the Irish Government in Civil Affairs appears to be that he is a routine clerk . . . The Chief Secretary is entirely unconcerned with the exploration or settlement of the problems which the Irish administration exists to solve . . . with the Chief Secretary skied on Olympus and his top permananent official hewing wood in the remotest valley the natural expectation is that essentials will suffer . . . the heads of the RIC and DMP respectively seem to be mediocrities, and while the morale of the former force is getting shaken the latter force has apparently lost it entirely . . . the office under its present management has lost its grip on the country.[6]

The report, while accurate in many respects, nevertheless only dealt with the symptoms of the Irish disease, not its causes. For instance the reason for the impotence of the Under Secretary, Sir James MacMahon, was at least in part his religion. He was a Catholic, and the Castle was riven by sectarianism and by Freemasonry. What Sir Warren Fisher was talking about was not merely bad administration; he was in fact describing the outcome of a political vacuum. The population of Ireland had voted in successive elections by majorities of the order of five to one for Home Rule. The ballot box was unambiguous in its verdict. But that verdict did not count against the manoeuvrings of the Tory/Orange caucus at Westminster.

The electoral vacuum was to be demonstrated yet again within days of Collins' return to Dublin from Woodfield. On 20 January Count Plunkett, the father of his old leader in the GPO, Joseph Plunkett, was formally expelled from the Royal Dublin Society because of his family's connection with the Rising (his other two sons George and John were at the time still undergoing penal servitude in England), an action which caused a good deal of resentment outside the *ancien régime* circles of the RDS itself. The Count announced his intention of standing in a by-election that had arisen in North Roscommon. Collins saw the possibility of using the campaign to do more than test public reaction to the attitudes of the RDS. North Roscommon could be a platform from which both to deliver a rebuff to the Irish Parlimentary Party and to derive some nationwide publicity for the aims of the physical force school. He travelled to Roscommon and campaigned vigorously for the Count. Collins and those who thought like him were quite clear as to where they stood. What they were not clear about was where Plunkett stood on the great issue of abstention. If elected, would he take his seat in Westminster, or would he abstain? There was a good reason for the uncertainty. Plunkett himself had not made up his mind and did not declare for abstention until a meeting of his supporters was held in Boyle after the election result was announced and it was found that he had defeated his Irish Parliamentary Party opponent by 3,022 votes to 1,708.[7]

As Collins himself wrote afterwards, his decision

was not received very enthusiastically by some of the most energetic of his supporters. They had returned a man, it was said, who did not intend to represent them anywhere . . . there was at this stage no unity of opinion on the policy of abstention among the various elements which formed the opposition, which was joined together only in opposition to the Redmondites.

On 19 February Collins became Secretary to the Irish National Aid Fund. The Fund had been set up by Mrs Kathleen Clarke to alleviate distress amongst the dependants of those killed or imprisoned as a result of the Rising. It was funded both by public subscription and by money from the Clan na nGael in America. The Christmas release of internees and the less heinously regarded prisoners from Reading, including Arthur Griffith, meant that suddenly a great deal more work became attached to the post so it was decided to make it salaried, at the princely sum of £2 10s a week. Collins was the favourite candidate. When I interviewed Mrs Clarke,[8] she spoke warmly of 'Mick's' drive and efficiency which reminded her of Sean

MacDiarmada. She obviously took pride in having done well by her executed husband's and brother's memories in passing on their contacts and any secrets she held for them to Collins. His IRB friends also campaigned for him though without his knowledge or consent, and he got the job after a pro-forma interview during which he showed himself so certain of the outcome that throughout it he sat not at, but on, a desk swinging his legs, 'altogether too cocksure', sniffed one of the lady interviewers. However the cocky one was to prove himself one of the all-time great administrators in a field in which the Irish have traditionally excelled, relief dispensation, wherein industry and efficiency have to be tempered with humanity and an ability to empathise with the aid recipients, whether these be in a third-world country or a Dublin back street. And with that extraordinary point–counterpoint nature of his, wherein humanity and generosity ran side by side with the most ruthless militarism and political chicanery, it was the National Aid Association, with its network of friends and contacts, that put Collins into a position of national influence only nine months after he had lain out in the open all night in Parnell Square, trying to keep Tom Clarke alive. Apart from running the National Aid Association with great efficiency, Collins took an active part in the reorganisation of the Volunteers, the IRB and Sinn Fein, and established strong links with Clan na nGael through John Devoy in New York. He also began making trips to various centres in England such as London, Liverpool and Manchester, setting up the arms-smuggling network which was later to work so spectacularly well. In London his main agent was his old friend Sam Maguire. In Liverpool it was another Frongoch friend, Neil Kerr, who apart from having a key position as a purser in a transatlantic shipping line, was also Head Centre of the IRB there, and in Manchester, Patrick O'Donoghue, whose large house in a comfortable suburb he would one day use to hide the Marchmont children whose kidnapping would gain him a priceless source of military intelligence. Even more importantly, as time progressed, he made secret contact with figures who as we shall see later, would be of crucial importance in the coming onslaught on Dublin Castle – four of its trusted detectives, Joe Kavanagh, James MacNamara, David Neligan and above all, Ned Broy.

Most of this activity was hidden from the public. What people saw was a powerfully built, extraordinarily efficient young man with a big heart and sometimes, a big mouth. One description of the time says:

It was a joy to watch Collins at his work. He was most methodical in everything; had an extraordinary aptitude for detail; always knew exactly what he wanted to do, and disposed of each particular task without a moment's hesitation.

He never missed an appointment. Never lost a file, or a piece of paper. Kept meticulous accounts and, most important of all, the fund's beneficiaries were treated like heroes of the revolution, not objects of charity. It was in the National Aid Association's offices in 10 Exchequer St that, building on his GPO and and Frongoch reputations, his mythic status began to emerge. One fatal lineament of that outline, a disregard for menacing firearms, showed itself the day a man flourished a revolver at the Association's president, Alderman Corrigan. Collins bore down on the gunman and kicked him down the stairs. His only comment as he threw down the gun and picked up his pen again was 'those bloody fellows'.

Insofar as the public was concerned, the banner under which Collins and his cohorts marched was that of Arthur Griffith's Sinn Fein. But as Wolfe Tone Republicans they supported only part of the Sinn Fein policy; abstention and self-sufficiency were acceptable, but two of Griffith's cardinal principles were not: his belief in the superiority of moral, as opposed to physical, force, and his recognition of the British Crown. Nor was his opposition to the Rising properly understood. Griffith, who feared that the country had not the physical or mental resources to withstand an unsuccessful attempt at insurrection, had in fact made his way to the GPO at the outbreak of the rising. Here he had spoken with Sean MacDiarmada who, as part of the general IRB policy of infiltration of all potentially useful organisations, had become business manager of Griffith's paper, *Nationality,* and who advised him to return home. Griffith would be needed in the Ireland that would emerge from the ruins of the Rising. The public thought increasingly highly of this gifted journalist and patriot who chose to live in poverty in Ireland for most of his life, rather than leave for America and a lucrative offer of a career in journalism. Hitherto he had been little known outside a relatively restricted circle of writers and intellectuals through his various newspapers, The *United Irishman, Eire, Nationality* and even, when the censor struck, his accurately named publication, *Scissors and Paste.* Now, in the wake of the Rising, a re-issued *Nationality* did reach a wider audience as MacDiarmada foresaw. Influenced in economic philosophy by Frederick List, who advocated protectionism and tariffs behind which to build up industry, Griffith added an Irish gloss to these doctrines, preaching that Ireland was a separate nation and must develop all the best resources of that nation whether these be in literature, language, afforestation or manufacturing, acceptable ideas whose hour had struck. Hundreds of Sinn Fein Clubs were springing up around the country and his theories were much discussed. He had been putting forward the idea of a dual monarchy for Ireland since 1904 when his great work, *The Resurrection of Hungary*, was first serialised in the *United Irishman* and later published in book form. Ironically, at the time it was the Fenians who thought that the people would never support his central theory, that Irishmen should do as the Hungarians had done in Vienna – withdraw from the Imperial Parliament and set up their own parliament and subordinate bodies. The type of parliament he was aiming at, representative of 'the King, Lords and Commons of Ireland', was based on that extinguished by the Act of Union which followed Wolfe Tone's rebellion. Now in 1917, after their own rising, it was the Fenian standard-bearers who objected to his proposal that the King should be retained in an independent Ireland so as to reassure loyalists, particularly Northern loyalists.

In an effort to resolve these differences and chart a new policy, Count Plunkett convened a meeting of public bodies and interested parties on 19 April in the Mansion House. Plunkett proposed to start a new organisation which would scrap all the existing national organis-ations, including Sinn Fein. Griffith suggested that each group should keep its identity but that a joint executive be formed which would include Sinn Fein, Labour, the Volunteers, and Plunkett's followers, on a programme of abstention and appealing to the Peace Conference after the war, which America had just entered. This was defeated, and he announced that Sinn Fein would continue as it was. Then, as a split loomed, a private session was held and in Collins' words: '. . . the divergence of opinion was so great that, to avoid a split, it was announced that there should be no greater union than a loose co-operation.'[9] The 'loose co-operation' was applied almost immediately to one of Collins' current projects, the winning of another by-election on 9 May 1917, this time in Longford where he was backing the candidacy of a 1916 prisoner in Lewes jail, Joseph McGuinness, a member of a well-liked Longford family.

The by-election had more significance for Collins than the election of McGuinness. For it was during the campaign that he stayed in The Greville Arms, run by the Kiernans – 'four beautiful sisters and their brother . . . lovely glamorous girls . . . had all the right ideas'.[10] According to Sean MacEoin Collins fell in love with one of the girls, Helen, who chose to marry a solicitor, Paul McGovern. Frank O'Connor claims 'on the night before her wedding he went to her hotel and pleaded with her not to go through with the marriage' and that during the speeches he was so agitated he shredded his handker-chief. Collins transferred his affections to another sister, Kitty, whom Harry Boland was already in love with, a fact which may have had a bearing on his subsequent relationship with Collins. (A third sister, Maud, was courted by the tragic Thomas Ashe.)

McGuinness was advised not to stand by the prisoners' leader, Eamon de Valera, who wrote: 'As regards the contesting of elections question, it is so extremely dangerous from several points of view that most of us here consider it unwise.'[11] This was the first occasion on record that Collins decided not to be bound by de Valera's wishes. It would not be the last. De Valera's stated attitude was based on a doctrinaire separatism that refused to acknowledge the British Parliament, and on fears of a loss of face for the men of 1916 if the candidate were defeated. He promptly forgot such arguments later when a candidate himself. Collins went ahead without McGuinness' permission in a campaign whose message was summed up by a poster showing a man in prison uniform with a caption saying: 'Put him in to get him out'. It succeeded, but only just. On the first count the Irish Parliamentary Party candidate, Patrick MacKenna, was declared elected. However, as Beaslai puts it, 'a bundle of uncounted votes was then discovered' and McGuinness won by thirty-seven votes.

Many years later, Alasdair MacCaba, by then the much-admired Chairman of the Irish Educational Building Society, gave me his version of how the discovery came about. 'I jumped up on the platform, put a .45 to the head of the returning officer, clicked back the hammer and told him to think again.' Whatever the worth of MacCaba's intervention, Lloyd George now most certainly had to think again. Count Plunkett, with the benefit of a sympathy vote, had been a blow to the Irish Parliamentary Party. Joseph McGuinness, a common criminal serving a jail sentence, was a blow to a British Government constrained by the circumstances of the war to be mindful of Irish-American opinion.

There is a well-established British tradition for dealing with such problems. Buy time, be seen to be doing something, set up a tribunal, a commission, a forum, an assembly, a convention. The history of Ireland is strewn with such milestones. Lloyd George chose the convention option. It met on 25 July, allegedly representative of all shades of Irish opinion to 'recommend a settlement of the Irish problem'. In fact, however, the Convention members were nominated by the British Government. It was the political equivalent of an expedient normally reserved for Irish political trials, the packed jury. Sinn Fein were allocated 5 per cent of the membership, but Griffith declined to attend unless the delegates were elected by the Irish people. So although the Convention might have been represented in a good light in America, in Ireland, where Sinn Fein support was rising by the hour, it was doomed from the start. However it was accompanied by another move which was to have far-reaching effects. With a view to 'creating a favourable atmosphere for the Irish Convention' Bonar Law announced on 15 June that the remainder of the 1916 prisoners still in England were to be released unconditionally.

The prisoners held in Lewes Jail had been agitating for prisoner-of-war status. A huge protest meeting on their behalf in Beresford Place, the site of the *Helga*-blasted Liberty Hall, which the British had proscribed, had gone ahead anyhow on 10 June, resulting in the first death of a member of the crown forces since 1916, a police inspector killed by a blow from a hurley stick. Both Cathal Brugha and Count Plunkett were arrested as a result. Consequently when the Lewes men landed back in Dublin they received a tumultuous welcome. The cheerful pugnacity of Frank Thornton's account of the triumphant journey home reads very differently from that of his post-Rising departure from Dublin. He says:

The British had issued us with 3rd class tickets. However feeling in a first-class mood, Eamon de Valera decided that we should all travel first class . . . the ordinary passengers [gave us] plenty of moral support. The Captain, concluding that discretion was the better part of valour, decided to leave us there . . . Having won our point we spent our journey . . . with a crowd of British Tommies trying to teach children 'The Soldiers Song'. . . . there was a terrifically enthusiastic crowd on the pier at Dunlaoghaire . . . We were escorted to our carriages on the train and when we arrived at Westland Row our real trouble started . . . the crowd nearly tore us asunder. Every man was trying to carry some other man out to the coaches outside. . . . We were carried out to the open brakes outside Westland Row and escorted though the city by a huge crowd of people up to Flemings Hotel in Gardiner Place. Here a royal feast awaited us . . . we were back in Dublin with a determination. The surrender of 1916 was only a breathing space between that and the commencement of war proper for the freedom of the country . . .

The first shot in that campaign was fired on the afternoon of the prisoners' return. At a meeting in Exchequer Hall, Exchequer St, they found a linen scroll prepared for their signatures. It was addressed to the President and Congress of the United States and contained a quotation from Wilson's recent statement to Russia, 'The right of each people to defend itself against external aggression, external influence, etc. . . .' After signature it was immediately taken to the United States by a member of the IRB, Dr Patrick MacCartan. The second shot was the selection of Eamon de Valera to contest a by-election in East Clare caused by the death in action in France of Major William Redmond, brother of the Irish Parliamentary Party leader.

De Valera made such an impact on the voters of East Clare that he was to hold the seat for nearly forty years. His appeal has never adequately been defined. His grasp of the Irish psychology, particularly in the days before TV or widespread education brought more sophistication to the electorate, his study of Machiavelli's doctrines, and his 1916 reputation formed a formidable political arsenal. This was added to, rather than detracted from, by his studied aloofness and his actual self-confidence, his harsh Limerick accent and his striking appearance. Over six feet tall, angular, with staring eyes, he had a prison-pale complexion that he often deliberately accentuated by wearing a black cloak. People voted for him out of a spirit summed up by the true story of his meeting with an old man during a Clare election campaign in the twenties.[12] Seeing the old man at the side of a road, de Valera stopped the car and attempted to engage him in conversation. 'Are you one of them political gentlemen come down for the election?' the old man asked suspiciously. De Valera replied that he supposed one could say that such was the case, whereupon the old man spat on the ground and walked off saying, 'You're wasting your time. We're all for de Valera down here.'

De Valera's victory, on 10 July by 5,010 votes to 2,035, over P. J. Lynch, the Parliamentary Party candidate, was significant for two reasons. Firstly it marked his emergence into a leading role on the national political stage. Secondly, for the first time since the rising, the Volunteers appeared as an open, disciplined force, wearing uniforms, acting as election workers, and, most importantly in a contest in which feelings ran high, maintaining order, at both candidates' meetings, albeit armed only with sticks.

With the return to Ireland of the Lewes men the cast was now complete. To the names that have already flitted across these pages were now added figures like William T. Cosgrave, who had fought alongside Cathal Brugha during 1916 and was also given life imprisonment after the Rising, who won another by-election in August of that year, in Kilkenny, and later went on to become the country's prime minister for ten years, and Piaras Beaslai, journalist and polemicist, who later was Collins' biographer. Curiously enough Collins did not take part in the Clare campaign. It may be that as Beaslai says, the return of the 122 prisoners 'most of whom had to be provided for' created a new work-load which kept him in Dublin. But in view of his intense involvement in other by-election campaigns, one is tempted to regard it as a significant omission. Collins' normal attitude to work was summed up in an observation to Terence MacSwiney: 'It is my experience that people who are very busy are never so busy that they cannot do something extra.'

And certainly, in mid-summer 1917, Collins was 'very busy'. He transferred his offices to 32 Bachelor's Walk and continued to use these premises, relatively unscathed, until the end of the Anglo-Irish war some four years later. His fellow Committee member Diarmuid Lynch said Collins did 90 per cent of the drafting of the revision of the Volunteer Constitution and records that '. . . very few changes were made in the draft as submitted by him.'

These were swirling, reckless days. Friendships were made and enmities formed. After Frongoch Collins' closest friends were the three Corkmen Gearoid O'Sullivan, Diarmuid O'Hegarty, and 'the medieval page', Joe O'Reilly. O'Hegarty, an acknowledged administrator, played a vital part in organising the IRB while Collins was still in Frongoch. He was later to become Secretary to the first native Irish Government, set up at least in part as a result of his efforts.

O'Reilly, from Bantry, County Cork, had known Collins in London and had been with him in Stafford and Frongoch. Collins bumped into him in Dublin about six months after their release and immediately ordered – not offered – him a job as his assistant. O'Reilly's devotion to Collins was legendary. Frank O'Connor wrote that 'no one except O'Reilly himself could do justice to it or to the strange flavour of romance that surrounds it and makes one think of a mediaeval tale. He was courier, clerk, messenger boy, nurse and slave.'

After Lewes Collins added Thomas Ashe and Harry Boland to the friends. Ashe, a brave and steadfast man of strong religious feeling, was the second officer of the Dublin Brigade in seniority, after de Valera, to survive the Rising. He had played a leading role in the Asbourne engagement outside Dublin, where a party of police were ambushed and overwhelmed in the sort of attack which was to form the pattern of the future. Ashe had one of the Volunteers' few successes, and had supported Collins against de Valera in the Lewes debates over McGuinness' candidature. Outside prison he was one of the first to proclaim Collins a man of unusual ability and formed a strong, if short-lived friendship with him. Harry Boland, a tailor by trade, was simply Collins' partner in crime. They were two of a kind, brave, energetic, unscrupulous, jolly buccaneers. Boland had considerable political talent of the 'vote early vote often' variety. As Frank O'Connor observed, when the pair of them got their hands on a list of candidates for an executive or an election panel there was little danger of moderation showing its hideous fangs. Without their partnership the Sinn Fein effort would have collapsed.

However these friendships and others, like that with Liam Tobin, were heavily offset through Collins incurring the wrath of Cathal Brugha. Given the differences in their attitudes to almost everything that mattered Collins would inevitably have had to clash with the formulaic, rule-book approach of the older man. Brugha was a 'static warfare' man. He still thought of fighting in GPO terms. It's doubtful if he ever seriously believed they could win the war. For him, carrying on the fight was the important thing, keeping faith with the men who had raised the standard in other generations. He opposed Collins over ambushing. Their military differences were compounded by Collins' unfortunate tendency to bait people, particularly fish that rose to the fly, and he, O'Sullivan and O'Hegarty used to delight in maddening the older man at occasions such as Gaelic League meetings with nit-picking questions about accounts. In a very literal sense Brugha would one day settle accounts with Collins. A man of 'adamantine simplicity' he had been hit by rifle fire, bomb fragments and bullets from a Colt automatic during his defence of the South Dublin Union in 1916 but refused either to die or to surrender. Instead, the squat little long-lipped man propped himself up against a wall after his colleagues had retreated and punctuated bursts from his 'Peter the Painter' revolver with the chorus from A. M. Sullivan's 'God Save Ireland':

'God save Ireland!' said the heroes;
'God save Ireland!' said they all.
'Whether on the scaffold high
Or the battlefield we die,
O, what matter when for Erin dear we fall!'

Hearing him sing his comrades returned and fought beside him until the surrender. He escaped a firing squad because he was thought to be dying anyhow. But the fitness engendered by Volunteer training and earlier years of swimming and boxing saved him. After the Rising, as the Volunteers started to reorganise, a meeting of some fifty representatives from different parts of the country was held in Flemming's Hotel. Brugha turned up on crutches and presided over the gathering which hailed him as a 'modern Cuchullain'.

Cuchullain too propped himself up *in extremis*, his enemies knowing it was safe to approach only when a raven had perched on the dead warrior's shoulder. Brugha, after the failure of 1916, detested the IRB and, despite his fearsome reputation, viewed the Volunteers as a defensive, not an offensive, body, but one which should be used only if the British made an attack on the population such as an attempt to enforce conscription. He didn't think the organisation had the capacity to initiate a successful campaign.

De Valera made common ground with Brugha over the IRB issue, arguing unsuccessfully with prominent IRB men like Harry Boland and Austin Stack that they should leave the Brotherhood. He claimed that his objections were based on the church's teachings regarding secret societies. Later, as the struggle progressed, both men did become supporters of his.

In that first week of release from prison de Valera displayed two of the enduring traits of his career. One was an ability to wrestle with his conscience and win. He had only barely arrived home to be reunited with his family, before, despite his scruples over MacGuinness contesting elections, he was on his way to Clare. Secondly he demonstrated his talent for bringing divergent viewpoints together. He insisted that Eoin MacNeill, the man who had opposed the Rising, should be on his election platforms, thus ensuring support not only from the Volunteers, but from the wide circle of academic and Gaelic League intellectuals who admired the polymath MacNeill. Even Pearse, in his 1916 statement of surrender, had gone out of his way to note that 'both Eoin MacNeill and we have acted in the best interests of Ireland'.

However by the end of that year of aftermath and regrouping de Valera had also demonstrated another vitally important facet of his character. He would be a unifying force only when he was in control of whatever movement it was required unifying. In October 1917 the two largest and most important bodies were Sinn Fein and the Irish Volunteers. The Volunteers' aim was the Republic contained in the Proclamation of 1916 but Sinn Fein stood for Griffith's 'restoration of the King, Lords and Commons.' If the two organisations were not to go in separate directions a compromise was obviously necessary.

De Valera and Griffith met over coffee in a Grafton St café a week before the Sinn Fein Convention was due to be held in the Mansion House on 25 October. De Valera insisted that he should control Sinn Fein as he had the Volunteers and the IRB behind him. He urged Griffith not to contest his nomination for the presidency, saying that if there was a contest he, de Valera, would win in any case. This was very far from being the case as the ballot for the Executive subsequently proved. Griffith's supporters headed the list and the IRB-supported candidates came in at the bottom of the poll, Collins himself being the last to be elected.

However there was one essential difference between Griffith and de Valera. Griffith wanted influence, de Valera wanted power. Despite the fact that Sinn Fein had suddenly mushroomed into a huge organisation which showed every sign of achieving the results he had hitherto only dreamed of, when the Convention met Griffith announced that he was retiring in favour of de Valera, 'a soldier and a statesman'. Plunkett then withdrew his candidacy also. Griffith became Vice- President and, secure in office, de Valera stated 'we are not doctrinaire republicans' and obtained support from both the Sinn Fein and Volunteer camps for the following policy declaration:

Sinn Fein aims at securing the international recognition of Ireland as an independent Irish Republic. Having achieved that status, the Irish people may, by referendum, freely choose their own form of government.

The other important decision taken at this open Ard Fheis, or convention, was that at the next general election every seat would be contested and that any Sinn Feiners elected would form themselves into a new national Assembly, Dail Eireann. When these political deliberations concluded a secret convention of Volunteers was held on 27 October at the Gaelic Athletic Association's ground at Jones's Road, Drumcondra. The IRB dominated these proceedings, securing de Valera's election as President of the Volunteers, Collins' as Director of Organisation and placing two important IRB men Diarmuid Lynch and Sean MacGarry, in the key posts of Director of Communication and General Secretary respectively. Lynch, a member of the IRB's Supreme Council, had been sentenced to death for his part in 1916, but his American citizenship saved him. McGarry, also a Supreme Council man, had reorganised the IRB with Hobson and McCullough.

The Dublin Executive of the reorganised Volunteers was also taken over by the IRB. One Volunteer post which the Brotherhood did not win was that of Chief of Staff; Cathal Brugha was elected on his Cuchullain reputation. Subsequently de Valera again refused to join the Brotherhood, remarking darkly that he suspected Collins was 'organising more than the Volunteers'. De Valera had made a calculation that his best road forward was on the high public ground of his 1916 popularity. The secret routes of the IRB would not advance his ambitions. Nor did it please him to see anyone working to improve those routes. 'Curse all secret societies,' he exclaimed once. In effect that meant 'curse Michael Collins' too.

Electorally, 1917 was a triumphant year for Sinn Fein. Apart from taking seats from the Irish Parliamentary Party by way of by-election, they were actually presented with one when Laurence Ginnell, who had been a stalwart champion of the Frongoch men in their agitations, added to the excitements of Clare and Kilkenny by resigning and later becoming treasurer of Sinn Fein.

But behind the cheering at the hustings it was brought home to Collins that there was a harsher side to the power struggle. It was an aspect of this that first brought him to the public's attention. To counter the growing disaffection in the country the authorities made copious use of the Defence of the Realm Act (DORA) which amongst other provisions allowed for deportations, and trial by court martial for offences such as illegal drilling or making speeches likely to cause disaffection. In August three prominent Sinn Feiners, Thomas Ashe, Austin Stack and Fionan Lynch, were arrested on the latter charge. Collins was friendly with all three, particularly Ashe, with whom he shared public platforms and private IRB activity, and Lynch, who lived with him at 44 Harcourt St.

The Ashe trio followed the increasingly common practice of refusing to recognise the court and received sentences of a year, eighteen months and two years respectively. However, the relatively light sentences masked that fundamentally serious issue which erupts so continuously on to the Anglo-Irish legal landscape, the question of political status. As the trio saw it they had been tried under a particular Act, before a particular type of court, charged with a particular type of offence, yet as soon as the jail gates closed on them they were classed as common criminals.

There were already about forty DORA victims in Mountjoy. It was mutually agreed that they would all go on hunger strike for political status. Austin Stack was elected leader and the strike began on 20 September. As this was a breach of prison discipline the authorities retaliated by taking away the prisoners' beds, bedding and boots.

After five or six days of lying on a cold stone floor the prisoners were subjected to forcible feeding. On 25 September Fionan Lynch saw Ashe being carried off to receive this treatment and called out to him, 'Stick it Tom boy.' Ashe called back, 'I'll stick it, Fin.' It was the last time they spoke to each other. Ashe was carried back, blue in the face and unconscious. He was removed to the Mater Misericordiae Hospital where he died within a few hours.

A combination of spontaneous feeling and IRB organisation made his death the subject of a national demonstration of mourning and protest. Clad in a Volunteer uniform, the shirt of which had been given to him by Collins, the body lay in state while some 30,000 people visited the hospital to pay their respects. Public bodies from all over the country were represented at his gigantic funeral. It was the Volunteers' greatest show of strength since the Rising. For a short time, as they marshalled the crowds, and marched in the funeral procession wearing their Volunteer uniforms, the Dublin Brigade, under the command of Dick McKee, took over the city. McKee, for a period was, after Collins, arguably the most important man in the Volunteers until his death in 1920. A printer by trade, he is spoken of as having natural leadership qualities and, following his release from Frongoch, he played a vital role in reorganising the Volunteers all over the country. Under him the Dublin Brigade became the most formidable in the country.

At the graveside three volleys were fired and then Collins, in Volunteer uniform, stepped forward and made a short and revealing speech in Irish and English. His English words were: 'Nothing additional remains to be said. That volley which we have just heard is the only speech which it is proper to make above the grave of a dead Fenian.'

He was observed weeping bitterly afterwards, but soon dried his tears. For a very great deal that was 'additional' remained to be said. The inquest for instance, on 1 November, censured the Castle authorities, the prison authority, spoke of 'inhuman punishment' and condemned forcible feeding. As it had taken three weeks to reach this verdict during the public hearing of a variety of witnesses, including Lynch and Stack, the impact on public opinion was considerable. The immediate official reaction to Ashe's death was that the Mountjoy prisoners were first awarded a special category status and then, after they had been transferred to Dundalk, giving rise to another hunger strike, released on 17 November.

A more lasting effect was created by the circulation of thousands of copies of 'The Last Poem of Thomas Ashe'. Written in Lewes Jail, its grace notes of sacrifice, sentiment and religion struck a sharp and powerful chord in the unsophisticated Catholic Ireland of 1917:

Let me carry your Cross for Ireland, Lord!
My cares in this world are few,
And few are the tears will fall for me
When I go on my way to you. . .

Let me carry your Cross for Ireland, Lord!
For Ireland weak with tears,
For the aged man of the clouded brow,
And the child of tender years.
For the empty homes of her golden plains,
For the hopes of her future, too!
Let me carry your Cross for Ireland, Lord!
For the cause of Roisin Dhu.

Nevertheless, despite the fact that widespread outcry at the manner of Ashe's death belied his prophecy that 'few are the tears that will fall for me', 1918 began with a reversal of Sinn Fein's electoral fortunes. The party lost two by-elections for a change. One was in South Armagh on 1 February where the Parliamentary candidate was backed by the Ancient Order of Hibernians and helped by the fact that the Unionist candidate stood down in his favour. The other was in Waterford on 22 March. This vacancy, which was filled by his son, was caused by the death of the Irish Parliamentary Party leader, John Redmond, earlier in the month. A broken and disillusioned man, his biographer truly said of his life that it 'will stand for ever as a symbolic tragedy of a greatly gifted and disinterested statesman, who trusted overmuch in the efficacy of Parliamentary agitation.'

Michael Collins did not trust that form of agitation 'overmuch'. That fateful March he made a contact which, more than any other, made the form of 'agitation' he did have faith in, physical force, a reality. At No. 5 Cabra Rd, Dublin, the householder, Michael Foley, introduced him to the celebrated detective Eamonn Broy. Three and a half years later in London as the British and Irish delegations met for negotiations which, in no small measure, his information helped to bring about, this is how Broy appeared to one observer:

. . . a strongly-built, broad-shouldered, stiff-backed man entered the room. I found it difficult to believe that this gauche, ill-at-ease, obsequious person was Ned Broy, the famous 'G' man who had turned traitor and wilily double-crossed his British masters. But not for long: soon I was convinced that his hard, cruel, green eyes were indicative of his character.

Some fifty years later after he had retired following a controversial but highly successful career, during which he became Commissioner of Police under de Valera, I asked the still superficially deferential Broy why he had acted as he did and he told me:

I come from Kildare. We were reared in a grimmer tradition than most. We remembered '98, the Yeomanry and what they did. There was a church once near where I was born and the Yeos rounded up the women and children, locked them in and set fire to the church. We remembered that, the pitch-capping and the flogging. And we talked about Wolfe Tone and the Fenians. The Fenians were riddled with informers. After 1916 I felt it was time we learned the lesson.

Collins thought so too. Before meeting Broy he and Harry Boland had talked with the old parliamentarian, Tim Healy, who had represented the Mountjoy prisoners at the Ashe inquest, and Healy had told them that their ideas of physical force were 'stark mad', though at the same time he conceded that 'there wasn't the ghost of a chance of getting anything out of the British Parliament.'[13] Broy, however, frankly told Collins that the RIC would 'have to be dealt with. You'll have to shoot.' Collins received this intelligence without demur. Since the Rising, Broy had been passing on information to Sinn Fein, via the O'Hanrachain family who had had a son executed and he thought that therefore he 'could rely on them to be bitter'. But nothing seemed to come of his efforts.

Of the other three Castle detectives who helped Collins significantly, two, Joe Kavanagh and David Neligan, had the same experience as Broy in that their initial offers of help were turned down before Collins got to hear of them. Joe Kavanagh had first tried to help the prisoners after the 1916 Rising, offering to take messages for them, or to do any kindness he could, but he was spurned in the belief that he was simply another 'G' man using different methods to get results. However he was friendly with a Sinn Fein sympathiser who ultimately put him in touch with Collins. This was Thomas Gay, the librarian of the Dublin corporation library in Capel St. Kavanagh was married, with a family, and his actions took unusual courage. Collins realised his worth when Kavanagh, through Gay, sent a message corroborating a warning Broy had given concerning what became known as the 'German Plot' swoop which, as we shall see, was of crucial importance to Sinn Fein.

Kavanagh worked for Collins for about a year before dying, of natural causes. But by then he had recruited another detective to take his place, James MacNamara, whose family were prominent loyalists, and who was regarded by the Castle authorities as one of their most trusted men, being brave, tough and a dead shot. He informed for Collins until almost the end of the war until, one day, he was suddenly sacked without reason. Prudently he did not seek one. As Collins said to him on hearing the news of his dismissal, 'You're lucky. If they had anything on you you'd have been shot outright.'

David Neligan made up for the loss of both Kavanagh and MacNamara. One of the most remarkable figures of the period, he was drawing five pensions when I first met him in the sixties – an old IRA pension, one from the RIC, the Irish Police force, the Irish civil service – and the British Secret Service.[14] He had sent offers of help to Sinn Fein through Patrick Sheehan, who became secretary to de Valera, but Sheehan returned with the dispiriting advice that he should resign from the force as his brother Maurice, a trade union organiser, was advising him to do at the time, May 1920.

Neligan duly resigned, but then Collins, who had not been told of his offer, got to hear what had happened and sent word to him in Tralee, County Kerry, where he lived, asking him to come to see him in Dublin where he asked him to rejoin. Neligan, who hated the Castle, offered to help by joining a flying column instead but Collins replied: 'We have plenty of men for columns, but no one can fill your place in the Castle.' Reluctantly, Neligan agreed, arranging that he be sent bogus threatening letters which he showed to the authorities, as the reason for his change of mind. After a few months working for Collins as a 'G' man he took advantage of the British shortage of knowledgeable personnel to apply to the Secret Service and was accepted, remaining undetected until after the British left Southern Ireland.

Initially Collins kept his contacts so compartmented that they did not know each other. He used to meet Kavanagh and MacNamara in Thomas Gay's house in Clontarf unknown to Tobin who fed the documents and information they provided into his system without knowing where they came from. But, as the war progressed and personnel changed, this proved more difficult to do. Neligan came into contact with Tobin immediately. By then the strain had changed Tobin from the light-hearted young man who once accompanied Collins on a hair-brained mission to Westminster Abbey, to see if they could steal the Stone of Scone, to a figure whom Neligan described wonderingly:

Tall, gaunt, cynical, with tragic eyes, he looked like a man who had seen the inside of hell. He walked without moving his arms and seemed emptied of energy. Yet this man was, after Collins, the Castle's most dangerous enemy.[15]

Collins, in the midst of the horrors, however, struck Neligan as having:

. . . a winning smile, a ready laugh and cheerful manner. He had a trick of turning his head swiftly and then the resolute line of his jaw showed. He was a friendly man with the fortunate manners of putting one at ease.[16]

Broy had a similarly good first impression of Collins. Like Broy himself, Collins 'was athletic. He was light on his feet. You could see he was fit'. This appealed to the non-drinking, non-smoking Broy. Between his views on the RIC and on sport Collins immediately struck Broy as 'the man I was looking for'. Although he claims that he did say to 'Mick', who was dressed in breeches and leggings, 'you'll have to change your clothes.' Collins accepted the advice. 'After that he dressed like a company director. This had a tremendous effect, a psychological effect on lads from the country. They felt everything was all right if a man wore a clean collar and tie!' So, it may be remarked, did the average member of the British security forces. One reason Collins got away from so many checkpoints subsequently was simply because the troops didn't think that terrorists dressed in neat grey suits.

Collins was of course quite clear on the central role of the police in the British system. What Broy brought to him, however, was a detailed, inside knowledge not only of how the system worked in its political aspects but how the men involved were trained, thought and felt. By 1918 he had been a policeman for seven years. At that time the DMP oath still included: 'I swear I will not belong to any secret society, the Society of Freemasons excepted.' The police force was divided into six divisions, 'A' to 'F'. 'G', the political wing, had three sections, political, ordinary crime, carriage supervision. 'G' Division was directed at all national movements. Anyone suspected of being disloyal to the British connection had an 'S' placed after their name. There were 'G' men at all boats and railway stations and the movements of all 'S' people were watched while in the city, and the relevant RIC barracks were notified as to their movements and whom they met. Back at home the movements of 'S' persons were similarly monitored and the details forwarded to Dublin. Each 'G' man had his own notebook and its contents were transferred at night to 'a very large book'. In 1915 Broy had been appointed a confidential clerk in the headquarters of 'G' Division, Gt Brunswick St Police Station, now Pearse St. This meant that for a large part of each working day he was alone with the 'very large book'. A copy of every secret report crossed his desk. By the time he met Collins the flood of reports was less than it had been because, following the Rising, the authorities had been cutting down on the normal complement of some forty 'G' men thinking that the executions had successfully cowed would-be rebels. As Collins saw immediately, 'The British could replace a detective. But he couldn't step into the dead man's shoes and his knowledge.' Also, as Broy pointed out to him, while, after three weeks' training 'a big change came over the simple country lad', the recruit was still Irish and susceptible to an appeal to patriotic instincts. In the depot and at mealtimes these men discussed politics honestly and openly and showed themselves quite nationalistic on the Home Rule issue and on topics like the latitude allowed to the Ulstermen to drill and arm. Later, as the struggle developed, it was this factor properly used, as much as intimidation, that accounted for the number of 'Good night, Mick's or 'Good day, Mr Collins's with which DMP men passed unhindered the most wanted man in Ireland. The myth of Collins, 'The man they couldn't catch', was born in No. 5 Cabra Rd.

Collins being a different man to so many different people, it was probably inevitable that descriptions of him vary greatly. Though he was fair-complexioned and brown-haired, Beaslai notes with puzzlement: 'A great many people who saw him received the impression that his hair was black or very dark.'[17] Beaslai gives a description of a man 'about five foot eleven inches in height . . .', with a face

intensely mobile and expressive, changing rapidly from a scowl of anger to a broad grin of enjoyment, now showing scorn or defiance and now the sunniest good humour. His restless energy showed itself in a series of abrupt jerky movements, and in an explosive brusquerie of manner which often offended the pompous and pretentious, and those sedate persons who disliked hurry. He always dressed well, and was particularly neat and tidy in his habits. His suits were generally of dark grey.

He had a funny patois of his own that he sometimes used with close friends, broadening his West Cork brogue so that 'eggs' came out something like 'ogs'.

Frank O'Connor describes a figure of raw genius, whose behaviour ranged through that of business tycoon, military expert, compassionate charmer, especially where children, the downtrodden, or old people were concerned, to that of a hooligan whose antics could sometimes resemble those of berserkers at play.

A network was set up so that Broy could pass messages to Collins undetected and vice versa. At Kingsbridge Station there was Pat Treacy, a relation of Broy's. In Capel St there was Thomas Gay. Broy could call there quite innocently in the evenings. Just as during the mornings he could drop in for a healthful glass of buttermilk to a little dairy in Parnell Square where the circuit between himself and Collins could be closed unsuspectedly, appropriately enough by passing on messages to Sean Duffy, who travelled all over the city in his job as an electrician.

Dairies were a particular feature of Dublin at the time and one of the most important intelligence and weaponry clearing houses in the city was Phil Sheerin's 'Coolevin Dairies', situated under the loopline bridge in Amiens St, close to the railway station. Couriers from Belfast, generally railway employees, could drop messages there without difficulty and it was also conveniently near the docks for sailors or dockers bringing in arms. Collins had one of his offices in the back rooms. The place was raided several times, but nothing was ever found and Sheerin survived unscathed throughout the war. Messages were also left in Harry Boland's tailoring shop in Middle Abbey St and in 'The Bookshop' in Dawson St where the studious Miss Susan Killeen had taken a job. The Bookshop became a veritable Collins post office as indeed did many another shop around the city. Broy commented, 'I felt my own little office surrounded by police to

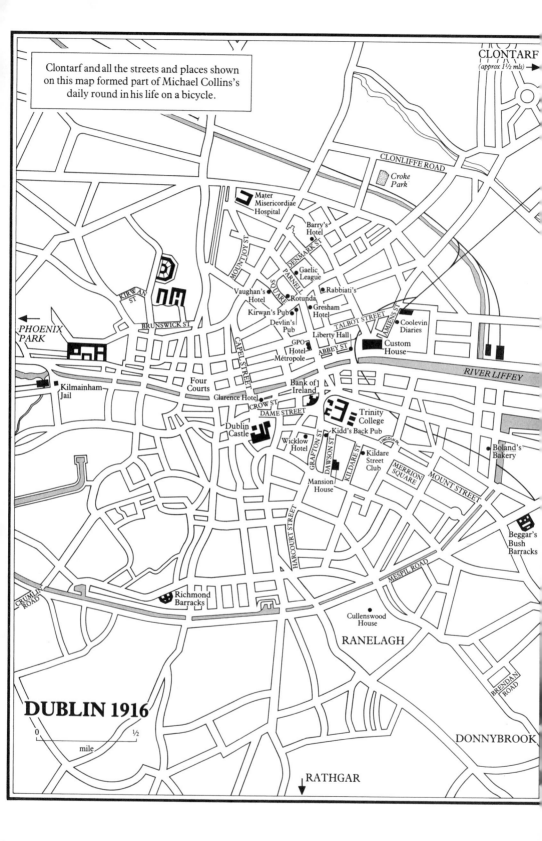

Clontarf and all the streets and places shown
on this map formed part of Michael Collins's
daily round in his life on a bicycle.

CLONTARF
(approx 1½ mls)

CLONLIFFE ROAD

Croke
Park

Mater
Misericordiae
Hospital

Barry's
Hotel

DENMARK ST

Gaelic
League

MOUNTJOY ST

PARNELL SQUARE

Vaughan's
Hotel

Rotunda

Rabbiati's

Kirwan's Pub

Gresham
Hotel

BRUNSWICK ST

KIRWAN ST

Devlin's
Pub

TALBOT STREET

AMIENS ST

Coo111evin
Diaries

Liberty Hall

PHOENIX
PARK

GPO

ABBEY ST

Custom
House

Hotel
Métropole

RIVER LIFFEY

CAPEL STREET

Four
Courts

Bank of
Ireland

Kilmainham
Jail

Clarence Hotel

CROW ST

DAME STREET

Trinity
College

Dublin
Castle

Kidd's Back Pub

Wicklow
Hotel

GRAFTON ST

DAWSON ST

KILDARE ST

LINCOLN PL.

Kildare
Street
Club

Boland's
Bakery

Mansion
House

MERRION
SQUARE

MOUNT STREET

HARCOURT STREET

Beggar's
Bush
Barracks

MESPIL ROAD

CRUMLIN ROAD

Richmond
Barracks

Cullenswood
House

RANELAGH

BRENDAN ROAD

DUBLIN 1916

0   ½

mile

DONNYBROOK

↓ RATHGAR

protect me was a kind of base for penetrating the British Government. Always they boasted of their informers. Now we could think of our informers.'

Collins was able to destroy Castle rule because the system was far less secure than it appeared. One of his principal agents in the Castle, Thomas Markham, a senior civil servant, prepared a report for him which gave a an insider's account of 'how it really worked':

The British system was based on:

(a) The grasp of human weakness and vanity.
(b) A correct appreciation of the value and use of duplicity and Pecksniffianism.
(c) A clear conception of the truth that success in governing depends on well-contrived antagonisms in the economic and social structure of the state.

A new Chief Secretary is powerless to alter the system fundamentally, or even 'materially'. Yet all departures [in policy] went to him. All staff are vetted by the police with exhaustive descriptions of family tree in all its hues and activities.

Belfast staff is very carefully selected as to loyalty. Numerical strength makes it a Staff-in-Waiting prepared to work for the whole Irish service if and when the opportunity arises.

Dealing with police and politics were the pivotal props of the system. . . . The Royal Irish Constabulary, organised in Counties, Districts . . . During his training his vanity, ignorance and intelligence were each subjected to the treatment designed to make the British Government his servant and his God. The RIC had something to do with every phase of governmental activity.

The constable records everything in his diary. What he frightens from the child and coaxes from the cailin. What he hears, sees, infers. The sergeant transfers the constable's report, never abbreviating. It is not his part to select. The policeman moves in a social atmosphere, he writes down everything, gossipy servants, what the RIC pensioner says. A 'someone' whose name is never written down. He's a 'reliable source'. He could be the publican. The rail spy could be the inspector. He frequently is.

The road to the Castle is paved with anonymous letters, deriving from the besetting Irish sin, jealousy. The depth and widespread nature of this treachery would make a good Irishman despair. The local loyalist could have a good post and be merely a disreputable spotter . . . what was said at a Volunteer meeting; where arms were kept; the eavesdropping prison warder; the opening of letters in the post.

Ambiguity and elasticity are the marked features of the system enabling the Administration to sanction in Belfast what it refused in Dublin. The exact standard of Irish morality, public and private, was taken, and rule measured in accordance. Ideology was ignored.[18]

Ideology was certainly ignored in the case of the recruitment of one of the most startling additions to the Collins network, his cousin

Nancy O'Brien. One day Nancy was sent for by Sir James MacMahon and told that in view of the worsening situation it was imperative that the Castle's most secret coded messages be in safe hands and that he was putting her in charge of handling these messages for him! Collins' first reaction on hearing of his cousin's new job was to exclaim, 'In the name of Jasus how did these people ever get an empire?!' His second was to ensure that Nancy's new role was exploited to the full, unmercifully, until the end of the struggle.

Nancy was one of the unsung heroines of the time. She had a good deal of Collins' intelligence and daring, though not his temper. In view of the demands he made on her she could hardly have worked with him if she had. Many of her lunch hours were spent in the GPO lavatory copying out decoded messages which she then smuggled out to him in her bodice. During her working hours she would frequently get disconcerting messages to check on something which might entail a hurried journey up steep stairs through the GPO labyrinth seeking information in some office where she had no right to be. When she complained to him that the climbing and the lack of lunch was wearing her out his reaction was to give her a pinch and say, 'Yerrah, ye can well afford to lose a bit of that.'

Her flat in Glasnevin was used as post office and staging post by everyone from members of the active service units to warders from Mountjoy. Often after the former's visits, she would have to pick up bullets that had dropped on a carpet or had been left lying on a dressing table – evidence every bit as incriminating as the guns she had hidden. Her looks and personality once attracted assistance with heavy luggage from a friendly British officer on a train to Cork, he not realising that the weight of her baggage came from the rifles she was ferrying.

On one occasion Collins subjected her to an inquisition over an important letter he thought she should have received. She denied having seen it; the only message she had recently seen had been some gibberish from an unknown admirer referring to 'Angelus bells and the light glinting in her hair.' He blew up. 'What sort of a Gligeen ejit are you anyway? That's the message I'm looking for. The warders change at six o'clock and our man will be in his room when the light goes on!' Nancy broke down in tears and told him where and how to deal with his messages in future.

That night 'well after midnight' Nancy was awakened by stones thrown at her window. There was Collins, in defiance of the curfew, standing in the front garden beckoning her down. 'Listen,' he told her, 'I'm sorry for what happened. I shouldn't have said it. I'm under the most terrible strain. Here's a little present for you,' he said, placing something on the garden wall. With that, the most wanted man in Europe disappeared into the darkness leaving behind him – a bag of bullseyes.[19]

Another vitally important agent was Lily Merin, a cousin of Beaslai's, who worked in the Castle as a WAAC typist. Collins' first test query to her was did she know a 'ginger-haired typist'?[20] A letter written on stolen Dail Eireann notepaper which gave indications of the existence of a death squad operating from the Castle had fallen into Collins' hands. The only clue as to the identity of one of its members was a sentence in the letter which said, 'X has a ginger-haired typist. Ginger for short.' After learning the officer's name, with subsequent fatal consequences for him, Collins briefed Merin on intelligence details such as the fact that carbon paper can be deciphered.

He then gave her the key to a house in Clonliffe Road used by one of his intelligence officers and she used to visit it regularly over a period of two years, letting herself in, going to a specified room and using the typewriter there to make her reports, which were placed in sealed envelopes and left on the typing table to be picked up by Collins. In all the time she used the house she never saw any of the other occupants, nor did the intelligence officer ever meet her or even know of her existence.

As the war intensified Dame St and Grafton St swarmed with British agents of all sorts, many of them Army Intelligence Officers dressed in mufti. Merin used to walk up and down the streets, ostensibly window-shopping on the arm of either Frank Saurin or Tom Cullen, identifying these agents for the Squad. She also provided Collins with the names and addresses of several officers who lived out of barracks in civilian digs while engaged in under-cover operations. She survived undetected until the ending of hostilities, but was suddenly dismissed without explanation after the Truce came into operation, an indication of how the British were able to breach IRA security once the Volunteers came into the open and of how the Collins network would have been dealt with had hostilities recommenced.

The British were also responsible for placing another woman, Josephine Marchmont, in a position where Collins was able to mastermind an extraordinary scheme which resulted in her being turned into an IRA agent.[21] She was employed at the HQ of the 6th Division in Cork Military Barracks with the rank of a foreman clerk, as confidential secretary to a Captain Webb who was the principal staff officer to the commander of the division, Major General Sir Peter Strickland. Strickland controlled the key areas of Cork, Kerry, Waterford, Wexford, South Tipperary and Kilkenny.

She was trusted implicitly. Her father had been a Head Constable in the RIC. Her husband had been killed in the First World War. But one day an orderly in the canteen, noticing that she appeared to be depressed, asked what was wrong and discovered that she was pining for her children, two little boys, who were in the custody of her mother-in-law, a formidable lady apparently, at Barry, South Wales.

This information was passed on to the alert Adjutant of the Cork No. 1 Brigade of the IRA, Florrie O'Donoghue, who in later life would become a noted commentator on the period, and one of the greatest collectors of its military history. He in turn informed Collins and as a result of this slight piece of intelligence Josephine Marchmont was eventually made an offer she could not refuse. She would be reunited with her children if she agreed to work for the IRA.

Collins oversaw the arrangements whereby O'Donoghue and a prominent Volunteer called Sean Phelan, who was later killed in an attack on a train at Upton, County Cork,[22] organised the kidnapping of the children, with the help of Patrick O'Donoghue of Manchester (no relation) and got them safely to Cork, where they were reunited with their mother and lodged with the families of friendly farmers. Marchmont's subsequent information alerted the IRA to the details of impending troop movements, such as raids and sweeps, and enabled the IRA to plan many a successful ambush, execute spies, and weed out 'stool pigeons' placed in internment camps amongst captured Volunteers. She came under suspicion following the killing of three British Intelligence officers in November 1920, but an act of kindness she had done saved her from exposure.

A soldier whom she had assisted in 'subbing' his pay tipped her off one lunchtime that all female staff were to be searched that evening on their way home, most particularly herself. She promptly returned the copied documents she had intended bringing out with her and escaped detection. Though her activities were curtailed after that she continued to supply information throughout the war, at the end of which she married – Florrie O'Donoghue.

Proposing a vote of sympathy to O'Donoghue on Josephine's death in 1966, which was seconded by the Lord Mayor of Cork, Alderman Sean Casey, TD, Dr Seamus Fitzgerald paid tribute to Josephine's 'significant part in the national struggle' but indicated that even at that stage the nature of the dead woman's contribution was still such a delicate subject that he could 'only leave references to her important activities in this field to those in higher authority'.[23]

In the spring of 1918 the struggle, though still comparatively mild in comparison with what was to come, had taken a turn that brought Collins two brushes with the police. Sinn Fein, both as part of its general muscle-flexing and because of folk memory of famine, became concerned at the war's acceleration of the flow of food out of the country and took a number of steps to reduce it. In the west, cattle were driven off grazing land and the ground was parcelled out for tillage by the local Sinn Fein Clubs. The rents were then passed on to the landlords; at least that was the theory of the thing. The cattle-driving and ground-breaking were occasions of great local excitement, often accompanied by bands and marching Volunteers. The

Volunteers were controlled from Dublin by a General Headquarters Staff (GHQ), which included Cathal Brugha, Chief of Staff, Richard Mulcahy, Deputy Chief of Staff, Collins, in a variety of roles, and Dick McKee. Slightly disturbed by the socialistic whiff of these activities GHQ issued a directive that they were 'neither of a national nor a military character'. However, coupled with the arms raiding which some Volunteers were also engaging in, the drives produced a response of a military nature. It was forbidden to carry arms in Tipperary, Galway or Clare, and Clare was declared a fully-fledged military area on 27 February. Persons wishing to enter or leave the county were issued with passports. The *Clare Champion* was suppressed. Extra troops were drafted in and mail and telegrams were subjected to miltary censorship.

In Dublin, Diarmuid Lynch, the Sinn Fein 'Food Director', ordered that the herd of pigs en route to England be impounded at the North Wall, slaughtered and sold to local butchers. The proceeds were handed over to their owners, but Lynch, an American citizen, was arrested and sentenced to deportation. He wanted to get married before being deported so as to assist his fiancée with her passport application but the authorities refused him permission. However while held in Dundalk Jail he was married in his cell by a priest who had ostensibly paid him a routine visit in the company of his fiancée and some friends.

The jail wedding created a sensation and to compound the publicity his bride accompanied him on the train to Dublin and deportation. The Lynches were met at Amiens St Station by a huge crowd and followed to the Bridewell by a party of friends, including Collins, who coolly entered the jail and spent a long time talking with Lynch, arranging communication routes between Ireland and America. A few days later he was in jail himself. He was arrested outside his Bachelor's Walk office on 3 April by 'G' men. At first he resisted fiercely, to the cheers of a large and sympathetic crowd. But another IRB man, Joe McGrath, turned up and negotiated with the police to such good effect that he and Collins were allowed to walk together over O'Connell Bridge to Brunswick St Station with the 'G' men following behind. From Brunswick St he was brought to Longford, charged at the Assizes with making a speech 'likely to cause disaffection' at Legga, near Granard and remanded to Sligo Jail.

From Sligo he wrote to Hannie on 10 April: '. . . Sad! Sad! Sad! . . . Before me the prospect of a long holiday . . . I'm very anxious to know what Lloyd George has done about Conscription for this country. If he goes for – well he's ended . . .'.

Lloyd George did go for conscription and thereby unleashed forces which meant that from the time of the so-called 'German Plot' arrests on 17 May 1918 until the summer of 1919, Boland and Collins, principally Collins, were the main motor forces in the Irish revolutionary situation. Both men were tough, intelligent, unusually energetic and courageous plotters. Between them, they achieved a great deal. But it was a tragedy for them, and for Ireland, that decisions taken elsewhere meant inevitably that most of their achievement was to lie in the realm of violence. The bloodshed they became involved in was made inevitable by the political warfare that broke out at a committee table they probably knew very little about. This was the Irish Committee of the British Government which, following a decision of the Cabinet to set it up on 11 April, met only four days later on Monday 15 April 1918 to draw up 'as soon as possible' a Home Rule Bill for Ireland. Alas, the speed at which the committee came into being was not to be paralleled by the speed with which it followed its instructions. In the world of politics wherein a week can be a long time, 'as soon as possible' turned out to be a very long time indeed. It wasn't for want of 'clout'; practically all the stars of the British firmament took part in its deliberations from the time of its first meeting, under the chairmanship of Walter Long. On the first day those present included Lord Curzon and General Smuts. The following day Austen Chamberlain joined the Committee and before the Irish tragedy bled itself to a temporary halt figures such as Balfour, Birkenhead, Churchill and Lloyd George would all have worried at the bone. The proceedings were sometimes clouded in such secrecy that no minutes were issued for months at a time.[24] The Committee issue which preoccupied Balfour and Churchill was the problem already outlined, the interaction of Unionist and Tory sentiment.

The dilemma of the Coalition Government, which was, of course, dependent on Unionist support, is perfectly highlighted in the contrasting views of Viscount Grey, the British Foreign Secretary, and Arthur Balfour, one of the Unionists' principal spokesmen. Viscount Grey cabled from Washington:

A real amelioration of American feeling may result from a policy of self-government for Ireland on good lines. I continue to take the line that Unionists have given up Unionism and Home Rulers have come to recognise that the Protestant area of Ulster must have separate treatment and that a fresh start is to be expected.

Some of the feeling of America arises from the belief that the Irish policy of the Government is directed by Carson. An important member of the administration told me the other day what this point of view was. They regard it as unfair that Carson should have been allowed to import arms into Ulster from Germany. Arms which were to have been used against the policy of the British government. They regard it as very unfair that these arms should not have been seized or molested, while arms used by Nationalists are seized. . . . They also point to the fact that Carson has twice been taken into the Cabinet . . . and that the other day the first announcement in the American papers that the Cabinet was considering a new Irish policy contained the statement that Carson had been called into consultation with the Cabinet.[25]

However 'a settlement on good lines' was anathema to the Balfour faction. Balfour submitted a markedly different viewpoint:

I admit that for many reasons, amongst which the British party system is not the least important, the Unionist policy has not succeeded . . . The only really workmanlike alternative to preserving the Union is the excision from it of the south and west of Ireland. . . . I gathered, however, that the Cabinet, while agreeing with the Committee that Ireland as a whole may have Dominion status, if she wants it, are unalterably averse to granting independence from any of its parts . . . had strong exception to the doctrine that Ireland, all Ireland, has a separate national existence . . . as a single, undivided political unit . . . On the one hand, they make it as easy as possible for Ulster to join itself with the rest of Ireland in forming a 'dominion' state. On the other hand, they give it no power whatever to remain what it is, and as I think ought to be, an integral part of the UK.

. . . is it tolerable that we should take by force from our loyal fellow countrymen for no better reason than that they should live in the same island with those who proclaim their disloyalty in every quarter of the world?[26]

On the conscription issue the underlying approach of the Government was summed up in October 1917 when the Cabinet was told that with Europe 'in anguish', Ireland 'had no real grievances', but that 'actual rebellions and seditious acts were being promulgated'.[27] The proceedings of the Irish Committee, as it were the Cabinet's private instrument for the introduction of Home Rule, the Convention, its public evidence of activity, and the bedevilling factor of conscription produced a hopeless thrombosis of policy. What was missing at the Committee table (and, indeed, at the Cabinet table, if one exempts Unionists from Northern Ireland who were mainly concerned with frustrating the Government's plans for Southern Ireland) was any sense of empathy with or real understanding of the position in Ireland. While maintaining the fiction that what was being discussed was an integral part of the United Kingdom, none of the elected representatives present ever seems to have reflected on the irony of the fact that of all the views and arguments put forward, none was prefaced by the simple expression 'my constituents . . .'. In France the British Army was under fierce pressure along a fifty-mile front. In London Lloyd George was under almost equally fierce pressure from Sir Henry Wilson not to allow an estimated 150,000 'recalcitrant Irishmen' to shirk the responsibilities being borne by the two and a half million strong army then engaged in several different theatres of war. Sir Henry won the argument. Despite warnings from President Wilson himself of the possible effects on American public opinion the Cabinet decided to bracket the introduction of the Military Service Act to Ireland with the publication of the Convention's report, hoping that the latter would meet the American difficulty.

In fact it solved nothing. The Convention reported on 5 April 1918, proposing a version of Home Rule whereby Ireland would get a parliament which would have no control over the Army and Navy, or over the postal services, customs and excise until the British Parliament decided it should have them. All matters concerning the Crown, peace and war were fully reserved to the Imperial Parliament and 40 per cent of the seats in the lower house were to be given to Unionists. There was also a Minority Report which proposed to concede a watered-down form of 'Dominion Home Rule' which in effect would have given Ireland less than the autonomy enjoyed by the existing Dominions.

It wasn't much of a signpost along the long and bloody road to Home Rule at the best of times. In the perfervid condition of the country at that moment, to include conscription in the directions meant that it pointed inevitably to disaster. However the Government pushed the Military Service Bill through the House on 16 April. The Irish Parliamentary Party withdrew in protest, never to return. A chapter in the British/Irish relationship of 118 years duration, stretching back to the Act of Union, was now irrevocably closed.

Two days after the withdrawal a huge meeting was convened in Dublin at the Mansion House by the Lord Mayor, Laurence O'Neill. Every strand of Irish Nationalist opinion, including Labour, was represented. The meeting agreed the terms of two statements drawn up by de Valera. The first was an anti-conscription pledge for signature at church doors the following Sunday:

Denying the right of the British Government to enforce compulsory service in this country, we pledge ourselves solemnly to one another to resist conscription by the most effective means at our disposal.

The second, a declaration for immediate publication, affirmed the call to resistance and foreshadowed the form that resistance would take by saying flatly: 'The passage of the Conscription Bill by the British House of Commons must be regarded as a declaration of war on the Irish nation.'

The meeting also appointed a deputation including representatives from Sinn Fein, The Irish Parliamentary Party and Labour to call on the Catholic Bishops, who were meeting at Maynooth Seminary on the same day, to issue a statement on conscription. The Bishops did so in terms somewhat less fire-eating than de Valera's:

We consider that conscription forced in this way upon Ireland is an oppressive and inhuman law which the Irish people have a right to resist by every means that are consonant with the law of God.

However their Lordships' statement had an enormous impact throughout the country. The Mansion House pledge was signed at every Catholic church door in the country. The day after the Mansion House meeting the Irish Parliamentary Party withdrew its candidate in a by-election in County Offaly and the Sinn Fein candidate was returned unopposed. This was a dramatic reversal of the trend in Sinn Fein's electoral fortunes which, only two weeks earlier, had seen yet another Sinn Fein candidate, Sean Milroy, defeated by his Parliamentary Party rival in East Tyrone. The week after the Offaly by-election Labour declared a one-day general strike and the whole country, with the exception of Belfast, closed down on 25 April.

During the conscription turmoil the Volunteers' Executive met in secret to decide its response to the crisis and took a number of decisions that were to have lasting implications for Collins. The British were trying to square the circle of keeping trouble out of the prisons while keeping trouble-makers out of the way by employing what was known as the 'cat and mouse' Act. Prisoners were released only to be pounced on again. A short while after Collins was picked up, Fionan Lynch and Austin Stack, for example, were re-arrested in this way, to finish serving their sentences, even though they had been freed after their hunger strike at the time of Ashe's death.

It was no time for dogma and the Volunteers' GHQ decided that the policy of not recognising the courts was playing into the enemy's hands. Collins was too valuable to be left in prison. He was told to give bail and did so, driving first to Granard where the streets were lined with people to welcome him to freedom. On his return to Dublin he persuaded another young man who was holding out against recognition to give bail also and installed him in his office at Bachelor's Walk. This was Tom Cullen, a captain in the Wicklow Volunteers who, with Thornton and Tobin, completed the intelligence team which broke the Castle's spy system.

In March the Volunteers had decided on a very drastic method of responding to conscription which necessitated a reorganisation of GHQ. Cathal Brugha, who had been Chief of Staff, went to England to link up with figures like Neil Kerr in Liverpool and Sam Maguire in London in drawing up contingency plans for assassinating members of the British Cabinet. So far as GHQ was concerned, if conscription were foisted on an unwilling people it would be tantamount to a massacre of civilians, justifying similar retribution on its authors' heads. Prior to the Executive meeting which confirmed the new Chief of Staff, Dick Mulcahy, another IRB man, Mulcahy and Collins conferred as to which of them should take the post. It was decided that it should go to Mulcahy as he had worked in Dublin for several years prior to the Rising and knew the city, whereas Collins had only arrived there in January 1916. However in addition to being Director of Organisation, Collins also became Adjutant General. Dick McKee commented on the arrangement, to Collins, 'You'd be too impetuous for a Chief of Staff.'

Yet it was Collins' caution that saved the emerging nationalist movement two months later. Lloyd George, realising that strong measures would be needed to carry conscription through, began by putting in strong men to execute them. The Irish Executive, or Government, had been going through a period of changing times since the Rising. Now it was shuffled once more to weed out any vestige of weakness or pro-nationalist sentiment. The Lord Lieutenant, Lord Wimborne, was replaced by Field Marshal Lord French with the new title of 'Lord Lieutenant-General and General Governor of Ireland'. The Chief Secretary, Henry Duke, was replaced by Edward Shortt, Sir Bryan Mahon went from the Military Command in favour of General Sir Frederick Shaw and other changes were made down the line.

According to Sir Henry Wilson, 'Lloyd George impressed on Johnny the necessity of putting the onus for first shooting on the rebels.'[28] Throughout the summer every conceivable use was made of DORA to further this aim. Apart from banning drilling and the carrying of arms, manifestations of Irishism such as language classes, football matches, dancing competions and athletic meetings were also prohibited. A major crack-down on Sinn Fein began with the 'German Plot' arrests of 17 May. The pretext for these was the capture of one Joseph Dowling, a member of Casement's ill-fated Irish Brigade, on an island off Galway on 12 April. The Germans had landed him from a submarine on their own initiative, hoping that he would set up links with Sinn Fein. No one on the Sinn Fein Executive had ever heard of him, though Collins and some of the other GHQ staff knew of the approach. However on Wednesday 15 May Broy got a list of prominent Sinn Feiners to Collins warning him that everyone on the list and many others, were due to be arrested shortly, probably the following Friday. On that day, from the Castle, Kavanagh corroborated the rumour; a series of raids was being planned for that night.

There was a meeting of the Volunteer Executive at 44 Parnell Square that night, and Collins, who had earlier circulated the arrest rumours to those on the list, warned everyone present, including de Valera, not to go home. De Valera vacillated for a time but eventually did go home and was arrested in Greystones. Most of the Sinn Fein leadership was also picked up during the night, Arthur Griffith, Darrell Figgis, Count Plunkett, William Cosgrave, Mrs Tom Clarke and Countess Markievicz. Markievicz, a member of a famous

Anglo-Irish family the Gore-Booths, who had married a Polish count, had also taken part in the 1916 Rising. Collins with Harry Boland and Eamonn Duggan had called in at Vaughan's Hotel and stayed until after midnight, thus getting to their homes after the raiders had called. Realising what was happening, Collins cycled out to Clontarf to warn the General Secretary of the Volunteers, Sean MacGarry. Finding that the Secretary had already been arrested he decided that lightning would not strike twice and slept in MacGarry's house. He woke up to begin his 'life on the bicycle'. The British Government felt that a good day's work had been done in carrying out the swoops, even though it was agreed that the evidence on which these were carried out, supplied by Admiral Hall, proved German intention rather than action. Looking at the situation caused by the 'German Plot' crack-down, and the subsequent sorry showing of British Intelligence during the ensuing war, one can understand why a leading British civil servant, Sir Mark Beresford Sturgis, confided to his diary after listening to Hall on another occasion: '. . . it would be more alarming if the pink paper prophecies had produced a winner or two in the past of which I cannot remember a single instance.'[29]

In the event Ireland saw neither Home Rule nor conscription. Throughout the summer and autumn of 1918 the Government hesitated over introducing either in the general climate of unrest. The signing of the Armistice removed conscription from the Irish agenda, though not the effect that its threat produced, but the Home Rule issue remained as pressing as ever. On Armistice Day itself the Cabinet received a telegram from the Washington Embassy containing a serious warning from Cardinal O'Connell, the 'dominant figure among Irish Americans'.[30] The Cardinal said that 'all Irish-Americans were in a state of ebullition which would soon break out into hostile utterances against England unless some definite action were taken about Home Rule.' A principle of self-determination had been recognised by all. England could not refuse it to Ireland, the Cardinal said. By way of underlining the Cardinal's warning, the 'state of ebullition' in Dublin took the form not of 'hostile utterances', but of real hostilities towards the Armistice celebrations which were attacked by the Volunteers acting under orders from GHQ. Collins subsequently described the outcome to Stack in rather callous terms:

As a result of the various encounters there were 125 cases of wounded soldiers treated at the Dublin hospitals that night. . . . Before morning, 3 soldiers and 1 officer had ceased to need any attention and one other died the following day. A policeman too was in a very precarious condition up to a few days ago when I ceased to take any further interest in him. He was unlikely to recover. We had a staff meeting and I wasn't in any of it . . .[31]

The German Plot swoops and the outcry over conscription created a situation which Collins and Boland manipulated to the full. They went over with a fine toothcomb the list of candidates chosen to represent Sinn Fein at the General Election on 14 December which followed the Armistice to ensure that only those who favoured a 'forward policy' were selected. This short-term success would plague Collins in the long term, because the voice of moderation was muted in the National Assembly when he desperately needed it in support for the Anglo-Irish Treaty. But that day lay ahead. For the moment the country was so grateful for the defeat of conscription that it obliterated the Irish Parliamentary Party and gave Sinn Fein a majority in all but four counties, Antrim, Derry, Armagh and Down. Sinn Fein won 73 out of 105 seats. The Irish Parliamentary Party was reduced from 80 to 6 seats. The Unionists, whose voices sounded so loud at the Council Chambers of the mighty in London, made a fainter sound in Ireland, securing 315,394 votes out of a total of 1,526,910. But this was not the customary four-fifths majority for Home Rule. In this election, the electorate had cast their votes for a party that said it stood for an All-Ireland Irish Republic, sovereign and independent of England. Collins, for example, told the electors of South Cork:

You are requested by your votes to assert before the nations of the world that Ireland's claim is to the status of an independent nation, and that we shall be satisfied with nothing less than our full claim – that, in fact, any scheme of government which does not confer upon the people of Ireland the supreme, absolute and final control of all this country, of all the affairs of the country, external as well as internal, is a mockery and will not be accepted.[32]

Interestingly, Collins' address never mentioned the word 'Republic'. He was unequivocal in stating that if elected he would not attend the British Parliament, believing attendance there would be 'wrong in principle, in practice a ghastly failure' which had 'wellnigh landed us in disaster until sixteen of the noblest men that this or any generation in Ireland produced, by their calm and unflinching self-sacrifice redeemed the national situation.' He concluded his appeal with the ringing declaration that he accepted Wolfe Tone's dictum:

To subvert the tyranny of our execrable Government, to break the connection of England – the unfailing source of all our ills – and to assert the independence of my native country . . . these were my objects.[33]

And Collins wound up by saying, 'Today these are my objects.' Unquestionably, therefore, the people of South Cork and of Ireland got a clear indication of the intentions of Collins, the fiery patriot. But Collins was pragmatist as well as patriot. Though he broke out his flag on the highest possible campsite nearest to the stars, he was prepared, when it came to it, to camp somewhere lower down the mountain once he was assured of a secure base from which to proceed further at a later date. However, to those who thought like Cathal Brugha the

Republic proclaimed by 'sixteen of the noblest men' had to be fought for, literally to the death.

Where the British Cabinet was concerned, the eruption of a crowd of ravening Sinn Fein Republicans on to the Imperial political landscape immediately raised the issue of whether or not to permit the opening of the Parliament which the Sinn Feiners proposed to set up for themselves in Dublin, not whether or not to grapple finally with the Irish problem. In fact, they long-fingered all of these. One of Chief Secretary Shortt's most trusted Irish appointees was the Right Hon. Justice O'Connor[34], to whom he wrote in the New Year: 'I am afraid that while the Peace Conference is sitting it will be impossible to get Lloyd George to appreciate the situation . . .' And he gave a fairly broad hint that his own ability to do anything in the Prime Minister's absence was severely limited. 'Obstruction, jealousy, stabs in the back all contribute to make the life of a Chief Secretary a rather heart-rending business.'

Shortt proved an accurate prophet. The opening of the post-war Great Power Peace Conference in Paris effectively took Lloyd George's mind off the Irish issue for several crucial months in 1919, during which the initiative passed from the British Cabinet table into the hands of the Irish revolutionaries and, in particular, Michael Collins.

4

The Twelve Apostles

'I am the Lord of the dance, said he,
And I'll lead you all, wherever you may be.'

From hymn by Sydney Carter

Michael Collins, in 1918–19, was responsible for a number of initiatives: the setting-up of two underground newspapers, the building of an intelligence network, an arms smuggling route, the organisation of a national loan, the creation of his elite hit unit, the 'Squad', a bomb-making factory, and a variety of other schemes.

Merely to get around to all his offices each day on a bicycle would have taxed the strength of most men, but when Collins got to his offices, or to Vaughan's Hotel at night, he would in a normal day deal with anything up to a hundred letters to and from all parts of the country. It was not unusual for a colleague to get as many as five or six communications from him in the course of one day. The people and projects he dealt with included everything from smuggling in coke for the bomb factories, to shooting spies. From organising a by-election campaign, to getting a few rounds of ammunition or a rifle or two for a hard-pressed country unit. From ensuring that loan receipts were sent promptly to making intelligence contacts with people whose identities will probably never be known.

Kevin O'Shiel, his friend and legal advisor, has left an unpublished account[1] of an incident which occurred after hostilities had ceased which sheds light on how the underworld war was fought. Collins and O'Shiel had been involved in meetings with Lloyd George and Churchill and Collins had sent O'Shiel ahead to Euston with instructions to (a) procure a bottle of Jameson's whiskey and (b) ensure that they had a compartment to themselves. O'Shiel was guarding the door of the compartment when a 'spruce, well-groomed fellow' approached him and told him to inform Collins that 'Major Shore (or Shaw) of the Auxiliaries was next door'. Despite O'Shiel's protestations that Collins was seeing no one the Major replied 'with great cocksureness', 'Oh, he'll see me alright.'

When O'Shiel told Collins someone wanted to see him 'he was

mad' – at first. For when he heard the name he picked up the bottle and said, 'Yes, we'll certainly see him.' There followed 'one of the most interesting nights' O'Shiel ever spent. The major, who had also provided himself with a bottle of whiskey, turned out to have been one of Collins' principal adversaries. The anecdote which lodged with O'Shiel most strongly concerned one of the several informants which it emerged both had employed as double agents. Neither had trusted the man in question. 'That fellow was your man always', said Collins. 'No,' said the major, 'he was yours. He tried to lead us into an ambush one night.' The spy had told the officer that if he raided the home of the woman Austin Stack later married, in Lansdowne Terrace, he would get 'the whole Sinn Fein Cabinet'.

Collins asked the major for the date, and after consulting his diary told him 'after a chuckle' that had he come that night he would have 'collared the whole Cabinet and IRA chiefs as well.' 'My God,' exclaimed the major, 'What a miss! I might be Sir Shaw [or Shore] now!' Collins told the major that he always trusted the judgement of the man who had warned him against the double agent, but that after hearing his story he now trusted him a hundredfold. Later he told O'Shiel who it was that had given the warning – Liam Tobin.

That true story helps to explain why Collins used to mark certain files 'DBI', meaning Don't Butt In. Woe betide an associate who disobeyed the instruction, but he himself cheerfully crashed through everyone else's sphere of operation. Still 'running the show', as in his boyhood days at Woodfield.

He had little foibles like hating the use of pencils or rubber stamps, but he never forgot an appointment, or a promise. He kept a mass of detail in his head, from the time friendly warders came on duty, when a co-operative postman made his rounds, exactly when and where a parcel might be collected. He made up his mind instantly and an order, once given, was rarely changed. In the midst of the vortex he forced himself to study politics, literature, other countries' methods of economic development, anything which might benefit the country once he reached his objectives. Particularly in his last few years of life he continually worked to develop a philosophy for himself. And, throughout all this, he made it a point to visit friends or helpers who had been wounded or fallen ill. As the pressure intensified he tried to train himself to do without sleep and made a point of giving up smoking and drinking. 'I'll be a slave to nothing,' he boasted.

Collins' demoniacal energy can be said to explain how he managed to bring his extraordinary gifts of concentration and intelligence to bear when he got to his various work centres, while the daily brushes with death which he experienced en route probably go a long way to explain also the dreadful bouts of horseplay he engaged in like a pressure cooker giving off steam. British propaganda, which continually portrayed him as a hulking thug, probably played a part in saving his life. The young tommy who turned to his mate on Newcomen Bridge, after Collins had greeted him cheerily, and said, "E's a decent sort, wished me good dye 'e did', wasn't programmed for the broad smile and friendly word that got 'the decent sort' through without being searched. Nor was the officer at a road block who was engaged in sympathetic conversation by a fine-looking young man who got out of his car to keep him company while the other passengers were being searched. Had he had the charming conversationalist frisked he would have found documents on him which would have hung Collins. On another night he stepped out of a car which also contained Neligan, MacNamara and Broy, with whom he had been conferring at Thomas Gay's house, and while they showed their detective passes, commiserated with the officer in charge on 'these dreadful ambushes'. Broy called to him, 'Step in, Sergeant' and 'Sergeant' Collins got back in the car bearing documents, passed over to him earlier that evening, which would have accounted not only for him, but for the other three as well.

Joseph Plunkett's extraordinary legacy of the idea that if he didn't think of himself as being on the run, then he wasn't a fugitive, worked for him time and again. Michael Collins moved through his various worlds – including making trips to England – like a businessman, not a spy. The only indication of espionage activities I ever came across in his papers was a set of tiny envelopes which he used for sending messages. At the time of writing few people are left who knew him well, but one of these, Pat Murphy, like Collins a West Cork man, but one of Ascendancy background, singles out the 'no-fugitive' quality as being one of his outstanding characteristics. The other was his extraordinary quality of making allies of people within seconds of meeting them.

Murphy was at the time working for *Freeman's Journal* as a night reporter. He met 'a big fellow with a West Cork accent' in a doorway near the *Freeman's Journal* where both were sheltering because a tender full of Tans was prowling the street. Murphy invited 'Carroll', as he called himself, back to the office for Bovril. But the *Freeman* was raided almost immediately and Murphy was given the job of showing a search party round the office in pursuit of 'a big fellow of about thirty, called Carroll, who is known to be on the premises'. No one was found and Murphy returned to his Bovril thinking that his visitor had managed to leave the building.

As he poured out the boiling water he heard a noise behind him and turned to find 'the big fellow' stepping onto his desk from a skylight. 'Thanks for the Bovril,' he said. 'If I ever make any money I'll leave you some shares in Bovril.' Murphy had grown to know 'Carroll' quite well over the next few weeks before he discovered who he was.[2]

One of Collins' and McKee's ploys was to hold 'Irish classes' around the country. The effect of these camps was to bring young country lads into touch with the leadership from Dublin and to give Collins and the others an estimate of who the good men were. At the Coosan camp near Athlone, for instance, Terence MacSwiney distinguished himself and in his memoirs Mulcahy recalled Austin Stack did not.[3] At Glandore in County Cork, Liam Deasy was impressed by the 'incredible example' of Dick McKee, who in six days turned 'raw amateurs into trained guerrillas'. These 'amateurs' had to be trained to make the leap of the imagination necessary to conceive of actually taking on the RIC and, behind this force, the British Army, in a heavily garrisoned area, poorly armed themselves, and with the tradition of viewing both the police and the army as not only omnipresent, but omnipotent.

Volunteers were unemployed and depended for food, shelter and clothing on the local population, and it was remarkable how this support held up right through the war, despite the pressures of incessant raids by the military and the activities of the inevitable informers. It was this spirit more than the IRA's armaments, or even the tactics of guerrilla warfare, which brought the IRA whatever success it achieved. Neither Collins nor the Volunteers would have survived without the country-wide network of women supporters who acted as intelligence agents, couriers, secretaries, providers of meals, shelter and nursing services. One must take note of the Trojan work done by women who never talked and were known only to a relatively small circle. Peig, the family maid at Woodfield, was a courier, adviser and nurse, who saved many a life, carried many a message, helped to plan many an ambush even. It was only after her death, while still in the service of the Collins family, when from all over the country famous figures from the fight for independence came to her funeral, that her story came to be more generally told.[4]

Sinead Mason, Collins' intelligence secretary, worked a twelve-hour day for him throughout most of the war and holds secrets for him no one can even guess at (she was still alive as this book was being written). For a time it was thought by friends such as the O'Connors and Nancy O'Brien that he might marry Sinead,[5] who was described by Sister Margaret Mary as being 'a merry, pretty girl, and very sensible'. Sinead Mason lived near the O'Connors with her aunt at 23 Brendan Rd. Collins sent her down to Woodfield for a holiday when the strain of war began to tell on her. A celebrated story of the period had Tom Cullen waltzing around the office with Sinead one day when suddenly Collins' footstep was heard outside. Sinead was promptly hurled into a chair and Cullen buried himself in a newspaper. Wasting time was a mortal sin in Collins' eyes. But wasting it with Sinead Mason . . .

Another major concern of Collins was the importance of jail and jail-breaking to the Republican tradition. The most sensational prison escape was that of de Valera from Lincoln Jail on 3 February 1919, which was to have important consequences for the course of Irish history, as we shall see later. But a number of other break-outs, from Mountjoy, Strangeways, Usk (in Wales) and Cork, had a significant bearing on developments also.

Collins organised the escape of Robert Barton from Mountjoy Jail, Dublin on 16 March 1919. He smuggled him in a file with which to saw through the bars of his ground-floor cell and arranged for a party of volunteers to throw a rope ladder over the twenty-foot prison wall and then catch him in a blanket when he jumped from the top. Barton was then brought to safety to the home of Collins' friend, Batt O'Connor.

Barton, a County Wicklow landowner, was a cousin of Erskine Childers. He had distinguished himself in Collins' eyes by his kindness to prisoners and their relatives in the aftermath of 1916, while he was an officer in the British Army. Later, when the Dail set up a land-bank, Barton became its Director[6], working closely with Collins whom he subsequently accompanied to Downing Street to negotiate the Anglo-Irish Treaty. When Batt O'Connor exulted over the escape, Collins replied: 'That's only the beginning. We're going to get Beaslai and Fleming out next.'

Beaslai, a Gaelic scholar, poet and playwright, was useful, both as a public speaker and as editor of *An tOglach*. Fleming was in a different category, a hero of jail resistance in the O'Donovan Rossa mould. Collins wanted him out, both for his publicity value and as a token of recognition for the struggle he had put up in jail. He had been sent to Maryborough Jail (now Portlaoise Jail) for five years by a court martial on a trumped-up charge on 9 March 1917.[7] He was christened 'Samson' because it took so many warders to put the prison uniform on him each day.[8] Eventually he was given political status and transferred to Mountjoy, having somehow managed, not only to break up his cell, but also systematically to destroy the 'muffs', a type of straitjacket used for insane prisoners, with which he was habitually spancelled by teams of warders, who also used iron manacles and leather belts to truss him up so tightly that his stomach could not accept food. Once he literally burned the straitjacket off his body by first using the manacles to smash the thick glass on his gas jet and then tearing off the pieces of the 'muff' as they burned.

For Beaslai's escape a rope ladder was again favoured, and, this time, eighteen other prisoners followed Beaslai and Fleming over the top, while on the ground below, Paddy Daly, later Commander of Collins' elite 'Squad', called out the names of the men who were to escape and five other prisoners with their hands in their pockets clutching what appeared to be revolvers kept the warders at bay. The 'revolvers' were, in fact, spoons, which added hugely to the public's enjoyment of the escapade when the news broke.

Collins himself broke into a fit of laughter when O'Reilly, whom he had stationed outside the jail with three bicycles, a measure of the total he expected to escape, rushed into the Wicklow Hotel to tell him: 'The whole jail is out.' Later that evening, as he worked at Cullenswood House, he was seen to throw down his pen several times to chuckle over the escape.[8]

Beaslai would give him further cause for amusement the following October when, having been picked up again in May, he made another escape, this time from Strangeways Prison in Manchester. Austin Stack was one of those who made up the party of six escapees on this occasion.

Stack and some of his companions had been transferred to Strangeways following another jail drama, the great riot in Crumlin Road Jail the previous Christmas. This almost touched off a sectarian riot outside the jail in Belfast as 'Orange' mobs gathered during the Republicans' defiance which lasted for the best part of two weeks. It began on 22 December 1918, when Stack ordered that a Volunteer, John Doran, who had just been tried, be taken by his colleagues into the Republicans' wing, and not the criminal section where the authorities wanted to place him. It continued until it was unofficially agreed that Doran would be considered 'political' after sentence. Stack had planned the protest with care, and prior to the seizing of Doran the prisoners had laid in food and were able to resist efforts to break them such as denying them provisions and shutting off the gas. The only breaking which occurred was of prison property.

The Strangeways breakout on 25 October 1919 was a particularly audacious affair. Collins himself crossed over to talk to Stack about the arrangements beforehand, using an assumed name. Prominent GHQ personnel like Rory O'Connor and Peadar Clancy also took part in the final breakout which necessitated having volunteers from Liverpool and Manchester holding up the traffic while six prisoners climbed down a ladder propped up against the outside of the prison wall.

Collins was also behind the escape of Denis MacNeilis from Cork Jail the previous year, on Armistice Day, 11 November 1918. MacNeilis was one of the first Volunteers to take a shot at a policeman and was in jail for wounding an RIC man, an activity of which Collins approved mightily.[10] However, he was correspondingly aghast at the unexpected escape of four 'German Plot' detainees from Usk on 21 January 1919. He feared, needlessly as it turned out, that the escape would interfere with a far greater coup he was planning, freeing de Valera.

In jail, de Valera had succeeded in getting another prisoner, Sean Milroy, to draw a postcard showing a drunken man with a huge key outside his hall door saying, 'I can't get in'. On the other side of the card a year later the same man was shown, in jail, looking through a carefully drawn keyhole saying 'I can't get out'. To avoid suspicion the card was sent out in the name of a third prisoner, Sean MacGarry. Both key and keyhole were replicas of the actual lock and master key. De Valera had got the wax impression of the key for Milroy by borrowing the chaplain's master key from the sacristy while the priest was saying Mass. De Valera, who was serving the Mass, had earlier melted down the stumps of altar candles, and he warmed the wax thus obtained with the heat of his body and took impressions of the key. In Dublin a key was fashioned from Milroy's drawing by Gerry Boland, Harry's brother, and smuggled back into the jail in a cake. The first key didn't work, but a second key and cake later, on the evening of 3 February, de Valera, MacGarry and Milroy were able to unlock every gate they came to without difficulty until they arrived at the outer wall of the prison, where they encountered disaster.

Collins had brought a duplicate key with him. When he fitted it in the outside of the door it broke in the lock. So near and yet so far. De Valera and the others were now on one side of the door; Collins and Boland, who had had to cut through the barbed wire of an outer, perimeter fence to get to the last obstacle, were on the other. Beaslai gives an interesting account of what happened next:

Boland, in describing the scene to me, dwelt on the feeling of utter despair which seized on him at that juncture. Collins said, in a heart-broken tone, 'I've broken a key in the lock, Dev.' De Valera uttered an ejaculation and tried to thrust his own key into the lock from the other side. By an extraordinary piece of luck, he succeeded in pushing out the broken key with his own and opening the gate.[11]

And so the prisoners were freed, completing their escape by Boland wrapping his fur coat around the gangling de Valera, putting his arm around him, as though they were a courting couple, and passing several genuinely courting British soldiers and their girlfriends from a nearby military hospital with cheery good wishes. Fortunately for the escapees, collective passion appears to have been such as to render the couples oblivious to the fact that the burly Boland, the supposed 'woman' had a remarkably deep voice. Curiously, in his official biography, compiled at a time when, of course, both Collins and Boland were long dead, de Valera plays up the role of Boland and Brugha in organising it, and says it was Boland who broke the key in the lock.[12] He does not refer at all to a far more important detail – the controversy over his decision to go to America immediately after his escape.

Leaving de Valera hidden in Manchester, MacGarry and Milroy in Liverpool, Collins went to London, spent a day there meeting contacts and, after thirty-six hours without food, returned to Liverpool, meaning to spend the night with Neil Kerr. Finding there was a boat leaving for Dublin, he immediately forgot about food and sleep and set out for Dublin where he reported to GHQ on de Valera's intentions. Beaslai describes the reaction:

The statement was received by all of us with dismay. We felt that de Valera's departure would be a fatal mistake, that the country would misunderstand his motives and regard it as a selfish, or even cowardly, desertion. When this view was expressed, Collins replied, 'I told him so, but you know what it is to try to argue with Dev. He says he had thought it all out in prison and that he feels that the one place where he can be useful to Ireland is in America.' The meeting took the view that the place for an Irish leader was in Ireland wherein the strength of the fight put up would determine the support in America, and it was decided to send Brugha to England to urge de Valera either not to go at all or, failing that, to show himself first in Ireland so that the publicity value of his escape should not be dissipated.[13]

Beaslai says, 'Brugha accordingly went to England and succeeded in persuading de Valera not to go straight to America, but first to return to Ireland.'

De Valera's version of the visit is that Brugha 'stayed from Friday, 7 February until the following Sunday, bringing him up-to-date with the progress made to establish an Irish legislature and conditions in Ireland.' De Valera would have us believe that it was subsequent to Brugha's visit and his weighing up of the chances of getting a hearing at the Peace Conference in Paris that he began to think that the place in which he could best work for Ireland was the USA where he could bring pressure to bear on President Wilson.[14] In any event his American decision shows how his priorities changed since he wrote feelingly to Sinead from jail telling her that he was memorising Merriman's lengthy erotic love poem, 'The Midnight Court', in Irish, so that they could read it together:

I am getting the 'Cuirt an Meadón Oidce' all off by heart. . . . If you read it I know you would like it. It is the nicest poem I have met in Irish. One of the principal pleasures I have in doing Irish poetry is to be able to read it with you when we are together.[15]

Even a few months before he was sprung from Lincoln, de Valera was protesting how much he wanted to be with his wife and children:

I cannot tell you how I feel being unable to be at your side just now. I am ever thinking of you . . . one of my resolutions . . . was that I would strive to be more with you and the children than in the past, but these matters are in God's hands.[16]

He was certainly more lyrical in prose style than Collins, but less direct in either style or action. In fact he left the resolution of the question of how he spent his freedom on release from Lincoln Jail not 'in God's hands', but in those of Michael Collins, who was charged with getting him to America.

Padraig O'Keefe, a particularly abrasive Corkonian[17], also told a story about de Valera's American trip which conflicts with the Authorised Version. De Valera pulled him aside one day in the Sinn Fein offices, shortly before he departed and, according to O'Keefe, said to him, 'Paddy, did you hear they're sending me to America.'

'Bejasus they are not', replied O'Keefe. 'It's your own [sanguinary] idea to get over there out of the trouble.'

Collins arranged for de Valera to be brought back to Dublin aboard the *Cambria* from Liverpool on 20 February and found him a hiding place in the Gate Lodge of the Archbishop of Dublin's house in Drumcondra, where he occupied himself for much of March drafting a statement for the Peace Conference in Paris. Collins, meanwhile, busied himself by arranging a public welcome for him at the end of the month, embroiling himself in general controversy as a result. An announcement was published that Sinn Fein were organising a reception for de Valera's return. It was proposed that he would be met by the Lord Mayor and presented with the keys of the city at his springboard to fame – the bridge at Mount Street which had been defended by Michael Malone in 1916. The keys to the city were an honour normally reserved for royalty. De Valera liked the idea and prepared a suitably fiery speech.[18]

O'Keefe also said that during this period Collins had turned over his own office to de Valera. Not knowing this callers continued to come asking for the 'Big Fella'. De Valera flounced out angrily one afternoon asking, 'What's all this about a Big Fella?' That evening there was a Sinn Fein meeting at which a chair was left vacant for de Valera as Chairman. When Collins asked him to take it he replied, 'Let the Big Fella take the Chair'.

De Valera's fiery speech was never delivered and this brought into the open the difference between those in Sinn Fein who, like Collins, espoused a 'forward' policy, and those who, like Darrell Figgis, were in favour purely of passive resistance and the efficacy of moral force. At the previous Sinn Fein Convention in October, it had been decided that so many of the Executive were in prison that an election should be held in which the candidature would be confined to persons at liberty, and to hold another election if and when the prisoners were released. The October decision resulted in the selection of an executive which was too pacifist for Collins' liking, 'moderates' generally receiving more votes than Volunteers. Ironically, it was Cathal Brugha's poor showing which aroused Collins' greatest wrath:

Cathal Brugha is a white man. There he is half crippled with English bullets, away from the meeting because he is doing work that they would never dare to think of, and they vote for Mr X and Mrs Y and leave Cathal near the bottom of the list. [Brugha was absent in England making arrangements to assassinate members of the British Cabinet if conscription was introduced.][19]

De Valera's escape, and the publicity bombshell it set off, interacted with the effects of the great influenza epidemic which swept through jails, as it did through the rest of Europe at the time. One of those whose life it claimed was a prominent Sinn Feiner, Pierce MacCan, from Tipperary, who came of a good family and was liked by everyone who knew him. His death caused great ill-feeling in Ireland. The prison doctor at Gloucester Jail urged that the entire prison be evacuated and the authorities reacted with unwonted measures of alacrity and clemency to his suggestion. Another factor in the decision may have been the fact that amongst those who contracted the illness, but recovered, was Arthur Griffith. At all events, the prisoners were returned to Ireland and Griffith presided over the meeting called to discuss the Sinn Fein reception issue. Darrell Figgis led the charge by demanding the minutes of the Executive which decided to honour de Valera. Figgis describes what happened next.

Michael Collins rose. Characteristically, he swept aside all pretences, and said that the announcement had been written by him, and that the decision to make it had been made not by Sinn Fein, though declared in its name, but by the 'proper body, the Irish Volunteers'. He spoke with much more vehemence and emphasis, saying that the sooner fighting was forced and a general state of disorder created through the country (his words in this connection are too well printed in my memory ever to be forgotten) the better it would be for the country. Ireland was likely to get more out of the state of general disorder than from a continuance of the situation as it then stood. The proper people to make decisions of that kind were ready to face the British military, and were resolved to force the issue and they were not to be deterred by weaklings and cowards. For himself, he accepted full responsibility for the announcement and he told the meeting with forceful candour that he held them in no opinion at all, that, in fact, they were only summoned to confirm what the proper people had decided. He had always a truculent manner, but in such situations he was certainly candour itself. As I looked on him as he spoke, for all the hostility between us, I found something refreshing and admirable in his contempt for us all. His brow was gathered in a thunderous frown, and his chin thrust forward, while he emphasised his points on the back of a chair with heavy strokes of his hand. He was a great foeman when he fought thus – a worthier foeman than when he manipulated organisations. But, by his contempt of his audience, he had touched the combative in Griffith.[20]

Griffith declared himself strongly opposed to the reception proposal, but said that he would accept the decision of the meeting and of 'no other body'.[21] The meeting adjourned while Griffith conferred with de Valera and, ultimately, a letter was published from de Valera in which he said:

I think you must all agree with me that the present occasion is scarcely one on which we would be justified in risking the lives of citizens. I am certain it would not . . . We who have waited know how to wait. Many a heavy fish is caught even with a fine line if the angler is patient.

Michael Collins was no patient angler. He wrote to Austin Stack:

. . . it is bad and very bad. The chief actor was very firm on the withdrawal, as indeed was Cathal. I used my influence the other way, and was in a practical minority of one. It may be that all arguments were sound, but it seems to me that they have put up a challenge which strikes at the fundamentals of our policy and our attitude.[22]

In a nutshell, Collins was willing to go to war, but as Griffith, de Valera and Figgis correctly divined, the public was not, and it would take several more months of repression and British policy blundering before the shooting of detectives and officials could be countenanced. Ironically, one of Collins' victims would be a brother of the doctor who had got the prisoners evacuated from Gloucester Jail – the Examining Magistrate, Alan Bell.

The Mount Street reception having been cancelled, a meeting of the first Dail was held on 10 April 1919 to enunciate Sinn Fein policy. Some of the Dail's principal architects were absent, organising the Lincoln Jail escape when 'the first Parliament of the Republic of Ireland' was set up in Dublin in the Lord Mayor's official residence, the Mansion House.[23] Presided over by Cathal Brugha, it met in an atmosphere of great dignity and make-believe. The roll call of members deemed to have been elected to the parliament, or 'First Dail', as it is more generally known, included the Unionists who had been returned to Westminster in the 'Khaki' election the previous December, figures like Edward Carson, Colonel Sir J. Craig and E. M. Archdale. These were declared to be '*as lathair*' (absent), a not unreasonable relationship for them to have with a Sinn Fein assembly, one would have thought. Nor would one have been surprised at the lack of response from Irish Parliamentary figures such as Captain W. Redmond or Joseph Devlin. Of the Sinn Fein representation, some forty were either '*ar dibirt at gallaib*' (deported by the foreigner) or '*fe glas ag gallaib*' (jailed). In fact, of the 104 names called, only 28 were '*i lathair*' (present). Nevertheless this quorum proceeded determinedly with the business of the First Day.

Some high-minded declarations were promulgated: A Message to the Free Nations of the World, a Declaration of Independence, and a Democratic Programme. Fraught and swirling words were uttered in French, Irish and English. The Declaration of Independence, for instance, contained the following:

We the elected representatives of the ancient Irish people in the National Parliament assembled do, in the name of the Irish nation, ratify the establishment of the Irish Republic and pledge ourselves and our people to make this Declaration effective by every means at our command.

We ordain that the elected representatives of the Irish people alone have power to make laws binding on the people of Ireland, and that the Irish Parliament is the only Parliament to which that people will give its allegiance.

We solemnly declare foreign government in Ireland to be an invasion of our national right which we will never tolerate, and we demand the evacuation of our country by the English Garrison.

The foregoing was, of course, no more and no less than a declaration of war, but lest there be any doubt remaining abroad as to what the insurgents' intentions were a Message to the Free Nations of the World was also read stating that Ireland was calling

upon every free nation to uphold her national claim to complete independence as an Irish Republic against the arrogant pretensions of England founded in fraud and sustained only by an overwhelming military occupation and demands to be confronted publicly with England at the Congress of Nations in order that the civilised world, having judged between English wrong and Irish right, may guarantee to Ireland its permanent support for the maintenance of her national independence.

There is no record that Collins ever found fault with any of these sentiments, but he did take exception to parts of the Democratic Programme as being 'too socialistic'.[24] Amongst the Programme's provisions was a declaration that 'all right to private property must be subordinated to the public right and welfare'. 'Every citizen' was to have 'an adequate share of the produce of the Nation's labour'.

The proceedings were conducted in a dignified fashion undoubtedly, but one wonders at the wit of The Times correspondent who wrote: 'The proceedings throughout were orderly and dignified, not a word being uttered that could produce ill-feeling.' Goblet, the French historian, was a more realistic analyst. He wrote: 'A new epoch was beginning, and one that would be terrible.'[25] As if to underscore his words, while the Dail was sitting, a party of Volunteers, imbued with the spirit of Collins rather than of Figgis, held up a party of RIC escorting a load of gelignite at Soloheadbeg, County Tipperary, and cold-bloodedly shot two of them dead. In their way, the killings, which were unsanctioned by Volunteer HQ, were literal translations of what the words uttered in the Mansion House actually meant.

It was after the sitting of the First Dail that, with an instinctive appositeness, the public began to refer to the Volunteers as the Irish Republican Army, soon shortening the term to IRA. Sean Treacy, the Tipperary IRA leader, and another firebrand, Michael Brennan of Clare, both of whom had served terms under the Defence of the Realm Act, DORA, had met earlier in the month and decided that whatever happened they were not going to spend any more time in prison. They would carry weapons and fight to resist arrest. Treacy warned Brennan that they were in fact declaring war on the British Empire by this policy and that they had better check their finances first. Brennan had one shilling and sixpence, Treacy fourpence.[26] Nevertheless Treacy, watching the Volunteer numbers dwindle as the threat of conscription receded, decided to go to war anyway. He echoed Collins' view as he marched into captivity after 1916: 'We'll have to get the British to organise us. We'll have to shoot.' Accordingly he took part in what is generally regarded as the firing of the first premeditated shots from the Volunteer side.

Collins attended all the April Dail sittings, although he was now on the run and hotly pursued, a warrant having been issued for his arrest a few days earlier as a result of his failure to turn up in court after giving bail. Efforts were made to arrest him as the Dail sat, but he was forewarned by Broy and got away. De Valera was elected President of Dail Eireann, or Priomh Aire, in Irish, First Minister in English. Later during his tour of America, he allowed himself to be described as 'President of the Irish Republic', a concession to American nomeclature which had important political and psychological implications for him later. Collins was appointed by de Valera as Minister for Finance in an eight-man Ministry: Arthur Griffith, Home Affairs; W. T. Cosgrave, Local Government; Countess Markievicz, Labour; Eoin MacNeill, Industries; and Robert Barton, Agriculture. The Dail also gave its blessing to the opening of 'embassies' in France and Washington, under Sean T. O'Kelly and Dr Pat MacCartan respectively. These appointments, and the proceedings which followed on 10 April, at a subsequent meeting of the Dail, were characterised by a good deal of waffle, mutual admiration and unreality.[27] Nevertheless, as with all functionings of this national parliament, decisions were taken which had severely practical results.

De Valera proposed that, 'members of the police forces acting in this country as part of the forces of the British occupation and as agents of the British Government be ostracised socially by the people'.[28] The motion was seconded by Eoin MacNeill who said that, 'the police in Ireland are a force of spies. The police in Ireland are a force of traitors, and the police in Ireland are a force of perjurers.' It was carried unanimously.[29] De Valera made another important announcement that day:

'It is obvious that the work of our Government cannot be carried out without funds. The Minister for Finance is accordingly preparing a prospectus which will shortly be published for the issue of a loan of one million pounds sterling – £500,000 to be offered to the public for immediate subscription, £250,000 at home and £325,000 abroad, in bonds and such amounts as to meet the needs of the small subscriber.[30]

Collins was to do more than 'issue a prospectus'. He was to be responsible for the entire organisation of the loan, its advertising, collection and the issue of receipts. The British declared the loan to be illegal but, despite continual harassment, Collins carried through the project successfully at a time when he was holding down four major positions in a full-scale guerrilla war, of which he was the main architect. His diligence seems all the more remarkable in view of the fact that he evidently disliked much of the loan work. Writing to Boland a year after de Valera's announcement, on 19 April 1920, he said:

I append a draft statement of the loan results in a general way up to date. These figures are the figures received at the Head Office only. The enterprise will certainly break my heart if anything ever will. I never imagined there would be so much cowardice, dishonesty, hedging, insincerity, and meanness in the world, as my experience of this work has revealed.

He had another experience during the April 1919 sittings which aroused considerably more enthusiasm in him, though it was also highly revealing of 'cowardice, dishonesty, insincerity and meanness'. Broy smuggled him into Detective Headquarters in Brunswick Street, where he spent the night going through the 'G' Division records. As with many of the turning points in his life, he approached the escapade in a light-hearted fashion. Encountering his old Frongoch companion, Sean Nunan, en route, he impulsively brought him along 'for the crack'. Nunan, who later became a director of the *Irish Press*, told me about the Brunswick St visit on more than one occasion. His abiding memory was the fright he got during the small hours of the morning when a drunk broke a window in their wing, and he feared that the police would come to inspect the damage. However, they dealt with the offender, a soldier, without coming near Broy's sanctum. Nunan remembered Collins chuckling over the contents of his own file which began, 'He comes of a brainy Cork family.' But the Brunswick St experience was no laughing matter. Collins had had the entire *modus operandi* of the RIC's intelligence system laid out before him. He saw both what he was up against and how to combat his enemy, the first Irish revolutionary to do so. Initially, he gave no sign of the importance of the discovery, turning up at the following day's Dail sitting 'with no great sign of fatigue considering his busy, sleepless night'.[31]

Then, on 9 April, he took the first steps towards implementing the lessons of Brunswick St. Acting on his orders, a number of 'G' men were accosted by Volunteers and warned against an excess of zeal. 'G' men who did not comply would pay for their stubborn courage with their lives, thus inaugurating a new and bloodier phase of the Anglo-Irish struggle. For the moment, Sinn Fein policy was largely directed towards a peaceful goal, the Peace Conference between the great powers who had fought in the First World War then meeting in Paris.

Collins had been active on the Peace Conference front, as he was in every other phase of Sinn Fein activity. In the New Year, he had been part of a delegation which went to London hoping to see President Wilson as he passed through on his way to Paris. When it was pointed out to him that his chances of seeing Wilson were slim, he replied with characteristic insouciance: 'If necessary we can buccaneer him.'[32] Wilson was not for buccaneering and he went on to Paris without seeing the Irishmen.

Undaunted, Collins accompanied O'Kelly and Gavan Duffy, who had defended Casement and had an extensive law practice in London, to a house in Kensington to draw up a submission to the American President. It was the home of a couple with whom Collins was to have a significant relationship thereafter, Crompton and Moya Llewelyn Davies. Moya, who was Irish-born, 'made some helpful suggestions' to the draft.[33]

Kathleen Napoli MacKenna was friendly with Moya Llewelyn Davies who spent a good deal of time during the Anglo-Irish war living in Furry Park House in Killester, north County Dublin, an eighteenth-century mansion which in those days was entirely surrounded by trees and fields running down to the extensive sand dunes and slob-lands fringing the sea at Clontarf. In a letter to Kathleen about evenings in her London home where, amongst others, her husband Crompton – Solicitor-General to the British Post Office and a former ally of Lloyd George's in land reform and other social issues – was in the habit of entertaining distinguished guests such as Bertrand Russell, Moya said:

The Irish trait is very strong in me, and when I moved in the highest circles, intellectually, in England, and had the greatest living philosopher and greatest living mathematician to dinner, in the course of the evening I would escape to the kitchen, and sit by the fire and talk to Ellie, the cook from Tipperary.[34]

Moya's 'Irish trait' caused her to involve herself in Irish affairs in many ways – writing pamphlets and articles, studying Irish, and later translating the classic tale of island life, *Twenty Years a Growing*, into English. Furry Park, with its sweeping staircases and panelled halls, its marbled fireplaces and gracious drawing rooms, must have been a place of enchantment in those days. A romantic vantage point from which a young wife surveyed the revolution sweeping through her country while her cultivated, studious, and older, Welsh husband attended to his duties in London.

Napoli MacKenna describes how Moya looked one night when she arrived unexpectedly at Furry Park with a message. Collins, whom

Napoli MacKenna likened to 'Siegfrid, the personification of joyous, powerful youth', was in the grounds watching for a 'tout' he had spotted. In anything but joyous mood Siegfrid let himself in the back door and left Kathleen standing in the rain at the hall door.

Moya herself, tall, thin, agile, extremely elegant in a brown, gold-brocaded tight-fitting frock with long clinging sleeves, carefully-groomed, her well-chiselled head Eton cropped, a cigarette in a long holder between her slender tapering fingers opened the door . . . calling me Caitlin . . . I admired her wide-open, wonder-filled eyes that shone like stars . . .

The friendship which formed between Collins and the Llewelyn Davieses gave rise to controversy on the grounds of both politics and sex. Politically, it was alleged by Republican critics that the Davieses and Sir James Barrie[35] were part of a British Intelligence plot, because both Barrie and John Chartres, whom Collins also saw at the Llewelyn Davieses' house, had been in Intelligence during the war. Chartres became part of the Irish team during the Anglo-Irish Treaty negotiations on Collins' invitation and he also assisted Collins with drafting advice.

It was also freely rumoured that Collins and Moya became lovers, an impression which Moya, as we shall see, appeared keen to further, although her first impressions of Collins do not appear to have been overwhelming. He appeared to her to be 'pasty' and too much given to smoking and bombast.[36] Nevertheless, she was to show herself prepared to do a lot more for Collins and the Irish situation than was President Wilson.

Wilson was not insensitive to the Irish issue. Irish-American leaders had begun to lift their heads up over the parapet again immediately the war ended, freeing them from the taint of helping Germany with their agitations. Wilson sent an emissary to Ireland to investigate matters, George Creel, who talked to Boland and Collins, amongst others. The President also gave ear to the views of Sir Shane Leslie and was in touch personally with Sir Horace Plunkett in the latter's capacity as Chairman of the Irish Convention. But he was not prepared to quarrel with his war-time allies over seating Ireland at the Peace Conference, as the Irish-Americans so stridently demanded. He needed British support in many areas, not least for the League of Nations which, *inter alia*, he hoped to use to advance Ireland's case. But many Irish-Americans were suspicious of the League, with its commitment, as they saw it, to involvement in foreign wars, and they were unenthusiastic about the Treaty of Versailles which gave neither promise of a new world order, nor restoration of the old.

Creel reported to Wilson on 1 March on his Irish visit, saying that an

Irish settlement was imperative in view of the Irish-American lobby. He thought Home Rule was no longer an option and that an offer of Dominion status would be accepted. But he warned against the British Prime Minister's bona fides over Ireland and that delay would mean 'that sentiment in Ireland and America will harden in favour of an Irish Republic'. It would indeed.

Three days after Wilson got Creel's report a resolution (which Wilson opposed) in the name of Thomas Gallagher of Illinois was passed by the House of Representatives by 261 votes to 41. It read as follows:

That it is the earnest hope of the Congress of the United States of America that the Peace Conference now sitting at Paris and passing upon the rights of various peoples will favourably consider the claims of Ireland to self-determination.

The importance of the resolution was widely oversold in Irish circles, so much so that a de Valera historian[37] would write later, 'The American people had instructed their President to support Ireland's claim.' In fact, nothing of the sort had occurred. The resolution was passed too late to be dealt with by the Senate and so did not have the full approval of Congress. Yet it was a shot across Wilson's bows. He got another that evening when a delegation appointed at an Irish Race Convention in Philadelphia the previous month saw him in New York to present him with resolutions passed at the Convention (held on 22 and 23 February). The meeting took place in a poor atmosphere. Wilson only agreed to it finally on condition that the Clan na nGael leader, Judge Cohalan, withdrew from the delegation. His German contacts at the time of 1916 and prior to America's ending the war were still not forgiven. The President told the delegation that he was unable to intervene in the domestic policy of other governments. He did, however, take a more supportive attitude to another of the Race Convention's decisions – the appointment of a three-man delegation to the Peace Conference to attempt to secure a hearing for Ireland.

On 12 April 1919, Collins proposed a motion, which was seconded by W. T. Cosgrave and passed by the Dail:

The elected Parliament and Government of the Irish Republic pledge the active support of the Irish Nation in translating into deed the principles enunciated by the President of the US at Washington's Tomb on 4 July, 1918, and whole-heartedly accepted [by America]. We are eager and ready to enter a World League of Nations based on equality of rights, in which the guarantees exchanged neither recognise nor imply a difference between big nations and small, between those that are powerful and those that are weak. We are willing to accept all the duties, responsibilities and burdens which inclusion in such a League implies.

In this motion Collins was signalling the general implicit recognition by his colleagues of an Irish Republic; his party's faith in Wilson's declaration of support for the aspirations of 'small nations'; and Sinn Fein's opposition to Article 10 of the Covenant of the League of Nations:

The High Contracting Powers undertake to respect and preserve against external aggression the territorial integrity and existing political independence of all State members of the League. In case of any such aggression the Executive Council shall advise upon the means by which this obligation shall be fulfilled.

This could be taken as recognising the territorial status quo of League members and it certainly posed a very large question as to how a self-proclaimed Irish Republic, which Great Britain did not recognise, might hope to find itself at the Paris negotiating table confronting 'the arrogant pretensions of England'. That confrontation could only come about if England, which at the time regarded all Ireland as an integral part of her imperial status quo, gave her permission for it to happen. The unlikelihood of this occurring did not worry Collins greatly. He had a number of other successes on his mind. The day after he successfully moved the motion, he wrote on 13 April to his sister, Helena:

The week that has passed has been a busy one for us – perhaps it has been a historical one for very often we are actors in events that have more meaning and consequence than we realise. At any rate – permanent or not – last week did, I feel, mark the inception of something new. The elected representatives of the people have definitely turned their backs on the old order and the developments are sure to be interesting. Generally the situation is working out to the satisfaction of Ireland – that is the foreign countries. At home we go from success to success in our own guerrilla way. Escapes of prisoners, raids against the enemy etc.[38]

The last session of the Dail which de Valera attended before he departed for America was held on 9 May in honour of the three-man American delegation appointed by the Irish Race Convention, which visited Ireland en route for Paris. During the proceedings Collins greatly impressed the Irish-Americans, both with his power of oratory and as an escapologist. They were already somewhat overwhelmed by their kaleidoscopic Irish visit which lasted for ten days, beginning on 3 May. Everywhere they went, they were treated to traditional Irish hospitality. Apart from being invited to address the Dail, they attended several civic receptions, including one at which they received the Freedom of the City of Limerick. The only rebuffs they got occurred in the north, where the Lord Mayor of Belfast refused to see them. Their speeches along the way greatly heartened nationalists, but they so infuriated the decision-takers in London that even the King wanted Lloyd George to demand from Wilson 'a disavowal of the action of these American citizens'.

Wilson's own view of the trio was that they had:

behaved in a way which so inflamed British public opinion that the situation has got quite out of hand, and we are utterly at a loss how to act in the matter without involving the Government of the United States with the Government of Great Britain in a way which might create an actual breach between the two.

The three were in no way wide-eyed or visionary. Frank P. Walsh, a Kansas City lawyer, was a former Joint President of Wilson's War Labour Conference Board. Edward F. Dunne was a former Mayor of Chicago and Governor of Illinois, and Michael J. Ryan was a successful Philadelphia lawyer. But a combination of their empathy with the land of their forebears and their and Wilson's differing interpretations of what they were meant to be doing in Ireland put paid to any lingering hopes which may have existed for a Sinn Fein presence at the Peace Conference. The Senate had passed a resolution on 6 June asking that the Irish be admitted to 'present the case of Ireland'. Further, the Senate expressed sympathy with the aspirations of the Irish people 'for a government of their own choice'. This resolution, which was also hailed by the Nationalists, was largely a sham.

The Irish Committee was informed[39] by a telegram from the British Embassy in Washington three days later that the influential Senator Lodge had informed the Embassy that he was 'certainly not' in favour of an independent Ireland. The resolution was, in fact, an attack on Wilson and the League of Nations.

Accordingly, when the trio met Wilson in Paris on 11 June and pressed him on his celebrated war-time aim of self-determination for small nations, he made the heartfelt reply: 'You have touched on the great metaphysical tragedy of today'. By then he was suffering from the pressures of having to crush the hopes aroused by his words in places as far removed as Africa and Korea. The 'revolutionary situation' prevailing in the country, which the delegation described to the President, can be understood by a study of the table[40] compiled by Arthur Griffith the month before the Americans toured Ireland:

	1917	1918
Arrests	347	1107
English raids	11	260
Meetings suppressed	2	32
Deportations	24	91
Courts martial	36	62
Bayonet or baton charges	18	81
Sentences	269	973
Death from prison treatment	5	1
Newspapers suppressed	–	12

The figures were compiled with propagandist intent, but they were accurate and contrasted with Assizes Judges' comments at the time about the lack of ordinary crime in the country. All the foregoing offences related to speech-making, military display, having or issuing papers likely to cause 'disaffection' and so on. One person was jailed for 'whistling derisively at the police'.[41]

The Dail, meeting in honour of the American delegation, was surrounded by armed soldiers looking for Collins just after he had made a lengthy and powerful speech detailing the extent of British financial malpractice and over-taxation in Ireland. (This contained ideas for reparation which found expression first in the Anglo-Irish Treaty negotiations and later, ironically enough, in de Valera's successful prosecution of an 'economic war' against Britain in the 1930s that led to the abolition of some of the objectionable clauses which Collins was forced to concede in the Treaty.) When the proceedings concluded, the soldiers and detectives, led by Detective Daniel Hoey, entered the Mansion House looking for him, but he escaped via a ladder provided by O'Reilly. After a three-hour wait in a dusty building nearby he emerged in a filthy condition. Showing an instinct for publicity he sent O'Reilly to fetch his Volunteer uniform. Resplendent in this, he turned up at the reception for the Americans, the only man not in mufti, and created a sensation. The Most Wanted Man appearing in uniform! The creation of the Collins legend was well under way.

'Actors in events that have more meaning and consequence than we realise . . .' The letter which Collins had written to his sister, Helena, was truer than he knew. De Valera's decision to go to America still stood, and it was decided that Boland would go over in advance to make arrangements for him. It meant a parting of the ways for the hitherto inseparable friends. Boland would go with de Valera in more ways than one.

A factor which could be overstressed, but hardly overlooked, in assessing the reasons for Boland and Collins' estrangement is the fact that both fell in love with the same girl, Kitty Kiernan. She eventually preferred Collins and although, before she made her choice, Boland said he was sure the 'triangle' as he termed it (see page 281) would never spoil their friendship, he would hardly have been human if he had not felt some resentment afterwards. Indeed, it seems to have been confidently expected at one stage that it was Boland, not Collins, she planned to marry. Boland's mother seems to have been so certain of this that she actually wrote[42] to congratulate Kitty who, it appears, had not told Boland that it was Collins she loved. Boland, who at that stage was going on another lengthy trip to America, was still talking of honeymoon plans to Kitty.

In many ways the Boland/Collins relationship is symbolised by

Mrs Batt O'Connor's reminiscence[43] of seeing their two heads on the pillow, fast asleep in the moonlight. The Roland and Oliver image is limned by the knowledge that she could see them only because the bedroom door had been left open in case of a raid, and that Collins' bare arm rested on a bedside table – between two revolvers.

Beaslai, who shared a room with them in Vaughan's, recalled an argument in which Boland took the unexpected position that the use of force in pursuit of a principle lowered its value. Collins agreed with Beaslai who quoted Shaw's Armourer: 'Nothing is ever done in this world unless men are prepared to kill one another, if it is not done.' But Boland held to the precept that to live by the sword was to perish by it. They had another memorable night in Vaughan's to mark Boland's departure for the US and Boland enthusiastically joined in the applause for Collins' rendition of 'Kelly and Burke and Shea', the final verse of which is:

'Oh, the fighting races don't die out
If they seldom die in bed,
For love is the first in their heart, no doubt,'
Said Burke, then Kelly said:
'When Michael the great Archangel stands
The angel with the sword,
And the battle's dead from a hundred lands
Are arranged in one big horde,
One line that for Gabriel's trumpet waits,
Will stretch three-deep that day
From Jehoshaphat to the Golden Gates,
Kelly and Burke and Shea.'
'Well, here's thank God for the race and the sod,'
Said Kelly and Burke and Shea.

Today it is easier to laugh at such doggerel than to comprehend its meaning for the men in Vaughan's Hotel that night. For Kelly and Burke and Shea, one could read Beaslai and Boland and Collins. They were of the 'fighting races' and they knew the line 'they seldom die in bed' could apply to them. It did. Beaslai was arrested the day after Boland left for America, but of the three he was the only one who lived to write about the night in Vaughan's. The real tragedy of the gascons was that they died on opposite sides, Boland forgetting to leave his bedroom door open, Collins, too, neglecting elementary precautions.

The preparations being made for smuggling de Valera to the US aboard a liner by two of Collins' agents, were such that very little notice could be given. De Valera was actually at home in Greystones, preparing to celebrate his wife's birthday, when Collins and one of the agents, Dick O'Neill, appeared to tell him that he'd have to leave that night, Sunday 1 June 1919.

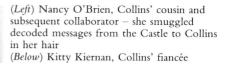

(*Left*) Hazel, Lady Lavery

(*Far left*) Edith, Lady Londonderry

FACING PAGE

Life on a bicycle: two leading players in Collins' undercover war were his Dublin Castle 'mole', Dave Neligan (*far left*), and British Intelligence Officer Captain Hardy (*below left*), whom Collins called a 'notorious murderer'

(*Foot*) Key men in the Volunteers, Seamus Robinson, Sean Treacy, Dan Breen and Michael Brennan

THIS PAGE

(*Above*) 'Apostles' Joe Slattery, Joe Dolan (second and third left) and William Stapleton (second right), Dublin Brigade members Joe Leonard (far left) and Charlie Dalton (far right), and Adj. Gen. Gearoid O'Sullivan (standing)

(*Below*) The infamous Cairo Gang (the two on the extreme left and the one in the middle are Irish)

Proving it more potent to endure than to inflict: Thomas Ashe, Kevin Barry (top right), Terence MacSwiney (below right); a woman with her child outside Mountjoy Jail while her husband is hanged, 1921

De Valera and O'Neill made the Holyhead crossing together. He was recognised aboard by a Fr McCarthy who had been a prison chaplain in 1916. He wanted to bring de Valera to a stateroom to meet another traveller, Sir James MacMahon, the Under Secretary for State for Ireland. De Valera knew MacMahon. They were both members of the same confraternity of St Vincent de Paul in Blackrock, but he decided this was no time to be discussing the corporal works of mercy and declined the invitation. They were followed by detectives at Holyhead but shook them off and de Valera was safely smuggled aboard the liner *Celtic*.

And so, stowed away and seasick, to New York went the 'President of the First Republic', pausing only to write a reassuring note to the long-suffering Sinead:

A Cuisle – I hope you were not too anxious yesterday. It may be the beginning of that birthday gift you prayed for.

I have made arrangements with S. Nunan to put to your account whatever is left after certain payments are made, with the exception of £25.

I trust you will not allow yourself to be lonely. It will be but for a short time.

I have only a minute or two. Kiss the children.
                                                Dev
Le gradh mo croidhe[44]

In fact, de Valera spun out that 'short time' for eighteen months and, during his absence, Collins' reputation acquired heroic proportions. He too became a President shortly after de Valera departed, though not a publicly announced one. The IRB do not announce the results of their elections. Sometime during June or July Collins was elected President of the Supreme Council of the IRB.[45]

The departure of Boland initially widened the breach between Collins and Sinn Fein. Boland's nominee for his position as Joint Honorary Secretary was spurned. Collins wrote to Stack in a fury:

The position is intolerable – the policy now seems to be to squeeze out any-one who is tainted with strong fighting ideas, or I should say I suppose ideas of the utility of fighting. Of course, any of the Dail Ministers are not eligible for the Stan. Cttee. and only 1/3 of the entire numbers may be members of the Dail. The result is that there is a Standing Committee of malcontents, and their first act is to appoint a pacifist secretary and announce the absence of H.B. Our own people give away in a moment what the Detective Division has been unable to find out in five weeks.[46]

Next day, still simmering at the disclosure of Boland's whereabouts, he again wrote to Stack:

. . . it seems to me that official Sinn Fein is inclined to be ever less militant and ever more political and theoretical . . . There is I suppose the tendency of all revolutionary movements to divide themselves up into their component parts. Now the moral force department have probably been affected by British propaganda.

But having said the position was 'disheartening' and had him 'awfully fed up', Collins characteristically concluded with one of his favourite quotations from Wolfe Tone, ''Tis in vain for soldiers to complain.' All he learned about British police methodology, all his own sources of information drove Collins to a realisation that if he wanted to put his knowledge to use then there was a grim logic to the situation.

Collins formally faced up to the implications of that logic with the formation of the 'Squad', which was officially founded on 19 September 1919 (though by that time it had been operative for two months and members of the Squad had two killings to their credit) at 46 Parnell Square, the meeting place of the Keating branch of the Gaelic League. The Squad was a group of assassins, a specially selected hit-squad directly under Collins' orders. The first recruits were warned by Dick McKee that their work would not be suitable for anyone with scruples about taking life, so they had no illusions as to what they were going into. Collins impressed on the Squad members that no organisation in Irish history had had a unit to deal with spies and the members of the Squad regarded themselves as being part of an elite. Its first leader was Mick McDonnell, a former Frongoch man, who was later succeeded by Paddy Daly.[47]

The first members of the Squad were Joe Leonard, Sean Doyle, Jim Slattery, Bill Stapleton, Pat McCrae, James Conroy, Ben Barret and Daly. Then in January 1920 Collins added Tom Keogh, Mick O'Reilly and Vincent Byrne. The expanded Squad became popularly known as the 'Twelve Apostles'.

Vinnie Byrne told me:

We were all young, twenty, twenty-one. We never thought we'd win or lose. We just wanted to have a go. We'd go out in pairs, walk up to the target and do it, then split. You wouldn't be nervous while you'd be waiting to plug him, but you'd imagine everyone was looking into your face. On a typical job we'd use about eight, including the back-up. Nobody got in our way. One of us would knock him over with the first shot, and the other would finish him off with a shot to the head.

Collins was a marvel. If he hadn't done the work he did, we'd still be under Britain. Informers and drink would have taken care of us. But our movement was temperate. Collins would meet us from time to time and say, 'You're doing great work, lads.' There was no formality about him. I remember after the Irish Government was set up I was on guard duty at Government Buildings, and he was Commander-in-Chief. He saw me and came over to me and put his arm around me and said, 'How are you going on, Vinny?'[48]

As explained earlier, the lynchpin of the British Intelligence system was the 'G' Division. When Collins began killing off its members, he paralysed the service.

Collins was very careful about the shooting of policemen. Once an order was given he was ruthless. It had to be carried out. Vinnie Byrne told me: 'You got your orders. He was your target. That was your job and it was up to you to see that it was done however you went about it.' But Collins 'went about it' cautiously. Broy remembered that 'Collins would always work out how the public would react to the shooting of a 'G' man first. And then he'd hang back for a while before he'd have another one shot. He tried to warn them off first without killing them.'[49]

Within two days (9 April 1919) of being shown the secret of Brunswick St, Collins began warning off detectives. One, Detective Sergeant Halley, was called on by a party of Volunteers at his home. Another, Constable O'Brien, was gagged and tied to the railings at Brunswick St Police Station. The 'G' man emerged unhurt from his ordeal, and, according to Broy, afterwards remarked that merely being warned was 'damned decent' of Sinn Fein. He took no further active role against the Volunteers. However, others were not so amenable. 'The Dog' Smith, for example, was a courageous man, as the son of a man sent to warn him told me afterwards: 'He told Dad that he appreciated him coming to tell him to lay off. He knew he was doing it because we were neighbours, but he said, "I'm not letting any young scuts tell me how to do my duty".'

The 'young scuts' were Boland and Collins who had tried unsuccessfully to get him to drop charges against Beaslai who had been arrested in possession of incendiary articles for *An tOglach*. The Squad waited for him for several nights before managing to waylay him near his home in Drumcondra, on 30 July 1919. A running battle developed, with Smith firing on his attackers and succeeding in getting in through his own front door even though hard hit. The Squad members were amazed to see him keep running. Collins did not merely weigh up the reaction to the subsequent death from wounds of the unfortunate Smith; he analysed the reasons why the detective 'kept running', and from then on the Squad was armed not with .38 but .45 revolvers.

The authorities responded to Smith's shooting by banning Sinn Fein and thereby creating a fertile climate for Collins' extremism. The Dail was banned on 12 September and Sinn Fein HQ at No. 6, Harcourt was raided. Collins reacted by having another detective shot, Hoey, a deeply religious man, who had, however, picked MacDiarmada out for the firing squads after 1916.

The Squad took a pride in its work. Daly remembers arguing with Collins on his positioning in a stake-out of one important quarry, (Assistant Commissioner Redmond, see page 129). It seemed that neither Daly nor his companions Leonard and Doyle were to go any-where near their intended victim and that other members of the Squad would account for him. ' "Are we to wait for the Stop Press?" I asked him,' Daly recalled. 'Collins replied: "The goal-man often gets more of the ball than the rest of the team . . .".' Actually as events turned out, it was Daly who felled Redmond with a single shot to the head. Even a glimpse of some of the detail of the Squad's activities as recounted by Daly still makes chilling reading today in a world accustomed to the horrors of war on a far greater scale: '. . . As he went down I heard him say, "What have I done to deserve this treatment" . . . Tom Keogh spotted Brooks at Westland Row station by accident and got him . . . Hugh said, "Kells is up there if you want him? . . ." "Where?" "On the footpath." "The fellows who went after Sergeant Revill will do a bit of crowing tonight".' (This last said of the team which had apparently hit another target successfully; in fact he lived.)

The obvious ruthlessness of the killings was balanced by strict instructions to the Squad that no one was to be shot except under orders or in self-defence when on active service. For instance, Daly's wife died the year the Squad was formed and he was left to raise a family which included a daughter with a deformed hand. A neighbour, an RIC man, maltreated the girl during a search of the Daly home and it was said afterwards, wrongly, that Daly intended to shoot the policeman. Collins heard the story and sent for Daly in a rage. 'What's this? Any man who has revenge in his heart is not fit to be a Volunteer.'

Not only was the Squad absolutely convinced of the rightness of their actions, they were soldiers fighting a far stronger enemy by the only means at their disposal; others, sometimes in highly significant places, shared this view. Byrne, for example, remembered going to confession to 'a great priest, Father Moriarty of South William Street. I told him: "I shot a man, Father." "Did you think you were doing right? Had you no qualms about it?" he asked me. I told him I didn't have any qualms, I thought I was doing right, and he said, "Carry on with the good work," and gave me absolution.'

Other helpers the Squad were able to count on were figures like 'Ninepence O'Connor' (so nicknamed because he was 'only as tall as ninepence worth of coppers'), who used to hide guns for Dick McKee behind a church altar. And there was also a well-known figure, 'the Black Man', a former boxer who perpetually walked the streets of Dublin. After a job the Squad would drop their guns in his pockets as they ran past. One inevitability of the Collins strategy was war, because as the police system crumbled, the British were forced to replace it with a military one.

As the war developed and grew in intensity, so too did the demand for the deadly ministrations of the Apostles increase, and their ranks grew also.

By 6 November 1919 the Irish Committee finally issued a report[50] (with an accompanying request for special secrecy) that contained the bones of the settlement which the British actually came to in 1921. Had the Report been acted on promptly and in the spirit it advocated, 'that the Government should make a sincere attempt to deal with the Irish situation once and for all', Ireland would have been spared a great deal of agony. The Committee agreed that:

. . . in view of the situation in Ireland itself, of public opinion in the Dominions, and in the United States of America, they cannot recommend the policy either of repealing or of postponing the Home Rule Act of 1914. In their judgement it is essential, now that the war is over, and the peace Conference has dealt with so many analogous questions in Europe, that the Government should make a sincere attempt to deal with the Irish question once and for all.

The Committee found two problems:

On the one hand the Government was committed against any solution which would break with the unity of the Empire. On the other, it was committed that Ulster must not be forced under the rule of an Irish parliament against its will. The first condition therefore excludes any proposal for allowing Ireland, or any part of Ireland to establish an independent Republic. The second again precludes them from again attempting what has so often failed in the past, the establishment of a single parliament for all Ireland on the lines of the Home Rule Acts of 1886, 1893 and 1914.

The stipulations in the last paragraph obviously made it inevitable that the type of Home Rule which would be agreeable to Britain was going to be very far short of the All-Ireland Republic which the Sinn Feiners had declared for themselves at the beginning of the year. The logic of the thing was clearly a separate state for 'Ulster', apart from any limitations as to the precise form of Home Rule which would be offered to the Southern nationalists. And on 24 November the Committee duly recommended to the Cabinet that two parliaments be set up in Ireland, linked by a Council of Ireland. The powers reserved included the Crown, Foreign Affairs, the conferring of dignities and questions of treason. A large measure of autonomy it clearly was not, nor was it intended to be. Discussing the Committee's Report two weeks earlier, on 11 November, Lord Birkenhead, the then Lord Chancellor, said:

I assent to this proposed Bill as effecting an ingenious strengthening of our tactical position before the world. I am absolutely satisfied that the Sinn Feiners will refuse it. Otherwise in the present state of Ireland I could not even be a party to making the offer, for I believe the Sinn Feiners, if they accept their parliament, would use it only for the purpose of forwarding separation.[51]

Birkenhead was a cynical but accurate prophet. The Cabinet was given a knowledgeable assessment of their Irish handiwork by Chief Justice O'Connor in a letter dated 24 December 1919:

I am sorry to say I can hear no good word for the Home Rule scheme . . . a parliament for the Nine instead of Six Counties would be less objectionable than the scheme as outlined, but even the changes will not make it acceptable, nor have I much hope that it will be honestly worked, if passed. I wish I could give you a more favourable view for all the decent people in this country (who I believe form the majority of the population) and all they want is peace.[52]

But peace did not come to Ireland.

5

The Year of Terror

'We have murder by the throat.'

Lloyd George

The year 1920 is remembered in Ireland as the Year of the Terror, the year the dreaded Black and Tans came. It was the year when the phase of daring escapades, of raids and rallies, gave way to the inevitable grimmer phase when the implications of the war began to strike home to everybody. On the one hand the Irish began to prove the truth of the assertion that successful revolutions are in fact no more than the kicking down of an already rotted door. The tiny handful of Volunteers – probably no more than three or four thousand strong countrywide – with their revolvers and shotguns began to paralyse the entire British system, or so it seemed. What in fact happened was that the British position was so untenable morally that they could not use their Army properly and were never able to put forth their full military might. Like a powerful wrestler whose own strength is used against him by a smaller opponent in judo, Lloyd George was forced to forgo his big battalions and attempt to combat Collins in his own underground world of Intelligence. And in that world Collins had something more important than weaponry, or even his ferocious drive and initiative. Behind his handful of detectives, his porters and clerks and postmen and warders and train drivers, his Tobins and his Cullens, he had the spirit of the people. Florrie O'Donoghue summed it up after a visit he paid to his native district in Cork to inspect the aftermath of British reprisals. Writing to the woman who had become his wife in extraordinary circumstances, he spoke in awed terms of what might be termed the Mujahadeen factor.

The calm undaunted fate of those people looking at the ruins of their own homes. I am not referring to my own people merely. I saw and spoke to them all, and I am convinced that there was something supernatural in the unshakable courage and olden Gaelic simplicity of these people. Truly the hills of Ireland could be levelled to the ground and all her children driven out upon the seas of the world before England can conquer us while we have such faith and courage.[1]

In Dublin the same spirit prevailed. Thornton expressed it in less high-flown language:

. . . the ordinary 'five–eight' common citizen was marvellous. Time after time when our men were watching houses, watching individuals, or watching for ambushes, men and women came along and quietly told them to look out that there was somebody watching them from a door or a street corner, and even after ambushes, we had women who were out shopping virtually grabbing grenades and revolvers from men who were in danger of being captured and coolly walking through the enemy lines. This spirit prevailed right throughout the country, but here in this citadel of British Imperialism the assistance given by the ordinary man and woman was simply marvellous and was responsible in the main for the success of our fighting services.

Put another way, what both O'Donoghue and Thornton were saying in effect was: because of her history, subversion in Ireland can only successfully be dealt with through military methods by the Irish, never by the British. But it was largely by military means that Lloyd George sought to proceed: nasty means at that. The British too had their 'squads'. Each side used the other's terminology: 'murder gangs'.

During 1919, the more active IRA leaders throughout the country had been itching for a fight. In Clare the leader of what was probably the first, and certainly one of the most successful, of the Flying Columns[2], Michael Brennan, was hauled over the coals 'very roughly'[3] by Mulcahy for unauthorised militarism. Tomas MacCurtain, head of the Volunteers in Cork, and Terence MacSwiney, his second-in-command, backed the idea of a 'revolving rising',[4] seizing a strongpoint in Cork one week, in Galway the next and so on throughout the country, holding out for as long as they could before going down to a glorious defeat which would have the effect of arousing the populace of the various areas, as 1916 had done. The 'static warfare' approach of course conflicted with Collins' ideas. But as 1919 ended GHQ felt that the Volunteers had grown sufficiently in strength to be allowed to go on the offensive. MacSwiney and MacCurtain were given instructions to attack a number of barracks in their area, and to be back at work the next morning 'as though a dog hadn't barked'.[5] Accordingly, on 1 January 1920 three barracks in the Cork area were successfully attacked, thus inaugurating a new phase of the struggle. Similar activities spread in the succeeding days to other parts of the country and Wexford, Waterford and Kilkenny were placed under martial law. In the midst of this uproar municipal elections were held under the authority of the Castle on 15 January. Sinn Fein repeated its triumph of the 'Khaki elections' to Westminster. The party's victories in Northern Ireland were particularly significant. Even the reduced Six-County area which the unionists were now resignedly seeking to agree on for exclusion from Home Rule showed Sinn Fein majorities in two counties, Fermanagh and Tyrone. Most disturbingly for the membership and organisers of the old Ulster Volunteer Force, Derry, the Covenanters' 'Maiden City', returned a Catholic Mayor, H. C. O'Doherty. In all, out of a total of 206 councils, Ireland gave 172 to Sinn Fein. As we shall see, this election result was an important factor in turning the militant Ulster Protestants from ballot to bullet as a means of holding their position.

But for the moment the point to note is that these councils promptly began cutting their links with the Castle and declaring their allegiance to the Dail. Many of the new councillors were IRA men. Amongst them was Tomas MacCurtain, who was elected Lord Mayor of Cork; Terence MacSwiney was appointed his deputy. A few days later, on 20 January, a policeman was shot in Thurles and that night, in a pattern that was to become all too familiar throughout the year, police and military shot up the town in reprisal. The editorial reaction of Lloyd George's own newspaper, the *Daily Chronicle*, was ominously significant:

Nobody can fail to deplore such occurrences, but equally obviously nobody can wonder at them. Indeed it is obvious that, if these murderous clubs pursue their course much longer, we may see counter clubs springing up, and the lives of prominent Sinn Feiners becoming as unsafe as prominent officials.

Reprisals had made their appearance; counter-insurgency 'murder clubs' as the *Chronicle* called them were on the way. Through one of his post office agents Collins was given sight of a letter written by a British Intelligence officer (in the St Andrew's Hotel, Dublin, on 2 March) to a colleague in the War Office who was about to join him. It contained the following:

Have duly reported and found things in a fearful mess, but I think I will be able to make a good show. Have been given a free hand to carry on, and everyone has been very charming. Re our little stunt, I see no prospects until I have got things on a firmer basis, but still hope and believe there are possibilities.[6]

MacCurtain received a threatening letter on 16 March: 'Thomas MacCurtain prepare for death. You are doomed.' It was written on Dail Eireann notepaper, seized in a police raid on 76 Harcourt St. A number of similar death notices were sent to other prominent Sinn Feiners, apparently with a view to making it appear that the rebels were now murdering each other. Four nights later, after a policeman had been shot dead near Cork, police cordoned off an area around MacCurtain's home. Around 1 am a party of armed men with blackened faces forced their way into his house and shot him dead in the presence of his wife. IRA intelligence subsequently established the fact that a group of civilians entered King St RIC barracks shortly afterwards. One of the group was further identified as looking suspiciously like the man in a photograph which Crow St provided of the officer to whom the 'little stunt' letter was written.

Collins was hard-hit by the death. He wrote to MacSwiney, 'I have not very much heart in what I am doing today thinking of poor Tomas. It is surely the most appalling thing that has been done yet.'[7] It was also a thing which would have far-reaching consequences in another highly sensitive part of the country, Northern Ireland. Collins took no retaliatory action until after the inquest which was in effect a trial of British policy. Despite efforts by Lord French and Lloyd George to claim that MacCurtain was murdered by his own extremists the jury, which had been selected by the police, brought in a verdict that was a comprehensive indictment of both Westminster and Dublin Castle:

We find that Alderman Tomas MacCurtain, Lord Mayor of Cork, died from shock and haemorrhage, caused by bullet wounds, and that he was wilfully wounded under circumstances of the most callous brutality: and that the murder was organised and carried out by the RIC officially directed by the British Government.

We return a verdict of wilful murder against David Lloyd George, Prime Minister of England; Lord French, Lord Lieutenant of Ireland; Ian MacPherson, late Chief Secretary of Ireland; Acting Inspector General Smith of the RIC, Divisional Inspector Clayton of the RIC; DI Swanzy and some unknown members of the RIC.[8]

They didn't stay unknown very long. When he was sworn in to succeed MacCurtain, MacSwiney said, 'We do not abrogate our function to demand and see the evildoers and murderers are punished for their crimes.'

Neither the death of MacCurtain nor the awful vengeance for his death which followed put a stop to the murdering of Lord Mayors. In Limerick the following year, on 6 March 1921, three leading citizens with nationalist sympathies, Joseph O'Donoghue, George Clancy and Michael O'Callaghan, were murdered during curfew hours in circumstances identical with MacCurtain's killing. Clancy was the Mayor at the time and O'Callaghan had preceded him in 1920. The killings were so outrageous that General Gough, of Curragh mutiny fame, wrote: 'Law and order have given way to a bloody and brutal anarchy . . . England has departed further from her own standards, and further from the standards even of any nation in the world, not excepting the Turk and Zulu, than has ever been known in history before.'[9]

While these events were taking place Britain was changing its team in Ireland. In March a new Commander-in-Chief was appointed, General Sir Nevil Macready, son of the famous actor, with experience behind him as Commissioner of the Metropolitan Police in London, of ruthlessness against miners in Tonypandy in Wales, and of service in Belfast during the Ulster gun-running crisis. None of this left him with a predisposition to win friends and influence the people of Ireland in his new posting, by other than approved methods of military efficiency. He was shortly to be joined by General Hugh Tudor as head of a reconstituted police force. The Cabinet was well aware from the time of the Fisher report that efficiency was sadly lacking in Dublin Castle. Lord French, who 'skied on Olympus' in the viceregal lodge, also made sure that the Government was kept continually aware of the position.[10]

Accordingly, in April, one of England's most distinguished civil servants, Sir John Anderson (later Viscount Waverley), was sent to take over the administration with two able lieutenants, Mark Beresford Sturgis and, most significantly, a Lloyd George man, Alfred (Andy) Cope, a former customs detective whose talents the Prime Minister had discovered in, of all places, the Ministry of Pensions. More importantly, Cope had helped to draw up the Fisher Report. During this exercise he had met Sir James MacMahon, the Catholic Under Secretary of under-utilised talents and, more importantly to Cope, of under-utilised contacts in Nationalist circles. While both open and undercover military methods were employed to crush Sinn Fein, covertly Cope sought to find a political path for Lloyd George out of the Irish morass. Not for nothing did the Welsh wizard sleep under a framed, embroidered text from the Book of Job: 'There is a path which no fowl knoweth and which the eye of the vulture hath not seen.'[11] Under the new men MacMahon was treated with greater respect[12] and it was probably he who ultimately put Cope on the road to meeting Collins. With the administrative and military wings taken care of, Lloyd George made political alterations also. Sir Hamar Greenwood was appointed Chief Secretary in place of MacPherson. A hard job called for a hard man and certainly few political figures of the time could have stood over the activities of the next actors to enter the scene as brazenly as did Hamar Greenwood whose name was to pass into Irish folklore – 'telling a Hamar' – as a synonym for lying. The actors, who also earned an unenviable niche in Irish history, were the specially raised corps known as the Black and Tans and the Auxiliary Cadets.

The former owed their existence to a combination of the increasing ineffectiveness of the RIC under the weight of the Sinn Fein moral and physical onslaught; the shakiness of Britain's moral position in the eye of world opinion; and the influence of Sir Henry Wilson, zealous for the reputation of the Army as Chief of the Imperial General Staff and a rabid Unionist. The Cabinet listened to his urging 'with all my force the necessity for doubling the police and not employing the military'.[13]

From the end of 1919 advertisements were placed in English papers for men willing to undertake 'a rough and dangerous task'. The task was to carry out the 'shoot-to-kill' policy outlined by Lt Colonel Smyth (see p. 150). From around March, when the first successful respondents to the ads began arriving in Ireland, the Tans carried out the Smyth policy with the full rigour of the lawless in two particular regards: the assuaging of their collective thirsts, and of the itch in their trigger fingers. Frank Thornton was in Limerick in March, with his comrade Joe Dolan, when the Tans made their debut in the city in a manner that was typical of their behaviour all over the country:

They arrived in a string of lorries and proceeded to shoot up the city, left, right and centre. Both Dolan and I were staying in the Glentworth Hotel, which is on the main road to the railway station. Just past the Glentworth stands Tate's Clock, standing at least 120 ft high and brilliantly illuminated at night. We were awakened by shooting at about 12.30 to 1 am and on looking through the window we saw thirty or forty Black and Tans all lying on the road and having a cockshot at Tate's Clock with their rifles.

After a bit they were organised by someone in control and they proceeded to shoot in regular relays at the clock. Getting tired of this after a bit, they then forced their way into the Glentworth and insisted on the management opening up the bar . . . after carousing downstairs for about an hour they made their departure.

The Tans were not, as was said, the scourings of the jails of England, they were merely encouraged to behave as if they were. They were ex-servicemen, generally unemployed, to whom the official offer of ten shillings a day and the unofficial assurance that they would be given a free hand in making Ireland a 'hell for rebels' were attractive baits. They owed the 'Black and Tan' description to the unattractive black and brown combination of khaki and police clothing provided for them by the British by way of uniform, resulting in the Irish giving them the nickname after a famous pack of hounds.

To ensure that the Tans' morale kept up, and to counter the effect of the *Irish Bulletin*, the Castle published the *Weekly Summary* from 5 May. In an editorial headed 'Black and Tans' published on 27 August the *Summary* said:

They did not wait for the usual uniform. They came at once. They were wanted badly, and the RIC welcome them. They know what danger is. They have looked Death in the eyes before, and did not flinch. They will not flinch now.

They will go on with the job – the job of making Ireland once again safe for the law-abiding, and an appropriate hell for those whose trade is agitation, and whose method is murder.

Suffice it to say that the Tans, as the Tate's Clock episode indicates, made Ireland safe neither for the law-abiding nor for anyone else for that matter, but made of the country a most inappropriate hell for an entire population.

Churchill is credited with thinking up the second force, the Police Auxiliary Cadets, who were mostly ex-officers, with a view to both bolstering the RIC and controlling the Black and Tans while at the same time avoiding the appearance of all-out military conflict. In the event the Auxiliaries, who were paid £1 a day as befitted their status as officers and gentlemen, were set up and maintained as an autonomous force, wearing a distinctive blue uniform with a Glengarry cap and, generally, the even more notably distinguishing trademark of a brace of revolvers worn strapped to the hip, wild-west style. The 'Auxis', as they were popularly known, were more formidable than the Tans, a tough, ruthless, energetic and courageous force who showed themselves ready, willing and able to use those guns. 'Time and time again the Volunteers testified to their bravery, but too often the mangled corpse of a woman or an old man did as much for their savagery'.[14] Walter Long accurately informed the House of Commons (3 June 1920) when he said that there was no foundation for the suggestion that the Irish police were not allowed to shoot. He was 'glad to say that the police had not only shot, but had shot with extremely good effect, and he hoped they would do it again'. They did. Several towns and villages were shot up by the police, including Limerick, Fermoy, Thurles, Killmalock, Kilcommon and Lismore. Curfew was imposed and khaki became the predominant colour in cities like Cork and Dublin.

Kathleen Napoli MacKenna described how Dublin looked one Sunday morning in July, a time when the streets would normally be more or less empty save for Mass-goers:

. . . citizens were thronging to hear Mass through streets filled with British Regulars carrying rifles with fixed bayonets, Auxiliary Cadets, Black and Tans and, here and there, broad-shouldered plainclothes men distinguishable as members of the 'G' Division of the Dublin Metropolitan Division engaged in political espionage. A tank was ambling along Bachelor's Walk, military lorries, filled with armed-to-the-teeth troops, their rifles at the ready, were racing through O'Connell St, and military cordons were drawn with barbed wire around the entrances to Grafton St from Nassau St and College Green.[15]

Along with this visible menace there were the hidden dangers of the British Secret Service and its attendant squads of assassins.

One of the agents sent against Collins was described by Sir Basil Thompson as 'one of the best and cleverest Secret Service men that England ever had'.[16] Plump, sharp-featured, middle-aged, of average height, his knee-length boots were the only distinguishing thing about the man known as Jameson, though he was apparently born Burns, the son of a police officer from Limerick. He had worked in intelligence in India before the First World War and during it somehow managed to elude detection in Germany. Afterwards he had been an *agent provocateur* during the London police strike. In Dublin his cover story was that he was a salesman of musical instruments with an interest in bird-watching. He began by infiltrating Irish circles in London by posing as one of the fiery communist speakers whose podium adjoined the Irish Self-Determination League's platform at Speakers' Corner in Hyde Park. As the communists supported the Irish revolution these Sunday morning occasions were friendly affairs through which Jameson had easily become acquainted with Sean McGrath and Art O'Brien. The consequences may be gauged from a despatch of Collins' to O'Brien: 'Jameson: has duly arrived and has been interviewed by 3 of us. I shall report developments later on.'[17]

The 'developments' were intended to centre on two of Jameson's stated objectives, firstly to provide the IRA with arms, as he had earlier done through O'Brien as evidence of good faith, and secondly to foment mutiny in the British Army and Navy, in both Ireland and England. In fact things fell out in fatally different fashion from what was expected. Jameson's visit was to cost England the lives of two of her best agents, that of Jameson himself and that of Assistant Commissioner Redmond, mentioned earlier in Chapter 4.

The Jameson incident gives another glimpse of Collins' extra-ordinary network of agents. The story shows that Collins had penetrated right into the heart of the British Secret Service. Collins had him watched in London as well as Dublin and one day in January sent a warning to Art O'Brien:

Jameson: What I have to say with regard to him will probably be somewhat of a thunderbolt to you. I believe we have the man or one of them. I have absolutely certain information that the man who came from London met and spoke to me, and reported that I was growing a moustache to Basil Thompson. I may get some more information. In the meantime will you get in touch with him somehow and show him my paragraph on himself in the other memo.[18]

The other paragraph was a decoy written in the tone of Collins' note to O'Brien on Jameson of December. Hand-written on the memo is a message asking O'Brien to 'find out from Jameson what addresses I gave him so that I can warn. I am not quite certain as my note is not very clear.' So obviously Jameson had succeed in prising some information out of Collins before he was unmasked. But the really remarkable thing is that Collins had obviously succeeded in placing someone close to Basil Thompson himself.

Collins at first took to Jameson and had him introduced to members of GHQ who also seemed to find nothing wrong with him. For no apparent reason, however, Tom Cullen took an immediate dislike to the agent and described him as a 'crooked English bastard', perhaps sensing that he and Jameson were in the same line of work. This feeling transmitted itself to Thornton and Tobin and they decided to lay a trap for Jameson. Meanwhile Jameson was also setting traps for Collins, traps which very nearly succeeded in their objective.

Collins brought him to lunch at Mrs O'Connor's, to have her vet him. He relied on her instinct and judgement so much that he adjudged it worth while exposing her to the risk of identification as one of his agents, for a detective had been posted outside at a safe distance.[19] Seeing Jameson come out again with another man, he cycled off to alert a waiting contingent of detectives and police. Incredibly he misinformed them, telling them that the bird had flown, not knowing that the bird was still in the house where Mrs O'Connor was telling him that she did not like her visitor. The man with Jameson was Liam Tobin. Collins was soon informed of the detective's mistake; one of the men in the police party had been MacNamara.

MacNamara had also been present in the Castle the previous day when Redmond, an able man who had been brought down from Belfast to reorganise the demoralised detective division, made what proved to be a fatal remark while dressing down subordinates: 'You were supposed to be looking for Collins. You have been after him for months and never caught sight of him, while a new man, just over from England, met him and talked to him after two days.'

However it was one thing to know that Redmond was a force to be reckoned with. It was another thing to identify that force. Collins sent Thornton to Belfast[20] where he linked up with the Belfast equivalent of Broy, a Sergeant Matt MacCarthy from Kerry, who operated from one of the most strongly loyalist centres in Ireland, Chichester St Barracks. Describing Thornton as his cousin, McCarthy installed him in the barracks for the night, the occasion of the police boxing championships. Every policeman who could was attending, including the District Inspector. Thornton was able to enter his office and remove a photograph of Redmond from his files. The photograph was in Collins' hands next day.

This Sergeant McCarthy helped Collins out of a tight corner in Kirwan's one night. He had come down from Belfast to hand over the latest police codes to Collins when the place was raided. His police pass caused the Auxiliary to relax and offer the pair a drink – without searching Collins, who had the codes on him. The barman put away the .45 he was preparing to use on the Auxiliary and poured a round of pints. Redmond had led a raid on Mrs O'Connor's house after which he had assured her that he would not trouble her again. He spoke truer than he knew. Paddy Daly was to shoot him dead three days later, outside the Standard Hotel in Harcourt St which he was due to vacate shortly for the safety of rooms which were almost ready for him in the Castle. One of the unfortunate Redmond's last acts of police work was to spend the night of the raid on O'Connor's staking out the house in a futile vigil for Collins in the company of another detective – MacNamara. On his death the Castle offered a reward of £10,000 for information leading to convictions in what was by then a total of fourteen dead DMP and RIC. The toll would go higher, but the reward would not be claimed.

Meanwhile Jameson returned to England where Collins was able to secure a report on his briefing to Sir Basil Thompson. With extraordinary courage the spy then returned to Dublin and contacted Crow St, which now proceeded to lay a trap for him. The spy arranged to hand over a portmanteau of revolvers to Thornton at 56 Bachelor's Walk, Dublin, the home of both the New Ireland Assurance Company and of a famous Dublin tobacconist, Knapp and Peterson's Ltd. Thornton accepted the revolvers, but instead of going up to the New Ireland offices, which were frequently used to plan activities that the British would certainly have wished to insure against, he went downstairs to Knapp and Peterson's basement while Tobin took Jameson away. Then Thornton sprinted down to the quartermaster-general's stores, run by Sean MacMahon at 32 Bachelor's Walk. The strain of trying to keep the underground army supplied had turned MacMahon's hair white by the time he was thirty. To him bullets were as precious as diamonds. When he read a newspaper account of some soldiers being 'riddled with bullets' he was furious. 'Riddled! Blast them, where do they think we'll get them.'[21] The revolvers were naturally warmly welcomed and should have guaranteed Jameson's bona fides. However, Thornton had earlier asked MacNamara to let him know if any special raids were planned by the Castle that day. A few hours after the revolvers were handed over word came that 56 Bachelor's Walk was to be raided at three o'clock.

It was, watched from across the river by Tobin, Thornton and Cullen. All the raiders found in the basement was a Volunteer's cap which convinced them that they were on the right track. After midnight they returned and dug up floors and knocked down walls looking for secret passages. Not surprisingly Jameson again went back to the drawing-board. He returned to London to report, and, showing remarkable courage, went back to Dublin yet again, still trying to see Collins.

Joe O'Reilly told Jameson that his wish to meet Collins was about to be granted.[22] He was collected by two of the 'apostles', Paddy Daly and Joe Dowling, and brought by tram to the back entrance of the Albert College in Ballymun. Here Paddy Daly told him that he was a spy and that he was doomed. There are differing accounts of what Jameson said in reply but all agree that he stood to attention and clicked his heels while the hammers of the .45s cocked. As Daly was 'close . . . as the killer is close one moment to the man he kills', I give his recollection of the agent's last words: 'That's right. God bless the

King. I would love to die for him.' An iron cross he had given Tobin was hung in his memory on the walls in Crow St alongside pictures of other agents who had either shared or, it was hoped, would share his fate.

One of the most important of these was an Irishman, H. Quinlisk, a former corporal in the Royal Irish Regiment, who, as a German prisoner of war, had enrolled in Casement's Brigade. It was probably Quinlisk who first gave the Castle an accurate idea of the extent of Collins' influence. On his return to Ireland he received assistance from Sinn Fein and from Collins who gave him money, bought him a new suit and got him a place in his lodgings at Miss MacCarthy's, 44 Mountjoy St, which by then he generally only used to keep his clothes in. Quinlisk apparently reciprocated by having the place raided. Collins put it down to happenstance. Apparently he thought that Quinlisk's knowledge of German and his military experience could be put to some use by the Volunteers. That wasn't what Quinlisk had in mind.

On 11 November 1919 he wrote to 'The Under Secretary, Dublin Castle' telling him that he had decided to tell 'all I know' of Sinn Fein and of 'that scoundrel Michael Collins' who had 'treated me scurvily'. The letter resulted in an interview in Brunswick St, an account of which was given to Broy to type and a copy sent along to Collins. Quinlisk lived like a caricature of a Greene/Le Carré portrait of an agent manipulated for some three months before his end. Unknown to him, his treachery was widely known. Kathleen Napoli MacKenna recalls seeing

a well-dressed young man [at 6 Harcourt St], with frank open countenance and nonchalant air sitting smoking, his legs dangling, on a console-table in the inner hall. I noticed the colours of his regimental tie. Fitzie[23] stopped to talk to him; I walked on to the hall-door and as I awaited her I could hear their chatter and laughter.

'Darn nice lad, that: pity he's up to no good in here', Fitzie remarked carelessly when she joined me. 'Who's he?' I enquired. 'Quinlisk, an ex-member of Casement's Irish Brigade on the make for blood money.'

MacKenna thought no more of the incident, imagining Anna FitzSimons meant something to do with recompensing Quinlisk for his Brigade activities. But the following February FitzSimons asked her if she remembered the day in the hall and told her Quinlisk had just been found shot dead in Cork. Collins had sent him on a false trail, letting him believe that he was going to be in Wren's Hotel, Cork. The result was that a message in code went to the RIC District Inspector in Cork from the Castle instructing him to surround Wren's Hotel and arrest Michael Collins. Quinlisk himself travelled to Cork and made a beeline for Wren's so as to be on the scene to collect the £10,000 offered after Redmond's shooting. Instead the Cork IRA found him and he was discovered dead in a ditch on 18 February 1920. Napoli MacKenna wrote:

The event impressed me deeply and threw a new light on the bitterness of the struggle in which I was now taking my part. From it I realised . . . how ruthless Collins could be when necessary. He had played up to, and trapped, this Irish Judas who for hard cash was prepared to betray one of Ireland's most valuable leaders.

It would be impossible to chronicle the individual killings carried out by each side as the war intensified but a few other examples of that 'ruthlessness' which suddenly dawned on Napoli MacKenna may be noted to indicate the nature of the war. Before doing so it is necessary to understand the importance of the Dublin institution known as 'Kidd's Back'.

As we saw, Neligan had managed to get himself accepted as a member of the British Secret Service. He then proceeded to introduce Tobin, Thornton and Cullen to his Secret Service colleagues. They generally met either at the Rabbiatti Saloon in Malborough St or in 'Kidd's Back', a famous bar off Grafton St at the back of what is now the Berni Inn in Nassau St. The British *modus operandi* was to have each member of the Secret Service surround himself with a number of touts, or minor informers. Some must have been worse than useless to their employers. They were generally English and completely at sea. One day in Rabbiatti's, Cullen and Thornton found themselves sharing a table with a group of them, one of whom suddenly exclaimed wonderingly: 'Gor blimey, how did you learn the Irish brogue. We're here in Dublin for the last twelve months and we can't pick any of it up. You fellows have it perfect.' The Irishmen solemnly explained that there was an art in such matters.

The more senior British Intelligence officers patronised Kidd's Back, and Willie Beaumont and Neligan introduced Cullen, Saurin and Thornton to some of them, pretending the three Irishmen were their touts. (Collins literally charmed Beaumont into joining the British Secret Service. He induced Beaumont's brother, Sean, to arrange a meeting between the ex-British officer, who had publicly announced his intention of 'getting' Collins, and himself. Beaumont was 'so impressed . . . that he offered his services to us.') The three became habitués of this mecca of British Intelligence. As Thornton says, 'a lot of our information was picked up by taking a very big risk.' Some of the most dangerous men in Europe met in that bar, from both sides. One day some of the British agents were chatting with the three Irishmen when an officer suddenly said to Cullen: 'Surely you fellows know Liam Tobin, Frank Thornton and Tom Cullen. These are Collins' three officers and if you get those fellows we should locate Collins himself.' That conversation in Kidd's was a tribute to the effectiveness of the campaign Collins and his men were waging against the Castle's hitherto invincible intelligence system. At least one of the battles in that campaign was fought out in Kidd's.

Liam Tobin used to drink with Fergus Brian Mulloy, a sergeant in the British Army who worked for Colonel Hill Dillon, Chief Intelligence Officer at Parkgate St. Neither he nor Dillon suspected Lily Merin, who was working as Dillon's secretary! Mulloy also met Thornton and Cullen and whether through the snobbery of the British officer system, or the confusion and rivalry between the various British forces, he never succeeded in fingering his new acquaintances to the representatives of the units who shared the bar with him. Auxiliaries, Secret Service, Military Intelligence, police officers, all sat drinking within arm's reach as Mulloy drank with Tobin.

Yet Mulloy seems to have been under no illusion as to whom or what he was dealing with. After his death it became known that he had written to his sister in America that if he were murdered 'a man named Tobin' would have been responsible. His cover story was that he intended joining the British Secret Service in order to help the IRA and he promised to get arms and an army pass for Tobin and company. These never materialised and he eventually proposed that Thornton and Cullen should accompany him into the Castle one night and he would make it possible for them to copy out secret documents. The pair had a shrewd notion that if they got into the Castle they stood a very poor chance of getting out again and counter-proposed that Mulloy assist them in shooting Colonel Hill Dillon who lived outside Parkgate in civilian quarters. The Colonel promptly disappeared into safer lodgings.

Then, in another well-known Dublin rendezvous, the Café Cairo, Mulloy suggested that Tobin give him some information to show his superiors to prove that he was achieving something – perhaps the names and addresses of some Sinn Feiners who were prominent but whose removal to jail would not seriously damage the movement, say, Countess Markievicz or Count Plunkett? 'Write the addresses and I'll be trusted with more secrets', he said, handing Tobin a sheet of captured Dail Eireann notepaper. Tobin had an apocalyptic vision of one of both of the two being found murdered with a sheet of Dail Eireann notepaper beside them containing the handwriting of Michael Collins' right-hand man. It would enable the British to make the sort of claims Lloyd George and French had come out with after MacCurtain's murder four days earlier. The interview terminated and that evening, going up the stairs of Vaughan's, Tobin was heard to say to Collins, 'We'll have to shoot that fellow.' Collins replied simply: 'Well shoot him so.' Mulloy died on the pavement of Wicklow St on the following evening, 25 March 1920.

Collins also discovered that the hall porter of the Wicklow Hotel,

William Doran, was an informer. Joe Dolan described what happened:

The Squad made several attempts to get him but were unsuccessful. At last Mick Collins sent a dispatch to Liam Tobin to hurry it up, as he was doing a lot of damage. Tobin asked me to do it as I knew him. Dan McDonnell and myself entered the Wicklow Hotel one morning about nine o'clock, shot him dead in the hall, and walked away. I was back there at 1 pm having my lunch.

Not knowing who had had him shot, his destitute widow applied to the Sinn Fein for a pension. For the sake of the children, Collins directed that she should be paid.

Amongst assassins on the other side the names of Captain Hardy and Igoe stand out. Hardy was the liaison officer between Dublin Castle and Special Intelligence Office, Scotland Yard. He was involved with the UVF in ways that even today the Northern Ireland authorities wish to keep secret.[24] These schemes included a plot to kidnap Arthur Griffith. Collins himself described Hardy as a 'notorious murderer'.[25] Crow St had a long list of killings to debit to Igoe and his men. Torture was added to the scale of horrors awaiting anyone who fell into such hands. Watching the forces pile up against him Collins summed up the position in a memorable letter: '. . . to my mind it is now a question of our nerves. There is no doubt a great deal of punishment ahead of us. It is a question of the body wearing longer than the lash.'[26]

The punishment did come, but so did a great deal of assistance in bearing it, from all sorts of unexpected quarters. One such was a publican, Liam Devlin, who had returned from Scotland to buy a pub in Parnell Square, directly opposite the Rotunda. Devlin, who had been active in Sinn Fein in Scotland and was put in touch with Collins through the IRB, now offered a means of protection to Collins, the use of his pub as an office and meeting place. It was an ideal cover, centrally situated in a busy part of Dublin, so that Collins and his contacts were able to come and go unremarked. Devlin's became

Mick's unofficial headquarters. 'We used Devlin's extensively and every night Mick, Gearoid O'Sullivan, Liam Tobin, Dermot O'Hegarty, Piaras Beaslai, Frank Thornton, Tom Cullen and Joe O'Reilly met there, the events of the day were discussed and plans were made for the following day. Any particular Column leader or Brigade Officer arriving in town was generally instructed to report to Devlin's. . . . Mrs Devlin acted in the capacity of a very generous hostess. Visitors from the country never left without getting a meal and in quite a large number of instances a bed for the night.[27]

The Devlins wanted Collins to use a large comfortable room at the front of the house, but he preferred to sleep at the back, where he could hear the sound of horses in a nearby stable.[28] Possibly the sound of breaking furniture was less audible from the back of the pub also! In exercise Collins would push the sofa at an opponent, throw the wash jug, the basin – 'a broken lock meant as little to him as a broken vessel'. The Devlins gave Collins an ordinary furnished room. As O'Connor notes,

within a month it was a wreck. There was scarcely a chair with a back to it; the delph had disappeared, yet when one of the gang, hearing a tumble and thunder from the sitting room in which Collins was lashing out with a chair, apologised to the Devlins, they merely smiled and said: 'It eases his mind'. They spoke with the understanding of love, for it was in this savage lashing and straining that all the accumulated anxiety was released.

The rollings on the floor with Liam Tobin, Gearoid O'Sullivan and Tom Cullen were roisterings between men who were taking life and knew that at any second their own could be snuffed out. The heaving mass on the floor striving for 'a bit of ear' was after all the hunted Leadership of the Irish Republican Army.

One of Collins' worst faults was his habit of baiting people, most notably O'Reilly and Tom Cullen. Once, in the emotional firestorm he always experienced before or after the carrying out of one of his killings, or 'jobs' as those involved always referred to them, he was so outrageous to O'Reilly that the unfortunate man broke down and wept, and said that he could take no more, he was going home. Collins snarled at him: 'All right, take some despatches for me on your way', and the selfless O'Reilly, worn out from sleepless nights and ceaseless Trojan work for Collins, took the despatches to the girl for whom they were intended. He had obviously been crying, and when she asked him why, he broke down again and gave her the reason, at which she flew into such a rage that she went immediately to Collins and read him the Riot Act for insensitivity to the amount of work O'Reilly did.

Collins stormed back at her, 'You mind your own fucking business. I know how O'Reilly works', and poor O'Reilly was back at work the following morning for some more of the same treatment, which so enraged at least one observer that years later Ernie O'Malley would write:

He had a habit of baiting Tom Cullen . . . and a few of the Dublin men that I hated. I could understand, take or make use of a tell-off, but the prodding got on my nerves. One day I told Collins and left the room in a rage. He never baited anyone in my presence afterwards.[30]

Joe O'Reilly once uncannily recreated both the horror that gripped Collins on the eve of a 'job' and the hold he exerted on O'Reilly's imagination. It happened when Frank O'Connor and Dr Richard Hayes were interviewing him one evening a dozen years after Collins was killed. By then O'Reilly had matured from a harassed drudge into the polished, golf-playing man who became ADC to W. T. Cosgrave, then President of the Executive Council (effectively the Prime Minister), and an important official in the Board of Works. After some hours O'Connor asked him, 'How did Collins behave when he had to have someone shot?' O'Reilly 'seemed to collapse . . . Something had gone wrong with him . . .' Seemingly some kind of auto-hypnotism occurred for he suddenly went into the Collins war-spasm. O'Connor writes:

. . . he suddenly jumped up, thrust his hands into his pockets and began to stamp about the room, digging his heels in with a savagery that almost shook the house. Finally he threw himself onto a sofa, picked up a newspaper, which he pretended to read, tossed it aside after a few moments and said in a coarse country voice, 'Jesus Christ Almighty, how often have I to tell ye . . . ?' It was no longer Joe O'Reilly who was in the room. It was Michael Collins, and for close on two hours I had an experience that must be every biographer's dream, of watching someone I had never known as though he were still alive. Every gesture, every intonation was imprinted on O'Reilly's brain as if on tape.[31]

The depth of the imprintation shocked O'Connor almost as much as it did O'Reilly. He said, 'You could see not only Collins, but also the effect he was having upon a gentle, sensitive boy, and it made you want to intervene between a boy who was no longer there and a ghost. I did it even at the risk of breaking the record.' At one point in the hypnosis, O'Reilly began recreating the scene when the girl-next-door stormed into Collins to protest at his cruelty. O'Reilly was beginning to describe Collins' response in normal tones when, O'Connor writes, 'suddenly Collins was back in the room again: "I know his value better than you do. He goes to Mass for me every morning. Jesus Christ, do you think I don't know what he's worth to me?"'

Generally when O'Connor writes of Collins, a sense of affection, of love almost, emerges, but he concludes his account: 'When O'Reilly left, the handsome, sprightly young man had disappeared. In his place was an elderly, bewildered man, and you could see what he would be like if Collins had lived.'

Against this description of Collins' methods one must balance that of another contemporary who, like O'Malley, later fought against Collins: Oscar Traynor, who succeeded Dick McKee as OC of the Dublin Brigade during some of the fiercest fighting of the Anglo-Irish war. To Traynor,

it was like a breath of fresh air to meet him or to talk to him. He was always full of ideas. His ideas were good too. You got the impression of eventual success. This man wasn't beaten. This fellow didn't think we were finished, nor did he give the impression of being finished himself. Mick Collins was very easy on men. He'd talk nicely to them, even if he didn't think much of them. After raging he'd come back and apologise.[32]

These methods maintained discipline on a force of young men

bound together more by idealism than training. Unpunctuality, for instance, sent him into a fury in which he would swing his watch so violently as he enquired why the —— he had been kept waiting that recipients of this treatment feared they were going to be struck by the timepiece. The point was that split-second timing was essential for the successful carrying out of his raids, meetings and ambushes. Even though he went about Dublin deliberately refusing to wear disguise, or to allow the ever-increasing strength of the enemy to interfere with his movements, he was at risk every second of the day. The solicitor Michael Noyek, called to a meeting with Collins in Kirwan's pub in Parnell St one day, received the usual indication of his whereabouts, an imperceptible nod of the head and a movement of the eyes to indicate where Collins sat in the snug, and there was the most wanted man in Europe 'sitting calmly, working away in a crowd of dealers'.[33]

That little anecdote is a testimonial to Collins' success. Those stallholders from nearby Moore St knew perfectly well who Collins was, but not one of them, in a class not normally associated with aversion to turning a quick penny, thought of betraying him, and, business with Noyek finished, Collins was apt to come up suddenly behind someone in the street and invite him to join him immediately in blowing up a barracks! Apart from the sudden shock of such a practical joke on an already strained Volunteer, there was the fact that they never knew when he might be serious.

Collins' personality was such that some of his practical-joking side rubbed off even on the gentle O'Reilly. Knowing that Sean Nunan and Frank Kelly, both friends of Collins, were looking for a flat in the Howth area, O'Reilly took time off from the revolution to concoct an advertisement offering rooms at a dream rent, and stipulating that the tenants would have to care for a parrot. Nunan and Kelly boned up on parrot-lore and then had a long, fruitless cycle, trying to locate a non-existent address. O'Reilly was suitably consoling when they returned muttering inadvisabilities about 'that stupid bitch of a landlady and her parrot'.[34]

On one occasion, Collins got word that Lord French would be passing through College St a little later and he got himself a gun, rounded up anyone who happened to be nearby, and set off to lead an ambush,[35] his extraordinary magnetism being such that he was joined on that hare-brained occasion by men who could hardly hold a weapon, never mind know anything about ambush techniques. Another time a friend rushed in to Devlin's to tell him that Mulcahy and Diarmuid O'Hegarty were trapped by police at a meeting in Parnell Square. 'I'll get Tobin and some of the boys and we won't be long getting them away', was Collins' reaction. Then he ran upstairs, whistling, to get his gun, and he and the friend headed up the square without waiting for Tobin. The case was less grievous than reported.

Mulcahy and O'Hegarty were coming down the square towards them. 'Can ye bloody children not look after yourselves yet?' was his salutation. As the four of them strolled down O'Connell St on a Sunday morning a policemen, who obviously knew who they were, looked up as they passed. 'Good morning boys.' Collins burst out laughing. 'The comic war', he said.[36]

Liam Deasy, one of the leading Cork IRA men, put his finger on one of the major reasons for Collins' success – his accessibility to, and concern for, men who came up from the country with some problem. He could be generous in time and effort to make either the humblest recruit or the most senior officer feel that his efforts were appreciated, albeit in his own alarming fashion. Deasy, who had come to Dublin on IRA business after a period of intense, savage, guerrilla warfare, recalls a memorable Easter with Collins.[37] Collins met him at Devlin's and ordered a taxi in which he took Frank Thornton, Gearoid O'Sullivan and Deasy to the Phoenix Park races.[38] In the grandstand enclosure they met a thunderstruck colleague who enquired incredulously on seeing them, 'Are ye mad?' Collins replied, 'We'll show ye country fellows how to work and enjoy yourselves,' and they spent the afternoon shoulder to shoulder with British officers, Intelligence agents, civil servants and loyalist supporters of Dublin Castle, who would cheerfully have joined in hanging all four of them. Before they left, Collins paid their bookies' debts.

At Vaughan's Hotel that night, Collins was warned that it would be curfew time in twenty minutes, and he replied, 'To hell with curfew and them that enforce it.' 'We finished our business twenty-five minutes after curfew and the two of us walked along an empty Parnell Square to Devlin's, the awestruck Deasy recalled. The next morning, Easter Sunday, Deasy went with Collins from Devlin's on foot right across Dublin to Harcourt St, where they had a meeting with James MacNamara. After this, Collins had some business to transact in the Commercial Buildings in O'Connell St from whence the pair went back to Devlin's at a 'four miles an hour walk'. From Devlin's they took a taxi to Rathmines. They were stopped at a checkpoint and a suspicious policeman ran his fingers through Collins' hair, twisting his head around in an effort to recognise him, but they were let go and proceeded on to lunch with Mrs O'Donovan where Collins' contribution to the talk of his escape was to tell his friend Tadgh O'Sullivan, 'You bloody country fellows are too careful.' Then he hired a horse and sidecar and took O'Sullivan with himself and Deasy out to the well-known hostelry on the foothills of Dublin, the Lamb Doyle's at Sandyford, where he had a small sherry. The sidecar dropped them off at Palmerston Park, Rathgar, where there followed four hours of serious discussion of the IRB's role in shaping events. After this, everyone who had attended the meeting was tired and most of the participants went to bed. 'They may as well have stayed up,' Deasy recalls, 'Collins went to every room and started a pillow fight. By four o'clock when he at last dropped off from sheer exhaustion, there was nothing to be seen in any room but feathers from floor to ceiling.' Sean Dowling has left another impression of Collins:

I knew Maureen Power, who was high in the movement. She was at a meeting attended by Sean Treacy shortly before he was shot. . . . Collins was going full pelt with the language. Treacy jumped up. 'How dare you go on like that in front of a lady.' It stopped him; he recoiled at once and apologised to both of them.[39]

This was the same Collins who, when Batt O'Connor was knocked down by a car, called at the house every evening to comfort his wife and family through a period when it seemed that Batt might not live. 'We saw the real man then,' said Sister Margaret Mary. His weekly visits to the de Valera family at Greystones, bringing money and solace, meant that the family were not split up as they had been after the 1916 Rising. Collins, the man who was seen in Greystones playing with the de Valera children, not the pillow-fighting hooligan, was the man the O'Connors saw in their hour of need.

The most peculiarly Irish form of weapon used in the conflict was that of hunger-striking. Long before the British came to Ireland there was a custom whereby a man would sometimes retaliate on a powerful enemy by starving himself outside his door. It was inevitable therefore that the tactic of hunger-striking would be employed in a struggle between two such unequal protagonists. Apart from the strikes involving Ashe and Stack mentioned earlier, there were major strikes at Mountjoy Jail in Dublin and at Wormwood Scrubs in England. The Mountjoy strike began on 5 April 1920 for a familiar Republican demand, the right to be recognised as prisoners of war, or failing that, for release. Because of the relatively unknown nature of hunger-striking the affair mushroomed into a state of national anxiety over what was universally believed to be the prisoners' imminent demise. Labour leaders called the general strike on 12 April and it was so widely observed that the prisoners were released unconditionally, three days later. Victory celebrations were held throughout the country, their impact on public opinion being sharply heightened by the action of police and military in Miltown Malbay in County Clare who shot up a bonfire crowd without warning, killing three people and wounding nine. A military inquiry was held but the results were never published. The second hunger-strike broke out amongst the Sinn Fein prisoners in Wormwood Scrubs less than a week after the Mountjoy men were set free. Their strike began on 21 April and continued until release was secured eighteen days later. This strike too was marked by violence. London mobs attacked the Irish crowds praying and demonstrating outside the jail. The police did not interfere.

A number of bodies wore out very quickly under 'the lash' of the Terror. As Sean Lemass noted:

... the time the Black and Tan War became active the numbers began to shrink very rapidly. The enormous companies that we commanded during the conscription period began to dissipate very quickly when it became a different type of operation. Some of them had quite conscientious objections to the type of work we were engaged in and dropped out for that reason.[40]

The 'type of work' the Volunteers were engaged in was killing people, notably spies and informers. For though there was very evidently a war in full swing in Ireland from the end of 1919, intensifying throughout 1920 and reaching a crescendo prior to the Truce of 1921, it was rarely a pitched battle affair. The Irish engaged the British successfully on two fronts, propaganda and intelligence and held them to a draw in the military field, largely through the use of their 'flying columns'. These columns, very poorly armed and generally numbering no more than fifteen to twenty men, lived 'on their keeping', staging an ambush here, a barracks raid there, perhaps after a night, or nights, spent out in the open, 'laying on', that is waiting to set up an ambush. Very often afterwards they would strike out in the depths of an Irish winter, through fog and bog, to a billet in a barn or a farm, perhaps twenty miles away. Denied the status of belligerents, the Volunteers knew that they fought in the likelihood of execution if captured under arms, or even without them, depending on whose hands they fell into. But they put up such a fight, particularly in Cork, Clare, Tipperary, Longford, Limerick and Mayo, that they tied up well over 50,000 troops and drove the RIC out of all but the most strongly fortified barracks in the larger towns.

The Cork IRA was certainly up against some formidable military opponents. There was Brigade Major Montgomery, later Field Marshal Montgomery of El Alamein, who wrote of his Irish experiences: 'My whole attention was given to defeating the rebels. It never bothered me a bit how many houses were burned.'[41] He told his father: 'Any civilian or Republican soldier who interferes with any officer or soldier is shot at once.' Montgomery set up a special 'Cork City Intelligence Unit' and prepared a special manual on how to deal with the rebels – sanguinarily – but his intelligence efforts were not in Collins' class, one Josephine Marchment being worth a score of his best intelligence agents, while his heavy-footed Western Front methodology could never hope to combat the fast-moving flying columns with their advantages not only of mobility, but also of motivation and local support.

Of course, had the British Army been used in a more all-out fashion, concentration camps, air raids, artillery bombardments and the rest of it, the result might have been different. But Lloyd George never felt secure enough to adopt such a policy and place the various forces in Ireland under a unified command as both the generals and the revamped Irish Executive demanded. In vain did Sir Henry Wilson plead for the introduction of methods such as drawing up lists of prominent Republicans and 'shooting by roster'. He felt that if the Sinn Feiners were to be murdered the government should be seen to do the murdering. But as he recorded in his diary Lloyd George 'fairly danced' when it was proposed to him that the government should take responsibility for reprisals.[42] He felt that no government could take responsibility for such activities. The dogs were only to be allowed off the leash in the murky underground of the war between two secret services that developed from the time Collins began having agents shot. But even in this limited arena, on the face of it, the British would appear to have had the advantage. Practitioners of what Kipling termed 'the Great Game', espionage, with all the resources of empire at their disposal, they were confronted by a group of country lads, led by a twenty-nine-year-old ex-post office clerk, 'from a brainy Cork family'. But Collins won, notwithstanding the combination of national spirit, his associates' talents, his own gift for intelligence work and all the rest of it, by his ability not only to endure, but to inflict, as an unpublished account by Sergeant Mannix, one of his principal contacts in the Dublin Metropolitan Police recalls:

I also attended a number of meetings at Williamstown, Booterstown, and at Rathgar Avenue which were convened for the purpose of passing the death sentence on a number of spies. The death sentence was passed on 9 or 10 informers for a date not fixed. The following are the names of those who sat at that meeting. . . . Michael Collins, Frank Thornton, Mr M. Byrne, Mr James Sullivan and myself . . . I also secured information pertaining to a cheque which was being received from the British Secret Service by 'Andrew Knight' who was employed as a Tram Inspector on the Dalkey line . . . he was taken off a tram car, taken out to Killiney Golf Links and shot.[43]

Collins took no pleasure in killing. There are in fact well-authenticated stories, in addition to O'Reilly's vision, of the tension and horror that gripped him before a 'job' was to be carried out. But with his knowledge of the Castle regime he realised that one spy was more dangerous to him than a regiment of soldiers. So too, according to Flor Begley, the Assistant Brigade Adjutant of Cork No. 3 Brigade, did the men in the field.[44] In theory the shooting of spies was supposed to be authorised by GHQ. Cathal Brugha, as Minister for Defence, wanted documentary proof of guilt to be provided beforehand so as to be able to satisfy an international commission (which he visualised being set up after hostilities had ended) that the Volunteers had acted correctly. In Cork however, Volunteers, hunted from pillar to post, felt this an inappropriately bureaucratic procedure which if carried out would allow a certain spy to continue his work while Brugha was deliberating. They appealed to Collins saying that they felt sure of their ground and the spy should be shot out of hand. According to Begley, Collins replied, 'Shoot him and say nothing about it.' 'No use, must let would-be spies know of it', was the reply. Collins agreed. 'Shoot him and label him if ye want to.' This provided further friction between Collins and Brugha, but it was the method which was adopted. Tom Barry calculated that his brigade shot some sixteen spies in this fashion.[45] The calibre of these wretches may be gauged from the fact that one was a man found drunk in a ditch by Volunteers. Befuddled by the spoils of his blood money he babbled on to them after being woken up, in the belief that they were British soldiers, until he realised too late that he was talking himself into another, longer, sleep.

One of the bedevilling factors of the Volunteer campaign was land hunger, a desire on the part of some unscrupulous people to profit from the disorders of the time. A letter to Collins from a priest in Rosmuck, in Connemara, in the west, for instance, dated 10 March 1920, spoke of widespread agrarian outrage and of intimidation on the part of locals styling themselves Volunteers and 'pressing young fellows into the Volunteers', thus getting the movement a bad name and costing some £1,000 in lost loan subscriptions. The same considerations were present in urban areas too, of course. One of the reasons the Belfast 'confetti' (rivets) was bespattered around with such energy was the fact that the expelled Catholic workers had their jobs taken by unemployed Protestant ex-servicemen.

Brugha continued to run his candle-making business during the war, and rarely came in contact with the rank and file and the realities of their existence. Liam Deasy was one of those who attended a significant meeting, presided over by Brugha, on 1 August 1920 in Dublin to discuss the IRA's tactics.[46] The attendance included Collins, Mulcahy, MacSwiney, McKee and a Catholic priest, Father Dick MacCarthy, representing the OC of West Limerick, Sean Finn. Ambushing was one of the main items on the agenda. Brugha argued against ambushes, preferring what Deasy termed 'straight fights'. He wanted the ambushers to call on the Auxiliaries or Tans to surrender before fire was opened. The Cork OCs pointed out that if they did this they would be robbed of their principal weapon, surprise, which they badly needed against a numerically superior and more heavily armed enemy. GHQ's initial plan for dealing with the Auxiliaries, who were quickly identified as a more dangerous foe than the Tans, was to confine them in towns by the use of overlapping formations of Volunteers. Terry MacSwiney pointed out that they didn't have the guns for this and it was decided to leave decisions on ambush methodology in the hands of the local OCs. A few days later, on 23 August the result of this decision was seen in a trend-setting ambush at Macroom in which six police were shot and a quantity of rifles seized.

But Brugha never got over his antipathy towards ambushing. It became a grisly joke in Volunteer circles. Oscar Traynor told Ernie O'Malley that he became particularly upset when a woman, the mother of three children, was accidently killed in crossfire while she was shopping.[47] He tried to have it laid down that ambushes would henceforth be banned on Saturdays, shopping day for most Dublin families. The only result, however, was that some wits in the Dublin Brigade began to inform their colleagues solemnly that 'the Saturday ambush has been postponed until Monday.' It was a miracle of either luck or marksmanship on both sides that civilian casualties were not far higher. Ambushes became so frequent in parts of Dublin that an area of Camden St was christened the Dardanelles. The Tans and Auxiliaries tore about the city in lorries seated back to back with their loaded guns pointing outwards. Neither they, nor the citizenry, knew when something nasty might suddenly be propelled from, or into the lorries. Joe Leonard, a member of the Squad, described how the IRA found a

partial cure for their greater activity, in the number 9 bomb manufactured in our National Munition Factory at Denzil Lane and which some of our 'Littlers' were very adept at introducing into their tenders causing the Tans to leave same in a state of undress.[48]

Sean MacBride, one of the 'littlers', showed me over his own company area of Pearse St and Westland Row one night and described how he operated:

We'd walk up and down on opposite sides of the street. And when we'd see a patrol or a lorry coming along we'd fire on it, or lob a bomb and fire on them when they'd jump out. Then we'd run like hares, dump the revolvers and I'd get back to college. The professors weren't too keen on what we were doing, but it didn't matter. So long as I got back quickly to Earlsfort Terrace I could pretend I was attending classes when the ambush took place. I remember one evening myself and another Volunteer were pinned down on the railway line by Tans firing on us. I could see the sparks from the bullets striking the tracks. I noticed blood coming from my friend's head and suddenly I realised he was dead. I had to see his parents and go to the wake and that sort of thing. It was my first experience of death. I was about sixteen at the time.[49]

At a Cabinet meeting held in Downing St on 31 May 1920, the Cabinet began holding its cloak over a form of reprisals policy, a 'plan whereby Irishmen were made to feel the effect of the campaign of murder and arson along economic channels'. The meeting sought recommendations from the Irish Executive on 'the best method of imposing fines on Irishmen in an affected area' and on the 'best method of interfering with the everyday facilities of an affected area'.[50] Policy calmly formulated in public-school accents behind closed doors can manifest itself in very raucous and savage proceedings when translated into action. The 'best method' turned out to be burning creameries, bacon factories and mills. One of the largest creameries destroyed – by uniformed RIC men – at Knocklong, County Limerick, on 22 August, was owned by Sir Thomas Cleeves, a Unionist.

'Telling a Hamar' probably reached its highest point in October after a bad day's work in Tubercurry, County Sligo. This began with the shooting of a popular RIC Officer, DI Brady, with, it was claimed, expanding bullets. Following the killing the RIC went berserk, shooting up the town and burning down the local creamery. The reprisal created such outrage that the Castle took the hitherto unprecedented step of issuing a communiqué which admitted that the men had 'broken out of hand' and that:

Reprisals continued till early in the morning, despite the efforts of the officers. The men were eventually got into the police lorries, and while final instructions were been given by the officer, the lorries moved off, and a creamery in the neighbourhood was burned.[51]

The outrage spread to England. There was a debate in the House of Commons on a censure motion put down by Arthur Henderson, Deputy Leader of the Labour Party, who wanted an official investigation into the reprisals policy. What he got was a full-blooded defence of the policy from Greenwood. He did admit that there had been a reprisal but with justifiable provocation. 'They knew him, they loved him. Soldiers and policemen trained under the British flag love their officers.' However, despite the Castle's communiqué, reluctantly based on the first-hand accounts of its own agents, he denied the creamery burning. In fact he said he had 'never seen a tittle of evidence to prove' that the security forces had ever done any such thing, leaving his hearers to marvel at the nationwide tendency towards spontaneous combustion in Irish dairy produce.

Greenwood had more to defend to Henderson and the world than creamery destruction. Britain's entire policy was on the line. He was clearly identifying himself with the concept of police war as envisaged by Lloyd George and Churchill. He had predicted on 20 September: 'we'll win out quickly if we pursue our firm and consistent policy.'[52] That night the doctrine of firm consistency was to be demonstrated in the north County Dublin town of Balbriggan in spectacular fashion. Greenwood told the House that it was 'impossible' to find out who was responsible for either shootings or burnings amongst the 150 men who broke out from the nearby Black and Tans' encampment, following a brawl in a pub in which two Tans were shot. But it was easy enough to see what they did. The Tans burned a hosiery factory, forty-nine houses and four public houses and killed two local people during hours of drunken looting and indiscriminate firing. The following day the reprisals policy had another airing in County Clare. As a reprisal for an IRA ambush the police shot up the towns of Ennistymon, Lahinch and Miltown Malbay, killing four people and destroying Lahinch Town Hall and a score of other buildings. In the south, the towns of Fermoy, Thurles, Lismore and Mallow were amongst those sacked. Sir Henry Wilson noted in his diary for 23 September:

At Balbriggan, Thurles and Galway yesterday the local people marked down certain SFs as in their opinion the actual murderers or instigators and then coolly went out and shot them without question or trial . . . Winston saw very little harm in this but it horrifies me.[53]

The execution of this economic policy was accompanied by a parallel destruction of human life. According to one authority[54] over 200 unarmed persons were killed by Crown forces in 1920. These included women and children. 'Sixty-nine were persons deliberately killed in the streets or in their own homes; thirty-six were men killed while in custody, the rest were the victims of indiscriminate firing by military and police'.[55] Some of the individual cases reverberate even today.[56] At Bantry a hunchback boy was shot after Tans failed to find his father in a raid. Ellen Quinn of Kiltartan, County Galway, was killed sitting on her garden wall holding a child in her arms when a policeman took a pot shot from a passing lorry. Two priests were shot. A young curate in Galway, Fr Griffin, was fished out of a bog hole with a bullet in his head, apparently because he had been imprudent in showing his Volunteer sympathies. Canon Magner, of Dunmanway, County Cork, got a note from the Tans telling him to toll his bell on Armistice Day or else. He refused and the bell tolled for him on a quiet road near Bandon on 15 December. An Auxiliary shot one of the two men he had been talking to as the Auxiliary lorry approached. Then the canon was asked for his name and having given it was immediately shot dead by the same Auxiliary. The third man was left shocked but otherwise unharmed as the bodies were dragged into a ditch and robbed. He, however, was a Resident Magistrate who insisted on an inquiry, with the result that the murderous Auxiliary was found guilty – but insane.

Six Volunteers captured, unarmed, by Black and Tans at Kerry Pike near Cork City were identified by their clothes only when their bodies were handed over to their relatives. One had had his heart cut out, another his skull battered in, a third his nose cut off, a fourth his tongue. I have seen pictures[57] of the bodies of the two Loughnane brothers, Patrick and Henry, from Gort, County Galway, after they had been pulled out of a pond. All I will say is I hope the fire which destroyed the lower parts of their bodies was not started before they died.

Apart from random savagery, arising from a controlled lack of discipline, torture was systematically employed to extract information from prisoners. The 'intelligence room' at Dublin Castle became a place of horror in Volunteers' imaginations.[58] But the horror was not confined to Dublin Castle, as Tom Hales and Pat Harte found out to their cost when they were surprised and captured by Major Percival of the Essex Regiment on 26 July 1920 near Bandon. Percival, who later rose to be a general and lived to experience the humiliation of surrendering Singapore to the Japanese, was also in charge of the raiding party that later burned Collins' home in Woodfield. He had a habit of driving about the countryside in the mornings in an open touring car so that he could 'have cockshots at farmers working in the fields'.[59] On capturing Hales and Harte he first ordered that they be stripped and beaten.[60] After this he had them dressed, bound with leather straps and caused a charge of guncotton to be placed on their backs. The detonators failed to go off and the prisoners were made to run while being prodded with bayonets. They were then thrown into a lorry and on the way to Bandon Barracks were again beaten with rifle butts, Harte receiving a particularly severe blow to the temple from which he apparently never recovered.

At the barracks they were handed over to the Intelligence Officer, Captain Kelly, an Irishman, who ordered a firing squad and had the prisoners stood against a wall. He told Hales to hold up a Union Jack and 'salute it at the peril of your life'. Hales refused and was beaten unconscious. As he recovered he saw Harte receiving the same treatment, ultimately holding the flag just long enough for another officer to take a photograph. Another beating followed and they were thrown into a room, still strapped and bleeding, at 6.30 pm. Hales said that 'until ten o'clock there was a continual howl for our blood.' At ten o'clock he was taken upstairs to a room where there were six officers seated around a table, including Kelly and Percival. He was again stripped and bound and Kelly, who referred to him as a 'murdering bastard', instructed two of the other officers to beat him with canes, which they did, one standing on each side, until they 'drove blood out through him'. Then pliers were used on his lower body and to extract his finger nails, so that Hales says, 'My fingers were so bruised that I got unconscious.'

On regaining consciousness he was questioned about prominent figures including Michael Collins. He gave no information and two officers took off their tunics and punched him until he fell on the floor with several teeth either knocked out or loosened. Finally he was pulled by the hair to the top of the stairs and thrown to the bottom, where he was again beaten before being dragged to a cell. Hales recovered. Harte, however, suffered brain damage and died in hospital, insane.

There are two points worth noting about the Hales incident. One, the supreme irony of the fact that having endured such punishment to protect Collins he later played a prominent role in encompassing his death. Secondly that he, like O'Malley, held out. Others who could not were then put in peril from their comrades. A typical case was Vincent Fourvargue, a member of the Third Battalion of the Dublin Brigade. Under duress he gave away the names of some of his unit. The British responded by staging a fake ambush in Dublin's South Circular Rd which allowed him to escape. He then made his way to England, but Collins wasn't fooled and had him shot in London, on 3 April 1921.

In the case of Harte and Hales, Collins also showed the Avenging Angel/Angel of Mercy sides of his character. His correspondence to Art O'Brien[61] contains several enquiries after Harte's health and suggestions for medical treatment and, when he was subsequently in London for the ordeal of the Treaty negotiations, he made time to visit him in Pentonville Prison. But he also tried to have Percival killed. Finding that he could not be got at in Cork, he sent a hit squad to follow him to England when he went on holiday in March 1921. Percival, however, remained out of reach in a military barracks. On 16 March he arrived at Liverpool St Station in London at 3 pm but the waiting Squad members were forced to pull out a few minutes beforehand when Sam Maguire turned up to warn them that Scotland Yard was on the way. Percival's luck continued. The following month, in Cork, on 19 April, a raiding party led by him killed one of the men Collins placed outside the station, Tadhg O'Sullivan.

As we have seen, Collins' special genius for intelligence work lay in the speed with which he could evaluate and act on any possibility of making contact with potential allies. RIC Sergeant Gerry Maher of Naas, County Kildare, was a typical example. Sean Kavanagh, then the newly appointed Intelligence Officer for County Kildare, had heard that Maher had passed on a warning to local Volunteers that their homes were about to be raided.[62] He mentioned this to his friend, Michael Staines, who told Collins. Kavanagh promptly found himself summoned to the Gaelic League HQ at 46 Parnell Square to meet Collins, who explained to Kavanagh that Maher could be of immense use in his job as County Inspector's Chief Clerk. As Confidential Clerk, Maher had access to the key of a new police code, the circulation of which was restricted below County Inspector rank. That evening, after dark, Kavanagh called on Maher and told him frankly what his mission was. Maher's reply was, 'You're the man I've been waiting for for years', and, says Kavanagh, he 'went on to explain that he had tried to establish contact but that nobody had tried to get in touch with him.' Maher duly turned over the key to the code then in use and Collins provided him with wax so that he could take an impression of the actual key used by the County Inspector to open the safe in his office. Kavanagh brought this to Collins and in a few days Maher had his own key to the safe. Kavanagh's subsequent description of how his own and Maher's operations worked is a perfect illustration of how the Collins network worked, not only in Naas, but all round the country.

Kavanagh visited Maher's house two or three times a week, always at night, either to collect Maher's information or to pass on queries from Collins. A railway courier system was established by which written messages to or from Collins could be sent via the ticket collector at nearby Sallins within a few hours. The collector handed letters to one of four sympathetic guards on mainline trains which were then delivered to Sean O'Connell, a clerk at Kingsbridge Station, Dublin.

The code was changed periodically, RIC sergeants being sent all round the country with a new cipher to each County Inspector. In Kildare the County Inspector's messenger was met at Sallins, and almost invariably a copy of the new cipher passed to Collins via Maher and Kavanagh. Maher was able to recruit another RIC man, Constable Paddy Casey, who took over Maher's duties whenever the latter was absent on leave, or through illness. During all the time the Maher–Kavanagh network operated Kavanagh was under orders from Collins to have no dealings with the local IRA. The only man who knew officially of his work was the local Battalion OC, Tom Harris. Kavanagh reported directly to Collins at Vaughan's Hotel.

How all these snippets of information which Collins received bore fruit may be judged from some memos concerning the MacCurtain killings. Item No. 8 in a list of dispatches to the Adjutant of the Cork No. 1 Brigade (O'Donaghue) on 20 July read: 'Enclosed is a memo regarding Constable Ashe. Please let me have your observations.' The memo (signed by Mulcahy using the Irish form of his name Risteard Ua Maolcatha) read as follows:

D/Information.
With regard to the report of Brig. Com. Wexford that Const. Ashe who is now at Gorey is probably one of those who was on the MacCurtain job – he states that this information was given him by John MacCarthy, Strand St, Kanturk.

R. ua M.

Another report about a second police officer, chilling for the implications of what even a child's remark can lead to in wartime, reached Collins towards the end of the month. It came from Monaghan on 30 July:

Head Constable Cahill came to Monaghan about 3 weeks after the murder of Thos. MacCurtain. He came from King's St Barracks, Cork and was escorted by 4 armed police men. One of his guard remarked to one of the older men in Monaghan Bk, He, (meaning Cahill) is a good man. He is not afraid of them (meaning the Volunteers). One of his children (about 10 years of age) remarked in the Barrack a short time after they came, 'When I grow up I won't murder Lord Mayors.'

He passed various remarks to the other men and Sergeant Faughan about what way to suppress sedition, and said that the proper way to do so, was to shoot them down.

From this and various remarks he made he gave me the impression he had to do with the murder of Thos. MacCurtain.[63]

The most terrible repercussions of all, literally on a national scale, followed the unearthing of DI Swanzy whom Collins traced via Belfast, through Sergeant Matt MacCarthy, who located Swanzy in the predominantly Orange town of Lisburn to which he had been transferred immediately after the MacCurtain killing. It was a point of honour with the Cork No. 1 Brigade to avenge their Commandant and members of the Brigade vied with each other to be sent north on the mission. This was turned down on the grounds of impracticability because the Cork accents would have been an instant giveaway. Instead, one Cork Volunteer, Sean Culhane, Intelligence Officer of the Brigade, who knew Swanzy, was sent north with MacCurtain's gun to link up with Belfast Volunteers who accompanied him to the assassination scene in a taxi on Sunday 22 August 1920. Culhane picked Swanzy out from a large crowd of churchgoers and was given the honour of firing the first shot. Swanzy went down and Culhane and one of his escort jumped back into the taxi. The second man, Roger McCorley, was so keen to take a hand in the killing that he was almost left in Lisburn:

I was the last to leave the spot where Swanzy fell as I delayed long enough to put another shot into him. The taxi started off before I reached it . . . but as they opened the door opposite to that on which I was running I was forced to grab the handle of the door on my side, open the car and throw myself in. As I still had my finger on the trigger of my gun and as I landed in a heap on the floor I accidentally fired a shot in the car.[64]

McCorley was luckier than most of the Catholic population of Lisburn. A UVF revival begun in the wake of the municipal election results enabled Protestant outrage at the Swanzy shooting to be translated into an organised pogrom in the town. Banbridge had also experienced prolonged anti-Catholic rioting during the previous month because of an IRA shooting, that of Lieutenant Colonel Bruce

Smyth VC, a native of Banbridge and Divisional Commissioner of the RIC for Munster.

Colonel Smyth's death, like that of MacCurtain, has to be understood against the larger, though hidden, backdrop of the British policy response to the IRA's growing strength. The Colonel's killing was brought about through his spelling out of part of that policy to an RIC garrison in Listowel on 19 June 1920. A sworn statement of his remarks on that occasion was given to Arthur Griffith by one of his hearers and published in the *Irish Bulletin*. Kathleen Napoli MacKenna reproduced part of it in her memoir:

Well, men I have something to tell you, something I am sure you would not want your wives to hear. Sinn Fein has had all the sport up to the present and we are going to have it now . . . We must take the offensive and beat Sinn Fein at its own game. Martial Law, applying to all Ireland, is to come into operation immediately. In fact we are to have our scheme of amalgamation completed on 21 June. I am promised as many troops from England as I require, thousands are coming in daily . . .

If a police barracks is burnt, or if the barracks already occupied is not suitable, then the best house in the locality is to be commandeered, the occupants thrown out into the gutter. Let them lie there, the more the merrier. Police and military will patrol the country at least five times a week. They are not to confine themselves to the main roads, but make across the country, lie in ambush and when civilians are seen approaching shout 'Up hands'. Should the order not be obeyed at once shoot and shoot to kill. If the persons approaching carry their hands in their pockets, or are in any way suspicious-looking, shoot them down. You may make mistakes occasionally, and innocent persons may be shot, but that cannot be helped, and you are bound to get the right person sometime.

The more you shoot the better I shall like you and I assure you that no policeman will get into trouble for shooting a man.

Hunger-strikers will be allowed to die in gaol – the more the better. Some of them have already died and a damn bad job they were not all allowed to die. As a matter of fact some them have already been dealt with in a manner their friends will never know about.

An emigrant ship left an Irish port for a foreign one lately with lots of Sinn Feiners on board: I assure you men it will never reach port.

We want you to carry out this scheme and wipe out Sinn Fein. Any man who is not prepared to do this is a hindrance, and had better leave the job at once.

One sequel to this address which may be noted illustrates the quite fiendish nature of some of the undercover operations of the period. The 'emigrant ship' of whose doom the Colonel apparently had foreknowledge was apparently the *Viknor* whose fate was also alluded to in a highly significant despatch from the British Admiralty which the Collins network captured. It is addressed to Sir Charles Cooke and signed by the celebrated intelligence expert Captain R. C. Hall. It says: 'I am afraid the *Viknor* has gone down. She had some very important prisoners aboard and I badly wanted their papers.'[65]

That was the underground background to the Smyth address. As the Napoli MacKenna memoir notes, the public sequel to this address was as 'unique, dramatic, and seemingly impossible as would have been a mutiny in the King's bodyguard'. The Colonel asked one of the men if he was prepared to co-operate, which was the signal for the men's previously chosen leader to step forward. Napoli MacKenna describes what the constable said and did:

'By your accent I take it you are an Englishmen, and in your ignorance you forget you are addressing Irishmen.' The Constable removed his cap, belt and arms and laid them on the table saying: 'These too are English. Take them and go to hell with you, you murderer.'

Worse was to follow for Colonel Smyth. When he ordered the arrest of the mutineer he was informed by the other men that if a hand were laid on their comrade 'the room would run red with blood.' A month later, in the County Club of Cork, an IRA Volunteer walked up to Smyth and said, 'Your orders were to shoot on sight. You are in sight now. So make ready.'[66] The Colonel tried to escape but was shot dead. In the wake of the MacCurtain, Smyth and Swanzy killings, the existence of a strong, well-organised force of Ulster Protestants emerged once again as a factor in the struggle between Irish Catholic Nationalists and the British Empire.

Mutinous Irishmen emerged in another part of the British Empire nine days after the Smyth speech. At Jullundur, in the Punjab, on 28 June, 250 men of the First Battalion of the Connaught Rangers also laid down their arms in protest against the news from Ireland.[67] The affair created a sensation. Sixty-two Rangers were court-martialled and death sentences plentifully bestowed; though ultimately only one soldier, James Daly, was actually executed, many underwent penal servitude until long after the Anglo-Irish war ended.

During October 1920 Collins' admiration for fighting men involved him in one of the grimmest incidents of the war. He had encouraged the Soloheadbeg men, Dan Breen and Sean Treacy, to stay around Dublin a good deal rather than in their native Tipperary. They assisted the Squad on various jobs which suited Collins and Treacy in particular because he had a girlfriend in the city. But it was a highly dangerous place for two such wanted countrymen; since Soloheadbeg, both were scarcely less sought after than Collins himself. They were sleeping in the home of a Professor Carolan in Whitehall in north Dublin on the night of 11 October 1920 when British Intelligence located them.

Somehow, even though they were found in bed, Breen and Treacy fought their way out, killing two of the undercover men in the process. One of these subsequently turned out to be associated with a number of shootings of the Lynch type (see page 157). Major Smyth, brother of the colonel who caused the RIC mutiny in Listowel, was serving in the Middle East. He came back to avenge his brother and was himself killed. Breen was badly cut in falling through a glass conservatory roof, and finally had to take his chances in knocking on the door of a strange house and asking for sanctuary, because he was suffering from loss of blood. Luckily for him, the occupants, though not in sympathy with Sinn Fein, adhered to the Irish tradition of shielding the fugitive and he was transferred to the Mater Misericordiae Hospital where the nuns ensured that he recovered safely by wheeling him into the maternity ward during raids. Treacy too got away but Professor Carolan was put up against a wall of his house, shot through the head and left for dead. The raiders put out a story that he had been killed by one of Breen's bullets. The Professor however recovered long enough to tell what had really happened.

Collins had been informed that top British military personnel like Generals Macready and Tudor were to walk in Smyth's funeral procession and the Squad, including Sean Treacy, were placed in readiness. However the generals thought better of attendance and the Squad dispersed harmlessly but Treacy, who apparently actually had gone to the funeral to pray for the man he had shot, was recognised in the doorway of the 'Republican outfitters', Peadar Clancy's shop in Talbot St. There was another raid, which missed Dick McKee, but netted Joe Vize, Collins' Director of Purchases, head of arms smuggling, a loss which would later cost Collins dear. Treacy and one of the British Intelligence officers were killed.

Two RIC sergeants who knew the Tipperary men were brought to Dublin to identify the corpse and to assist in searching the hospitals for Breen. Neligan told Collins of this and one of them, a Sergeant Roche, was actually shot dead by the Squad as he was chatting with Neligan on a Dublin quay. Neligan told me, nearly fifty years later, that he still prayed for Roche every night. The other detective was also shot dead. Neligan came under suspicion, because another policeman had seen him talking to the Squad men just prior to the Roche shooting, a particularly horrific affair. Joe Dolan described the shooting thus: 'I fired six shots into him. Tom Keogh and Jim Slattery fired a few more into him for luck.' Neligan was able to discredit the badly shocked policeman's story, but subsequently he found that he was being followed by a suspicious detective. One night, after curfew, the shadowing stopped in a dark alley. Neligan shot and killed his colleague.

The ending of the Breen/Treacy saga is described by Breen himself in his colourful book.[68] He had been removed from the Mater

Misericordiae Hospital to a safe house when Collins got word that his hideout was surrounded by soldiers and Black and Tans. He called out the Squad to lead a rescue attempt personally, which in the circumstances would have been almost certainly suicidal. Breen saw him from a window standing outside the cordon with 'a few of the boys':

Their services were not needed. The soldiers raided almost every house in the locality, including the house next door, but never came into the house where I was. All the same I felt grateful to Mick. As I have already explained, he was the only member of GHQ who stood by us consistently.

While the major IRA effort was of course confined to Ireland, Cathal Brugha's urgings that the war should be carried to England resulted in some spectacular operations in the UK, particularly in Liverpool, where seventeen warehouses were burned on the night of 28 November 1920. Burnings also took place in various other UK centres under the direction of Rory O'Connor. Collins produced a list of the home addresses of Black and Tans and some of these were also attacked and destroyed by fire. O'Connor drew up somewhat unrealistic plans for incendiary attacks in London, Birmingham, Sheffield, Newcastle, Manchester and Liverpool, the destruction of railways, tube stations, reservoirs, the Ministry of Pensions and the homes of figures like General Tudor and Lord FitzAlan. By way of evaluating the IRA's capability to carry out this programme, however, it should be noted that his proposals were accompanied by a report on the state of the IRA in London which said:

I find that things are in a very serious way. Owing to the unemployment, in many cases our men have had to sleep on the Embankment, and in one case, one of the men has only been able to have four dinners per week . . . various Irish societies have apparently done nothing towards relief of distress . . . the QM practically extracted money from the members of the G.A.A.[69]

Several key figures in the Collins network were picked up just before the November burnings, including Neil Kerr and Steve Lanigan in Liverpool and Paddy O'Donoghue in Manchester, and the Brugha/O'Connor offensive had a damaging effect on the arms-smuggling routes Collins had built up. But by the following May he had repaired the damage to the extent that he was arranging for a ton of potassium chlorate per week to be sent from Liverpool under the guise of bread soda.[70] In fact had a raid not driven Mulcahy to escape across the roof-tops of his hideout in Longwood Avenue, leaving his papers behind, seconds ahead of the Auxiliaries, very large-scale operations would have taken place in Liverpool and Manchester during April 1921. These would have included the destruction of all British shipping in Liverpool and of Manchester's electricity supply. But the capture of the Mulcahy papers alerted the authorities and created a sensation in England when they were released to the press, not so much for the revelations about IRA strength and ruthlessness as for the fact that included in the papers was a proposal made by an eccentric for infecting horses' feed with glanders. This was taken up by the press as evidence of a fiendishness on a far greater scale than merely blacking out a city and destroying a shipping fleet!

One of the most tragic aspects of the struggle was the execution by both sides of prisoners and hostages who were often people of quite remarkable calibre. Collins, who played such a notable part in bringing about and conducting the war, was keenly aware of his role in these events. On the Irish side the religious fervour of some of the prisoners executed was such that it had a bearing on changing papal policy in Rome (see Chapter 7) To this day one of the most popular Irish rebel ballads is 'Kevin Barry', describing the capture, torture and hanging of Barry, an eighteen-year-old student.

Barry was captured after a raid on a British Army party who were collecting bread from a bakery in Church St, Dublin on 20 September 1920. Learning that the raid was to take place at 11 am he calculated that he would have plenty of time to take part and still attend his medical examinations at University College Dublin which were scheduled for 2 pm. The intention was merely to hold up the tommies and take their rifles. But shooting broke out and three of the soldiers died. Barry was subsequently captured and sentenced to hang. Because of his youth the case attracted enormous attention. Collins saw to it that it received the maximum publicity. In the Fenian days men had frequently been executed with no word from their leaders and little outside protest. Moya Llewelyn Davies coined a memorable phrase for Collins to describe the campaign to have Barry reprieved. He declared that there would be 'no more lonely scaffolds in our time'.[71] But despite widespread protests at the fact that Barry had been maltreated after capture and pleas for mercy, a Conference of Ministers presided over by Lloyd George in Bonar Law's rooms in the House of Commons on 28 October decided that they could not recommend any commutation of the death penalty.[72]

Amongst those taking part in the Conference was Sir Hamar Greenwood, so it need not surprise us that 'it was pointed out . . . that it was precisely young and irresponsible men of this type who were the main cause of the present disturbances in Ireland.' Barry had made an altar in his cell at which he received two Masses on the morning of his execution.[73]

Outside the jail a crowd of some 5,000 said the rosary and sang hymns, watched over by soldiers and armoured cars. The crowds were a causative factor in Collins' last desperate hopes of a rescue attempt being abandoned. This would have involved the use of explosives to blow a hole in the jail wall. Barry's guards were under instruction to shoot him if any rescue attempt was made, so the attempt, had it been made, was fairly certain to have ended unsuccess-fully and in bloodshed anyhow. Collins realised this all along. 'His intense, painful ability to enter the victim's mind placed him under intolerable strain.'[74] The night before the execution the gathering in Vaughan's Hotel saw Collins in a state of depression. He remained brooding the whole night, taking no part in the conversation, the only words he uttered being: 'Poor Kevin Barry'. Frank O'Connor says 'his face was drawn with agony, his long lock of hair drooping.'

Along with the Barry execution another moral turning-point of the period was the last great hunger-strike of the time, that involving Terence MacSwiney. When he was sworn in to succeed MacCurtain the previous year, MacSwiney had made the prophetic statement: 'It is not those who can inflict the most, but those that can suffer the most who will conquer.' He began to demonstrate the meaning of that utterance on 12 August 1921, having been arrested at City Hall, Cork, presiding over an IRA meeting. Having refused to recognise his court martial (for possession of documents likely to cause disaffection), he went on hunger-strike for release and was transferred to Brixton prison. The ten Volunteers arrested with him also went on hunger-strike in Cork Jail. Like the other members of GHQ,[75] Collins was uneasy at the strike-for-release policy, though he had no objection to a strike for political status or for the remission of grievances, but he felt release was too dangerously large a demand. In the case of the Wormwood Scrubs' prisoners the men had only been held on suspicion. MacSwiney was too big a figure for the British to give way easily. Nor did they. The Cabinet agreed with Balfour at a meeting held in Downing St on 23 July[76] that the release of MacSwiney would be a fatal blow to the policy of coercion to which the government was committed.

MacSwiney endured until 25 October before dying, a fast of seventy-four days. One of the Cork ten, Michael Fitzgerald, had already died on 17 October; another, Joseph Murphy, died a few hours after MacSwiney. The other eight acceded to Arthur Griffith's request that they should come off the protest at that stage. These sacrifices had an incalculable effect on world opinion. The transfer of MacSwiney to Brixton focused world opinion on the Lord Mayor and elevated the Sinn Fein cause to a moral plane higher than much of what was happening in Ireland would ever have done. Londoners lined the streets to pay their respects as the body was taken through the city accompanied by a guard of honour of Volunteers wearing their illegal uniforms. Robed bishops and priests accompanied them. Sir Henry Wilson, however, spoiled the last stage of the journey by persuading Lloyd George to have MacSwiney's brothers and sisters removed from the boat train at Holyhead and to divert the coffin to Cork, so as to forestall Sinn Fein's plans to derive political advantage from a huge public reception for the remains in Dublin. But the Field Marshal was unable to prevent the country practically closing down in answer to Dail decree that the day of MacSwiney's burial, 31 October, should be observed as a day of national mourning.

MacSwiney's burial, coupled with the execution of Kevin Barry the following day, might be taken as ending a phase of endurance. Such happenings moved Eoin MacNeill to compose a much quoted epigram:

> In prison we are their jailers;
> On trial their judges,
> Persecuted their punishers,
> Dead their conquerors.

Lloyd George made speeches at Caernarvon, on 9 October, and at the Guildhall Banquet, on 9 November, which clearly backed the policy of reprisal and hanging. At the Guildhall he summed it up by saying:

There is no doubt that at last their [the police] patience has given way and there has been some severe hitting back . . . let us be fair to these gallant men who are doing their duty in Ireland . . . it is no use talking about this being war and these being reprisals when these things are being done [by the IRA] with impunity in Ireland.

We have murder by the throat . . . we had to reorganise the police. When the Government was ready we struck the terrorists and now the terrorists are complaining of terror.

In Ireland it was realised that 'murder by the throat' meant throats like Barry's. Michael Collins also interpreted Lloyd George's speech differently from the Guildhall audience. He knew why the Prime Minister felt his murder gang policy was working and he was laying plans to prove him wrong.

6

The Sky Darkens

'It is not those who can inflict the most, but those that can suffer the most who will conquer.'

Terence MacSwiney

That winter of 1920–21 was to see some of the most horrific deeds of the entire war on what became known ever afterwards as 'Bloody Sunday', 21 November 1920. As the 'Kidd's Back' war intensified Collins began to realise that the British were improving their intelligence network in Dublin. Hitherto the British approach had been somewhat amateurish, as some of the spy episodes recounted will have indicated. Captain Hardy himself, 'the notorious murderer',[1] who afterwards became a novelist, wrote that for all the hope the various agents initially sent over had of remaining undetected at their Dublin addresses they 'might as well have worn uniforms'. But from 11 May onwards things had begun to improve on the British intelligence front. Colonel Ormonde d'Epée Winter, code-named 'O', arrived in Dublin. Mark Sturgis described him as looking 'like a wicked little white snake . . . probably entirely non-moral'. David Neligan however described him as being 'a decent old fellow'. And Collins welcomed him to town by having him ambushed in Thomas St as he drove to pay his first call on the Viceregal Lodge. Appropriately enough the attackers waited in a butcher's shop but only succeeded in wounding him in the hand.[2] However, though in the end Collins defeated Winter, 'O's arrival did do something for British counter-insurgency operations, hampered as they were by poor information and internecine rivalry between the hydra-headed British security efforts.

A group of intelligence officers, known as the 'Cairo Gang' because of their Middle-Eastern experience, rather than the fact that some of them frequented a Dublin haunt known as the Cairo Café, began to augment their spying activities by carrying out shootings in Dublin. Collins was particularly annoyed by the death of John Lynch of Killmallock, County Limerick, who was shot in his bed at 2 am in the Exchange Hotel, Dublin, on 23 September. The Castle's cover story was that he had resisted arrest and fired on police. In fact Lynch never carried a gun. He may have been mistaken for Liam Lynch, the Cork IRA leader, but he was not a Volunteer and was unconnected with the IRA beyond the fact that he was a Sinn Fein loan organiser and had come to Dublin to hand over some £23,000 to Collins.

By 5 October Collins had compiled a report on the shooting for Arthur Griffith which included the following:

At 1.35 am on the morning of the murder a 'phone message was received by Captain Baggelly, General Staff, Ship St Barracks . . . to send a car. A car was sent . . . members of the RIC force picked up a small party of military . . . and proceeded to the Royal Exchange Hotel.

At 2.15 am a 'phone message passed from the Headquarters of the Dublin District to College Street Station, giving the information that the RIC had been to the Royal Exchange Hotel and shot a man named Lynch.

There is not the slightest doubt that there was no intention whatever to arrest Mr Lynch.

Captain Baggelly was one of those whose fate would illustrate the danger of being mentioned in dispatches by Michael Collins. The Cairo Gang, though they made mistakes like those over Lynch, were getting closer. October saw all three of Collins' top intelligence agents picked up and released after questioning, Thornton being held for ten days before being released. Tobin and Cullen also got away with a grilling after being detained in Vaughan's. Collins knew that it was only a matter of time before they and he were finished. But just as the Gang were closing in on him he was closing in on them.

Information had come from various sources which showed that the British had set up an intelligence network working on 'proper continental lines with a Central Headquarters and other houses forming minor centres scattered all throughout the city'.[3] Here the sister of an IRA man had told her brother that some of the gentlemen in the house where she worked spoke with English accents, went out after curfew, and kept odd hours. Then one of Lynch's killers got a fit of conscience in drink and told a girl what he had done. Sergeant Mannix of the DMP station at Donnybrook was particularly valuable. In his own words he 'secured names and addresses of British Secret Service Officers who were shot on "Bloody Sunday"'. As a result Collins was able to get an IRA hall porter placed in one of the houses and hall door and room keys were obtained for all the others. Detailed reports were prepared on each agent. Thornton's job was to collate the information. He also got:

the very unenvious [sic] job of presenting my full report to a joint meeting of the Dail Cabinet and Army Council, at which I had to prove that each and every man on my list was an accredited Secret Service man of the British Government.

At the head of his list were the Gang's leaders, Colonel Aimes and Major Bennett, two men with whom he had become 'great friends' in Kidd's Back. The joint meeting sealed their fate and that of the others on Thornton's list. Sunday 21 November was decided on both for speed and because there was a big football match on in Croke Park that day and Dublin would be unusually crowded.[4] On the night of the 20th Collins went to the Gaiety Theatre with a group which included Dave Neligan. He happened to speculate as to what sort of men they were whom he had consigned to doom the next day. Neligan told him to look into the next box where he could see some of them for himself. After the show Collins went to Vaughan's where a meeting was held to put the finishing touches to the plans for the next day. Amongst those present were Peadar Clancy, Dick McKee and a young Gaelic scholar from Clare called Conor Clune who had nothing to do with the Volunteers but had come to the hotel to see Beaslai about Irish language projects. There was a raid by Auxiliaries – all the IRA men got away safely, but the raiders took Clune with them. Clancy and McKee were asleep in their hideout in nearby Gloucester St when it too was raided later in the night. Both were captured, McKee barely having time to destroy the list of intended victims before the raiders burst into the room. Captain Hardy would have one of the greatest triumphs of the British undercover war effort. McKee, Clancy and the innocent Clune would pass one of the most hellish nights imaginable. For Clune there was the terror of the uninitiated, for the others, the horror of the too-well-informed. They were in the hands of the torturers and the plans they had helped to formulate would give their captors an added incentive for brutality.

Next morning, shortly after eight o'clock, groups of Volunteers, members of the Squad augmented by the Dublin Brigade, converged on eight different addresses in Dublin. Nineteen soldiers, one or two of them probably not agents, were roused from their sleep and shot, some in the presence of their wives, and girlfriends, some in bed, others standing against a wall. One was 'shot in his pyjamas in the back garden'.[5] Captain Baggelly, who died at 119 Lower Baggot St, never knew that one of the three-man party which shot him would be a future Irish Taoiseach, Prime Minister Sean Lemass.[6] The killers were all young men, generally of religious sensibility, and most of them didn't find their work easy. One, Mick O'Hanlon, recalled, 'When we got in we found our man had a girl and that he was covering the door and the landing . . . none of us fired as she was in bed with him and she covered him with her arms . . .'[7] But this moment soon passed. Following the hesitation O'Hanlon notes simply, 'Mick Flanagan shot him.'[8]

Some didn't hesitate. O'Hanlon also recalled that one of the victims, 'an old major', had a meal prepared. 'Mick White ate the breakfast.' Joe Dolan was so disgusted at finding that one prime target, Major King, a colleague of Hardy, was missing when he burst into his room, that he took revenge by giving his half-naked mistress 'a right scourging with a sword scabbard', and setting fire to the room afterwards.[9] But in general the spirit of the morning was accurately summed up by Charlie Dalton:

In the hall three or four men were lined up against the wall, some of our officers facing them. Knowing their fate I felt great pity for them. It was plain they knew it too. As I crossed the threshold the volley was fired . . . the sights and sounds of that morning were to be with me for many days and night. . . . I remembered I had not been to Mass. I slipped out, and in the silence before the altar, I thought over our morning's work and offered up a prayer for the fallen.[10]

There would be further reason for prayer before the day was out. The Volunteers got away from most of the death sites without incident but those involved in the Mount St and Pembroke Road areas had to fight their way through encircling Auxiliaries in a series of running battles. Somehow they managed to do this successfully and despite being greatly outnumbered and out-gunned, got away with their wounded. Only one member of the entire operation was captured, Frank Teeling, and Collins would soon engineer his escape. He sat in Devlin's waiting for news as O'Reilly cycled round the city collecting reports. The city was filled with horrific accounts of what had happened. At Masses priests advised their congregations to go straight home and remain indoors for the rest of the day.

Collins was 'white and defiant with no expression of pleasure'[11] as O'Reilly reported. He asked, 'Any casualties?' and, Teeling's capture not being known at the time, was told 'no'. His reaction to this was, 'there'll be no football match today', and he sent O'Reilly to warn the Gaelic Athletic Association that the afternoon's game between Dublin and Tipperary should be called off. The GAA sent back word that it was too late. Crowds would be congregating in the area of Croke Park whether a match was played or not. As the morning progressed Collins began to get uneasy about the whereabouts of McKee and Clancy. They had helped to wind up this particular clock. Why weren't they in Devlin's to hear how it struck? O'Reilly was sent to find out. Nearing their lodgings he was met by a boy who told him he had a message for Collins: 'They were captured last night.'

When Collins heard the news he sank back in his chair and exclaimed, 'Good God. We're finished now. It's all up.' When he recovered, frantic messages were sent to MacNamara and Neligan to locate the captured men. MacNamara heard that two men resembling them had been taken into the Bridewell. Collins ordered Neligan to go down and check and Neligan showed extraordinary courage in obeying. He went through every cell in the place, telling the sergeant on duty he was looking for a cousin. Had they been there the Squad might have got them out. But eventually their location in the Castle became known and Collins realised they were beyond hope. He went for his usual Sunday lunch at O'Donovans', cycling back and forth across the terror-filled city as he normally did. He had to sit with what was in effect a *memento mori* during the meal, for not knowing what had happened Mrs O'Donovan had set Dick McKee's customary place. Meanwhile the Auxiliaries and Tans made arrangements to surround Croke Park while the match was in progress, ostensibly to search the crowd for known Sinn Feiners. Later it was claimed in their defence that IRA men in the crowd fired first. But it is not denied that the security forces opened up on both crowd and playing field with rifles and machine-guns causing bloodshed and panic. Fourteen people died and hundreds were injured, none of them Tans or Auxiliaries. The stand in which each year the Sam Maguire cup is presented is named after one of the dead, Hogan, the Tipperary player who was shot on the playing field.

That night most of the prisoners held in Dublin Castle were transferred to Beggar's Bush. Clancy, Clune and McKee were left in the guardroom beside the canteen where, MacNamara reported, the Auxiliaries were 'drunk and thirsting for vengeance'. Later that night the three were 'shot while attempting to escape'. Neligan and the other friendly detectives reported to Collins that all three had been tortured and that, when their bodies were being loaded on to a lorry, the officer responsible had battered their faces with his torch.

Collins was beside himself at the news. Contemporary accounts speak of him swaying in anguish as he relived the tortures, continually repeating that all was over. He caused uproar by insisting that the bodies be dressed in Volunteer uniforms. Even the bravest of men thought he was mad and some refused to accompany him to the mortuary chapel in the pro-cathedral. However he pushed his way through the small crowd of detectives and spies who were hanging around the gate to see who would turn up and stood in the chapel as doctors opened the coffins to examine the bodies. The stories had been so awful that the investigators were almost glad at what was revealed. Badly battered faces certainly, and bayonet thrusts, and bullet wounds, but not the mutilations expected. He took part in dressing his comrades in Volunteers' uniforms and accepted the verdict of the clergy that the coffins should be closed again because of the condition of the faces. Next morning he also attended the funeral Mass and, with no one present knowing from one moment to the next whether the Auxiliaries might suddenly burst upon the scene, made his last gestures of friendship and defiance. First, wearing a trenchcoat, he stepped out of the crowd, which, because of the threat of the Auxiliaries, was unusually small for such an occasion and pinned an 'in

memoriam' message on the coffin: 'In memory of two good friends –
Dick and Peadar – and two of Ireland's best soldiers. Miceal
O'Coileain, 25/11/20.' Then he helped to carry the coffins. An *Evening
Herald* photographer got a picture which appeared in the early edition,
but the Squad visited the paper and the block was taken out for later
editions. Copies were bought up around the city and the Castle missed
getting a good picture of their chief enemy. He went to Glasnevin for
the burial also and was recognised by a woman. 'There's Mick
Collins,' she exclaimed. He turned round and snarled at her, 'You
bloody bitch.'[12] It was the same date as that on which, in London, the
men Collins, Clancy and McKee had had shot the previous Sunday
were laid to rest. Years later, in his novel *Never in Vain*, J. L. Hardy[13]
had his hero, Andrew Kerr, receive another note: 'Andrew Kerr. This
is to warn you that you have been sentenced to death for the brutal
murder of Clancy, McKee.' Hardy wasn't writing fiction. In the copy
of the novel Liam Tobin, the man who sent him the original of the
death threat, at Collins' instigation, has written: 'Hardy on arrival in
Dublin lived in Harcourt St. He was responsible for many murders
including those at Drumcondra and McKee, Clune, Clancy.'

In the aftermath of Bloody Sunday, quite a number of people either
felt like sending death threats or sensed that they were under threat.
The immediate reaction was for the agents who had escaped, and
despite all the planning a number were missed, to pour into the Castle
seeking sanctuary. Within hours of the shootings the various small
houses and apartments within the Castle's walls were filled with
shocked men and hysterical women who had barely paused to fill a
suitcase before seeking shelter. Collins might be coming for them
next. The O'Connor children discovered that a neighbour of theirs,
the father of one of their playmates, 'a boy called Percy Smith',[14] had
been shot. A Protestant, and a loyalist, his house, No. 117
Morehampton Rd, had been the scene of two shootings (a Captain
McClean and a man known as 'Caldron'). Emerging from a downstairs room at the sound of the shots, Smith was killed because the
gunmen thought he was trying to prevent their escape. British
propaganda made what it could from the death, trying to elicit
sympathy for the dead army men, not mentioning that they were
spies, glossing over Croke Park and putting the number of officers
shot at a reduced figure, generally fourteen or less. Thornton,
however, gives twenty names in his memoir, including one who
escaped. In each case he gives the officer's name, rank and the address
at which the shooting took place. Sir Henry Wilson was furious at the
fate of 'the poor murdered officers' and said after the funeral that he
wondered that Churchill, Greenwood and Lloyd George 'did not
hang their heads in shame'.[15] Interestingly, in his diary for 25
November, Erskine Childers talked of the funeral of the 'murdered

officers'.[16] The account given to the Cabinet of the events of Bloody Sunday, not for the first time in the Anglo-Irish war, makes one wonder how much the Government were kept informed by the military of what was really happening in Ireland:

The motive for these terrible crimes . . . is hard to explain, but the fact that several of the murdered officers were engaged on work connected with the preparation of cases for courts martial suggests an endeavour on the part of desperate criminals to strike back at the men who were thought to be specially concerned in bringing them to justice.[17]

No indication was given by Greenwood that the men were an elite, undercover 'hit' unit. Croke Park was passed off as a search operation intended to capture

men belonging to the Tipperary units of the Irish Republican Army . . . most desperate characters in that organisation [Tipperary were of course playing]. The police were fired upon by armed Sinn Fein pickets at the entrance to the field . . . the police returned the fire . . . there is no doubt that some of the most desperate criminals in Ireland were amongst the spectators. The responsibility for the loss of innocent lives must rest with those men, and not with the police or military who were forced to fire in self-defence and used no unnecessary violence . . . a civilian and a boy of ten were . . . shot in the streets of Dublin . . . and three prisoners who were being detained in a guard room at the entrance to Dublin Castle were shot while trying to escape.

Churchill subsequently stated at a Cabinet meeting[18] that no reprisals had taken place after the Dublin murders. However the initiated amongst the ranks of British decision-takers knew that Collins had probably struck the most damaging blow of the entire undercover war. The Cairo Gang had had one instruction, to locate and destroy Collins and his organisation.[19] They had failed and the implications of that failure were well understood.

It was Collins' most testing hour. The atmosphere in Dublin was so terrible that many trusted agents and couriers feared to leave their homes. William Cosgrave, one of the steadiest men ever to come into Irish public life, was so intimidated that he donned a soutane and took refuge for a period in a Borstal run by the Christian Brothers in Glencree in the Dublin Mountains. Cosgrave was not acting unwisely. Anything might have happened. General Boyd, GOC of the Dublin District, ordered Arthur Griffith arrested without consulting the Chief Secretary. Lloyd George was angered by this but Boyd justified his action by saying that if he hadn't arrested Griffith there might have been more murders, because there was such feeling amongst the regimental officers.[20] He felt it advisable to be seen to be cracking down on prominent Sinn Feiners as a result. However the man in the eye of the storm, Michael Collins, refused to let himself be cowed. When couriers' nerves failed he got on his bicycle and went himself to pick up despatches or to get the latest news from the friendly sources in the Castle and the DMP. If change may be said to be effected by a combination of will and circumstances then in that ghastly November, with the memory of the battered faces of McKee and Clancy before him to remind him of what lay in wait for himself, Collins both showed the former and created the latter. He later described the elimination of the Cairo Gang in the following terms:

My one intention was the destruction of the undesirables who continued to make miserable the lives of the ordinary decent citizens. I have proof enough to assure myself of the atrocities which this gang of spies and informers have committed. Perjury and torture are words too easily known to them.

If I had a second motive it was no more than a feeling such as I would have for a dangerous reptile.

By their destruction the very air is made sweeter. That should be the future's judgement on this particular event. For myself, my conscience is clear. There is no crime in detecting and destroying in wartime the spy and the informer. They have destroyed without trial. I have paid them back in their own coin.[21]

A week after Bloody Sunday, on 28 November, there came the news of the Kilmichael ambush by Tom Barry and his flying column. The Auxiliaries had suffered their greatest losses to date, seventeen killed in the attack. Sean Collins (equally known as Johnny), Collins' brother, had played a part in its planning. Collins' depression lifted. The fighting races had not died out.

The year ended with the most spectacular reprisal of all, that on portions of the city of Cork on 11 December. Following an ambush, shops were looted, civic buildings set alight, including the City Hall and half of the principal street of the city, St Patrick St, was gutted. Two brothers named Delaney were murdered in their beds for good measure. Hamar Greenwood gave a virtuoso performance in the House of Commons − 'there was no evidence that the fires were started by the Crown Forces.' He said that the City Hall had been destroyed after flames spread to it from St Patrick St. To do this the fires would have had to spread for half a kilometre, crossing the River Lee and leaving the intervening streets untouched. A more convincing verdict on the Cork example of the 'police war' policy and of the utilisation of such a policy generally comes from within the ranks of the Auxiliaries themselves. It gives a good idea of the difficulties experienced by those in the front line who had to operate the policy:

16.12.20   Aux. Division, RIC,
                                                                        Dunmanway,
                                                                        Co. Cork.

My darling Mother,
    . . . we came here from Cork and are billeted in a workhouse – filthily dirty.

Half of us are down with bronchitis. I am at present in bed . . . recovering
from a severe chill contracted on Saturday night last during the burning and
looting of Cork in which I took a reluctant part. We did it all right never mind
how much the well intentioned Hamar Greenwood would excuse us. In all
my life I have never experienced such orgies of murder, arson and looting as I
have witnessed during the past 16 days with the RIC Auxiliaries. It baffles
description. And we are supposed to be officers and gentlemen. There are
quite a number of decent fellows and likewise a lot of ruffians.

    On our arrival here from Cork one of our heroes held up a car with a priest
and a civilian in it and shot them through the head without cause or
provocation. We were very kindly received by the people but the consequences of this cold-blooded murder is that no one will come within a mile of
us now and all shops are closed. The brute who did it has been sodden with
drink for some time and has been sent to Cork under arrest for examination
by experts in lunacy. If certified sane he will be court-martialled and shot.
The poor old priest was 65 and everybody's friend.

    The burning and sacking of Cork followed immediately on the ambush of
our men. I, as orderly sergeant had to collect 20 men for a raid and then left the
barracks in the motor cars. I did not go for I was feeling seedy. The party had not
got 100 yards from barracks when bombs were thrown at them over a wall. One
dropped in a car and wounded eight men, one of whom has since died.

    Very naturally the rest of the Co. were enraged. The houses in the vicinity
of the ambush were set alight. And from there the various parties set out on
their mission of destruction. Many who witnessed similar scenes in France
and Flanders say, that nothing they had experienced was comparable to the
punishment meted out to Cork. I got back to barracks at 4 am.

    Reprisals are necessary and loyal Irishman agree but there is a lot which
should not be done . . .[22]

    While Collins' daily routine was a chapter of near escapes, some
stand out as being particularly hair-raising. His 'life on the bicycle' had
given him severe stomach trouble, necessitating special food, and
Eileen O'Donovan, then a girl of fourteen, was up before dawn on
Christmas Eve, 1920, to prepare his breakfast of curds and whey. That
evening, for the first and only time in her life, she saw him drunk on
raw whiskey. His condition had been brought on, not by Christmas
spirit, but by the Auxiliaries. He always enjoyed Christmas and the
day was a busy one with a myriad of visits and present-giving to a long
list of people ranging from friendly sailors to hostesses who had fed
him and his men during the year. Poor O'Reilly nearly had the pedals
worn off his bicycle going around the city delivering them all. Collins
decided to stand a dinner in the Gresham Hotel, in O'Connell St, one
of the best-known places in Ireland. Too well known. Neligan nearly
had a seizure when he was invited and turned down the invitation with
a few appropriate comments on the subject of suicide.

    When the party arrived at the Gresham, they discovered that all the
private rooms were taken as Collins would surely have reckoned on

beforehand, had his normal foresight and instinct for danger not gone on Christmas holiday. They sat at a table in the public dining room, Collins, Rory O'Connor, Gearoid O'Sullivan, Tobin and Cullen; the Castle could not have imagined a more welcome Christmas present. It was very nearly delivered. A party of Auxiliaries raided the hotel. Collins was searched and a bottle of whiskey discovered in his hip pocket. 'For his landlady', he said. Less convincing was his explanation for one of the entries in a notebook which was also discovered. 'Rifles', said the Auxiliary. 'Refills', said Collins. Understandably, after that exchange he felt a need to relieve himself and was taken to the lavatory under escort. When he didn't return Tobin became alarmed and went looking for him. He found him held under one of the bright hand-basin lights while an Auxiliary officer tousled his hair and compared his likeness with a photograph of Collins he held in his other hand. Collins had despairingly made up his mind to make a grab for the officer's revolver when suddenly he was released and he and Tobin were allowed to return to the table. It was still touch and go. Collins whispered to Tobin to 'be ready to make a rush for it.' But in his absence his whiskey bottle had helped to ease the atmosphere. O'Connor had offered the Auxiliaries a drink and a second bottle of whiskey was ordered into the bargain. John Jameson spread a benign glow over the Auxiliaries and they departed without the Castle's five-man Christmas present. The Castle might have taken some small comfort from the episode had they known of the cosmic hangovers the five proceeded to inflict on themselves. They finished the whiskey – and their wine – and then repaired to Vaughan's. Diarmuid O'Hegarty, who had not been at the Gresham either, was horror-stricken at the prospect of a raid on Vaughan's and implored them to go home, with conspicuous lack of success. Delayed reaction, and John Jameson's, had taken over and there were wrestling matches and tumblers of whiskey before the warriors were decanted into a car and poured into some of Mrs O'Donovan's beds for the night.

On New Year's Eve, 'O' struck Collins a more serious blow than the fright of Christmas Eve had been. One of the most prominent Sinn Fein women, Eileen MacGrane, a lecturer in the National University, was in her bath, in her flat in Dawson St, when 'O's men burst in. Collins was furious at their subsequent behaviour. Writing to Art O'Brien later he said . . . 'gallant British officers bandied her name around with every low suggestion, please do everything possible.'[23] It wasn't only Eileen MacGrane's modesty that suffered. Some of Collins' most valuable files were captured in a room in her flat which he rented. These included documents that eventually led to the arrest of Broy. In his book, Neligan criticises Collins for not being careful enough in protecting his sources.[24] This is the incident he is referring to. In fact Collins was extraordinarily careful and secretive in his protection of people, but his work method involved keeping such detailed records for checking and cross-checking that he left himself open to a discovery of this sort. Eileen MacGrane had a rough time of it in jail in England, but Broy would have been tortured and killed had his role been even guessed at. Though he was arrested on suspicion, as some of the documents found had obviously been typed by him (Collins had also kept the day-book he took from Brunswick St) it proved possible to muddy the waters.

Firstly he sent a warning to Broy's superior officer who, not wishing to appear on Collins' hit list as Broy's accuser, destroyed any incriminating evidence he could lay his hands on. Next Collins got another detective, who shared Broy's office, to disappear suddenly out of the country, partly through inducement, partly by threat, which automatically deflected suspicion on him. (Collins saw to it that this man was sent a return ticket when the Truce was signed.) Finally he wrote and signed a letter which he sent into the Castle, arranging for its discovery. It purported to be an inquiry to an unnamed contact asking what was behind the fuss about this man Broy who had never been any good and was always an enemy of the IRA. These stratagems and the coming of the Truce saved Broy's life. But the MacGrane raid[25] meant that Collins found out for himself just how true was his own saying that the British could replace a detective, but not his knowledge. Although Neligan continued to operate successfully Broy was irreplaceable.

Broy's seizure initiated an era during which Collins, even by his own standards, was incredibly lucky to escape capture. The common factor which saved him in each case was loyalty. The night Broy was caught, Christy Harte, the hall porter at Vaughan's, was taken to the Castle. After several bad days he was put in a darkened room and told that if he betrayed Collins he would be given £5,000 and a new start in life anywhere in the world. However Harte, a poor man, continued to maintain that he did not know Collins. Eventually he was released – to make a full report to Collins.

A little later the military raided a house in Brendan's Rd close to O'Connor's where Collins was staying. An officer rummaged through the love letters of the occupant, a girl, and was so abashed when she berated him for his lack of chivalry that he dropped the list of the addresses he was supposed to be raiding. He rang up the Castle to be given the addresses of the houses he had yet to raid, but was told that such information was not for transmission over the telephone and to return at once to the Castle. Next morning the girl found the list and gave it to Batt O'Connor; the only house on the list still unraided was No. 23, where Collins had spent the night.

He had an even nearer miss some weeks later, on Friday 1 April, when one of his helpers, Eileen Hoey, made an April Fool out of a party of Tans and detectives at No. 5 Mespil Rd, which was one of his intelligence centres. Hoey talked her way out of an incriminating revolver find by blaming it on a mythical lodger in the house. Then, after a gruelling in the Castle, she was driven back in the small hours of the morning to Mespil Rd where the Tans proceeded to set up a week-end-long stake-out for Collins who, unknown to the Tans, had been due at nine o'clock that Saturday morning.

But after saying the Rosary for inspiration, Hoey got her mother to fake a heart attack and persuaded the Tans to accompany her to a neighbouring doctor, whom she never attended, but who was preferable to her mother's loyalist physician. The doctor, correctly divining *Uisce fé Talamh* (water under the ground), came to the house, 'treated' the mother in private and agreed to get a message to Collins who was duly stopped by a scout within an ace of Mespil Rd. The stake-out produced a valuable haul of papers for the Castle and landed Hoey in jail where she was subjected to 'shocking ill-treatment'[26] but released after the Truce.

The raid on his papers hit Collins hard. He said afterwards, 'The raid was much worse than I thought. Practically the entire record is gone.'[27] His methodology, which incensed Neligan, necessitated keeping so many records that their discovery was inevitably damaging. Nevertheless his incredible resilience showed itself yet again. By now even the British were coming to admire him. Lloyd George's right-hand man, Cabinet Secretary Tom Jones, wrote to Bonar Law at this stage: 'The tenacity of the IRA is extraordinary. Where was Michael Collins during the Great War? He would have been worth a dozen brass-hats.'[28] Collins recovered sufficiently to take part in a notable 'first' the following month (May 1921), the first use of the Thompson sub-machine gun in warfare.

Clan na nGael had organised the purchase of a large consignment which the US Customs seized on 16 June 1921, underlining the difficulty of smuggling large-scale supplies of armaments to Ireland undetected by Britain or her allies. However a few dozen had got through the previous month. Two Irish-American ex-American Army officers from Chicago, Captain Cronin and Major Dineen, also arrived safely and conducted Thompson training sessions. Collins was delighted with the new toy and so enthusiastically tested one in the grounds of the Christian Brothers at Marino, County Dublin, that a Brother came out to warn him that the noise would attract the enemy.[29] The guns were actually used in a number of Dublin ambushes and had a psychological effect, but did not materially affect the war.[30]

Tom Barry, one of the men Collins introduced to the Thompson, recalls that the sound of the weapon was not the only danger to accrue from Collins' behaviour at the time. He wrote about an occasion when Collins acted drunk and succeeded in bluffing both of them safely out of a death trap.

One night we ran into a hold-up by about fifty Auxiliaries. . . . I was next to Collins and he put up such a fine act, joking and blasting in turn that he had the whole search party of terrorists in good humour in a short time.[31]

After a perfunctory search they got through safely, but Barry berated Collins for not having scouts out in front of them. The reaction he got was:

Mick as usual guffawed and chaffed me about being a windy West Cork buggar . . . Failing to see the joke, I told him crossly that it was quite true, I was a windy beggar, as I had a wholesome regard for my neck.[32]

Barry in fact was one of the bravest men in the war and probably the most successful field commander. Apart from his victory at Kilmichael he achieved a spectacular success at Crossbarry, County Cork, on 19 March 1921. In a day-long engagement, encouraged by the traditional pipes of Flor Begley, Barry and a force of about a hundred men broke through a more heavily armed British encirclement of ten times that number and got away safely, inflicting heavy casualties as they went. Barry bore Collins no grudge but the same combination of Collins' style and the difficulties created by another unsuccessful attempt at large-scale arms shipments, this time from Italy, did create a good deal of hostility towards Collins in other circles both during, and indeed long after, the Thompson period.

The long-running Italian arms saga, which actually began in 1920, was finally abandoned a year later, in 1921. Apart from illustrating the kind of difficulties Collins' style brought on him, it conclusively proved the impossibility of getting any large-scale arms shipment through British Intelligence. The Rector of the Irish College in Rome, Monsignor Hagan, and Monsignor M. J. Curran, Vice Rector, had introduced Donal Hales and a colleague to Italian War Office officials, possibly even the War Minister. Collins' subsequent letter to Hales indicated that:

The reports were so satisfactory that the Trade Department say they are sending another friend out shortly, who is interested in the same business, but has new ideas to develop . . . the new visitor hopes the way will be well-paved for him when he gets there.[33]

Collins had been involved in the Italian affair for several months before he told the Cork IRA what he had in mind. He acknowledged to Hales on 13 August 1920 that he had received:

. . . the important communication on the subject of Italian Cabinets and such antiques in this country. This is a matter which requires very careful organisation so that there may be no loss. You will understand that although the finances are not exactly limited yet a loss would render further dealings uninviting.[34]

One of his September despatches to Art O'Brien read as follows:

ITALIAN FURNITURE: Joe Vize is away at the moment, so I cannot give you any details, also I have not yet gone into the matter quite fully with Liam. I am doing so however. You will be fully advised as to how things go ahead.[35]

But as far as Liam Deasy and Florrie O'Donoghue were concerned the Italian gun-running idea had only taken shape at a meeting with Collins in Barry's Hotel, Dublin months later, on 16 December 1920. Deasy and O'Donoghue were impressed and, in view of the importance of the project, O'Donoghue suggested a man 'we could ill spare' as a pilot, Mick Leahy, Vice OC Cork No. 1 Brigade, because he had qualified as a marine engineer.

It was decided that Leahy, the 'new visitor' Collins mentioned to Hales would be sent to Italy and that arrangements for the actual landing would be placed in the hands of the Vice-OC of the Skibbereen Brigade, Patrick O'Driscoll. A site screened from the sea was picked out not far from where Collins grew up, the channel inside Rabbit Island, about 400 yards off Myross Strand. Dumps were constructed. A flotilla of small boats was arranged and special boxes provided with ropes bound round them so that they could be filled with arms and then lowered from the Italian ship into the boats and thus brought ashore. Meanwhile all the roads and lanes leading to the landing beaches were to be guarded by a strong force of Volunteers.

Leahy was suitably impressed when he was instructed by his OC Sean O'Hegarty, to go to Dublin on 2 January 1921, in order to make arrangements with Collins for a passport to Italy. He was to become progressively less impressed.[36] In Dublin he met Gearoid O'Sullivan, at that stage Adjutant General, and was taken on a 'very lengthy journey through many streets, and eventually fetched up at Devlin's in Parnell St 'only the length of O'Connell St from where we started. . . . I had the feeling it was all done to impress me, the boy from the country.' Worse was to follow. Leahy goes on:

When we entered Devlin's pub, I was surprised to find nearly all the GHQ Staff assembled and a merry party in progress, this despite Gearoid's protestations that Dublin was a dangerous place for the likes of him. My choice of lemonade when whiskey was being pressed did not go down too well with Michael Collins who seemed to be master of the revels. Dick Mulcahy was in Devlin's, but was quiet in comparison to a number of them and left early . . .

The Devlin's affair had been Tom Cullen's stag party and Leahy was put out to find that no one took any interest in his mission until after the wedding breakfast next day. Then, having being sent to

London by Collins to get a British passport, he found that he was expected to make the arrangements himself. He finally found his way over the Swiss border into Italy, at Modane, on 28 March.

He linked up with Donal Hales, who taught at Genoa University and was married to an Italian. Hales was friendly with both d'Annunzio and Mussolini, and introduced Leahy to d'Annunzio before bringing him to the gun-running ship, the *Stella Maris*, a four-masted barque, with a 'ballast' of rifles, machine-guns, revolvers and ammunition. But the money for the shipment failed to arrive from Dublin, and Leahy's own money began running out. Collins wrote to Hales on 7 March:

The arrangement made for the transfer of the money was a bad one, as of course it would be obvious what it was meant for – I have a better plan if I can work it out properly. It is to pay the amount for the credit of the Branch – not for any individual. You could then make application at your end. [37]

The money never got through. In desperation Leahy set out for Paris and Sean T. O'Kelly, who suggested that Leahy make his way to London where Art O'Brien would have more direct contact with Collins. All O'Brien could get for Leahy was an instruction to return home, which he did on 23 April 1921.

Collins gave him no satisfaction. He said he had got his messages but that the project was out of the question. 'The British knew all about it.' Tom Hales said:

. . . failure remained a mystery to my brother for a long time . . . in my view members of the Cabinet, not Collins, were not too hot about the under-taking, and as time went by, on to April 1921 all possibly became worried about the success of this undertaking. It may also be governed by a third factor, you remember when the ease off was suggested . . . [38]

Hales, one of the most knowledgeable men about IRA affairs of this period in the country, was almost certainly putting his suggestions in a deliberately tentative fashion – it's a celebrated Cork characteristic! Both he and O'Donoghue knew that the 'ease off' reference referred to de Valera's proposal on his return from America (see Chapter 7). But Leahy himself probably contributed to the aborting of the mission inadvertently, possibly through being identified by British Intelligence. Collins sent Hales a cheque for his expenses in the matter on 7 July 1921 with a letter which said:

The business, I think, should be kept in view, but unfortunately it has not been found practicable. We were not very satisfied with our messenger in the latter stages of the procedings, and we consequently had to change plans temporarily at any rate. You should be very reticent in any reference you make to this . . . [39]

Hales was duly 'reticent'; so was Collins himself, and his silence, combined with his flamboyance at the Cullen party, injured his reputation in some circles for many years.

One consequence of the increasing intensity of the war was that some seventy persons were found shot as spies between January and April. Though all were labelled, 'spies and informers beware', or somesuch, it is very doubtful if the IRA did in fact execute them all. Some were the work of criminals, some of the 'Dirty Tricks Brigade', units like the Igoe gang and others. The IRA did however carry out some executions which Collins regretted. In Cork, an elderly loyalist landowner, a Mrs Lindsay, gave away an ambush. Six Volunteers were captured and sentenced to death as a result. Cork No. 1 Brigade kidnapped Mrs Lindsay and her chauffeur and sent word to the British that she would die if the Volunteers did. The Volunteers were executed and the Cork men shot the old lady and her driver without sanction from GHQ. The usual thing in such cases was to burn the informant's house. One captive of the period who had a happier experience was General Lucas who was captured by a party of Volunteers under Liam Lynch in July 1920, while fishing on the Blackwater. He was moved around for almost a month before his last custodian, Michael Brennan, the Commander of the East Clare Brigade, engineered his escape. Brennan,[40] who liked Lucas otherwise, got tired of buying the General his daily bottle of whiskey, out of his own pocket. Moreover it was impossible to mount attacks on British patrols while at the same time guarding a British general in secrecy.[41] To keep fit Lucas played tennis and made hay while in captivity. Collins' network saw to it that letters to and from his wife were delivered. The only time Lucas expressed fear was when his captors offered to take him salmon poaching on the River Shannon one night. The thought of being found 'stroke hauling' salmon by the bailiffs worried him greatly. He was both relieved and astounded to find that his IRA boatman on the poaching trip was the Chief Bailiff. Lucas' troops shot up Fermoy and a number of other towns in reprisal for his capture. After escaping he lectured them for 'an over-zealous display of loyalty'. Displeased at his allowing himself to be captured, the Army authorities made no use of Lucas' services thereafter.

Collins was said to be opposed to the shooting of women. Even in one case very close to him, a neighbour of Batt O'Connor's, a Mrs Maud Walsh, escaped with her life despite activities of a more serious nature than those which claimed the lives of other spies.

This does not appear to have been his attitude always, to judge from a story concerning my father. According to this he and another Volunteer were sent out by Collins to shoot two young women, who had been consorting with British soldiers and had apparently given away information. But my father decided that the girls 'were very young and very beautiful' and made up his own and his companion's mind that they should not be shot. For once Collins does not àppear to have been too concerned about the non-fulfilment of a 'job'. My father was promoted to more congenial duties concerned with intelligence and the operations of the underground Sinn Fein Courts. But the ferocity of the struggle in Cork militated against kindly feelings.

In February 1921 a group of Volunteers were given away by an informer at Clonmult and surrounded by Tans, Auxiliaries and regular troops. After a two-hour fight the thatch on the cottage they were sheltering in was set alight and they surrendered on being promised fair treatment. However when the Volunteers emerged with their hands up the Auxiliaries fell on them 'like wild beasts' and nine were battered to death.[42] The six who survived, through the intervention of a regular officer, were subsequently executed by order of a court martial. The Cork No. 1 Brigade again seized and shot a hostage, a Major Compton Smith, a man whose character greatly impressed his captors. His last letters were sent to Collins, who wrote to Art O'Brien after Greenwood had made capital out of the shooting in the House of Commons urging him to publicise the fact that Compton Smith in his last letter to his wife said that he had been treated 'far better than Englishmen would treat an Irishman in the same circumstances'.[43] His final letter to General Strickland urged that there be no reprisals, and he said that the men who captured him were no murder gang, but men filled with a sense of high duty.

Collins' sister Mary described the morning the Clonmult prisoners were shot in Cork City. Tomas MacCurtain's widow had erected an altar outside the barracks wall and the women, including the mothers of the condemned men, prayed there under the shadow of a tank. They heard a volley and prayed until an ambulance emerged:

and just as we were about to disperse we heard another volley of shots . . . instead of shooting the six they had arranged to kill them one by one. In another 15 minutes there was another volley . . . was again repeated after an interval . . .

I cannot describe the wonderful patience and heroism, almost to the point of elation, displayed by these bereaved mothers. . . . The reaction, no doubt, came later but that day they each felt it a privilege to have raised a son for God and Ireland.[44]

Reaction of a different sort did come that day. Mary Collins-Powell describes hearing that afternoon that:

there had been six British soldiers shot in various parts of the city as reprisals for the morning executions. Some of them were mere children with gooseberries and sweets in their pockets, a few walking with the colleens . . . I was sorely stricken with sympathy for those boys and also for the very young Volunteers . . . who got orders to shoot unarmed men . . . Freedom, what crimes are committed in thy name.

While these tragedies were occurring in the foreground of Collins' life, in the background he had to contend with a vendetta that Brugha conducted against him and which de Valera literally presided over. It was so intense that it caused him to think seriously about quitting his highly successful underground war in Dublin and taking to the hills with the Cork IRA.

Brugha at this stage, March 1921, was pursuing Collins over what he described as irregularities in the Scot accounts for arms purchase. His allegation seems to have been, not so much that Collins was embezzling money, but that he was using IRA funds for IRB purposes. For once Collins was not able to produce his usual meticulously prepared accounts. Tom Cullen had left a bag of papers with a friend who was raided and the papers seized. They had included the accounts Brugha was now querying almost a year later. Collins wrote to Michael Staines[45] in Mountjoy, who with Eamonn Duggan was one of the prisoners' principal leaders, on 16 March, unaware that Brugha had already carried his campaign into the prison, which with executions taking place within its walls, was an unlikely venue wherein to conduct a squabble about petty cash. Collins' letter gives an indication of his pressures and thoughts that week:

There was a Dail meeting on Friday and consequently I was rushing all day on Thursday. Then there was a lot of men from the country on Saturday and Sunday, so I had not the slightest opportunity of writing you a word. You don't know how I feel for you all. It is dreadful to think of you remaining in your cells and just thinking and brooding when the poor lads were being taken to their deaths. May God help every man to bear it as they bore it . . .

Enclosed is a letter from Cathal. He is making an awful fuss and rumpus generally about accounts. It is so intolerable that I am thinking seriously of getting away to Cork No. 3. I would get a run for my money there anyway . . .

Staines replied the next day, 17 March 1921:

. . . I enclose . . . a note from . . . C. [Brugha] If I could have a chat with Cathal I am sure I would be able to satisfy him that everything is alright but it is a different matter putting my thoughts on paper. If I say what I think I will probably get his rag out and we cannot afford that at the present critical juncture. As he is such a crank and you know exactly how the a/cs stand I would be glad if you will suggest the wording of my reply.

As you are aware I know practically nothing about the a/cs now and T.C. [Tom Cullen] didn't lodge the money with my knowledge except in this way that he was my assistant for a certain time and during that time had the right to act for me. I don't remember signing cheques for any of this money. Since we were appointed treasurers you always kept the a/cs and during that time I was satisfied that all the money was accounted for and I am satisfied still.

Above all things I will depend on you not to let Cathal know that I sent you his letter. Did T.C. lodge the money in No. 1 joint a/c or did he open a social account for it?

It was terrible here on Sunday looking at the Boy's (*sic*) friends coming to say their last goodbye, but when the visits were over our sorrowful feelings gave way to a feeling of pride that they were facing death so bravely and we kept up communication practically all night. They sent us messages for their friends in this world and so sure were they that they were going straight to heaven that we gave them messages for our friends there. Their last message to the boys was 'carry on the fight we will watch over you and pray for you in heaven'. . . .

. . . For goodness sake get that Cork No. 3 idea out of your head. You are required where you are at present. Don't take C. too seriously and rub him the right way an odd time . . .

Collins's reply is dated the 21st:

Yours of the 17th reached me on the morning of the 19th or rather late on the 18th. There was not an opportunity of sending in a reply since, although I was very anxious to reply to that particular communication of yours . . .

Yes the lads were great weren't they. A fellow prisoner of yours . . . in a letter to me, put the thing in the following beautiful way: 'Monday morning was very terrible, but pride afterwards took the sadness away, and they were so certain of heaven that death became not only unfeared but desired. They one and all stepped across the threshold joyfully.'

. . . Enclosed is a little statement which will help you in replying to Cathal. In replying to him it would be well to point out the difficulty of getting anything more than general details in view of the seizures of books etc. This is the thing that has nettled me most in reality – he expects every sixpence to be accounted for, nothwithstanding all we have gone through in the way of raids, etc.

Collins pointedly does not reply to Staines' admonition about his 'Cork No. 3' idea. This may be because Staines had given him an opportunity of drafting a reply which temporarily deflected Brugha. The intensity of Brugha's hatred may be gauged from the mere fact that he would send such a request in to Staines during the octave of the execution of men who, in Mother Dodd's words, were 'strong in the conviction that the fight for country was a fight for Faith'.[46]

Sean Dowling summed it up tellingly:

Cathal Brugha hated Collins like poison. It was pathological . . . Brugha was Minister for Defence but he never did anything. He was not able, but he was never on the run. He continued to work as manager for Lalor's candle factory on Ormond Quay . . . Collins was so energetic that he had usurped many of Brugha's functions: he sure was hated by him. . . .[47]

Brugha's hatred for Collins actively interfered with the war effort. Payments for arms were held up, as letters from Collins to P. G. O'Daly in Liverpool show: 'I am very sorry about the matter of funds.

That is not my fault. I thought the little man had arranged to send you on what you required. I shall mention the matter to him.'[48]

Next day he wrote again:

You will understand that I could forward you some money for your own use, but the way things are going here at present I don't like doing that. It is up to these people who are making so much fuss to attend to things. Nothing like it happened when I was in charge of a certain number of details. It should not happen now either.

The same shortages occurred elsewhere. Mulcahy wrote to the Director of Purchases, Liam Mellowes, complaining that: 'in the hearing of the QMG's staff, just returned from Scotland, 9,000 rounds of .303 offered for sale were refused for lack of money . . . we would be lynched down the country if this were known.'[49] Mulcahy was not exaggerating. At the time 'men were dying for lack of the few rounds of ammunition to defend themselves'.[50] But Mellowes, who had been in America with de Valera, was inclined to take sides against Collins. He wrote back:

It is quite possible that the situation reported to you by QMG as existing in G [Glasgow] is quite correct. In fact I am so informed myself. As the M/D has stated relative to London and Manchester . . . he will debit me with amounts unless I can show goods on hand and I was not, and am not, going to put myself in the position of adding to the Glasgow muddle by making further disbursements until I saw my way clear.[51]

That particular round in the Brugha-Collins feud was brought to a close by means of a highly embarrassing inquiry presided over by de Valera. Dowling described the scene:

Collins came, he brought books and receipts and was able to account for all of it except maybe a hundred pounds . . . Austin Stack told me the story afterwards in Waterford. He found it very embarrassing. Collins was so upset by the accusation that he openly wept. 'Now,' said de Valera, 'it is quite clear that these charges are groundless.' Brugha arose without a word and left the room. Stack rushed after him: 'Come in, shake hands'. But Brugha angrily turned from him; 'You'll find him out yet,' he spat. He stamped out.[52]

Ultimately Brugha's dislike of Collins came down to simple jealousy. De Valera remarked to Mulcahy that it was a great pity that a man with Brugha's many fine qualities should be guilty of 'a dirty little vice like jealousy',[53] as though he were immune from it himself. Collins had taken such a grip on the British imagination that the first question raiding parties often asked on entering a house was, 'Where's Michael Collins?' Frequently different raiding parties at opposite ends of the city would smash into homes yelling, 'Where is he? We know he's here.' Other men too had hair's-breadth escapes, indeed all the leading figures in Sinn Fein and the Volunteers were constantly harried, but Collins was the one who most caught the popular imagination, and Brugha resented press labels on Collins such as 'the Irish de Wet'. *He* was the Minister for Defence; Collins he saw as a mere subordinate manipulating press coverage to gain an undeserved notoriety.

Collins' notoriety was such that while Auxiliaries were tearing houses apart looking for him in Dublin, he was said to be involved in escapades in other parts of the country. In one such, a shoot-out at Burgatia House, near Rosscarbery, on 2 February 1921, he was supposed to have taken part mounted on a white horse and to have been killed. Commenting on the *Daily Sketch* report of this, he wrote to Celestine:

Yes indeed, the English papers have been giving me plenty of notoriety – a notoriety one would gladly be rid of, but they must make a scapegoat. The *Daily Sketch* had a gorgeous thing one time – 'Mike', the super hater, dour, hard, no ray of humour, no trace of human feeling. Oh lovely! The white horse story was an exaggeration. I have not ridden a white horse since I rode 'Gipsy', and used her mane as a bridle.[54]

Collins had other things to worry him during this period (March/ April 1921). As part of the reprisal policy the security forces broke up fairs and destroyed the agricultural machinery and farm buildings of suspects. Collins' old home, Woodfield, at the time occupied by his brother Johnny's large family, was amongst those which were razed. Collins' own account of the burning has survived:

Col Commandant Higginson, the Commanding Officer of a brigade at the Cork City Headquarters of the 6th Division ordered the destruction as an official reprisal for the attack on Rosscarbery. It should be understood that my brother's place was four miles from Rosscarbery. The enemy force came bringing with them several of the neighbouring civilians as hostages – some of the civilians were forced at the point of the bayonet to bring hay and straw into the house. The hay and straw were then sprinkled with petrol (also forced). On arrival of the English forces the house was occupied by a maiden lady, a maid and eight little children (ages from twelve years downwards to a little child of less than twelve months). It should also be explained that quite a short time prior to the burning the mother of the children had died.

She had been in bad health for nearly twelve months and, no doubt, a succession of raids by British forces contributed to hasten her untimely end. My brother, the father of all the children, was attending a County Council meeting in Cork and was not present at the time of the burning. The little children were without anyone to protect them. The English forces proceeded to throw them out of the house and having done this proceeded with the burning.

The dwelling house itself, and every out-office (with the exception of one stable) were completely destroyed. The hayshed which contained some hay, was likewise destroyed. A farmhand was ploughing in a field near the house – the English forces went to the horses, took the harness off them and threw it into the fire. The net result therefore was that eight young children were left homeless and there was no person or nothing left to carry on the ordinary work of the farm, so that of course production suffered.

To complete the story my brother, himself, was arrested on his arrival at the Railway Station at Clonakilty – the timing of the arrest practically coincided with the burning of his house.

He is at present at Spike Island, was visited on Friday last and is likely to lose the use of his right hand as a result of medical neglect. The above are the details – there were in fact other, minor, points of brutality which cannot be told until all the evidence is available. The important thing is that the case is no exception.

My brother was over military age, but he had always been an advanced Irishman. He was a member of the Cork County Council. Being over military age he devoted himself to this work and to general Local Reconstruction.[55]

Collins was right. The case was no exception; four other houses were burned in the same area that night (16 April 1921) alone and hundreds were burned throughout the country, but his letter is remarkably dispassionate considering the impact the burning had on him. 'They knew where they could hurt me most,' he said and went into one of his black moods for days. With no home or family of his own, Woodfield had always been his anchor. Now he brooded on an old forecast that around the beginning of the Twentieth Century there would be no Collinses at Woodfield, and on the new and more pressing realities of how to cope with the burning's aftermath. Johnny's family had to be farmed out amongst neighbours and in the terror of the time it was hard enough to get all the children placed for fear of further reprisals. Liam Collins, the baby mentioned, suffered ill-health all his life as a result of the hardships of those days. Johnny did not lose his hand, which had been injured in an accident on the farm, but due to the absence of medical facilities at Spike Island Prison, or, it was suspected, the unwillingness to provide any, the hand did suffer permanent damage and he had to give up farming and leave Woodfield. So the old prophecy came true. However neither Collins nor the country at large had much time to ponder such things.

The IRA countered the farm-burnings by destroying the homes of loyalists. Sean Hales, whose Brigade operated in the Woodfield area, summed up the counter-burning policy to the seventy-year-old Lord Bandon – whom he had surprised in bed with a young lady not his wife – as he prepared to sprinkle the petrol: 'You burned my castle last week. Now I'll burn yours.'[56] The Hales treatment repeated throughout the country caused such reaction from loyalists that the reprisals policy was abandoned by the Cabinet. In order to save face Army officers were instructed to tell their subordinates that the decision was not 'because of the vapourings of some insignificant member of the House of Commons', but, 'largely due to His Majesty's influence, so that in that case we can all be perfectly happy about the decision.'[57]

Throughout the burnings period Collins was attempting to use his influence to make a friend of his, Sean MacEoin, 'perfectly happy'.[58] The lengths to which he was prepared to go to get men out of jail were never better exemplified than in the case of MacEoin. Few fighting men excited Collins' admiration to the extent Sean MacEoin did. A blacksmith, from Ballinalee, County Longford, he took charge of the Longford brigade at Collins' request. Amongst his exploits was a reprisal upon a reprisal party of Auxiliaries and Black and Tans who looted and burned several shops and houses in Granard, County Longford on 5 November 1920 after the IRA had carried out an ambush a few days earlier. On the way home from the reprisal, the Auxiliaries and Tans, who outnumbered the IRA by five to one, were attacked by MacEoin and twenty Volunteers who created terrible slaughter amongst the drunken reprisalists. As many as twenty deaths and several times that number of injured are believed to have been inflicted, but the exact casualties were never given. MacEoin had a reputation for chivalry. When he was surrounded in a cottage near Ballinalee the following January, he came out of the shelter of the house to make his stand because there were women inside. Once outside he killed the police officer in charge and put the rest of the party to flight. In another ambush in February, he and his column forced a larger party of Auxiliaries to surrender after a hard-fought engagement. He congratulated the surviving Auxiliaries on their courage, and did what he could for the wounded before sending them back to base in one of the captured lorries. Three of the Auxiliary party paid tribute to him at his court martial in June of that year. The court martial came about as a result of one of Cathal Brugha's obsessions.

From the first, Brugha had wanted to counter the reprisal policy by bringing the war to England, first by assassinating members of the British Cabinet and then by actions such as machine-gunning cinema queues. Collins had blocked the assassination scheme, pointing out that England could always replace a Cabinet, and telling Brugha flatly, 'You'll get none of my men for that.' Brugha had replied icily: 'That's all right Mister Collins, I want none of your men. I'll get men of my own.'

He didn't find them that easy to get. The Donegal Commandant, Joe Sweeney, told Mulcahy that he found Brugha's proposal 'completely immoral'. Eventually, around the beginning of March 1921, Brugha sent for MacEoin who could hardly find his way around Dublin, never mind London, and arranged that he would remain in Dublin under Brugha's direct command. Emerging from the interview however he bumped into Collins and there were emissions of sulphur before Collins managed to arrange with Mulcahy, as Chief of Staff, to countermand the orders of the Minister for Defence, and repoint the blacksmith in the direction of Balinalee.

However MacEoin had been identified in Dublin, by the RIC. He was taken off the train at Mullingar and, in an attempt to escape, was shot through the lung and beaten with rifle butts. As a doctor only gave him an hour to live, a party of Black and Tans decided they had better make the best use possible of the time available and beat him up savagely. Various efforts to rescue him miscarried.

In one, Collins had smuggled in a change of clothes, a watch and a hacksaw, soap and oil. MacEoin used his gifts to work all one Thursday night and Friday morning, cutting through the bars of his downstairs cell and obliterating the marks of his handiwork in preparation for an escape on Friday evening.

Recovering from wounds as he was, MacEoin had driven his temperature sky-high by his sawing exertions and when the prison doctor put in an unexpected appearance he attributed MacEoin's fever to the damp of the ground floor cell and ordered him moved immediately.

Next, Collins attempted to make use of the fact that every morning a British armoured car drove to the Dublin abattoir to collect meat. He decided to have the crew held up and the car used in an attempt on Mountjoy Jail. Emmet Dalton and a group from the Squad were entrusted with the rescue. Each morning Dalton's younger brother Charlie sat in a window overlooking the abattoir watching the armoured car. Nearby, personally checked each time by Collins himself, the rescue party, dressed in army fatigues, waited for the signal that would show all the tommies had come out of the car. One morning they did emerge. Dalton lifted the blind, the tommies were surrounded and their vehicle commandeered. Emmet Dalton and Joe Leonard, dressed as British officers, climbed in, Dalton carrying an official-looking letter marked OHMS. At the jail gate Dalton, who had been an officer in the British Army during the war, gave the correct salutes, waved his OHMS envelope and in imperious fashion demanded entry on important business. Once inside, the driver, Pat McCrea, managed to turn the armoured car in the narrow passageway so that it blocked both inner gates, while Dalton and Leonard headed for the Governor's office, where it was hoped MacEoin would be waiting. But on this particular morning the changing of the guard was late and he was informed that he would have to wait.

Dalton's cover story, and the written authorisation in the letter, was that he had been sent by the Castle to collect MacEoin. He was arguing with a suspicious Governor and staff that he should be allowed to proceed to his cell with the Chief Warder to collect the prisoner when, outside, a sentry opened fire.

The rescue team kept their heads. One, Tom Keogh, shot the sentry, and then coolly held up an approaching party of soldiers as a machine-gun mounted high up in the gate turret rained bullets down on the armoured car. Leonard and Dalton tied up the Governor and his staff with their own ties. The raiders remounted the armoured car despite the machine-gun fire and made off safely through an approaching party of soldiers who were misled by the sight of the officers' uniforms.

Collins' next attempt was still-born. He planned to get a revolver in to MacEoin so that during his court martial he could hold up the officers of the court and throw himself out of a window of City Hall, beside the Castle, where the court martial was to be held. Michael Noyek, MacEoin's solicitor, was perfectly willing to do the smuggling, and MacEoin was prepared to try for the window, though the fall would very likely have killed him, but Collins abandoned the idea when Noyek pointed out that all the court martial officers were armed. He finally got MacEoin out, as we shall see, by refusing to stop the war until the British released him.

MacEoin was luckier than one of Kevin Barry's prison friends, a Volunteer called Frank Flood who, a few months after Barry was executed (on 14 March 1921) told a nun, Mother Patricia Dodd, of Barry's last wish for him. 'He wanted me to have a long and prosperous life – here I am again.'[59] 'Here' was a condemned cell. Flood was one of a number of Volunteers sentenced to death by court martial for the 'Bloody Sunday' killings. As so often happens in such cases none of the accused was in any way involved. The one man who had taken part in the shootings, Frank Teeling, escaped with Ernie O'Malley and Simon Donnelly from Kilmainham. Collins, who had planned the escape, wanted a Volunteer called Paddy Moran to accompany them, but knowing he was innocent and not wanting to make trouble for those who had given evidence on his behalf, Moran refused to breakout, believing he was sure to be acquitted. The court martial decided otherwise however. On the eve of his execution he invited Mother Dodd to come and stay with him and his comrades in heaven in which, like his comrades, he felt assured of the 'highest, highest place', as the nun described it. The one note of regret she seems to have encountered was struck by Volunteer Bernard Ryan who spoke of his young wife whom he had 'loved for years and only married now when he could keep her'. By contrast another Volunteer, Tommy Whelan, informed her: 'I have just told my mother that just as a priest starts a new life at ordination so on Monday I will start a new life that will last for ever.'

But apart from eliciting a sigh from the tender-hearted over the Karma of the British and Irish peoples, which so often apparently dooms them to torture each other, the manner in which these men met their deaths had a most important historical consequence, at the critical time when the Anglo-Irish Treaty was hanging in the balance.

Paddy Daly was appointed as OC of the Squad and the corps was expanded. So did its work, as the British began sending in fresh undercover agents to replace the shattered Cairo Gang. A member of the Squad also disposed of one of their existing agents, Shankers Ryan, the man who betrayed McKee and Clancy to Hardy's clutches. He was shot not long after their deaths as he sat drinking close to the place they were captured in Gloucester St.

After the Cairo Gang one of the Squad's principal enemies was the Igoe Gang, an effort to meet like with like run by a Head Constable from Mayo. Igoe, who would have made an ideal member of the Squad himself, was held to be responsible for several deaths. He and his men, RIC personnel drawn from different parts of the country, patrolled the streets of Dublin in plain clothes, looking for wanted men. Igoe developed a simple but very effective trick of doubling back on his tracks so that scouts who had gone ahead to alert the Squad to ambush him almost invariably lost him. On one such occasion the Squad, including members of GHQ, were stationed in St Stephen's Green waiting for Igoe to come up Grafton St when he and his men suddenly wheeled into Dame St. Here they chanced on two Volunteers, Charlie Dalton and Sweeney Newell of Galway, neither of whom was carrying a gun. Dalton they let go, not knowing of his role in Bloody Sunday or the fact that, while still only seventeen, he had taken on an entire patrol of rifle-carrying British tommies single-handed and put them to flight, wounding two of them with his revolver. Newell, however, they held on to for a time, releasing him unharmed from the Bridewell later that afternoon. But as he walked along the unusually deserted streets congratulating himself on his luck he was 'fired on from all sides'.[60] He was taken to hospital, where he hung between life and death for a long time, eventually recovering, though lame in one leg, which, it was subsequently discovered, had had a large safety pin sewn into it.

On one occasion the Squad was on the point of opening up on Igoe and his men in Thomas St when a patrol of soldiers appeared up a side street behind the Squad and advanced towards them in extended order. Vinnie Byrne, a typical Dubliner, though the occasion called for an appropriate song and began to sing, 'Do I want to see my mammy anymore? Do I? Yes I do.' The Squad leader agreed that if fighting started the chances of any of his men seeing their 'mammies' again were slim and the .45s remained undrawn. The only time that the Squad and Igoe's men met face to face the Squad got the better of the encounter, which took place in Parliament St, 'where a running fight took place in which three of the gang were shot, the rest running away. For some reason or another, after this incident at Parliament St, we saw less of Igoe's gang on the streets', Thornton writes.

But the lack of visibility does not appear to have indicated a lack of activity on Igoe's part. When he appeared before a Whitehall tribunal seeking compensation for his services in Ireland the tribunal gave

. . . considerable attention to Head Constable Igoe's case. Col. Winter gave evidence on Igoe's behalf and emphasised the H/C's loyalty and devotion to duty and his quite exceptional danger which may involve him in frequent removals from one part of the globe to another. The tribunal also saw Igoe himself: he created a favourable impression. One feature of hardship is that Igoe will never be able to return to a 43-acre farm in Ireland to which he had hoped to retire when he left the RIC. Col. Winter considers £1500 the least that Igoe deserves. He suggests annuity and lump sum.[61]

The most spectacular, though less sanguinary, aborted operation of the whole period involved Lloyd George personally. The Auxiliaries and Tans responded to the 'littlers' campaign of bombing their lorries by having posts erected in the vehicles to which they tied captured Sinn Fein TDs (*Teachtarai Dail*, or Dail Deputies). 'Bomb us now,' they called cheerily as they careered about with the terrified hostages aboard. By way of retaliation Collins decided for once to fall in with Brugha's oft-expressed wish to carry the war to England. While Lloyd George, Hamar Greenwood, Bonar Law, Balfour and the rest of them were debating in the House of Commons whether or not to introduce martial law to Ireland in the wake of Bloody Sunday, Collins was planning to kidnap and hold twelve members of the Government including, if possible, some of the men mentioned above, as hostages against the hostage-taking in Ireland. Three top men were sent to London early in 1921 to liaise with Sam Maguire and Reggie Dunne: George Fitzgerald, Sean Flood and Frank Thornton.

Thornton describes the job as being 'colossal'. The movement of every member of the Government had to be checked so as to be able to say with certainty who did what at regular time each night. This process threw up 'some very interesting sidelights on the private lives of members of the British Government'. It also provided the names of not twelve, but twenty-five MPs 'who did a regular thing on the same night every week'. Each of the twenty-five was then pointed out to IRA men in London so that they would know whom to swoop on when the time came. Everything was in readiness – men, transport and intelligence – when for some reason the practice of hostage-carrying ceased in Ireland and the London kidnappings were called off.

During the planning stage Thornton and Flood were involved in an episode which shows what notions of security were in those days. They were going to Acton to check up on some of their arrangements and entered the Westminster tube station to find the lift gates just closing. Flood challenged Thornton to race him to the platform and the pair set off at top speed, Flood in front. Then:

around the second-last bend I heard a terrific crash and on coming round the corner I fell over two men on the ground, one of whom was Sean Flood. We picked ourselves up and both assisted to his feet the man whom Sean Flood had knocked down. To our amazement two other men who were with him ordered us to put our hands up.

We more or less ignored them and started to brush down the man and apologise to him when to our amazement we discovered that the man we had knocked down was Lloyd George, Prime Minister of England.

Lloyd George told the guards to put their guns away which they were loath to do, pointing out that he had obviously been felled by Irishmen. Lloyd George replied, 'Well, Irishmen or no Irishmen, if they were out to shoot me I was shot long ago.' Profuse in their apologies, Thornton and Flood took a tube in the opposite direction to Acton and spent the next few hours looking over their shoulders to check that they really were not being followed.

Another slaughter was avoided on the eve of the truce. Collins had made preparations which would have put Bloody Sunday in the shade. This time he had the names and addresses of some sixty fresh agents whom the British had been pouring into Dublin in increasing desperation and, in addition, there were plans to wipe out the Kidd's Back confraternity and the groups which habitually patrolled Grafton St. Throughout Dublin, groups of Black and Tans and Auxiliaries had all been targeted for being mown down when, half an hour before the operation was due to begin, it was called off. Lloyd George had sent word that he wanted peace.

7

Peace Comes Dropping Slow

'At 8.00 pm we held up four soldiers and searched them,
but found no arms. We took them to a field in our area
where they were executed before 9.00 pm.'

Report of OC, H Co., Cork No. 1 Brigade,
on eve of Truce, 10 July 1921.

Peace moves continued intermittently throughout 1921 until a truce was arranged in July. Many of the initiatives were either English or English-inspired. Art O'Brien's Irish Self-Determination League pricked some consciences. Others were stirred by the activities of Lord Henry Cavendish-Bentinck's 'Peace with Ireland Council' formed amongst English Catholics. And writers of the stature of Belloc, Chesterton and Shaw added their voices to the chorus of protest raised by some influential newspapers, including *The Times*, but most frequently by the *Manchester Guardian* and the *Daily Herald*, the organ of the Labour Party. The Labour Party-sponsored British Labour Commission presented a report on Irish conditions to a Conference at Caxton Hall on 29 December which said that the Auxiliaries and Black and Tans were 'compelling the Irish people – men women and children – to live in an atmosphere of sheer terrorism'. The Conference called for negotiations, echoing a previous resolution passed by the Labour Party on 11 November, and endorsed by the Irish Labour Congress on 16 November. Independent Liberals, including Asquith, also added their voices to the chorus expressing disquiet about the trend of British policy in Ireland.

None of these public initiatives of themselves bore any fruit, though they helped to set the scene for a private attempt that stimulated further movement. Brigadier General Cockerill MP drew up a memorandum for Lloyd George suggesting that the Irish problem

could be solved only by a Conference of fully accredited plenipotentiaries, representing Ireland and Great Britain, equal in number, and untrammelled by restrictive instructions and empowered by means of negotiation to make the best peace possible. . . . Pending the negotiation there should be a truce and amnesty. Once the provisions of the new Constitution were agreed, they should be submitted for final acceptance or rejection, but no amendment, to the parliaments of the contracting peoples.[1]

The Brigadier also sent a letter to *The Times* outlining these proposals on the day on which he sent his memo to Lloyd George. His letter appeared on 8 October 1920 and aroused considerable interest. Publicly, Arthur Griffith welcomed the idea of direct negotiations with no preconditions. Privately, a contact of Griffith's, Patrick Moylette, a London-based Irish businessman, got in touch with Cockerill on 21 October to tell Lloyd George that 'he could have peace with Sinn Fein, whenever he wished', on the lines of Cockerill's letter. Cockerill made a note of the substance of his message:

. . . accommodation could be had on the various contentious points. A new Constitution could be agreed between the parties which would be acceptable in Ireland with peril neither to the authority of the Crown nor the security of the British Isles nor the liberties of Ulster. The word Republic should be interpreted with understanding. What other word could be used to express the idea of a revolt from the existing form of Constitution. Ireland had always been a kingdom – they had not looked elsewhere for a king and had never uttered a word of disloyalty to the crown. If Ulster would join with them in a spirit of conciliation to seek a settlement by consent there was practically no limit to the concessions they would be prepared to make . . . As regards the question of the Army and Navy, Sinn Fein had no ambitions in those directions. Ireland could not afford such luxuries.[2]

Cockerill duly passed all this on to Lloyd George with an addition which sounds more as though it came from Moylette than either Griffith or Collins. 'He agreed with me that Ireland should retain, as at present, some share of control over the direction of the armed forces of the Crown. Her own safety demanded it.' Moylette may either have been giving his own opinion on military matters or quoting only what he thought was Griffith's view, for certainly Collins would never have given up the chance of setting up the first standing Irish Army. But Moylette was correct in telling Cockerill that he could stress to Lloyd George that the chief merit to Sinn Fein of Cockerill's Conference proposal was 'its spirit. If there is ever to be a true union of the four nations, its terms of peace must be negotiated, not directed'. All this was a far cry from the sort of settlement which the Irish Committee in its deliberations argued about *conferring* on Ireland. The Cockerill parameters were largely those within which the Treaty settlement was finally agreed. But the Cockerill initiative was significant in two other ways. By the introduction of Moylette to the dialogue it opened up the principle of talking to Sinn Fein. This, though subsequently temporarily abandoned in favour of a resumption of the policy of frightfulness, meant that the unthinkable became first thinkable and then ultimately do-able. The second consequence of the Cockerill memorandum lay in the introduction of the Roman Catholic Church to the peace process which, though initially unsuccessful, ultimately resulted in Collins' character being brought to the Pope's attention in a manner which, as we shall see, proved highly advantageous to the Irish at a crucial juncture.

As Lloyd George was well aware, Moylette was by no means a centre-stage figure in Sinn Fein councils. Moreover there was a strong body of opinion in the Cabinet against contact with Sinn Fein. Reacting to Tory hostility to Cope's activities in Dublin, the Irish Committee had decided that 'no person serving in the Irish Government should in any circumstances be permitted to hold communication with Sinn Fein'.[3] Nevertheless, Lloyd George saw Moylette, even on the day after Bloody Sunday, to discuss a letter from Griffith on the 16th, agreeing to a truce 'unhampered by preliminary conditions'. Surprised that Lloyd George did see him, in the circumstances, Moylette's first words to the Prime Minister were, 'Well, I suppose this ends all further hope?' To which Lloyd George replied, 'Not at all, they got what they deserved – beaten by counter-jumpers.'[4] At the time, Lloyd George was also using Alfred Davies MP and John Steele, the London Correspondent of the *Chicago Tribune*, to send signals through to Sinn Fein. Word was sent to Griffith, in the aftermath of Bloody Sunday, not to break off the contacts and to 'keep his nerve'. In the circumstances Griffith might well have felt that Lloyd George was the one with nerve, seeing that it was Lloyd George's men who had locked him up. Nevertheless he sent back word, via Steele, that he would do what he could to reduce the level of violence but that the British would have to taper off the reprisals.[5] Either was easier said than done, but Lloyd George was serious about wanting talks and was genuinely annoyed at Griffith's unauthorised arrest, which he saw as an intrusion of the military arm into the area of political prerogative.[6] He told George Russell (AE)[7] that it would be impossible for him politically to talk to either Collins or Brugha but that he was prepared to negotiate 'anything short of a Republic'. As we shall see, his opportunity to do so arose at a lunch party held in London the next day, 30 November 1920. But before examining the further course of peace negotiations it is time to pick up the threads of the progress of another main player in Anglo–Irish events who has been absent from these pages for some time, but who is shortly to make a significant re-entry, Eamon de Valera.

De Valera's lengthy stay in the US (from June 1919 to December 1920) was a spectacular combination of success and failure. His activities were summed up by the historian Francis M. Carroll as follows:

De Valera spoke before State legislatures, conferred with Governors, was given the freedom of several cities, and received two honorary doctorates . . . always, he addressed large public audiences . . perhaps de Valera's travels throughout America, more than any other event since the 1916 Rising, dramatised for the American people the dimensions of the Irish struggle.[8]

But there were hidden costs to this triumphal progress. De Valera concerned himself with four issues during his protracted stay in America: the raising of money; the securing of recognition of the Irish Republic; the defeat of the League of Nations; and the recognition of himself as the supreme spokesman and arbiter of policy on Ireland by the leaders of the existing Irish-American organisations. He succeeded best in the first objective, and probably deserves to be regarded as one of the first 'junk-bond' salesman. So-called 'bond-certificates' were issued from January 1920, the name being decided on after Franklin D. Roosevelt had been consulted on the law against issuing regular 'bonds' in the name of a Government not recognised by the US. Irish-Americans whom the *Wall Street Journal* (4 February 1920) scornfully described as 'Irish domestic servants, and others of like or lower standards of intelligence',[9] subscribed a total of $5,123,640 to the bond-certificates. De Valera only allowed something over half of this to come to Ireland, the rest remaining in American banks from which source he eventually succeeded in getting control of sufficient funds to found what became his family's newspaper empire, the Irish Press Group. Why he did not send all the money on to the Ministry of Finance in Dublin, or pass it on to the American White Cross, must necessarily remain a matter of conjecture. One would have thought Alan Bell's fate said all that was required about Collins' determination to safeguard loan funds. The British brought Bell, a senior police official, out of retirement to find out how and where Collins was depositing the loan's proceeds. Bell set up a kind of Star Chamber for bank managers in Dublin Castle which seriously threatened the loan until one spring morning in 1920. Collins ordered the Squad to take him off the tram bringing him to work, and to shoot him dead in front of the horrified commuters. Nevertheless Boland wrote to Collins from New York on 22 September 1920:

The Chief . . . is particularly anxious that you at home be satisfied that you can safeguard the money. There is roughly speaking three million dollars available for dispatch to Ireland. . . . will you in your next dispatch assure him that you can safeguard the funds . . .

De Valera's fund-raising attempts in the States were hampered by diversions amongst the Irish-American organisations, both those which he helped to create and those which existed before his arrival. The linked issues of the German Peace Treaty and the League of Nations were of course useful for focusing anti-British, Irish-American sentiments. But these issues were targeted by many other groups in the United States, the Republicans, for example, finding them a handy stick with which to beat the Democrats. And though the Senate defeated the ratification of the German Peace Treaty as early as March 1920 it was July 1921 before a truce obtained in Ireland. Yet in his first public report to the Dail on his return from America, de Valera claimed that Article 10, which was represented as committing the US to defending the territorial status quo of its allies, specifically that of the British in Ireland, had been his prime objective in the US. He allowed speakers to praise him as though he had forced America to adopt the League only on condition that Ireland was a consenting party. He completely failed to secure recognition of the Irish Republic at either the Democratic or Republican Convention, in large part because of his last failure, that of getting himself recognised as the sole leader of the Irish-American opinion. He wrote to one of his rivals:

I am answerable to the Irish people for the proper execution of the trust with which I have been charged. I am definitely responsible to them, and I alone am responsible. It is my obvious duty to select such instruments as may be available for the task set me. It is my duty to superintend every important step in the execution of that task.[10]

His two principal adversaries were Judge Cohalan, the head of the Friends of Irish Freedom, the most important of the open Irish-American organisations, and John Devoy, editor of the *Gaelic American*. Devoy was the man behind such notable episodes in Fenian history as the rescue by the whaler *Catalpa* of Irish prisoners from Western Australia on Easter Monday 1876 and the even more spectacular gesture of defiance in Dublin on Easter Monday of 1916. They were formidable opponents. Cohalan, a judge of the New York Supreme Court was closely associated with Tammany Hall (the notoriously corrupt headquarters of the Democrats in New York) and Devoy was renowned as a 'difficult' man. They came from a background of 'Bossism', the tough, brawling world of Irish-America, formed, in the New World, by deprivation and the antagonism of nativist and Wasp groupings, and in the Old, by attitudes summed up in two sayings that were part joke, part precept: 'If there's a government, I'm against it' and 'Look after your own'. Questions of personality aside, Devoy and Cohalan favoured a policy of working for Irish independence as Americans and through the American system. They had seen how the taint of being pro–German had weakened the Irish-American movement during the war. They wanted no suspicion of un-American activity attaching to their post-war agitations. Collins, who had considerable dealings with Devoy on IRB matters, was under no illusions as to the character of the two men, and was aware of differences of approach within the Irish-American firmament even before de Valera arrived on the scene. But he favoured co-operating rather than feuding with the Irish-American leaders. He wrote to Sean Nunan at a relatively early stage in the personality clash, 6 October 1919:

From the very beginning and indeed prior to anybody going out I knew very well what to expect from the people in command in the U.S.A. However,

the best not the worst must be made of them, and there is little doubt that
eventually things will be all right.

'Eventually', however, things became far from 'all right'. De Valera
said of Cohalan, '. . . big as the country is, it was not big enough to
hold the Judge and myself'.[11]

At an early stage in the De Valera tour one Irish-American leader,
watching the tensions build up, commented that the best thing to do
with de Valera was, 'turn everything over to him. He will make a
failure of it, but a failure is better than a split. And a split is certain
unless De Valera can have his way.'[12] Events certainly bore out the
truth of the statement. The internal power struggle came into the open
during February over an interview De Valera gave to the *Westminster
Gazette*. He likened the position of Cuba *vis-à-vis* America to that of
Ireland in relation to England and suggested that a British version of
the Monroe doctrine would both concede Irish independence and
guarantee British security. As Americans understood the reality of
Cuba's position to be that of a political slum, dominated by the US, de
Valera's analogy was badly received. John Devoy attacked the
interview in the *Gaelic American*, arguing that de Valera was falling
prey to moderation and abandoning the claim for an Irish Republic. In
March de Valera sent MacCartan back to Dublin to put his side of the
case before the Sinn Fein decision-takers. He also wrote to Cohalan
saying that 'to ignore the article in the *Gaelic American* would result in
injury to the cause I have been sent here to promote'.[13] Cohalan
replied telling him that he was not responsible for Devoy's opinions
and pointing out that freedom of opinion was one of America's
'fundamental liberties. We have no law of *lèse-majesté* here.'[14] De
Valera thought it wiser not to reply to Cohalan after that but he sent a
highly charged letter to Griffith, timed to coincide with MacCartan's
lobbying effort on his behalf:

A deadly attempt to ruin our chances for the bonds, and for everything we
came here to accomplish, is being made. If I am asked for the ulterior motives
I can only guess what they are. 1) To drive me home – jealousy, envy,
resentment of a rival – some devilish cause I do not know what prompts. 2)
To compel me to become a rubber stamp for somebody.[15]

In fact the 'purpose' cannot have been too 'deadly'. The bonds raised
some $600,000 in New York, Cohalan and Devoy's power base. De
Valera himself said the dispute was not about fundamentals. 'The
trouble is purely one of personalities. I cannot feel confidence enough
in a certain man to let him have implicit control of tactics here,
without consultation and agreement with me.' A month later de
Valera also sent Boland home to explain his position. He arrived on 27
May and Collins and he greeted each other as cordially as at any other
time, Collins not suspecting that in America Boland had surrendered

to de Valera's charisma and now gave allegiance to him. In the circumstances, forced to choose between Cohalan and Devoy and their own elected President, both Griffith, who had stood down for him, and Collins, who had arranged for him to get into the States, backed de Valera over the Cuban interview, even though Brugha, Count Plunkett and Countess Markievicz were prepared to repudiate him at that stage. But Griffith and Collins persuaded the others to accede to de Valera's request that Boland should bring back to America a 'declaration of solidarity with de Valera'.

The cost of de Valera's ego became disastrously clear during the Presidential Conventions of the Republican and Democratic parties. De Valera led his own delegation to the Republican Convention in Chicago where the Resolutions Committee turned down by eleven votes to one a 'plank' approval by him calling for recognition of an Irish Republic, adopting one proposed by Cohalan, calling for 'recognition of the principle that the people of Ireland have the right to determine freely, without dictation from outside, their own governmental institutions, and their international relations with other states and peoples'. This resolution was accepted by a majority of seven votes to six. But de Valera said he wanted a Republican plank or nothing. Nothing is what he got. Faced with two delegations and two planks the Resolutions Committee decided to have no plank at all. De Valera felt his pride demanded no other course. He wrote to Griffith saying that he had undermined the Cohalan initiative lest people assume that the judge was 'the power behind our movement – the man to whom they would have to go. Were I to allow myself to appear thus as a puppet, apart from any *personal pride*, the movement would suffer a severe blow.' It seems to have escaped his attention that the movement *had* suffered a severe blow. Undeterred he moved on to the Democratic Convention, held a few weeks later at the end of June in San Francisco. Here he completed a double by failing to get the Democrats to adopt a resolution. The cost of the Convention fiascoes in money terms may be guessed at from the fact that on 29 June 1920 the Dail voted de Valera a 'sum not exceeding $500,000 as he may require in connection with the election campaign for the Presidency of the United States of America', and 'a sum not exceeding $1,000,000 to obtain the recognition of the Irish Republic by the Government of the United States'. None of the million-dollar vote was to be spent 'unless the recognition was assured'. Nevertheless these sums make the figure of $1,000,000 voted to the Ministry of Defence actually to fight the war seem paltry. De Valera's antagonism towards Devoy and Cohalan cost the services of at least two good men. Diarmuid Lynch, the National Secretary of the Friends of Irish Freedom, resigned both his secretaryship and his Dail seat in disgust. He followed James O'Mara who had already given up his work for the National Loan in America through finding it impossible to work with de Valera.

In both these cases Collins sided with de Valera. He wrote to Griffith showing a typical concern for detail: 'I wonder if you have stopped the *Bulletin* going to him [Lynch]. I think this is absolutely essential. It will give them a power out there to use against the President.'[16] O'Mara's defection hit Collins particularly hard. He wrote to Harry Boland grieving both at the loss of one of the best financial brains to come into the Sinn Fein orbit and at such petty feuding when issues of, quite literally, life and death were being fought out all round him. This supportive attitude, which makes a stark contrast to that shown by de Valera, was no isolated matter for Collins.

Though he thought Boland 'mad to put the idea in Sinead's head', Collins saw to it that Sinead de Valera's wish to join her husband in America was granted within a few days because 'she's had a bad time'. The only warning he issued before smuggling her across the Atlantic concerned her habit of praising him: 'Don't take any notice of her, she's so grateful'.[17] Sinead may have been motivated to join her husband by the spate of rumours circulating in Dublin concerning an alleged affair between de Valera and his secretary, Kathleen O'Connell, who was travelling with him in the States. However, to judge from the friendly tone of correspondence between Sinead and Kathleen after Sinead landed in America, she found no evidence of an affair and Kathleen remained de Valera's respected secretary for several decades. But the visit was not a success. Sinead missed her children and did not like either the boredom of hotel life or the razzmatazz of American public life. She returned home in September 1920 after about six weeks, leaving the biographer to speculate whether the attention Collins gave de Valera's family would have been seen by that student of Machiavelli as cause for gratitude, or as a source of suspicion that Collins was attempting to gain some influence with him via his family circle.

In the month of Sinead's arrival in America, August 1920, Devoy invoked Collins' name in his feud with de Valera. Collins had given an interview to the syndicated columnist Carl W. Ackerman in which he had said, 'there will be no compromise and no negotiations with any British Government until Ireland is recognised as an Independent Republic'. Pressed by Ackerman as to whether he would consider accepting Dominion Home Rule as an 'instalment', Collins replied:

I see you think we have only to whittle our demand down to Dominion Home Rule and we shall get it. This talk about Dominion Home Rule is not prompted by England with a view to granting it to us, but merely with a view to getting rid of the Republican movement. England will give us neither as a gift. The same effort that would get us Dominion Home Rule will get us a Republic.[18]

Devoy, anxious to make the comparison between Collins risking his life in Ireland while de Valera toured America in luxury, used this interview in the *Gaelic American* to praise Collins. On one occasion a large picture of Collins appeared on page one captioned 'Ireland's Fighting Chief'; on another he printed an editorial entitled 'Michael Collins speaks for Ireland.'[19] Collins wrote to both Boland and de Valera condemning the publicity.

Collins and Boland used to write to each other using the noms de plume of W. Field (Collins) and J. Woods (Boland). In November Mr Field in Dublin told Mr Woods now back in New York that the Supreme Council would abide by any decisions which Mr Woods took in the dispute.[20] Armed with this carte blanche Boland took the extremely radical step of breaking with the American wing of the IRB a few weeks before Bloody Sunday. He made the break public by writing to the *Gaelic American* and other sections of the Irish-American press, a step Collins was decidedly unhappy with. His conspirator's soul revolted at the thought of a secret society airing its differences with a powerful ally in the press while locked in a vicious war with an even more powerful opponent.[21] Nevertheless, he loyally stood by de Valera, writing to Boland only two days before Bloody Sunday, 'Practically everybody here had accepted in the face of recent developments the inevitability of the steps taken.' His attitude, despite his unhappiness over the publicity, was still what he had written to Devoy two months earlier: 'Every member of the Irish Cabinet is in full accord with President de Valera's policy. When he speaks to America he speaks for us all.'[22]   Collins later apologised to Devoy for taking this position. He sent him a message[23] saying:

Our idea was to have some sort of a world-wide Irish federation, each separate part working through the Government, and in accordance with the laws of the country where it had its being, but all joined by common ties of blood and race. Unfortunately some of those we sent to America did not understand the vital principle of that idea.

De Valera finally decided that the answer to 'the *Gaelic American* difference' was to set up his own Irish-American organisation which he did at a meeting in Washington on 16 November 1920, The American Association for the Recognition of the Irish Republic. He was fully aware that American politicians were not going to concede recognition to an Irish Republic. Indeed he said as much to the Dail on his return: 'If I were President of the United States I could not, and would not, recognise Ireland as a Republic.'[24] But still smarting from having left himself open to a charge of being 'soft' on the Republic, de Valera was determined to stake out the most extreme position possible to safeguard himself from further attack. Then, leaving his newly formed organisation feuding merrily with those led by Cohalan and Devoy, much to the detriment of concentration on the struggle in Ireland, he arranged to have Collins smuggle him home so as to be in on the peace moves then gathering force.

The peace moves owed their origin to the lunch party referred to earlier (page 187). The lunch was given in London on 30 November for the Clare-born Archbishop of Perth, Joseph Clune. It was to afford Lloyd George an opportunity of furthering the peace process but more importantly to lead to a sort of moral turning-point insofar as the Vatican's view of Ireland was concerned. Clune had been Chaplain General to the Australian Army during the war but he was also an uncle of Conor Clune who was done to death in the Castle after Bloody Sunday. The Archbishop had been staying with Bishop Fogarty in Ennis when the Black and Tan reprisal occurred in Lahinch and his account of what transpired so appalled the guests at the lunch that one of them, Joe Devlin, the Nationalist MP, arranged for him to meet Lloyd George, which he did the next day, to give him the details. Lloyd George professed himself shocked at these happenings, denounced all reprisals and asked the Archbishop to act as a mediator if Cabinet sanction could be obtained.

There followed what the Archbishop later described to his secretary, Father John MacMahon,[25] as a 'Gilbertian situation'. Lloyd George informed him the next day that although he had obtained the approval of a majority of his Cabinet, over the strong objections of a minority, the difficulty now arose as to how the Archbishop's safety in Ireland could be guaranteed. Father MacMahon said:

So completely had the Auxiliaries been given a free hand to do what they liked . . . that neither the Government nor the ordinary military command in Ireland could control this irresponsible and undisciplined corps of truculent adventurers. Mr Lloyd George admitted the situation to the Archbishop and quoted the advice received from the official military officials in Dublin that they could not guarantee the safety of Archbishop Clune if it became public that he was going to Ireland to interview the Sinn Fein leaders. Never for a moment would they consent to a safe conduct for the Sinn Fein leaders to meet the Archbishop.

At this stage a further element of farce entered the proceedings. At that stage the worst clerical thorn in the side of the British establishment was Dr Daniel Mannix, the Archbishop of Melbourne, whom the Government had sent a destroyer to intercept on the high seas to prevent him landing in Ireland. He had led the MacSwiney funeral cortege through London and was unrelenting in his denunciation of British policy in Ireland. He too was in London at the time and Clune consulted him about furthering Lloyd George's request. Mannix put him in touch with Art O'Brien, who gave him a letter for Collins and Mannix himself telegraphed Bishop Fogarty in Ennis: 'Archbishop Clune crossing to Dublin tonight. Meet him Gresham Hotel on important business.' That telegram saved Fogarty's life.

Clune stayed as 'Dr Walsh' in the home of Sir John O'Connell, a leading Dublin Catholic lawyer. Mannix's advice to contact Art

O'Brien bore fruit in the form of meetings with Joe O'Reilly which resulted in an appointment to meet Collins on 7 December at the home of Dr Farnan in Merrion Square. Collins had sent O'Reilly cycling the ten miles to hilly Killiney with a letter for Clune. O'Reilly noticed detectives in the area of the house and entered by a back way. He warned Clune about the detectives. 'This upset his Grace a bit,' O'Reilly noted. 'He realised the danger to which he was exposing Michael Collins and he discussed whether it was worth the risk to continue his mission. I remained silent until he made his own decision.' The next day O'Reilly again met Clune in the Gresham, and gave him Dr Farnan's address. O'Reilly warned Clune about being followed and told him not to go near the Castle to try calling the detectives off. The value of Collins' capture to the authorities would outweigh the worth of any promise he might get.

Meanwhile Bishop Fogarty had had cause to be thankful for the Clune mission. When he got Mannix's telegram he decided at first not go to Dublin. He telegraphed Clune accordingly, prepaying the reply. Clune intended to tell him not to worry about coming up but forgot to send the prepaid wire. Getting no reply, Fogarty set off for Dublin, feeling that Clune must have some good reason for contacting him. That night a party of Auxiliaries with blackened faces and drawn revolvers came to his house looking for him. They refused to believe he was not at home and searched thoroughly, even looking under the beds. No damage was caused, other than a bad fright for the servants and the loss of some papers and whiskey.

The attempt on Fogarty's life was one of the reasons the head of the Auxiliaries, Brigadier General Crozier, resigned his command. He later wrote:

At Killaloe I received further evidence the hidden hand was still at work and was told in confidence that instructions had been received to kill the Roman Catholic Bishop of Killaloe, Dr Fogarty, by drowning him in a sack from the bridge over the River Shannon so as to run no further risk of detection by having his body found.[26]

Clune, too, had several near escapes from violence during his visit. On one occasion he was upstairs in Farnham's house talking with Collins when a lorry-load of Auxiliaries drew up outside and there was a knock on the door. It turned out that one of the Auxiliaries had a message from his wife for Farnan, a leading gynaecologist. A second lorry passed by another day as Collins and the Archbishop came down the stairs while Farnan hailed a taxi for Clune from across the road. Collins stepped behind the open hall door, drew his revolver, closed the door and got out the back as the lorry turned. He picked up his bicycle from the tobacconist's in Merrion Road, where he always left it during the negotiations, and cycled away safely, leaving the lorry patrolling up and down outside Farnan's house.

Ironically the least-interrupted negotiations Clune had in Dublin were conducted in the lowering atmosphere of Mountjoy Jail where he handed over Mannix's letter to Griffith. Cope made the necessary arrangements for Fogarty and Clune to see not only Griffith, but also MacNeill and Staines. Griffith was the most enthusiastic of the three for a truce and Cope impressed the Bishops with his enthusiasm for a settlement also. Fogarty subsequently told MacMahon that 'alone among the die-hards in Dublin Castle, he kept Lloyd George's interest in the truce alive'. At his suggestion Clune drew up proposals for a truce and forwarded them to the Castle. The terms were not well received. There were two major sticking points. One was the fact that the IRA proposed holding on to their weapons and the second was immunity for Collins and Mulcahy during the truce. There was a third reason for the military heads not wanting a truce – they thought they had the IRA and Sinn Fein on the run. A party of them crossed from Dun Laoghaire on the mailboat to put this view to Lloyd George. Clune, who was on the same boat, only discovered their mission when Cope materialised on deck and pointing to a group of officers said very dejectedly:

I don't like to see these fellows crossing in such strong numbers. They have convinced themselves that they have the boys in the hills beaten and they want no talk of Truce to interfere with them now. But the Prime Minister may not listen to them. Who knows? I still have hopes of that Truce.

His hopes were not realised. Apart from the Castle contingent, the weight of the Conservative wing of the coalition and the ever-present influence of Sir Henry Wilson, another factor now entered the equation – an apparent willingness on the part of significant sections of Sinn Fein to sue for peace, or as the British saw it, to cave in. A letter from Roger Sweetman, the Sinn Fein Deputy for Wexford North, which appeared in the press on 30 November, proposed a conference of public bodies to formulate truce proposals. Six of the thirty-two members of Galway County Council not in jail or on the run, met on 3 December and discussed, though did not pass, a resolution calling on the Dail to negotiate a truce. A telegram was sent to Lloyd George from Fr. O'Flanagan, the Vice-President of Sinn Fein, who had accompanied the Chief Justice, James O'Connor, on the latest of his peace attempts to London that very week, saying: 'You state you are willing to make peace at once without waiting till Christmas. Ireland is also willing to make peace. What first steps do you propose?'

Collins himself described what happened next:

the intermediary . . . returned to the Prime Minister of England, and the latter had three things in his hand (the letter, resolution and telegram). 'Now Dr Clune,' he said, 'this is the white feather and we are going to make these fellows surrender.' The first time he [Lloyd George] saw Dr Clune he did not know of the letter to the press . . . it was when he went back that he was confronted with these things. He did not want to suggest for one moment that Lloyd George was sincere. Indeed, when Dr Clune came back Lloyd George made the excuse that he could not control his Cabinet . . . but it was wrong to give him the chance to bolster up his actions by the ill-timed actions of persons who ought to have hesitated before they leaped.[27]

One of the statements which surfaced in the press of the time was that if negotiations did take place Collins' own safety was to be guaranteed. Collins issued a statement saying that Fr. O'Flanagan had acted without authority and that so far as he was concerned himself: 'No person in Ireland or anywhere else, had any authority to use my name. My personal safety does not count as a factor in the question of Ireland's rights. I thank no one for refraining from murdering me.'

Another suggestion was that Griffith arranged to be arrested so that he could negotiate more freely and safely. Collins dealt with this in a second statement which the *Independent* was afraid to publish having received a visit from revolver-brandishing Auxiliaries after publishing the previous statement (on 6 December).[28] He asked: 'Does anyone think that Mr Griffith would be so foolish as to negotiate with anybody from behind prison bars, away from his followers and from his movement?' Griffith was neither caving in nor asking for a truce. If one was offered he would not reject it, but he had not initiated the truce suggestions. 'Everyone in Ireland,' Collins wrote, 'has reason to be mistrustful of English politicians of all schools and we have learned to be more distrustful of their promises than their threats.' It was in this statement that he first publicly used the phrase that became his hallmark, 'Let us drop talking and get on with our work.'[29]

Clune told Collins that Lloyd George's main interest seemed to lie in meeting the amazing escapologist 'Mick' as he always referred to him. He took a mischievous delight in the rage of 'the Castle contingent' at their inability to lay hands on Collins when the Archbishop could apparently see him at will. However, behind the Welsh charm and puckishness there lay the steel that had carried Lloyd George through the First World War. He sent Clune back to Dublin on 11 December with a message to say that the Dail would be permitted to meet openly to discuss peace terms but, and it was a very big but, neither Collins nor Mulcahy could attend and arms would have to given up. On hearing the terms Collins wrote to Griffith:

It seems to me that no additional good can come from further continuing these discussions. . . . We have clearly demonstrated our willingness to have peace on honourable terms. Lloyd George insists on capitulation. Between these two there is no mean; and it is only a waste of time continuing.[30]

The pacific Griffith agreed with him. He told Clune that the terms amounted to surrender and that 'there would be no surrender, no matter what frightfulness was used'.[31] The burning of Cork had occurred during the course of the Clune initiative and both Griffith and Collins were concerned that the British were using the talks as a smoke screen behind which they stepped up their campaign. Clune believed that Lloyd George was more circumscribed by Cabinet restraint than did Collins. He wrote to Art O'Brien that this view was 'too credulous'. He said:

My own feeling about Lloyd George is that we should not allow him to disassociate himself from his public actions, as head of his cabinet. Particularly on this side, there is too great a tendency to believe that Lloyd George is wishful for peace, and that it is only his own wild men that prevent him from accomplishing his desires.[32]

Nevertheless he was anxious to go as far as possible along the road to peace. After Clune had had further talks with Lloyd George and the Castle administration he obtained from Griffith a draft peace formula which the Archbishop and he went over at a lengthy meeting on 18 December before Clune returned to London to see Lloyd George for the last time. The final draft of the Irish proposals was:

The British Government undertakes that during the truce, no raids, arrests, pursuits, burnings, lootings, demolitions, courts martial or other acts of violence will be carried out by its forces, and there will be no enforcement of the Martial Law Proclamations. We on our side undertake to use all possible means to ensure that no acts whatever of violence will occur on our side during the period of the truce. The British Government on their part and we on ours, will use our best efforts to bring about the conditions above mentioned, with the object of creating an atmosphere favourable to the meeting together of the representatives of the Irish people with a view to the bringing about of a permanent peace.

The proposal foundered, not on its prose, but on something it did not contain, the question of the surrender of arms. At their final meeting, in Downing St, on 21 December, Lloyd George upheld the military viewpoint that arms must be handed in. He told Clune that the military were confident of mopping up the IRA, 'some hundreds of men on the hills', and saw no reason for giving Sinn Fein a new lease of life by declaring a truce during which they would be allowed to hold on to their weapons.

Lloyd George met his Cabinet on Christmas Eve[33] and reported on Clune's mission. He told them that, after the Archbishop had interviewed various leaders, 'he found Michael Collins the only one with whom effective business could be done'. Collins, he reported, wanted peace but the stumbling block on his part was the handing in of arms and, on theirs, the fact that Collins was the organiser of murder. Surprisingly, the Cabinet was also informed that arms were being surrendered 'in some quantities'. The report stiffened the Cabinet's resolve to 'do nothing to check the surrender of arms' and it was decided to hold a major review of the Irish situation, with all the Irish Executive present, as soon as possible after Christmas. Clune was asked to stay in London for the outcome of the meeting.

The meeting,[34] which went on over two days (29 and 30 December), was more instructive of how the military perceived the situation in Ireland, and filtered information accordingly, than for an insight into the state of Irish public opinion. General Tudor admitted that drink was a problem with the Auxiliary Divisions but said that 'anyone who has seen the Black and Tans on parade must admit that their discipline was very fine'. When Lloyd George brought up the bad effect on public opinion of steps such as the arrest of Arthur Griffith after Bloody Sunday the Cabinet Record notes that: 'Mr Churchill interposed that it was fair to remember that no reprisals had taken place after the Dublin murders.' Nobody mentioned Croke Park, though it was stated that publication of the report into the burning of Cork 'would be disastrous for the Government's whole policy in Ireland'. The consensus amongst generals Boyd, Macready, Strickland and Tudor was that another four months at the present rate of favourable progress would bring victory but that a truce would give Sinn Fein a chance to re-group, particularly in the intelligence field. Sir Henry Wilson, present in his capacity as CIGS, drew the meeting's attention to 'the decent peasant', who was nearly on the Government's side but who would go over to Sinn Fein if a truce were declared. He felt that if military law were applied to the whole of Ireland, in six months perhaps 90 per cent of the people would be on the side of the Government. Macready thought that if an election were held in the forthcoming three to four months, under the terms of the Government of Ireland Act, 'there would be a general boycott, at the point of a pistol, on the word of Michael Collins'. To which Lloyd George replied feelingly that if Michael Collins could stop three million people using their vote, it did not say much for the success of the policy they were pursuing. But in the circumstances it was not surprising that Clune was not asked to continue his efforts and the Cabinet decided on the military option. However there was one point at which the Archbishop's influence was to have an effect not guessed at by the men around the table.

Sir John Anderson said everything would depend on 'the line it was possible to get the Church to take.' The question of the Church's influence was a not unfamiliar theme in Cabinet. Various efforts had been made either to enlist the aid of the Vatican directly in support of the British position, or to silence critical clerics, most noticeably Mannix. The Cabinet's main preoccupation was to secure from the Pope a condemnation of the Irish insurgents and Curzon exerted considerable pressure on the British representative in Rome, Count de Salis, to secure this. The Count enlisted the support of two influential cardinals for the British initiative, Merry Del Val, Secretary to the Congregation of the Holy Office and Gasquet, Archivist to the Holy Roman Church. As a result a Papal condemnation was prepared. Not knowing this, Clune summed up the position, in a letter to Fogarty, on New Year's Day 1921, describing a visit to him by Sir Philip Kerr, Lloyd George's Private Secretary. He told Fogarty that the Government:

. . . had come to the conclusion that it was better to see the thing through as was done in the American and South African wars unless meanwhile the Sinn Feiners surrender their arms and publicly announce the abandonment of violent measures; that the Government felt sanguine that the new Home Rule Bill when studied and understood would be worked . . . He then added a few gracious compliments from the Prime Minister. My first comment was that I felt sure that the Holy Ghost had nothing to do with such a decision which sent him off exploding with laughter. What is the source of this strange optimism about all classes working the Home Rule Bill in harmony within a few months I can't make out.

The Government's determination to carry on the policy of frightfulness to the bitter end may be bluff. I think it is not; and hence I believe that the position needs further reconsideration in the light of this considered declaration of policy on their part. The secretary incidentally mentioned that from my conversations the Prime Minister had a higher idea of the gunmen . . . through the working of the Home Rule Act practically every English official could be sent out of Ireland in a few months, etc, etc . . . ought our boys to allow themselves to be butchered to make a Saxon holiday? Ought they not rely on passive resistance?

The Archbishop had indeed given high praise to Sinn Fein in Lloyd George's presence, a fact which led to world headlines. Sean T. O'Kelly, the Dail's Representative in Paris, gave a lunch for Clune as he passed through en route for the Vatican. At this Clune told journalists that he 'admired the courage' of the Sinn Feiners. He then went on:

During the negotiations, when my taxi would stop before the house where I was to meet one of the leaders I was exposing him to certain death. I never saw one of them tremble. When Mr Lloyd George, the Prime Minister, in my presence spoke of them as 'assassins' I corrected him, saying; 'No sir, not assassins but the cream of their race.'

The phrase 'the cream of their race', went round the globe and Clune went on to Rome. He was deeply torn by the calls of race and his outrage as a churchman at the taking of human life. Like Fogarty, he had been chilled by the psychological impact of Mountjoy 'where so many of our brave boys were held'. He had been reassured in meeting Collins, Mulcahy, O'Higgins, Fitzgerald and the others, as to the calibre of those leading the Irish struggle. However this was not the view of certain other members of the Irish Church. Such a one was Dr Cohalan, the Bishop of Cork, who pronounced a decree of excommunication on 12 December 1920. In fact the Bishop was extremely even-handed and judicious in his condemnation of violence. His quite lengthy exposition of the circumstances leading up to his decree contained the following:

We are face to face with the crimes of individuals and with Government crimes. The crimes of the Government in Ireland are on a different plane and are infinitely greater than the crimes of a private military organisation, because it is the duty of the Government, through its servants, to protect the lives and property of the citizens, especially the innocent, unoffending citizens.

But it was the statement's concluding paragraph which the British fastened on and which, *inter alia*, has made the Bishop's name execrated by the IRA ever since. It said:

Besides the sinfulness of the acts from their opposition to the law of God, anyone, be he a subject of this diocese or an extern, who, within the diocese of Cork, shall organise or take part in ambushes or kidnappings, or shall otherwise be guilty of murder or attempted murder, shall incur by the very fact the censure of excommunication.

Clune arrived in Rome in the wake of the publicity over this decree and a growing belief, fostered by the British, that some priests were preaching that it was not a sin to shoot policemen. In fact the British were not entirely wide of the mark as the following letter to Florrie O'Donoghue, on Cohalan's edict, from the Chaplain to the Brigade shows:

An excommunication . . . may be inflicted only for the external and grievous (or mortal) violation of the law (Canon 2242) . . . kidnapping, ambushing and killing obviously would be grave sins or violation of the law. And if these acts were being performed by the I. V. as private persons (whether physical or moral) they would fall under the Excommunication.

But they are doing them by and with the authority of the State – the Republic of Ireland. And the State has the right and duty to defend the lives and property of citizens and to punish even with death those who are aiming at the destruction of the lives or property of the citizens or itself. It has moreover a right and duty to protect by every means in its power the liberty of the State and its citizens against the Army of Occupation of a Foreign Power unjustly present in the country.

Hence these acts performed by the I. V. the Army of the Republic are not only not sinful but are good and meritorious. And therefore the Ex-communication does not affect us. There is no need to worry about it. Let the boys keep going to Mass and Confession and Communion as usual. There is no necessity for telling a priest in Confession that you went to Mass on

Sunday so there is no necessity to tell him one is in the I.R.A. or that one took part in an ambush or killing etc.

My love and blessing to all the Brigade staff. God keep and protect you all.
DOC
Bde Chapn.

For their part some Protestant clergymen were equally staunch in their support of the forces of the Crown. I have a copy of a list of informants in Ireland drawn up by Captain Hall[35] which includes the names of several Protestant clergymen. *Guns in Ulster*, a sympathetic study of the B-Specials by Wallace Clarke, singles out a number of clergymen for special praise because of their work in organising and openly patrolling with the Specials. But such pre-ecumenical considerations were absent from the minds of the Irishmen as they prepared to meet the Pope. They were unaware that since the previous summer, when Balfour had visited Rome, British pressure for a Vatican condemnation of IRA violence had been growing.

The day after the Cabinet chose the hard-line option, an instruction to de Salis to make 'more pressing and insistent representations' was sent in which he was to be mindful of the recent example of Dr Cohalan who had called for excommunication.[36] Sir John Anderson's words had borne fruit. When Clune met Pope Benedict he discovered that a Papal condemnation of all violence in Ireland had been drawn up in terms that would fall most heavily upon Sinn Fein. The Pope specifically mentioned the rumour about priests preaching it no sin to shoot policemen. His interpreter was Father Patrick Murray, the Superior General of the Redemptorists, the order to which Clune had belonged before becoming an Archbishop. A man used to the emollient language of Vatican diplomacy, Murray, as he afterwards told MacMahon, was amazed by the plain-spoken way Clune reacted to this news:

He told the Holy Father amongst other things that such a pronouncement would be a disaster for the Church, not only in Ireland, but in every country where there were descendants of the Irish race. In fact his language was so strong that when I, as his interpreter, translated it into Italian, I had to excuse him for speaking so strongly as the matter was so grave. His reasons seemed to make a great impression on his Holiness.[37]

So great an impression in fact that the condemnation was shelved. Mrs Gavan Duffy, wife of the Sinn Fein representative in Rome, sent Art O'Brien an account of what happened. When she arrived to see the Archbishop off he 'had very grave news':

He then told me that a condemnation had been drawn up and that his audience alone had postponed its publication. One justification was the lie about priests preaching that it is not a sin to kill policemen and I should imagine that Cohalan of Cork was another . . . From many different sources

I have heard that the Pope was immensely impressed by Dr Clune, the murder of his young nephew, his admiration for our leaders, in particular Mick Collins, his testimony of the religious faith of the Republicans – all made a very deep impression on Benedict . . . Roger's supposed diary [Casement's diary, depicting homosexual activity] has been sent over here to show the Vatican the type of leader we follow.[38]

When Collins passed this dispatch on to de Valera, who by this stage had arrived back in Dublin, he made one significant omission, his own name, and made a joke about being all right now in the care of the Holy Father. He had already learned in the few weeks since de Valera's return that praise of 'The Big Fellow' was not welcome to 'The Long Fellow'. Clune's opposition to the threatened condemnation was strongly supported. The secretary of the Irish Hierarchy, Dr O'Doherty, issued a very broad hint to the Vatican 'that Ireland will not stand another Parnell pronouncement'[39], that is, no Papal Rescript and, amongst other protests, the American Archbishop Hayes warned that taking sides against 'our people would be like a spark applied to the American powder magazine'.[40] Accordingly, when Mannix also saw the Pope a month later, the Pope, far from dressing him down, took his advice that he should make a public contribution to the White Cross, an American charitable relief organisation active in Ireland, accompanied by a letter for publication.

The White Cross organisation was a highly reputable body which disbursed some five million dollars collected by the American Committee for Relief in Ireland in the spring and summer of 1921, far more than de Valera's efforts at the time resulted in. It was strictly non-partisan. Collins personally ensured that the White Cross' work remained aloof from politics, issuing strict orders that the IRA should not benefit from White Cross funds.[41] The Relief Committee acquired such stature in the US that, despite hostile reports from the pro-British Consul in Dublin, Dumont, Warren Harding wrote approvingly to its Chairman, Judge Morgan J. O'Brien: 'It was powerful boost that lent a degree of credibility and official approval which the Irish movement had never enjoyed in the United States.[42] It was also to have some significant implications for Anglo–American relations.[43] Collins was later to call on the assistance of the White Cross in drawing up Ireland's first Constitution. The Pope went on to ask Mannix to submit a draft of the type of letter he felt should be issued. Having passed through many hands it duly appeared on 22 May with the basic Mannix hand still discernible:

We are most especially concerned about the condition of Ireland. Unflinching even to the shedding of blood in her devotion to the ancient Faith and in her reverence for the Holy See she is subjected today to the indignity of devastation and slaughter . . . neutrality . . . by no means prevents us from wishing . . . that a lasting peace . . . may take the place of this terrible enmity

. . . we do not perceive how this bitter strife can profit either of the parties, when property and homes are being ruthlessly and disgracefully laid waste, when villages and farmsteads are being set aflame, when neither sacred places nor sacred persons are spared, when on both sides a war resulting in the deaths of unarmed people, even of women and children, is carried on. We exhort English as well as Irish to calmly consider . . . some means of mutual agreement.

This missive, the first time the Pope had spoken on the Irish question, was highly unwelcome to the British. Curzon thought it 'just the sort of casuistic performance that might have been expected from the Vatican'. Collins was correspondingly delighted. Efforts to get a similar pronouncement from the Irish hierarchy had proved fruitless.[44] He immediately wrote to de Valera:

I was specially informed that it would be a good thing for you to write to His Holiness acknowledging his beneficent remarks about Ireland thanking Him for His subscription. I know this will strike yourself, but it's a message that came directly from Dr Mannix immediately he had finished his audience with His Holiness. It might be as well if our representative in Rome specially delivered this communication of yours.

The British delivered a 'communication' of their own to the Vatican making a vigorous protest at the Pope's not only failing to condemn the IRA but actually making a partisan statement which 'put HMG and the Irish murder gang on a footing of equality'. The Vatican riposted by offering the services of Cardinal Gaspari, the Secretary of State, as a mediator. But the British, although uneasily aware that the military men's 'four months' was up with no end in sight to the policy of 'frightfulness' which had disturbed Benedict, had had enough of clerical mediators for the time being. The next time a priest was called upon it was to introduce an Englishman to de Valera.

Collins had had de Valera met by Tom Cullen and Batt O'Connor[45] when his ferry docked at the Customs House Dock. The meeting set the tone for much of what happened subsequently. De Valera asked Cullen how things were going. 'Great,' replied Cullen with more enthusiasm than caution, 'the Big Fellow is leading us and everything is going marvellous'. De Valera reacted by slapping his hand on the guard rail and exclaiming, 'Big Fellow! We'll see who's the Big Fellow.'[46] Cullen took him to Dr Farnan's house, where Brugha was his first visitor. Collins did not meet him until 5 am the next morning, Christmas Eve 1920, the day that nearly ended so disastrously for him in the Gresham. It is not being unduly fanciful to see a certain symbolism in that sequence of visits, for de Valera's first major initiative on returning to Ireland was to try to get Collins out of the country, to America. He sent Collins a lengthy letter on 18 January outlining a variety of tasks which he wanted Collins to carry out in the US. One of these was to 'see to the building up of a system of communications through which despatches and material can be sent with increased safety at regular intervals between the two countries'. As de Valera had first-hand experience of the efficiency of Collins' existing system of communication, having been safely smuggled back and forth across the Atlantic himself, this desideratum seems a trifle odd. But no more so than point 'F' which was:

to examine the possibilities of the US from the point of view of supplying material to the Minister of Defence. To make a report and recommendations to the Minister on this head and as far as possible to execute any commissions which that Minister may give in relation to his own Department.

In other words to take orders from Brugha.

Not surprisingly, Collins was both angered and hurt at de Valera's suggestion. 'The long whore won't get rid of me that easily', was his original reaction according to Frank O'Connor,[47] but both Broy and Oscar Traynor told O'Malley that he was deeply wounded by the attempt. Broy described him as being practically in tears and Traynor thought the idea disastrous. 'I know it's all bullsology,' Collins told him, 'but if I'm ordered I'll have to go.' No order came. De Valera found that his proposal met with a hostile reaction from everyone apart from Brugha and the Minister for Home Affairs, Stack. Collins had come to symbolise the entire struggle to the fighting men, including the British fighting men. The British made such an ogre figure out of him that he came to have a correspondingly heroic stature in the minds of the Volunteers. Collins' larger-than-life personality magnified his deeds so that they outshone everyone else's. De Valera made it abundantly clear however that he wasn't going to let Collins outshine him. Even though Collins had been Acting President while he was in America, on his return he appointed Stack as his President-designate.[48] But de Valera was not only virtually demoting Collins, he was doing so for a man of far lesser capacity. Stack was viewed as a 'dud', a by-word for inefficiency in the underground ministry.[49] His want of ability sometimes jeopardised the lives of Volunteers.[50] By not having a separate police force to call on the active Volunteers in the flying columns were often put at risk through trying to fit in police duties, such as supervising fairs, or guarding courts when they should have been lying low between staging raids and ambushes. Stack's proposal to meet this difficulty was that 'Collins' intelligence agents should be used to distribute circulars about district courts'.[51]

In addition to these drawbacks Stack apparently felt that he suffered in GHQ's eyes for the sins of a close friend of his, another prominent Kerry IRA man, Paddy Cahill, the Commander of the Kerry No. 1 Brigade. Because Cahill tended to concentrate his efforts on his own area, the Tralee, Castlegregory district, Mulcahy made a memorably scathing comment on his conduct of the war: 'Paddy took his column up Sliabh Mis and stayed there.'[52] De Valera's nomination of Stack as President-designate thus seems to have been a calculated rebuff for Collins.

De Valera arranged with Collins to preside over his first meeting of the Dail on 21 January 1921. But Brugha argued that it might result in everyone being captured and, despite Collins' feelings to the contrary, the meeting was deferred for four days. When it was held, differences of approach on the military front immediately surfaced between Collins and de Valera. De Valera proposed a formula which, if accepted, would have contained two conflicting proposals: that they should have no public change, continue as they had been and try to keep their people together, and that they should try to ease off as far as possible, consistent with showing the country that they were in the same position as before.

Collins took issue with the 'ease off' approach which to him smacked too much of the sort of policy which was also advocated at the same meeting by Roger Sweetman. He said:

the enemy were repeating the very same things they had practised in Ireland in other days. It was not in the strong places the deepest terror was, but in the weak places. Where the fight was carried on hardest, except in Cork, these were the safest areas . . . it would be better work to give the Volunteers the necessary moral support than to be finding fault with the men carrying on fighting against odds never before known.[53]

Collins' force and eloquence carried the day but de Valera wanted to exert his authority, to prove that he was back in charge. He continued to develop his theories of a different form of warfare, one fought with an eye to public relations. He felt it would be better to change from hit and run guerrilla tactics to having a series of battles with the British. The one operation of this nature in which de Valera did get his way was, both a publicity success and a military débâcle, the burning of the Custom House on 25 May 1921. Urban guerrillas used to blazing off six shots (at best) at an enemy before disappearing into a crowd could not easily be metamorphosed into a standing army. The account given by Joe McGuinness of the ASU (see page 209), a survivor of the Custom House attack, makes this abundantly clear. That morning he and his comrades were told:

the 2nd Battalion under Tom Ennis would enter the building and destroy it by fire . . . the ASU would act as a covering party on the outside, in conjunction with the Squad . . . We were further instructed that we were not to fire on any British lorries unless they fired on us first. We were given a revolver, four or five rounds of ammunition each.

What McGuinness did not know as he was being briefed was that

Michael Collins was deeply unhappy about the 'static warfare' operation. 'It remained a Dublin Brigade Affair and "Collins' outfit" kept out of it, though the Squad and the Active Service Unit were reluctantly allowed to lend a hand *outside* the building.'[54] However, disapproving or not, Collins was not a man to let his men go into battle unremarked. McGuinness notes: 'As we were about to leave our mobilisation place at Strand St, Michael Collins came to the doorway on a bicycle and wished us luck.'

The reasons for Collins' apprehensions can readily be deduced from McGuinness' description of what followed:

We saw the blaze starting . . . at about this time . . . an armoured car crossed O'Connell Bridge . . . it was followed by three or four armoured Lancia cars . . . this party opened machine-gun fire on the windows of Liberty Hall [the Volunteers were still inside] . . . another party of Black and Tans who were stationed in a hotel on the quays, came towards the Customs House at the double . . . we opened fire on them . . . I threw my hand grenade at a lorry. The Tans opened fire on us . . . other lorries arrived almost immediately . . . when our ammunition was used up we withdrew.

The operation yielded a world-wide propaganda success. Not only was the finest building in Dublin destroyed, local government administration and the collection of income tax were paralysed. However, from the military point of view, it was a disaster. Six Volunteers were killed, twelve wounded and some seventy of the best IRA fighters of the time were captured. The attack also served to erode Collins' power base somewhat because a few days later, ostensibly to make up for the losses, the ASU, Intelligence and the Squad were all amalgamated into the Dublin Brigade, which gave Brugha and de Valera more control over 'Collins' outfit'.[55]

De Valera's theories of warfare were completely inapplicable to the situation. Even the flying columns in the most successful rural districts didn't know what it was to have more than thirty rounds of rifle ammunition per man.[56] One of the outstanding countrymen, Ernie O'Malley, has left a vivid picture of the impression de Valera made with his theories and of the tensions which these unleashed:

de Valera was tall, his lean, stringy build over-emphasised his height . . . He looked worn. He smiled with his eyes. The lines on his face broke as if ice had cracked. His voice rumbled from the depth with harsh, but not a hard dryness . . . there was a sense of sternness about him, dignity, a definite honesty and a friendly way of making one feel at ease . . .

I pointed out posts and barracks, outlined our battalions' areas, gave, as far as I could remember, our armaments and told him the support the people gave us. He had not the human qualities of Collins, 'The Big Fellow'. 'Dev' was more reserved, the scholarly type. He was cold and controlled. Collins might solve a problem boisterously by improvisation, solve it by its own development. The talk lasted for nearly three hours. He shook hands . . .

I sat in a smaller room with Mulcahy and Collins. 'What did you think of the interview?', asked Collins. 'He did not know much about the army in the south,' I said. Both laughed as if amused. Collins mentioned some of the questions the President had asked. They laughed again. I felt uncomfortable. Dev was the President. After all, I thought, how could he be expected to know the military situation thoroughly? Cathal Brugha the Minister for Defence, did not know his senior officers well. He worked as a traveller, whilst his deputy was paid his salary. The desire to work without pay was understandable, but his position as MD needed all his energies. Many members of the GHQ staff did not know the country . . . I resented their jokes at the expense of 'The Long Fellow'.[57]

As 'Big Fellow' and 'Long Fellow' began moving towards their inevitable estrangement, the Ireland de Valera was familiarising himself with was beginning to suffer the results of Lloyd George's choice between two men 'on the spot'. One was James O'Connor, the Chief Justice, who wrote to the Prime Minister saying:

you may compel Ireland to pass under the Caudine Forks, but I put it to you that it is not wise. The people are stubborn – I wish they were sagacious for, if so, they might accept your suggestions of working the Act and asking for extensions – and they are suspicious, for which there is warrant enough in the history of both countries.[58]

There would be further warrant. O'Connor was in fact an extremely well-informed observer whose opinions deserved to be treated with respect.[59] But Lloyd George opted to accept the advice of another correspondent from Ireland, Hamar Greenwood, the Chief Secretary. Greenwood was disturbed by the fact that O'Connor's friend Fr O'Flanagan was trying to get peace talks going. He wrote to Lloyd George:

In my opinion, you ought not to see de Valera . . . I urge you not to be rushed into negotiations that are certain at this stage to be abortive. Leave things to me I am here on the spot . . . the tide has turned against Sinn Fein.[60]

Lloyd George decided to continue on the basis of Greenwood's analysis, part of which was based on the fact that the Chief Secretary thought it a good sign that some twenty Sinn Feiners were then facing death sentences – readers will have gained an insight in Chapter 6 as to what the effects of these were on Sinn Fein support. From the burning of Cork, the British instituted a system of official reprisals. The army began formally to destroy houses in the wake of IRA activities. Seven houses were destroyed in Midleton, County Cork, on 1 January 1921 after three RIC men were killed in an ambush. This policy was rigorously enforced in what was known as the 'Martial Law' area, the province of Munster and Leinster counties of Kilkenny and Wexford. The policy boomeranged badly on the British when the IRA began destroying Loyalist property in retaliation.

In the general escalation of hostilities, a new 'Active Service Unit' (ASU) was formed early in 1921, comprising some fifty members of the Dublin Brigade. Like the Squad these were full-time operatives and were paid between four and five pounds a week. The ASU was the hit-unit of the Brigade in the same way that the Squad carried out the Intelligence Department's 'jobs'. Both the Squad and the ASU were amalgamated shortly before the Truce in July 1921, becoming known as the 'Guard'. When a National Army was formed, the 'Guard' became the 'Dublin Guards', the first regular unit of the Irish Army. The Volunteers began attacking trains and troop lorries in the street. Many civilian casualties were caused this way. One of these casualties was the Moylette/Steele peace initiative. The way of the peacemaker is hard in any land, but particularly so in Ireland. In a memo to de Valera, O'Hegarty described their efforts in disparaging terms: 'The impression I gathered from Moylette was that he was the paw, that Steele was the cat and that Sir Philip Kerr was the monkey. In other words, that Steele is a tool of Lloyd George. I think M. C. has somewhat the same opinion.'[61]

The 'Irish Businessmen's Conciliation Committee', which struggled through the thorns from March to 21 May, had little better luck. The committee was composed of a group of leading Unionist businessmen, including Andrew Jameson, Sir William Goulding, Sir Walter Nugent and a number of other people with a stake in the country, like Major Bryan Cooper.

A more tenacious, more successful entrant in the peace lists was the unlikely figure of Andy Cope, who extended himself so thoroughly on Lloyd George's behalf that Mark Sturgis wrote in his diary: 'GHQ regard Andy as a complete "Shinner" and believe him no more or less than they would believe Michael Collins, so anything he says they regard as ipso facto, something to be resisted and yielded, if at all, only after a struggle.' Where and how Cope met Collins is still a subject of controversy, but it may have a bearing on a curious correspondence that took place between Sir John Anderson and General Macready in March and April of 1920.

One of the legends about Michael Collins is that he had a price of £10,000 on his head. But this does not appear to have been the case. Macready wrote to Anderson on 5 March 1921[62] suggesting that:

rewards should be offered for Michael Collins and certain other people. The following is suggested:

	£
Charles Burgess (otherwise Cathal Brugha)	10,000
Michael Collins	10,000
Richard Mulcahy	10,000
William Cosgrave	3,500

Gerald O'Sullivan	3,500
Austin Stack	3,500
Joseph McDonagh	3,500

De Valera's name does not appear on this list because, realising that he was less of a problem politicking in relative freedom than languishing a martyr in jail, the British had directed that he was not to be arrested on his return from America. Anderson replied on 9 March objecting on three grounds: 1. Rewards do not make a difference. 2. They make heroes. 3. What about state servants? (meaning why should a state servant be paid for turning someone in in the line of duty). He went on to make the following significant observation: 'You may not be aware that it has already been made known quietly in what seemed like likely quarters that liberal reward, though not on such a scale as your letter indicates, would be given for valuable information leading to definite results.'

Seemingly someone failed to bring this reply to the general's attention for Macready tried again on 8 April:

My Dear Jonathan,
You have never replied to the query I put to you some time ago about offering 'head money' for Michael and others. I do not suppose for a moment it will be done, but what about it?

To which Anderson replied:

I put the question immediately to Ministers, but they were not disposed to move for reasons such as I indicated to you in my letter of March 9.

There may have been more reasons than Anderson indicated for not putting a public price on Collins' head. Lloyd George was playing a very deep game at the time trying either to best or cajole Sinn Fein to the conference table in his public 'Hamar-and-olive-branch' stance, but privately Cope was clearly being encouraged to go further than the Tudor Tories and the militarists would have wished. Hypersensitive, highly intelligent, and a workaholic, he had Lloyd George's complete confidence. Everything Cope did was done with official but unacknowledged sanction.[63]

As a result of Cope's activities Collins was forced to confront charges such as 'Collins is a drunkard and spent the time during the truce boozing with Cope.'[64] Sean T. O'Kelly denied making the allegation but admitted that he had 'joined with others' in telling pre-truce Collins–Cope stories, including one in which Collins 'on one occasion carried him to bed'.[65] Angered, Collins replied: 'I don't know who told you that I met Cope before the Truce and I should like to meet the man who says it, or repeats it, and I may say that I consider the man who repeats it just as bad as the man who said it.'[66]

However Mrs Larry Nugent, a prominent Sinn Feiner, met Cope at

Judge O'Connor's and, surprised to find that he seemingly wanted only to meet de Valera, Stack and Brugha asked, 'Do you not want to meet Michael Collins?' According to Mrs Nugent he replied: 'No. I meet Michael every night.'[67] Mrs Nugent later put a date of 3 May on a subsequent meeting with Cope. Even this later date was more than two months before the Truce. From all we know of Collins' life and his method of operation it seems quite possible that he and Cope could have got together. They seem to have been kindred spirits insofar as lack of formality was concerned. A month after the Truce we find Sturgis sniffing into his diary:

I cursed Andy for avoiding the Royal Box at the Horse Show – he goes down the main drain, not only for business, but for pleasure; spends most of his evenings with 'shinners' of various sorts and seems to dislike all other society. They remember, if he seems to forget sometimes, that he is a highly placed British official with much of the dignity of England in his hands and I worry sometimes that his sympathies will encourage them to think they will get through him all they can.[68]

The peace offensive quickened throughout April and May. Collins was interviewed again by Ackerman and again turned down Dominion Home Rule:

When I saw you before I said the same effort which would get us Dominion Home Rule would get us a Republic. I am still of that opinion and have never had so many peace moves as we have had since last autumn. Our Army is becoming stronger every day, its morale is improving and its efficiency is increasing.[69]

The IRA was in fact in very straitened circumstances. However, it was still making such inroads into the military prong of Lloyd George's 'peace-and-war' double approach that he had a Liverpool priest, a Father James Hughes, contacted in a further peace initiative which had the result of putting Lord Derby in touch with de Valera on 21 April in Dublin. Though these talks yielded nothing of substance they had the effect of encouraging Lloyd George in two other initiatives. In one he gave an interview to New York's *Herald Tribune* on 11 May 1921 in which he said: 'I will meet Mr de Valera or any of the Irish leaders without conditions on my part and without asking promises from them. It is the only way a conclusion can be reached.' In the other he gave his blessing to Cope to set up a meeting in Dublin between de Valera and Sir James Craig. Nothing came of it. Craig afterwards told Emmet Dalton, who brought him to the talks, that de Valera was 'impossible'.[70]

The elections called for by 'The Better Government of Ireland Act' were held on 24 May. In an effort to sweeten the atmosphere, Lloyd George replaced Lord French as Viceroy by a Catholic, James Talbot, Lord FitzAlan, the first in Irish history, as hitherto Catholics were debarred from representing the Crown in Ireland. However the general reaction to this would-be conciliatory gesture was 'We would as soon have a Catholic hangman.' As early as January of that year Collins, anticipating the elections,[71] had sent a very detailed memo[72] to de Valera on the subject of elections. He analysed the returns for Parliamentary, County Council, Rural and Urban District Council and Board of Guardian polls and said: 'It is my opinion that candidates should be put forward, and put forward in every division. The programme will be abstentionist from the Northern Parliament and Assembly with their colleagues.'

Sinn Fein did adopt the abstentionist policy. De Valera entered into a pact with the Nationalist Party, led by John Dillon in the South and Joe Devlin in the North, whereby each contested the election on a ticket of abstention and self-determination and, under PR, each gave its first vote to its own side and second vote to the other. Nationalists returned included Collins, de Valera, Griffith, Sean O'Mahony, Sean Milroy and Eoin MacNeill. There would have been a greater Nationalist return but for the gerrymander of constituencies. The elections in the North were marked by ferocious violence, person-ation and gerrymandering by the Unionists, who won forty seats.

A number of other points may be made about the election's outcome. Firstly the election, which made Craig the Six Counties' first Prime Minister (Carson had relinquished the leadership due to his age) had the more important long-term result of definitely and unmistakably releasing the scent of Partition into the Irish electoral air. Secondly, though the Unionists gained a large majority, the orange cloak would henceforth have to hang most uncomfortably over some spots of green. Armagh, for instance gave two of its four seats to anti-Partitionist candidates. Thirdly, in the South, Sinn Fein recorded an even larger victory than it had done in 1918 in the wake of the Rising. After years of warfare and terror the electorate declared itself unequivocally in favour of Sinn Fein. The party won 124 seats unopposed and the four seats allocated to the National University went to Sinn Feiners also. Southern Ireland's pro-Unionist support consisted solely of four Trinity College seats and two senators.

Although there was as yet no line on a map to mark a border the country was *de facto* partitioned, the division in the country was unmistakable – as were its challenges and opportunities.

Lloyd George was faced with the simplest and most complex of choices, war or peace. He was now assured by Macready and Wilson that full-blooded Martial Law would be necessary to crush Sinn Fein. The four months was conveniently forgotten. If victory were not quickly assured it would be necessary by October to relieve most of the troops then in Ireland. For Martial Law to succeed all normal life would have to be suspended. Banks, post offices, newspapers, transport, even bicycles, all would have to come under the control of the military who would then, with the rebels immobilised, have to carry out a 'foul job for any soldier'. It was an even fouler one for any statesman who had to reckon with public opinion. Nevertheless Churchill urged Lloyd George to go for 'a tremendous onslaught'.[73] Chamberlain, who had succeeded the fatally ill Bonar Law as leader of the Conservatives, agreed with Churchill but felt that a new offer of peace should be made on the basis of a larger form of self-government for the South than had been contained in the Act which had caused the election.

If this did not work the way was clear for 'the most unlimited exercise of rough-handed force', as Churchill put it. The Cabinet decided on 26 May that if the Southern Parliament was not in operation by 12 July then Martial Law was to be proclaimed throughout the South.

Then, to use a most abused phrase, fate took a hand in the person of a man bearing a name one might not have expected to find taking part in negotiations involving the British and the Irish – Tom Casement, brother of Roger. As he says in his diary, 'I had kept in touch with my old friend General Smuts, Prime Minister of the Union of South Africa and had promised to meet him on his arrival in London for the Imperial Conference.' On 13 June 1920 Casement left Galway to travel via Dublin to London to meet Smuts at the Savoy Hotel. In Dublin he was met by de Valera. Casement notes:

de Valera rode up on a bicycle and introduced himself. He asked me why I was going to London to see Smuts and that I had no authority from him or any official message from him. That was understood but he told me he would like Smuts to know what was required and that he would meet him if I could arrange a meeting . . . during our talk I told him that Smuts could not stand for an Irish Republic, as he was Prime Minister of a Dominion, de Valera frankly told me that a Republic was out of the question. All he wanted was a Treaty between two nations. I saw that point and told him that I would put it before Smuts.

That diary entry throws an interesting light on de Valera's psychology. Years later Casement sent de Valera a copy of his diary and after the entry for 14 June 1921 de Valera wrote:

this is not accurate. I might have said that I was aware that it was out of the question to demand that Smuts should accept the Republican position as a condition precedent to seeing me. It is probable that I indicated that the line to be pursued in seeking a settlement was that of a treaty between the two countries.[74]

It is curious, in view of the fact that the note was obviously written for the historical record, that de Valera in his authorised biography did not advert at all either to Casement or to the differing interpretation of his remarks. Smuts is introduced to the scene with the comment: 'After much preliminary spadework initiated by de Valera, Smuts and his secretary arrived in Dublin on July 5th.' In fact the spadework had been initiated by King George V himself and had borne fruit on the day that Casement met de Valera when, unknown to either of them, Smuts sent what turned out to be an historic letter to Lloyd George. Smuts had been invited to Windsor on 12 June by the King who was disturbed by happenings in Ireland. He had been invited by Craig to open the new parliament in Belfast but he feared that to do so 'might look like a deliberate affront to the South'.[75]

Smuts realised that, as the King had never opened a subordinate parliament before, to do so at that juncture could appear partisan, but he suggested that the King might do more than 'open a small parliament. He might address all Ireland – address a message of peace to all Ireland – and to the Dominions too.' The King liked the idea and suggested that Smuts put his thoughts on paper. Smuts did so and sent a copy to Lloyd George who invited him to a Cabinet meeting on 17 June to discuss the King's speech. The occasion was stage-managed superbly by Lloyd George who explained Smuts' presence by saying the latter had written him an interesting letter on Ireland. According to his biography Smuts found that the draft submitted by Lord Stamfordham, the King's Secretary, was the speech he had written at Windsor. However, 'nothing was said about my being the author. They innocently consulted me and I innocently answered them. But imagine the interesting position'. Smuts centred his arguments on the need to produce an appeal to the Irish in America because 'the real solution of our defence problem, which was now a Pacific problem, was to draw the United States and Japan closer together'.[76] He impressed his hearers by pointing out that the forthcoming Imperial Conference was concerned with this matter and a settlement in Ireland would produce a good climate both in the Conference and between the Conference members and the Americans. The line of reasoning influenced the meeting towards his draft rather than towards one prepared by Balfour. A newspaper report adverted to by Smuts' biographer described this as a 'bloodthirsty document amounting to a declaration of war against the South'. However when the King spoke, on the 22nd, his speech, although it retained some Balfourisms also contained the following:

I speak from a full heart when I pray that my coming to Ireland today may prove to be the first step towards the end of strife among her people, whatever their race or creed.

In that hope I appeal to all Irishmen to pause, to stretch out the hand of forbearance and conciliation, to forgive and forget, and to join in making for the land they love a new era of peace, contentment and goodwill.

It is my earnest desire that in Southern Ireland, too, there may, ere long, take place a parallel to what is now passing in this h.ill; that there a similar occasion may present itself, and a similar ceremony be performed. For this the Parliament of the United Kingdom has in the fullest measure provided the powers. For this the Parliament of Ulster is pointing the way . . .

The divisions and contradictions in British policy-making and execution almost wrecked the good effect this speech created. For on the same day that King George spoke, British troops arrested de Valera. They did not know who he was initially. When Cope found out he had him transferred from jail to officers' quarters while he fought to have him released. He succeeded a day later. Meanwhile, in London, Casement had seen Smuts and the South African delegation. He told them that he could arrange a meeting with de Valera, but that a truce was essential. Smuts, who was said by his delegation to be 'raising hell with Lloyd George',[77] passed this on to the Prime Minister. Various intense Cabinet meetings followed including one to which all the relevant civil servants and military were summoned and Cope was called upon to give his advice and opinions. He confided to Sturgis afterwards that the 'sweat poured off him' as he stood before this formidable array and argued so forcibly for peace that Hamar Greenwood interrupted him to tell him to 'curb his Sinn Fein tendencies'.[78] But the days of the Greenwood analysis were numbered. Lloyd George sent a public appeal to de Valera proposing a peace conference so that 'the King's appeal for reconciliation, for peace in Ireland shall not have been made in vain'. He proposed that de Valera should bring any colleague he wished with him under safe conduct and proposed a meeting in London with Sir James Craig. De Valera temporised, replying on 28 June that 'we most earnestly desire . . . a lasting peace, but see no avenue by which it can be reached if you deny Ireland's essential unity and set aside the principle of self-determination.' Five days later, on 30 June 1921, Casement crossed again to Ireland with Captain Lane, Smuts' Private Secretary, whom he introduced to de Valera at the Mansion House. Casement suggested to Cope that Griffith, Barton, and MacNeill should be released to help the negotiations. The three, along with Eamonn Duggan and Michael Staines, were released and when Casement met them, at Farnan's house, 'they all appeared happy . . . a good sign.' The reason for the gathering at Farnan's house was a visit by Smuts to whom de Valera explained his ideas. Significantly, in view of what was to come. Collins was not amongst those present.

De Valera began his talks with Smuts by stating that his demand was for a Republic. If a Republic were forthcoming the Irish would give the English any guarantees they sought as to defence. If Ireland was only offered Dominion Status she would not be prepared to limit herself by such defence stipulations. When Smuts argued that it would be a mistake to seek a Republic de Valera's response gave him grounds for hope. He said, 'If the status of a Dominion is offered to me I will use all our machinery to get the Irish people to accept it.'

A rash of peace-making broke out on both sides of the Irish Sea. The Southern Irish Unionists were brought into the process. The Earl of Midleton, Sir Maurice Dockrell, Sir R. Wood and Andrew Jameson met Lloyd George in London and de Valera and Griffith in Dublin. But not the Northern Unionists; Craig was conspicuous by his absence. He told Sturgis that he would 'sit on Ulster like a rock. Let the PM and Sinn Fein settle it. He was satisfied with what he'd got.' The military men on both sides were brought into the conference, Macready being cheered by a Dublin crowd as he turned up at the Mansion House. He and Colonel Brind negotiated truce terms with Duggan and Barton:

1. No incoming troops, RIC and auxiliary police and munitions. No movements for military purposes of troops and munitions, except maintenance drafts.
2. No provocative display of forces, armed or not armed.
3. It is understood that all provisions of this Truce apply to the Martial Law area equally to the rest of Ireland.
4. No pursuits of Irish officers, or men, or war material, or military stores.
5. No secret agents, noting descriptions or movements, and no interference with the movements of Irish persons, military or civil and no attempt to discover the haunts or habits of Irish officers and men.

Note there are other details concerning courts, motor transport etc. to be dealt with later.

On the Irish side it was agreed:

1. Attacks on Crown Forces and civilians to cease.
2. No provocative display of force, armed or unarmed.
3. No interference with British Government or private property.
4. To discountenance and prevent any action likely to cause disturbance of the peace which might necessitate military interference.

There were differing interpretations of the Truce on both sides, but it meant in practice that the IRA retained their weapons and the right to drill and train, a major advance on the 'surrender weapons' policy of seven months earlier. The IRA were secretly circulated by Mulcahy with an instruction, dated 9 July 1921, that 'active operations by our troops will be suspended as from noon, Monday 11 July'. Collins took no chances. On 8 July the *Freeman's Journal* carried a House of Commons report denying that any reward had ever been offered for Collins. He cut it out and wrote under it, 'Tudor offered £4,000 to any of his men who'd bring me in dead. Even up to 12.30 tomorrow I'm sure the offer will be honoured.' Certainly the IRA kept up the offensive to within minutes of that noontide.[79] On some it had a galvanic effect. Knowing that retribution could not occur after the

11th, many literally eleventh-hour warriors now took the field. For others, used to hard fighting, the harshness engendered by war was summed up by the matter-of-fact cold-bloodedness of this IRA report: 'At 8.00 pm we held up four soldiers (2 Royal Engineers; 2 Staffs) and searched them, but found no arms. We took them to a field in our area where they were executed before 9.00 pm.[80]

The men who had undergone that harshness were not all overjoyed to hear of the Truce. Liam Deasy, OC Cork No. 3 Brigade, described his feelings when a meeting he was presiding at was suddenly interrupted by the arrival of the *Cork Examiner* bearing news of the coming truce:

The news was received in silence. There was no enthusiasm. The feeling seemed to be that this was the end of an epoch and that things would never be the same again. Even in retrospect, after more than fifty years, I well remember that my personal feeling was one of disappointment and I must admit I foresaw defeat and trouble ahead.[81]

It was not in Collins' nature to foresee defeat but he could certainly see trouble coming. He told Moya Llewelyn Davies that the Truce was 'only the first move. The days ahead are going to be the truly trying ones and we can only face them with set faces and hearts full of hope and confidence.'[82] He had had sight of the British plans for Martial Law and he had been sufficiently impressed by them to send de Valera an accurate warning (on 27 June) that Martial Law would be 'of the most rigorous kind and . . . will be supported by three times the present military strength.'

Had the Truce not come into effect Collins had retaliatory plans of his own drawn up. Apart from the wholesale shooting of agents and Auxiliaries mentioned in Chapter 5 he outlined a ruthless scheme to de Valera on 26 June which the Cabinet subsequently adopted but did not implement.[83] Collins advocated 'a regular all-round, thought-out onslaught on all the departments which operate on behalf of foreign Governments in Ireland. In my opinion, the proper way to start this, and the proper basis to start it on is legislation.' Collins suggested that once his proposals were adopted notices should be issued to 'all parties concerned that it was illegal for anyone to support or dispense English law in this country. After a fixed date . . . they would be liable to certain penalties . . . no English connection should be tolerated . . .' The fact that the Cabinet would adopt such a sanguinary policy during the period of Truce and peace talks indicates the extent of the doubts on the Irish side concerning the prospects for peace. Collins in particular had good reason for taking a sombre view of the future. He commented, 'once a truce is agreed, and we come out in the open, it is extermination for us if the truce should fail . . . We shall be like rabbits coming out from their holes.' He knew better than

anyone else in the country what the real strengths and weaknesses of
the IRA were. Even Dorothy Macardle, a historian favoured by de
Valera, has conceded that the state of the Volunteers at the coming of
the Truce was parlous in the extreme.[84]

In Collins' own immediate sphere of activity just before the Truce
the Dublin Brigade had suffered a body blow in the Custom House
operation. He suffered one himself immediately after it. De Valera
agreed to go London on 12 July to see Lloyd George, but he
deliberately left Collins out of the delegation he took with him.
Collins protested but got no satisfaction. Griffith, Stack, Barton,
Childers and Plunkett were to accompany the President to London,
but not Michael Collins. De Valera later told his biographers that his
reason for excluding Collins was that he did not want the British to
obtain photographs of him. We are not told how he squared this
reasoning with the fact that if Collins had gone to America as he had
wished several months earlier, the British would have had unrivalled
opportunities for taking pictures. (They could also have obtained the
picture of Collins published in the *Gaelic American* as a result of de
Valera's feud with Devoy.) But we can readily understand Collins'
mood as he penned this note sitting in his Harcourt St office in Dublin
while de Valera prepared to meet Lloyd George in London the next
day:

Agreement is a trifling word or so I have come to look on it as such. At this
moment there is more ill-will within a victorious assembly than ever could be
found anywhere else except in the devil's assembly. It cannot be fought
against. The issue and persons are mixed to such an extent as to make
discernibility an utter impossibility except for a few.[85]

Collins' depression was totally at variance with the mood of the rest
of the country. Indeed, as Frank O'Connor commented, there was 'far
too great a feeling of confidence'.[86] O'Connor, who lived through
those days, understood why this should have been so. The British had
sued for peace. Their officers had had to treat with Volunteer officers.
'Terrorised by landlords, bullied by policemen, magistrates and
soldiers, shipped like cattle to the American boats, the people had
never known their veins to run with pride before'.[87] Now as in the
first days of the French Revolution it was 'bliss . . . to be alive'. The
Thermidorian reaction lay around the corner unseen as parties,
marriages, heroes' welcomes greeted the return home of the men on
the run. As one warrior I have knowledge of put it rather ruefully,
'My wife, an angel, was one of the many young ladies who developed
a condition for which marriage was the only cure.' Egos popped like
champagne corks. Even the Black and Tans joined in the general
relaxation that glorious summer. They could be seen here posing for a
souvenir photo with a former adversary in the Volunteers, there

'scurrying about, still in their cages, but with towels framed all around the railings to show they were on pleasure bent. The sun warmed us and the sun of freedom was rising on the horizon, warming our hearts.'[88]

But it rose too slowly. One of the tragedies of that summer was the amount of time let slip before a treaty was concluded. On the one hand the belief took hold that peace was now secure. There would be no return to war. On the other, the numbers in the Volunteers mushroomed. Guns poured into the country, expectations of what could be won from the British soared. And, of course, Collins and his associates became visible and traceable to their opponents, 'rabbits, out from their holes'. O'Connor could well have been right in his judgement that 'there was only one hope: negotiation broad and brief'. But with de Valera, one of the great procrastinators of Irish history, a speedy settlement was impossible.

Lloyd George made one fundamental miscalculation throughout the early part of 1921. He continued to regard Collins as the extremist and de Valera as the more moderate of the two. In fact Dr T. Ryle Dwyer has the evidence of history on his side when he judges that: 'Unlike the President who tended to portray a moderate public image while privately advocating a more hardline approach, Collins tended to do the opposite. Privately he was much more moderate than was generally believed.'[89]

De Valera met the hard-line approach by appearing to sound conciliatory so as to make it appear in the eyes of the world that it was the British, not the Irish, who were the hard-liners. He talked, not about an Irish Republic, but about self-determination, for which America and England had fought in the First World War. 'If England should concede that right there would be no further difficulties, either with her or with the Ulster minority. If Ulster should claim autonomy, we would be willing to grant it.' He showed himself willing to accept Dominion status, quoting Bonar Law to show that the Dominions had 'control of their whole destinies . . . We are thoroughly sane and reasonable people, not a coterie of political doctrinarians, or even party politicians, Republican or other.'[90] He told Harry Boland:

In public statements our policy should be not to make it easy for Lloyd George by proclaiming that nothing but so and so will satisfy us. Our position should be simply that we are insisting on only one right, and that is the right of the people of this country to determine for themselves how they should be governed. That sounds moderate but includes everything.[91]

It did indeed 'sound moderate' to the British, especially in view of the tough-line utterances Collins made to Ackerman. Just as the British tried to keep de Valera in a position where he might become of use to them there appear to have been two strands to their approach to Collins. On the one hand he would certainly have been killed, with or without torture, had he fallen into the hands of one segment of the Castle's forces, those referred to by Griffith as 'the Camerilla', in an article in the *Bulletin* on 11 December 1919:

There is a 'Camerilla' in Dublin Castle directing the present outrages against the Irish people. The organ of the Camerilla in the English Press is the London *Daily Express* which prints, day after day, from its Dublin correspondent, a series of concocted falsehoods forged in Dublin Castle. Two of the members of the Camerilla were formerly employed under Arthur Balfour in 1888 as secret agents to sustain the Piggott forgeries against Parnell . . . the members of the Camerilla, together with a couple of members of the British Cabinet, have as object the provocation of the Irish people into an armed uprising.

The hawkish element which in 1921 had an equally hawkish Chief Secretary to turn to would certainly have used their Hardys and their Igoes to dispose of Collins. But the 'Peace Party', headed by Anderson, Cope, MacMahon and Wylie, the Law Officer, who were responsive to Lloyd George's anxiety for a settlement, may have preferred to see him alive and in a position to 'deliver' on a solution to the Irish problem. To some extent this judgement has to be a matter of conjecture. To this day the Irish files are amongst the most closely guarded of the British State papers. Hundred-year rules hang over the papers of key figures like Colonel Winter. Not only mysteries, but more importantly in Ireland, a land of long memories and long-tailed families, names remain to be revealed.

It is a matter of record that Lloyd George and his circle thought highly of Collins during the war, ironically, more highly then they came to do during the peace. Worthington Evans expressed his admiration of Collins' military genius to Wilson at a dinner, and the two nearly came to blows as a result.[92] Lloyd George's feelings were of course not based on abstract admiration. His concern was how best to make use of Collins' position which he was able to gauge with some accuracy from the information passed on by the various British moles and listening posts. He told the Cabinet on 27 April that 'de Valera and Michael Collins have quarrelled'. Years later de Valera would allow his biographers to admit that it was from April 1921 that 'Collins did not accept my view of things as he had done before and was inclined to give public expression to his own opinions even when they differed from mine.'

Lloyd George was wrong in his assessment of the reasons for the quarrel. He told the Cabinet, Collins 'carries a gun and makes it impossible to negotiate. De Valera cannot come here and say he is willing to give up Irish Independence, for if he did he might be shot.'[93]

Lloyd George had no moral objections to meeting Collins: 'No doubt he is the head and font of the movement. If I could see him a settlement might be possible.' The question for Lloyd George was political: 'Whether the British people would be willing for us to negotiate with the head of a band of murderers.'[94] He had not made up his mind on the issue a few weeks later when he told Cabinet that his information was that de Valera was opposed to 'the gun business', but was in the grip of the militants led by Collins.

And so the British political and military machine remained poised before the Sinn Fein mouseholes like a giant cat that knew where the mice were, even if it wasn't quite sure what each of them was doing, but was afraid either to pounce or to let them go because of the conflicting pressures coming from those in favour of an Irish settlement and 'Tudor Toryism'.

Though he had brought a strong team with him de Valera began his July meetings with Lloyd George by insisting on meeting him alone. The Prime Minister, who apparently discovered, like many another man before and after him, that de Valera could be disarmingly likeable when he chose, subsequently reported to his Cabinet:

After three [there were actually four in all] interviews with Mr de Valera, aggregating several hours, I found it difficult to see exactly where the Irish leader stood . . . What he wanted was a Republic, but this the Prime Minister had said was impossible, being inconsistent with the Monarchy. Mr de Valera, however had not admitted this inconsistency . . . as the conversation progressed, it became increasingly clear that Ulster was the real difficulty.[95]

De Valera made a show of keeping Collins informed from London. He wrote to him on 15 July saying 'the meetings have been between us two alone as principals . . . you will be glad to know that I am not dissatisfied with the general situation . . . the proposal will be theirs – we will be free to consider it without prejudice'. Collins wrote back the next day saying that 'things and people here are splendid – everything going on magnificently, fine spirit, fine confidence, and although there was a little more relaxation than I should have liked, everybody is working *fairly* hard again.'

Eventually, Lloyd George told the Cabinet, de Valera had said that he had to consult his own Cabinet, as only two members of it were with him in London and asked for a draft of the British proposals to bring back to Ireland with him. Lloyd George said that he had given de Valera 'a very serious warning' that if the talks broke down the resumed war

would bear an entirely different character, as Britain's reduced military commitments around the world meant that more troops were available to be sent to Ireland where a great military concentration would take place, with a view to the repression of the rebellion and the restoration of order.

The draft which Lloyd George drew up, in consultation with Balfour and Chamberlain, offered the twenty-six Southern Counties a type of Dominion status in which Ireland could have an army, but no navy. Britain was to have whatever facilities she might require in time of need. There was to be free trade between Britain and Ireland but partition was to be acknowledged. The twenty-six county State was to allow for full recognition of the existing powers and privileges of the Parliament of Northern Ireland which could not be 'abrogated except by their own consent'.

There had already been a skirmish in London the day before over partition, as Craig had publicly announced that 'it now merely remains for Mr de Valera and the British people to come to terms regarding the area outside of which I am Prime Minister. I go back to Ireland to carry on the practical work of Government.'

De Valera wrote immediately to Lloyd George complaining that the claim that he only spoke for the area outside of the North was 'wholly inadmissible' and saying that before going on with any further talks he wanted a 'definite statement as to whether your Government is in agreement with Sir James Craig and intends to support his view'. Lloyd George replied: 'I am responsible neither for Sir James Craig's statement to the Press, to which you refer, nor for your statement to which Sir James's purports to be a reply.'

On 19 July de Valera wrote: 'Things may burst up here suddenly, so all should be prepared.' Collins was seemingly unperturbed and proceeded to give de Valera a description of a two-day trip he had just made through Cork.

The spirit animating the enemy in Cork City and in the parts of the County I visited is arrogant and provocative. They are trying to regard the position not as a truce but as a surrender on our part. For instance, the car in which I was travelling was held up in Clonakilty by regular troops although they have no power whatever to undertake such action. I was not in it at the time . . . The first exciting incident I had was a few minutes after leaving Cork City, going southwards. We very nearly ran into one of our own trenches. I said to the driver that if anything happened it would be the irony of fate.

I would like you to know that while I was down in Cork yesterday we intercepted messages from Bandon – that's the CI's office – DIs, Macroom, Bantry, Clonakilty, Castletownbere and Skibbereen. The purport of the message was as follows: 'Submit return at once of rough estimate of No. of males between ages of 16 and 50 in your district.' Skibbereen said, '7,000 males'. Bantry and Clonakilty replied, 'letter by next train'. Macroom replied '3,000 males'. Castletownbere replied, 'roughly 1,500 males'. I can't judge what this could mean, unless it is an enquiry with a view to arrangements for a round-up. I think it well that you should know this. That wire was handed in at Bandon at midday yesterday.

Wires have also been issued to the effect that in the event of negotiations breaking down the enemy forces would be confined to barracks, and will get a further cipher as to the next step. Generally speaking, I fancy the idea is to have preparations made to attack us the moment they decide to finish their offers. I don't know whether anything really tangible has been referred to up to the present, but I should say that in the final result it would be worthwhile stipulating that no matter how bad the terms are they would be submitted to a full meeting. You will know my object in this.

De Valera and Lloyd George continued their shadow-boxing, with de Valera pretending that he was so shocked by the British proposals when he had sight of them that he at first refused to take them back to Dublin. Then he sent a messenger for them, but let it be thought in Dublin that the British had forwarded them. Behind the shadow-boxing however there now lay one ineluctable truth which Collins more than anyone else would have reason to ponder bitterly. After his lengthy tête-à-têtes with Lloyd George, Eamon de Valera knew better than any man alive how slim was the prospect of a Republic and what sort of a settlement he and his colleagues were likely to get.

Collins had correctly analysed the mood of the British military and the steps being taken to resume hostilities. The Cork preparations were replicated in every county in the country and the members of the Cabinet had to consider very firmly whether or not their acceptance or rejection of British proposals meant peace or war, not just horse-trading. If it had to be either, it was important that the Dail was shown to be informed and united on the issues. But Collins also wanted a 'full meeting' in order to secure the release of imprisoned Deputies, amongst whom was Sean MacEoin. He visited Mountjoy Jail himself to see MacEoin, on 14 July, using the name James Gill. He also walked out of a Cabinet meeting in fury after de Valera had stated his reluctance to jeopardise the Truce for one man. The British announced that they would release all prisoners, except MacEoin, on 6 August but Collins promptly broke into print with a statement in the *Irish Times* on 8 August saying flatly: 'There can and will be no meeting of Dail Eireann until Commandant Sean MacEoin is released. The refusal to release him appears to indicate a desire on the part of the English Government to terminate the Truce.'

Much as he disliked being upstaged, de Valera had no option but to follow Collins' initiative and say that he could go no further with the negotiations until MacEoin was set free. MacEoin was released that evening and must have wondered, at least temporarily, if he were not better off in jail. As he started up the steps of the hotel where Collins was waiting for him Collins, forgetting about his wounds, made a welcoming dive at him and the pair fetched up in a heap on the floor. MacEoin survived to deliver a speech in Irish which Collins had written out for him, proposing de Valera as 'President of the Irish Republic' when the Dail met to consider the British proposals.

Nevertheless, a despatch which Art O'Brien sent to Collins, on 20 August, was nearer the mark than O'Brien evidently realised at the time: 'Attached another cutting from the *Daily Express* about Dev. You will see at the end that they tried to work in the old stunt of divisions in the ranks.' The *Express* may have been actuated by malice in its report about divisions but it was not without accuracy.

A step taken by de Valera at this stage is worth noting since it shows how acquiescent the Dail was towards him. He formally rejected Lloyd George's offer on 10 August after consulting with the Cabinet. He wrote, 'on the occasion of our last interview I gave it as my judgement that Dail Eireann could not, and that the Irish people would not, accept the proposals of your Government. I now confirm that judgement.' In fact, the Dail did not meet until almost a week after that letter went to Lloyd George and then its function was merely to rubber-stamp de Valera's action.

Collins seemingly saw little wrong in this for he wrote to Art O'Brien on the 17th saying:

I think we may still be pleased enough with ourselves. Although LG's words looked big you will notice a few peculiarities in his statement – peculiarities which do not look as if he felt himself very happy about the thought of resuming, his insistence on the Dominion status offer is peculiar also . . . it may mean that by constantly repeating Dominion Home Rule he may reconcile his people to it.

De Valera was attempting similar reconciliation at the time. Having met Lloyd George he obviously realised that partition might have to be accepted. He told the Dail on 22 August, 'they had not the power, and some of them had not the inclination, to use force with Ulster'. He did not think that policy would be successful. They would be making the same mistake with that section as England had made with Ireland. He would not be responsible for such a policy . . . for his part, if the Republic were recognised he would be in favour of giving each county power to vote itself out of the Republic. Otherwise they would be compelled to use force. This went even further than he had gone in his 10 August rejection of the British proposals in which he had said: 'We do not contemplate the use of force . . . if your Government stands aside, we can effect a complete reconciliation. We do agree with you that no common action can be secured by force.' He was now conceding to Ulster sufficient autonomy and recognition to allow it to opt out of the state he was hoping to set up. If the use of force was eschewed there was no other possible means of bringing Belfast under Dublin rule. The following day de Valera made another highly significant statement. He pointed out that the title 'President of the Republic', though accepted, had 'never been constitutionally created'. As a matter of fact the President was President, not of the Republic, but of the Ministry of Dail Eireann. This point, which never seems to have troubled him in his travels to the United States, did not stop him allowing Collins and MacEoin to co-operate in proposing him for the position, which he seems to have seen as a kind of political blank cheque. He told the Dail on 23 August: 'I am no longer to be looked on as a party leader. I am representing the nation and I shall represent the whole nation if I am elected to office and I shall not be bound by any section whatever of the nation.' The real significance of his assumption of the 'Presidency of the Irish Republic', prior to the start of negotiations which he knew from his talks with Lloyd George were highly unlikely to yield a Republic, only emerged later. It was a classic example of how de Valera outmanoeuvred his closest colleagues without their being aware of it. In the minds of an electorate predisposed towards 'follow-my-leader' the title naturally had a bearing subsequently on the widespread support he attracted to his views.

The diplomatic sparring continued right throughout September with de Valera and Lloyd George exchanging more than a dozen letters and telegrams. One of those hit a snag on 9 September when Lloyd George refused to accept de Valera's assertion that 'our nation has formally declared its independence and recognises itself as a sovereign State. It is only as the representatives of that State, and as its chosen guardians, that we have any authority or powers to act on behalf of our people.' Harry Boland and Joe McGrath went with this missive to the Gareloch in Scotland where Lloyd George was on holiday, despite Collins' warning that 'you might as well stay where you are'. He was proved right. Lloyd George immediately cancelled the arrangements which had been proceeding for a conference. As Lloyd George had already told de Valera that he could not entertain any claim to enter into negotiations on the basis that Ireland was 'an independent and sovereign State', this reply cannot have been unexpected. The British never abandoned that position in subsequent exchanges of letters and telegrams. For example, on 18 September Lloyd George specifically stated that unless a paragraph in another letter of de Valera's (dated 12 September) affirming independence as an independent State was withdrawn, 'conference between us is impossible'. He pointed out that de Valera had made no such condition when he came to see him in July, but had come as 'the chosen leader of the great majority in Southern Ireland', and continued:

From the very outset of our conversation I told you that we looked to Ireland to own allegiance to the Throne, and to make her future as a member of the British Commonwealth. That was the basis of or proposals, and we cannot alter it. The status which you now claim in advance for your delegates is, in effect, a repudiation of that basis.

De Valera tried to head off the inevitable on 19 September by trying to slip into conference with the plea:

We have had no thought at any time of asking you to accept any conditions precedent to a conference. We would have thought it as unreasonable to expect you, as a preliminary, to recognise the Irish Republic, formally, or informally, as that you should expect us, formally, or informally, to surrender our national position . . . We request you, therefore, to state whether your letter of 7 September is intended to be a demand for a surrender on our part, or an invitation to a conference free on both sides and without prejudice should agreement not be reached. If the latter, we readily confirm our acceptance of the invitation and our appointed delegates will meet your Government's representatives at any time in the immediate future that you designate.

Lloyd George's reply was ten days in coming and contained no give whatever on the recognition issue. It said:

His Majesty's Government . . . cannot enter a conference upon the basis of this correspondence. Notwithstanding your personal assurance to the contrary, which they much appreciate, it might be argued in future that the acceptance of a conference on this basis had involved them in a recognition which no British Government can accord. On this point they must guard themselves against any possible doubt . . . The position taken up by His Majesty's Government is fundamental to the existence of the British Empire and they cannot alter it. My colleagues and I remain, however, keenly anxious to make in co-operation with your delegates another determined effort to explore every possibility of settlement by personal discussion . . . We, therefore, send you herewith a fresh invitation to a conference in London on 11 October, where we can meet your delegates as spokesmen of the people whom you represent with a view to ascertaining how the association of Ireland with the community of nations known as the British Empire may best be reconciled with Irish national aspirations.

It was obvious that the self-recognition game was up although de Valera's reply of 30 September, which Griffith drafted for him, was posed as merely a letter of acceptance rather than one of capitulation:

We have received your letter of invitation to a Conference in London on October 11th 'with a view to ascertaining how the association of Ireland with the community of nations known as the British Empire may best be reconciled with Irish national aspirations.'

Our respective positions have been stated and are understood, and we agree that conference, not correspondence, is the most practical and hopeful way to an understanding. We accept the invitation, and our Delegates will meet you in London on the date mentioned 'to explore every possibility of settlement by personal discussion'.

Collins later judged that

the communication of Sept. 29th from Lloyd George made it clear that they were going into a conference not on the recognition of the Irish Republic . . . if we all stood on the recognition of the Irish Republic as a prelude to any conference we could very easily have said so, and there would have been no conference . . . it was the acceptance of the invitation that formed the compromise.[96]

Robert Barton, one of those who took part in the conference with him, and fell out with him over its outcome, nevertheless agreed with this assessment. He said:

in these preliminaries the English refused to recognise us as acting on behalf of the Irish Republic and the fact that we agreed to negotiate at all on any other basis was possibly the primary cause of our downfall. Certainly it was the first milestone on the road to disaster.[97]

It was a milestone certainly, but one has to go back in time to decide whether the formation of the UVF or the failure to concede Home Rule were the real culprits. One thing is certain however. The day of reckoning was at hand. On 20 August 1921, he held a long argument-ative session with Collins (at which Harry Boland was present) about who should go to London for the continuation of the peace process. Having left Collins at home while he teased out from Lloyd George what was on offer, he now, having found out, began to steer Collins towards the negotiating table in Downing St. The man who had felt his place was in America during most of the Tan war felt he must stay in Dublin during the coming diplomatic offensive in London. Collins, who thought of himself as a soldier, not a politician, resisted bitterly. He wanted de Valera to go. So did Griffith and Cosgrave, but Barton, Brugha and Stack backed de Valera who then used his casting vote in the Cabinet to get his way over staying at home. It took more than a casting vote to get Collins to go. Pointing out that he was universally regarded as the epitome of the Republican gunman he argued that if he stayed at home this reputation would be of value because the delegates who did go would be able either to seek concessions on the pretext of placating him, or at worst buy time by saying they would have to refer back to him.

In dealing with de Valera this was the worst possible line he could have taken because in the 'Long Fellow's' view there was only one figure in Ireland to whom all must defer, himself. Collins com-pounded the error by pleading with de Valera 'for three hours one night after the decision had been made to send the delegation to London' that:

for several years (rightly or wrongly made no difference) the English had held me to be the one man most necessary to capture because they held me to be the one man responsible for the smashing of their Secret Service Organisation and for their failure to terrorise the Irish people with their Black and Tans . . . the important fact was that in England as in Ireland, the Michael Collins legend existed. It pictured me as mysterious active menace, elusive, unknown, unaccountable, and in this respect I was the only living Irishman of whom it could be said . . . Bring me into the spotlight of a London conference and quickly will be discovered the common clay of which I am made. The glamour of the legendary figure will be gone.[98]

If de Valera had any doubts about either the morality or the practicality of what he was doing those were not the arguments to reinforce them. In the end it was not de Valera but Batt O'Connor, whom de Valera instructed to convince Collins, who in fact persuaded him to go. Obviously there were very few people still alive as this book was being written who had first-hand knowledge of this aspect of the story, but a daughter of Batt O'Connor's, Sister Margaret Mary, was one such. A member of the enclosed order, the Carmelites, whom I had to get special permission to visit, she was a girl of twelve when Collins arrived at her home for the fateful colloquy. She was sleeping in a downstairs room in Brendon Rd, because of an ankle injury which ruled out stair-climbing. Collins and her father were next door.

Daddy brought out the bottle and they talked for hours and hours. I could hear Mick's light voice arguing. Mick didn't think it right that he should go, because he was a soldier. De Valera should go, he kept saying. It's not my place. He sounded terribly upset. But daddy kept arguing 'You'll have to go Mick. It's the one chance you'll get. Think of how it will look in America if you miss this opportunity. Think of what this could do for Ireland. It's your duty. It's a great opportunity. Think of what you can lose if you don't go.'

Batt O'Connor himself painted a similar picture:

I will never forget his agony of mind. He would not sit down, but kept pacing up and down the floor, saying that he should not be put in that position. It was an unheard-of thing that a soldier who had fought in the field should be elected to carry out negotiations. It was de Valera's job, not his.[99]

It was the worst single decision of de Valera's life, for himself and for Ireland. Instead of the experience and prestige of the most revered political figure on the Irish side being made available to parley against the English, de Valera's full force was ultimately to be turned against his fellow countrymen. The consequence of his decision was to drive him to an extremist position in which he helped to unleash a hurricane of violence and destruction on Ireland. He knew that any agreement brought back from London would be a compromise. He admitted to the Dail when announcing his decision to stay in Dublin that 'he knew fairly well from his experience over in London how far it was possible to get the British Government to go'.[100] Even as he took part in those Dail proceedings he had had the implications of his letter of agreement to enter into conference spelled out to him. Mary MacSwiney stated forcefully that unless the British received the Irish on their terms the alternative was war:

a settlement within the Empire . . . was impossible. Association with a community of nations known as the British Empire might be reconciled with Irish aspirations outside but not inside that Empire. An association that would involve any allegiance direct or indirect to the British Crown – that was one point on which they could never give in . . . Their allegiance was to the Irish Republic. They had taken an oath to the Irish Republic . . . they had no *arrière-pensée* when taking that oath, they meant a Republic not a Dominion inside the Empire.

With Brugha and Stack standing balefully in the wings ready to denounce anything that Collins signed, de Valera knew that if dissent was to be kept to a minimum his signature would be an essential to any Treaty document. Even a rejection of terms would have been more palatable to the public if he were part of the team which did the rejecting.

De Valera later gave several different reasons why he did not go. Amongst these, he made the claim that his staying at home was 'generally accepted' and only became an issue when the Treaty was signed.[101] This is not true. Cosgrave formally proposed a motion that the President should go with the delegation, as Chairman, because of his 'extraordinary' experience in negotiations, and the advantage of being in touch recently (with Lloyd George).[102] The British would have their Head of State on their delegation, yet the Irish were sending over a team 'leaving their ablest player in reserve'. Collins also said he felt the President should go and said bluntly that he did not want to go himself and would very much prefer not to have been chosen.

It is not unduly fanciful to imagine the shade of Machiavelli nodding approval at his pupil's elbow as de Valera proceeded to scuttle these arguments. Insofar as Collins' objections were concerned he declared that from the personal contact he had with him he felt and he knew the Minister for Finance was a man for that team. He was absolutely vital to the delegation. He said that he himself would go if he were not the President, the 'symbol of the Republic'. The 'symbol' should be kept 'untouched' . . . not compromised by any arrangements which it might be necessary for plenipotentiaries to make. He was sure the Dail realised the task they were giving to them – to win 'what a mighty army and navy might not be able to win for them'. It was not a shirking of duty, but he realised the position and how necessary it was 'to keep the Head of State and the symbol untouched and that was why he asked to be left out'. Left out he duly was. Cosgrave's motion was defeated. Collins must have thought dark thoughts about what his few words of Irish for Sean MacEoin had helped to bring about. 'You might say the trap is sprung',[103] he wrote later to Joe O'Reilly. The Presidency of the Republic was indeed being used to ensure that the President was not going to be bound by any sector of the nation.

The Dail then unanimously passed a motion put down by Liam de Roiste: 'that if plenipotentiaries for negotiations be appointed, either by the Cabinet or the Dail, such plenipotentiaries be given a free hand in such negotiations and duly to report to the Dail'. De Valera made it quite clear to the Dail that he fully supported de Roiste's contention that the plenipotentiaries should go without their hands being 'tied in any way'. But he later tried to override the Dail motion by attempting to limit the plenipotentiaries' freedom of action by issuing them with letters of instruction which said:

1. The plenipotentaries have full powers as defined in their credentials.
2. It is understood before decisions are finally reached on a main question, that a despatch notifying the intention to make these decisions will be sent to members of the Cabinet in Dublin, and that a reply will be awaited by the plenipotentiaries before final decision is made.
3. It is also understood that the complete text of the draft treaty about to be signed will be similarly submitted to Dublin, and a reply awaited.
4. It is understood the Cabinet in Dublin will be kept regularly informed of the progress of the negotiations.

The plenipotentiaries, apart from Collins, were Griffith, Barton, Duggan and George Gavan Duffy. Erskine Childers was the official Secretary to the Delegation. Brugha and Stack were invited to go but refused and, unlike Collins, were not subject to any pressure to reconsider. De Valera later admitted to Joe McGarrity 'for your eyes only' that he had deliberately built division into the negotiating team in his selection process. He told McGarrity[104] that he had expected that Collins and Griffith would ultimately accept the Crown. However he reckoned that Barton and particularly his cousin, Childers, 'an intellectual Republican',[105] would oppose them on this. Duffy and Duggan he said were mere padding, chosen for their legal training; both were solicitors. Brugha he had not chosen because he would have caused wasteful rows and he knew that Griffith and Collins would not work with Stack. That sort of *divide et emperor* reasoning, a balancing of opposites, might work in Cabinet selection, under a strong leader. To send such a delegation overseas while the leader stayed at home was not merely inviting, it was guaranteeing trouble. But de Valera told McGarrity that he had intended that 'the Cabinet at home should hang on to the delegation's coattails', leaving everything safe for a final 'tug of war'. That final 'tug of war', according to the de Valera grand design, was to come not by, with or from a Republic, but on an idea of de Valera's, the External Association formula.

In return for recognition by Great Britain and the Commonwealth of an independent Irish State, Ireland was to become an external associate of the British Commonwealth. According to Barton the delegates had 'only a hazy conception of what it would be in its final form' but were said to be clear that 'no vestige of British authority would remain in Ireland. The compromise would be as regards our foreign relations.'[106] Griffith, who was supposed to be the leader of the plenipotentiaries, gave a celebrated account of how he first heard of External Association to P. S. O'Hegarty:

The first I heard of External Association was when Dev was pressing me to go over as a plenipotentiary. I went in to him one day and found him with Cathal and Austin at his desk, all three sitting. I was standing. He told me he wanted me to go to London. I said to him; 'You are my Chief, and if you tell me to go, I'll go. But I know, and you know, that I can't bring back a Republic.' Then he produced this External Association idea – the first I ever heard of it – and after half-an-hour's persuasion, Cathal gave a reluctant consent to it. Stack said nothing, but sat there, sullen. I said nothing. Then the other two left, and left me alone with him. I said, 'Look here Dev, what is the meaning of this External Association idea? What are you getting at with it?' He replied by getting a pencil and paper and drew the line thus: [At this point Griffith too produced paper and pencil and drew a line AB at a sixty degree angle.] 'That,' said he, 'is me, in the straightjacket of the Republic. I must get out of it.' Then he drew another line, a curved line [from A] AC. 'That,' said he, 'is External Association. The purpose of it is to bring Cathal along.' Then he drew another straight line. [Here Griffith drew the line AD] 'That,' said he, 'is where we'll eventually get to.' Then I was satisfied, and said no more about it.[107]

De Valera in fact had first embodied the External Association idea in a memorandum he prepared, but did not send, to Lloyd George after his return from the July talks. He gave it to the plenipotentiaries as Draft Treaty A, not to be confused with Draft Treaty B which he also gave them, in an equally unfinished state. The idea behind B was to use it for propaganda purposes if the negotiations broke down, as containing the terms which Ireland was prepared to accept. What exactly the plenipotentiaries were to accept was not spelt out. They were expected to produce that draft themselves. 'We must depend on your side for the initiative after this', de Valera wrote to Griffith.[108] It was understandable in the circumstances that it was another remark de Valera made at the time which lodged more weightily with Collins than the details of External Association: 'We must have scape-goats.'[109] Wearily Collins told Sean O'Muirthle, 'Let them make a scapegoat, or anything they wish of me. We have accepted the situation, as it is, and someone must go.'[110] He was quite clear that he was enmeshed in a web of intrigue and hostility. Shortly after the Truce was signed, not realising that his old friend had, in America, become a member of the de Valera camp, he wrote to Harry Boland warning him that things had changed for the worse in Dublin:

I don't intend to dwell overmuch on what to me are issues more vital than truces. But I think it right that you should be warned of the changes here. There's something about which I don't like, and I have the impression that the whole thing is pressing on me. I find myself looking at friends as if they were enemies – looking at them twice just to make sure that they really are friends after all, I mention no names. After all it may be a wrong impression that's got into me. Frankly, though, I don't care for things as they are now.[111]

That was in July. Later that month, on the 29th, Brugha seized on another opportunity to embarrass Collins. He raised with the Cabinet the fact that Tom Cullen had caused an Englishman called Robbie to be expelled from the country as a suspected British agent. Collins, obviously feeling that Cullen may have been in the wrong, wrote to Tobin:

Will you please caution Tom that he is not to be making use of sweeping remarks in places where they may be taken up wrongly . . . not slightest particle of real evidence . . . reports must be submitted by my staff to you. We've seen what results of talking to other Departments has been.[112]

In September Brugha made a serious attempt to embarrass both Collins and Mulcahy. He tried to appoint Stack as Deputy Chief of Staff to Mulcahy. When Mulcahy objected, Brugha tried to sack him, sending him a letter reeking of animus towards both him and Collins:

Before you are very much older my friend, I shall show you that I have as little intention of taking dictation from you as to how I should reprove inefficiency or negligence on the part of yourself or the D/I [Collins, Director of Intelligence] as I have of allowing you to appoint a Deputy Chief of Staff of your own choosing.[113]

Mulcahy immediately sent the file to de Valera 'to draw your attention to the attitude of the Minister for Defence to myself and to at least one other member of the General Staff'. This produced a meeting between Brugha, Mulcahy and de Valera[114] which ended as unsatisfactorily as the meeting in the spring over the Glasgow accounts. Brugha burst into tears and walked out exclaiming that he 'could do no wrong'.[115]

In fact in August Brugha had returned to the charge over the accounts. Stack backed him saying 'a serious charge had been made which should be probed to the bottom'. De Valera managed to do nothing in a way which indicated to Collins that if he were to be a target for mud-slinging de Valera, while he might not join in throwing, would do nothing to obstruct the throwers.[116] Collins admitted later that he had acted against good advice, from Tim Healy amongst others, in going. 'I was warned more times than I can recall about the ONE. And when I was caught for this delegation my immediate thought was of how easily I had walked into the preparations. But having walked in, I had to stay.'[117] One could hardly imagine a worse background of suspicion and mistrust against which to begin negotiations of any sort, let alone talks of such historic importance.

Well might Collins and Griffith agree when they got to London, that they did not know 'whether they were being instructed or confused from Dublin'.[118] They also agreed that Collins would become the *de facto* leader of the delegation. Years of overwork, poverty, strain and imprisonment had taken their toll of Griffith, now in his fiftieth year.[119] Knowledgeable contemporaries[120] have left descriptions of Griffith in his last years, having to borrow a pound to take a guest to lunch; of sitting in his office in his stockinged feet while his boots were repaired; of being so abstracted that he used to ruin Kathleen Napoli MacKenna's hair, while dictating his *Bulletin* articles. He had a habit of standing behind her, smoothing down her hair while he concentrated, his eyes on the middle distance, which caused Desmond Fitzgerald to joke that 'when Kathleen washes her hair there is enough copying ink in the water for another day's *Bulletin*'. Winston Churchill summed him up as having the appearance of a 'tired scholar'. Accordingly Collins took on a major share of the negotiating donkey-work. Apart from wearing drafting and side conference sessions with his own colleagues he took part in seven plenary sessions, nine meetings of the sub- committees set up by the Plenary Conference and almost all of the twenty-four meetings of the sub-conferences to which the plenary sessions gave way after 24 October. In addition there were various informal meetings with Tom Jones, Secretary of the Cabinet. Apart from conference business, he continued to discharge a good deal of his normal workload.

It is quite clear that though Collins was negotiating for peace, he was also making certain to do what he could to prepare for war. One note[121] shows him arranging a meeting of the English centres of the IRB, another[122] puts Paddy Daly in touch with a Liverpool police sergeant because he can 'tell you of the instructions that have been issued regarding the protection of houses of relatives of Black and Tans here', and there were many other such missives. Another example of Collins' activities during the talks is recorded in a 'note' in an important compilation of Treaty documents I have had access to.[123] There is a widespread belief in Ireland, which I have frequently heard expressed, that once the delegation landed in London, there was little or no contact with Dublin until the Treaty was signed and presented as a *fait accompli*, thus helping to bring about the civil war. In fact as the 'note' states with regard to the 'Instructions to Plenipotentaries':

These were adhered to rigidly so far as the delegation as a whole was concerned.

Until the date of the signing of the Treaty every week one or more delegates returned to Dublin and reported to members of the Cabinet. Michael Collins returned almost every weekend.

Collins is known to have met de Valera on several of these visits[124] and to have kept in touch with the IRB. In fact Collins secured the IRB's prior approval for the wording of the Oath[125] which he eventually assented to in the Treaty.

In London Collins stayed in 15 Cadogan Gardens, while Griffith and the other delegates stayed in 10 Hans Place. It was generally assumed at the time that he wanted to be on his own so that he could receive his intelligence agents in privacy, but in fact he had a large household. The publicity department was housed at Cadogan Gardens, as was Diarmuid O'Hegarty, one of the secretaries to the delegation and other prominent figures such as Joe MacGrath, Dan MacCarthy and Sean Milroy. Collins did have his own intelligence agents and bodyguard with him. Liam Tobin, Tom Cullen, Emmet Dalton, Ned Broy, Joe Guilfoyle and Joe Dolan all accompanied him, which would have effectively ended both the anonymity and the usefulness of the Crow St team, had hostilities recommenced. In fact this was thought such a likely outcome that Dalton arranged for an aeroplane to be purchased by friends with a Canadian Air Force background ostensibly 'to inspect forests', in reality to fly Collins out in an emergency. One key agent whose cover remained intact was Dave Neligan whom the British brought to London in his Secret Service capacity to spy on Collins and company, all of whom travelled separately from the Hans Place contingent. This included Griffith, Barton, Childers, Duggan, Gavan Duffy, their wives and two of the assistant secretaries to the delegation, Fionan Lynch and John Chartres. The secretarial assistants included Lily Brennan, the Lyons sisters, Alice and Ellie, and Kathleen Napoli MacKenna. When they arrived at Euston by special train a huge crowd waited for them – the King and Queen had just passed through and the Irish spectators and the royalists combined to cheer, and chair, the party to their cars, which were preceded all the way to Hans Place by a pipe band.

Kathleen Napoli MacKenna painted an equally animated picture of the day the negotiations opened, Tuesday 11 October 1921:

The precincts of Downing St presented an impressive scene with men, women and children kneeling in prayer across the thoroughfares. The paths were lined along the route with Irish exiles, including nuns and clergymen, reciting the rosary, singing hymns, exclaiming good wishes, pouring blessings on the difficult undertaking. There were tricolours, banners, flags, lengths of cloth and cardboard with wishes and slogans in Gaelic and English.

But there was a darker side to the picture which Napoli MacKenna, a keen chessplayer, also captured. She struggled through the crowds 'just in time to see my little "pawns" – taut, rigid, serious – entering the Battle Field . . . Liam Tobin . . . near to the railings of No. 10, and Emmet Dalton . . . handsome as a Wild West cinema star, the butt of a

service rifle [*sic*] peeping from his hip pocket, standing all alert.'
Though she intended no irony, in the circumstances in which the Irish
delegation was chosen, Napoli MacKenna's 'pawns' is a not inappropriate description. They were 'standing all alert' inside Downing St
too. The credentials which the Irishmen were issued by de Valera read
as follows:

TO ALL WHOM THESE PRESENTS COME, GREETINGS

In virtue of the authority vested in me by Dail Eireann, I hereby appoint:

Arthur Griffith, TD	Minister for Foreign Affairs.
	CHAIRMAN
Michael Collins, TD	Minister of Finance
Robert Barton, TD	Minister of Economic Affairs
Eamonn J. Duggan, TD	
George Gavan Duffy, TD	

as Envoys Plenipotentiary from the Elected Government of The REPUBLIC OF
IRELAND to negotiate and conclude on behalf of Ireland with the representatives of His Britannic Majesty, George V, a Treaty or Treaties of
Settlement, Association and Accommodation between Ireland and the
community of nations known as the British Commonwealth.

IN WITNESS WHEREOF I hereunto subscribe my name as President.

With this remarkable document de Valera was trying to recover
both the self-recognition of the Republic which he had lost in agreeing
to the negotiations in the first place, and to have it tacitly accepted that
the delegates' business was to come to an accommodation with the
Commonwealth, not to sign a Treaty agreeing to take an oath of
loyalty to the Crown. Lloyd George reacted by killing it and two
other birds with the same stone. There had been some fears of
awkwardness on the British side about 'shaking hands with murder',
that is, Michael Collins, and on the Irish at having to take the hand of
Hamar Greenwood. Lloyd George solved the problem by greeting the
Irishmen individually at the door of the conference room and then
escorting them to their side of the large table across which he
introduced them to their opposite numbers so that handshakes and the
production of credentials were rendered equally superfluous. The
'Welsh Wizard' had begun as he intended to continue.

8

Settling This Old Strife

'Blessed are the Peacemakers.'

Gospel according to St Matthew, V, ix

Michael Collins was thirty years of age when, at eleven o'clock on the morning of 11 October 1921, he sat down to negotiate with one of the most formidable political teams that England ever assembled. Facing him were David Lloyd George, Lord Birkenhead, Austen Chamberlain and Winston Churchill. Alongside them were Sir Gordon Hewart, the Attorney General, Sir Lamington Worthington Evans, the Conservative Secretary for War and Sir Hamar Greenwood, the Chief Secretary for Ireland. Though not of the calibre of the Big Four, these three alone would have constituted a useful team in their own right. Taken together, the English negotiators, backed up inside the chamber by two of the most brilliant public servants of the century, Lionel Curtis and Tom Jones, and outside it by the resources of an imperial civil service, presented an obstacle of Himalayan proportions to Irish Republican aspirations.

Collins established an extraordinary friendship with one of his adversaries during the struggle to surmount that obstacle, courageous, fractious, noble, and foredoomed as the attempt was.[1] Apart from his affinity to Collins by virtue of their shared realism, audacity and courage, Birkenhead was in his heyday a great athlete and visitors to his estate were exposed to a daily routine of golf, riding and tennis. Like Collins (as we shall see in Chapter 9) Birkenhead loved women, and social drinking – though he seems to have eschewed the bottle for most of the negotiations – and one could well imagine the pair, had Birkenhead been younger at the time, enthusiastically fighting, and biting, for 'a bit of ear'. Birkenhead, like Collins, had an 'X' factor behind the ruthlessness, the patronising, baiting, put-down demeanour which he carried like a weapon. The factor in both cases was patriotism, a patriotism which so often seems to be the Karma of the Anglo-Irish relationship that the one appears as the obverse of the other's medal: freedom-fighter/terrorist; law-giver/oppressor.

Austen Chamberlain afterwards wrote that Birkenhead had managed to 'enter Michael Collins' mind, won his sympathy and secured his confidence. The very fact that to him life was a gallant adventure created a link between him and Michael Collins without which we might never have reached agreement.' It was an extraordinary turn-around for 'Galloper Smith', who as the rising lawyer and Tory politician, F. E. Smith, had acted as Carson's 'galloper' at the great anti-Home Rule rallies in Ulster. Whether he had come to his new position through expediency, because it was the way the compass of empire was now set, or for any other reason, Birkenhead's conversion was so complete that in the Treaty debates on Ireland he became Carson's principal, and most successful, adversary in the House of Lords.

Lloyd George was described by Lord Longford as being able to:

talk to perfection the jargon of nationalist aspiration. . . . He believed in the paramount necessity of settling the Irish question . . . but . . . he was a politician, not a philanthropist or international philosopher . . . His own reputation was endangered anyway by negotiations. It would be blackened inevitably by the consequences of another recourse to war, but it would be destroyed once and for all by any surrender that Parliament judged one of principle, say for Ireland to retain her Republic.

Austen Chamberlain of course was the son of Joseph Chamberlain, a man whose name in Irish history will be forever synonymous with opposition to Irish Home Rule. He had followed in his father's footsteps where Ireland was concerned for much of his political career and even to agree to confer with Irishmen on Dominion Status was a major departure for him. But concession on any form of Irish Republic, whether internally, or Externally Associated, would not have been a mere alteration of policy, it would have been an abandonment of principle. 'And when principle was touched, he would yield to no Irishman in devotion.'[2] However he had one friendly connecting link with the Irish delegation. Arthur Chamberlain, his cousin, was chairman of a firm called Kynoch's, a munitions factory which was the largest employer in the County Wicklow town of Arklow. Arthur had met Griffith as early as 1907 and had impressed the founder of Sinn Fein as having a genuine interest in furthering Irish industrialisation. By the time the negotiations were over 'Austen Chamberlain came to have a great admiration for Arthur Griffith'.[3]

Finally, of the Big Four, there was the Great Warlord himself, W. S. Churchill, the archetypal representative of the Officer and Gentlemen class who could understand and defend war fought along conventional lines with uniformed battalions and thundering heavy guns. Organised slaughter, conducted by people who had the status of belligerents, was one thing. But he could never bring himself to empathise with the ideals and aspirations of peasants who fought out of uniform and shot men in their beds. Yet though the gulf between Chartwell and Woodfield was practically unbridgeable, Churchill's cousin, Shane Leslie,[4] who himself played an honourable and constructive role in trying to bring about a settlement of the Irish issue, has written that without Churchill there could have been no Anglo-Irish Treaty. Certainly it was Churchill who piloted the Treaty through the House at several junctures when storms across the Irish seas seemed certain to wash it away. But much of Churchill's work on the Treaty to which Leslie refers took place away from the conference table, in private meetings with Collins at the home of Sir John Lavery, the painter, in Cromwell Place, and there is, of necessity, an element of speculation surrounding its evaluation. There can be no doubt that he, after Lloyd George, was the man whom the Irish viewed with most suspicion. His espousal of the Auxiliaries, his pre-war Home Rule speeches and his floor-crossing from the Conservative to the Liberal Party in opposition to Balfour and the Free Trade issue were dubious credentials for entrusting him with negotiations with Irish rebels seeking to dismember the British Empire.

The secretaries of the two delegations were almost as interesting as their principals. On the Irish side, Erskine Childers is the best-remembered, as much for the doom which the Treaty brought on him, as for his manifold qualities as a writer, draftsman, and highminded human being – the man who gave England the book *The Riddle of the Sands*, and Ireland the Howth gun-running. But Diarmuid O'Hegarty, Fionan Lynch and John Chartres were outstanding men also. The first two we have met before, helping Collins to revivify the IRB after 1916. Chartres was Collins' protégé. A barrister, Collins had him brought to London from Germany. Republican mythology has subsequently tended to cast him as 'the mystery man of the Treaty',[5] who may have been a British spy.[6]

Chartres came to Dublin in 1916 to do business with the Kynoch factory for the British War Office and apparently, fired with post-1916 Irish nationalism, contacted Griffith in 1917, subsequently becoming an important *Nationality* contributor, writing leaders and articles under the pseudonym HI (Haud Immemor, 'Let them not be forgotten'). It is said that none of the Irish leaders, including de Valera, was aware of his *Who's Who* entry which contained the following:

Chartres, John; son of late Surgeon-Major Chartres, M.D. 8th Hussars . . . m. Anne Vivanti . . . Educated Wellington College, Germany, University of London; Barrister of Middle Temple (Powell Prizeman in Common Law); Chief of Intelligence Section of War Office Armaments Output Committee, 1915 transferred to Ministry of Munitions same year; organised and for nine years directed the Intelligence Departments of *The Times* . . .

In fact Collins was well aware of the entry and what it portended.[7]

The 'intelligence work' for the Armaments Committee consisted of circulating information concerning its work throughout the War Office and the *Times* job consisted of re-organising the Library. His wife, Madame Annie Vivanti, a Piedmontese, also worked for Sinn Fein. Collins described her as 'this brilliant writer,' who 'has been a great accession to our cause in France as well as her native Italy.'[8] Chartres himself worked for four years with Collins prior to the Treaty:

Whatever he asked of John Chartres was done without argument or fuss, whether it was to convey a machine gun to Dublin, to obtain plans of certain offices in Dublin Castle, or to live in an hotel resorted to by Auxiliaries for the purpose of picking an acquaintance with them and their friends and acquiring scraps of information for the IRA Intelligence Department . . . John Chartres . . . could be trusted absolutely and whose abilities were as great as they were varied.[9]

In fact the irony of Chartres is that he was unhappy with certain aspects of the Treaty and after Collins' death felt that his successors were lacking in Republican philosophy, so much so that he was dismissed from an Irish Government post in Berlin over a strongly Republican article, published on 27 July 1922, by a contributor to an official journal he was responsible for.[10]

The fact that allegations against Chartres persist to this day indicates something of the intensity of feeling caused by the rifts in Dublin, interacting with the profound philosophical differences which arose amongst the Irish during and after the Treaty negotiations. For example, Moylette, the businessman who helped to initiate the Clune peace attempt, told me once that Childers was 'an improver' sent in by the British to 'improve' a revolutionary situation to the point where it would explode prematurely to the detriment of the revolutionaries. 'They did it all the time in India,' he told me solemnly. Curtis and Childers had been to the same school, Haileybury, and had fought against the Boers. But there, except in ability, the resemblance ended. Curtis stood for the ennobling qualities of the British Empire, Childers for the oppressed struggling to be free. Curtis was the spirit behind the *Round Table* journal, Childers animated the *Irish Bulletin*. The other English Principal Secretary, Tom Jones, animated everything. He was the Cope of the negotiations (Cope himself was also hovering in attendance throughout the talks), the go-between between Lloyd George and Griffith and Collins. He knew Ireland well, having first been Barrington Lecturer travelling the entire thirty-two counties, and subsequently Professor of Economics at Queen's University, Belfast. If it could not be said that he used his knowledge to mislead the Irish delegation, it can certainly be shown that he used it to lead them in the direction Lloyd

George wanted them to go. There was another ally on the British side, tradition, the conscious use of pomp, psychology and setting as an adjunct in negotiation. As they trod the corridors of power in Downing St, or the richly carpeted warrens of the Houses of Parliament, adorned by bookcase and portrait recalling great deeds and personages of the past, the effect on that small handful of Irishmen, contesting with the heads of an empire at the height of its power, must have been awesome. Robert Barton recorded:

It was clear from the start that the English interest was centred on Michael Collins. We Irishmen were nervous and ill at ease, it was our first introduction to Diplomacy. The English were at home and confident in surroundings where they had met and out-manoeuvred or intimidated their opponents in a hundred similar struggles. On the walls hung portraits of past prime ministers, the builders of Britain's Empire. Opposite to me was the portrait of Sir Robert Walpole and beneath it sat Winston Churchill.[11]

Formidable psychological pressures indeed for an Irish delegation that would soon be torn by internal dissension, and weakened by the need to refer and, in Collins' case, to travel incessantly back to Ireland. He above all of them would have to cope with a growing certainty of enmity and suspicion of treachery in Dublin. The British also had a reasonably good grasp of the state of public opinion in Ireland, and of the disunity in the Irish camp, as is made clear by an intelligence report which was circulated to the British negotiators a little after the Conference opened:

The Sinn Fein Party, or moderate section of Dail Eireann, as represented at the Conference by Arthur Griffith, fear that during the 'Truce', British politicians may possibly become acquainted with the real feeling of the Irish people on the Irish question, and realise they are most anxious to have peace. They also fear that British public opinion will assert itself and induce the P.M. to withdraw part of the offer already made.
    . . . They will boggle considerably at taking the Oath of Allegiance to the Crown, but will take it if the Government will not give way. They feel that the people as a whole will compel them to accept the compromise.
    They fear that we know much more about their domestic troubles than we actually do, as the possession of this information might induce the British Government to reduce the offer to them.
    They are doing their utmost to prevent people talking about the many subjects of disunion, as they fear that if it gets to the ears of the Conference it will weaken the hands of their own delegates.[12]

As to the calibre of those delegates, the British reckoned that Collins was 'the strongest personality of the party'. Griffith, 'more clever than de Valera, but not so attractive, is the real power in Sinn Fein'. George Gavan Duffy was 'vain and self-sufficient, likes to hear himself talk'. Eamonn Duggan was 'completely under the influence of Michael Collins', but it was at least conceded that he 'recognises that he is not one of the strong men'. Poor Barton on the other hand was dismissed out of hand for having 'no outstanding quality'.[13]

Barton, so summarily dismissed in this profile, has left a good picture of the opening of the proceedings.[14] Lloyd George began with a general review of the situation, stressing the importance of the negotiations for both countries and emphasising England's desire to conclude a peace treaty, but acknowledging that both sides had limitations beyond which they could not go. 'If these limitations prove insuperable, then the responsibility for failure will rest, not with those at the council table, but with *others*.'[15] From the outset the Prime Minister was using the tactics of dividing the delegation from those at home, the 'others', the impossibilists. Griffith replied, unemotionally, but impressively, that 'England's policy in the past has been to treat Ireland as a conquered and subject country. If there is a change in the policy of subordinating Ireland to English interests, then there appears to be a possibility of peace.'[16] He then went on to follow the line which the Irish delegates hoped to focus on. Barton said:

I was struck at this time and on many others by the adroit manner in which he succeeded in making the discussion pivot upon Ulster and the relationship of the 6 Counties to the rest of Ireland and keeping the relationship of Ireland to the Crown in the background . . . his determination to . . . find the possible points of agreement before we touched at all upon the points of the Crown and allegiance.

Away from the conference table, another pattern, a cleavage in the delegation, was established that day. Barton and Duffy were rebuked by Griffith for 'being too emphatic and creating the wrong atmosphere' in exchanges with Lloyd George, Churchill and Birkenhead over trade and neutrality. Overall however Griffith was pleased and wrote to de Valera:

The meeting today has left on my mind the impression that the English Government is anxious for peace and also that this question of naval defence re the coasts of Ireland is a fixed idea of theirs – that they believe it vital to their lives.

The question of the Crown and Ulster did not arise. When they do, the sailing will be rough. Today they were amiable and both sides were quite polite to each other. The report herewith states what occurred. But, of course, the discussion had very many minor points of interest, amusement and instruction. Ll. G. is a remarkably suave and astute man, but on the whole we have scored today, although the most difficult part has yet to be discussed.

Barton commented on this letter: 'poor Griffith! He always scored when he fell for the baited trap.' Collins did not feel that anyone had a particular advantage. Thinking of his colleagues and opponents in London, his adversaries in Dublin, he wrote, on the night of the first day of talks, to one man he knew he could trust, the faithful Joe O'Reilly:

You know the way it is. Either way it will be wrong. Wrong because of what has come to pass. You might say the trap is sprung. This could be a good thing. Enough has been said to put behind as waste the strife of other days. But that's the way it is. Neither I nor anyone else can end or mend it.

At this stage a certain amount of, if not quite speculation, then at least reconstruction becomes necessary. Between 11 and 24 October seven Plenary Sessions took place. Somewhere in this period it appears that Collins decided that he and Griffith would have to go it alone in making the best deal they could. Dominion status was as far as he could hope to go. Face-to-face contact with the British leaders had confirmed this view. He also knew the limits of the support or direction he could expect from Dublin. A set of letters he wrote[17] during the talks gives an indication both of his thinking and of the problems he and Griffith faced in negotiating:

(4 November) . . . Not much achieved, principally because P.M. [Lloyd George] recognises our over-riding difficulty – Dublin. Plays on that. On the other hand we fight every word, recognising that to betray ourselves would mean disaster for us.
    G [Griffith] said, 'What do we accept?'
    Indeed what do we accept? If we accept at all it will be inferred as a gross betrayal or a similar act of treachery. What have we come for? I ask myself that question a dozen times a day.

(15 November) . . . I do believe it is L.G.'s ambition to kill two birds with one stone (G & me). If so, he didn't succeed. I looked at G. and he looked at me. We nodded and then plunged into the fray. I prefer Birkenhead to anyone else. He understands and has real insight into our problems – the Dublin one as much as any other. Dublin is the real problem. They know what we are doing, but I don't know exactly the state of their activities. No turning back now.

(Also November, undated) . . . Rather the years that have gone before with all their attendant risks than the atmosphere that is part of this conference. Who should one trust – even on my own side of the fence? Griffith. Beyond Griffith no one. As for C [Childers] it would be better that he led the delegation. He is sharp to realise how things will have due effect in Dublin – and acts accordingly.
    To go for a drink is one thing. To be driven to it is another.

(Undated) G and I had a lonely meeting – a house almost empty of customers – and talked and talked.
    He confessed that he was far from well and asked me to assume leadership of our party, even if unofficial. He and I recognise that if such a thing were official it would provide bullets for the unmentionables.
    I agreed G is in poor health and further burdens will do no more than grossly worsen his condition.

We came to the topic for the thousandth time of the Dublinites. I have often said that Brugha commanded respect and I still say the same. I respect a fighter and B. is one. Only he is misguided. Yet even in enmity he is capable of sincerity – which is more than I can say of the others.

Several writers, amongst them, from opposing perspectives, the uniquely well-placed Lord Longford and Barton, tend to portray the Treaty negotiations as being the inevitable outcome of superior British statecraft. Of course this factor did have a marked bearing on the outcome of the talks, but the two factors above had an even greater bearing. British diplomacy defined the parameters of the agreement. It was Collins' decision to have an agreement at all that prevented the talks from breaking down.[18]

I believe that the record, particularly that concerning Northern Ireland, bears the interpretation that in deciding to conclude a treaty Collins had more radical long-term strategic goals in view than either his colleagues or the British suspected. He decided to go for the maximum degree of independence he could achieve through negotiation and then, once he got control of an army and saw the British safely out of Dublin Castle, he would set about removing any restrictions imposed by the Treaty – by fair means or foul. My reasons for advancing this thesis will become clearer in Chapter 11 on Northern Ireland.

So far as the bulk of the Irish delegation was concerned, a procedural change was proposed from the British side when the seventh session was reached which had the effect of transferring the main business of the negotiations to sub-conferences.[19] The Irish in London and in Dublin reluctantly accepted the proposal although very soon critical voices would be raised against it. Barton said: 'from the moment Griffith and Collins met Lloyd George and Chamberlain alone their power to resist weakened. They became almost pro-British in their arguments with us and Duffy and I often felt that we had to fight them first and the English afterwards.'

In fact Barton, Lord Longford and the rest of the Irish team were misled as to the source of the sub-conference proposal. The real authors of the proposal, Griffith and Collins, were only named[20] when Tom Jones' Diaries were published, long after everyone concerned was dead. By now Collins and Griffith had an interest in common with the British. Both sides wanted to get rid of Childers. Griffith mistrusted him and thought that as an Englishman he had had far too much trust reposed in him. Collins disliked his pre-occupation with detail and his theoretical approach generally. On 13 October 1922 he and Childers were engaged with Churchill and Admiral Beatty on a sub-conference on defence which Childers opened with the remarkable statement: 'Now, Gentlemen, I mean to demonstrate that Ireland is not only no source of danger to England, but from the

military standpoint is virtually useless.' Churchill and Beatty exchanged glances and the following dialogue occurred:

Childers: 'Take the matter of Irish bases for English submarine chasers. From
the viewpoint of naval expediency Plymouth is a far better base than any port
on the Irish coast.'
Beatty: 'You really think so?'
Childers (having stood by the claims of Plymouth): 'For instance (tapping the
map) supposing Ireland was not there at all . . .'
Beatty (smiling): 'Ah, but Ireland *is* there . . .'
Churchill (very definitely *not* smiling):'And how many times have we wished
she were *not!*'

To compound the emotions generated by these proceedings Collins
also discovered that Childers was sending back secret reports to de
Valera.[21] Quite possibly the British may have done so too, but
certainly they regarded him as a fanatical opponent of any settlement
along Dominion lines and a 'renegade Englishman'.[22] And it was true
that, insofar as their influence really counted, Worthington Evans and
Greenwood were unsympathetic to Irish aspirations. Thereafter
Childers was excluded from all but one meeting of the sub-
conferences, Barton attended four, and Gavan Duffy three. Collins
and Griffith, whether separately or together, attended all twenty-four
sub-conferences, various meetings with Birkenhead, Lloyd George
and Churchill and at least nine 'informal meetings' with Tom Jones.
Thus, however one views their achievement, Michael Collins and
Arthur Griffith have to be regarded as the two Irishmen most
responsible for contemporary Ireland's political architecture.

As Collins' correspondence shows, he and Griffith felt that they
faced worse problems with Dublin than across the conference table.
While at this remove it might appear to be axiomatic that a delegation
from a small country entering crucial negotiations with the world's
largest empire needed all the expert help it could get, de Valera did not
act as though this was his view. He behaved as if the paramount
requirement was that his needs, and his lines of authority, should be
met and obeyed. Within a few days of talks opening he was telling
Griffith that he 'would be very glad'[23] if Diarmuid O'Hegarty were
sent back to Dublin. 'Please do not keep him an hour longer than is
necessary.' Three days later he was writing[24] to make a complaint on
Brugha's behalf that military advisers had not been chosen through
the Minister for Defence. Collins had brought over Eoin O' Duffy,
Emmet Dalton and Ginger O'Connell. Brugha and de Valera were at
the time engaged in reorganising the Volunteers for their own
purposes, as we shall see shortly, and Brugha had earmarked
O'Connell for a role in this process. Two points might be noted here
on the question of experts. One, de Valera had already made a
suggestion that Stack be invited to London to help the delegation in a

wrangle that developed with the British (during the session on 13 October) over the functioning of Sinn Fein courts.[25] Stack had refused to join the delegation in the first place and Collins and Griffith did not take up the suggestion which would have had the effect of installing one of Collins' most bitter critics at the talks in a position of power without responsibility. The second point is that Griffith had already tried, and failed, to get de Valera to send him over an expert of his own choosing, his friend and ally Darrell Figgis.[26]

But while de Valera demanded that the delegates should act in consultation with him he had no compunction in acting without consultation with them, even when they were directly involved in the consequences of his action. On 20 October 1921 he deliberately engaged in a controversy with the Pope in a manner which may have been the final straw in deciding Collins and Griffith to adopt the sub-conference option. The next day, on the morning of the Sixth Plenary Session, 21 October 1921, the text of a telegram from de Valera to Pope Benedict appeared in the press criticising the Pope for remarks he had made in a congratulatory telegram to King George V:

We rejoice at the resumption of the Anglo-Irish negotiations and pray to the Lord with all our heart that He may bless them and grant to your Majesty the great joy and imperishable glory of bringing to an end the agelong dissension.

The King's reply was:

I have received the message of your Holiness with much pleasure and with all my heart I join in your prayer that the Conference . . . may achieve a permanent settlement of the troubles in Ireland and may initiate a new era of peace and happiness for my people.

In his telegram de Valera said:

The people of Ireland . . . are confident that the ambiguities in the reply sent in the name of King George will not mislead you into believing that the troubles are in Ireland, or that the people of Ireland owe allegiance to the British King. The independence of Ireland has been formally proclaimed . . . The trouble is between England and Ireland and its source that rulers of Britain have endeavoured to impose their will upon Ireland.

British press reaction to this communication may be gauged from the leading article in *The Times*; 'Towards the Pope himself it is an act of impertinence; and towards the King it is unmannerly to the point of churlishness.' De Valera conceded to Griffith that his telegram was 'somewhat disconcerting' but he went on to make a remarkable statement:

We cannot expect the Vatican to recognise us, but we have a right to expect that it will not go out of its way to proclaim its denial of recognition as it did by *addressing King George alone* as if he were the common father, so to speak, of both disputant nations . . . the Vatican recognised the struggle between Ireland and Britain as purely a domestic one for King George.[27]

In plain language, de Valera was resurrecting the self-recognition issue and insulting the British King into the bargain at a time when Collins and Griffith were engaged in sensitive negotiations with the British Prime Minister.

When the Sixth Session opened Lloyd George allowed the Irish to make a complaint about British military occupation of County Council offices in Sligo and then launched into a tremendous attack over the telegram, armed with the timely discovery of two major Irish attempts at gun-running. The German police had impounded a shipload of weapons at Hamburg and the British police had aborted a Brugha–Mellowes plot to bring in armaments by an arrest at Cardiff which promised to yield some embarrassing evidence. The Truce was being taken advantage of, Lloyd George claimed, to 'accumulate destructive stores' in a manner which was having a 'serious effect' on Parliament. De Valera's telegram, 'offensive to the King', and the gun-running were combining to 'make our task almost impossible'.

Few negotiators in history can have had a more awkward corner to argue their way out of. But somehow Griffith and Collins managed it. Griffith began[28] by dealing with the arms issue: 'My conception of the Truce does not mean that your military forces should prepare . . . for the end of it and that we should not.' He argued that de Valera was *compelled* to take note of the phrase in the King's message referring to 'troubles in Ireland'. The trouble 'is not a trouble in Ireland, but is one between Ireland and Great Britain'. A sturdy defence for a man who privately disapproved of the telegram.

Collins went one better. He had the audacity to argue that the fault in Cardiff lay in the fact that the British police force 'took advantage of a condition which did not exist prior to the Truce'. Understandably puzzled Lloyd George asked, 'In what way?' To which Collins replied, '*Because our people took less precautions!*' On Hamburg he refused to accept that the ship was destined for Ireland at all because the British had issued a similar false report on 24 April 1918 (the 'German Plot' affair) to the effect that two submarines loaded with arms from Germany were on their way to Ireland. 'Unfortunately there was no truth in that.' But he had the documents in his possession. Somewhat dazedly, one guesses, the British negotiators then turned to a document Collins had earlier submitted on defence. Churchill found it 'of marked ability'. The only problem was that it was also a 'reasoned and deliberate refusal of every article which we made out for the defence of our security'! And so, between the concentration on defence and interpretations of the Truce, the Irish managed to sidle away from the implication of the telegram during that session.

After it, Collins took action on the Hamburg and de Valera fronts.

He sent Sean MacBride[29] to Hamburg. MacBride, who was still in his teens, found the ship under guard, but managed to have the arms transferred to another ship. He told me that he accomplished this near-impossible feat because of anti-British feeling amongst the German police. However Collins had less luck with de Valera. He returned to Dublin after the Sixth Session to ask him to join the delegation, but was refused. The sub-conference procedure was adopted the following week.

Griffith sent de Valera an important report of a conversation with Lloyd George and Chamberlain after the Seventh Plenary Session, on 24 October, in which, interestingly enough, he did not mention the sub-conference arrangement, stressing the significance the British attached to the Crown:

They pressed me to say that I would accept the Crown provided we came to other agreements. It was evident they wanted something to reassure themselves against the Die-hards. I told them I had no authority. If we came to an agreement on all other points I could recommend some form of Association with the Crown . . . I told them the only possibility of Ireland considering Association of any kind with the Crown was in exchange for essential unity – a concession to Ulster . . . They always fell back on the impossibility of peace except on acceptance of the Crown.

After his tête-à-têtes with Lloyd George the contents of the letter can hardly have surprised de Valera but his reply certainly surprised Collins and Griffith. More importantly it angered them. The first paragraph contained the following:

We are all here at one that there can be no question of our asking the Irish people to enter an arrangement which would make them subject to the British King. If war is the alternative, we can only face it, and I think the sooner the other side is made to realise it the better.

It created a scene when it arrived in London. Collins was furious and told the full delegation that he was going home. Dublin was trying to put him in the wrong and 'get me to do the dirty work for them'.[30] Griffith also threatened to go home unless his hands were left free. It was decided to send a letter of protest to de Valera signed by all the delegates. Collins refused to sign this at first, probably because the letter offered de Valera a way out of coming to London 'to do his own dirty work', by suggesting that he should only come over if he could do so without publicity, which was clearly impossible. On Collins' refusal Duffy and Barton also refused to sign, saying that it would appear that everyone except Collins was prepared to give allegiance. 'Eventually,' says Barton, 'Griffith induced Collins to make his protest by signing instead of returning home'.[31] The incredibly hidden nature of the Collins–de Valera power struggle is underscored by Barton's final word on the episode: 'I do not today quite understand what was the cause of Collins' extraordinary outburst.' It was the comment of an honest, intelligent man, albeit something of a political innocent, who through being in prison had been away from the unfolding of most of the drama which followed de Valera's return from America.

When de Valera got the delegation's letter he obviously realised he had gone too far and sent a temporising reply which mollified those in London, but left his position on Association unchanged. The delegates had stated that they considered that his letter was 'tying their hands in discussion and inconsistent with the powers given them on their appointment . . . it is obvious that we could not continue any longer in the conference and should return to Dublin immediately if the powers were withdrawn.'

De Valera replied:

There can be no question of tying the hands of the plenipotentiaries beyond the extent to which they are tied by their original instructions. Of course a Cabinet decision cannot be withdrawn or varied except by the Cabinet as a whole . . . the delegation must understand these memos of mine, except I explicitly state otherwise, are nothing more than an attempt to keep you in touch with the views of the Cabinet here on the various points as they arise. I think it most important that you should be kept aware of these views, for when the delegation returns there will be a question of a Cabinet decision as a policy.

Where at least one of his Cabinet colleagues was concerned Collins had little need of memos to find out how he felt. While the talks were moving exhaustively, and exhaustingly, towards their climax he was involved with Cathal Brugha in no less than three distracting controversies during the month of November. The first was bound up with the question of the Courts and manifestations of Sinn Fein activity during the Truce, in this case the continuation of the IRA practice of collecting levies from the public to maintain the Volunteers. The British had agreed to turn a blind eye to the substance provided the style was changed. 'Levies' would cease; 'collections of money' would continue. However the wording of Brugha's circular instructing officers that 'levies' were now illegal created fears that officers who had been collecting levies hitherto were now considered to have been acting illegally. Mulcahy suggested that retrospective approval be granted. Brugha refused saying:

If the local Officers send us a full list of the monies received and the manner of its expenditure we will credit the subscribers with having contributed to the National Exchequer and take the sums into account as a set-off in calculating the amounts due from them in the case of further taxation, or refunding the amount as may be decided.[32]

Mulcahy then consulted Collins, as Minister of Finance. Collins immediately wrote back vetoing Brugha's scheme: 'It is a proposition which would be wholly impracticable [and] raises a tremendous question, so far as the liability for levies by the Government goes.'[33]

The second incident was a bungled IRA arms raid on Windsor Barracks on 23 November in which an Irish Guardsman, a Sergeant Roche, was found to be implicated. For a moment both Truce and talks trembled. The British thought Collins was responsible. Collins thought Brugha had planned the raid so as to embarrass him. He nearly went berserk and instituted an inquiry which found that Brugha had not being trying to undermine him.

Brugha had given Michael Brennan, OC of the 1st Western Division, £1,000 to buy arms. Brennan selected Michael Hogan and Ned Lynch, who had lived in London for years, to make the purchases. Brennan said:

We knew there were many agents in London who would sell anything for cash and the only problem was how to get in touch with them. Lynch was certain he could make the necessary contacts through his acquaintances . . . In justice to Cathal Brugha . . . there wasn't even a suggestion of getting arms anywhere except by purchase.[34]

Hogan and Lynch bumped into Roche, a fellow Clare man, in a pub. He offered to place the resources of Windsor Barracks at their disposal. Scotland Yard intervened and in Brennan's words: 'my first news of their scheme was the newspaper reports of their arrest. Neither Brugha nor I had any knowledge of the scheme to get the arms of a military barracks . . .' On hearing this Collins cooled down. Not only did he succeed in convincing the British that no one except those directly involved in the raid knew about it beforehand, he subsequently managed to secure the release of Hogan, Lynch and Roche. The raid, however, had occurred on the eve of the last act in a long-running plot by de Valera and Brugha[35] to undermine the influence Collins exercised on the Army through the IRB, going back to the previous March. Having tried to tighten his hold on the Army by every means possible, de Valera finally attempted a 'surrender and re-grant' policy towards both officers and men that brought him into direct conflict with the GHQ staff on 25 November.

Prior to this there had been friction over Brugha's attempt to have Austin Stack appointed Deputy Chief of Staff. Mulcahy wrote on 1 November 1921 that he would take no responsibility for 'any position' if Stack was appointed Deputy Chief of Staff. Mulcahy admired Collins whom he regarded as the 'outstanding leader with all the qualifications for the only system of war which could beat the British' and as Chief of Staff, and he had helped to blunt Brugha's attacks on Collins. As a result Brugha made two unsuccessful attempts during the Truce to sack Mulcahy using issues such as the Robbie affair and the O'Connell appointment.

De Valera did not study Machiavelli merely for enjoyment. He was adept at concealing his moves from public view – there is no mention of the O'Connell and New Army controversies in his authorised biography – and the Brugha–Stack animosity to Collins was so well-established as to be accepted as part of the normal order of things so far as the senior members of the IRA and IRB were concerned.

To judge from various anecdotes preserved in the Collins family,[36] Collins had a great respect for de Valera, deriving in part from his respect for teachers going back to his Denis Lyons days and in part from the soldier's respect for authority. He had certainly shown this earlier in the year, in March, when the curtain went up on the first act of the Army reorganisation drama, the taking over of Army control by the Dail. Without Collins' influence the IRB would never have amended its Constitution so as to cede to the Dail the Government powers of the Supreme Council. This meant in effect that Collins as President of the IRB handed over power to de Valera. Now, in November, as the battle for the Treaty raged in London, de Valera persuaded the Dail to agree to a scheme of offering all officers fresh commissions subject to them and their men taking an oath of loyalty to the Dail.

The real reason for reorganising the 'New Army' at that juncture was obscured by pointing out that 25 November was 'the anniversary of the founding of the Volunteer force in 1913'. However, though Collins undoubtedly respected de Valera and found him, in Mulcahy's term, 'disarming', there was a limit to how disarming he would allow him to be. He wrote to Mulcahy on 23 November in terms which both demonstrate the power he could exert when he wished and the fact that he did keep his IRB colleagues generally informed throughout the Treaty negotiations:

I have heard from Mr Griffith that the Cabinet has been summoned for the 25th to meet the GHQ Staff of the Old Army (it reminds me of Napoleon). The members of the Cabinet at present in London have been asked to be present. I think *we ought to have a meeting of the GHQ Staff very early Friday morning* [author's italics]. I would strongly suggest that we should have associated at that meeting Directors of the Staff who operated for a certain time in the Old Army. I mean Directors who really did operate, not nominal Directors . . . Staines, Hegarty . . . wide knowledge of the Staff and the things that were done during the days when it was hard work to organise and to run the Old Army

Enclosed I am sending you a copy of a letter which was written yesterday by Mr Griffith [Giving details of Lloyd George's and Birkenhead's reception of the Irish proposals for a Treaty] to the President. You will *treat this in the usual fashion.*[37]

The fruits of that letter were seen two days later. Mulcahy had proposed that before the 'Old Army' was disbanded the GHQ staff should be brought in, thanked for their past services, and told what was in prospect. This ceremony was delayed for several hours while Collins and Griffith explained to the Cabinet in Dublin what was on the table in London. They had actually left on the tiring boat and train journey back to London when de Valera called in the waiting officers. He had suggested to Mulcahy that he could have his choice for Deputy Chief of Staff, Eoin O'Duffy, provided that Stack also be appointed so as to be 'Brugha's ghost on the staff'. But not one member of the GHQ staff found the reshuffling and the 'New Army' proposals acceptable. Ginger O'Connell summed up the way he and his colleagues felt. They were he said 'a band of brothers'. He thought no change was necessary. Neither did Eoin O'Duffy who said he found the proposals personally insulting. De Valera realised he was being checkmated. Collins might not be present in the room, but his influence was. The President interrupted O'Duffy: 'Rising excitedly, he pushed away the table in front of him and, half screaming, half-shouting said: "Ye may mutiny if you like, but Ireland will give me another army," and dismissed them all from his sight.'[38] But even a man with de Valera's ego had to acknowledge, if only to himself, that with the Truce hanging in the balance, it would be lunacy to proceed with an attempt to reorganise the GHQ staff against its wishes. He let it be known a few days later that there would be no 'New Army', but that the new commissions should be accepted. This took the heat out of the army controversy, but it can have done little to cool Collins' suspicions of his leader. These Dublin-based pressures playing about Collins and Griffith may fairly be regarded as part of the 'why' of signing the Treaty, the text of which can be examined in the appendix. An insight into the 'how' may be gained from the sonorous language of a British memorandum[39] of 27 October 1921:

1. THE CROWN . . . The Crown is the symbol of all that keeps the nations of the Empire together. It is the keystone of the arch in law as well as in sentiment . . . The British Government must know definitely whether or not the Irish Delegates are prepared that Ireland should maintain its ancient allegiance to the Throne, not as a state subordinate to Great Britain, but as one of the Nations of the Commonwealth, in close association with the Realm of England, Scotland and Wales.

2. COMMON CITIZENSHIP . . . No man can be a subject of two States. He must be either a subject of the King or an alien, and the question no more admits of an equivocal answer than whether he is alive or dead. The essence of common citizenship is that all who enjoy it are at peace or at war together . . . it is not compatible with neutrality in any form . . . His Majesty's Government must therefore know whether or not the Irish Delegates will acknowledge this common citizenship and the full partner-ship in the fortunes of the fraternity of nations known as the British Empire which it entails.

3. DEFENCE . . . Of supreme importance . . . Ireland will have no Navy

and no Air Force, and it is manifest that Great Britain, to whom will belong the vital task of Naval and Air Defence, must have, for that definite and limited purpose, and by agreement beforehand, such facilities of access and the like as are required for the competent discharge of that task.

4. TRADE & COMMERCE . . . Neither side shall impose protective duties or other restrictions upon the flow of transport, trade and commerce between all parts of these islands. [The British sought a 'definite assurance' on this point.]

5. FINANCE . . . Ireland shall assume responsibility for a share of the present debt of the United Kingdom and of the liability for pensions arising out of the Great War.

The Irish reply, dated 29 October, 'accepted the principle that the naval and air defence of the Irish coasts would be a matter of common concern to Ireland and to the British Commonwealth'.[40] This was in line with de Valera's thinking on such matters as revealed in his controversial Cuban interview with the *Westminster Gazette*. But he made no comment on defence, concentrating instead on the proposal in the final paragraph of the reply from the Irish delegation which became known as 'The Chartres Crown':

The unimpaired unity of Ireland is a condition precedent to the conclusion of a Treaty of Association between Ireland and the Nations of the British Commonwealth. Subject to this, and . . . agreements on . . . other issues the Irish Delegates are prepared to recommend that the elected Government of a free and undivided Ireland, secured in absolute and unfettered possession of all legislative and executive authority, should, for the purposes of the association recognise the Crown as symbol and accepted head of the combination of signatory states.

De Valera wrote to Griffith: 'We are not quite certain what exactly the last three lines may involve, and accordingly refrain from making any comment. You know the views here from my despatch No. 7.' This was the letter which had provoked the all-delegation complaint about the attempt to curtail their powers. So with a stroke of the pen de Valera had both managed to maintain his hard-line position without drawing any further remonstrance from the delegation and, as Collins suspected, stitched it into the record that, whatever anyone else might commit themselves to, *he* was not countenancing any retreat from the Republic.

It is important to remember that throughout this period, as Longford notes,[41] there was serious discontent in the pro-Unionist, Die-hard, or extreme right-wing, section of the Conservative party, which was appalled at the prospect of the Government talking to Sinn Fein and had a motion of censure down for debate in the House of Commons on 31 October 1921, the night before Collins and Griffith were unexpectedly invited to meet Lloyd George at Churchill's house at 9.30 pm.[42] Longford describes the talk which ensued as one of the most important of the entire negotiation; 'some would say the most important in the whole negotiation'. It was explained that the Prime Minister was preparing his speech for the Die-hards and wanted to elucidate the Irish reply of the previous day to the British proposals. At Churchill's house the British immediately suggested a division of forces.

Accordingly Griffith had 'about three-quarters of an hour' with Lloyd George upstairs; downstairs Birkenhead and Churchill saw Collins alone and subsequently all five talked together. One historian has described the evening as 'something of a turning point for Collins'.[43] What exactly was said we shall never know, but the upshot of the night, in Griffith's words, was that Lloyd George said 'the bias of his speech had to be peace or war with Ireland'.[44] If Griffith would give him 'personal assurances' on the Crown, *free partnership* with the British Empire and coastal naval facilities he would 'smite the Die-hards' and would 'fight on the Ulster matter to secure essential unity'. Lloyd George duly smote the Die-hards, the censure motion was easily defeated and Griffith then moved to give form to the assurances Lloyd George sought. He called a meeting of the delegates and told them he intended to send the Prime Minister a letter which contained the following:

Provided I was otherwise satisfied I was prepared to recommend a recognition of the Crown . . . the formula to be arrived at in a similar discussion at a later stage . . . I similarly agreed to recommend free partnership with the British Commonwealth, the formula . . . to be arrived at . . . later . . . the British Navy should be afforded facilities for coastal defence . . . mutual obligations our common security . . . this attitude of mine conditional on the recognition of the essential unity of Ireland . . . on no account would I recommend any association with the Crown of Empire, if the unity of Ireland were denied in word or fact.

Griffith made the significant observation that he intended the letter to be a personal one 'because he was very anxious to shield Collins from attacks that might be made on him at home as a result of its being sent'.[45] The letter caused uproar. Barton did not know whether Collins had seen the letter before the rest of the delegation but he was suspicious and angry. 'It was in our opinion stating a false case. Going much further than either we or the Cabinet at home were prepared to go.'[46] After 'ugly scenes', in which Griffith is said to have used some 'very abusive language', Duffy, Barton and Childers 'decided that in no circumstances would we permit this letter to be sent as a personal letter, or in the form submitted to us'.[47] Duffy got up specially early the next morning to prepare a memo to Griffith expressing the dissidents' objections:

That letter will necessarily be read by Lloyd George as indicating a weakening from the last memorandum of the delegates [that of 29 October]. We had in the last memorandum very carefully limited the recognition of the British Crown that we would recommend, your letter abandons that nor have we yet made any fight at the Conference against entertaining it. [48]

Duffy, who obviously did not realise that the sub-conference had become permanent, went on to argue that until they got an answer from Lloyd George to their memorandum it was wrong to send him a letter, very likely for use in Washington as well as with Craig and company, which 'cuts up that memorandum'. Griffith bowed to the pressure; the letter was re-drafted and signed by Griffith as Chairman. Then, on the morning of 2 November, Collins and Griffith took the letter down to the House of Lords where they met Birkenhead, who tried without success to get the Irish to accept alterations in the Crown and Empire references. Another conference on the document took place in Downing St that afternoon, involving Collins and Griffith, Lloyd George, Chamberlain and Birkenhead. Further changes were proposed from the British side and Collins and Griffith argued with their colleagues until these were accepted 'very reluctantly' and, around midnight, the final draft was sent to Downing St. It now contained this passage:

I was prepared to recommend a free partnership of Ireland with the other States associated within the British Commonwealth, the formula defining the partnership to be arrived at in a later discussion. I was, on the same condition, prepared to recommend that Ireland should consent to a recognition of the Crown as head of the proposed association of free States.

This was of course contingent on 'essential unity' being secured. But 'within the British Commonwealth', went further than the draft that the delegates had objected to in the first place. That had merely recognised a partnership 'with the British Commonwealth'. Within meant *within the British Empire*. Despite Duffy's legalism, confusion and mistrust, arising out of the problems with Dublin, had done their work. Barton commented afterwards: 'In my opinion, these Conferences between the English and Griffith and Collins on 30 October, 1 November and 2 November sealed the doom of the Republic.' [49] The Republic was probably doomed from the moment de Valera accepted the invitation to send Barton and the others to London. But Barton would have felt confirmed in his view, had one other detail been known to him at the time he was arguing with Griffith. He thought, as did Childers and Duffy, that Griffith had drafted the 'assurances' letter in the first place, which was bad enough. But had they known that it was, in fact, drawn up by Tom Jones[50] before Collins and Griffith even met Lloyd George in Churchill's home they would probably have gone home there and then. In fact Collins and Griffith were well aware of the agenda *before* it was called. The letter may be seen as a by-product of the sub-conference methodology. It eventually proved to be the hinge on which the entire Treaty swung, and its genesis is therefore of historic importance. Significantly, there is no record of any meeting with Tom Jones entered in the official log of 'Informal Meetings with the Cabinet Secretary' until 8 November, almost two weeks after he gave Griffith and Collins the draft. Collins and Griffith did not falsify the record, they simply did not record all of it. The Treaty could well have been voted down if the full circumstances of the letter and the sub-conferences were known.[51] The reason that Jones' handing over of the missive to Collins and Griffith does not appear in the listing of sub-conferences is that he did not give it to them – he passed it over to Duggan. Most writers on the Treaty tend to write Duggan off as a mere cipher of Collins' but in the background he did what he had done in Ireland, liaison work. Cope, who does not figure in the sub-conferences either, also worked hard behind the scenes, only occasionally showing up – albeit as a figure of influence – in Longford's pages, for instance. Sturgis in his diaries, however, recorded during the negotiations that the word from London concerning 'Andy' indicated that he was doing Trojan work, but he does not indicate its nature. There was a great deal more going on in London than Brugha, de Valera or Stack knew.

The letter, in Jones' writing and initialled by him read as follows:

Dear P.M.,
You can appreciate the difficulty of conducting negotiations by means of written documents, which in the event of a breakdown, might be made public and be used by one side against the other. For that reason it is natural that the formal reply which we have sent you today may seem to be couched in terms of such diplomatic caution, as to conceal our genuine desire for peace. We therefore give you this personal assurance that in essence the meaning of our reply is that we are prepared to be free partners in the British Commonwealth, to recognise the golden limit [?link] of Crown as its head and to have unity of control in all matters of the naval defence of these islands. All this to be subject to our securing the unity of Ireland as a condition precedent or incorporated in whatever Treaty is made.

At its head Jones had written 'Draft of private letter of assurance which I suggested to Mr Duggan that Arthur Griffith might give to Prime Minister. T.J.'. By coincidence I happened to read the document an hour or so before I lunched with a friend in the House of Lords. As I walked down the corridors, thinking of Griffith and Collins being shown into Birkenhead's room to argue over the letter, Barton's description of the British at the start of the talks seemed particularly apt, 'at home and confident in surroundings where they had met and outmanoeuvred or intimidated their opponents in a hundred similar struggles'.

But, for all its appositeness, Barton's comment only illuminates part of the picture. Incontestably Collins wanted the best deal he could get for Ireland. He did not trust Lloyd George or his associates, as a letter of his makes clear:

This is a real nest of singing birds. They chirrup mightily one to the other – and there's the falseness of it all, because not one trusts the other. Lloyd George's attitude I find to be particularly obnoxious. He is all comradely – all craft and wiliness – all arm around shoulder – all the old friends' act. Not long ago he would joyfully have had me at the rope's end. He thinks that the past is all washed out now – but that's to my face. What he thinks behind my back makes me sick at the thought of it. [52]

But, as he said to C. P. Scott, whom Lloyd George had sent along to try to soften him up two days before the meeting in Churchill's home, 'surely it would be a discredit to us all if after coming together in conference we did not manage to agree.' [53] Hence the willingness to give Lloyd George the 'assurances' letter. And hence Griffith's willingness to be accommodating in the next decisive step of the Die-hards saga, the Unionist Party Conference at Liverpool on 17 November 1921. Collins and Griffith came to the conclusion that decisions had to be taken and that it was up to them to take them. Here is the political balance sheet which both men drew up in London:

M.C.: What will be the outcome if the present talks break down. 1, a declaration of war by the British. 2, Cessation of hostilities on our part. We have, mistakenly, put all our cards on the table; we have laid ourselves open to the British. 3, Perhaps a continuation of efforts by the British to find a solution. This because world opinion is with us – proving that the British dare not engage us in full scale war.

Comment by Griffith: No declaration of war by the British. Point number three is the most likely.

M.C.: How best to reconcile our ideas with the fixed ideas at present held by certain members of the Cabinet? I will not agree to anything which threatens to plunge the people of Ireland into a war – not without their authority. Still less do I agree to being dictated to by those not embroiled in these negotiations . . . If they are not in agreement with the steps we are taking, and hope to take, why then did they themselves not consider their own presence here in London? Example: Brugha refused to be a member of the delegation.

Comment by Griffith: It is not so much a question of who dictating to whom. It is a question of powers invested in us as representatives of our country. Sooner or later a decision will have to be made.

Comment by Collins: Exactly. What are our powers? Are we to commit our country one way or the other, yet without authority to do so?

M.C.: The advantages of Dominion status to us, as a *stepping stone* [author's italics] to complete independence are immeasurable.

Comment by Griffith: Agreed, but with one question. How far can we trust the signatures of the British delegation in this matter? Once signed we are committed. But are they?

M.C.: No we are not committed – not until both the Dail and Westminster ratify whatever agreement is made.

Comment by Griffith: Ratification by the Dail means what precisely? That a certain amount of power is still in the hands of those we know will be against anything which treats of Empire status.

M.C.: I agree in part to the above. Supposing, however, we were to go back to Dublin tomorrow with a document which gave us a Republic. Would such a document find favour with everyone? I doubt it.

Comment by Griffith: So do I. But sooner or later a decision will have to be made and we shall have to make it – whatever our position and authority.[54]

Three points about that exchange of views are worth noting. One, Collins, the man who more than any other impelled his country into war, is now setting his face against a repetition of that course, despite de Valera's 'we can only face it'. Collins knew with certainty, however, that he would be a marked man, his intelligence service was laid bare and armaments to carry on the fight were in very short supply as the Italian episode demonstrated. Sean MacEoin reckoned that he now had 4,000 men, but only one rifle for every fifty men, about enough ammunition to keep them supplied for 'about fifty minutes per rifle'.[55] Though they inclined to the third option, Collins and Griffith felt that if they could rely on their British counterparts, the way forward was onto Collins' 'stepping stone'. It might carry them to Ulster which, combined with their uncertainty about Dublin, is inextricably bound up in the next decisive step taken in the treaty negotiations where once again Tom Jones enters the picture.

For a brief moment after Griffith had managed to get Jones' brainchild – a brainchild that was certainly well baptised by Lloyd George before Duggan saw it – returned to the British under the guise of his own 'assurances' letter, all was sweetness and light. Collins and Griffith paid another visit to the House of Lords at Birkenhead's invitation where they were informed that the letter was greatly appreciated as a 'document upon which they could deal with Craig'.[56] So much so that in fact the British were prepared to resign if Ulster proved unreasonable and, as Griffith wrote to de Valera, in such a case 'no English Government is capable of formation on a war policy against Ireland'. He went on:

The tactical course I have followed has been to throw the question of Ulster against the questions of Association and the Crown. This is now the position. The British Government is up against Ulster and we, for the moment, are standing aside. If they secure 'Ulster's' consent we shall have gained essential unity and the difficulty we shall be up against will be the formula of association and recognition. You will observe my wording, which they accept, is consistent with external association and external recognition.[57]

But, as readers will remember, Griffith's phrase in his letter to Lloyd George, which was the basis for this hopeful analysis, spoke of association *within* the British Commonwealth' which was hardly 'consistent' with *external* association. More inconsistencies showed up in the next five days. Carson and Bonar Law were not dissuaded from opposition and Craig, who was continually in touch with his 'Tudor' advisers, refused to budge. He had his Six-County area. Dublin and London could come to any arrangement they wished, so long as they left him out of it. Thus the Prime Minister was confronted not only with an impasse in the Irish negotiations but with his own promise to resign. He escaped from his dilemma with a classical piece of Welsh wizardry. Jones met Collins and Griffith at an 'informal meeting' in the Grosvenor Hotel to tell them that unless the Ulster Government accepted Lloyd George's proposal that they hold their Six-County area, but under an All-Ireland Parliament, he would resign and undoubtedly be replaced by a militarist government, hostile to Ireland. Then, giving it as his own idea, Jones suggested the following:

Supposing the Twenty-Six Counties of the South were to be given all the powers under discussion, and suppose Ulster were to be not only restricted to existing powers, but also submitted to a Boundary Commission set up to 'delimit' her area? How would that strike them?[58]

It struck them that, as Griffith wrote to de Valera next day, it would give them 'most of Tyrone and Fermanagh, and part of Armagh, Londonderry, Down etc.' However he adopted the attitude that it was 'their look-out for the moment'. But Jones obviously gathered from his meeting that there was some enthusiasm for the Boundary Commission in the Irish camp because he returned the next day with a further gloss on the idea. Craig 'had become far more intractable as a result of certain interviews in London.'[59] But rather than go out of office, if Ulster refused the Boundary Commission, as Jones and the Irish agreed they probably would, and so expose beloved Ireland to the horrors of Bonar Law, Lloyd George would stay in office and call a full Cabinet meeting to get the backing he would need in order to rally public opinion against Ulster, which would be made to appear 'utterly unreasonable in insisting [on coercing] areas that wished to get out'.[60]

Jones expressly asked if the delegation would support such a move.

Griffith replied that the proposal would be a British, not an Irish one and was therefore not binding, but said 'we realised its value as a tactical manoeuvre and if Lloyd George made it we would not queer his position'.[61] The big Unionist Conference in Liverpool was approaching and Lloyd George wanted to make sure that no one else queered it either, before that date. He had a voluminous correspondence with Craig which yielded one important proposal from the Ulster man on 11 November, as a 'lesser evil than being included in an all-Ireland Parliament'[62] namely that the Northern state should have the same powers *as those proposed for the South*. In effect, though the term was not used, 'They proposed Ulster should be formed into a Dominion and pay none except voluntary contribution to England.'[63] Dominion status was certainly beginning to peep above the negotiating horizon. Significantly Lloyd George showed this letter to Griffith at a meeting on 12 November in Sir Philip Sassoon's house in Park Lane at which he again sought and received reassurances that Griffith would not repudiate him if he proceeded according to the Jones formula, which now seemed even more coercive of the Ulstermen through stipulating that the part that remained after the Boundary Commission had done its work would have to 'bear the same taxation as England'.

Taken together with the assurances given by Griffith in his earlier letter, and on the night he talked with Lloyd George in Churchill's house, after Jones had revealed what was on the table, we have now come to the real turning point in the whole Treaty negotiation saga. For Lloyd George interpreted the assurances as meaning that if he confronted Ulster along the lines suggested, Griffith as a quid pro quo would not subsequently break off the negotiations on Ulster. Jones drew up a memorandum on the British proposals which he showed to Griffith the following evening, appropriately enough, the 13th. Griffith is thought not to have given them much attention on that occasion. He 'briefly indicated his assent'[64] to the memo's contents. Collins was not present at the time, but the overriding shared belief of Collins and Griffith that they could not look to Dublin for guidance and that it was up to them to make a settlement, coupled with the Boundary Commission proposal, meant that in practice from then on the Irish delegation could not break on Ulster. If they did so Griffith, though he wrote nothing down himself, could be accused of reneging on written proposals. Longford holds that in this phase of the negotiations the Irish were manoeuvred towards committing themselves into giving partition *de jure* as well as *de facto* status. Were they in fact manoeuvred, one wonders, or did they bow to the inevitable, as they saw it, and, in a sense, connive at a set-up? In any event Chamberlain and the other Unionist leaders accepted Lloyd George's interpretation and, thus fortified, went on to defeat the Die-hards at

Liverpool. The Conference turned down Colonel Gretton's motion of censure – for parleying with Sinn Fein at all – in favour of an amendment which said:

That this Conference expresses its earnest hope that consistent with the supremacy of the Crown, the security of the Empire and the pledges given to Ulster and the safeguarding of the interests of the minority in the South of Ireland, a solution of the Irish difficulties may be found in the Conference now in progress which will bring peace to Great Britain and Ireland, and strength to the Empire.

And so the talks went on. Was there ever any possibility of their conceding to Irish nationalists either a united Ireland or one delimited by a Boundary Commission, as Jones and Lloyd George indicated? Almost none, I should say. The strength of Unionist sentiment in England at the time may be gauged from three happenings in the week that Griffith was manoeuvred into or, possibly, acquiesced in giving his assurances to Lloyd George.

In a secret meeting Birkenhead induced the Liverpool Unionist leader, Salvidge,[65] to sponsor the amendment which defeated Gretton, by assuring him that 'a settlement was almost reached' which would involve no coercion of Ulster if she refused to co-operate in Dominion Home Rule, but which would guarantee the Crown, British naval interests and keep Ireland within the Empire.

Secondly, neither Lloyd George's promises to resign nor talk of Cabinet backing for a 'strong position' against the Ulstermen were practical politics. The 'full Cabinet meeting' which Jones spoke to Griffith about was held on 10 November. The record contains no hint whatever that he ever contemplated resignation. But what it does say is that [author's italics] *'emphasis was laid upon the importance of exercising the greatest patience in the conduct of the negotiations with the Cabinet of Northern Ireland'.*[66]

Thirdly, very powerful figures in decision-taking England were actively conniving at steps to ensure that the Six Counties would be strong enough militarily to frustrate any moves towards a united Ireland. On the very day of the Liverpool Conference the *Irish Bulletin* carried a report of a highly significant circular issued by Colonel Wickham to senior officers of the Ulster Special Constabulary.

Away from the rarefied atmosphere of Cabinet and Conference, the circular dealt with the unacknowledged, but all too real interaction of the supposedly illegal loyalist para-militaries of Northern Ireland with the forces of 'law and order' that set off the historical chain-reaction which in our day led, amongst other things, to the formation of the Provisional IRA. It said:

Owing to the number of reports which have been received as to the growth of unauthorised loyalist defence forces, the government have under consider-

SETTLING THIS OLD STRIFE

ation the desirability of obtaining the services of the best elements of these organisations.

They have decided that the scheme most likely to meet the situation would be to enrol all who volunteer and are considerable in Class C of the USC and to form them into regular military units . . .

The force is intended to be a military one only, to be called out in grave emergency to act in a military capacity. They will not of necessity be utilised for local defence but may be drafted to any theatres of operation within the Six Counties. It is not intended that this force should interfere with or replace Class B Special Constabulary who remain as a local force for local protection . . .

The 'C' scheme therefore applies mostly to towns and cities where there is a population surplus to 'B' requirements. The most suitable class for this force are ex-soldiers . . . what is required is to ensure that every unit recommended for formation can be constituted from a reliable section of the population.

The circular, which was of course yet another illustration of the doctrine 'Ulster will fight and Ulster will be right', was a clear breach of the Truce. The seriousness of the incident, coming at a time of delicately poised negotiations, may be gauged from Sir John Anderson's wire to the Chief Secretary:

Matter seems to me most serious. Wickham, while an officer of the Imperial Government, has not only constituted himself the instrument of another authority in a most delicate matter involving big political issues but has done so in terms which suggest that in so acting he was carrying out instructions of the Government which employed him. I cannot understand how any British officer could get into such a position and can only suppose that he received assurances on which he relied that the action he was taking would not be disapproved.[67]

Wickham was in fact acting on instructions from Sir Henry Wilson and Worthington Evans. Despite a flurry of indignation and dis-avowal from Lloyd George, Wickham went on to become head of a new force recommended by Wilson, The Royal Ulster Constabulary, partly because the RIC was deemed to contain too many Catholics.[68] Worthington Evans was one of those who counselled 'patience' with the 'Ulster Government' at the Cabinet meeting of 10 November. The meeting expressed 'satisfaction with the results which had been achieved in the negotiations with Sinn Fein'. But there was very little 'satisfaction' on the Sinn Fein side. The one limited area in which progress was made lay in quelling some Southern Unionist fears. On the eve of the Liverpool Conference, Griffith saw a delegation consisting of Lord Midleton, Dr Barnard and Andrew Jameson. He gave them assurances on land purchase and income tax and on the provision of a Senate in the proposed Irish Parliament to allow their voices to be heard. Though he would not discuss Ulster with them, Griffith told de Valera 'we parted on cordial terms'.[69] But there was little cordiality and much bickering and suspicion in the Irish camp. Griffith's health was not good. As the talks neared their end Collins wrote: 'More and more responsibility rests with me. What responsibility it is.'[70]

He had just come through an especially bad patch. In Dublin he was faced with the 'New Army' manoeuvre, and in London there had been a furious row and Duffy had been sent home to complain about the way the leaders of the delegation were conducting the negotiations. The Irish had had to put on paper their reply to the British proposals, which were now based on Dominion status within the Empire, on the lines of Canada, with an Oath of Allegiance to the King and guarantees on defence.

A memorandum by Childers had been submitted to Collins and Griffith in Barton's name, 'owing to the animosity which Mr Griffith had shown to any proposals put forward by Childers'.[71] On 22 November the whole delegation met, reworked the Barton–Childers formula and sent it to the British, calling it a 'Memorandum by the Irish Representatives'.

This 'Memorandum', the first formal statement of the Irish claim to be submitted, reflected the ambiguity of the position of the Six Counties in its preamble which stated that the proposals were put forward 'upon the *assumption* that the essential unity of Ireland is maintained'. Legislative and executive authority were to be derived 'exclusively from the Elected Representatives of the Irish people'. Ireland would agree to be 'associated with the British Commonwealth for all purposes of common concern, including defence, peace, war, and political treaties; and to recognise the British Crown as Head of the Association.' To mark that recognition Ireland proposed to make an annual contribution to the King's personal revenue.

Barton described the British as being 'bitterly disappointed' with this document and as having 'the dogs of war ready to unleash' as a result.[72] That was their public face; privately they unleashed Jones and somehow yet another conference was arranged to bridge the divide between the British minimum requirement of Dominion status and the Irish demand for External Association. This meeting, on the 23rd, at Downing St, resulted in a further conference being arranged with Birkenhead, Collins and Griffith on the basis of the 2 November letter of assurances from Griffith, ostensibly to prevent what Lloyd George called 'the tragedy' of a break-up 'on any verbal or technical misunderstanding'. But by so limiting the conversation the parties involved managed to exclude the voice of de Valera – Barton, who was present at the Downing St meeting. Birkenhead's suggestion that they bring a constitutional lawyer with them meant that Chartres, not Childers, accompanied Collins and Griffith to the meeting, in Birkenhead's room in the House of Lords on 24 November.

Chartres argued that in Ireland the Crown would not function, but that externally it would be recognised as the head of the aggregate of states. The Irish required a symbolism acceptable to themselves. However Birkenhead stipulated that the British also had their own symbolism. It was made clear that failure to recognise the Crown would mean war. Birkenhead did come to one momentous agreement on nomenclature with Griffith. Griffith proposed that the British might prefer to translate *Saorstat Eireann* as 'Free State', rather than as 'Republic'. Birkenhead agreed that the title Free State would go into the Treaty.

External Association therefore had been fully aired with the British and had been found unacceptable to them. What next for Collins and Griffith? They decided to return to Dublin to consult their Cabinet colleagues. All the Cabinet could come up with was to approve unanimously that Ireland 'should recognise the British Crown for the purposes of Association, as symbol and accepted head of the combination of associated states', and to repeat the offer of an annual subscription to the civil list. In the de Valera camp Childers held that Dominion status on the Canadian model was out because in Canada, though the law said otherwise, the fact was that distance made Canada independent of her nominal subordination to England. In Ireland the law would be the fact because of Ireland's proximity to England. Griffith and Collins both vigorously argued this contention but, having handed in Dublin's reiteration of External Association on Monday, 22 November 1922, and, predictably, found it unacceptable to the British, they were favourably inclined towards a compromise proposal which emanated from Lloyd George following upon the rejection, but which may have initially come from Collins.

Throughout the negotiations, Collins had been studying authorities on Dominion status: Duncan Hall, Berridale Keith, Josiah Wedgwood and Jan Smuts (probably under the tutelage of Crompton Llewelyn Davies). To him Dominion status represented the only possibility of compromise between the Crown and the Republic. He developed his ideas in a 'personal and unofficial memorandum' that in view of the Lloyd George offer now appears highly significant. Collins' memorandum said:

The Colonies as full-grown children are restive under any appearance of parental restraint, though willing to co-operate with the parent on an equal footing in all family affairs. Ireland, as a separate nation, would be also restive under control from the neighbouring nation, but equally willing to co-operate in free association on all matters . . . of common concern . . .

The problem on both sides can only be solved by recognising without limitation the complete independence of the several countries, and only on that basis can they all be associated by ties of co-operation and friendship. The only association which it will be for Ireland to enter will be based, not on the present technical legal status of the Dominions, but on the real position they claim, and have in fact secured.

It is essential that the *de facto* position should be recognised *de jure*, and that all its implications as regards sovereignty, allegiance and constitutional independence should be acknowledged. An association on the foregoing conditions would be a novelty in the world. But the world is looking for such a development.

Chamberlain's comment on this memorandum to Birkenhead was: 'extraordinarily interesting though sometimes perverse and sometime Utopian. Who outside our six [the British delegation] would guess the name of the writer?'[73]

However if Collins' Dominion status ideas were merely 'perverse' to Chamberlain, to Lloyd George de Valera's External Association proposal was 'impossible'. He said that 'any British Government that attempted to propose to the British people the abrogation of the Crown would be smashed to atoms'. But on Dominion status he introduced a most important 'sweetener'. The Irish could insert in the Treaty 'any phrase they liked which would ensure that the position of the Crown in Ireland should be no more in practice than it was in Canada or in any other Dominion'. As Griffith wrote to de Valera the next day this effectively 'knocked out my argument on the document they sent in – that the Crown in the Dominions was merely a symbol but that in Ireland it would be a reality'.[74] That offer in fact became the cornerstone of all subsequent Irish Dominion constitutional advancement.

The following day an important meeting was held in Downing St, to which Duggan was brought, but not Barton. The Downing St meeting confirmed the Chequers offer about the Canadian analogy in the Treaty and came to one crucial decision, namely that Griffith would get the final draft of the British proposals before Craig got his copy. Longford suggests that the Irish 'did themselves a disservice by this policy'.[75] His argument is that without it Collins and Griffith 'would have been in the same position as was de Valera towards the terms handed him in July. There would have been no ultimatum. There would have been plenty of time to discuss the terms in Dublin and reach a decision there.' But did Collins and Griffith believe that a 'decision' was possible in Dublin? Or rather did they believe it possible to get a decision they could agree with? From what has passed so far I believe it is not unreasonable to speculate that the 'the ultimatum' could well have suited them because it gave them the opportunity of producing a *fait accompli*, as opposed to further hair-splitting and politicking in Dublin which they feared would only result in losing Ireland an historic opportunity.

On 1 December Downing St was a-hum with people coming and going as further meetings and sub-conferences ensured that various changes were embodied in the draft. These included a stipulation that the Oath only imposed allegiance to the Crown 'as head of the State and Empire' and that naval defence would only be an exclusively British prerogative 'until an arrangement has been made whereby . . . the Free State undertakes her own coastal defence', a highly significant concession which introduced the principle that Britain's defence stake in Ireland would not be permanent and made possible Ireland's neutrality in the Second World War. The tension and bitterness which the Treaty was to cause in Ireland is foreshadowed in Childers' diary description of the final document:

It is July 20th 'in practice' minus army recruiting, and plus Boundary Commission. Impossible to accept [Oath as before] . . . point by point discussion of clauses . . . Griffith . . . flared out at me with some vague charge . . . I protested at such vague nonsense. M.C. instead of backing me up said he thought I implied a wider criticism. Refused to withdraw . . . M.C. made a ghost of a suggestion of an apology after the meeting. A.G. in favour of going to Dublin 'to carry out instruction to ask Cabinet before a grave decision was made.'

Childers was unimpressed:

They don't understand the meaning of half of them [points] the English worked on these skilled draughtsmen . . . Cope urged me to support peace . . . I thought of the fate of Ireland being settled hugger-mugger by ignorant Irish negotiators and A.G. in genuine sympathy with many of the English claims.

When the final English draft arrived at Hans Place, Childers comments: 'A.G. muzzy with whiskey, succeeded in getting some copies from him . . . Bitterly dissatisfied. Went to bed at 2 am. What a day!'

'Muzzy' or not, Griffith was en route for Ireland at 8.30 am that morning (2 December). Collins stayed back for a final discussion at the Treasury on financial matters with the Chancellor of the Exchequer, Sir Robert Horne, and Lionel Curtis. Childers accompanied him. Later in the day there was a second Treasury meeting attended by Lloyd George and R. G. Hawtrey of the Treasury, an economist described by Longford as being 'already competent to dazzle and befog beyond the common run of economists'. Collins attended this meeting alone.

Childers's diary indicates why:

when shown British draft on income tax for Ulster I blew the whole thing to pieces by pointing out not only the gross impropriety of a provincial fund but the grotesque results which might follow Ulster receiving too much from central funds. Horne's answer was 'Ulster would not come in without that clause.' M.C. did not understand the subject or only imperfectly.

Apart from their mutual tensions, fate too worked against Collins and Childers. As they were returning to Dublin with Duffy for the vital Cabinet meeting on the British terms, the mailboat collided with a trawler in the Irish Sea at 3.30 am. By the time the mailboat re-crossed the Irish Sea and berthed at Dun Laoghaire it was 10.15 am.

The wracking night coming at the end of the exhausting negotiations was the worst possible preparation for a fractious Cabinet meeting that began at 11 am, less than an hour after the boat had docked. In Collins' case the effect of the night was particularly severe. He had to contend with the effects of not one meeting but two.

Collins had intended to see O'Muirthle, the man who had played a key role in organising the IRB in and after Frongoch, and other members of the Supreme Council of the Brotherhood, before entering the arena with Brugha, de Valera and Stack, so that he could acquaint the IRB with the details of the British offer. As matters turned out he had to phone O'Muirthle from the Mansion House to arrange for him to pick up a copy.[76] O'Muirthle then consulted with the IRB during the morning and Collins and he met during the lunchtime adjourn-ment of the Mansion House conclave. The IRB's objections may be summarised as centring around the Oath, for which an alternative form of wording was proposed; defence, and the provisions govern-ing the Six Counties.

These reservations can hardly have been either surprising to, or welcomed by, Collins, embattled as he was at the time, but they were at least based on the document's merits. However, two words may be used to sum up the seven hours in the Mansion House: acrimony and confusion.

Brugha asked who had been responsible for the sub-conference arrangement – having done nothing when Duffy reported on it to Dublin weeks earlier – and on being told 'the British', remarked that they 'selected their men'. Collins contained himself well[77] while Griffith stalked over to where Brugha was sitting and demanded that he retract the allegation. Collins' comment was, 'If you are not satisfied with us, get another five to go over.' It was Barton's sense of honour that saved the day. Although he had strongly disapproved of the sub-conference idea, he intervened to say that he refused to have the private proceedings of the delegates discussed and pointed out that Collins and Griffith had gone to the sub-conferences with the delegation's full knowledge and consent. Duggan interjected to say that there had been meetings afterwards at which proceedings were reported. Childers notes in his diary, 'Nobody contradicted this.' Brugha subsequently asked that the remark be withdrawn. Childers commented: 'It was an unpleasant scene.'

This was one of the most important Cabinet discussions ever

conducted by any Irish political party but, remarkably, no proper record was taken.[78] Colm O'Murchadha, the acting secretary to the Cabinet, Childers, Stack and Barton made some notes but the public's main source of information came from subsequent Dail debates during which various people gave accounts of what they said they had said. De Valera took pride in this. At pains to show the Dail that he was not in any way responsible for the Treaty's signing he said: 'I did not give, nor did the Cabinet give, any instructions to the delegation as to any final document which they were to put in.'[79]

In fact there was particular confusion over what de Valera said, or intended. He clearly objected to the Oath and Ulster clauses, but thought that with amendments the document could be acceptable. Without them the delegation, whom he conceded had done their utmost, should show the British 'they were prepared to face the consequences, war or no war.'[80] However Collins subsequently thought that 'de Valera had proposed an oath consistent with Dominion status.' Childers noted that he had said, 'King of the Associated States'.[81] De Valera later claimed that he had said Association, not Associated States. O'Murchadha's official note of the Oath the President proposed was:

I . . . do solemnly swear true faith and allegiance to the constitution of the Irish Free State, to the Treaty of Association and to recognise the King of Great Britain as Head of the Associated States.

On top of this de Valera subsequently gave two more differing versions of the Oaths he proposed.[82] Given the circumstances of the time it certainly explains the irritation Collins and Griffith expressed over being unable to tell whether they were being instructed or confused from Dublin. They were expected to face-down the British, 'war or no war', for the sake of hair-splitting. Later, nearing the close of the meeting, Childers asked de Valera if scrapping the Oath in the draft meant scrapping also the first four clauses in the Treaty, those dealing with Dominion status. 'Yes', replied de Valera. This bit of by-play, which would of course have meant aborting the entire agreement, later caused trouble between Collins, who had not heard it, and Childers, who wanted to implement the President's wishes.

Griffith said that he didn't like the document[83] but that he did not think it dishonourable. It practically gave a Republic. The first allegiance was to Ireland. If it were to be rejected the people were entitled to know what the alternative was. The country would not fight on the question of allegiance. There would be a split. He would not recommend the Government to accept, but thought the plenipotentiaries should sign and leave it to the President and the Dail to reject. According to Stack's memoir[84] a significant exchange then occurred.

Brugha interrupted: 'Don't you realise that if you sign this thing, you will split Ireland from top to bottom?'

Griffith pondered this and replied, 'I suppose that's so. I'll tell you what I'll do. I'll not sign the document, but I'll bring it back and submit it to the Dail and if necessary to the people.' This exchange is said to have persuaded de Valera not to join the delegation. Certainly, he later told the Dail that he would 'probably' have gone but for it.[85] But in the afternoon session O'Murchadha records Griffith as saying that he would not take the responsibility of breaking on the Crown; that when as many concessions as possible were extracted, and when accepted by Craig ['Accepted' was obviously misheard, or uttered unthinkingly] he would go before the Dail. The Dail was the body to decide for or against war.

The most eloquent statement of the day was embodied in Collins' silence. As Childers notes in his diary, 'M.C. difficult to understand. Repeatedly pressed by Dev but I really don't know what his answer amounted to.' O'Murchadha however noted that he said that the non-acceptance of the Treaty would be a gamble, as England could arrange a war in Ireland within a week. He thought the sacrifices to North East Ulster justified for the sake of essential unity. He felt further concessions could be obtained on trade and defence. The Oath of Allegiance would not come into force for twelve months, the question therefore was – was it worth taking the twelve months and seeing how it would work? He would recommend the Dail should go to the country on the Treaty but would recommend rejection of the Oath. He obviously threw in enough question-marks and savers to prevent de Valera bringing his thoughts into the open. Duggan followed his lead. Duffy and Barton were unequivocally opposed.

The divisions at the meeting were underlined when the delegates went back to London on separate boats, Collins and Griffith from Dun Laoghaire, Barton, Duffy and Childers from Dublin. They also went with separate ideas as to what they were supposed to be doing. O'Murchadha records the meeting as deciding that the delegates were to carry out their original instructions with the same powers. The existing Oath could not be subscribed to and the Cabinet was prepared to face war as a result; Griffith was to say the document could not be signed and to try to break on Ulster. Childers noted that amendments to the trade and defence clauses were not mandatory but merely 'suggestions'. A majority of the Cabinet, including de Valera, but not Brugha and Stack, were in favour of the delegation trying to see Craig in London. And it was stitched into the record that de Valera was not joining the delegation 'at this stage of the negotiations'.

The general air of unreality and lack of a sense of proportion that hung over this day of bickering is symbolised by the fact that the delegates were being sent back to create a risk of war, not over the dismemberment of their country, but on the wording of the Oath. The British very soon became aware of this folly and it played its part in the enshrinement of partition.

En route to London, Barton's party encountered Cope and Tim Healy.[86] Barton gave Cope no information but, with Diarmuid O'Hegarty, had a two-hour conversation with Healy, who was aghast at the prospect of war, strongly in favour of the terms on offer, and was meeting Lloyd George the next day. After seeing the Prime Minister Healy had a 'long interview' with Collins, after which he told Barton that Collins was 'the only sensible man amongst us'. He had probably given the same opinion to Lloyd George, and perhaps more besides, for a Cabinet meeting, the following Monday, was informed that 'Mr Arthur Griffith and Mr Michael Collins were greatly disappointed at the rejection of the British proposals. The latter appeared to be not unwilling to accept paragraphs 1, 2 and 3 (Dominion status) though he would have preferred an immediate decision on Ulster and would have remitted the question of Ulster safeguards for discussion between representatives of Ulster and the rest of Ireland.'[87]

Before that meeting was held the Irish had again quarrelled amongst themselves over what to put in the document summarising their position as a result of the Dublin Mansion House meeting. Collins was of course beside himself at the thought of going back to Downing St yet again with External Association. 'I did not go to this conference for the reason that I had in my own estimation fully argued all points.'[88] Eventually Griffith, who had been as enraged as Collins at the proposals, decided to accompany them so as to lessen the appearance of dissension.

For someone totally out of sympathy with his mission Griffith 'played up like a man and fought as hard as we did', Barton noted afterwards. It was 'one of his greatest efforts in debate. Considering that a few minutes before he had been refusing to come at all his force and conviction were astounding.'[89] Trying all the time to keep the break point centred on Ulster he asked, in view of his own promise concerning Association in relation to 'essential unity', for a similar letter on 'essential unity' from Craig. The British told him that there would be no letter. Craig would refuse the proposals, nevertheless they would persevere with them, hand over Dublin Castle, withdraw their troops, pass a ratifying act in the next few days . . . glittering vistas were opening up and then Duffy intervened to say: 'We should be as closely associated with you in large matters as the Dominions, and in the matter of defence still more so, but our difficulty is coming into the Empire.' That was the slip the British were waiting for. 'That ends it,' cried Chamberlain and he was on his feet as he spoke. With that appearance of spontaneity which only orchestration can bring, his colleagues joined him. They would send the final proposals tomorrow and inform Craig that the talks had broken down. The journey back to Hans Place was enlivened for Gavan Duffy by Griffith's informing him of matters concerning his ancestry he had not previously been aware of. The result of his support for Barton and Duffy had been the loss of his opportunity to break on Ulster. The night of Sunday 4 December 1921 was not a pleasant one in Hans Place.

Then 'in the early hours of the morning' Jones re-entered the picture yet again.[90] He claims that he found Griffith 'labouring under a deep sense of crisis'. Griffith is said to have told him that he and Collins would accept the Treaty, but something fresh was needed to get it through the Dail, even a 'conditional recognition of Irish unity, however shadowy, in return for the acceptance of the Empire by Sinn Fein'. For this, Jones says, Griffith would give 'Ulster' any safeguards required, including scrapping the Boundary Commission. They agreed that Collins would see Lloyd George later that morning. The meeting took place at 9.30, fifteen minutes later than arranged because, we are told,[91] Collins' objections to going were only overcome at the last moment. According to Collins' own record[92] of what transpired he told Lloyd George that he was 'perfectly dissatisfied' with the British proposals for the Six Counties. He repeated Griffith's argument of the previous day, saying that Craig should state his terms for either rejecting or accepting unity, in writing.

Lloyd George's reaction to this, says Collins, was to counter-attack. The Prime Minister said:

I myself pointed out on a previous occasion that the North would be forced economically to come in. I assented but I said that the position was so serious owing to certain recent actions that for my part I was anxious to secure a definite reply from Craig and his colleagues, and I was as agreeable to a reply rejecting as accepting. In view of the former we would save Tyrone, and Fermanagh, parts of Derry, Armagh and Down by the Boundary Commission, and thus avoid such things as the raid on the Tyrone County Council and the ejection of the staff. [Since the end of November the Craigites had been cracking down on Sinn Fein-controlled county councils which were disputing the authority of the new 'Ulster' Government.] Another such incident would, in my view, inevitably lead to a conflict, and this conflict, in the nature of things (assuming for instance that some of the Anglo-Northern police were killed or wounded), would inevitably spread through Ireland. Mr Lloyd George expressed a view that this might be put to Craig, and if so the safeguards would be a matter for working out between ourselves and Craig afterwards.

Lloyd George also expressed willingness to show some flexibility on financial, trade and defence matters and to consider a new oath – if the Irish accepted Dominion status. Says Collins:

The conversation ended with Lloyd George saying that if Clauses 1 and 2 of the Treaty were accepted (Dominion status) he would be in a position to hold up any action until we had, if we desired to do so, submitted the matter to Dail Eireann and the country. I left it at that saying that unless I sent word to the contrary some members of the delegation would meet him at 2 o'clock.

Thus, although there was nothing new of substance produced from Lloyd George's side, Collins effectively got the talks restarted. The Conference duly entered its last phase that afternoon. Significantly Collins and Griffith brought Barton, the most resolutely Republican of the team, on this penultimate visit to Downing St. The generally accepted account of what happened there is that Griffith was confronted with his pledges given prior to the Liverpool Conference. The Conference adjourned, there was an anguished debate amongst the Irish who eventually agreed to sign the Treaty, and the fate of Ireland was decided in the small hours of 6 December. This interpretation is true insofar as it goes. But, as these pages should have by now made clear, this appears to be only part of the story. From the time de Valera accepted the invitation to negotiate in September, both Collins and Griffith seem to have decided that compromise was inevitable. They realised they would not be supported by de Valera in facing that inevitability and, having explored the British offer, they then embarked on the sub-conference route to settlement.

The confusions of 3 December in the Mansion House and the subsequent differing interpretations in preparing for the following day's meeting with the British could only have confirmed them in the view they were being 'confused not directed'. The seeming breakdown of Sunday over Gavan Duffy's blunder may not have been all it seemed. It was certainly portrayed as a most serious crisis in all the London papers that mattered on the 5th and 6th. But, significantly, Lloyd George's own mouthpiece, the *Daily Chronicle*, carried headlines and comment (6 December) which said: 'Irish Crisis, chances of getting round it – if the negotiators are still unable to sign a compact let them adjourn their negotiations for a fixed period of weeks.' Moreover just as it was generally believed that the sub-conference idea emanated from the British not the Irish, it was also widely believed[93] that it was the British who asked Collins to have the morning meeting with Lloyd George which put the conference back on the rails. In fact, as Jones' diaries revealed long afterwards, it was Griffith who asked Jones to arrange the meeting.[94]

According to Collins' memorandum on the meeting with Lloyd George, the Prime Minister opened by telling him that he was informing his colleagues later in the day that the conference had ended. The *Daily Chronicle* that morning (5 December) had carried a report headlined 'Grave Irish outlook — little hope of settlement now entertained'. The headline next day indicates that both paper and Prime Minister received new information between one edition and the next.

Certainly there is no indication of breakdown in the Cabinet record of the meeting Lloyd George had with his colleagues after seeing Collins. Two highly significant things were said however:

1. . . . there were indications that the division of opinion which had manifested itself among the Irish Representatives in London, also existed in the Irish Cabinet . . . a majority of the members of that Cabinet had rejected the terms and submitted counter-proposals.
2. Attention was drawn . . . to the fact that the document contained no counter-proposals regarding Ulster, from which it would appear that no Sinn Fein objection would be forthcoming to the proposals regarding Ulster.[95]

Thus the British were fully aware of the divisions in the Irish ranks and could fine-tune the last moves accordingly. Furthermore the document produced from the shambles of the Mansion House, containing the distilled wisdom of the allegedly most extreme All-Ireland, Republican wing of the Nationalist movement, indicated that the British could, in real terms, disregard further protestations about Irish unity.

Whether they needed any encouragement to do so is a moot point, but they certainly adopted that policy when on the afternoon of 6 December 1922, Arthur Griffith started off on the familiar path about further progress being contingent on learning Craig's intentions concerning Irish unity. He was promptly accused of going back on his promises not to let Lloyd George down over the Boundary Commission. Collins then took up the running. He pointed out[96] that the delegation's fighting position would be surrendered if they agreed to sign without Craig's agreement on unity and recalled that every document ever given to the British on Association with the Commonwealth was contingent on unity. While Collins was speaking Lloyd George administered the *coup de grace*.

He had left the room for a few moments to rummage amongst his suits for the document Jones had shown Griffith the previous month outlining the Boundary Commission proposals. On finding the correct pair of trousers he returned with both the document and a real or simulated show of anger at what he characterised as the Irish attempt to break on Ulster whereas their real problem lay in Dublin. Barton, who of course had never heard of the memorandum, had no idea what was going on and he whispered to Collins: 'What is this letter?'

'I don't know what the hell it is,' was the reply.

Lloyd George rubbed salt into the wounds. 'Do you mean to tell me, Mr Collins, that you never heard of this document from Mr Griffith?'

Collins said nothing and Lloyd George went on to say that he had assumed that both were party to the memorandum. 'I took the risk of breaking my party. You in Ireland often bring against us in England the charge of breach of faith. Now it is for you to show that Irishmen know how to keep faith.'

At that Griffith capitulated: 'I said that I would not let you down on that and I won't', he replied. Further argument on the Six Counties was now denied him, but he did remonstrate that it was unfair to tie his colleagues to his promise. The conversation then switched to trade, defence and the Oath, the very topics Collins had indicated at the Mansion House that movement might be forthcoming on. There was movement on all of them, almost as if he guessed or knew, possibly from Birkenhead or Cope, that there would be. The Oath which Collins had prepared after his IRB consultations was accepted with insignificant changes. Collins also secured agreement, over Lloyd George's objections, to a reduction in the period allowed to the Six Counties within which to decide for or against joining the Free State. He thought a year was too long and got it reduced to a month because he felt a year would allow life to be made impossible for the Nationalists. To prove this contention he cited both loyalist outrages and instances of partisanship on the part of the British Army towards loyalists and of corresponding bias against Nationalists. Reluctantly Lloyd George accepted the 'Ulster month'.

Britain no longer sought the exclusive right to defend Irish coastal waters and Ireland was to be permitted to build and maintain vessels for revenue and fisheries protection. Furthermore the two governments were to meet after five years to review the 'undertaking by Ireland of a share in her own coastal defence'. Finally, Lloyd George proposed that if the Irish agreed to sign the Treaty he would drop Britain's demand for free trade.

Griffith again repeated that he would sign, but said again that it was unfair to ask the others to do so before they knew Craig's position. Lloyd George replied: 'Do I understand, Mr Griffith, that though everyone else refuses, you will nevertheless agree to sign?'[97] There was a pause as Griffith no doubt struggled with a vision of the contumely his answer would bring upon him, and then he replied simply, 'That is so, Mr Prime Minister.' Austen Chamberlain said afterwards, 'A braver man than Arthur Griffith I have never met.'[98]

As we have seen, Lloyd George knew that Collins was in favour of signing. Barton, who had been invited to make a rare appearance in sub-conference that now seems more than coincidental, was thus the one to convince. Ultimatum time had arrived. Lloyd George bent all his formidable array of psychological weaponry on him. 'That is not enough, if we sign we shall sign as a delegation and stake the life of our government on our signature. Is the Irish delegation prepared to do the same?'

Barton's report says: 'He particularly addressed himself to me and said very solemnly that those who were not for peace must take the full responsibility for the war that would immediately follow refusal by any delegate to sign the Articles of Agreement.' Having let that sink in the Welsh Wizard continued to weave his spell in a manner more theatrical than ethical. 'I have to communicate with Sir James Craig tonight,' he said, holding up two envelopes.

Here are the alternative letters which I have prepared, one enclosing the Articles of Agreement reached by His Majesty's Government and yourselves, and the other saying that Sinn Fein representatives refuse the Oath of allegiance and refuse to come within the Empire. If I send this letter, it is war – and war within three days. Which letter am I to send? Whichever letter you choose travels by special train to Holyhead, and by destroyer to Belfast. The train is waiting with steam up at Euston. Mr Shakespeare is ready. If he is to reach Sir James Craig in time we must have your answer by ten pm tonight. You can have until then but no longer to decide whether you will give peace or war to your country.[99]

That was some weight of responsibility to have deposited on the shoulders of a young man, by the leader of what was then still the world's largest empire. Lloyd George was of course bluffing for Barton's benefit. He had promised to give Collins more time to consider just that morning and he was only committed to sending Craig a copy of the proposals, nothing else hung on their despatch. But getting the Treaty through Dublin hinged on getting all the delegates to sign in London.

Barton was not the only one with a load on his shoulders. No one knew better than Michael Collins himself that he was going to have to carry the burden of the Treaty with his countrymen. Churchill's famous description of Collins recalls his agony at that moment: 'Michael Collins rose looking as though he were going to shoot someone, preferably himself. In all my life I have never seen so much pain and suffering in restraint.'[100] He had kept his cards so close to his chest that when, on the way back to Hans Place, he told Barton that he intended to sign, Barton was astounded. But he acknowledged Collins' motives in taking the step. 'He knew that physical resistance, if resumed, would collapse, and he was not going to be the leader of a forlorn hope.'[101] Forlorn or no, Barton would not give in easily. For hours he and Duffy held out, bolstered by Childers.

Griffith spoke 'almost passionately for signing'[102] and there was much putting on of coats and threats of departing to Downing St with or without Barton and Duffy. A remark of Collins' lodged with Barton and helped to tip the scales. Collins had pointed out how few active Volunteers there had been. 'Do you want to send them out to be slaughtered?' he asked. Duggan had added to this by saying: 'Barton, you will be hanged from a lamppost in Dublin if your refusal to sign causes a new war in Ireland.' And then, suddenly, Duggan broke down and began recalling the deaths of Moran, Flood and the others.

He described Mountjoy, on the morning 'when I saw the hangman who was to hang our young lads there'. Childers records: 'There was long and hot argument about committing our young men to die. Die for nothing. What could G.D. (Gavan Duffy) get better? G.D. assented quietly. Bob was shaken. Asked me out and I said it was principle.' And here Childers inadvertently gave the scales of decision the final touch. He added, 'and I felt Molly was with us'. This had the opposite effect on Barton to what was intended. The idea of resolving his tumult of conscience on the basis of what Childers' American wife had to say about the situation angered Barton. He replied, 'Well I suppose I must sign.'

Judging from Kathleen Napoli MacKenna's reminiscences Collins had gone to Cadogan Gardens while most of this discussion was in progress. She was told to go to Hans Place and set off there with Broy. There was an air of menace about that was not due only to the fog:

We were conscious that figures were sheltering everywhere in the shadows . . . three or four thugs stepped out unexpectedly before us and, without uttering a syllable, blocked our way. One flashed an electric torch in Broy's face, and by its light I could see pistols glinting. They scrutinised Broy thoroughly, passing the torch over his head, face and body, then slunk silently away.[103]

Collins came to Hans Place with Tobin and Cullen. Outside, says Napoli MacKenna:

the vicinity was bristling with Scotland Yard men. Mick was irritated to find the other delegates had not as yet come down to the hall. He stalked nervously up and down the dining room, his attache case in his left hand, his old mackintosh dangling untidily over it . . . Tom poured him out a sherry . . . he sent Eddie upstairs to tell the others he was waiting . . . outside Diarmuid O'Hegarty, Desmond Fitzgerald, Eamonn Broy . . . were waiting in the cars . . .

Collins was informed that the discussion upstairs 'gave no sign of terminating.'. . . Like a wild beast in a cage he paced up and down the room, morose, silent and sullen; then plumped down in a dining-room chair that happened to be placed in line with that part of the stairs down which those who were to join him would have to come . . . he fell into a short profound sleep. Poor 'Big Fellow!' As I gazed my heart ached with anguish at the thought of what his mental torture must be. I appreciated the weight of responsibility placed by events beyond his control on his young generous shoulders . . . suddenly those going to Downing St came down the stairs.

In Dublin detectives and Auxiliaries had suddenly reappeared on the streets also. They stopped pedestrians and searched them. Memories of the pre-truce terror flooded back. Was it war again? In Downing St the same question was asked. 'We had doubts as to whether we would see them again', said Lloyd George. He thought they would, 'provided that Michael Collins has as much moral courage as he has physical courage . . . but moral courage is a much higher quality than physical courage and it is a quality that brave men often lack.'[104] Suddenly a message came that the Irish were on their way back. Pulse rates increased sharply. The Irishmen marched in. It was

clear from their faces that they had come to a great decision after a prolonged struggle. As before they were superficially very calm and quiet. There was a long pause, or seemed to be; then Mr Griffith said: 'Mr Prime Minister, the delegation is willing to sign the agreements.'

At 2.30 am they did so after a final frenzy of last-minute argument, redrafting and re-typing.

Birkenhead turned to Collins after putting his name to the document and said, 'I may have signed my political death-warrant tonight.' The younger man replied, 'I may have signed my actual death-warrant.'

9

Fighting the Waves

'For forms of government let fools contest.'

Alexander Pope

Now the waking nightmare began. Cathleen ni Houlihan, Yeats' synonym for Ireland, would show herself as an envious, strident, venomous bitch throughout the Treaty debates conducted both in and outside the Dail. One of the mildest epithets hurled at the delegates was 'traitors'. Griffith and Collins were reckoned to have been drugged or drunk when they signed the Treaty,[1] but Collins was singled out for special treatment, on the grounds of both drink and sex. Countess Markievicz regaled the Dail with a rumour that Collins had broken up a royal romance![2] She said that the Governor Generalship, 'the centre of English immorality and divorce', had been earmarked for a member of the royal family until Collins came along. As a result 'Princess Mary's wedding is to be broken off . . . the Princess Mary is to be married to Michael Collins who will be appointed first Governor.'

This nonsense came at a particularly bad moment. Collins had fallen in love and planned to marry Kitty Kiernan. She had visited him in London during the talks but the strain and uncertainty of his position, and her Catholic conscience, seem to have made the visit a stormy one. She wrote to him saying:

. . . why not marry the one I really love, and what a cowardly thing of me to be afraid to marry the one I really want, and who loves me just as well as any of the others I thought of marrying.

Then London came. I should not have gone. It gave rise to such talk. People got to know about it and I thought it better from a girl's very conventional and narrow point of view that we had better have something definite, and so we have drifted . . . now don't think by this that I want a row or want you to end it. Not likely. I want you only not to think bad of me when we had those scenes.[3]

Collins wrote back on 5 and 6 December sending her a two-part letter. The first part said:

If the question were of no interest at all to me surely I could not blame you for having concern for your own future and your lifelong happiness. When it does so very closely concern you I cannot blame you more. This is really my straightforward and genuine point of view.

He was interrupted then by the alarms and excursions attendant on the signing of the Treaty and resumed the letter to express hopes doomed to be unfulfilled:

To bed about five, and up to go to Mass and didn't (need I say it) forget your candle. My plans in regard to home are as yet uncertain. I don't know how things will go now but with God's help we have brought peace to this land of ours – a peace which will end this old strife of ours for ever.

He met the Countess Markievicz's charge in typically Collins fashion, cutting through the rumours and uncertainties to make his engagement public knowledge, while still safeguarding his fiancée's identity. His statement of rebuttal delivered with stilted, old-world courtesy drew loud applause:

I do not come from the class the Deputy for the Dublin Division comes from; I come from the plain people of Ireland. The lady whose name was mentioned is, I understand, betrothed to some man. I know nothing of her personally, I know nothing of her in any way whatsoever, but the statement may cause her pain and may cause pain to the lady who is betrothed to me (Hear! Hear!). I just stand in that plain way, and I will not allow without challenge any Deputy in the assembly of my nation to insult any lady either of his nation or of any other nation. (Loud applause.)

He rounded this off by sending Kitty an express letter that evening (3 January 1921):

My Dearest Kitty,
    This will reach you before the letters I sent today. My dear, dear Kitty, see the references to yourself and Princess Mary of England.
                    My betrothed,
                    My fondest love,
                    Michael.

Incredibly enough, 'Princess Mary' type accusations, however understandable amidst the hopes and hates of revolution, were still being levelled at Collins as this book was being written. So much so that Dr T. Ryle Dwyer came to the defence of his reputation, pointing out that pursuing 'a piece of ear' rather than 'a piece of ass' did not make a man either a homosexual or a 'rampant philanderer'.[4] Sharing beds with other men, or staying at the homes of single women was a necessary concomitant of a life on the run in which a bed anywhere was a prize. Both Collins and associates like Tobin and Cullen knew what it was to spend nights in the open, literally within seconds of death. In one raid on Vaughan's Tobin and Cullen escaped by hanging by their fingertips from a window ledge. In another, Collins and other Vaughan's habitués got out ahead of a raiding party but were trapped inside a cordon and had to spend the night in the meagre shelter afforded by the buttresses of a nearby church. As they shrank back against the cold stone, armed sentries walked up and down within feet of them. Sanctuary, not sex, was the priority in such conditions.

In the film Cathal O'Shannon made of his life, Emmet Dalton, then an old man,[5] said of Collins, 'I loved him. I use no other word. I loved him as a man loves another man, with pure love.' Dalton, Tobin, McKee, all Collins' close companions had the close bonding of men in war. That did not make them homosexual. Yearnings for women must have been overwhelming at times – after leaving the arena gladiators traditionally sought release – and I know from contemporary testimony[6] that some men on active service needed to have a woman after a 'job'. But that did not make them womanisers. The majority of Volunteers afterwards settled down to the strictly observed Catholic marriages of the time.

Nevertheless the rumours about Collins' sexual activities had gained fresh currency the year before Dr T. Ryle Dwyer's book was published (1989) following the screening of an important, two-hour-long, award-winning documentary on Collins for RTE (Radio Telefis Eireann) in 1989, which subsequently became a best-selling video.[7] Amongst those who took part was Mr Eoghan Harris who had written a film script which gave rise to stories about Collins being homosexual. Mr Harris said amongst other things that Collins was 'cruel, calculating, devious, two-timed a lot of women and was probably hypocritical in the sense that he went to Communion a lot while carrying on an affair with two women at the same time.'

He based these statements on a large file, 'the best American money can buy. Every person he ever spoke to, every document, diaries, bits of paper he left around, they're all here, all the facts.' This collection, said Mr Harris, was 'compiled by Mr Arthur Schlesinger Jnr, great historian, and may be sixteen others.'

As Arthur Schlesinger[8] is the only one of the seventeen scholars referred to at this point, I got in touch with him. He told me he was 'surprised'[9] and wrote: 'I would never dream of posing as an authority on Michael Collins . . . I have never said or thought that Collins was a hypocrite and a womaniser who received Holy Communion while taking advantage of different women.' In fact Dr Schlesinger was so horrified at the idea of being associated with such a theory that he authorised me to 'deny these statements', and made a similar rebuttal on behalf of Alexandra [his wife, the expert on Collins in the family].[10] The interest generated by Mr Harris' remark is an example of the way in which myths about Collins are generated today.

Women did play an important part in the Anglo-Irish war, much more so than the role they were accorded in the political life of the state they helped to create. Collins was constantly in the company of courageous, passionate women, some of them very beautiful, his cousin Nancy for example. She was doubly related to him.[11] Nancy told Liam O'Donnachadha, also a cousin, 'All the girls were mad about him.'[12] Was Nancy 'mad' about Collins? Some members of the family think so, but his affections turned elsewhere and in 1922 she married his brother, Johnny, and reunited the large family scattered after the burning of Woodfield. Nancy's calibre may be gauged from her attitude towards the youngest stepson, Liam, who suffered a multiplicity of illnesses as a result of hardships sustained while still an infant after the Woodfield break-up, amongst them bad eyesight. When he got older he wanted to be a lawyer, but couldn't read the text books. Nancy sat up 'every night for four hours and in her beautiful, Civil Service, copperplate handwriting she copied out every single book'.[13] Liam became a solicitor and built up one of the largest practices in Cork.

It is certain that by the time the Treaty negotiations began, insofar as women in Ireland were concerned, everyone else, including Susan Killeen, had faded from the centre of Collins' affections in favour of Kitty Kiernan. He was still friendly with Susan but, as the following letter[14] indicates, hardly intimate:

Madam,
   None of your impudence. I want to know what I asked about No. 9. Keep in touch and see if the place is raided. I gave you 4/6 for that damned ticket you sent me but I don't suppose I'll go. Other people are like cats too but not because of the number of their lives.
Do dtuigeann tu bas me [Trans: do you want to kill me?]
                    Miceal

There is a story in Susan's family that she told Collins that he didn't want a wife, he wanted someone to cook and sew for him. She disagreed with Collins over the Treaty and of course about Kitty Kiernan. It is part of the family folklore that when Collins was agonising over whether or not to declare war on those who were defying him on the Treaty some of their mutual friends came to her and asked her to advise him. 'Why should I tell him what to do?' she is said to have replied. 'If he wants advice, let him ask Kitty Kiernan!' Susan was however destined to be happier than Kitty Kiernan and, ironically enough, in Granard, Kitty's home town, where she went to live with her bank manager husband and large family.

Kitty Kiernan was to experience tragedy and unhappiness for most of her life, civil war claiming the lives of two men who loved her and illness ruining her later days. She must have caused some unhappiness too, judging from the tone of a letter Harry Boland wrote to her before setting off for America:

Pulse of my heart . . . How I can leave you even at the order of 'the Chief' [de Valera]. I do not know, and I'm asking myself all the time if I have not made a great mistake in leaving you behind . . . I would just love to have you come to America where we will spend our honeymoon in perfect bliss!

Mick and I spent the last night together. He saw me home at 2 am, and as I had to catch the 7.35 am I bade him goodbye – only to find him at Kingsbridge as fresh as a daisy to see me off. I need not say to you how much I love him, and I know he has a warm spot in his heart for me, and I feel sure in no matter what manner our Triangle may work out, he and I shall be always friends.[15]

The triangle was to 'work out' in death. Although in America Boland's first reaction on hearing the news was to welcome the Treaty, he soon swung behind the de Valera line and on 15 December 1921 telegraphed the Dail, in his capacity as a Deputy for Roscommon-Mayo, rejecting the Treaty. However his distancing himself from Collins in this way appears to have been politically, not romantically motivated. Kitty does not appear to have told him about her engagement plans. This news seems to have come from Collins himself on Boland's return from America to take part in the Treaty debates. A note from Boland to Kitty[16] on the subject contrasts markedly with his lyrical letter on departure:

Kitty,
     I want to congratulate you. M. told me of your engagement, and I wish you long life and happiness,
                              Ever yours,
                              H. Boland

Collins and Kitty appear to have talked about marriage during the London negotiations. They made a pact that they would write to each other every day and the lovers' letters literally fill a book, named after the phrase that appears in most of his, *In Great Haste*. As his life entered its last turbulent phase many of the letters he wrote to Kitty contain things like: 'I read over all your letters again last night and I started writing to you sitting up in bed but I had to give it up. Positively I was too worn out to write legibly,'[17] and 'I'm so tired that I can scarcely remain awake. This is just a line to tell you so.'[18] Kitty however wrote passionately and open-heartedly at times: 'I almost shudder at the thought of the strength of my love, what I do believe I am capable of feeling and that without you, life held nothing for me. Nobody mattered to me, not even myself, if you were not with me.'[19] She writes about wishing that she could be near him so that she could make 'sacred and profane love'[20] to him and apparently got her wish later in the month when she recalls a night of passion:

Last night was a real wedding night for you and me. Didn't you feel that way too, but couldn't put it into words? I *wanted* to run away with you. That must be the feeling with people who do run away like that. We had it last night. That was our night. Glad today, *for both you and me*, that I did not go.[21]

Kitty did not hesitate to put intimate thoughts on paper. She describes going to bed early and lying awake thinking of him:

. . . madly passionately in love with you, to use your own words . . . I found myself promising you faithfully that I'd never had a real row, nor fall out with you at all, no matter what you did, 'if' first, you are sympathetic to me (now don't laugh, because I'm real serious), if you are not too rough, and don't hurt me when we are just playing, just fooling and a few other little ifs.[22]

By contrast his letters are guarded, stilted, the work of a man who is constantly aware of how easily ones innermost thoughts can fall into the hands of others. His letter to Kitty on the night of the Markievicz attack, restrained though it was, was one of his most expressive. Collins, the world's expert on interrupting the mails, is now hoist with his own petard. He warns her about the need to take care with their correspondence, urging her to put a letter into an inner envelope, marked personal, and worries that some of her letters are falling into the hands of his enemies on the anti-Treaty side.[23]

Another reason for this hesitancy to express himself may have been her lack of interest in politics, except insofar as they involved following his doings in the newspapers. For example when she heard of his military appointment during the civil war, after they had been apart by force of circumstance for some three weeks, she wrote: 'You are C. in Chief now. What does this mean? More trouble I suppose. Will it ever end? But God is good. I wish that we were already married, and that the very next time we'd meet was on our honeymoon.'[24]

An overview of the correspondence gives one an impression of a want of intellectual communication between them. There is little doubt that he reciprocated her passion, as references like the night 'you really wanted me', make clear but his suspicions about tampering with his mail – which, as we shall see, were to have fatal consequences for one suspect, Noel Lemass – confined his mode of address to 'dear' rather than Harry Boland's lyricism. Kitty talks of being ill a good deal. There are also frequent references to rows and misunderstandings. A combination of her natural hot temper and her edginess, caused possibly by Bright's disease, from which she seems to have died ultimately, would certain explain these.

Sister Margaret Mary told me that she and her sisters all thought that he was going to marry Sinead Mason. 'She was very nice, but he was a great ladies' man.' They were filled with curiosity about Kitty when she was suddenly introduced to their circle. A story is told of a shopping expedition on which Kitty bought a large hat which she asked him to carry. His reaction to this was 'blast ye, woman, I'm not going to be seen carrying *that*!' And Kevin O'Shiel said that Collins' comment when Kitty put on the hat was: 'The cartwheel's bigger than the cart!'[25] After Collins' death her life became something of an emotional wasteland. She read and re-read his letters and when she finally married, to Felix Cronin, then Quartermaster General in the Army, installed his portrait in her living room and called the second of her two children Michael Collins Cronin.[26] She died in 1945, the years preceding her death punctuated by stays in nursing homes.

Both Collins and Kiernan were deeply religious. *In Great Haste* contains several references to prayer and attendance at Mass and Communion. Her last letter to him[27] mentions the possibility of going together to make the severe Lough Derg pilgrimage, which involves sleeplessness, bare feet, fasting and continuous prayer over a three-day period. During a period of great difficulty with the English in May 1922 his piety made such an impression on a Passionate Order priest giving a mission in Greystones that the Missioner, Ignatius CP, wrote after Collins' death to his sister Lena:

Michael was very busy in Dublin, worked and worried almost beyond endurance. He got to Greystones one night very late, and very tired . . . He got up next morning as early as 5.30 am, came to the church and made a glorious General Confession, and received Holy Communion. He said to me afterwards, 'Say the Mass for Ireland and God bless you, Father.' He crossed an hour or so later to London.[28]

On the one hand Collins' defenders have traditionally argued that this piety preserved him from any female entanglements, on the other his critics say it renders him a hypocrite if he did yield to the urgings of the flesh. It's a very Irish type of debate, though less common now than it used to be, and one that shows a very superficial understanding of human sexuality.

Much is revealed in Collins' response to a letter from a parish priest which included this advice:

Will you attend Mass and receive Holy Communion every morning as long as the Conference lasts? You will I am sure, when you know you have not only Ireland's temporal destiny but her spiritual one as well in your hands. That is a dreadful responsibility remember. Beware too of English hospitality, live retired after conference in your hotel. Remember there is a danger and pardon me for pointing it out. You will be watched and criticised and your every smallest action shall be held up before the world and it may possibly happen that a set shall be put on your track and lead you astray and spy upon you. Be on your guard.[29]

Collins was very struck by this letter. The points about temporal and spiritual destiny and the phrase 'dreadful responsibility' are underlined in blue pencil, that about 'English hospitality' in red. After acknowledging the letter through his secretary, Collins himself wrote thanking the priest for his information about British intentions and saying:

You will remember the other advice you gave me. Believe me, I know fully the English method in these matters; I didn't live so long among them without finding it out. The other part of your advice is being attended to also though not – for certain essential reasons – quite fully. You needn't worry, I will tell you the whole story some time.[30]

The 'not quite fully' could refer to either receiving the sacraments daily or accepting British hospitality. As we know he did make an effort to attend the sacraments with some frequency, it is more likely that he was giving an explanation – before he might be asked for one – as to why he would be attending certain houses outside the strictly Irish-Ireland circle that the rest of the delegation confined themselves to. Even on a visit to Chequers, Griffith would not accept hospitality. His drinking was confined to Hans Place or the homes of Irish friends. The houses Collins visited were those of the Laverys and the Llewelyn Davieses.

Collins' friendship with the Llewelyn Davies family caused them great anguish in the months before the Truce. In March 1921, through no fault of Collins but because of what he called a 'frightful example of carelessness and thoughtlessness'[31] premises were hired for the propaganda department under a false name, Moya's, and when the premises were inevitably raided this fact highlighted Collins' relationship with Moya. She was arrested and imprisoned and her husband was promptly dismissed, losing an income of £2,500 a year.[32] She was in some respects lucky, because at the time of the raid there were no guns in the house. She normally kept them in open hat-boxes, concealed only by scarves or underclothing. On top of this, either because of Crompton's friendship with Lloyd George, or possibly because the Government simply found the affair embarrassing, there was very little publicity about the dismissal. It was not raised in Parliament until just after the Truce had come into effect[33] and only rated one paragraph in the Irish papers the next day.

Collins obviously took the arrests and dismissal to heart. He made repeated efforts to get Crompton employed by the Dail as a legal expert in terms which are indicative as much of his concern for the future as for his friend:

It seems to me that we have to take things now on a permanent basis. This is a time when precedents are being made and when much thinking ahead is necessary. Establishments that at the moment may look threatening are in my opinion going to have a permanent character. Therefore it is important that right lines are laid down at the start.[34]

There was some resistance. Art O'Connor agreed that it would be 'worth many thousands a year in order to get the foundation of our land system and policy right',[35] but went on to say that 'some of their colleagues' might regard the appointment as 'a needless expenditure'. Crompton, who was 'a bit broken up',[36] ultimately found himself a partnership in a London firm of solicitors specialising in international law. He did in fact help Collins considerably with research and drafting during the Treaty negotiations and with speech writing thereafter.[37]

In Dublin, Collins used his network of warders to see to it that everything possible was done to make prison life easier in Mountjoy for Moya and her two companions, his helpers Eileen MacGrane and Patricia Hoey. 'Mick saw to it that little comforts such as woollen rugs, good books, food, China tea, which she preferred, sweetmeats were smuggled into her and her companions,' writes Kathleen MacKenna. Collins himself said, 'I'm in very close touch. She keeps in tip-top form . . . I fancy it could easily be arranged [if Crompton went to work on 'certain liberals'] that she might be released quietly.'[38] All three were released soon after the Truce and 'Moya went immediately to her husband and children in London.'[39] The next time Kathleen and Moya met was in Cadogan Gardens, Collins' headquarters during the Treaty negotiations. But were Collins and Moya lovers? Does it matter? One might well ask in 1990, but in 1921 the question could sometimes carry with it insinuations of espionage and conspiracy concerning the Treaty's signing and it therefore has to be addressed. There is strong, but not conclusive, circumstantial evidence that Collins and Moya were indeed lovers. Two anecdotes about now-vanished manuscripts certainly point in that direction. Both are redolent of the atmosphere of menace and conspiracy that accompanied so many of Collins' activities.

The first was related to me by Valentine Iremonger, the distinguished poet, playwright, translator of Irish literature and former diplomat.[40] Iremonger, who during the mid-1950s was Counsellor to the Irish Embassy in London, paid a visit to Rex Taylor in Lancashire while he was writing his biography of Collins.[41] Taylor showed him research material, which included Collins' diaries and day-books and a collection of Moya Llewelyn Davies' letters, some of which indicated a love affair. Taylor agreed to send 'small parcels at a time' to the Embassy so that Iremonger could have them copied and place the copies in the National Library with a thirty-year prohibition on publication. But following a subsequent conversation on an open telephone line, 'two men in bowler hats, acting for the firm of solicitors who represented the Llewelyn Davieses, showed up with authorisation to repossess the documents and took them away'.

The second anecdote came from Sister Margaret Mary, Batt O'Connor's daughter. Moya, who had helped Batt O'Connor with the publication of his book on Collins, showed the manuscript of her autobiography to Batt and his wife. Mrs O'Connor was aghast to read her account of her relationship with Collins and decided something must be done. She summoned some of his closest associates, including Liam Tobin and Frank Thornton, to a reading. It was generally agreed that the book contained material concerning their dead leader that should not be printed. They decided to send the unfortunate Moya an anonymous death threat. The crude censorship worked, the book never appeared and the manuscript has been lost sight of.

Poor Moya never suspected the conspirators. She recalled: 'it was put up to Mick that he should allow the Army to be canvassed as the other side was doing, and he refused. His attitude in that first week was that if the people didn't want the Treaty he had no wish whatever to force it upon them. They could take it or leave it.'[42] Moya believed that Collins had made 'no attempt to persuade you' [Thornton] or any of 'his extremists of the IRB'. She recalled the enormous satisfaction that Collins got from receiving a letter signed by Tobin, Cullen, Thornton and the others telling him they were 'with him' in that first uncertain week after the Treaty was signed. Collins' pleasure was of course quite genuine. Moya clearly did not realise that Collins had kept the IRB suitably informed before signing the Treaty.

Obviously, therefore, for all his genuine solicitude for Moya and her husband during her imprisonment, whatever their degree of intimacy was (the *Sunday Press* of 23 August 1987 discussed a rumour that Collins and she had a child) it did not allow her either to share his thoughts fully or to understand the fierce, primitive, clannishness that surrounded him.

Collins' reputation has also suffered because of his friendship with Sir James Barrie at whose house it was wrongly believed that he first met John Chartres. Kathleen Napoli MacKenna has left an account of the Llewelyn Davies connection which, though affectionate, nevertheless clearly shows how the suspicions arose. Moya brought Kathleen to meet Crompton, 'Bertrand Russell, Sir James Barrie and other intellectuals' and told her something of their background:

In his youth Jimmy Barrie loved a girl named Sylvia with a spiritual love similar to that of Dante for Beatrice. Sylvia married a Llewelyn Davies and, on her early demise, Barrie took care of the education of her two sons, and wrote for them the tales of Peter Pan and Wendy . . . In turn Jimmy Barrie was the confidant and bosom friend of 'The Welsh Wizard' Lloyd George who, when a Liberal taking his first steps on the road to political fame, was sponsored by Crompton. In the evenings Lloyd George visited Barrie's flat where, according to himself, 'he let his nerves relax and drew completely aside the curtain of his soul', disclosing plans, tactics, opinions, comments and so on! Naturally wily Lloyd George knew all about Moya's political associations, and of Barrie's friendship with Moya's husband.[43]

Some republicans to this day believe that the entire Barrie/Llewelyn

Davies/Chartres connection were spies who kept 'Ireland's principal war leader . . . dangling upon a line held firmly from Downing St.'[44]

The sheer importance of the Treaty for Ireland, would of course account in part for the explosion of myth and gossip. But there was also the Lilliputian factor. The impact of emerging out of the cabins and the small houses, the world wherein their soldiers were not accorded belligerent rights, into the world of the denizens of the big houses, was such that it inevitably expressed itself in the tones of envy and small-mindedness. The houses where the delegates stayed were not especially grand by London standards but consider the effects of the following description of a party at Hans Place (on 10 November 1921) on the imaginations of flying-column men who slept fifteen or twenty to a room in wet clothes – and made sure they broke nothing and, if they could, paid for everything before they left.

When the feast was at its height Mick with Liam Tobin, Tom Cullen, Emmet Dalton, Joe Guilfoyle and Joe Dolan joined us. They were jovial boisterous men who preferred horseplay to formalities. It was not long before they began throwing cushions at one another, then tangerine oranges, apples and nuts from the table, and finally coal from the coal-scuttles![45]

Some people took to such scenes with less indulgence than did Napoli MacKenna. Sean O'Hegarty, OC of Cork No. 1 Brigade, for instance, wrote[46] to Liam Lynch, OC of the 1st Southern Division purporting to be dismayed at the report of a Brigade officer after a visit to London. O'Hegarty relayed tales of 'rowdy and drunken conduct at Hans Place continuously'. Such conduct was 'particularly bad' when 'a dance or dances were held, or some form of entertainment ceremony'. These functions had been known to result in the 'smashing of a chair and door panels'. O'Hegarty notes 'the name of Michael Collins bandied about as central figure in alleged orgies'. But worse than all this a 'Fr. Dempsey had gone three times to see Michael Collins and discovered him "half cocked" on two occasions and "worse on the third".' A clear note of envy is struck as O'Hegarty grimly records that the drink bills from 'two houses' for one week were £300 and £200 and states that it is 'not clear whether the "two houses" means from two public houses for Hans Place establishment or has reference to the two establishments which I understand are being maintained in London for the delegation'.

When O'Hegarty, whom Mulcahy refers to as being 'always a snarly gob'[47] was pressed to substantiate his allegations, he replied that the officer who had supplied him with the information was 'not now available being despatched on a special mission'.[48] O'Hegarty believed it was 'his duty' to make such a report but having made it said 'the responsibility for the matter passes from me'.

Of course the reports also passed all round Ireland and very easily became intertwined with talk of treachery and espionage, especially when beautiful women could be mentioned (legitimately) in the same context. One of the most beautiful women in London at the time was Hazel Lavery, wife of the Belfast-born portrait painter, Sir John Lavery. She came from a branch of a well-known Galway family, the Martyns, which had settled in Chicago. In 1910 she married Lavery, who was nearly twice her age, and became one of London's most-talked-of society hostesses.

The writer Shane Leslie, first cousin of Winston Churchill, who was once in love with Hazel Lavery himself, said:

> . . . of Hazel's achievement in bringing about the Irish Treaty of 1921 I know no historical comparison save the Princess Dorothea de Lieven's diplomatic cleverness amongst the statesmen of the drawing room in bringing about the Treaty of London in 1827 by which the Powers recognised the Independence of Greece. It was from her salon which was also her husband's studio that Hazel set out to inveigle English and Irish statesmen from the summits to descend and know each other personally as well as politically. Many such as Winston Churchill and Lord Birkenhead or Michael Collins and Arthur Griffith had reason to remember number five Cromwell Place (an ironical name for omen) during the twenties.[49]

This is an accolade indeed, but a more prosaic approach is taken by another authority on the period, Terence de Vere White,[50] in his biography of Kevin O'Higgins. He gives the then orthodox view amongst Collins' associates and admirers of the relationship between Hazel and Collins:

> Lady Lavery developed a romantic attachment to Michael Collins which was notorious. Rumour gave colour and exaggeration and Lady Lavery, it must be confessed, gave rumour wings – to what was, after all a fancy on her part. Collins was unaware of the role which he played in the lively imagination of his hostess. He was engaged to be married . . . Lady Lavery persisted in the belief that Collins was unattached, and put on widow's weeds which only the firm tact of a friend prevented her from wearing at his funeral. Letters from Collins were shown to Lord Birkenhead by Lady Lavery and he noticed that the occasional romantic passages were interpolated in a woman's hand-writing, valiantly, if unsuccessfully, disguised. It was all very odd, very unreal but not unpleasant, when one became accustomed to it and accepted the romantic convention. O'Higgins was destined to take the place of Collins in Lady Lavery's romantic imagination.[51]

But was it only a 'romantic imagination'? The truthful answer appears to be almost certainly not, however unconsummated the affair may or may not have been. The RTE documentary film, by Colm Connolly, shows close-up shots of her wearing deep mourning black and very obviously devastated by grief. Shane Leslie made a more complex analysis of the relationship of Hazel Lavery to both Collins and Kevin O'Higgins, whom Kathleen Napoli MacKenna termed 'the Irish Robespierre'.[52] Writing to Lady Audrey Morris about her proposed biography of Hazel he said that if their relationship

> were truly portrayed there would be war in Dublin and much protestation. Both men were hopelessly in love with Hazel in the style of Tristan with the wife of King Mark because they had drunk a poisonous drug not intended for them. I had a sip myself so I know what it was like. The Republicans intercepted her letters to Collins and decided to shoot them both. Their three ambushes in August 1922 failed but Collins was shot a week later owing to those letters, as his enemies boast.
>
> Collins' own letters to Hazel were of a type – full of half educated half romantic stuff but ending up with vital messages to the English Cabinet which were shown to Winston, Charlie [Lord Londonderry, Edith's husband] and others. It was on the strength of these letters that the Treaty was made. Hazel was proud of the letters and carried them about unwisely in a bag and was inclined to show Collins' love for her. Here she told me that she brought them on a party here and was convinced they were rifled by another guest called Dixon [a prominent Unionist]. This is given colour too by the names in the visitors' book. Every letter that would enable the Orange Party to frighten and blackmail the cowardly English Government had disappeared. John did not mind how much Collins and Kevin adored Hazel. He knew she was playing pityingly and ambitiously with men. He sent for me the night after Kevin was shot and took me for the first and only time to Hazel's bedroom. I held her for some hours while she shook and sobbed in my arms. She was aghast. She cried out that every man who loved her with true love was bound to die. She had killed her first husband and Collins and Kevin. She cursed herself as a curse to men.
>
> She showed men's letters to each other. She actually gave me a copy of the pathetic love poems which Kevin wrote her. We all did! She showed one of my prose poems to Collins which he took and wrapped around her miniature. They were returned soaked with his blood after his death . . .
>
> I think that as far as liaisons it was what the French call 'Le cas de Madame Recamier'. Do you know what I mean.[53]

It was all very different from the world in which Collins and O'Higgins were brought up and it is understandable that an unexpected draught of the sophisticated 'drug' which Leslie describes would have worked powerfully on young, idealistic men who had never before encountered such sophistication.

It says much for Hazel Lavery's alchemy that she should have captivated O'Higgins as well as Collins. Kevin O'Higgins, newly-wed, was a devout Catholic, an austere, spiritual man who fasted for six months before his marriage in October of 1921 to Bridget Cole, a teacher and daughter of T. E. O'Sullivan, the man who wrote the song 'God Save Ireland'.

His best man was Rory O'Connor, whose execution he sanctioned in 1922. When assassins fatally wounded him in 1927, amongst his last words were 'I forgive my murderers', and he joked with his wife, picturing himself sitting on a damp cloud with a harp and arguing politics with 'Mick'.[54]

But no man can hold himself immune from love as one of the 'pathetic' poems Shane Leslie refers to indicates:

H   How can I tell you – I unskilled to sing –
A   All the deep nadirs of despair I know –
Z   Zeniths of joy that from remembrance flow
E   Evening may fall before our torches glow,
L   Love of my life, for time is on the wing.[55]

After Collins' death O'Higgins favoured Lady Lavery for the post of Governor General of Ireland. But by then the tide of revolution had ebbed and the thoughts of his colleagues were flowing in more mundane directions. The Laverys were not appointed to the old Viceregal Lodge[56] and Hazel's reward for her service to Ireland was to have her portrait printed on the Irish banknotes, where it appears to this day, although in recent designs, only as a watermark. Apart from helping to smooth the Treaty negotiations Hazel appears to have come to Collins' assistance on at least one other occasion. Although the precise date is not known it probably occurred in May or June of 1922 when relations between Collins and Churchill were particularly strained (see Chapter 11). Churchill was taking a tough line with Collins, for, amongst other things, the latter's North of Ireland activities and his refusal to crack down on former comrades whose activities were causing Churchill considerable embarrassment with the Die-hards.

Collins, who needed arms and continued British support at that stage, called with Hazel Lavery to Sir Philip Sassoon's home at Lympne where Churchill was painting. But Churchill refused to leave the easel. 'Young men must learn patience'[57] was his message to the butler. However, Hazel persisted. Shane Leslie, although he may have overstated its value, nevertheless authenticates her description of the situation at this juncture:

matters were looking desperate in the Irish troubles, so I arranged for a special meeting of Collins with Winston Churchill . . . at Sir Philip Sassoon's house at Port Lympne. At first Churchill was hesitant about coming to the meeting. But I impressed upon him the urgency of the situation, and he finally agreed . . . This meeting, arranged while Michael Collins was on a forty-eight-hours visit to England, really saved Ireland, and brought about the creation of the Irish Free State.[58]

A number of items concerning Hazel were found on Collins' body after he was killed. One was a transcript of a description by Shane Leslie of three portraits by Lavery in the Grosvenor Gallery, Collins, Hazel and Dennison Ross. Entitled 'To a Portrait of Hazel as Leda or Rose O'Grady' it included:

What feathered denizen of the sea or hills, what proud plumed lover from the mountain or the lake did Lavery suspect when he painted that flowing fluttering trembling view of your surprised and passionate Beauty? . . . or was it some amorous flamingo who broke through his bars at the Zoological Gardens or some dreadful nighthawk who clawed and dropped you ere he could carry you to his eyrie or was it some fierce 'wild goose' of Ireland that passed crying in the night.[59]

Others are fragments of letters which passed between them. One[60] is dated the day he was killed, 22 August 1922, and Hazel has written on it: 'Note written the day he was killed – found in his pocket – also small ruby brooch belonging to me which he wore in his scapular case. These and his note case were given to me after his death through his sister Johanna.' The Collins note says, 'must face realities . . . so goodbye – I read your letter again this morning before going to sleep. When I woke the pages were by my side. God bless you, I am *mombuirnin* [Irish term of endearment, 'my darling'] yours, M.' Another fragment[61] also said to be written by Collins but with a different pen from that used in the previous remnant, says, 'Hazel My Dear Dear Hazel I too wish it was "tomorrow" – with all my love, yours M.'

If Hazel did make romantic interpolations in Collins' letters in a disguised hand, as Birkenhead averred, it is not impossible that others may have done the same, perhaps to an even greater extent. A portion of a celebrated letter, said to be from Collins to Lady [Edith] Londonderry[62] which was quoted by Montgomery Hyde in his book *The Londonderrys*[63] raises the possibility that Collins may have had yet another relationship with a society figure. The quotation is as follows:

Forgive me. I bitterly regret my outburst at L. You are very kind to arrange the meeting and I am very well aware that I was miserably minded to listen to W. Churchill.

It is all very well to tell me as you do that he has no 'interest' in you. But how can you expect me to believe that, feeling as you know very well how I feel. So you must forgive my bitterness, and try to imagine what it means to be a man like myself entirely self-made, self-educated, without background and trying to cope with a man like Lord L., a man who has every advantage I lack . . .

I feel savage and unhappy, and so I blame you for a situation for which I alone am to blame, but I contrast myself with my uncouthness, with his distinction, my rough speech and his unconscious breeding, and the worst of it is I like and admire him, and feel he is brave and honest.

On one point alone I believe myself his superior.

Edith Londonderry was one of the great English political hostesses. From her Park Lane eminence, Londonderry House, far above the social torrent, she ran the Ark, a celebrated social grouping. She was married to Charles Stewart Henry Vane Tempest-Stewart, 7th

Marquess of Londonderry, a descendant of Castlereagh, father of the Union which Collins had done so much to undermine. Educated at Eton and Sandhurst, and a more enlightened figure than normally found in Unionist circles, Londonderry was a reforming Minister for Education. Lord Londonderry was a very proper person for a Catholic Nationalist leader to get to know. But the Londonderrys never forgot where the seat of their power and wealth lay, the British connection, particularly the right wing of the Tory party, as we shall see in Chapter 11. The Ark's membership included the Duke of York (later George VI), the Prince of Wales (later Duke of Windsor) and the Duke of Gloucester, to say nothing of Balfour, Carson, Lord Hailsham, Ramsay MacDonald, Churchill, Neville and Mrs Chamberlain, and a spattering of figures such as Elinor Glyn and Sean O'Casey.

It was certainly all a long way from Woodfield. Would a conspirator of Collins' calibre have written such a letter therefore? The first answer is he might have, given the 'out of my country and myself I go' atmosphere of London society that obviously affected both himself and Kevin O'Higgins where Hazel Lavery was concerned. Also, judging from notes accompanying it, the letter was regarded by the Londonderry family as coming from Collins.

However, though the notepaper seems to be genuine, headed from the Lavery's Cromwell Place home, it carries no date, no signature and is written in pencil. Collins hated pencilled notes and I do not remember seeing any from him in the vast number of his letters I have gone through. The writing does not look like his. Nor is there any signature. What does accompany the letter is a transcript in Lord Londonderry's handwriting which, judging from the rusted paper clip, was pinned to the pencilled original around the time both were written. Was the letter shown to Lord Londonderry by his wife, whose attitude to politics was swayed by the head, not the heart, out of interest? Or to compromise Collins? If the former, it indicates a greater degree of empathy between husband and wife than the contents of the letter would suggest. The second would be in line with the political antagonism of Collins and the Londonderrys where Northern Ireland was concerned. Or, a third possibility, was the letter copied from Lord Londonderry's transcript? The obvious way to settle the question would be to consult a handwriting expert. Unfortunately the North of Ireland Public Record Office would not allow a photostat of the letter to be made under the rules governing the collection. It must be said that if the Londonderrys ever did have plans to 'set up' Collins these would not appear to have survived Londonderry's first meeting with him:

I can say at once that I spent three of the most delightful hours that I ever spent in my life . . . and I formed a conclusion of the character of Michael Collins which was quite different from the one I would have formed if I had only known him as I had heard of him before this particular interview.[64]

Both Hazel Lavery and Moya Llewelyn Davies openly claimed to have had sexual relations with Collins. Moya said that on the night he learned that de Valera was going to reject the Treaty: 'He was so distressed that I gave myself to him.'[65] And Hazel, who claimed that he rang her up the night he signed the document and said, 'I've signed your damned Treaty', wrote a letter about their last encounter which may have had fatal consequences. Certainly his last dinner party with Moya seems to have had. It was given in Furry Park, by Crompton and Moya, some days before Collins was killed.

The guests are said to have included George Bernard Shaw, the Laverys, Desmond Fitzgerald and his wife, Horace Plunkett and his wife, Piaras Beaslai and Joe O'Reilly. It was a pleasant, animated gathering. Bill McKenna was then fifteen years of age and the memory of the scene at Furry Park that night remained with him for the rest of his life.[66] McKenna had been sent to the house with a message for Joe O'Reilly. Word had been received of an assassination attempt on Collins. O'Reilly wanted Collins to move away from the windows while the grounds were searched but, careless of danger as ever, Collins refused. Both O'Reilly and Hazel Lavery then sat in the window to shield him. Eventually the search party in the grounds found a sniper, a man called Dixon, an ex-Connaught Ranger, perched in a tree. A number of attempts had been made on Collins' life shortly before this. Accordingly, as inside the house gaiety continued, outside it Collins' bodyguard took Dixon through the darkened fields, down to the sloblands and shot him dead.[67]

The shooting of the sniper sounds authentic; the problem is, when did it occur? Lennox Robinson wrote to Lady Gregory telling her about a dinner at Horace Plunkett's house, Kilteragh, in Foxrock on the Saturday before Collins was killed. Lady Gregory noted in her journals (pp. 180–1) that Robinson said: 'Kilteragh on Saturday. He came in Lady Lavery's train, or rather she in his, for she is his abject admirer. The Shaws were there too. G.B.S. was in great form on Sunday afternoon.' Shaw certainly met Collins that weekend, as a famous letter[68] he wrote to Hannie on his death shows. It is not impossible that he went to both houses on the same night, or that the dinners occurred on different nights, nor is it impossible that a number of the same guests were at the different houses. But the uncertainty leads one to be cautious about what is supposed to have been said at those dinner tables. In a letter to Collins Kitty Kiernan made a comment which is all the more relevant for having been made during the week in question. She had heard of 'a society woman – don't know if she's a girl – in London that her only idea in life now is to get spending a night with Mick Collins. One night will do her, just for the "notoriety" of it.'[69]

Hazel afterwards said that Collins asked her to go away with him that weekend.[70] According to her story, which she repeated widely, he stopped outside her bedroom window in a car. The horn sounded. She got out of bed and looked down at him and then at her elderly, sleeping husband. Her conscience smote her and, as she told it, 'the car drove away with a mournful sounding of the horn.' The story may or may not have been wishful thinking on Hazel's part.

Certainly Collins' busy schedule that weekend did not allow for any elopements. He left for the country at 6 am the following morning, Sunday. And as his correspondence shows he was in his office for at least part of the previous day[71] before spending a large part of Saturday evening at Furry Park and/or Kilteragh. At all events, the week after he was killed Hazel wrote a letter of sympathy to Emmet Dalton[72] telling him that Collins and she had been together at the weekend in terms which suggested intimacy and mentioning that he had been worried that the anti-Treaty forces were learning of his movements through opening her letters. She said that he suspected Noel Lemass, a prominent anti-Treaty intelligence officer, of being responsible. The contents of the letter became known to others. It was decided that the case called for more than a mere death threat. In July the following year, after the civil war had ended, Lemass was kidnapped and murdered by unknown men.

So much for the romantic web of fact and fiction woven around Collins and the circumstances leading to the signing of the Treaty and its aftermath. After Collins' funeral Oliver St John Gogarty told Lady Leslie: 'We had Lady Lavery in widow's weeds, full of confidences of Collins. Lady Fingall made her go home and leave the arena to Kitty Kiernan.'[73] It is time now for us too to leave the arena of romance to return to the political arena and the storm that burst over Ireland after de Valera learned of the signing of the Treaty.

The delegates were given a send-off as exuberant as their welcome on arrival in London to start the negotiations. At Euston, 'Mick was chaired, and lost his trilby in the delightful hurly-burly,' writes Kathleen Napoli McKenna. But when she got home herself the next day she found a very different atmosphere in Dublin. Gearoid O'Sullivan was amongst the group which met her party:

A strong dust-laden wind was blowing as they accompanied us to a waiting car. We at once noticed that O'Sullivan was black in the face with rage, and, while looking ahead, his eyes fixed on space, whistling between his teeth in an annoying fashion he had, we managed to gather from him: 'the fat's in the fire; the so-and-so and his so-and-so buddies, Stack and Brugha, won't accept what the Big Fellow signed; the Country will be quartered; nothing can prevent a split in the army, and the outbreak of civil war!' We were nonplussed.

Collins had not been sanguine leaving London. As Dr T. Ryle Dwyer has observed, 'He had realised that de Valera would oppose the agreement, if only on selfish grounds.'[74] It was a compromise, but it was not de Valera's compromise. As he prepared to preside at a Dante Commemoration ceremony in the Mansion House on the evening of 6 December, Austin Stack showed de Valera a copy of the *Evening Mail* with the terms. These should not have got out so soon as, according to the arrangements arrived at in London, neither side was to publish until eight o'clock, by which time the couriers, Duggan and Fitzgerald, would have had time to get an official copy to the President. They managed to get him a few minutes after he had read the *Evening Mail*. He was in a 'towering rage'. Duggan handed him the Treaty and, noticing that he was taking no interest in it, asked him to read it.

'Why should I read it?' was the reply. Taken aback, Duggan told him about the publication arrangement and pointed out that it was then nearly eight o'clock. 'What,' exclaimed de Valera, 'to be published whether I have seen it or not – whether I approve or not?' Beaslai, who was one of the speakers at the Dante Commemoration, says: 'I was astonished at the state of suppressed emotion under which he seemed to labour. And all this time he had not taken the trouble to study the Treaty. Apparently the fact that a Treaty had been signed without first being referred to him was the source of his agitation.'

The next morning de Valera summoned a Cabinet meeting of the members available in Dublin and announced that he was calling for the resignations of the three absent members, Collins, Barton and Griffith. Cosgrave stood up to him, saying he ought to wait to see what the three had to say first. 'This was the first indication that Cosgrave was not in agreement with him. Caution was necessary', says his official biography.[75] Realising that if Cosgrave went with Collins and the others he would be outvoted in the Cabinet, instead of calling for scalps he decided to issue a press statement. When Fitzgerald saw it he pointed out that it might be construed as meaning that de Valera was opposed to the settlement. He was surprised and puzzled, because at that stage, he, like a lot of other people judging de Valera on his published statements, regarded him as a moderate. He was soon disabused of his impression. 'That is the way I intend it to read. Publish it as it is,'[76] was the answer. The statement said:

In view of the nature of the proposed treaty with Great Britain, President de Valera has sent an urgent summons to the members of the Cabinet in London to report at once so that a full Cabinet decision may be taken. The hour of the meeting is fixed for 12 noon tomorrow, Thursday. A meeting of the Dail will be summoned later.

That was the first open step taken in the direction of civil war. By it the public learned, amidst a rapturous chorus of press approval for the

Treaty, that more ominous notes were being sounded. Peace was not assured. The IRB put on what Childers termed 'an organised Army reception'[77] for Collins and Griffith when they arrived at Dun Laoghaire. Collins took advantage of it to ask Tom Cullen, 'What are our fellows saying?' Cullen replied, 'What is good enough for you is good enough for them.' It was far from good enough for de Valera, Brugha and Stack. Childers arrived to find de Valera 'head in hands reproaching M.C. for signing'. De Valera was to speak at great length that day. He centred his opposition mainly on the fact that the delegates had not referred back to him before signing as Griffith had promised to do, claiming that he would have gone to London had it not been for Griffith's promise not to sign without referral back. And he recalled the fact that he had replied 'yes' when Childers asked him if the first three clauses should be scrapped.[78] His subsidiary argument was that he had always worked for Association which would not have given up the Republic and would have been acceptable to 'the Cathal party' as Childers termed it. But now all was thrown away without an effort, without permission of the Cabinet, or even consultation.

Barton 'strongly reproached the President'[79] and said the whole situation had arisen because of de Valera's 'vacillation'. He had had his chance of going to London and had refused. The disaster was that 'we were not a fighting delegation'.[80] There was much discussion as to whether or not the delegation had signed under 'duress'. Collins said that the position was that in a contest between a great empire and a small nation the settlement was as far as a small nation could go. Until the British Empire was destroyed Ireland could get no more. On that basis only was he intimidated. Kevin O'Higgins did not like the Treaty which he felt should not have been signed, but having being signed it should be supported. He stressed the absolute necessity for unity, unity being possible only on the Treaty. In the end Cosgrave decided the issue, voting with Collins, Griffith and Barton against Brugha, Stack and de Valera.

Diarmuid O'Hegarty made a strong appeal to the President not to oppose the decision publicly because of the consequences that would follow, but de Valera issued the following statement to the press:

The terms of this agreement are in violent conflict with the wishes of the majority of this nation, as expressed freely in successive elections during the past three years. I feel it my duty to inform you immediately that I cannot recommend the acceptance of this treaty either to Dail Eireann or to the country. In this attitude I am supported by the Ministers of Home Affairs and Defence . . . The greatest test of our people has come. Let us face it worthily without bitterness, and above all, without recrimination. There is a definite constitutional way of resolving our political differences – let us not depart from it, and let the conduct of the Cabinet in this matter be an example to the whole nation.

De Valera was back to his old tactic of taking an extreme course while sounding moderate. Beaslai[81] spoke for many when he said that the publication of the statement was akin to throwing a torch into a powder magazine. The Cabinet's example was followed, the country marched inexorably into civil war. De Valera's policy was quite deliberate. The next day he met the anti-Collins wing of the delegation, Gavan Duffy, Barton and Childers, in the Mansion House at three o'clock in the afternoon. Childers recorded in his diary that they discussed an 'alternative scheme' to the Treaty. It was a 'revelation' to Childers to discover that de Valera was not thinking of appealing to moderate opinion.[82] In order to defeat Collins and Griffith he intended to adopt a policy for which he would get 'extremist support' rather than 'moderate support'. Childers found 'his nerve and confidence are amazing. Seems certain of winning. Will put up a scheme productive of real peace . . .' At this remove de Valera's 'nerve' certainly does appear amazing. His courting of extremist support was to prove productive of the peace of the grave for many of his fellow countrymen.

For Collins that Christmas of 1921 was to prove only slightly less nervewracking than the previous year's when he had almost fallen into the clutches of the Auxiliaries. He literally had no home to go to and he stayed either in the Gresham, with friends, or in his old lodgings in Mountjoy St. Family considerations prevented him from going to Granard to spend Christmas with Kitty because Johnny was released[83] and there were details to be attended to, medical treatment for him, and the question of reuniting the family. But on the first occasion he met Batt O'Connor after the Treaty signing, 8 December, the night of the confrontation with de Valera in the Mansion House, he was so unnerved by the events of the day that he hesitated on the step after O'Connor had opened the door to him. Seeing him stand there 'with a strange expression on his face', O'Connor was puzzled and asked him, 'What are you waiting for?' Collins replied, 'I thought you would have no welcome for me, Batt.'[84] In the days that lay ahead there would be many who would agree with O'Connor who brought him in and told him:

You have brought back this Treaty. It is a wonderful achievement. The people want it. They must at least be given the chance to say what they think of it. Then if they reject it (only they will not reject it) you will have done your part, and will have no responsibility for the consequences.

That soothed Collins a little. He agreed that the people should have their say. 'I will accept their verdict.' But only a little. O'Connor describes him as being too filled with emotion to sit down. He strode up and down the room, the same room in which O'Connor had persuaded him to go to London in the first place, flailing his arms and threatening to leave Dublin and go back to Cork if the Treaty were defeated. 'If the fighting is to be resumed,' he said, 'I will fight in the open, beside my own people down there. I am not going to be chivvied and hunted through Dublin as I have been for the last two years.'

But for every comforting Batt O'Connor there were others like the woman who cut him dead in the street as he stopped to greet her and her husband.[85] When the Dail debate on the Treaty began, in University College, Earlsfort Terrace, because the Mansion House was occupied by a Christmas Fair, Collins knew he had the IRB behind him. But he literally had de Valera, Brugha and Stack in front of him, the division between the parties being brought into the open by the contestants sitting across the floor from each other. The subsequent debate calls to mind images from both Swift and Yeats. The former described a war fought over which end of an egg should be topped, the latter his hero Cuchullain being seized with madness, through the wiles of King Conchubar, so that he went out to spend his strength fighting the waves. Whether one sees Collins as Cuchullain and either de Valera or Lloyd George as Conchubar is really immaterial; the result was the same. The heroes fought the froth of the Oath and ignored the substantive flaw in the Treaty, which is still disturbing the peace of Ireland and bedevilling Anglo-Irish relations – the enshrinement of partition.

De Valera began[86] as he intended to continue, in Conchubar fashion. Speaking in Irish he explained that while he would like to deliver his speech in Irish he did not have enough command of the tongue to express himself properly and therefore he was going to continue in English. However when he spoke in English it was to begin by saying: 'Some of the members do not know Irish, I think, and consequently what I shall say will be in English.' What he had to say was said at enormous length. Apart from his formal speech of opposition his contributions to the debate came to a total of thirty-nine pages in the official reports. This compares with twelve for Collins and eight for Griffith. The debate lasted for thirteen days of private and public sessions during which de Valera behaved as if he were motivated, not by precepts of Republicanism, but by notions of the divine right of kings. One commentator has written: 'Whenever the President wanted to say something he seemed to act almost as if he had a right to determine his own procedure.'[87] In all he interrupted the proceedings more than 250 times.

His opening gambit was to try to convey the impression that the delegation had exceeded their instructions in signing. He read out the secret instructions with which they had been issued. At the same time he stressed that they did have plenipotentiary powers and while his audience was still trying to work out whether the signatories had or had not exceeded their instructions he moved that the press and public be excluded so that misunderstandings could be cleared up. Collins refused to let him get away with the ploy and read out the credentials which the plenipotentiaries had received, saying that the secret instructions should not have been read out without them. He objected to going into private session saying, 'I have been called a traitor . . . If I am a traitor, let the Irish people decide it or not . . . I do not want the issue prejudged. I am in favour of a public session here.' He pointed out that as with the British side, only the respective parliaments could ratify or reject the Treaty. However de Valera got his way with the private session suggestion.

He had two major objectives in following this course. One, he wanted Dail approval for the sort of draft treaty he felt should have been signed. Secondly, he returned to the charge of signing without permission:

I was captaining a team and I felt that the team should have played with me to the last and I should have got the chance which I felt would put us over and we might have crossed the bar in my opinion at high tide. They rushed before the tide got to the top and almost foundered the ship.

Collins' comment was: 'a captain who sent his crew to sea, and tried to direct operations from dry land'. He argued that as the document they actually signed was quite different from that rejected at the Cabinet meeting on 3 December, in fact Griffith had not broken his undertaking. This is stretching things somewhat, but de Valera could equally have been accused of exaggeration when he claimed that the only reason he had not gone over himself was a remark made not to him but to Cathal Brugha. However, he continued to use that argument not only in Cabinet but when trying to rally support outside the Dail, in the country and in America. In the end it was one of the few arrows he was left with in his quiver because his effort to win 'extremist support' with an alternative to the Articles of Agreement was a fiasco which turned hard-liners against him as being soft on the Republic and won no adherents from the Collins camp. Collins dubbed his proposal Document No. 2. It was a rehash of the proposals which the British had rejected on 4 December when Gavan Duffy provided the opportunity for a break.

Document No. 2 did not contain an oath. It provided that 'for the purposes of the Association, Ireland shall recognise his Britannic Majesty as head of the Association'. It resurrected External Association and practically replicated the Articles on partition, merely entering a demur that 'the right of any part of Ireland to be excluded from the supreme authority of the National Parliament and Government' was not recognised. On defence, the document proposed that after five years Ireland should be responsible for its own coastal defence 'unless some other arrangement for naval defence was agreed upon by both governments'.

Collins rejected these proposals, both for what they contained and because they had been tried before. For him, Document No. 2 was not worth fighting for.

However, his close friend and IRB colleague, the much-respected Sean Hales, very nearly let the cat out of the bag with his frank description of what he did think was worth fighting for, and, as we shall see in Chapter 11 secretly did continue to fight for. After pointing out that the people were for the Treaty and that for the moment the Volunteers were poor and exhausted, Hales went on to describe the situation he envisaged when the 'army of occupation' was withdrawn:

in a short time with the building up of the youth of the country, the training of their minds and the training of them as soldiers and the equipping, that day will soon be at hand when you could place Ireland to my mind in rightful place amongst the nations of the earth . . . when Sarsfield under duress signed that treaty with the English King foolishly enough . . . he honourably kept his word and they honourably broke it. Well the day is coming when we will pay that back . . . There is no fear that the soul of Ireland will die. Ireland's destiny is to be a Republic.[88]

Significantly, Hales did not use this argument in the public debate, confining himself merely to a declaration that he would support the Treaty. Whether he or Collins chose caution must be a matter of conjecture. The fact that de Valera was supported during the wearisome hours of public and private discussion (the Treaty debates fill two fair-sized books) by the women deputies and by Erskine Childers led to his support being dubbed the 'women and Childers party'. The women included Mary MacSwiney, Terence's sister, who was the most vociferous anti-Treatyite, Countess Markievicz, Tom Clarke's widow, Kathleen and Mrs Margaret Pearse, mother of Padraig and Willie. Sean Etchingham said of them, 'the women in the Dail will show they are the best men in it'. But de Valera realised that their support was not reflected by the public at large and he tried to have Document No. 2 withdrawn when the Dail returned to public session (on 19 December) having settled nothing in the private wrangle.

His manoeuvre drew from Griffith the icy and telling question: 'Am I to understand, Sir, that the document we discussed at the Private Session is to be witheld from the Irish people?' The document of course disclosed the fact that de Valera was not standing as 'the living symbol of the Republic' but as someone who favoured a compromise similar to the one on offer. A compromise, moreover, which Brugha and Stack had been prepared to accept. Griffith subsequently handed Document No. 2 to the press and resumed the public debate with a speech[89] in which he referred to 'the man who won the war' – Michael

Collins – and pointed out that not once was a demand made for recognition of the Irish Republic in the letters that preceded the negotiations. De Valera made a lengthy speech which never once mentioned partition, but it was Collins' reply which was regarded as the centrepiece of the day. He had a script before him but rarely used it. The press described him as 'passionate, forcible, and at times almost theatrical'.[90] Sometimes he stood erect, sometimes leaned forward to make a point. 'His flashing eyes, firm jaw, and thick black hair, through which he ran his fingers from time to time, were all revealed under the dazzling lights of the electroliers.' He drew applause when he dealt with the charge that he had been bluffed into signing. 'England put up quite a good bluff for the last five years here and I did not break down before that bluff.' He read out the correspondence between Lloyd George and de Valera which had preceded the negotiations and, having pointed out that Lloyd George had made it clear that they were not negotiating on a Republic, declared: 'If we all stood on the recognition of the Irish Republic as a prelude to any conference we could very easily have said so, and there would be no conference.' Recommending acceptance of the Agreement he said:

In my opinion it gives us freedom, not the ultimate freedom that all nations desire and develop to, but the freedom to achieve it . . . we have stated we would not coerce the North-East. We have stated it officially. I stated it publicly in Armagh and nobody has found fault with me. What was the use of talking big phrases about not agreeing to the partition of our country. Surely we recognise that the North-East corner does exist, and surely our intention was that we should take such steps as would lead to mutual understanding. The Treaty has made an effort . . . to deal with it on lines that will lead very rapidly to goodwill and the entry of the North-East under the Irish Parliament.

He wound up with a ringing declaration that he had stood over deeds which had caused excommunication, that he still stood over them, and appealed to people to stop quoting the dead. His objective was to achieve something which the dead, the living, and the children yet unborn would approve of.

Collins' speech had the impact he hoped for. Public and press reaction was clearly with him. The shrewd Tim Healy judged that his contribution was 'worthy of a lawyer as well as a politician. It was big enough for a trained statesman. I was surprised by its precision and detail, and rhetoric.'[91] However, in the emotional let-down that often follows such an effort Collins thought he had done badly and wrote to Kitty that 'it was the worst day I ever spent in my life . . . the Treaty will almost certainly be beaten.'[92]

The Dail recessed for Christmas on the 22nd. Between then and 3 January when the debate resumed Cosgrave as Minister for Local Government may have taken a hand in inducing no less than twenty

County Councils to pass resolutions of support for the Treaty proposals outside the Dail. Inside it, however, due in no small measure to the type of deputy whom Collins himself had been instrumental in getting selected by Sinn Fein, things were different. In Desmond Ryan's inspired phrase, there continued the 'long wrestle between ghosts and realities with all the stored-up spleens of five years flaming through the rhetoric'.[93] De Valera had also been active. He subjected deputies who announced their intention of voting for the Treaty to inquisitions for their threatened *lèse-majesté*.[94] In a letter to Joseph McGarrity, the Irish-American leader, who had originally hailed the Articles of Association until he learned of de Valera's rejection, he wrote of:

. . . an act of disloyalty to their President and to their colleagues in the Cabinet such as is probably without parallel in history. They not merely signed the document, but in order to make the *fait accompli* doubly secure, they published it hours before the President or their colleagues saw it.[95]

The reference to himself in the third person is indicative of the state of de Valera's ego at this period. Even though warned by close friends, such as Dr Farnan, that the country did not understand his alternative, Document No. 2,[96] he returned to the charge with it after the recess. Initially there had been hope that the contestants could bury their differences by means of a stratagem suggested by the Labour Party and supported by Collins. This would have involved the Dail passing legislation to set up a Provisional Government as a committee of the Dail. The Provisional Government would then proceed to draw up a Constitution, as would be necessary if the Treaty were accepted. But it would be an autochthonous constitution, one derived from the Irish people themselves, not an outside authority, such as the Crown. Thus those with reservations about taking the Oath could do so in the knowledge that they were swearing allegiance to the Free State's Constitution drawn up by Irishmen. De Valera however rejected the compromise.[97] He had revised Document No. 2 over Christmas and he proposed to put this as an amendment to the motion advocating Dail approval for the proposed Treaty. This manoeuvre was in fact an attempt at a filibuster. Had it been accepted, everyone in the house would have the option of speaking on the amendment, whether or not they had already spoken.

The ploy failed. Griffith revealed that de Valera's latest proposals were really Document No. 3[98] because he had materially altered the document from the one the Deputies had argued over for several days at the private session. De Valera tried to bluster his way out of this embarrassing revelation by saying, 'I'm going to choose my own procedure.' Griffith was outraged. He rose to his feet and said in a formal, even tone, 'I submit it is not in the competence of the President to choose his own procedure. This is either a constitutional body or it is not. If it is an autocracy let you say so and we will leave it.'

De Valera evidently considered it could be an autocracy when he saw fit. His answer was, 'In answer to that I am going to propose an amendment in my own terms.' It was after this scene that Griffith gave Document No. 2 to the press. Its publication cost de Valera a good deal of the hoped-for extremist support. Neither end of the egg, the Treaty or Document No. 2, appeared particularly appetising to the IRA. And the public at large could see so little difference between the two documents that it was hard to make out what all the fuss was about.

That night a group of pro- and anti-Deputies met at Sean T. O'Kelly's house to work out a peace formula. Again it showed the enormous respect de Valera was held in. The idea was based on the Labour Party initiative which he had already vetoed. In order that 'the active services of President de Valera should be preserved for the nation' eight of the Deputies (one, Liam Mellowes abstained) 'respectfully' recommended that de Valera 'might advise abstention from voting against the Treaty' provided: 'that President de Valera should continue as President of Dail Eireann. The Provisional Government would be permitted to function by the Dail, and would derive its powers from the Dail.' The Army and other services would also remain under control of the Dail. Griffith and Collins accepted the plan. Not so de Valera. According to one historian,[99] 'The whole nine Deputies then waited on de Valera, who, when he received it, flew into a passion, swore, and refused to accept the terms of the agreement, again urging the acceptance of his own pet document.'

His passion was added to by a broadside against him in the *Freeman's Journal* next morning (5 January) for his 'criminal attempt to divide the nation' by his Document No. 2 which the *Freeman* found 'much worse' than the Treaty. The editorial said that he 'had not the instinct of an Irishman in his blood'. The public were exhorted to 'put their fate in the hands of their own countrymen', that is, Collins, Griffith and Mulcahy. Collins wrote to the *Freeman*, protesting at the slur on de Valera. But the gesture had no effect on the Great Adamantine. For although, as one of the pro-Treaty members of the Committee, Joseph McGuinness, said in the Dail afterwards, 'the people on this side literally went on their knees to President de Valera to try and preserve the unity of the country,'[100] in private session the next morning (6 January 1922) de Valera thumped the table and said: 'There is no use in discussing it. The whole of Ireland will not get me to be a national apostate and I am not going to connive at setting up in Ireland another Government for England.'

When the Dail reconvened that afternoon in public session his reason for not accepting the joint appeal by the Deputies to avoid a split became clear. Gambling on the power of his own enormous prestige he moved the goalposts of the debate away from Treaty v. Document No. 2 to the question of his own resignation. He opened the afternoon session with a lengthy and oft-quoted speech[101] in which he portrayed himself as the Apostle of Unity who had for four years linked Sinn Fein, as represented by Arthur Griffith, to the Volunteers, as represented by Cathal Brugha. He read out his hard-line letter of 25 October to Griffith, thus making it abundantly clear that the letter had been written in the first place with an eye to the record. Dealing with the animadversions of the *Freeman's Journal* concerning Irish ancestry he said: 'I was reared in a labourer's cottage here in Ireland (applause) . . . and whenever I wanted to know what the Irish people wanted I had only to examine my own heart and it told me straight off what the Irish people wanted.'

What an examination of his heart on this occasion told him was required was his re-election so that he could pick a new Cabinet and 'throw out that Treaty'.

It may seem surprising at this remove that none of de Valera's opponents thought to ask the author of these republican-sounding propositions why he had not seen fit to mention the word 'republic' either in Document No. 2 or in its revised version, nicknamed Document No. 3. De Valera's stance appears very similar to his conduct at the Republican Convention in Chicago. There he was more concerned to show that he was the leader of Irish opinion than with the possible benefits to Ireland of the Cohalan-sponsored resolution. Now, on the second last day of the Dail debate as one authority[102] has described it: 'his attitude towards the Treaty was similarly influenced by his determination to show that he, not Collins, was the real Irish leader. Hence the President's refusal to accept the Treaty even under the terms urged upon him by Sean T. O'Kelly.'

The effect of de Valera's introducing the question of his resignation across the path of discussion angered Collins, as it prevented him analysing Document No. 2. He made a reference to 'Tammany Hall methods'[103] being employed by the Treaty's opponents and condemned the fact that the Sean T. O'Kelly initiative had not been pursued because the House had been prevented from getting a report on it 'by three or four bullies'. Asked to withdraw the term he paused for almost a minute before replying to the Speaker, Eoin MacNeill: 'I can withdraw the term, but the spoken word cannot be recalled. Is that right, sir?' At this Cathal Brugha, who had controlled himself well during the rest of the procedings, took offence:

I don't know to whom he referred when he mentioned this word 'bullies'. Possibly he may have referred to me as being one of them. In the ordinary way I would take exception and take offence at such a term being applied to me, but the amount of offence that I would take at it would be measured by the respect or esteem I had for the character of the person who made the charge. In this particular instance I take no offence whatsoever.

The atmosphere was further thickened when Harry Boland also took issue with the Tammany Hall reference. He had only joined the debate that day. He told Collins that 'if he had a little training in Tammany Hall, and reserved some of his bullying for Lloyd George we would not be in the position we are in today'.

Collins wrote to Kitty that night:

Saw H. last night. He was friendly, of course, and very nice. I'm afraid he was not so nice today, but not about you – I mean not on the subject of you. I'm afraid he wasn't fair in his homecoming in what he said about our side today. He's working like the very devil against us.[104]

The bitterness and the casuistry continued to the end. Seamus Robinson said that Collins' 'reputation and great deeds of daring were in existence only on paper'[105] and asked if there was 'any authoritative record of his having ever fired a shot for Ireland at an enemy of Ireland?' He thought that there was a prima facie case for 'the charge of treason' against the delegates, Arthur Griffith and Michael Collins. When Joseph MacGrath recalled that Harry Boland had been sent to America by the President to 'prepare the American people for something short of a Republic'[106] de Valera's reply was: 'Short of the *isolated* Republic.'

In general de Valera eschewed personalities, contending that the difference was purely one of principle. However the mask slipped during the course of one of his frequent protestations of high mindedness. Having declared that he was 'sick and tired of politics . . . I have only seen politics within the last three weeks or a month. It is the first time I have seen them and I am sick to the heart of them',[107] he went on to give another reason for wishing to resign: 'For instance there is the case in today's papers. Someone was kidnapped, and the Minister for Finance sent someone to make enquiries. He had no right to send anybody.'

A man who listened to him make this speech afterwards commented:

One of the most irritating features of Mr de Valera's behaviour at this time was, having used every device of a practised politician to gain his point, having shown himself relentless and unscrupulous in taking every advantage of generous opponents, he would adopt a tone of injured innocence when his shots failed, and assume the pose of a simple, sensitive man, too guileless and gentle for this rough world of politics.[108]

The wearing proceedings came to a conclusion insofar as a vote on the Treaty was concerned the following day, 7 January 1922, but not before Cathal Brugha delivered a particularly venomous attack on Collins.[109] He developed Seamus Robinson's innuendo about Collins not having taken an active part in the fighting, saying that he would not have done so had Griffith not made a reference to 'Mr Michael Collins as the man who won the war'. According to Brugha, Collins had merely been a 'subordinate in the Department of Defence', a seeker of notoriety, of whom the Press made 'a romantic figure, a mystical character such as this gentleman certainly is not'. He returned again to the charge that the British had selected their men during the negotiations.

Winding up for the Treaty side Griffith vigorously defended Collins:

He was the man that made the situation; he was the man, and nobody knows better than I do how, during a year and a half, he worked from six in the morning until two the next morning. He was the man whose matchless energy, whose indomitable will carried Ireland through the terrible crisis and though I have not now, and never have had, an ambition, about either political affairs or history, if my name is to go down in history I want it associated with the name of Michael Collins. Michael Collins was the man who fought the Black and Tans for twelve months until England was forced to offer terms.[110]

In theatrical terms he brought down the House. The psychological release, even on the anti-Treaty side, of being able to answer Brugha's invective by simple applause was amply availed of. It was some time before Griffith was able to continue. Yet the Collins reference only took up a fraction of an oration whose tone and content it is only possible to hint at in short extracts.

Although a procedural agreement between the pro- and anti-Treaty sides before the debate had given the last word to Griffith, de Valera tried to have the final say by making a melodramatic declaration that the 'document would rise up in judgement'[111] when compared to his 'explicit document'. Collins cut him off: 'Let the Irish nation judge us now and for future years.' And so the counting began, alphabetically. Ironically the first vote for the Treaty was cast by Collins himself on behalf of his Armagh constituency, a part of Ireland that was to be cut off from Dail Eireann by the terms of the Treaty. Neither he nor his colleagues who had been elected to more than one constituency voted twice. The result was sixty-four for and fifty-seven against. The Treaty had passed by seven votes. When the news filtered out of the chamber there was cheering in the streets, but little enough enthusiasm inside the House.

The first speaker after the announcement of the result was de Valera, saying that he intended to resign.[112] Collins appealed to his adversaries to help in preserving order, to form some sort of a committee to carry on because in times 'when countries change from peace to war or war to peace, there are always elements that make for disorder and that make for chaos'. For a moment there appeared to be a prospect that there might be a reaching out of hands and hearts but an obviously enraged Mary MacSwiney ended the moment:

This is a betrayal, a gross betrayal; and the fact is that it is only a small majority, and that majority is not united; half of them are looking for a gun and the other half are looking for the flesh-pots of the Empire. I tell you there can be no union between the representatives of the Irish Republic and the so-called Free State.

It was the authentic voice of those from whom he would require 'extremist support'. De Valera made no reply to Collins directly but called on his supporters to meet him the following day. Collins tried again for an 'arrangement' that would 'preserve the present order in the country, at any rate over the weekend'. But de Valera ignored the overture. He tried an oratorical flourish: 'I would like my last word here to be this: we have had a glorious record for four years; it has been four years of magnificent discipline in our nation. The world is looking at us now . . .' But his control failed him and he broke down. Brugha looked around the chamber, women crying, men trying not to, and then remarked: 'So far as I am concerned I will see, at any rate, that discipline is kept in the Army.' Collins gazed across at Harry Boland. There were tears in both men's eyes.

10

Wading Through Blood

'The Volunteers . . . in order to achieve freedom, will
have to march over the dead bodies of their own
brothers. They will have to wade through Irish blood.'

Eamon de Valera

Outside the encapsulated world of the Dail, preoccupied with Oaths
and formulae, the problem confronting both parts of the country was
not the difference between the Treaty and Document No.2, but the
growth of anarchy. The situation in the North was growing uglier by
the day. In the South, apart from the physical damage caused by the
war, there was the economic cost. Over 130,000 people were out of
work.[1] What industry there was, was in imminent danger of collapse,
and a million acres of land had gone out of cultivation. Commandeering and crime were rife in the country. The Volunteers, who should
have been policing the country, were wracked with dissension over
the Treaty. The people looked to the Dail for a restoration of peace and
progress towards prosperity. This was both the strength and the
weakness of Collins. A strength because, despite what was said in the
Chamber by the Treaty's opponents, outside it the people were
massively in favour of it. A weakness because, inevitably, to respond
to the feelings of the public at large meant a parting of the ways with
old friends in the IRA.

By trying to maintain the freedoms and potential offered by the
Treaty, while at the same time avoiding taking action against the
elements who wished to smash it, he set up terrible tensions within
himself and those around him. Time after time he attempted to bridge
the unbridgeable; by doing deals with irreconcilable opponents; by
trying to uphold the Treaty while at the same time fathering a
Constitution which, had it not been vetoed by the British, would have
subverted Dominion status; by postponing taking military action as
the South slid further and further into chaos. And, over and above all
this, throughout virtually the entire period he was risking bringing
everything to a crash by sponsoring undercover military action
against the Six Counties. In the last eight months of his life Michael
Collins was a man on the rack.

He had four major spheres of contention: the Twenty-six County political arena in which de Valera continued to be his principal adversary; relationships with the British Government; the position of the Army; and Northern Ireland. (The last is best examined separately and is dealt with in some detail in Chapter 11.) The first major hurdle for Collins and Griffith after the Treaty vote was the vote three days later (10 January 1922) on de Valera's resignation, which in effect was another vote on the Treaty. The result was a further defeat for de Valera, though by a narrow margin, sixty votes against fifty-eight. He left the chamber in protest, followed by all his supporters, thus leaving the country without a government. Griffith was elected in his stead, appointing a six-man team of Ministers: Finance, Michael Collins; Foreign Affairs, Gavan Duffy; Home Affairs, Eamonn Duggan; Local Government, W.T. Cosgrave; Economic Affairs, Kevin O'Higgins; and Defence, Richard Mulcahy.

The atmosphere in the Dail caused by the de Valera walk-out may be gauged from the following exchanges, though Beaslai in 1937 disputes the record (p. 352):

Collins:	Deserters all! We will now call on the Irish people to rally to us. Deserters all!
D. Ceannt:	Up the Republic!
Collins:	Deserters all to the Irish nation in her hour of trial. We will stand by her.
Markievicz:	Oath-breakers and cowards!
Collins:	Foreigners – Americans – English.
Markievicz:	Lloyd Georgeites.

Later on, after de Valera had made a reappearance, Erskine Childers made some criticisms of Griffith which caused that normally phlegmatic man to lash out uncharacteristically, 'I will not reply to any damned Englishman in this assembly.'

Against that sort of background it is not surprising that Collins should write to Kitty around this time in the following terms[2]:

My dearest Kitty,
  I am absolutely fagged out and worn out and everything, but I send you this note to give my little remembrance of you. If you knew how the other side is 'killing' me – God help me – we had to beat them again today. Please come up as soon as you can . . . In awful haste and trying to catch a post so that you'd know I was thinking of you,
  My fondest love,
  Kitty dear,
  Miceal.

The next major political development occurred a few days later at the Mansion House on 14 January when, under the terms of the Treaty, a Provisional Government was formed from the pro-Treaty members of the Dail and the four Unionists returned by Dublin

University. Until such time as the Free State Government contemplated by the Treaty was set up this was the body which would take over the administrative machine from the British. Collins became Chairman of the Provisional Government and Griffith remained President of Dail Eireann. De Valera refused to take any part in the setting up of the PG.[3] The Cabinet again included Duggan, Cosgrave and O'Higgins along with Joe McGrath, Eoin MacNeill, P.J. Hogan and Fionan Lynch. Collins thus took on responsibility for fourteen departments of Government; negotiations with the British, which entailed several journeys to London; the existing Dail Ministry of Finance; the explanation of Government policy to journalists and at public meetings all over the country; and a great deal of the negotiation over the increasingly troublesome IRA.

His first major task was to receive the hand-over of Dublin Castle on 16 January, a step of enormous practical and symbolic significance, tangible proof to the man and woman in the street that whatever might be said against the Treaty, it really had changed things. Characteristically there are differing accounts of what Collins actually said on this historic occasion. Two different anecdotes have an identical ring of truth. In one, a fussy official, perhaps the Viceroy, Lord FitzAlan, is supposed to have said, 'You're seven minutes late, Mr Collins.' Collins replied, 'We've been waiting 700 years, you can have the seven minutes.' In the other, James MacMahon, the helpful Under Secretary, said, 'We're glad to see you Mr Collins,' to which the West Cork accent responded, 'Ye are like hell boy!'

Collins probably took on so much administrative work himself at this stage that it had harmful effects on the day-to-day overseeing of the developing crisis in the Army. As so many of the significant IRA officers were also members of the Dail the political split over the Treaty was automatically replicated in the Army. Several of the most important GHQ and rural OCs were opposed to the Treaty. Liam Lynch stated, 'We have declared for an Irish Republic and will not live under any other law.'[4] Oscar Traynor said that the Treaty was 'not what the hungry and ragged men of the Dublin Brigade fought for'.[5] They were young, they were brave, they were fiery. Some felt they had beaten the British into conceding Dominion status in Round One. Round Two would bring the Republic. The Truce had been seen purely as a breathing space to gain strength before resuming the struggle. Many felt at the time they joined the Volunteers that they were taking part merely to keep alive the tradition of a 'rising in every generation', another gallant failure. They couldn't cope with the thought that they might have actually won something. It seemed dishonourable to stop now. For many, war had simply become a way of life.

The sheer size of the Army was another factor in the situation. It had probably comprised around 3,000 fighting men at the time of the coming of the Truce. But an unhealthy mushroom growth took place after that so that by 'the beginning of November 1921, nominal IRA strength was listed as 72,363'.[6] Many of these 'Trucilers' as they were called were poorly disciplined and (a great source of suspicion and tension to men who had fought all through the Black and Tan war) were former British Army men.

Within a few days all these sources of conflict had combined to make nonsense of Cathal Brugha's statement about maintaining discipline in the Army. The day after Mulcahy succeeded him as Minister for Defence (11 January 1922) a demand was served on Mulcahy that he should hold a Volunteer Convention, described as a Convention of the Irish Republican Army. Backing the demand were prominent IRA leaders like Rory O'Connor, Liam Mellowes, Oscar Traynor, Sean Russell and Liam Lynch. Eventually it was decided that a Convention would be held in two months' time. Meanwhile, at a meeting of both wings of the IRA in Parnell Square on 18 January, a watchdog Council comprising two from O'Connor's side and two from Mulcahy's was set up to ensure that 'the Republican aim shall not be prejudiced'.[7] By delaying the Convention – the proposed date had been 5 February –Mulcahy's side ensured that no open split occurred in the meantime, and that therefore there was no reason for the British to cease their evacuation. On the other hand the compromise of 11 January meant that from then on the British were handing over barracks to both pro–and anti-Treaty forces.

A similar rickety compromise was patched up on the political front at an Extraordinary Sinn Fein Ard Fheis held on 21 February to consider policy in the light of the Treaty's passing. Collins and de Valera came to an agreement whereby the Treaty was not put before the Ard Fheis,[8] and in return no change, that is, no split, would occur in the organisation and no election was to be held for three months. This last point was the important one. While the Ard Fheis, or Convention, would have gone overwhelmingly anti-Treaty, Collins' Provisional Government colleagues pointed out, correctly, that de Valera and his supporters would have been rejected by the public at large had an election been held. But against the forfeiture of this seemingly invaluable advantage Collins weighed up the possibility of staving off an open split and inevitable civil war. As we shall see shortly in the case of both the Army and the Sinn Fein Convention he was pinning his hopes on the same panacea for uniting pro- and anti-Treaty forces, the terms of the Constitution which, like the postponed general elections, was called for by the terms of the Treaty. He hoped that it would be possible to produce a Constitution which would be both acceptable to the British and Republican enough to prevent civil war.

The election would return party candidates to the new Free State Parliament wherein a government would be formed replacing both the existing Dail and the Provisional Government. Griffith was unhappy with the compromise at the outset and he and his colleagues soon had cause to be even more displeased, as the records of the Dail show. De Valera and his followers, while not recognising the Provisional Government, tried to have it both ways by putting down harassing questions for its members, who were also members of Dail Eireann, about PG activities.

Collins selected a Constitutional Committee which held its first meeting in Dublin on 25 January 1922.[9] Collins himself was its first Chairman though subsequently, because of his other commitments, he had to allow Darrell Figgis, who was the paid Secretary to the Committee, to act in his stead. However Collins laid down the guidelines for the Committee and all final decisions were taken by him. In a very real sense, 'Michael Collins was ultimately responsible for drafting the Constitution of the Irish Free State.'[10]

In many ways, the rarely illuminated story of the setting up and instructing of the Constitutional Committee[11] shows the nobler aspects of Collins' vision, the constructive thought for the future of a man who hoped it would be one of independence, democracy and peace. He told the Committee that what he wanted was 'a true democratic Constitution'; it was to contain 'not the legalities of the past but the practicalities of the future'. It was to be 'short, simple and easy to alter as the final stages of complete freedom were achieved'. He felt that the Constitution should omit anything already covered in the Treaty concerning Anglo-Irish relationships. Therefore the Oath should be left out. (His legal adviser, Hugh Kennedy, told him this was legal.) To put it in the Constitution would make it appear the Irish wanted it there. He further decreed that there should be no suggestion in the Constitution either of a Governor General, or that any power in Ireland derived from the Crown. The new Constitution 'must' be one which would guarantee Ireland's equality of status not only within the British Empire but amongst all the nations of the world.

Collins received regular progress reports from James Douglas, the Dublin businessman and humanitarian whom we encountered helping the activities of the White Cross in Chapter 7, an expert on constitutional matters, and from Kevin O'Shiel, a lawyer and expert on Northern Irish affairs.

Crompton Llewelyn Davies also gave advice and assistance. The first task for Davies and Hugh Kennedy, who afterwards became the Irish Chief Justice, was to go with Collins to London to get from Lloyd George the answers to two central questions raised by Douglas at the Committee's first meeting. Would the British ratify the Treaty before the Constitution was finalised? Would the Constitution have to be submitted to London for approval before being approved by Dublin? On the first, Collins succeeded in out-manoeuvring Lloyd George whose first instinct had been to tell him that prior ratification was impossible. Collins' reply was that he had not come to London to discuss the impossible but to inform the British Government that the Provisional Government was in imminent danger of collapse under anti-Treatyites' pressure and Lloyd George conceded on ratification but stipulated that the British would have to see the Constitution before Collins published it.

The British wasted no time in implementing promise number one. The Irish Free State (Agreement) Bill was introduced into the Commons on 9 February and, shepherded by Churchill in the House and Birkenhead in the Lords, passed all stages so swiftly that it received the Royal assent on 31 March. Whether one agrees or disagrees with the terms of the Treaty, it has to be conceded that Churchill's prowess in steering the ratification through his own constitutional and political minefields made a significant contribution to the creation of modern Ireland. But it was unrealistic of Collins to expect him to persuade Parliament a few months later to accept a Constitution which discountenanced all its symbols of authority. However, for the moment, Collins had bought time not only to bring his Constitution to fruition, but also in Churchill's phrase, to 'hold an election under favourable conditions at the earliest moment'. His Sinn Fein Ard Fheis agreement with de Valera was concluded in an attempt to create 'favourable conditions'. But militarily and politically the situation continued to develop inexorably towards a position which made the attainment of such conditions impossible.

Militarily, under the terms of the arrangement come to between the two wings of the IRA on 18 January, the 'watching Council' should in theory have prevented hostilities between those loyal to the Rory O'Connor faction and Collins' supporters, at least until the holding of the proposed Convention. But in fact the truce between the two wings was very like the truce between the IRA and the British the previous year; both sides used the lull in an attempt to improve their situation. As Collins and Mulcahy strove to consolidate their position from Beggar's Bush barracks, where Ginger O'Connell, who had American Army training, was trying to train up a new army as quickly as possible, the O'Connor forces were raiding for arms and transport all over the country. Figures like Ernie O'Malley and Seamus Robinson became virtual warlords in their own areas. Robinson, for instance, wrecked the offices and machinery of the pro-Treaty Clonmel *Nationalist* and threatened its editor with death.

From the end of February Limerick became a flashpoint. Sean Forde, an anti-Treaty IRA commander, issued a proclamation (on 18 February) repudiating Beggar's Bush and subsequently began arresting pro-Collins officers. Between 3 and 11 March, armed anti-Treaty forces took over buildings in the city. It seemed inevitable that the two wings would have to come into conflict, as figures like Griffith and

O'Higgins urged in Cabinet, but an agreement was hammered out, in the Mess of Beggar's Bush, largely through the mediation of Liam Lynch and Stephen O'Mara, the Mayor of Limerick, whereby in effect both sides withdrew from the city.

Although Mulcahy had calculated that the Army was simply not strong enough yet to dislodge the IRA from Limerick, some of his colleagues saw the Limerick compromise as little short of 'capitulation to mutineers'[12] and it was realised that a firmer line would have to be taken if the proposed Convention was not to result in an embarrassingly large vote for an anti-GHQ army. The Convention was banned. But O'Connor forced the pace. Asked at a press conference if he proposed to set up a military dictatorship he replied, 'You can call it that if you wish.' The banned Convention was then held despite GHQ on 26 March and a new Executive was set up with Rory O'Connor at its head. Underlying the sanguinary-sounding proceedings of the Convention there were two significant sub-texts. One, the same sort of disinclination Collins entertained against turning guns on old comrades and two, a lack of organisation and of political awareness.

But the public at large, knowing nothing of either factor, was understandably alarmed at reports of resolutions discussed at the Convention. These included 'the declaration of a dictatorship which would. . . overthrow the four Governments in Ireland opposed to the Republic – viz: Dail Eireann, Provisional Government, British Government and Northern Government.' Apart from this 'if there's a government we're against it', policy there was a great deal of talk about suppressing newspapers, drastically enforcing the Belfast boycott, and interfering with Provisional Government activities such as the building up of a police and courts system. The talk soon turned to deeds with the wrecking of the *Freeman's Journal*'s premises and presses on 30 March, because of its Convention reportage. From this there followed bank and post office raids, and the destruction of goods and sometimes premises in prosecution of the Six-County boycott, interference with mails, and seizures of state revenues such as excise duties and dog licence payments! Yet though the presence of two rival armies in the field made it inevitable that the guns would sometime begin to go off there was a reluctance on both sides to actually attempt to kill each other.

Watching the unresolved build-up of tension in Limerick, Churchill sent a telegram to Cope asking plaintively: 'Do you think there is any fighting quality in the Free State Government? Will anybody die for it or kill for it?'

Early in April a British naval vessel, the *Upnor*, allegedly en route to Portsmouth from Haulbowline Dockyard, was intercepted off the Cork coast by a ship commandeered by Cork IRA men and a large quantity of arms was landed at Ballycotton. Collins was convinced that there was collusion between elements on the British side and his opponents. Churchill rejected this charge but Collins accepted neither Churchill's denials, nor his estimates of the amount of arms seized.[13] There was speculation in London prior to the *Upnor* seizure, which was mentioned in the House of Commons, that the guns were to be made available to the IRA. Various reasons were advanced for this. Either it was intended simply to destabilise Collins' regime, with a view to facilitating a British return, or to strengthen forces held to be at the disposal of de Valera so that he could emerge as a strong man who, unlike the vacillating Collins, would restore law and order.

Collins cabled Churchill:

We do not charge collusion from high responsible authorities but we are convinced there has been collusion from subordinates. It is absurd to believe that a vessel containing such quantities of arms and ammunition be left open to seizure in an area where it is notorious our opponents are well armed . . . the fact that the Cork raid was talked of in London service clubs before it came off has been reported to us here. This corroborates Ward's statement [in a House of Commons query] and convinces us of collusion between some subordinates and our opponents.[14]

The War Office made an official estimate[15] of the strength of the *Upnor* haul as 381 rifles and 700 revolvers, which was much lower than that of the rumours current in Dublin. Churchill may have been deliberately misled. The War Office told him[16] that T. Barry and the Harbour Master, Cork Harbour Board, were responsible for the '*Upnor* business'. But Collins' sources of information were such that it is unlikely that he would have complained to Churchill if he thought that the *Upnor* affair was simply due to Tom Barry's outwitting him. 'Dirty tricks' departments are a familiar phenomenon in Ireland, as the collusion between some high-ranking British decision-takers and their Unionist confederates detailed in Chapter 11 illustrates.

Despite a universal urge towards restraint the first shots in the civil war were fired in April. Throughout that month, though casualties were light,[17] there were scores of clashes all round the country. The anti-Treaty forces attempted to seize barracks, commandeer lorries, and ambush rival troops for weapons. Speaking in Wexford, on 9 April, Collins described the situation bitterly but honestly: 'The humiliating fact has been brought home to us that our country is now in a more lawless and chaotic state than it was during the Black and Tan regime. Could there be a more staggering blow to our National pride, and our fair National hopes?'[18]

Then, on 14 April, O'Connor's men seized the nerve centre of Ireland's legal system, the Four Courts in Dublin, where they set up their headquarters. A number of other Dublin centres were also seized: the Fowler Hall, the Masonic Hall, Kilmainham Jail and the *ancien régime* Kildare St Club. These seizures conveyed sectarian overtones combined with a flouting of Provisional Government authority. But on this occasion, as on many others, Collins hesitated to assert his authority, even though he was personally involved in several potentially deadly incidents.

The military and political situations overlapped in his and Griffith's appearance at public meetings which the anti-Treatyites tried to prevent them addressing as a matter of set policy. Collins wrote to a friend around this time:

The opposition policy is making it almost impossible for us to hold useful meetings. The crowds assemble all right, but 20, or 30, or 40 interrupters succeeded in most places in preventing the speakers from being heard. That apparently is official policy accompanied by blocked roads and torn up railways to prevent the excursion trains from bringing the people to our meetings.[19]

He had first-hand experience of all the conditions he described. At Cork, on 14 March he was humiliated when a group of armed men refused him entry to the Republican burial plot. Subsequently he addressed a huge meeting in the city, possibly attended by as many as 50,000 people. Shots were fired throughout his speech. He told his listeners that those who accused him of betraying the national position could apply one simple test. Whoever ended in possession of the battlefield had won the war. The British were leaving, and would be gone altogether if de Valera and his friends would allow them to depart. Meanwhile outside the city a train bringing people to hear him was halted by armed men at Mogeely station. At Dungarvan a train he was actually speaking from was driven off in the middle of his address. He finally succeeded in speaking from a hotel balcony. At Castlebar he addressed a meeting which he had to get to over blocked roads and through cut railway lines. Many of his potential hearers were prevented from getting to hear him by armed parties on the roads, who held them up and sent them home. In Kerry, where his message was that neither the Treaty nor the Republic was worth the risk of civil war, he spoke in circumstances of great danger, as at both Tralee and Killarney his meetings were formally proclaimed by the IRA. He secured a hearing partly by negotiation with local commanders, partly through improvisation. At Killarney his platform was destroyed by fire but he obtained a brake. When the local anti-Treaty commander stepped in front of him, backed up by a force of armed men, as he strode towards the brake, he simply pushed past him and, turning his back on the gunmen, moved on to give his speech.

These were far from being his only brushes with gunmen. On the night of the Cork meeting in March he was on his way to the house of his sister, Mary Collins Powell, when a man with a revolver appeared in front of him shouting, 'Collins I have you now.' Before he could pull the trigger Sean MacEoin had him. After disarming him he asked Collins, 'Will I shoot him?'

'No. Let the bastard go,' was Collins' answer. The following month he drew his automatic on a party of riflemen who tried to seize his car outside Vaughan's Hotel. The pistol jammed but he grabbed one of the raiders and despatched him to Mountjoy.

Arthur Griffith showed similar, or possibly even greater courage in view of his age, and the fact that, unlike Collins, he had little experience of military confrontation. When it became known that he was going to address a meeting in Sligo on Easter Sunday, 16 April, it was proclaimed and the town was heavily invested by anti-Treaty forces. Bloody confrontation seemed inevitable. But Griffith did not flinch. He was already deeply critical of Collins' 'softly softly' approach and, Ernest Blythe recalled:

For the first and only time in my experience, he rose to his feet at a Cabinet meeting and made a formal speech. He spoke, I remember, under obvious stress and with a degree of passion I had never before known him to show. He wound up by saying that if we were not prepared to fight and preserve the democratic rights of the ordinary people and the fruit of national victory, we should be looked upon as the greatest set of poltroons who had ever had the fate of Ireland in their hands.[20]

The night before the meeting was due to be held he left his friends the Montgomery family with a letter to be opened in the event of his death. When some months later he did die the envelope was opened and the message was found to read: 'Let the people stand firm for the Free State. It is their national need and their economic salvation. Love to all the Irish people and to all my colleagues and friends.'

He arrived in Sligo in an armoured car surrounded by armed troops. At the eleventh hour the IRA commander, Liam Pilkington, who afterwards became a priest, stepped back from the prospect of fratricidal strife and the meeting passed off peacefully. But large-scale fighting broke out a few weeks later in Kilkenny where anti-Treaty forces made a Sligo-type investiture of strongpoints from which they were only driven after two days' fighting and the taking of 150 prisoners. Remarkably only two men were injured.

Cooler heads on both sides realised that that sort of luck could not last indefinitely and one last major effort at securing peace between the fighting men was made under the auspices of the IRB. Lynch and a number of top Cork IRA leaders including Tom Hales, Sean O'Hegarty and Florrie O'Donoghue were out of sympathy with the anti-democratic drift of the O'Connor-led Executive and, for their part, figures such as O'Connor, O'Malley and Mellowes were shrewd enough to realise that the prospects of military success without Lynch and the others were slim. Although an early proposal by Florrie

O'Donoghue failed, on 1 May an IRB-sponsored statement appeared, signed by Collins, Mulcahy, Gearoid O'Sullivan, Eoin O'Duffy for the pro-Treaty faction and for the other side by Dan Breen, Sean O'Hegarty, Florrie O'Donoghue, Tom Hales and Humphrey Murphy.

It called for a closing of ranks in the face of the 'greatest calamity in Irish history' and conceded that a majority of the people were for the Treaty. It called for an agreed election, Army unification and the forming of a government which would have 'the confidence of the whole country'. This was the last time the IRB played a major role in the developing crisis. It was largely unsuccessful. Rory O'Connor immediately issued a public statement repudiating the initiative as a 'political dodge intended to split the Republican ranks'.

But it did create a basis for a dialogue between the two sides. Lynch, Mellowes and Sean Moylan on behalf of the Executive agreed to a form of truce with three of Collins' nominees, O'Duffy, O'Sullivan and MacEoin. These six continued to meet and somehow, a truce more or less held between the sides until near the end of June, although raids and robberies directed by the Executive forces or their sympathisers continued all round the country. Then on 15 June O'Connor and O'Malley handed Mulcahy a document repudiating the six-man talks, which had been faltering over matters which the Cabinet obviously could not concede such as the Four Courts' men's demand that they appoint the Army's Chief of Staff. Three days later an Executive Convention was held in the Four Courts to consider the resolution, 'That this Executive Council of the IRA hereby decide . . . the only means of maintaining the Republic is by giving the English seventy-two hours' notice to evacuate the country.'

The Four Courts' men proposed:

The destruction of all barracks occupied by our troops, the attacking present port positions held by the English troops. The striking at English forces . . . wherever possible in areas which the pro-Treaty troops occupy so that they may be brought into collision with English troops.

O'Connor and his followers were in fact debating how best to embroil the two wings of the IRA in a renewed struggle against the British. The military path to civil war was now within a few days of its destination. At this stage we must turn to see how and by whom the political path to the same destination was constructed.

De Valera's decision not to go to London for the Treaty negotiations really rebounded on him and on the nation in the months following the vote on the Treaty. Certainly if he, Collins and Griffith had come back with their names on a document, opposition to it throughout the country would have been only a small fraction of what he stirred up against the Treaty. Even if he had gone without Collins, as he did in July 1921, in the words of Tom Hales, the man in charge of the ambush party that shot Collins, 'If Dev had come back with a document that Collins didn't like, there'd have been no civil war.'[21] The 'what might have been' tragedy for Ireland lay in the fact that in a very real sense it was de Valera who later proved the validity of Collins' 'stepping-stone' argument.

On the Irish scene, de Valera was a great figure, but the actions of great men, particularly on a small stage, can sometimes have far-reaching and harmful consequences, especially when they seek extremist support. He began by founding a new party (on 15 March) from amongst the anti-Treaty section of the Dail known as *Cumann na Poblachta* (League of the Republic). Then in addition to the election postponement of two months secured by the Sinn Fein Ard Fheis pact between himself, Collins and Griffith, he attempted to gain further postponement by trying to get the election held on a new register which, as Griffith commented when rejecting the stratagem, would have made 'an election impossible for the next six months'[22] and would effectively 'muzzle the electorate'.

De Valera's 'extremist support' policy then led him to launch himself on a course of inflammatory speech-making which became an ineradicable blot on his reputation. At Dungarvan, on 16 March, he said:

The treaty . . . barred the way to independence with the blood of fellow Irishmen. It was only by civil war after this that they could get their independence. If you don't fight today, you will have to fight tomorrow; and I say, when you are in a good fighting position, then fight on.[23]

In Tipperary he marked St Patrick's Day with two speeches which raised the spectacle of drowning the shamrock in blood. At Carrick-on-Suir, where it was estimated his audience included several hundred IRA men, he said:

If the Treaty was accepted the fight for freedom would still go on; and the Irish people, instead of fighting foreign soldiers, would have to fight the Irish soldiers of an Irish Government set up by Irishmen. If the Treaty were not rejected, perhaps it was over the bodies of the young men he saw around him that day that the fight for Irish freedom may be fought.[24]

He then went on to Thurles, where the composition of his audience may be gauged from the fact that hundreds of his hearers carried rifles, and repeated these statements, adding:

If they accepted the Treaty, and if the Volunteers of the future tried to complete the work the Volunteers of the last four years had been attempting, they . . . would have to wade through Irish blood, through the blood of the soldiers of the Irish Government, and through, perhaps, the blood of some of the members of the Government in order to get Irish freedom.

Next day in Killarney he said: 'If our Volunteers continue, and I hope they will continue until the goal is reached . . . then these men, in order to achieve freedom, will have, I said yesterday, to march over the dead bodies of their own brothers.'[25]

When he was condemned editorially by the *Independent* for these speeches de Valera riposted with a letter in which he said he had been misrepresented in a 'villainous' way that showed 'criminal malice'.[26] He said that his speeches were 'an answer to those who said that the London Agreement gave us "freedom to achieve freedom".'

After the seizure of the Four Courts, representatives of the Labour Party met him in an effort to avert the wading 'through Irish blood'. One of those who pleaded with him, Senator J. T. O'Farrell, afterwards told the Seanad that:

the only statement he made that has abided with me since as to what his views were was this: 'The majority have no right to do wrong.' He repeated that at least a dozen times in the course of the interview, in response to statements made to him to the effect that the Treaty had been accepted by a majority, and that consequently, it was his duty to observe the decision of the majority until it was reversed. He refused to accept it on the grounds that the majority had no right to do wrong.[27]

Far from repudiating the Four Courts' men de Valera greeted the seizure with a proclamation on 16 April which declared: 'Young men and young women of Ireland, the goal is at last in sight. Steady all together; forward, Ireland is yours for the taking. Take it.' At this stage Harry Boland was working for de Valera as his secretary and he was obviously relaying the thoughts of the Master when he wrote to Austin Stack: 'Civil war is certain unless Collins and Company see the error of their ways and come to terms with their late colleagues.'[28] Two days later (on 29 April) the Catholic Archbishop of Dublin, Dr Byrne, tried to bring the former colleagues together by convening a meeting at the Mansion House between Collins and Griffith and de Valera and Brugha. Brugha provoked a scene by telling Collins and Griffith that they were British agents. Collins jumped up and glared at him: 'I suppose we are two of the Ministers whose blood is to be waded through?' Brugha replied, 'Yes, you are two.' De Valera neither rebuked nor disowned him but, somehow, Dr Byrne managed to keep the peace.

Collins argued that 'every adult has a right to vote.'[29] But Brugha replied: 'No nation has power to part with its nationality or barter any part of national heritage.' Collins proposed a plebiscite but Brugha refused, saying no such issue should be put before the people while the threat of war was there.

De Valera did not want an election to be held either, but clothed his fear of facing any sort of national verdict on the Treaty in an objection to the 'stone age plebiscite' proposed. The idea was that people would congregate in certain areas, mainly at churches, and signify their preference by walking through gates or barriers. His real objection of course was that he was angling for 'extremist support' and the Four Courts' men were opposed to an election. So he had to follow the anti-democratic path, issuing a statement after the Mansion House débàcle[30] explaining his refusal by saying that 'Republicans maintain that there are rights which a minority may justly uphold, even by arms, against a majority.' He justified his refusal to co-operate in holding an intimidation-free election in June by counter-proposing a six-month postponement so that:

Time would be secured for the present passions to subside, for personalities to disappear, and the fundamental differences between the two sides to be appreciated – time during which Ireland's reputation could be vindicated, the work of national reconstruction begun, and normal conditions restored.

The 'fundamental differences' of course were those between the Treaty and Document No. 2, and as for the work of 'national reconstruction' it may be observed that the day before the statement appeared[31] the Four Courts' men organised countrywide swoops on Bank of Ireland branches – their section of the IRA was no longer being paid by Beggar's Bush – which netted more than £230,000. But far from appearing taken aback by this, de Valera, if anything, strengthened his hard-line approach in an interview with John Steele of the *Chicago Tribune* which he thought so highly of that it was reprinted in the paper published by his faction which Erskine Childers edited, *Poblacht na hEireann*. He assured Steele that: 'We all believe in democracy, but we must not forget its well known weaknesses. As a safeguard against their consequences the most democratic countries have devised checks and brakes against sudden changes of opinion and hasty, ill-considered actions.'[32] He pointed out that in America a Treaty needed a two-thirds majority to pass the Senate. As Ireland had not had 'an opportunity of devising constitutional checks and brakes', he said, 'The army sees in itself the only brake at the present time and is using its strength as such.' Looking back at this phase in his country's history the poet Yeats would one day write:

Had de Valera eaten Parnell's heart
No loose-lipped demagogue had won the day
No civil rancour torn the land apart.[33]

At this stage it becomes necessary for a moment to consider Griffith's attitude to de Valera. As these developments unfolded, his opinion of the 'Long Fellow' sank lower and lower. After the vote on the Treaty was taken he said, 'There is no man in Ireland I respect and love more'. Then he became a 'good man whom America spoiled'.[34] After the abortive Mansion House talks he told Ernest Blythe and others in private, 'that was the first time I really got after the "Long Fellow".'[35] In public he read out the following from *Poblacht na hEireann*: 'We'll not have this Treaty executed. Let us rather execute the man who signed it for us behind our backs.'[36] Griffith said of the article in which the foregoing occurrred: 'I say that is a deliberate incitement to the assassination of the plenipotentiaries and they won't get off with it . . . I know the atmosphere which is being prepared. You may assassinate us but you won't intimidate us.'

Griffith was sick and tired of the confusing two-hatted Dail/ Provisional Government position. He wanted an end to the make-believe and an election to a new, unambiguous parliament. Following the Sinn Fein Ard Fheis pact with de Valera this election was now scheduled for 16 June. But above all he urged Collins to take action to dislodge the Four Courts men. 'By God we will', Collins would say, thumping the table. But always he postponed the issue and tried to compromise.[37] We can image Griffith's dismay, therefore, when on 20 May 1922 his greatest compromise was unveiled. Under a formula devised by Harry Boland, Collins, acting independently of Griffith, entered into an electoral pact with de Valera.

The idea was that they should face the electorate together under an arrangement whereby the Treaty would not be an issue. However a coalition panel of candidates would be formed from both the pro- and anti-Treaty sections of Sinn Fein, each section having a number equivalent to its existing strength in the Dail. The Cabinet seats in the ensuing Government were to be apportioned on the basis of the election results.

It was a highly dubious arrangement, which, apart from anything else, cut across the interests of the other parties, the Farmers and Labour. Griffith was appalled when it was brought before the Cabinet. Asked if he would accept it, 'he spent three whole minutes reflecting, pulling nervously at his tie and wiping his glasses. The other ministers waited in silence for his answer for what seemed a long time, and when he did assent he no longer addressed Collins as "Mick", but with a noticeably formal "Mr Collins".'[38] In the few months of life left to the two men their former cordiality was not re-established. In London they had drawn close together because of de Valera; now they were driven apart because of him. Another admirer of Collins, Hugh Kennedy, the Law Officer, was also horror-struck when he learned of the pact's terms. He immediately sent him a 'lengthy memorandum in a spirit of helpfulness, and not of obstruction', setting forth the blatant illegality of the arrangement:

(a) The Provisional Government is, as far as the Treaty is concerned, the only Government with authority until the Parliament and Government of the Irish Free State has been established . . . until after the Constitution has been adopted.

(b) You cannot have a Coalition Provisional Government consisting of pro-Treaty and anti-Treaty members. Every member of the Provisional Government must accept the Treaty in writing.[39]

If that is how the pact seemed to an Irish friend of Collins' one can imagine how it looked to British critics. It is not generally known that Churchill had been well aware that something of the sort was likely and that he had written in very strong terms to warn Collins against concluding any such arrangement five days before the pact was announced:

I think I had better let you know at once that any such arrangement would be received with world-wide ridicule and reprobation. It would not be an election in any sense of the word, but simply a farce, whereby a handful of men who possess lethal weapons deliberately disposed of the political rights of the electors by a deal across the table . . . It would be an outrage upon democratic principles and would be universally so denounced . . . Your Government would soon find itself regarded as a tyrannical junta which having got into office by violence was seeking to maintain itself by a denial of constitutional rights.

The enemies of Ireland have been accustomed to say that the Irish people did not care about representative Government, that it was alien to their instincts, and that if they had an opportunity they would return to a despotism or oligarchy in one form or another. If you allow yourself to be misled into such an arrangement as is indicated, such action would be immediately proclaimed as justifying to the full this sinister prediction. As far as we are concerned in this country, we should certainly not be able to regard any such arrangement as a basis on which we could build.[40]

Collins ignored Churchill's letter and on 17 May began three days of negotiation with de Valera at University College, Dublin. Apart from hoping to secure an intimidation-free election, Collins had three other considerations in mind in going ahead with the pact in the face of the Churchillian warning.

First he still desperately hoped to avoid conflict with his former comrades with whom he still empathised to a greater degree than with many of his Cabinet colleagues. Sean O'Muirthle said of Collins at this period that he was not particularly worried about losing either de Valera's friendship or that of many of his political colleagues:

What troubled Collins was the split in the Army. There were men in the Army that he would go almost any distance to satisfy. He would rather, as he said to me more than once, have one of the type of Liam Lynch, Liam Deasy, Tom Hales, Rory O'Connor, or Tom Barry on his side than a dozen like de Valera. These were men of great energy and patriotic outlook down through the . . . Anglo-Irish War, and they had been faithful subordinates as well as personal friends, and the thought of turning the guns on such men was abhorrent to Collins.[41]

Secondly, he still hoped that his Constitution, now nearing

maturity, would bring peace. Judging from British intelligence reports analysed by Lionel Curtis it seems clear that he gave de Valera some indications that the Constitution would be sufficiently Republican to allow of the formation of a Coalition Government. Curtis commented: 'The possibility that this project may furnish the key to the Agreement cannot be ignored.'[42]

Thirdly, the hidden agenda to his pact with the anti-Treaty forces included agreement on a joint IRA offensive in Northern Ireland which was to commence a few days later.

How much either de Valera or British Intelligence knew of this component of the deal must be a matter for speculation. Apart from whatever Collins may have told him directly the former's relationship with Frank Aiken, the Northern IRA leader, who was central to the offensive, would certainly seem to indicate that he knew something of Collins' Six-County intentions. British Intelligence could hardly have gleaned as much as it did of Collins' constitutional scheming without picking up something of his military plotting also. On the other hand the fact that the gun-running which preceded the offensive was successful might indicate that the agents of his military plans were more security conscious than his political associates.

It must be conceded that the whole pact episode and its attendant manoeuvrings places Collins more in the light of a conspirator than a statesman. But though he might appear to have been merely either weak or simply attempting to throw a cloak of constitutionality over a preferred course of IRA activity, his vision of what he sought remained clear even in that maelstrom month of May. This was shown in a reply to a former close IRA associate in Liverpool whose letter of regret at parting from him well articulates the naive sincerity of many Republicans, both then and subsequently. Paddy Daly wrote to him saying:

I have put off writing this letter from day to day in the hope that some form of unity might be accomplished . . . Possibly you have already heard that I am against the Treaty. I needn't point out the path I have chosen is not an easy one and that my freedom could not last very much longer on this side . . . I want you to know I am following my conscience and am not influenced by any individual . . . believe me, I would rather be riddled a hundred times over than think I had helped in any way to harm you. On the contrary, I would defend you as your nearest friends would.

I say this because I know you are as sincere today as you were in Xmas 1920 when things looked black – sincere in the idea of an Irish Republic. I know also and believe that you are acting as you think in the best interests of Ireland . . . continue now and finish the fight . . . struggle for fifteen or twenty years, would be a forlorn consolation. The big businessmen and politicians will come forward when peace is established and perhaps after some years gain control. Their interests would never demand a renewal of war.[43]

The whole thing has given me more mental worry than I have ever experienced. . . .

Beannact De, a Naom muire leat, do cara, P.O'Dalaig, L'pool (The blessing of God and his holy mother on you, your friend P. Daly).

In the press of events Collins took nearly a month to reply:

Believe me the Treaty gives us the one opportunity we may ever get in our history for going forward to our ideal of a free independent Ireland. This cannot be gained without very much work yet – very hard work, *and perhaps more than hard work* [Author's italics]. And it is not by dissipation of the national energy that we can gain this. It is not by acts of suppression, and is not by denial of liberty that we can reach liberty.

At any rate I am perfectly conscious that you are influenced only by what you think right in the matter, and with an expression of very sincere appreciation of your past services, and a hope that we may work in the same company again, I leave the matter.[44]

Lloyd George and Churchill knew little of such partings of the ways, but they understood all too well that there was a strong likelihood of divergence from the Treaty's terms following the publication of those of the Collins–de Valera pact. The Treaty signatories were immediately invited to London and Cope was instructed to find out what was happening. Collins gave him a number of assurances[45]: (1) that Churchill would be quite happy when he heard what the delegation who were going over to London to explain the pact had to say; (2) that it would not breach the Treaty; and (3) that de Valera would not see the Constitution before the delegates, including Griffith, left for London. However he did not give Cope one important reassurance sought. He said there was as yet no decision as to whether or not the Constitution would be a Coalition measure. Most significantly of all he at first refused to go to London himself. It took a personal letter from Churchill in his own handwriting to induce him to travel: 'I learn from Mr Cope with great apprehension that you may consider yourself unable to come . . . Your absence would I fear be misunderstood. Certainly it would be deeply regretted.'[46]

It was a meeting, or rather meetings, of 'great importance'. Between Saturday 26 May and 15 June whatever slight hope there was of avoiding the Irish civil war evaporated. The Constitution on which Collins had pinned such hopes ended up being so altered as to bring it back into conformity with the Treaty. Collins did not join the talks until Saturday 27th, having spent the previous Friday afternoon arguing with Darrell Figgis who objected to Collins' decision to include in the Draft Constitution provisions for four 'Extern' ministers to join the Government by appointment which would have allowed de Valera and Childers, for example, to have joined the Cabinet without taking either the Oath or being subject to collective responsibility. Figgis' opposition indicates that he was reflecting the views of his friend Arthur Griffith whom the British regarded as 'the only Irish leader who appreciates his real obligations under the Treaty'; a break between him and Collins was therefore speculated on as a real possibility.[47]

Churchill made use of Hazel Lavery to let Collins know how the Cabinet viewed the Irish situation. In a handwritten letter marked 'private', he said:

My dear Hazel,
I had a very pleasant talk with M.C. this morning and hope to see him again on Monday. I am very glad he and his colleagues are dining with you tonight. I am sure your influence will be exerted in the cause of peace . . . I ought, I think, to let you know 'confidentially' that my colleagues take a most grave view of the Constitution.

The style of the Churchill–Collins meeting may have been 'very pleasant talk' but the substance of those May – June dealings was very tough. The gravamen of the British case on the pact and on the Constitution was as follows: the pact was a giving way to unconstitutional forces, '2% of the population' represented by 'Boland, de Valera's Secretary'.[48] Churchill developed the arguments contained in his letter of 15 May to Collins. The Provisional Government 'had made one surrender after another to the Republicans and had not obtained the free opinion of the Irish people' causing the British Treaty signatories to be subjected to a 'fierce scrutiny of our actions'. Churchill warned that: 'You will find that we are just as tenacious on essential points – the Crown, the British Commonwealth, No Republic – as de Valera and Rory O'Connor, and we intend to fight for our points.'

At first sight the Constitution struck Churchill as being of 'Bolshevik character'. After a more measured perusal Lloyd George termed it a 'complete evasion and complete negation of the Treaty'.[49] Adducing the opinions of Law Officers, the Lord Chancellor and the Lord Chief Justice, he told his increasingly depressed Irish listeners[50] that, amongst other things, the Draft Constitution was so far from its intended basis in the Canadian Constitution that it was

substantially a setting up of an independent Republic in Ireland. The Crown was only brought in under conditions very derogatory to its dignity. The Court, which constitutes the Empire, was expressly excluded . . . The British Empire was ruled out from the making of Treaties altogether . . . the Constitution was a complete going back on the provisions of the Treaty.

Days of frequently emotional exchange followed. At one meeting[51] Collins burst out at Lloyd George that during the Anglo–Irish war, the British had released Childers 'after half an hour because he was an Englishman', whereas had he fallen into English hands he would have been shot. The Prime Minister replied evenly that 'they would indeed have shot him'. Lionel Curtis was present at this meeting and after it he and Lloyd George discussed Collins. Lloyd George said that 'Collins was just a wild animal, a mustang'. Curtis compared negotiating with Collins to 'trying to write on water'. Lloyd George replied, 'Shallow and agitated water'.[52]

The Irish argued that without the pact[53] an election could not have been held, the British that the trouble came from Collins' failure to confront O'Connor. Collins' responses sometimes went to the outer limits of discretion. At one meeting he repeatedly told Lloyd George that he was willing to 'give Ireland back as a present'. Understandably, Lloyd George found this 'the most significant feature of the interview', which was described as being of 'great gravity and of a menacing character'.[54] Collins gave Lloyd George a dossier on atrocities perpetrated against Catholics in the North and demanded an inquiry. When he was asked if he got the inquiry he would disavow the IRA in Northern Ireland he replied that he was prepared to co-operate with Craig but that 'he was not prepared to hold up the hands of the Ulster Government while Catholics were being murdered'. One British Minister, Worthington Evans, took this as an outright indication that Collins was behind the IRA in the North.

One can say with certainty that few issues in the long, stormy history of Anglo-Irish relations produced such blunt speaking in Downing St, or so little positive result, as did Michael Collins' Constitution. On the question of an inquiry into the atrocities in the North of Ireland Lloyd George showed some sympathy with Arthur Griffith who had argued that arming the undisciplined Ulster Protestant Militia, the B-Specials, was like 'arming the East End'. He commented: 'The Fascisti in Italy would be a more exact analogy.'[55] Lloyd George told the Cabinet that he feared that Collins was manoeuvring him into a break over Ulster, not over the Constitution. He said that the British case on Ulster was bad in the eyes of world opinion. They had armed Protestants but Catholics had been murdered with impunity. If a break came on 'Republic versus Monarchy', England's case before the bar of world opinion was sure of 'solid support'. Accordingly it was decided to send for Craig with a view to setting up an inquiry. The futile outcome of this aspiration may be judged in Chapter 11.

The respective strengths of the two countries was symbolised by the attendance at the final meeting of the Irish and British negotiators at Downing St on 15 June, the day before the Irish General Election. Only Griffith and Kennedy were present on the Irish side. The British, by contrast, had strengthened their original nine-man team by the addition of Sir Frederick Liddell and Sir Francis Greer. The stronger side got the Constitution it wanted. Afterwards, Kennedy was congratulated by Churchill and the British Chief Justice, Lord Hewart, for his 'enormous service to the cause of the execution of the Treaty'.[56] Churchill was positively glowing in his 'admiration of Mr Kennedy's resource' and the speed with which he had been able to draft changes. In the legal sense the praise was well merited. The Irish Free State's Constitution *qua* Constitution was an admirable document. But in the eyes of Irish Republicans intent on armed defiance of the state it contained incitements to continue rather than inducements to change their minds. The word 'Republic' was so repulsive to contemporary British political thought that Kennedy noted amongst a list of British amendments he sent to Collins: 'They have also rendered "Uachtaran" as "President of the Executive Council"; the word "President" alone suggests a republic to their, at present, panicky minds.'[57]

When he got Kennedy's letter Collins made one last effort to get the Constitution through. He went immediately to London on the 12th, and tried without success to change Churchill's mind. He returned the next day in despair and went straight to Cork for solace. For there were many more concessions to 'panicky minds'. Collins' intention to keep the Constitution separate from the Treaty was frustrated. The preamble to the Constitution specifically stated that the Articles of Agreement were given the force of law and that any law passed or amendment made under the Constitution repugnant to the provisions of the Treaty was 'absolutely void and inoperative'. The Irish legislature was to consist of the King and two houses. Parliament was to be summoned and dissolved in the name of the King. His Representative, that is, the Governor General, was to sign any Bill passed by the two Houses, before it could become law. Right of Appeal to the Privy Council from the Irish Supreme Court was included, thus making it a superior court to any in Ireland. Above all the Oath of Allegiance contained in the Treaty was made mandatory on every member of the Irish Parliament.

The Southern Unionists were also unhappy with the Constitution. Agreement was not reached with their representatives[58] until 13 June. The Unionists argued that the Senate 'constituted as proposed by Popular Election and with powers so strictly limited' did not afford protection for minorities.

From Collins' point of view the only bonus emerging from the Constitution débâcle was the fact that it enabled him to outmanoeuvre de Valera on the eve of the election. On 6 June when the fate, though not the form, of the Constitution was already fixed, Collins and de Valera joined in a joint appeal to support the Pact because: 'many of the dangers that threaten us can be met only by keeping intact the forces which constituted the national resistance in recent years'.

De Valera was aware that the Constitution had run into trouble;

Poblacht na hEireann had printed speculation that it had 'been amended under British threats to suit British demands'.[59] On the same day the *Independent* carried a report that de Valera had been 'acquainted with matters requiring joint consideration and action'.[60] But he shrank from any repetition of the 'violent conflict with the wishes of the Irish people' proclamation with which he had greeted the return of the Treaty. That statement had sent a shock-wave through the country but his attempt to win extremist support had not impressed the Rory O'Connor faction and his 'wading through blood' speeches had cost him moderate support. So long as the Constitution was not published he did not have to take up a position on its terms. It was in his interest not to break with Collins as there might yet be electoral advantage in the pact. The mood of the public was such that any party standing against the Treaty would fare badly.

Accordingly he stayed silent. Collins, recovering in Cork from his unsuccessful encounter with Churchill, did not. Two days before the election, while de Valera was urging an audience in Kildare to support the pact,[61] Collins repudiated it in Cork. His speech, which was reprinted in all the major newspapers contained the following:

You are facing an election here on Friday and I am not hampered now by being on a platform where there are Coalitionists. I can make a straight appeal to you – to the citizens of Cork, to vote for the candidates you think best of, who the electors of Cork think will carry on best in the future the work they want carried on. When I spoke in Dublin I put it as gravely as I could that the country was facing a very serious situation. If the situation is to be met as it should be met, the country must have the representatives it wants. You understand fully what you have to do, and I depend on you to do it.

The Constitution was printed on the morning of the election, again too late for de Valera to be able to derive any advantage from its terms. Whether it would materially have affected the result in an atmosphere in which the issue was rapidly narrowing down to peace or war, is a matter of conjecture. Certainly the result was a severe blow to the de Valera faction which held only thirty-six seats, a loss of twenty-two. The Collins/Griffith party won fifty-eight seats, a loss of eight, but which taken with the pro-Treaty Labour Party's seventeen seats, the Farmers' Party seven, the six independents and the four Unionists represented a solid pro-Treaty majority. But the ending of the pact and the terms of the Constitution taken together clearly presaged a breach with the Four Courts Executive. The military paths and the political ones were fast converging. The convergence was completed by the assassination of Sir Henry Wilson on 22 June and the kidnapping of the Provisional Government General, J. J. 'Ginger' O'Connell, by the Four Courts men four days later.

The Wilson assassination and the reasons for it are dealt with in some detail in Chapter 11. Suffice it to say here that it caused

consternation in London. The British considered a move against the
Four Courts men who were, wrongly, held responsible for it. In the
House of Commons Churchill, in the teeth of a howling gale of Tory
outrage that would have intimidated anyone else, delivered a bellicose
speech:

The presence in Dublin, of a band of men styling themselves the Headquarters of the Republican Executive is a gross breach and defiance of the
Treaty. The time has come when it is not unfair, premature or impatient for
us to make to the strengthened Irish Government and new Irish Parliament a
request in express terms that this sort of thing must come to an end. If it does
not come to an end, if through weakness, want of courage, or some other less
creditable reason it is not brought to an end and a speedy end, then it is my
duty to say, on behalf of His Majesty's Government, that we shall regard the
Treaty as having been formally violated, and we shall take no steps to carry
out or legalise its further stages, and that we shall resume full liberty of action
in any direction that may seem proper, or to any extent that may be necessary
to safeguard the interests and the rights that are entrusted to our care.[62]

Collins' response to this was sulphuric. He 'spoke raging'.[63] Now
whatever he did to enforce the mandate received at the election would
be represented as being at the behest of the British. 'Let Churchill
come over here and do his own dirty work,' he snarled.[64] He had come
very near to deciding to dislodge the Four Courts men himself. A
note of his for a Provisional Government Cabinet meeting, held the
same day as Churchill spoke, reads as follows: 'Internal policy in our
own area. The restoration of ordinary conditions. Arrangements for
peace and order.'[65]

Collins was only too well aware that if he did not attack the Four
Courts the likelihood of the British doing so was growing by the
hour. This would mean a halting of troop evacuation with two very
unlovely possible side effects. One, that they might not resume
evacuation again. Two, that if the British did attack the Four Courts
the situation might escalate to a point where the Provisional Government troops might end up fighting alongside the British.

Despite his anger at Churchill, Collins was finally prompted to act
against his old comrades by these and two other additional,
secondary, but precipitative considerations. One, he believed
mistakenly that the Executive was split between the followers of
Mellowes, O'Connor and O'Malley and those of Liam Lynch. A
quarrel had taken place but had been patched up. The second
consideration arose when the Provisional Government arrested a
prominent Four Courts' man, Leo Henderson, on 26 June, while he
was commandeering transport for the dual purpose of use in Northern
Ireland and enforcing the Belfast boycott against the garage concerned, Fergusson's of Baggot St. Angered at this because they
believed the shared Collins/Executive anti-Six-Counties policy to be

still in place, O'Connor ordered the seizure of the popular Deputy Chief of Staff, Ginger O'Connell in retaliation.

Griffith, O'Higgins, and the rest of the Cabinet took the kidnapping as the last straw. Even Collins told Mulcahy that they would have to fight.[66] But then he agonised for one more day before agreeing that:

Notices should be served on the armed men in illegal occupation of the Four Courts and Fowler Hall that night, ordering them to evacuate the buildings and to surrender up all arms and property, and that in the event of their refusing to do so, the necessary military action should be taken at once.[67]

The ultimatum was received at about 3.40 am on Wednesday 28 June 1922 by a gentleman called 'Skinner' O'Reilly.[68] Given twenty minutes to surrender, the garrison decided not to send any reply but knelt down and said a decade of the Rosary in Irish.[69] Within minutes the Four Courts dome became a target for shells fired from across the Liffey by two eighteen-pound field guns borrowed from the British.

Arthur Griffith stood on the roof of Government Buildings watching the bombardment. As the smoke drifted up from the Irish Supreme Court he 'shook his fist at the clouds of gunsmoke and cursed de Valera'.[70] Ever practical, Collins realised that clean shirts would be hard to come by in the coming days. He called at Vaughan's Hotel to pick up his laundry and found someone else with the same idea, Harry Boland. It was the last time they met.[71]

The shells which the British supplied with the two howitzers were shrapnel, unsuitable for use against heavy masonry. Emmet Dalton, one of the few officers on the pro-Treaty side who knew how to fire the guns, was called back to his office, leaving an inexperienced gunner in charge of one gun. A short time later he received an urgent summons to Macready's HQ in the Royal Hospital. The Republicans were attacking. As his car screeched to a halt outside the HQ where Macready, very correct, very aloof in his full regalia awaited him, a shell burst a short distance away from the group. Aghast, Dalton hurtled back to the gun sites to find that the gunner was using the eighteen-pounder to fire at a sniper on the roof of the Four Courts dome. The shells were passing right through and exploding in the Phoenix Park.[72]

Apart from deficiencies in calibre, the stock of shells supplied by the British was too small and Macready delayed in sending Collins what he asked for to such an extent that Collins cabled Churchill on the 29th: 'Hampered by the continued lack of material . . . promised . . . but not available . . . Essential that action be taken immediately otherwise situation will become impossible.'[73]

Churchill was assuring Collins that 'ample quantities of ammunition are being despatched'.[74] In his eagerness to continue the attack successfully he cabled Collins that:

General Macready . . . has been told to place one of the six-inch howitzers at your disposal . . . can be fired from their positions in Phoenix Park . . . If necessary IFS officers can be by the howitzers and can actually fire them. It is absolutely vital not to break off the attack which having being started must surely be carried through in one way or another.[75]

The following day he urged 'essential to take the 60-pounder [*sic*], its gunners and its ammunition and most desirable to use the six-inch howitzer as well and all together'. He also cabled that 'aeroplanes manned by their own pilots will carry out any action necessary. They could be quickly painted Free State colours to show that they were an essential part of your forces.'[76]

However, without accepting Churchill's lethal largesse, Collins' assault succeeded to a point where at 3.30 pm on Friday, 30 June 1922, a white handkerchief was tied to a broom handle by the defenders. O'Connor had planned to take his men out through the sewers, but he had not allowed for the tidal Liffey.[77] O'Malley signed the unconditional surrender and threw his parabellum into the Liffey to show his contempt. Another, greater, demonstration of contempt resulted in two lorry-loads of gelignite exploding in the Public Records Office situated in the Four Courts complex. For hours after the explosion, the biggest ever recorded in Dublin, priceless manuscripts, some going back to the twelfth century, floated over the city. Miraculously no one was killed. Churchill's comment, contained in a most unwelcome message of congratulation to Collins, was: 'The archives of the Four Courts may be scattered, but the title deeds of Ireland are safe.'[78] The Free State was not safe yet; many casualties lay ahead, amongst them the shared anti-Six-County policy of Collins and the members of the Executive he had just blasted out of the Four Courts. Even while his men were shelling the Four Courts, Collins was securing governmental approval for protests to Churchill concerning two matters arising out of the Northern situation.[79] These were the British decision to give further assistance to the Protestant paramilitary force, the B-Specials, and the fact that an Irish officer, Commandant Hogan, attempting to negotiate with British counterparts over a crisis on the border had been: 'treated with the greatest discourtesy, and it was clear that the attitude of the British officers towards the inhabitants of the district was conducive to disorder rather than to peace.'

It is now necessary to examine how Collins' policy towards Northern Ireland arose and was implemented.

11

Setting up the Six

'Ulster will fight; Ulster will be right.'

Lord Randolph Churchill

One of the buzzwords in the Anglo–Irish dialogue is 'ambivalence'. This is generally used by British or Unionist commentators to indicate that Dublin and the Nationalists condemn the IRA in word but condone it in deed. Viewed from the Unionist standpoint Michael Collins, in the last months of his life, could be regarded as the supreme practitioner of this policy. Janus-faced he stood in Dail Eireann, arguing fiercely for the Treaty and the establishment of law and order in a democratic, independent Irish State, while at the same time he acted with the vigour, intent, and methodology of any chief of staff of the Provisional IRA to wreck the other state enshrined in that Treaty, 'Ulster'. He told northern IRA men that although the Treaty might appear to be the 'outward expression of Partition . . . Partition would never be recognised even though it might mean the smashing of the Treaty.'[1] However, the Nationalist also uses the term 'ambivalence' when he or she points to the methods by which the Northern statelet was set up and maintained. Collins was a Nationalist to the core. From prison camp he had written to Susan Killeen after the Rising of 1916 'anything but a divided Ireland'. He had also been intimately connected with the process by which Ireland was partitioned. Ironically, his killing of Swanzy had probably helped to accelerate the process, in which three fundamental steps had already been taken before he became Chairman of the Provisional Government. As Chairman he would encounter the final step, the refusal to introduce proportional representation into the voting system.

He resented each one of these steps, each one more bitterly than the last. The first was that involving the fundamental question of the area of the state itself. The Irish Committee unambiguously recommended to the Cabinet, on 17 February 1919, that:

the whole of the Province of Ulster should be included in the Northern Parliament. The Committee consider that a Northern Parliament consisting of the nine counties in Ulster is more likely to lead to the ultimate union of the whole of Ireland than if the Northern Parliament was composed of six counties only.

That this viewpoint was accepted and widely supported by the Cabinet is evidenced by the fact that at the end of that year an unusually well-attended meeting held in Downing St on 3 December 1919 agreed that 'the general feeling was that the ultimate aim of the Government's policy in Ireland was a united Ireland with a parliament of its own'.[2] This was subject to various provisos about Ulster's consent, but throughout that December it was made crystal clear[3] that British Cabinet policy *as a whole* favoured a united Ireland as the ultimate goal. But somehow the goalposts were moved. On 15 December the Cabinet was informed that 'the Ulster leaders were doubtful whether the Northern Parliament of Ireland would be able to govern Northern Ireland where there was a Nationalist Majority, and greatly preferred that the scheme should be limited only to the six Protestant counties.' On the same day Worthington Evans reported that Craig had suggested:

the establishment of a Boundary Commission to examine the distribution of population along the borders of the whole of the Six Counties, and to take a vote in those districts on either side of and immediately adjoining that boundary in which there was no doubt as to whether they would prefer to be included in the Northern or the Southern Parliamentary area.

This suggestion is of course of great interest in view of Sir James' subsequent attitude to the Boundary Commission but the major point to be noted here is that while they had accepted the principle of partition for reasons of political expediency, the more far-seeing British statesmen, including Churchill and Birkenhead, had perceived that it was in Britain's and Ireland's best interests to have a peaceful united Ireland (Dublin after all lies closer to Liverpool than to Belfast) athwart the Western approaches, but that Orangism, and more importantly their Tory spokesmen, notably Balfour, had decided otherwise. Ulster would not be Ulster, but six Protestant counties and in fact these Protestant counties had Catholic majorities in the city of Derry, and the counties of Fermanagh and Tyrone.

Lloyd George personally confirmed Craig's views with him and reported to the Cabinet meeting of 19 December 1919 that Craig was 'strongly in favour of the proposed Boundary Commission in order to define the precise boundary of the Parliamentary Area'. At that meeting it was again 'strongly urged' that the new state include 'the whole of Ulster'. But Craig's allies at the table saw to it that *realpolitik* set in with a thud. It was acknowledged that: 'the jurisdiction of the Northern Parliament over the whole of Ulster as a geographical unit was more logical and in many ways easier to defend in Parliament.'

But it was 'generally felt that it was *even more important* [author's italics] to get a scheme which, even though theoretically less perfect, would meet with general acceptance.'

The more far-seeing imperialists saw it otherwise. Birkenhead later pointed out to Lord Londonderry 'the admitted circumstances that if the political considerations allowed it the economic and financial interests of Ireland would be greatly benefited by union, however long postponed.'[4] But ad hocery carried the day and, as we have seen, two years later the Boundary Commission surfaced again under the guise of a Tom Jones idea during the Treaty negotiations. By then Craig was declaring himself vehemently *against* his own proposal.

It is of course easier to speak of change being inevitable than to have to experience it. The assimilation, marriage, blending, call it what one will, of what the Unionists termed 'Ulster' and the Nationalists scornfully referred to as Carsonia or, more accurately, as the Six Counties, with the rest of Ireland in 1921 might not have been a pleasant experience at the time. It would certainly have been viewed with fear, hatred and hysteria by a large number of Northern loyalists. How far these feelings would have been translated into action without the money and support received from the Tories, and the almost equally valuable reluctance of the British Army to open a second front with loyalists as well as Nationalists are amongst the 'ifs' of history. Nevertheless a state, like a company, a tree, or a family either grows or it dies. The tragedy, for 'Ulster', and Michael Collins, is that 'Ulster's' philosophy of government was founded on trying to ignore this inevitability.

This was seen clearly in the second major step in enshrining partition. The Cabinet proposed that 'Ulster' should have a bicameral system so that an upper house would be an integral part of the parliamentary system, so weighted as to be capable of discharging its conceived duty of safeguarding Catholic interests. However a Cabinet meeting presided over by Lloyd George, at which Balfour and Bonar Law were also present, held on 3 November 1920, was informed that: 'Sir Edward Carson and the Ulster Members were strongly opposed to a Second Chamber for the Northern Parliament and would use the whole weight of their opposition to endeavour to defeat the proposal.'[5]

The Cabinet was somewhat exercised at this. Nevertheless the proposals for a second chamber vanished into a portmanteau Council of Ireland compromise in which if either side (North and South) 'did not approve the scheme there would be no Second Chamber'. There was no second chamber.[6] However, to ensure that, in Craig's words, Northern Ireland would continue to have 'a Protestant Parliament and a Protestant state',[7] two more safeguards were required, the withdrawal of proportional representation from the area and the formation of the militia, generally known as the 'B-Specials'.

While generally speaking the 'Specials' grew out of the pre-war Ulster Volunteer Force (UVF) set up to frustrate Home Rule, they took their formal shape from developments in 1920. Sir Basil Brooke began organising Protestant vigilante forces in his native Fermanagh in April of that year. He had visited Dublin, where his wife was having a baby, in the aftermath of the 1916 Rising. The visit decided him to fight any attempt at a Sinn Fein takeover in the North.[8] Also in April, Carson urged Bonar Law to back the idea of recruiting loyalists into a special force to combat the IRA. He used the familiar Unionist argument that if these forces were not organised there might be unorganised retaliation which could bring loyalists into confrontation with British forces.[9] Helped, *sub scriptum*, by the Unionist hierarchy and in particular by pre-war UVF leaders like Colonel Wilfred Spender, a central figure in the pre-war raising of the UVF, and by Fred Crawford, the principal architect of the Larne gun-running, the UVF continued to grow in strength. Captain Hardy established underground contact with the force for use in his counter-insurgency activities. By 23 July 1919, after renewed pressures by Carson and Craig for the introduction of loyalist recruitment, Churchill wanted to know: 'what . . . would happen if the Protestants in the Six Counties were given weapons . . . charged with maintaining law and order and policing the country'.[10] He got a good insight into the likely outcome in Craig's memorandum[11] on the subject to the Cabinet on 1 September in which he complained about Catholic influence in the RIC and demanded the formation of a Special Constabulary from the ranks of the UVF forthwith. Otherwise the Unionists would have to: 'see what steps can be taken towards a system of *organised* reprisals against the rebels, mainly in order to defeat them, but partly to restrain their own followers from acts which are regrettable and in a large measure ineffective.'

Balfour backed the idea[12] and a surprisingly small but strongly pro-Unionist meeting of the Irish Committee[13] decided that not only should the Ulster Volunteers be enlisted as Special Constables, the whole of Ireland should be offered a chance of enlistment. The decision appalled both Macready and Anderson. Anderson wrote to Bonar Law:

I sincerely trust there is no foundation for the rumour that the Government contemplate recognising the Ulster Volunteers in any form. Macready has said in the plainest terms more than once that to do so would not bring relief to the Forces of the Crown but the reverse and I am convinced that he is right. Not only would party and religious feeling be intensified all over Ireland, but sooner or later the Regular Forces would inevitably come into conflict with the Volunteers called to their aid.[14]

However the 'Tudor Tory' influence of Balfour, Bonar Law and the rest was sufficiently strong at Westminster to override the advice of Britain's two top experts, military and civil, on the ground in Ireland. The formation of the Specials was announced on 22 October 1920. There were three categories, A, B and C. The A-Specials were full-time and received the same arms, equipment and high pay as the RIC. The B-Specials were a part-time body whose duties were to patrol, man road blocks and conduct searches. They were intended to operate only in their own localities. The C category was for calling out in emergencies and was mainly used for intelligence purposes.

The Specials were specifically designed as a sectarian force and were not well received in British Liberal and Labour Party circles, coming as they did against the murderous reaping of what the *Daily Herald* of 31 August 1922 termed the 'bloody harvest of Carsonism'. In order to counter 'the opposition of the Labour Party in England' to the fact that the Specials were to be chosen by all-loyalist selection committees UVF leaders,[15] who admitted that 'it is fully recognised that, at first at any rate, no Roman Catholics will respond', suggested an appeal to all 'well- disposed citizens' as 'the only means whereby this scheme can be put through'.

How well-disposed some of the citizens who came forward were may be gauged from the Cromwell Clubs which eventually were subsumed into the Specials. The Clubs were but one of the groupings formed to take the 'organised reprisals' of which Craig wrote. They were located mainly in Belfast. Each Club was armed with a Lewis gun, service revolvers, automatic pistols, rifles and night glasses. Lists of suspects were supplied by the local military intelligence. A Sergeant William MacCartney of the RIC who operated under the Belfast Detective officer DI Harrison, from Musgrave St Police Barracks was a principal organiser of the Cromwell Clubs, which had 50 to 100 members each, drawn from the ranks of loyalist ex-service men. At one recruiting meeting[16] MacCartney said that the object of the Clubs was to establish a system of terror amongst Catholics by shootings, ambushes and midnight visits to ordinary houses.

Such reports had a marked influence on Collins who obviously felt for the Northern Nationalists very profoundly. He would appear to have approached his North-Eastern brethren in liberal terms at the outset. Sean MacEntee, later to be a Minister, successfully proposed at a meeting in Dail Eireann on 6 August 1920 that in view of the pogrom against Catholics which was raging at the time 'an embargo be laid upon the manufactures of the . . . city of Belfast'.

Collins spoke against 'the attempt which had been made by two deputies (Blythe had seconded MacEntee) from the North of Ireland to inflame the passions of members. There was no Ulster Question'. As MacEntee had given the most appalling record of outrage and atrocity against the Catholic community of Northern Ireland one can only speculate as to why Collins spoke thus. Perhaps he simply underestimated the strength of resistance to Dublin which existed in Northern Ireland. His experience of Protestantism in Cork was very different to that of the North. He wrote to Art O'Brien: 'There is really only one small question in Ulster and it has its pivot in the Belfast shipyards. They are the spot from which the strength of intolerance comes.' During a famous speech he made in Armagh on Sunday, 4 September 1921, he said that religious intolerance 'was the product solely and entirely of British policy operating in Ireland'. It had been widely forecast that his appearance in Armagh would lead to serious trouble. He wrote to Moya Llewelyn Davies on 2 September: 'This damned meeting is making me feel nervous already. I should more gladly look forward to an ambush. But perhaps I'll have that also. The unity of Ireland is going to be my main idea I think.'

In fact, with appropriate symbolism, Collins got more of a scare in Dublin than he did in Armagh.[17] His secretary Ally Lyons worked late for him the night before the meeting. As he walked with her to a taxi, gunmen accosted them. A shot was fired as Collins immediately tackled the pair. It subsequently turned out that the two were only Republican police on patrol, but Ally, not knowing this, fled. When she reached home in a panic, thinking him shot, he was there with her father, checking if she was all right. 'What kept you?' he asked.

In Armagh he was greeted by one of the biggest and most peaceful crowds of the period.[18] He delivered a serious, well-researched argument on the 'Unity of Ireland' showing how Ulster had declined under British rule and appealed to his Protestant listeners 'to join with us, as Irishmen to come into the Irish nation . . . to come in and take their share in the government of their own country'. While the meeting itself concluded peacefully, the stones which whistled around his car as he drove home were his answer and by the New Year of 1922, just a few months later, he had changed his approach. 'Non-recognition of the Northern Parliament was essential.'[19]

In thus setting out to negate an essential part of the Treaty which he had done more than anyone else in Ireland to have accepted, Collins, and the British ironically enough, took their precedent from the same source, though as is usual in Anglo-Irish relationships, the two sides interpreted it differently. The Cabinet feared that the term 'Treaty' implied 'recognition of an existing Irish Republic and which it might prove impossible to resist in the case of India'.[20] However as Sinn Fein preferred 'Treaty' to 'pact' the Cabinet had decided to proceed on the basis that a precedent existed since the seventeenth century for the use of the word Treaty, the Treaty of Limerick. Anyone with a knowledge of Irish history could have told the Cabinet that the Treaty of Limerick is notorious in Ireland for having been broken by the British, a fact which Collins secretly made use of with devastating

TOM BARRY'S WEDDING PHOTOGRAPH, VAUGHAN'S HOTEL, 22 AUGUST 1921

Seated on ground: (far right) Gearoid O'Sullivan. First row, seated: (second left) Liam Deasy, the bride Leslie Price, de Valera – who insisted on sitting between bride and groom – Tom Barry; (from right) Countess Marcievicz, Mary MacSwiney. First row, standing: (far left) Sean Lehane, (fifth left) Jim Hurley, Ted Sullivan, Collins – his head is lowered because he suspected the photographer was a police informer – (tenth left) Dick Mulcahy, (12th left) Eoin O'Duffy, (16th left) Emmet Dalton, (15th right) Tom Cullen, (13th right) Rory O'Connor. Last row: (second and third left) Sean Hales, Liam Devlin, (far right) Joe O'Reilly

(*Right*) November 1920: after the 'sack of Balbriggan'

(*Centre*) The Propaganda war: two stills from a British newsreel purporting to show Sinn Feiners shot and captured by Auxiliaries after a Kerry ambush. In fact they show Vico Road, Killiney; (*Right*) The British Tommy, who had no part in the intelligence war, was generally not disliked by the people and the IRA

Michael Collins and Harry
Boland on the hurling field

(*Below*) Cathal Brugha

(*Above*) Richard Mulcahy

(*Right*) The 'Long Fellow' with Griffith,
London 1921

The bodies of Catholic publican MacMahon, his three sons and a barman, murdered in a sectarian raid with the connivance of the RUC, March 1921 – the youngest son, aged twelve, survived and was later noted for flying a Union Jack every Armistice Day

Field Marshal Sir Henry Wilson, the Chief of Imperial General Staff

effect. Eamonn de Barra described to me a highly significant incident which occurred at a moment when the Treaty was hanging in the balance. On 29 December 1921, he encountered Sean Hales, a staunch Republican, probably the most significant pro-Treaty figure in Cork after Collins himself. De Barra, who took the anti-Treaty side, dared to ask the legendary 'Buckshot',[21] who was several years older than he, why he had changed his mind. 'I agree with Mick. He says the British broke the Treaty of Limerick, and we'll break this Treaty too when it suits us, when we have our own army,' he replied. The de Barra incident was no isolated occurrence. Frank Aiken described Eoin O'Duffy[22] telling an IRA gathering in Clones around the same time that the signing of the Treaty with GHQ approval 'was only a trick' in order to get arms to continue the fight. Aiken demurred at the use of such tactics saying that if the Treaty went through the people who supported it would constitute an obstacle to independence. The attendance included some of the most senior IRA officers from the midlands and the north who realised O'Duffy was close to Collins (Collins told Batt O'Connor that he regarded O'Duffy as his successor[23]). They were impressed when O'Duffy repeated that he would never dream of taking an oath, or of asking anyone else to take it.

Collins didn't only use that argument in debate. He put it into practice. His 'stepping stone' was to be a jumping-off point for raids, kidnappings and gun-runnings into Northern Ireland. He also personally initiated policies of obstruction with every single Governmental agency through which the North dealt with the South. However before taking warlike action he gave peace a chance, or at least made an effort to find out what the North's government was thinking. A representative of the Provisional Government was given credentials and sent to ascertain the attitude of the Northern Government towards the South. The representative, Diarmuid Fawsitt, saw J.M. Andrews, the Minister of Labour, and reported his findings on 13 January 1922:

The official view and feeling is that understanding and co-operation with the South is desired by the Northern Government. The present mandate of the Northern Cabinet would not warrant a change in policy towards the South at the moment.

A meeting of the Ulster Unionist Council will be held on 27 January before which a full statement on the position of the Northern Parliament and Government will be laid, and a line of future political action will be submitted for consideration and adoption.

Pending a decision by the meeting of the Ulster Unionist Council on the programme, the Ulster Cabinet will take no steps towards an immediate arrangement with the Provisional Government of the Irish Free State.[24]

Despite this, Collins arranged to see Craig before the 27 January meeting in London, at the Colonial Office where Churchill was in charge of Irish affairs, having become Chairman of the Provisional Government of Ireland Committee which evolved from the Cabinet's earlier Irish Committee. Collins secured his own Cabinet's approval for his policy[25] of putting it to Craig that 'his Cabinet could stop all the outrages in the North if they set their hands to do so.'

His meeting with Craig was 'friendly' and resulted in a five-point agreement. It called for a conference of elected representatives 'for all Ireland' to draw up a constitution which would guarantee the North its autonomy. Most importantly, the Boundary Commission was to be scrapped and Collins and Craig were to work out the boundaries between them. Craig agreed to get the Catholic workers who had been driven out of their employment reinstated in their jobs and Collins promised to call off the Belfast boycott. The two men also agreed to meet again to thrash out the vexed question of Republican prisoners in Northern jails. It seemed that North–South relationships were improving.

But appearances were deceptive. Craig ran into such opposition to his boundary proposals at the Council meeting of 27 January that he had to assure the gathering that there would be no change that left 'our Ulster area any less than it is' and the all-Ireland conference was not even discussed. Yet when Collins and Griffith met a delegation of Northern Nationalists on 1 February, the day before he saw Craig for their progress report meeting in Dublin, he assured them that large transfers of territory from the Six Counties would be forthcoming under the terms of the Boundary Commission if that had to be invoked.

Collins was in an extraordinarily delicate situation, pulled between the machinations of de Valera to appeal to the increasingly militant Republicans on the one hand, and the British and Craig on the other. The bulk of the people in the twenty-six counties wanted a return to peace, not adventures across the border. This wish was amply reflected in the composition of his Cabinet, particularly in the views of figures like Griffith, MacNeill, O'Higgins, Hogan, Blythe and Cosgrave. Their priority was bringing the crisis in the South to a head so as to crush the 'Irregulars' as they both termed and thought of their opponents, before they grew too powerful. They were fully prepared to settle down to building what they could within twenty-six county confines, leaving the solution of partition to the future. Mulcahy was probably the only one at the Cabinet table who shared Collins' approach.

There is a tendency on the part of some contemporary historians to ascribe Collins' Northern policy merely to his desire to keep the South's Republicans in line. But it went deeper than that. Collins was not only the head of the newly formed twenty-six-county Irish state.

He was the head of the IRB, committed by conviction and by the oath administered to him by Sam Maguire to continue what was begun in 1916. He said as much publicly, and could hardly have been more explicit. Speaking at Wexford on 9 April 1922, he said:

the acceleration of cowardly and murderous violence in North-East Ulster allays an inexorable and unquestionable duty of every Irish patriot – a duty which is as definite and immediate as if the British were again violently threatening our Nation . . .

If the so-called Government in Belfast has not the power nor the will to protect its citizens, then the Irish Government must find means to protect them.

This is what he had to say about the Act which set up the six-county state: 'It is my own very strong view now that we should have refused to negotiate a Peace until that Act of Usurpation had been written off. But it is easy to be wise after the event. That Act is written into the Treaty.' And he then went on to speak words which we can see now contained a very ominous ring for Sir Henry Wilson:

We all know only too well the hopes and aims of Orange North-East Ulster. They are well expressed to the world with a lightly veiled brutality in the language of Sir Henry Wilson. They want their ascendancy restored . . . They want the British back . . .

British diehards and mischief makers of the Sir Henry Wilson breed are leaving no stone unturned to restore British domination in Ireland.

Collins' behaviour might well be termed duplicitous in his role as head of the fledgling Irish government, but those sentiments, and his subsequent actions, were entirely consistent with his position as head of the Irish Republican Brotherhood, the logic of attitudes inculcated by Santry and Lyons. After he had signed the pact with de Valera, on 20 May, Collins wrote a note to himself: 'Above all, Ulster'.[26] And certainly the appalling risks he took for the greater part of 1922 in attempting the impossibility of secretly conducting an aggressive policy against the new northern state indicate that he did in fact place this objective 'above all'.

Before meeting Craig for round two of their pact negotiations, and before meeting the Northern Nationalists with Griffith he laid down his policy to the Cabinet:

Non-recognition of the Northern Parliament was essential – otherwise they would have nothing to bargain on with Sir James Craig. He had suggested to Sir James that a meeting of all Irish representatives should be called to draft an Irish Constitution. He would put plainly to Sir James the advisability of the Northern people coming in under the Free State.[27]

But when he met Craig in Dublin on 2 February it was evident how far this approach was from the reality of Unionist sentiment. Collins produced maps showing how much of the Six-County area he felt would be restored to the twenty-six counties under the terms of the Boundary article of the Treaty. The meeting promptly broke down. The main purpose of the Cabinet in accepting the Treaty had been to remove Ireland from the British political agenda. Now, Collins' attempts to push the Treaty beyond its already unpopular parameters and bring 'Ulster' back centre-stage were anathema to the British Government. In his heart Collins had no faith in the Boundary Commission and was only using it as a ploy in his negotiations with the Unionists. Writing to Louis Walsh on 7 February 1922 he said:

You will have seen the map published in the papers yesterday. This map was the most argumentative map we used in conference, and it was for this reason I made use of the expression, 'forcing an open door'. I must confess, however, that I am no lover of partition, no matter in what form it appears. . . . It would be far better to fix our minds for a time on a united Ireland, for this course will not leave minorities which it would be impossible to govern.[28]

As he said to Walsh, Collins did have some faith in ending partition 'in an economic way. This intercourse will inevitably bring our views before the supporters of the others . . . people will wonder why they cannot agree on the bigger things.' But he also made it clear in his letter that he was pleased that in their recent conference Craig had angered British statesmen by sticking out for nothing less than a six-county state because 'we shall be in a much better position to resume the fight with them.' In a nutshell Collins' vision was of a united Ireland which if necessary would have to be fought for.

To the Unionists his activities were, inevitably, simply inflammatory. Carson had not conceded three Ulster counties and settled reluctantly for the six, which the Unionists knew they could control, to permit the precious six to be whittled down by any pact. Craig was not allowed to deliver on any of his five promises. The expelled Catholics were not re-admitted to their jobs. And the Unionist Council meeting stipulated that if relief payments were made to the destitute workers similar sums would have to be made available to unemployed loyalists.[29] There was no give whatever on the issue which was to precipitate the most drastic immediate response from Collins – that of Republican prisoners. But the initial reaction from the Republican side to the pact's breakdown was quite different. Mulcahy sent Collins a note the next day which is revealing of militant Nationalist sentiment in the North:

Mick,
Aiken was tremendously relieved yesterday at the Ulster hitch. Previously in the day he came to speak to me about the Ulster position generally and the following are points which he stressed very earnestly and asked me to stress with you:

A better consultative body regarding Ulster than whatever one at present exists is absolutely necessary for the Provisional Government . . . this body is absolutely necessary to preserve a link between a very strong body of Ulster Sinn Feiners and the Provisional Government.

In your future dealings with Ulster you should not recognise Joe Devlin or his clique . . . there can be no vigorous or harmonious policy on our part inside Ulster if his people occupy any position in our circle.[30]

Collins was to act on the Aiken suggestions in two important regards, the setting up of a North-Eastern Advisory Committee to advise the Provisional Government on Northern affairs, and the avoidance of Joe Devlin and his party. This was an inevitable but unfortunate development as Devlin, an able and intelligent politician, would have been a most useful ally for the Provisional Government. The old suspicion of Constitutional politicians was continuing.[31] Something else was continuing also: the old Collins preoccupation with IRA men in jail. On 14 January 1922 a group of Monaghan footballers including Major General Dan Hogan, OC of the 5th Northern Division, based in Monaghan, had been arrested in Dromore, County Tyrone, on their way to play in the Ulster Gaelic Football Championship. The party were carrying arms which they claimed they were entitled to do under the terms of the Truce. But the Unionists believed, rightly, that they intended to rescue three IRA prisoners in Derry Jail who were due to be hanged in early February.[32] The prisoners had been in jail since before the Truce and GHQ had sanctioned an escape attempt on 2 December 1921 stipulating that no firearms were to be used. Unfortunately chloroform was, and two warders were accidentally killed, one of them a friend of another warder, Patrick Leonard, who was assisting in the unsuccessful escape attempt. Fifteen prisoners were tried for murder and three, Leonard amongst them, were sentenced to hang.

Collins, who of course knew all about the escape plans, put pressure on both Churchill and Craig to have the Derry prisoners reprieved and the Monaghan men released. He wrote to Craig on 26 January 1922 reminding him that: 'I mentioned particularly to you the cases of these Co. Monaghan prisoners who were arrested at Dromore. I left you on the understanding that these cases would certainly be dealt with promptly with a view to release.'

On the face of it Craig responded reasonably and promptly, replying on the following day that if 'the prisoners will at once apply for bail, I will direct the Attorney General not to oppose . . . at the Assizes, the further necessary steps will be taken'. However this course raised the question of recognising the Northern courts. Collins wrote to Eoin O'Duffy, Chief of Staff of the newly formed Army, saying, 'I don't think it would do. Before I reply I would like a word with you.'[33] O'Duffy replied, 'No, Sir James's suggestion of bail will

not do. I have written to you today at some length in connection with
the action I propose to take in this matter, and hope to discuss it with
you further tonight.'[34] O'Duffy had indeed set down his proposals,
on official Army notepaper:

I have information from many sources this morning that there is grave
consternation in the counties of Monaghan, Cavan, Fermanagh and Tyrone
over the continued detention by the A-Specials of Commandant Hogan, and
the Officers of the 5th Northern Division, and they demand authority from
me to take immediate action to bring public opinion to bear on the
situation . . .

You understand that I have arranged for the kidnapping of one hundred
prominent Orangemen in Counties Fermanagh and Tyrone. This was to take
place last Tuesday, the 24th inst., but on account of the agreement arrived at
between Sir James Craig and yourself I postponed action until tomorrow,
Tuesday, 31st inst. and failing to hear from you to the contrary the
kidnapping will commence at 7 o'clock tomorrow evening . . .

The North and South Monaghan Comhairle Ceanntair jointly demand
that the Boycott be not lifted in Co. Monaghan until the men that did so
much to secure the present measure of freedom be released from the custody
of the pogromists. I am anxious to reply to my Monaghan friends tonight.

I should add that there are 54 affiliated Clubs in Co. Monaghan and each of
them are sending two delegates to the Ard Fheis. This means 108 votes fore
[sic] Monaghan for the Treaty . . .

Apart from squarely implicating Collins in cross-border hostilities
the letter from the Chief of Staff speaks volumes for the attitudes
amongst his own supporters with which Collins had to deal. O'Duffy
was telling him in plain language that if he needed those hundred
Monaghan votes to help him uphold the Treaty and, *ipso facto*, law and
order in the South, then, in the North, illegality and disorder would
have to be countenanced and the one hundred Orangemen would have
to be kidnapped.

In the circumstances 'ambivalence' is a term which hardly covers
the situation. But kidnapped a number of Orangemen duly were a
week later, ironically enough on the night of 7 February, the day that
the British reprieved the Derry prisoners, much to the disgust of the
Orangemen.

In all some forty-two people were kidnapped in the cross-border
raid well-described in the telegram that Craig sent to a startled Lloyd
George apprising him of the situation:

Large bands crossed frontier at Derry, Tyrone and Fermanagh. They
attacked and occupied houses of leading citizens on Ulster side of boundary.
Numerous leading citizens including a High Sheriff were wounded or
kidnapped and taken across border to the South. Bridges were blown up.
Twenty Ulster Specials at Rosslea (Fermanagh) were kidnapped and taken
across border. The Ulster police captured 11 men who were identified as
members of the IRA from Longford and Leitrim. They were armed with

bombs and revolvers and had transport. Sir J. Craig regards this as deliberate and organised attack on Ulster.[35]

Lloyd George, only too well aware of what the affair would do to a Coalition already creaking under the weight of the Treaty, reacted by sending a copy of the telegram to Collins accompanied by one of his own saying:

If anything approximating to this has happened H.M. Government take gravest view of the situation; such acts are a breach of the Truce and gravely imperil the Treaty. They will be glad to hear at once from you that you are taking immediate steps to ensure release of prisoners and to provide against any repetition of these grave outrages.[36]

Arthur Griffith, completely in the dark about what Collins and the IRB were doing, cabled Collins:

The diehards here are representing what appears to me to be the taking of hostages against the execution of political prisoners in Derry as an invasion of Ulster. I assume that since the 3 political prisoners have been reprieved – a decision which only reached me last night – every possible step will be taken to have these hostages released and to prevent the malign influences at work in England against the Treaty from scoring a success. Message from you to this effect will blunt widespread press attacks tomorrow.[37]

Collins in reply sent copies of his telegram to both Griffith and Lloyd George. To say that he economised with the truth is to understate the case very considerably:

Throughout yesterday I was extremely anxious as to what might happen in view of pending executions of the three men in Derry prison. I made special efforts to prevent acts of violence on the part of my people and as soon as I heard of reprieve last night I took steps to have information conveyed without delay to leading men on border in order to allay anxiety and to ensure against any untoward incident. The Provisional Government will do everything it possibly can to ensure the safety of the captured men and their early return to their homes.[38]

Whatever suspicions this response may have aroused in Griffith it convinced at least one influential observer of Collins' *bona fides*, Alfred Cope, on whom Lloyd George relied heavily. Cope joined in the fusillade of cables to implore that Craig and Collins be brought together again saying, 'Collins and his colleagues are doing their best but their difficulties are great . . . Collins has had great difficulty in holding in certain sections of the IRA who were out for hostages.'[39] The extent to which Collins had succeeded in masking his hand may be judged from another passage in Cope's telegram:

Please endeavour to get Craig to hold in check the special constables and also Belfast otherwise there will be pogroms. If he can do this there will be no more incursions from the South and Collins will have an opportunity of squaring up things. To think that the fruits of our long labours should be jeopardised by damn fools makes me sick. Let Griffith see Collins' statement. Could Griffith and Craig [Craig was also in London] meet at once and see what can be done . . . Collins has given very firm orders to his people against repetition . . .

To put it bluntly Collins was hoodwinking Cope. Far from making 'special efforts to prevent acts of violence' he had taken the most extraordinary steps to cause it. Prior to the Derry prisoners' reprieve he had called in two of his toughest Squad men, Charlie Byrne and Joe Dolan, and told them that 'at all costs' they were to shoot the two hangmen deputed to execute the Derry prisoners. Here, in his own stark terms, is Joe Dolan's description of what happened:

Charlie Byrne and myself were sent across to England to shoot Ellis and Willis, the two executioners, before they could reach Ireland. Mick Collins told us to get them at all costs, but if we were captured we could not expect any help from him, as we could not identify ourselves as part of the newly formed National Army.

. . . I went to Rochdale to get Ellis. . . . I saw Ellis' wife and made her come round the house with me while I searched it. She told me Ellis had gone to Ireland . . . I had to wait an hour for a train which was held up by a snowdrift, all the time expecting to have a fight for my life if the police came, but I think I frightened Mrs Ellis so much that she was afraid to leave the house. When I came back to Ireland I found out that the executioners had reached Ireland all right, but the prisoners had been reprieved.[40]

Much later in the year, on 12 July, Collins was still keeping up the fiction that someone else had done the kidnappings. He replied to a letter of Cope's on that day saying, 'Residents of the Six Counties alleged to have been kidnapped and were supposed to have been detained in the 26 Counties . . . I discovered that there were 10 Specials from Belcoo in custody (while on a visit to Athlone) Gearoid O'Sullivan also discovered 17 in Dundalk on 19th.'[41] But Craig too had his fiction of ferocity. He reacted to the kidnappings by demanding of Churchill whether there was any 'legal obstacle to our sending a flying column of 5,000 Constabulary to recover the kidnapped loyalists'. He wanted Churchill to reinvade the border area of the South and reoccupy a portion of territory for every person kidnapped until such time as they were all returned. Aghast, Churchill pointed out that such a policy would probably lead to the resignation of the Provisional Government, 'thus creating chaos and leaving the extremists in control'.

Reactions to the kidnappings were explosive. Three days after the O'Duffy raids a party of B-Specials travelled through County Monaghan in the South en route to Enniskillen in the North. During a stop at Clones Station a row broke out between the B-men and IRA Commander Fitzpatrick, who was shot dead. His colleagues retaliated by shooting four of the B-men and arresting the survivors. This precipitated a literal slaughter of the innocents in Belfast, where, amongst other ghastly incidents, a bomb was hurled into a group of Catholic children playing in a schoolyard, killing six of them.

The British responded by halting troop withdrawals from the South and by setting up a Border Commission on 16 February to monitor and control happenings along the border. Churchill told Collins that the Commission was an alternative to 'drastic steps which Parliament would otherwise expect me to take for securing the area of Northern Ireland'. Collins had little time for its mixture of IRA, British and B-Special observers and events bore him out; even Macready said the Commission was a farce.[42] The day after the Commission was set up he introduced a scheme whereby the Provisional Government assumed liability for the payment of teachers who refused to accept the authority of the six-county Government. In the preceeding fortnight he had also made it Government policy that local government councils in the North were also to be supported with funds if they refused to recognise the regime and he set in train a whole battery of minor obstructions. These included refusing to co-operate with the Northern Department of Agriculture, stipulating that trainee teachers from Northern Ireland who wished to take the customary examinations in Dublin would require a knowledge of Irish and stalling all requests from the Northern civil service for the transfer of files from Dublin to Belfast, as the Northern state set up its own departments and services.

All these dealings were unacknowledged at first. Dilworth, the Secretary of the Office of National Education, was instructed to reply to a query from his counterpart, McQuibban, at the Ministry of Education in Belfast, on 7 April, stating that he had 'no knowledge of the payment from Dublin of teachers in Northern Ireland'.[43] Dilworth was telling the literal truth. The £220,000 was paid from the Secret Service Estimate[44] 'not a penny' of which 'has been or is being spent on espionage . . . this money was required for a particular service.'[45]

Yet in correspondence with Lord Londonderry on the issue Collins blandly wrote on 10 April:

I fully agree with you that 'reasonable co-operation between the North and the South in educational matters' is very desirable. It seems to me that such co-operation on equitable terms could easily be arranged. For this purpose I suggest a conference between yourself and such others as you may desire.[46]

However, in education as in much else, 'reasonable co-operation' between Collins and the Northern Government could not 'easily be arranged'. The education issue in fact was almost a non-event compared to some of the happenings in Northern Ireland at the time.

In the conditions prevailing in Northern Ireland, the Truce between
the British and the IRA overall, signed in Dublin in July 1921, was
never closely observed by the Unionists in the North, to whom the
mere existence of the IRA was a provocation and a threat. A threat
made particularly fearful by the fact that with the coming of the Truce
the British dispensed with the services of the Specials. There were
several outbursts of sectarian rioting throughout the province and a
particularly vicious outbreak in Belfast in August which escalated
until it involved the IRA and the loyalist para-militaries directly. Each
side killed ten victims. Nevertheless the liaison arrangement for the
country as a whole obtained with varying degrees of success until 19
November 1921. GHQ continued to supply the various units in the
North with arms, money and training from figures like Emmet
Dalton, Dan Breen, Mulcahy and Eoin O'Duffy who actually set up
an office in St Mary's Hall in Belfast from which he directed
Republican activities. But in November, at a time of renewed rioting
in Belfast, the British handed over responsibility for Justice and
Security to the Six-County Government. Wilson was still Chief of the
Imperial General Staff and he and Worthington Evans saw to it that
Craig's government received considerable numbers of weapons and
ammunition to assist in bringing the Specials back on to the stage. The
new administration immediately put arms and men to use in cracking
down on the IRA. GHQ was particularly incensed by a raid on an IRA
training camp at Cranagh in the Sperrin Mountains on Christmas Eve,
1921. Until then no operations against Specials had been sanctioned
but the Derry prisoners issue had been causing temperatures to rise
and the pot boiled over with the arrest of the Monaghan footballers.
At the end of February, following the expiry of the date for handing in
all unauthorised arms, that is, those in Catholic hands, raiding by
Specials intensified and during a ten-day period in March Collins
sanctioned reprisal attacks against barracks at Pomeroy, Maghera, and
Belcoo in which a number of Specials were killed.

Along with the covert activities of Prescott Decies (see p. 353)
Collins also had cause for concern in the overt activities of Field
Marshal Sir Henry Wilson who, on retiring from the Army, had been
returned unopposed as the Unionist candidate for North Down on 21
February 1922 and was appointed Military Advisor to the Northern
Government on 14 March. Craig was enraptured by Wilson, telling a
group of businessmen[47] that he regarded him as 'my only guide as to
what steps are necessary. Everyone else is brushed aside. All
suggestions will be put before the Field Marshal, and if he recommends them I'll carry them out.' According to Wilson himself Craig
'put aside two millions to carry out my plan'.[48]

The plan involved disbanding the RIC and setting up a new force
known as the Royal Ulster Constabulary and 'stringent regulations'

concerning the carrying of arms. The law was to be 'strengthened in various ways for dealing with men found guilty of outrage'. The strengthening process included the introduction of flogging. Wilson got official British sanction for his plans. Macready promised to send in extra battalions of troops and Wilson's nominee, General Sir Arthur Solly-Flood, was put in command of the new force immediately after Wilson's appointment.

These developments coincided with the announcement by Dawson Bates that he had given instructions that there was to be no further liaison with the Border Commission and that the Government had ordered the police to refuse to recognise the IRA in any way. This announcement was underscored on the night of the circulation of Wilson's plans three days later, 18 March. The headquarters of the liaison committee, St Mary's Hall in Belfast, was raided, drawing a rebuke from the Provisional Government that 'the liaison arrangement between England and Ireland still holds good, and it is a pure breach of the Truce to take over the hall now.'

Both Churchill and Lloyd George had been strongly warned against issuing a political and military blank cheque to the Unionists before they allowed Wilson to take it to the bank. On 18 March 1922 two of the top civil servants concerned with Ireland, Lionel Curtis and Tom Jones, had drawn up a memorandum for the British Government on the Specials, following Craig's announcement that he was having nothing to do with the Boundary Commission. It said:

the whole of these Specials are Protestant . . . The British Government has armed and is paying for that force, but without question the Government of Northern Ireland controls it . . . The British Government has armed and is paying for forces which, it is told by the one who controls them, will in certain eventualities be turned against itself.[49]

Tom Jones followed this up with a note to Lloyd George saying, 'I feel strongly that you should not personally be drawn into conniving in the policy clearly hinted at . . . in Craig's speech when he implied his Government would resist any Boundary changes they did not like.'[50] But two days later Wilson presented his cheque by unveiling his plan for strengthening the North's forces. Next day it was announced in the Northern Parliament that the British would pay for the Specials. Collins was furious and wrote to Churchill saying that this made the British Government 'directly responsible for the situation in Belfast'. He warned Churchill that reaction in Dublin to what was happening in Belfast was generating pressures on the Provisional Government which were 'well-nigh overwhelming. In fact it is no exaggeration to say that the very existence of the Treaty will be gravely threatened.'[51]

As the split developed over the Treaty in the South it opened up in the North, with one important difference. In the North the debate centred not so much on questions of the Oath and the terms of the Treaty, but of whether Michael Collins or those opposed to him would be more reliable in helping the Northerners to throw off the yoke which still burdened them. Joe McKelvey (3rd Northern) and Charlie Daly (2nd Northern) ultimately went anti-Treaty, being subsequently executed by the pro-Treatites. They were replaced by Seamus Woods and Thomas Morris respectively. The complexity of the IRA's Northern organisation and the increasing pace of events caused Collins to sanction the formation of a Northern Military Council with Frank Aiken in command. Aiken, Commander of the 4th Northern Division, was a South Armagh man who had earned a formidable reputation during the Anglo-Irish war. He made notable efforts to avert the civil war before finally siding with the anti-Treaty forces, eventually becoming Chief of Staff.[52] His Deputy on the Military Council was Sean MacEoin. The objective of this Council was twofold: to prevent the Stormont Government from consolidating its position under the 1920 Government of Ireland Act and to protect the Catholics of Northern Ireland. As Mulcahy put it in a policy directive to the 4th Northern Division: 'The general aim underlying all operations in Carsonia is to disorganise the economic structure of the territory and to make the hostile inhabitants realise that aiding and abetting the activities of the Enemy does not pay.'[53]

O'Duffy's official memo to Collins confirming the setting up of a 'Military Council for the North' is dated 10 March 1922. In the memo[54] he also thanked Collins for sending him a letter from a correspondent, 'your Mr O'Driscoll', saying, 'I appreciate some of his suggestions particularly that in connection with widespread incendiary fires.' Other matters mentioned in the memo included the creation of a 'central dump in Cavan' for 'all supplies for the North'. In a sworn affidavit describing these activities[55] Thomas Kelly, Divisional Engineer of the 2nd Northern Division says: 'Michael Collins and General O'Duffy took a staggering risk in supplying . . . weapons and ammo because all were a part of the equipment handed over by the British Forces to the Provisional Government.' Collins attempted to minimise the risks involved in his clandestine operations by exchanging the weapons held by men in the anti-Treaty Southern Division, led by Liam Lynch, for the equipment he had received from the British. The most hair-raising experience was that of the 3rd Northern Division whose lorry broke down en route to Belfast outside the home of a British Army officer, a genial type who gave the IRA men tea and helped them to get the vehicle on its way again. The smoothest gun-running operation was that of the 2nd Northern. Thomas Kelly, who collected the consignment of 200 Lee-Enfield rifles with 100 rounds of ammunition each from O'Duffy, says in his affidavit:

These issues were made with the knowledge and approval of Michael Collins. The rifles and ammo were brought by army transport to Donegal and later moved into Co. Tyrone in a compartment of an oil tanker. Only one member of the IRA escorted the consignment through the Special Constabulary Barricade at Strabane/Lifford Bridge. He was Sean Haughey, father of Charles Haughey.[56]

O'Duffy was also authorised at a meeting at which Collins was present for the 'formation in Belfast of a Guard up to 60 men and the payment of £3 per week'.[57] Payments for the guard and twelve officers came to a total of only £216 per week. The rate of pay for officers in the province as a whole was Divisional officers £5 per week, Brigade officers £4. 10s and Battalion officers £4. In the 2nd Northern Division four Battalion officers were paid £2 a week instead of the £4 for two officers sanctioned by GHQ. An internal Free State civil service memorandum describing the conditions of the time says the decision to make payments was taken because:

the Volunteers were unable to carry on their daily work . . . and so as to obviate an exodus from the area. There was no organised attack on North of Ireland forces. The Volunteers [in Belfast] were daily however engaged in dealing with the riots or mob element . . . Orange mobs continually attacked the Catholic areas . . . Volunteers were almost exclusively confined to beating off these attacks. The police intervened when Volunteers pressed the attack into Orange areas and in that way Volunteers came into contact with them.[58]

During 1922 a Commission appointed by Belfast Catholics investigated some of the murders committed in Belfast.[59] Its report opened: 'there is little difference between these murders and the murders carried out in various parts of Ireland by the Black and Tans, except that in nearly all cases in Belfast, the bodies were mutilated.' One Head Constable[60] 'always used the bayonet on his victim' as he considered it prolonged his agony and 'he didn't believe in giving them an easy death.' The police murder gang had been active during the Black and Tan war. The Duffin brothers were murdered in their home in Clonard Gardens at 10.35 on the night of 23 April 1921. The gang included two District Inspectors, two sergeants and four policemen all of whom were identified. They used a silenced revolver, but ironically, says the report, left a dumb witness:

a dog belonging to the police barracks followed the Gang . . . In their hurry to fly the scene of their crime, the police slammed the door after them, leaving the dog in the kitchen. It was only next morning, about 9 o'clock, one of the police noticing the absence of the dog recollected what had happened.
     . . . two of the police were in a sulky mood, and both demanded that as it was [the] DI who organised the murders it was up to him to go back for the dog . . . at 9.30 he came over for the dog . . . seen by numbers of people

coming in by the back way and taking the dog away. His doing so, far from destroying traces of evidence, only added to it.

After the Tans had gone the police continued the killings. While Collins was arguing with Craig on one hand and trying to damp down the fires of civil war on the other, one of the most revolting murders in the North's history occurred, the murder of the menfolk of the well-off family of publicans, the MacMahons on the morning of Friday 24 March. A statement given by one of the survivors, John MacMahon, in the Mater Misericordiae Hospital, on the evening of the attack tells what happened:

This morning about one o'clock I heard the hall door being smashed in. Five men rushed up the stairs and ordered my brothers and myself and Edward McKinney out on the landing. Four of the five men were dressed in the uniform of the RIC but from their appearance I know they are 'Specials' not regular RIC. One was in plain clothes. They ordered us downstairs. When we got down they lined us up in the room below, my father, my four brothers, Edward McKinney and myself, against the wall. The leader said, 'You boys say your prayers', and at the same time he and the others fired volley after volley at us. I think I lay on the floor for half an hour before the ambulance came. Three or four regular RIC came too.

John MacMahon suffered wounds to the head and body; his youngest brother, aged eleven, crawled under a table and survived also; the others did not. The man responsible for organising the MacMahon massacre and many other lesser-known killings was Detective Inspector Nixon. Nixon and District Inspector Harrison, head of the Belfast Detective Division, were given a free hand in organising Specials and RIC into a counter-insurgency unit in East Belfast which killed Catholics with impunity, either in reprisals for IRA activity or simply to cow others into fleeing or becoming unwilling to help Sinn Fein. Affidavits testifying to Nixon's active part in a number of killings, obtained from Catholic members of the police force who saw him in action, were made available to Collins.[61] He also had the testimony of figures like Bishop Joseph MacRory of Belfast who later became a cardinal and who was so friendly with Collins that the latter brought him to a meeting of the Provisional Government[62] at which Northern policy was formulated. MacRory told the North-Eastern Advisory Committee[63] that Brown St Barracks at the foot of the Protestant Shankill Rd contained a 'number of notorious murderers' who were 'immune' from discipline. Collins, however, knew better. While he agreed with the bishop about Brown St he pointed out that it was not a question of 'immunity'. The Brown St men and their ilk in other police barracks were acting in 'collusion with their superiors who were acting on even higher instruction'.

Collins knew what he was talking about. His intelligence service in Northern Ireland was not as widespread as in the South but he had valuable sources nevertheless. Sergeant Matt MacCarthy was only one of a number of informants in the RIC who included, amongst others, the personal assistant to General Solly-Flood, the senior British officer commanding North of Ireland police operations. He knew that figures in the Northern establishment, including the respected Secretary of the Cabinet, Colonel Spender and of course the Minister for Home Affairs, Dawson Bates, were in favour of reprisals. Men like Igoe and Prescott Decies, who opposed 'parley with murderers' at the Liverpool Unionist Conference during the Treaty talks, were at work in the North. Even before the truce, IRA intelligence had established that Igoe had personally shot four Sinn Fein sympathisers near Newry on 6 July.[64] Brigadier General Prescott Decies, when he was a District Commissioner of the RIC in the Cork area, so dismayed Macready that he wrote: 'Strickland will have to watch the police very carefully for certainly Prescott Decies will think that martial law means that he can kill anybody he sees walking along the road whose appearance may be distasteful to him.'[65]

A background document prepared for Collins by the Catholic Commission for the NEAC meetings said: 'The official position of Prescott Decies in Belfast is a mystery. He is busying himself, apparently with the Ulster Ex-Servicemen's Association and taking a leading part in the anti-boycott campaign.' The ESMA was the para-military body most associated with driving Catholics from the shipyards in 1920 and with taking various actions against the employment of Catholics throughout Belfast. The anti-boycott campaign was directed at putting pressure on Catholics in retaliation for their co-religionists' activities in the South. A crude method of doing this was to burn out Catholic publicans, who were often found in Protestant areas, and see to it that when the business re-opened it did so in Protestant hands. The MacMahons appear to have fallen victim to an extension of this policy.

Sinn Fein temporarily buried its differences on the day of the MacMahon murders to hold a meeting in Dublin presided over by de Valera at which Collins was represented by Kevin O'Shiel. It passed a resolution:

That, just as when the nation was menaced by Conscription, common action was taken by parties fundamentally in disagreement on other questions, the Officer Board of Sinn Fein now appeal that common action be taken to bring the outrages committed in North-East Ulster before the public opinion of the world.

In London, on the same evening, the view that common action was called for also prevailed and the Government reacted to the murders by issuing a 'formal request' to Collins, Craig and their advisors to come to London to confer on 'every aspect of the situation'. Both parties accepted but there was a very acrimonious public exchange of statements between them before the Conference met in London on 29 March. Collins issued a lengthy point-by-point condemnation of Craig's failure to uphold the earlier pact saying that he 'had neither kept his undertakings with us nor done anything to meet us on the several points of controversy'. With the air of a man who had never even heard of a memo from O'Duffy about kidnapping Orangemen, never mind acting on it, he termed it an 'absolute fabrication' and an 'outrage' for Craig to have said in Parliament that the South was trying to 'coerce Ulster citizens and stir up strife here by bombing and sniping them'. Craig riposted by saying that Collins' interpretation of the Boundary Clause in the Treaty was a 'predatory attack' on Ulster and that Collins 'was not big enough to stick to his signature'. Collins drew attention to the provision of Clause 12 which stipulated that the boundary was to be determined in accordance with the wishes of the inhabitants 'so far as may be compatible with economic and geographical conditions'. He declared ringingly: 'I stand by my signature and the Treaty'.

Two points about the foregoing exchanges strike one.[66] One is that the strain of the Northern situation coming on top of his other problems can be guessed at from the emotional tone of Collins' language and the length of his public comments which are strikingly at variance with the terse style he used during the war. The second point is that, ironically in view of the great volume of publicity given to the terms of the Boundary Clause and its impact on the 'wishes of the inhabitants', this was the period in which the Northern Government introduced the deceptively styled Representation of the People Bill (No. 2). In fact its effect would be to gerrymander Counties Tyrone and Fermanagh so that the wishes of the Catholic inhabitants of those areas could not be electorally expressed.

But despite the background against which it took place the meeting was a success – on paper; so much so that Churchill caused Paragraph 1 of the Agreement, published on 30 March, to read: 'Peace is today declared.' It certainly sounded as though better days were coming. Both governments pledged themselves to co-operate in 'the restoration of peaceful conditions in the unsettled areas'. The police in Belfast trouble spots were to be Protestant, Catholic, or a mixture of both, depending on the area. An Advisory Committee of Belfast Catholics was to be set up to help select Catholic recruits to the Specials. There was to be a joint Committee of Protestants and Catholics set up in Belfast to investigate complaints of intimidation and violence. IRA activity was to cease. There were to be further meetings on the Boundary Commission. People expelled from their homes were to be encouraged back with the assistance of the Advisory Committee. The British Government was to vote £500,000 for relief works in Belfast, two-thirds for Protestants and one-third for Catholics. Subject to agreement between the parties, political prisoners were to be released, provided their crimes occurred before 31 March 1922, the day on which the terms of the pact were released to the press.

Privately Collins was far from optimistic. He wrote to Kitty Kiernan on 31 March:

We came to an agreement on certain things with Craig yesterday – I am not very sanguine about the future from any point of view. We have however secured release of all the prisoners – at least the agreement will mean that in the course of a few days and I am hopeful of getting the same result in favour of all the prisoners here. But the news from Ireland is very bad and 'the powers that be' here are getting very alarmed and there may be a burst up any moment. Were it not for the awful consequences I'd almost welcome it.

. . . When I think of how the position is given away behind our backs. Last week Belfast and the N.E. was dreadful to everyone here. A few things are done by our political opponents and all is changed they stand in with Craig again immediately.[67]

The reaction to the pact showed that Collins was right not to be too hopeful. Peace, though declared, was far from accomplished. Sir Henry Wilson, for one, was furious. He visited Ulster (14–22 April) and, at a Government meeting, he 'bit' his hearers by asking, 'Who is governing Ulster? You or Collins?'[68] Apart from the weight Craig attached to Wilson's opinions he knew from the reception that he had already received in Parliament[69] that the Field Marshal's views were widely shared by his followers. Some of these had shown their feelings in particularly grisly fashion the day after the Agreement was published.

A policeman was shot dead[70] at about 10 pm, at the foot of the Shankill Road and an hour or so later a group of uniformed police, led by DI Nixon, emerged from Brown St, the dead man's former barracks. They entered the nearby Catholic areas of Arnon St and Stanhope St, accompanied by a strong force of Specials and armoured vehicles, and broke into a number of houses. The occupant of one of them, Mrs Elizabeth Walsh, of No. 18 Arnon St, afterwards described what happened:

men broke in the front door of our house. My husband was in bed with two of the children. He was upstairs; I was sleeping downstairs with another child. They rushed upstairs . . . I heard the shots . . . When I went up I found my husband shot dead. His hands were over our two children. Bridget aged 1 year and 9 months and Michael aged 7 years; they too were shot.[71]

In all, three people were shot dead, one was battered to death with a sledgehammer and a child, one of a number wounded on the occasion, died some days later from gunshot wounds. Nixon and Harrison were folk heroes in Protestant East Belfast. In the atmosphere of the time neither Craig nor the British could or would prosecute or investigate such men without risk of a serious backlash amongst the Specials. Nixon, who had openly threatened the lives of his senior officers on occasion, was eventually dismissed on 29 February 1924. Collins telegraphed both Craig and Churchill pressing for an inquiry on two occasions (5 and 10 April) before meeting the North-Eastern Advisory Committee on the 11th and telling it that 'if we don't get an inquiry there is not very much use in going on with the pact', in other words pursuing the solution of the North-Eastern problem by political means. What other means should then be employed?

The proceedings of the inaugural Committee meeting,[72] which was held in private, and the status of those who attended it are important for an understanding of Collins' policy towards the North. The purpose of the Committee was to 'advise the Provisional Government' both on the Agreement and on 'all matters affecting the Six-County area'. On Collins' side the meeting, chaired by him, was completely representative of his Cabinet, with Griffith, Mulcahy, Fitzgerald, O'Higgins, McGrath and O'Duffy present. The Northerners included three bishops, a number of priests, Sinn Feiners of whom the most prominent was Cahir Healy, and some members of the IRA active in the Northern area. It did not include Joseph Devlin or any of his followers, which certainly left a gap in the representation of Nationalist opinion. The moderates, and the propertied Catholics, who tended to be found in the Devlin camp, were the very type Collins was depending on to push the Treaty through in the South. There were of course no Unionists present. The proceedings of the Committee were reflective of Catholic concerns only. How these impacted on Northern Protestants we shall see later.

It was open knowledge at the Committee that Nixon and company had refused to turn up for the identification parade at Brown St Barracks after Aron St. Collins proposed holding their own inquiry but Bishop MacRory told him that he would need a 'regiment of soldiers' to protect such an inquiry if it were held in Belfast. With characteristic truculence Collins replied, 'We could hold it all right!' He then read out his correspondence with Craig and said that he believed there would be no inquiry and that Craig would attempt to gloss over the pogrom and attempt to represent the situation as being a direct consequence of a Catholic invasion along the border. Griffith explained the dilemma of the Provisional Government:

We're sitting here as political cock-shots for our opponents and we are trying to defend the people of the North-East and our political opponents come along and call us traitors. We're quite prepared for that . . . I am quite prepared to advocate the breaking with Craig and take all the consequences. I want to know your views.

Views rather than policy were what he got. Bishop MacRory pointed out how helpless the Catholics were, hounded out of jobs and penned into their ghettoes with the Specials rampant, and suggested that if the state and the new police force were recognised to the extent of Catholics taking up the places allotted to them it would at least put arms in some 1,000 Catholic hands. Without the Treaty and the Agreement Catholics were totally defenceless and dependent on relief. At least under the Agreement the one-third of the £500,000 was available. Fears were expressed on all sides as to the debilitating effect of a split in the South over the Treaty in relation to the forces available for Northern Ireland. No one contradicted Mulcahy when he observed 'I take it that under the terms of the Treaty we recognise that Parliament in order to destroy it . . . to carry out all its terms will ultimately unify the country and destroy the Northern Parliament.' This was a strong underlying sub-text to the entire meeting, how to destabilise the Northern state rather than how to work with it, an approach which Devlin and his spokesmen would certainly have been expected to explore more fully.

Collins read out correspondence from Lord Londonderry which made it clear that he had lied point-blank on the payments to teachers.[73] He told him that as far as he was aware the Provisional Government was not responsible for the payments. The clerical representatives were not particularly enthusiastic about the payments policy. They were more concerned to have it understood that the schools would remain under Catholic church control. Archdeacon Tierney said firmly: 'We have come here *merely* to attend to the National aspect of things . . . What I would suggest is that schools under Catholic managers would get the right to adopt the programme and timetable of Southern Ireland. If we get that I would close with them at once.'

O'Higgins raised the uncomfortable point that the destruction of loyalist-owned property which was occurring in some areas in the South as an unsanctioned collateral of the Belfast boycott was giving the Orangemen a justification for their behaviour. Dr Russell MacNabb said, however, that the destruction of property made the other side 'uncomfortable' and remarked wistfully that there had been 'some beautiful fires in Belfast each night'. Collins said frankly, 'I know for a good many months we did as much as we could to get property destroyed. I know that if a good deal more property was destroyed . . . I know they think a great deal more of property than of human life. The whole thing again is what *is* proposed?' He did not get any clear answer. Nor was he able to give one to MacRory's fundamental query, 'Can you protect us?'

Collins decided on his own answer, a three-tier strategy of public, parliamentary and military pressure. In public, he continued his increasingly voluminous and acrimonious correspondence with Craig and, as the Provisional Government minutes for the time show, had little or no difficulty in carrying the Cabinet with him. On the 21st it was decided, because of the 'continuation of the outrages in Belfast', that Collins should wire Churchill informing him that unless Craig took immediate action 'to show his good faith' the Provisional Government would regard the Agreement as broken and it was also decided to tighten the screw of non-cooperation with the Northern educational authorities.[74] The Cabinet also backed him in preparing a tough reply to Churchill's answer asking Collins to meet Craig in London again. It would be 'useless' to meet Craig unless he showed 'some intention of abiding by the Agreement'.[75] He sent Craig a letter of almost six closely typed foolscap pages on 28 April, in which he found him guilty of 'the greatest want of courtesy', and went on to say:

Your entire letter has apparently been drafted with a view to keeping attention off the daily practice of atrocities and murders which continue uninterrupted in the seat of your Government. There is not space here to detail the abominations that have taken place in Belfast since the signing of our Pact, and I quite understand your desire to draw the attention of civilisation away from them.

Belfast was not of course the only place in uproar; the entire province was in convulsions, but Belfast was the worst-hit. In all twenty-four Catholics and eleven Protestants were killed in the city from 1 April to the date of Collins' broadside to Craig. On a day, 19 April, when Sir Henry Wilson was inciting an audience at Bangor, by drawing their attention to the dangers of Republican troops massing on the border 'while a supine British Government withdrew from Ulster,' the *Irish News* carried the following report of an attack on the Catholic Marrowbone area of Belfast, in which two women were killed, and fifteen houses burned down:

The match and petrol men operated with as much freedom as if they had happened upon as many deserted 'shanties' in the American backwoods 100 miles from the nearest civilised settlement, and all the time scores of men wearing the King's uniform were quiet witnesses of the scenes of destruction and many scores were within hailing distance, while the occupants of an armoured car could almost warm their hands at the flames.

The side-effects of the Northern convulsions on Catholic–Protestant relationships in the South were nothing like as horrific as in the North. The southern authorities actively worked to combat and overcome sectarianism. Nevertheless the South did have its share of atrocities. Ironically one of the worst outbreaks of sectarian killing was in Collins' own home district. It began when an anti-Treaty IRA officer, Commandant O'Neill, was shot dead when he called at a Protestant-owned farm near Bandon on 25 April. Three Protestants

were shot at Dunmanway and over the next week the latent sectarianism of centuries of ballads and of landlordism (described in Chapter 1)
claimed a total of ten Protestant lives. Tom Hales, Commandant of
O'Neill's Brigade (3rd Cork), ordered all arms brought under control
and issued a statement promising 'all citizens in this area, irrespective of
creed or class, every protection within my power'.[76]

Speaking in the Dail, Griffith echoed the sentiments expressed by
Hales, who was at the time actively engaged in armed opposition to
Griffith's government. He said:

Dail Eireann, so far as its powers extend, will uphold, to the full extent, the
protection of life and property of all classes and sections of the community. It
does not know and cannot know, as a National Government, any distinction
of class or creed. In its name, I express the horror of the Irish nation at the
Dunmanway murders.

However, the effect of the killings on the Southern loyalists may be
gauged from a letter from a Protestant lady in Crosshaven, County
Cork, Alice Hodder, to her mother in England, which was forwarded
to Lionel Curtis as Secretary of the Cabinet's Irish Committee:

For two weeks there wasn't standing room on any of the boats or mail trains
leaving Cork for England. All Loyalist refugees, who were either fleeing in
terror or had been ordered out of the country . . . none of the people, who did
these things, although officially reported as the rebel IRA faction, were ever
brought to book by the Provisional Government. And what is even more
sinister is that the worst murders and roughest evictions took place in
Clonakilty where Michael Collins comes from.

Then the murder of young Woods shook us all very much. Do you
remember him last summer? He used to bring us up lobsters and mackerel.
He was a bit of a ne'er-do-well and a bit mad but he'd done splendid work in
the war and was recommended for a VC . . . his aunt and uncle had been
subjected to a lot of persecution and feared an attack so young Woods went to
stay with them. One night about 2.30 am armed men . . . broke in . . .
Woods fired on the leader and shot him.

They . . . caught Woods . . . tried him by mock Court Martial and
sentenced him to be hanged . . . The brothers of the murdered man then . . .
gouged his eyes out while he was still alive and hanged him . . .

The letter went on to give details of Protestant farmers being turned
out of their farms by anti-Treaty IRA parties as part of a policy 'got up
by the Irish Transport Union, because all these people have brought
down their labour, owing to the slump in prices and the workmen
refusing to reduce wages.' Even though the pro-Treaty IRA always
reinstated such people Hodder commented, not surprisingly, 'you
never know when you've been reinstated what will happen next', and
enquired: 'When will the British Government realise that they are
really dealing with savages and not ordinary normal human beings?'
Curtis' comment appended to the letter was, 'This is rather obsolete.'

But the file already contained too many such protests to be ignored.[77] For example Carson was eliciting considerable anger and sympathy amongst Conservatives and in the Press, particularly the *Morning Post*, over 'the worst thing that happened', the case of an 'outraged girl' in Tipperary, a Protestant, whom raiders had 'forced to submit seven times'.[78]

On 13 April 1922 Collins sent Desmond Fitzgerald copies of two telegraphed despatches which the Dublin Correspondent of the *Morning Post*, Bretherton, had filed, with a note saying: 'You will observe that portions are what would be described as fair newspaper comment, but the strain of certain parts is very objectionable', and he suggested that Fitzgerald get one of his people to interview Bretherton. 'It need only be a friendly interview.'[79] One of the despatches (5 April) stated that 'Dublin swarms with youths wearing leggings and faces that the kindliest hangman would be glad to get to work on.' The other, describing a resolution passed by Waterford workers concerning the Belfast situation said:

What the Southern Bosthoon thinks, if the word think can be properly used in this connection, of the trouble in Belfast is well illustrated by the resolution passed last night (March 21st) by the Waterford and District Workers Council STOP

The time for the massacre to begin is clearly now STOP . . . This attractive resolution proceeds to declare 'Unionists in Waterford and the South of Ireland must shoulder responsibility for what is happening in Belfast . . . should the Unionists . . . not take requisite measures to discharge their serious responsibilities in the matter the Workers Council will accordingly act immediately STOP

Probably no brighter example of the typical Southern Irish mentality could be provided than these truculent and ignorant bolshies every one of whom is awaiting his chance to murder and some of whom have doubtless already assisted in murdering with all the circumstances of filthy brutality the loyalists whom they hate not merely because they are loyalists but still more because they are clean decent and industrious and have something that Bolshies can steal STOP.

Apart from whatever results might have been expected from this type of coverage, and their many other sources of disagreement, Craig and Collins had been exchanging letters throughout April over the seizure by anti-Treaty forces of the headquarters of the Loyal Orange Institute of Ireland in Dublin, which they used to house homeless Catholic refugees from the North. The prosecution of the Belfast boycott by anti-Treaty forces also resulted in the destruction of some Protestant businessess, and in fines and threats which sometimes caused Protestants, particularly in border areas, to flee northwards. County Leitrim, with a particularly bad history of poverty and bad landlords, was harshly affected in the latter regard.[80] But there is no doubt that in many other parts of the country, the land-hungry and predatory element which emerges from any revolution tried to take advantage of the times to seize what did not belong to it.

It was a time in which the newspapers' daily list of Northern outrages, the bulk of them directed against Catholics, took 'from about half a column to a column each day'.[81] Defending the conduct of the boycott, Sean Moylan had no hesitation in telling the Dail:

Raids and acts of obstruction have been enumerated and it was stated that this work has been done under cover of the Boycott. It has not been done under cover of the Boycott. It has been done as part of the Boycott work until this affair in the North – these murders and so on – is stopped.[82]

Accordingly, Curtis was instructed to write to the Provisional Government on 13 May inquiring about recompense for the relief expended by His Majesty's Government on 'the large and increasing number of persons who have been driven from their homes in Ireland by intimidation, or even by actual violence at the hands of men acting openly in defiance of the authority of the Provisional Government'.

Replying on 18 May, Diarmuid O'Hegarty accepted liability[83] in *bona fide* cases but warned that 'an organised movement' aiming at discrediting both governments was responsible for 'a considerable number of persons having left Ireland on the plea of compulsion without any justification whatever for that plea'. He urged the British to be vigilant in ensuring that only '*bona fide* cases' received assistance. O'Hegarty repeated guarantees already given to the Church of Ireland Synod that the Government would 'secure civil and religious liberty' and 'the restoration of their homes and property to any persons who have been deprived of them by violence or intimidation'.

This ecumenical approach was unquestionably Collins' also. But the Janus-faced approach inevitably led to perversions of it. At the Parliamentary level Collins privately explored every avenue open to him to bring down the Northern Administration. On 4 May he circularised every member of the Cabinet that they should:

get the advice of your experts on the exact powers and limitations of the Northern Parliament in the British Act of 1920 . . . You will need to watch carefully to prevent any extension of these powers. You will also need to have a scheme prepared for non-co-operation in every possible way with the Northern Parliament. And in addition, a scheme towards making it impossible for them to carry on.[84]

To impress upon his colleagues that he was serious in this proposal he again circularised them on the 15th and 16th emphasising 'the importance of not losing sight of this matter'. On the 16th he wrote:

I want a memo giving any points regarding the position of your Ministry in relation to the Six-County Parliament ie any matter troubling you, any point you want raised, or that you have anything particular to say about. This matter should be treated as very urgent.[85]

He did not circularise his colleagues on the third strand of his policy of 'making it impossible for them to carry on', his pact with the IRA to use force against the Northern Parliament in flagrant breach of the Treaty he was so desperately trying to uphold in the Provisional Government area.

Collins' idea in mounting the Northern offensive had been to give the British the impression that it was in fact a defensive operation, a reaction against the activities of the Specials. This fig leaf lost a good deal of whatever credibility it possessed when at the beginning of May the 2nd Northern Division went into operation on its own, apparently through a confusion over orders from GHQ. Attacks were launched on barracks in Derry and Tyrone in which six RIC and Specials were killed. However any lingering qualms Collins might have had about launching a more co-ordinated campaign would certainly have been dissipated by the proceedings of the Catholic Advisory Committee provided for by the pact. The Committee did not hold its first meeting until 16 May, two days before the large-scale offensive was due to begin. Solly-Flood made it quite clear that he was not going to give the Committee any reforming role where the Specials were concerned. Some of its members were in the IRA and he regarded the Committee as a device to gain information about the security forces. At the last meeting of the short-lived Committee, held on 7 June 1922, it was pointed out that its members were being arrested and their homes, including those of priests, were being shot up by the Specials.

By 7 June the Collins-sponsored IRA campaign in Northern Ireland was well under way. It may be considered to have begun formally on the morning of 18 May when Seamus Woods led an attack on Musgrave Street police barracks in Belfast. It was marked by confusion and lack of co-ordination.[86]

However the overriding reality was that the forces against the IRA were overwhelmingly superior in numbers and material. One IRA officer described 'three train loads of Specials coming into Belfast every day'. His recollections are of daring incidents rather than of a campaign that seemed likely to win ultimate success. Ernie O'Malley records the OC of the Belfast Brigade and a companion being followed through the streets of Belfast as 'we ran from a job. We only had forty-five rounds between us.' The campaign was short and sharp, practically over by the end of June except for Belfast, where amongst other pieces of destruction the colleagues were responsible for raiding the Custom House and 'sledging' an estimated 500,000

gallons of whiskey. Though 50,000 seems more likely, it was said that
the aftermath was such that: 'the drains couldn't take it all. Men were
drunk on the fumes.' In some circles that particular raid probably did
more to set back Orange–Green relationships than anything else.

All told, the IRA managed to cause over a million pounds worth of
damage by burning Unionist property, roughly half of it in Belfast.
The war did not seriously discommode the loyalists' decision-takers,
though it touched some of them. Belfast's Twadell Avenue today
commemorates the Unionist MP, W. J. Twadell, shot because of his
inflammatory speeches and involvement with the para-military
grouping, the Imperial Guards, which also became subsumed into
the Specials. The homes of the Speaker of the Six-County Parliament,
Sir Hugh O'Neill, and the hard-line Conservative MP, Captain
Ronald MacNeill, were amongst the properties burned.

But the reaction fell heaviest on Catholics. For instance, May saw
sixty-three deaths in Belfast alone. Of these, forty were Catholics. In
an effort to balance the sectarian scales the IRA made things worse. On
19 May after three Catholics had been murdered two days earlier, an
IRA party entered a cooperage in York St and enquired, 'Who are the
Mickies here?' The three Protestants present obligingly pointed out
their Catholic workmates and were promptly themselves shot dead.[87]
Next day, out of a total of thirteen killings, Protestant retribution
claimed twelve Catholic lives. It was the same if not worse in the
countryside. This was part of settled B-Special policy. The British
General, Ricardo, a founder member of the UVF, who later became
disenchanted with the force, described the Specials' *modus operandi* in
a memorandum prepared for the British Government:

The 'B' Head Constable . . . goes to the leading local nationalist . . . He tells
him that they have arms and mean to patrol at nights . . . the nationalist is
shown a list with his name at the top and is told that if any 'B' man is touched
the list will be attended to from the top. This is not an effort of the
imagination but is not an uncommon arrangement.[88]

In reacting to the IRA onslaught the Unionists made other
'uncommon arrangements'. Internment was introduced, the hulk, the
Argenta, moored off Larne, being used as a prison ship. Although
murders were running at a rate of two Catholics for every Protestant,
only Nationalists were interned. All Nationalist and Republican
organisations were banned, but no loyalist groupings were proclaimed. Curfew was introduced in Belfast and Craig said (on 23 May)
that as far as the North was concerned the Boundary Commission was
now finished. In Dublin, the Cabinet, most of whom were unaware of
Collins' part in these developments, backed him in a statement saying
that as the Treaty was entered into between Great Britain and Ireland,
the interpretation of its clauses did not lie with Sir James Craig.[89]

Churchill was displeased with Craig's repudiation of the Boundary Commission which he termed 'little short of a defiance of the Imperial Government'. The defiance was particularly unwelcome because it came at the same time as Craig was seeking what Churchill accurately termed 'enormous' financial and military aid in order to strengthen the Specials along lines advocated by Wilson and Solly-Flood. In money, Craig sought £5 million sterling, in weaponry, 23,000 rifles, 15,000 bayonets, 242 Lewis guns, 50 Vickers guns, mortars, grenades and other equipment such as uniforms and tents.

However Churchill took the view that the troubles in the North stemmed from the fact that:

two so-called divisions of the Irish Republican Army were located in Ulster, and these divisions were most improperly maintained as organisations in spite of the truce, in spite of the Treaty . . . the prime and continuing cause of all the horrors which have taken place in Belfast is the organisation of these two divisions of the Irish Republican Army in Northern territory and the continuous effort by extreme partisans of the South, to break down the Northern Government and force Ulster against her will to come under the rule of Dublin.[90]

In these circumstances Churchill, though he claimed to believe in long-term Irish unity, decided like his father before him that Ulster would fight and Ulster would be right. After some quibbling Craig got almost everything he asked for plus a bonus of 3,000 surplus RIC revolvers and ten million rounds of ammunition. Units of the Navy and RAF were also sent to Ulster and ex-officers recruited to help train the Specials. By contrast it may be noted that less than two weeks earlier Wilson had observed with satisfaction[91] that Churchill had vetoed a request from Cope to supply Collins with arms, lest they be used in the North. That day, 10 May, Wilson had made a speech in the House of Commons demanding that the four battalions of British troops then in Cork should be sent to Ulster. They were, bringing the total of British troops in the area to some 9,000 and the Specials to approximately 48,000. Churchill told the Cabinet:

We could do no less, having regard to the gathering of the forces from the South and the ferocious steps used against Ulster . . . [Collins] having joined hands with avowed republicans we could hardly wonder that the North has gone back to its extreme and violent position. I think we have to give them assurances of help.

Churchill gave more than assurances. He took drastic action in support of the Unionists in two territorial disputes involving a triangular section of Fermanagh that ran a little way into Free State territory. At one end is Pettigo, largely in Free State territory, though the border runs through some of the houses. Belleek is in the Six-County area, overlooked by a fort on the Free State side. The Specials commandeered a house in the Pettigo area belonging to the parish priest. On 28 May there was an exchange of fire between the Specials and Provisional Government troops under Divisional Commander Joe Sweeney who earlier had had to run for his life when Specials opened fire on him. One Special was killed and the rest evacuated.

Churchill, who was coming to view Collins as a 'corner boy in excelsis'[92] saw the triangle incidents as an opportunity to teach him a lesson. On 3 June he ordered into Pettigo 1,000 British troops armed with a battery of howitzers, and a number of armoured cars. The troops were told 'to inflict the greatest possible loss on the enemy'. The village was shelled, the gunners succeeding in killing three Irish soldiers and one Special. The commander of the garrison and fourteen of his troops were captured, and newspaper reports make it clear that had the other Irish troops not fled with the civilian population casualties would have been much higher.

Collins sent a telegram to London demanding an immediate joint inquiry and protesting at 'unwarranted interference with our forces in our territory. An extension of the trouble will be disastrous and will certainly imperil the whole situation.'[93] Churchill's reply next day, 6 June, illustrates the confusions and tensions of the period:

On Wednesday last information was received that armed republican forces had invaded the Northern territory and had entered both Belleek and Pettigo . . . We immediately brought this to your notice . . . You told us that these forces were not your forces, that you disclaimed any responsibility for them. I announced this in Parliament in your presence the same afternoon.

It is with surprise that I received in the Communiqué issued from GHQ Beggar's Bush that there were 'no other Irish troops' than 'our troops', ie Free State Troops, 'in the district now or then' and I shall be glad if you will explain the discrepancy . . .

British troops have also been ordered to occupy the village of Belleek . . . It must not be supposed that any part of the border can be kept in a continuous state of disorder and alarm either by raids or by fire directed from your territory and all persons and armed parties over whom you have any control should be warned by you that they will certainly be counter-attacked . . . There can be no question of any inquiry into these operations.

Collins replied to him on the same day saying that his telegram 'had made the situation very much worse'. He protested at the lack of warning, repeated his demand for an inquiry and pointed out that while Belleek was in the North the Barracks was in the South's territory. He finished by telling Churchill: 'You misunderstand the position and only immediate inquiry can put it right.' The Belleek–Pettigo situation was exacerbated by an attack on the Mater Misericordiae Hospital in Belfast by Specials which occurred on the night of the 5th. The Specials sprayed the Catholic hospital with machine-gun fire for some forty-five minutes. Then the hospital was raided by the police 'in search of arms'. Pelion was piled upon Ossa in Collins' view by the Northern Government which ordered the arrest of three members of the Police Committee that night. They were lodged in the Crumlin Road Jail alongside the Mater Misericordiae, for which he demanded military protection.[94]

For once Lloyd George sided with Collins. He had come to think that Collins had allowed himself to 'become obsessed with the Ulster situation'. But he also saw himself being drawn into a war for which he considered de Valera and Wilson responsible. He could see the Treaty collapsing and hostilities resuming, not merely in the North but with the Provisional Government. He warned Churchill that the Oath or the Constitution were the only grounds on which they could hope to carry public opinion for a break with Dublin. He said privately that he thought 'there was a strain of lunacy in Churchill'.[95] Nevertheless Churchill got his way by threatening to resign. All he conceded to Collins was a promise to 'discuss the border situation with Mr Griffith tomorrow in the light of your telegram'.[96]

Collins did not view the affair lightly. While he 'did not regard the Belleek position as being so serious . . . the whole position is unquestionably cause for gravest anxiety'.[97] In Dublin civil war loomed. A general election was due to be held within a few days. The last thing the Provisional Government needed or wanted was trouble on the border. The tension between Collins' secret activities and the views of his colleagues is reflected in the Minutes of a Provisional Government meeting on 'The North East Question', on 3 June. Paragraph 1 says:

It was decided that a policy of peaceful obstruction should be adopted towards the Belfast Government and that no troops from the twenty-six counties, either those under official control or attached to the Executive, should be permitted to invade the Six-County area.

Obviously, from the reference to 'official control', some members of the Cabinet had an inkling that their troops might have been used to 'invade the Six-County area'. Equally obviously, paragraph 2 is undiluted Collins:

Any extension of powers on the part of that Government should be strongly opposed and care should be taken to prevent it being granted powers other than those conferred on it by the 1920 Act.

The same dichotomy of approach was noticeable after the Cabinet met in agitation to discuss the Belleek incident. The first decision read:

It was arranged that the Minister of Defence should obtain daily reports from every post on the twenty-six county side of the Border, and that particular care should be taken to ensure that there would be no Border conflicts.[98]

From this it is evident that the other members of the Cabinet were unaware that the Minister of Defence, Mulcahy, was already receiving daily reports of what was happening in the North of a very different character from what was envisaged around the table.

The strain of these events was taking its toll on all concerned. Collins wrote to Griffith in London where he was attending one of the incessant meetings with Churchill, necessitated by the press of events, 'Duggan and O'Hegarty both laid up. I am a little better today.'[99] The object of the letter was to force an inquiry into the Pettigo attack from Churchill:

It appears to me that the position in the North-East gets steadily worse, and if we are ever to get anywhere there must be an enquiry about Pettigo. The whole incident must be gone into. All the incidents leading up to the final attack must be revealed.

But Churchill refused to concede any inquiry despite a particularly undiplomatic public call for one by Collins on 11 June in the course of which he said that while he would strain every nerve to avoid border clashes with the British it did not follow that his Government had not 'a very definite policy to put into effect as a last resort against that demoniacal barbarism which is aiming at the extermination of their people in the Six Counties'.[100] The two sides eventually came to an agreement to follow the practice 'adopted in Silesia with very great success'[101] and set up a sort of neutral buffer zone in the area. Churchill afterwards wrote that the triangle episodes:

gave me the opportunity of reassuring Ulster that if it came to an actual invasion they would certainly be defended. The IRA realised that we should not hesitate to levy open war and the Free State government knew that at any rate one line was drawn which would not be transgressed.

However there is a dimension missing from Churchill's policy considerations in this seemingly straightforward summation, that of the influence of Sir Henry Wilson on the growing disenchantment of 'Tudor Toryism' with the Coalition between the Conservatives and the Liberals. As Collins said in Wexford, plans were afoot for a new Die-hard party. Lady Londonderry had been canvassing the idea in the great houses of England for some time and as she plotted amongst the peers the right-wing backbencher John Gretton was taking similar soundings amongst his colleagues. As letters circulated amongst various lords[102] over Christmas, Northumberland had written to Lady Londonderry on 23 December asking her to stay with him to discuss the formation of the new party and the selection of a leader:

I quite agree about Salisbury. He has far more experience than anyone else in the Lords and would carry more weight . . . as to Horne I like him, and I think his instincts are Tory, but I'm afraid he has gone too far to turn back. He thinks Michael Collins is a very good fellow!!! He told me so the other day.

Wilson approved of these endeavours, noting after a lunch at Londonderry House in London at which only he and Lord and Lady Londonderry were present:

We discussed the possibility, necessity and probability of forming a real Conservative party. Lady Londonderry is working hard to this end with Salisbury, Northumberland, Carson, Ronald MacNeill and I am sure this is the right thing to do and I believe if they could get a fine leader it is a real possibility.[103]

The possibility had become considerably more real by mid–May 1922, when it was obvious that the Coalition was beginning to crack up. Wilson was addressing Die-hard meetings and more and more 'Tudors' were beginning to see him as the 'fine leader'. However he felt the time was not yet ripe for him to accept the leadership, and contented himself with attacks on the coalition for being 'increasingly inclined to work with the King's enemies'.[104] The Collins–de Valera pact played straight into his hands, Collins having said openly at the Sinn Fein Ard Fheis on 23 May that it would enable him to concentrate on the North-East. Churchill told a delegation of Catholic businessmen from Belfast on 2 June[105] that the pact adversely affected the relationship between Dublin and London. He said it also prevented Craig from working with a government in league with Republicans. Churchill described the pact as doubling the forces of evil and halving the forces of good. The power of Sir Henry Wilson was doubled he said, and told the delegation that 'you are being tortured by Wilson and de Valera'. Sir Geoffrey Shakespeare gives Churchill credit for 'keeping the Die-hards at bay and upholding Michael Collins'[106] but he was also concerned with upholding one Winston Spencer Churchill.

What Churchill did not tell the Catholic businessmen was that the previous day he had told the Committee of Imperial Defence's sub-committee on Ireland that 'in order to protect Ulster from invasion by the South' he wanted plans drawn up immediately whereby, when operations commenced, 'all our means of exercising pressure on Southern Ireland should be applied at once . . . we must act like a sledge-hammer so to cause bewilderment and consternation among the people in Southern Ireland.'[107] A version of the 'sledge-hammer policy' was duly applied over the Constitution and the Belleek–Pettigo area, but at this stage Churchill was still not sure whether Collins was going to break with de Valera or take steps to eject Rory O'Connor and his men from the Four Courts. 'Although the British could breathe a bit easier now, they could not abandon measures designed to conciliate the Provisional Government such as the pro-posed enquiry in Belfast.'[108] Accordingly, Churchill, having first got Balfour to test the waters, wrote to Craig on 10 June:

We gathered from Lord Balfour that at his interview with you last week you were not unfavourable to the setting up of a Commission of Enquiry on certain lines . . . such an enquiry would be of real value . . . show the provocation the Protestants have received and are continuously receiving as well as the bloody reprisals with which they repay it. I would not have been in favour of such an enquiry if the main constitutional issues which we have with the Irish Provisional Government were not now in a fair way of settlement.

Furthermore having shown quite clearly by the use of British military force our intention and our inability [sic] most faithfully to carry out our duty of defending your frontiers, and having supplied you with arms and financial aid for your own Police forces, I feel entitled in the general interest to make this request to you, and to make it seriously and definitely.[109]

However even in Craig had any real intention of holding an enquiry along the lines pressed for by Collins, Dawson Bates had not. He had a reputation for hostility to Catholics which included leaving them waiting for hours whenever they were forced to call on him on business. As Minister for Home Affairs, he had not attended any meeting of the Conciliation Committee set up by the Agreement. He had seen it purely 'as any voluntary committee'[110] without executive powers and had refused to grant it any expenses. Now he was even more opposed to the idea of an outside inquiry. He wrote to Craig:

It is impossible to agree to Mr Churchill's suggestion without gravely weakening the Government of Northern Ireland . . . the Executive of Northern Ireland and those who attempt to carry out the law must be supported at all costs. To set up an outside tribunal to enquire into the action which is found necessary from hour to hour, and to justify or condemn it would strike at the very roots of government.[111]

Armed with this, Craig was able to tell Churchill and Lloyd George, whom he met in Downing St on the 16th, that he was opposed to an inquiry the request for which did not come from Ulster. He was afraid that the new police force would get the idea that 'Dublin Castle methods' would prevail and that the identities of their secret service agents would be disclosed. Londonderry said that a public inquiry would only encourage the South to redouble their efforts to defeat partition. Instead, Craig proposed that some government official be sent over to decide whether or not an inquiry should he held. Churchill, who seems to have expected some such reaction, said that he wanted to have a Cope-like figure in Ulster and the meeting, which included Balfour, Chamberlain and Lord FitzAlan agreed to Craig's suggestion. The man suggested to the meeting to action Craig's proposal was Colonel Stephen Tallents, at the time a civil servant, private secretary to Lord FitzAlan, the Chief Secretary, with a record of achievement in organising food rationing and putting down Bolshevism in the Baltic. Now he was required, in effect, to put down the claims of Michael Collins for a public inquiry and to ration unpalatable truths.

Tallents very obviously got the message. In a letter accompanying his report[112] to the Under Secretary at the Colonial Office, Sir James Masterson Smith, he recommended that a permanent representative of the British Government should be appointed to Belfast. He was given the job in October 1922, Churchill having first got the report[113] he wanted in July. The stated brief was:

to enquire and report (for the information of Mr Churchill, as Chairman of the Irish Committee of the Cabinet) upon the extent to which effect has been given to the Agreement of 30th March signed in London by Representatives of the Government of Northern Ireland, and of the Provisional Government of Southern Ireland, and countersigned by representatives of the Imperial Government. In so far as effect may not have been given to that Agreement, you should report as to the reasons.

Tallents had high praise for the friendliness of the many and varied personages he met with in the Six Counties.[114] These were mainly Unionists, though he did meet MacRory. Interestingly enough, MacRory had just come back from a mission to the South which included calling on de Valera to intercede with him, Tallents said, in 'calling off the murder gang'. Obviously Collins had decided not to strain his relationship with the bishop by letting him know that he was better placed than de Valera to get the Northern campaign called off. Tallents did not attempt to see Collins or any representative of the Southern administration. He found that the 'failure to give effect to Clause 6 of the Agreement, which provided for the cessation of IRA activity in the Six Counties, was the major cause of its failure'. He deliberately lied in part of the report, Paragraph 26 of which stated: 'I am not aware of any responsible suggestion that the Provisional Government have promoted active measures by the IRA in Northern Ireland against the Northern Government.' The paragraph, in order to illustrate the difficulties confronting the Northern Administration, then went on to quote a document 'found in a Belfast house', and headed 'Headquarters 4th Northern Division' which stated: 'The immediate job which is up to us here in Ulster, no matter what happens in the rest of the country, is to get Ulster to recognise the principle of a united Ireland.' This document was part of a large and damning dossier supplied to him by Solly-Flood and other leading figures in the Northern hierarchy, proving conclusively that 'the Provisional Government is fully cognisant of the activities' of the IRA in Northern Ireland.

Tallents was welcomed by the Unionists, Spender writing[115] to him on 20 June to invite him to stay with him when he came to Belfast, referring to 'the pleasing rumour' that he was to be appointed liaison officer, the term used by Londonderry at the Downing St meeting. He got complete co-operation and it is quite evident from the material supplied to him in the form of captured IRA documents and intelligence reports that 'responsible suggestion' took the form of proof positive that Collins was implicated. Solly-Flood, for instance, supplied him with a breakdown of the 'connection between GHQ Beggar's Bush and the Northern Divisions'[116] and Spender, who was in charge of garnering the evidence from the various Departments, wrote to him on 29 June:

When you come to examine the facts you will have to admit that not only has there been a failure to co-operate but that the Southern Government has taken active measures to obstruct the Government of Northern Ireland in its normal functions and to undermine its actions . . .

Not only does our evidence show that the IRA in Northern Ireland is regarded as loyal to the Headquarters at Beggar's Bush, and, therefore, is presumably acting under the orders of the Provisional Government, but there is clear proof that there is active co-operation between the members of the IRA inside the Six Counties with members of that force outside the Six Counties who are undoubtedly representatives of the Provisional Government.[117]

Tallents therefore had all the relevant information but chose not to make use of it in the report proper, though he did make a vast amount of very revealing material available to his superiors. Churchill and his colleagues were under increased pressure from the Die-hards. To have produced a governmental report showing that Michael Collins, with whom the Treaty had been negotiated, was hand-in-glove with the IRA might have brought down the Government. Also, if a critical report had been published, the resultant spotlight would have shone not only on Michael Collins, but on the behaviour of the forces of law and order in the state he was trying to overthrow. Forces for which the British taxpayer had been committed unwittingly to writing a blank cheque, politically as well as economically.

The pressures of the Tories in London were however of greater moment to Churchill than those of Nationalists in Dublin on the Provisional Government. In the event Tallents wrote privately to Masterson Smith making a number of criticisms. He found that the 'Government has failed to perform the elementary duty of guaranteeing life and property.' Apart from that, however, he thought that it had 'made good progress'! He at first used the word 'disgusting' to describe the B-Specials' reputation but then substituted 'disquieting'.[118] And he was deeply critical of the manner in which Solly-Flood and Craig had been allowed to run up an establishment of 48,250 paramilitaries, costing nearly £5 million a year. 'A weapon is being forged which in time of crisis might be most dangerously used by other hands than those who now control it.' He thought Dawson Bates so bad that he was an 'asset' to the Republicans. He wrote wistfully,

If I had to choose a precise wish for immediate fulfilment in Northern Ireland, my first selection would be the kindly removal of the present Minister of Home Affairs to a less responsible Ministry. I am inclined to think that my second would be his replacement by Lord Londonderry.

Where Collins was concerned he noted

for future consideration that the system employed in the Agreement of inviting Mr Collins virtually to act as the representative of a minority in the territory of another Government both encouraged the Catholics in the North in their policy of non-recognition of the Northern Government and exasperated Sir James Craig's supporters.

In the circumstances he felt

sure that the idea of holding an independent judicial enquiry into events in Belfast, though it may have been feasible at one stage, should now be ruled out. I do not think it could secure any advantage and I am sure it would lead to a revival of propaganda about matters that are best forgotten.

Where his own report was concerned Tallents felt that 'Collins' inclination to interfere in the Six Counties needs no encouragement'[119] and that to send him either a copy of the report, or even a digest of it, would 'supply such encouragement without any corresponding advantage'. Churchill accepted this advice and the report was buried as finally and completely as either the MacMahons or the victims of Aron St. Churchill did allow a partial inquiry into one set of killings which occurred while Tallents was conducting his investigations, the shooting by B-Specials of three unarmed Catholic youths in Cushendall[120] on 23 June. Because of the involvement of British troops Churchill ultimately sanctioned an investigation by the Recorder of Hythe, F. T. Barrington-Ward, the month after Collins himself was killed. Barrington-Ward found that the Specials had cold-bloodedly shot the three youths without provocation. But the report was never published. The Unionists then conducted their own inquiry which exonerated the Specials. Both reports were pigeon-holed when the Unionists' allies, the Tories, were returned to Government after the fall of the Coalition.

Collins' Northern policy caused the assassination which led to the Cushendall deaths, that of Field Marshal Sir Henry Wilson. His name had been placed on a death list by the IRB in June 1921 but the Truce came shortly afterwards and the order was cancelled.[121] His shooting can only be understood against the terrible backdrop of the times and the bogey-man reputation which the former Field Marshal had built up for himself in Nationalist circles. When de Valera heard the news he said:

I do not know who they were who shot Sir Henry Wilson, or why they shot him . . . I know that life has been made a hell for the Nationalist minority in Belfast and its neighbourhood for the past couple of years. I do not approve but I must not pretend to misunderstand.

A colleague of Collins' was less circumspect: 'When Mick saw the pogroms he grew very angry and said: "We'll kill a member of that bunch".'[122] Wilson's involvement with every prominent anti-Nationalist and pro-Unionist cause from the Curragh mutiny to the foundation of the Specials would have been damning enough without his frequent attacks on Collins personally and the Treaty settlement in general.

The assassination was one of the most indefensible, inefficient, and hopelessly heroic deeds of its kind of the entire period. Wilson was shot on his own doorstep on the afternoon of 22 June by two ex-servicemen, Reggie Dunne and Joseph O'Sullivan, who had lost a leg at Ypres. Dunne was second-in-command to Sam Maguire in London, a friend of both Collins and Rory O'Connor, both of whom he had talked with on a visit to Dublin shortly before the shooting. The fact that he took a one-legged man with him on such a mission indicates what the split over the Treaty had done to the London IRA. One of the reasons for the shooting in fact was that it was 'hoped that it would bring about unity between the two sides'.[123] Dunne could easily have escaped, but he chose to stay with O'Sullivan and the pair were captured and beaten by an angry crowd in a fracas during which official tempers were worsened by a policeman being shot.

The Cabinet almost went into shock on hearing the news. Macready was told to confine his troops to barracks in Dublin (though not in Belfast) and ordered immediately to London. The revolvers used by Dunne and O'Sullivan and the documents found on them were brought to Lloyd George and his colleagues.[124] After examining these items the Prime Minister sent the following letter to Collins:

I am desired by His Majesty's Government to inform you that documents have been found upon the murderers of Field Marshal Sir Henry Wilson which clearly connect the assassins with the Irish Republican Army and which further reveal the existence of a definite conspiracy against the peace and order of this country.

The ambiguous position of the Irish Republican Army can no longer be ignored by the British Government. Still less can Mr Rory O'Connor be permitted to remain with his followers and his arsenal in open rebellion in the heart of Dublin in possession of the Courts of Justice, organising and sending out from this centre enterprises of murder not only in the area of your Government but also in the Six Northern Counties and in Great Britain. His Majesty's Government cannot consent to a continuation of this state of things and they feel entitled to ask you formally to bring it to an end forthwith . . .

I am to inform you that they regard the continued toleration of this rebellious defiance of the principles of the Treaty as incompatible with its faithful execution. They feel now that you are supported by the declared will of the Irish people in favour of the Treaty, they have a right to expect that the necessary action will be taken by your Government without delay.[125]

Collins was in Cork when the letter arrived, conducting an investigation into tampering with his votes which had raised the question of his seat being in jeopardy. In his absence Diarmuid O'Hegarty, as Secretary to the Provisional Government, replied with a masterpiece of instantaneous procrastination:

My Government have been profoundly shocked by the tragic and untimely death of Sir Henry Wilson and they hasten to place on record their condemnation of the assassination by whomsoever it was perpetrated.

The Provisional Government is gravely concerned with the statements in your letter as to information in the possession of His Majesty's Government revealing the existence of a conspiracy on the part of certain elements in Ireland to undertake attacks against life and property in England and in this country . . . It would appear however from your letter that your Government is in possession of information which leads them to conclude that a more serious state of affairs exists threatening serious consequences both in England and in Ulster.

The Provisional Government has no intention of tolerating such a situation of things and therefore requests your Government to assist them in dealing with the situation by placing at their disposal the information to which you refer. They will then be able to call upon the newly elected parliament which meets on the 1st proximo to support them in such measures as may be considered adequate.[126]

Churchill replied by wire, via Cope for Griffith: 'Information in our possession is at present of a highly secret character and cannot be disclosed. The Cabinet are awaiting the answer of Provisional Government to Prime Minister's letter.' The information Churchill referred to may have been secret intelligence reports concerning the IRA offensive against the North. It does not seem to have been given even to Macready at a crisis meeting on the 23rd. But I think I can say with certainty that the documents discovered on Dunne and O'Sullivan linking them to the IRA consisted principally of a lengthy letter smuggled out from an IRA prisoner in jail in England which could be construed as containing a fairly damning reference to Collins. After some coded references to guns and weaponry the following occurred:

Insist on a proper system. You are entitled to meeting. Now is the time to reorganise. If four of you go and see the Big Fellow he would arrange an election. And recruits – let 44 and 1 concentrate on the district around No. 1 and so on. The place Smith comes from needs attention. Put 84 and 85 there permanently . . . I shall write more later follow out *our old plan* of campaign if things recommence. Then all will be OK.[127]

For a few days after Wilson's death it appeared that war might break out again between the Irish and the English. Macready was instructed to draw up a scheme for attacking the Four Courts immediately. But he managed to delay matters until the Cabinet cooled down and reconsidered the consequences. On 25 June, 'word came through from London that the Government had reconsidered their original decision and that no action was to be taken against the Four Courts – I never ceased to congratulate myself on having been an instrument in staving off what would have been a disaster.'[128]

The Wilson assassination placed the Coalition under enormous strain. The *Morning Post* of 23 June said 'Mr Lloyd George, Mr Austen Chamberlain and Mr Asquith all shared in the murder of Sir Henry Wilson and are bedabbled with the stain of his blood.' When the House of Commons met to debate the issue on 26 June it did so, in William O'Brien's memorable phrase, 'hungry with anti-Irish fury'.[129] Had Collins not attacked the Four Courts garrison two days later the burden of probability is that the Conservatives would have either forced Lloyd George to do so, or moved to bring down the Coalition. In his death Wilson wielded more widespread influence than at any other time in his political career.

It was a foregone conclusion in the circumstances that Dunne and O'Sullivan would hang. They were sentenced to death at the Old Bailey on 18 July and executed on 16 August. Dunne was prevented from reading his reasons for their action during the trial. But their statement was subsequently published in the *Irish Independent* on 2 July. It said:

We took our part in supporting the aspirations of our fellow countrymen in the same way as we took our part in supporting the nations of the world who fought for the rights of small nationalities . . . the same principle for which we shed our blood on the battle-field of Europe led us to commit the act we are charged with. You can condemn us to death today, but you cannot deprive us of the belief that what we have done was necessary to preserve the lives and happiness of our countrymen in Ireland.

Sir Henry Wilson . . . was not so much the great British Field Marshal, as the man behind the Orange Terror . . . as Military Advisor he raised and organised a body known as the Ulster Special Constables who are the principal agents in his campaign of terrorism. You may, by your verdict, find us guilty, but we will go to the scaffold justified by the verdict of our own consciences.

Neither man ever went beyond that in explaining who or what motivated them.[130] But a deathbed crisis of conscience on the part of someone who played a small but vital part in the Wilson affair helped me to put together the hitherto unacknowledged details of the assassination.

The mother of a school friend of mine, Gearoid Johnston, as a girl worked for a small, elite group of couriers, whom Collins sometimes used for special missions. They were not allowed to join *Cumann na mBan*; the Women's Auxiliaries of the IRA, or any of the more obviously Sinn Fein-connected organisations. They operated from Leix House in Gardiner St, sometimes taking guns or ammunitions to country commanders, sometimes carrying messages. My friend's mother, Peig ni Braonain, before marriage, always knew when she was working directly for Collins, although no one ever specifically told her so. 'There seemed to be a tension in the air. Everyone took more care and something always seemed to happen afterwards', she told her son.

One day in June 1922 she was given an assignment in London by Pat Fleming, the famous jail escaper. She had never been out of the country before, but from the care taken with her instructions she sensed that they came from Collins. Fleming gave her a cover letter which purported to be the offer of a job as a waitress at Woburn House, a favourite London stopping place for Irish visitors. The real purpose of her journey was to bring a letter for someone who would meet her at Euston, 'a tall man called Tobin'. Peig duly carried out her instructions, and a week later Wilson was assassinated. She realised that she had brought the instructions for the killing. Years later as she came near death conscience assailed her, not for Wilson, but for Dunne and O'Sullivan. On her deathbed she told her son the story for the first time.

Liam Tobin, who was of course the 'tall man' of Euston, was back in Dublin when the news broke.[131] He received it with elation rather than remorse, and proceeded to tell Mulcahy 'that our lads had shot Wilson'. Mulcahy was far from elated. At first he refused to believe Tobin, then he reacted by saying he was 'going to resign'. At that Tobin began to realise the enormity of the situation and he made a beeline for Kingsbridge Station to intercept Collins as he returned from Cork. Worried as he was himself Tobin felt that Collins seemed even more so 'alone, carrying the weight of the Republic on his shoulders'. When he told him about Mulcahy, Collins replied, 'I'll make that all right,' and, said Tobin, 'It was all right, for it was never again mentioned.'

The Wilson shooting was in fact discussed by Collins on at least one other occasion that day, 23 June. One of his generals, Joseph Sweeney, remarked that he looked 'very pleased. The last time I had seen him look so pleased was when a DI was shot to his order in Wexford' (Lee-Wilson).[132] Sweeney asked, 'Where do we stand on the shooting?' and Collins replied, 'It was two of ours that did it.' Collins tried to have the 'two of ours' rescued and sent Tom Cullen over to make the attempt, but it was hopeless. Cullen reported back that rescue was impossible.[133] He did 'everything I possibly can' to secure a reprieve.[134] But the tragedy of what can happen to men caught up in large impersonal forces was highlighted in the result of his exhortation to Cosgrave to

'make an official representation that mercy be extended to these men'. [135]
The law officer duly drafted the appeal but at 9.45 am the following day,
we find Sinead Mason sending the draft to MacDunphy, the Government official who was to sign it, with a note saying: 'Draft was handed to
me last evening at 6.40 pm to get off but as you were not present to sign
the letter nor any typist available I could not possibly get it out. The
matter is urgent as Thursday is fixed for the executions.'

However, Edward Shortt, Principal Secretary of State for Home
Affairs, turned down the plea on behalf of the British Government,
and Dunne and O'Sullivan were hanged the following morning in
Wandsworth Prison.

The 4th Northern Division of the IRA, seeking a 'law-abiding and
united Ireland' by means of the unacknowledged Collins-assisted
offensive, carried out one of the worst atrocities of the period in June
1922. It occurred at a time of RUC activity in the area such as the
murder of two Catholics whose bodies were subsequently found on a
road deposited in holes which were originally dug by the IRA to plant
mines. At the beginning of the offensive Aiken had issued the
following directive to his men:

To all Brigade O/Cs – operations are to be continued all over the division
until further notice. These operations are to be:
(a) General destruction of enemy property, wires, bridges etc.
(b) Destruction of property owned by prominent Orangemen living or
   having residence in your Brigade area.
(c) Reprisal – all reprisals must be taken at once. Reprisal must be six to one,
   so as to prevent the enemy from continuing same.
(d) Spies and informers to be shot on sight. [136]

On the night of Saturday 17 June 1922, in pursuit of (c), Aiken's men
moved into the townlands of Altanaveigh and Lisdrumliska in South
Armagh, less than a mile from the major town of Newry, mining the
roads against interruption. In his unpublished memoirs John McCoy
tells what happened:

Seven or eight farm houses belonging to Unionists were attacked with bomb
and rifle fire and five of the inhabitants slain, two others dangerously
wounded and the residences of some burned. The dead:
   Thomas Crozier and his wife, James Heaslip, farmer (50), Robert Heaslip,
his son (17), James Lockhart, farmer, single (21), James Gray (17).
   Badly wounded: John T. Gray, William Lockhart, Joseph and Edward
Little. The houses of Thomas Crozier, John Heaslip and William McCullagh
were partly burned. [137]

Looking back on the period some sixty years later John McCoy
wrote:

The record . . . should be an object lesson to the people in the North who are
led to take offensive action against their fellow countrymen who have a

different political outlook or who worship at a different church. The resort to force is a two–edged weapon which has a persistent habit of recoiling on the user and which in the last analysis seldom achieves anything that could not be obtained by reason and peaceful means.

The only people who have thrived on discord in the North are a select number of the trouble-making politicians who have climbed to office and are today engaged in the old device of creating the canard that men of a certain religious persuasion are *ipso facto* disloyal . . . their own 'loyalty' has always depended on how far they were able to dictate British policy here. When their power was in danger they preached sedition and sowed rebellion with uncomfortable results.

Apart from the rejection of his demands for an enquiry into the North's security methodology and issues such as the Derry prisoners and the Belleek–Pettigo affair 'discord in the North' involved Collins in major controversies with the British on other matters, at least two of which deserve examination. They concerned banking and proportional representation.

The second of these issues we shall come to shortly, the first dropped on his desk in the form of a letter from H.S. Guinness, the Governor of the Bank of Ireland on 11 June 1922, a date that leads one to speculate that it was part of the general British screw-turning policy of the time. It said that the Bank had just been informed from London that the Treasury proposed to transfer to London and Belfast from Dublin the Register of Stocks and:

at an early date to seek Parliamentary authority for the discontinuance of the Register of British Government Stock at present maintained at the Bank of Ireland in Dublin and for the establishment of a Register at the principal office of that Bank in Belfast.

Collins immediately wrote to Griffith in London asking him to consult Kennedy about this:

. . . typical instance of how they load the dice against us at every turn. It shows also the vital necessity of settling with them at once and finally so that we won't have to be thinking of their politics on every occasion. Equally it is another of these moves calculated to strengthen enormously the position of the N-E. Naturally there are several retaliatory measures we could take and in fact must take if things of this kind go on.[138]

The Bank of Ireland directors had a stormy meeting with Sir Basil Blackett at the Treasury on 16 June[139] and learned that the Treasury 'had acted in the first instance at the request of the Northern Ireland Government'. Guinness signed a protest from the Bank saying that the Treasury's action could:

certainly be attributed to a favoured nation treatment of Northern Ireland and would further embitter the present unfortunate relations between South and North and the removing of the remaining stocks to London would have the appearance of prejudging the financial arrangements between Great Britain and the Irish Free State, to the detriment of the latter state.[140]

Guinness kept up a stubborn rear-guard action and the issue was finally resolved in Dublin's favour after Collins' death through the intervention of Tim Healy, then Governor General of the Irish Free State. Collins must have been relieved as well as gratified at the Bank's attitude. During the Black and Tan war his intelligence network had intercepted letters from Captain Hall at the Admiralty, giving lists of the Captain's spies, one of which had stated, 'In the Cos. of Cork and Waterford there are several Agents who work to me through the Governor of the Bank of Ireland'.[141] Sean MacEoin used to tell a story about Collins' first dealings with the Bank[142] in January 1922. MacEoin accompanied him on a visit to the Bank's directors to seek a loan to finance the fledgling Provisional Government. The directors at first demurred and Collins sprang up and began to pack his briefcase, saying to MacEoin, 'Right so! General, when we get back to the office, make immediate arrangements to have the guard removed from this building.' As they made for the door the puzzled MacEoin whispered, 'What guard, Mick?' To which the reply was a sotto-voce growl, 'Shut up you fucking eejit, a large whiskey they'll be after us before we're well out the door.' The pair hadn't even reached the door when there came an embarrassed cough and a 'Mr Collins, can we discuss this matter a little further . . .' Collins got the loan, MacEoin got his whiskey and, as civil war spread, the Bank did actually get a guard.

Collins' commitment to the Catholics of Northern Ireland was deeply felt. In his last two weeks of life he continued to fight their cause over the proportional representational issue. Churchill replied to an earlier protest of his (made on 28 June) on 31 July saying that during the month's delay:

the Bill has been exhaustively examined by His Majesty's Government. As a result it appears very doubtful whether under the system of proportional representation, which the Bill abolishes, the Catholic minority in the six Northern counties would obtain a more adequate representation on the county councils and other municipal and local bodies than they may expect to obtain under the system by which under the Bill proportional representation is replaced.

In any event I feel bound to observe that the continuing refusal of the Catholic minority to recognise the Northern Government robs of much of their substance and possible validity the arguments urged in your letter against the passage of the Bill.

Collins noted on the first page of the letter: 'It is a sentence of death or expulsion on every Catholic in the North.'[143] He took time out from his increasingly successful prosecution of the civil war to reply to Churchill on 9 August:

I have been very seriously disappointed by the decision indicated in your letter of 31st ultimo . . . The effect of this Bill is to prejudice the Catholic and Nationalist position in the whole of the North Eastern Counties. It purports to repeal the Local Government Act passed in the year 1919 against the most strenuous opposition from the Orange Members at Westminster. Your Government insisted upon that Act as a measure of justice for minorities everywhere in Ireland, but particularly where they most needed it – in the North-Eastern Counties.

Prior to the Act of 1919 (which Sir James Craig's Government has now repealed) what with the gerrymandering of constituencies, the system of direct voting produced a result which practically excluded Catholics and Nationalists from their rightful position in these Counties. Take Tyrone where there is an admitted Nationalist majority of over 15,000 – our people could never get a fair show there, largely by being thrown into one huge area, Omagh, which was treated as one constituency, while the Unionist areas were divided up into a number of constituencies. The Act of 1919 went a long way towards curing that state of affairs.

The Local Government Bill which has just been passed restores the bad system prevailing before 1919. This is flagrantly so in Tyrone and Fermanagh. Tyrone with its nationalist majority will now have an Orange council with an Orange majority.

Do you not see, or have His Majesty's advisers not disclosed, the true meaning of all this? Not merely is it intended to oust the Catholic and Nationalist people of the Six Counties from their rightful share in local administration, but it is beyond all question intended to paint the Counties of Tyrone and Fermanagh with a deep orange tint.

I therefore urge upon you that this Bill should not be allowed to pass into law.[144]

Cope backed him in his appeal as 'a necessary condition of a step in conciliation being taken by either side'[145] but proportional represent-ation was duly abolished and the results over the ensuing decades more than bore out Collins' predictions to Churchill about gerry-mandering.

After the triangle episode and the start of the civil war, which was also causing divisions in the Northern IRA, Collins knew that the Unionists could not be defeated by military means. Despite his brave words about 'definite Government policy' he knew that his Cabinet colleagues did not share his feelings on Northern incursions. The position of the Northern units may be imagined from the following report to GHQ concerning the state of affairs in Belfast, the only area still able to put up any semblance of a fight two months after the May offensive began:

Strength of Brigade – 800 men
Armament: 181 rifles and 11,600 rounds of ammunition. 308 service revolvers and autos, 7,400 rounds of ammunition. 5 Thompson guns and 1,220 rounds of ammunition.

Engineering material:	156 detonators
	12 stone war flour.
	20 lbs cheddar. [Home made explosives]
	12 lbs gelignite,
	20 ft time fuse.
	Enemy strength in area:
British military:	5,500
RUC:	2,650
Specials:	26,680
Total	34,830

For a period of three months previous to our resuming the offensive the enemy was running loose murdering and harassing our people, and as the Army was not very active the people were gradually losing the respect they had for the IRA. This respect had been won, not so much out of sympathy with our National aspirations, and our fight for National freedom, but more on account of the part the Army had played in defending the minority against organised attacks by uniformed and non-uniformed Crown forces.

When, however, we commenced a campaign of destruction of enemy property which hit the authors and promoters of the pogrom, and was having the effect of stopping the murder campaign, the sympathy and support of the people was slowly coming back to us.

As I have already reported to GHQ there was a small Executive following in Belfast and on the 31st May they attempted to shoot two Specials. Most of our officers . . . were attending a Brigade Meeting when this happened, and before they could get back to their areas the Specials ran amok, and shot up practically every Catholic area in the city; the death toll for that day was twelve and upwards of 50 were wounded. This was the hardest blow the civil population had got, and it almost broke their morale. Notwithstanding that we kept up our campaign of burning, and in a short time the enemy realised that they would require to change their tactics. They set about establishing a series of block-houses throughout our areas, and selected their men specially with a view to fraternising with the Catholic population.

This policy has met with great success as the people war-worn and long tired were glad of an opportunity of peace. Unfortunately however, the anti-Irish element of the population are taking advantage of the situation and are giving all available scraps of information to the enemy. Several of our dumps have been captured within the last few weeks, and in practically every case the raiding party went direct to the house.

. . . many officers and men are forced to go on the run, necessarily in their own restricted areas. They find it difficult to get accommodation with the people now and in a particular area, seventeen of our best officers and men had to sleep in a refugee home where they were all captured.

The enemy are continually raiding and arresting; the heavy sentences and particularly the 'floggings' making the civilians very loath to keep 'wanted men' or arms. The officers are feeling their position keenly. Recently a number of men were rounded up and detained in custody. The mother of one of the boys when bringing him food shouted out, in the presence of Crown forces, the name of local o/c and made a tirade against him for misleading her boy into this movement.

As I have mentioned before the economic position is very acute. To give a rough idea there are 171 married men with 405 dependants and 346 single men with 936 dependants. These figures are taken from cards returned by each company and where there were two brothers the number of dependants was divided. To relieve the situation it would require a grant of say £500 per week.

The men are in a state of practical starvation and continually making applications for transfer to Dublin to join the 'Regular Army' . . . under the present circumstances it would be impossible to keep our Military Organisation alive and intact, as the morale of the men is going down day by day and the spirit of the people is practically dead.

In the face of that report, from a brave man, not given to exaggeration, Collins knew that to attempt to continue the Northern activities with a civil war raging in the south would be disastrous. In the two years between 21 June 1920 and 18 June 1922, it was reckoned that 428 people had been killed in the North and some 1,766 wounded; 8,750 Catholics had been driven out of employment and, the object of the exercise, around 23,000 driven out of their homes altogether.[147] To have continued would certainly have made those figures worse. The one man in the Cabinet who shared his approach to the North, Mulcahy, said bluntly to Collins in a memo dated 24 July:

The people were for a peace policy and for a recognition of the Northern Government . . . They are even giving information to the Specials. Our officers seem to realise there is no other policy for the North but a peace policy of some kind, but the situation for peace or war has gone beyond them, none of them feel they are able to face the policy of one kind or the other.

By coincidence on the same day that Mulcahy wrote, Collins also heard from Markham in the Castle, who passed him an assessment of Carson by a senior Scotland Yard figure called MacBrien:

Carson dominates the British Administration and will continue to do so. He has Lloyd George, Churchill and Asquith in his power. All the monied classes are at his back. He has more to do with the dispensation of honours and jobs than any man in England. . .Carson is itching for an opportunity to lay Ireland in ruins.

How accurate the assessment was is a matter of opinion. But the continuation of the ineffective IRA campaign in Northern Ireland would certainly have given him an opportunity to vent any instincts he may have had towards laying Ireland in ruins. A meeting of officers of the Northern Divisions was convened in the Officers Mess in Portobello Barracks on 2 August to outline the new policy. It was to be a meeting of the defeated but, as Thomas Kelly's affidavit bears out, 'many and varied views were expressed, some quite heatedly'.

The only statement of importance now was the final summation and decision of Michael Collins. His final words remain clear and distinct in my mind to this day. He said: with this civil war on my hands, I cannot give you men the help I wish to give and mean to give. I now propose to call off hostilities in the North and use the political arm against Craig so long as it is of use. If that fails the Treaty can go to hell and we will all start again.

His intention to 'start again' communicated itself to everyone present as being sincere. The Belfast OC, Seamus Woods noted:

The late C-in-C outlined the policy we were to adopt – one of non-recognition of the Northern Government and positive resistance to its functioning. At the same time, from the military point of view we were to avoid as far as possible coming into direct conflict with the armed forces of the Northern Government, and any action on our part would be purely protective.[148]

The day after the Portobello meeting Collins was furious to hear news of the killing by the British military of two girls, one aged twelve and the other nineteen, in a raid at Edenappa, near the Jonesboro-Dundalk border on 23 July. He wrote to Cosgrave:

I am forced to the conclusion that we have yet to fight the British in the North-East. We must by forceful action make them understand that we will not tolerate this carelessness with the lives of our people. . . It is not individuals who are in charge of shooting parties or 'Hold-up' parties that are the guilty ones. The guilt lies with the high authorities, and we must face that.

He sent a memo to GHQ on 7 August which certainly indicated an intention to 'fight the British', rather than co-operate with them: 'at the present moment I think we ought to be making every possible effort to develop Intelligence system in North-East'.[149] However, Collins' Cabinet colleagues had no wish to 'fight the British' and by this stage were clearly making difficulties over aspects of his Northern policy. For instance there were problems in sustaining the payments to the teachers in the North and Cosgrave, who had taken over from Collins as Minister for Finance only two days earlier, noted on 14 July that

The question of payments in the Six-County area is in a pretty chaotic condition. . . There was no authority to spend money raised by taxing the South in the North. . .that the Northern Government may be enabled to avoid its own proper liabilities and this is done in such a manner that the Free State tax payer cannot tell that his money is being spent in this way.[150]

A change in policy was obviously taking shape as Collins became more and more immersed in the conduct of the civil war. More than a little disingenuously he had given an impetus to a policy shift himself by making peaceful noises in public while the IRA offensive he was sponsoring was still continuing. In an interview with the *Daily Mail* on 30 June he had said:

I think my attitude towards Ulster, which is the attitude of all of us in the Government, is not understood. There can be no question of forcing Ulster into union with the 26 Counties. I am absolutely against coer :ion of the kind. If Ulster is to join us it must be voluntarily. Union is our final goal that is all.

Kevin O'Shiel, the Government's civil service expert on the North, judged correctly when he wrote: 'The Army for a long time had one policy and the civilians another, or rather a series of policies that changed as quickly as the circumstances on which they were founded.' Collins, he said with massive understatement, 'tended to come to quick decisions without consulting many'.[151]

The Cabinet decided that there should be a civilian policy and that as many as possible should be consulted in its formulation. On 1 August a committee was set up 'to consider the question of the policy to be adopted towards the Belfast Government and with regard to the North-East Ulster question generally.' The Committee consisted of James Hogan, J. J. Walsh, Desmond Fitzgerald, Ernest Blythe and Michael Hayes. A copy of the governmental minute recording the fact of the Committee's formation was sent to Collins.[152] The two who actually prepared a report for the Cabinet were Blythe and Hayes. Blythe, an Ulster Protestant who had come south to learn Irish and join the revolution, had altered his views since he wrote in *An tOglach* that a British soldier 'merits no more consideration than a wild beast, and should be killed without mercy or hesitation.'[153] Hayes too was growing more constitutional by the hour. As Chairman of the Dail, it had been his duty to administer the Oath to its members. The joint report,[154] presented on 19 August, was in effect a condemnation and complete overturning of Collins' policy. The central recommendations were:

As soon as possible all military operations on the part of our supporters in or against the North-East should be brought to an end . . . The line to be taken now and the one logical and defensible line is a full acceptance of the Treaty. This undoubtedly means recognition of the Northern Government and implies that we shall influence all those within the Six Counties who look to us for guidance, to acknowledge its authority and refrain from any attempt to prevent it working.

The policy document set out at some length both the reasons for the *volte face* and the steps to be taken to achieve it:

The results of the General Election and the still more important results of the offensive against Irregulars put the Government for the first time in a position to decide freely upon its policy in regard to the North-East.
     . . . Nothing that we can do by way of boycott will bring the Orange party to reason . . . Their market is not in our territory. Our boycott would threaten the Northern ship-building industry no more than a summer

shower would threaten Cave Hill . . . the same may be said of the linen industry . . . pressure must be absolutely normal and constitutional. The use and threat of arms must be ruled out of the dispute . . .

The events of the past few months have done much towards fixing the Border where we cannot consent to its being fixed. It is full time to mend our hand. . . . Payment of teachers in the Six Counties should immediately stop. . . . We should stop all relations with local bodies in the Six Counties. Catholic members of the Northern Parliament who have no personal objection to the Oath of Allegiance should be urged to take their seats and carry on a unity programme . . . precautions should be taken to prevent border incidents from our side. Any offenders caught by us should definitely be handed over to the Northern authorities . . .

Catholics in the North . . . should be urged to disarm 'on receiving satisfactory assurances from the British'. Prisoners in the North should be requested to give bail and recognise the courts. The outrage propaganda should be dropped in the twenty-six counties.

Heretofore our Northern policy has been really, though not ostensibly, directed by Irregulars. In scrapping their North-Eastern policy we shall be taking the wise course of attacking them all along the line . . . The belligerent policy has been shown to be useless for protecting the Catholics or stopping the pogroms. There is of course the risk that the peaceful policy will not succeed. But it has a chance where the other has no chance. The unity of Ireland is of sufficient importance for us to take a chance in the hope of gaining it. The first move lies with us.

The Cabinet decided that 'a peace policy should be adopted in regard to future dealings with North East Ulster' and negotiations were authorised on outstanding educational matters, 'subject to . . . obtaining the approval of the Commander-in-Chief'. Collins was not present and may never have read the document. Notification of the 'peace policy' decision was sent to him on the 21st and he was killed the next day. The day after he was buried it was decided to circulate the memorandum 'to all Ministers'. It was adopted as Government policy both by the Provisional Government and, with minor alterations, by all administrations in Southern Ireland since. In practice the policy document was found to be erroneous in its judgement that 'the Treaty gives us a clear claim to at least two and a half counties of the Six. They can only dig themselves in if we help them by producing a state of turmoil and disorder'. The Northern authorities took full advantage of the opportunities presented by peaceful conditions after Collins' death to dig themselves in, using the mechanisms of law and legislature which they had fashioned expressly to achieve that purpose. The border remained unchanged and so until our day troubled 'Carsonia' remains a separate entity, neither properly in nor out of either England or Ireland. And now it is time to examine the final steps taken by Michael Collins to ensure the establishment of the Free State, and how these led to the two parts of Ireland acquiring the shape they still have today.

12

The Mouth of Flowers

What is that curling flower of wonder
  As white as snow, as red as blood?
When Death goes by in flame and thunder
  And rips the beauty from the bud.

They left his blossom white and slender
  Beneath Glasnevin's shaking sod;
His spirit passed like sunset splendour
  Unto the dead Fiannas' God.

Good luck be with you, Michael Collins,
  Or stay or go you far away;
Or stay you with the folk of fairy,
  Or come with ghosts another day.

Shane Leslie

(From poem written on seeing Sir John
Lavery's picture of the dead Michael Collins)

The worst fate that can befall a nation was about to strike Ireland: civil war. 'The safety of the Nation is the first law and henceforth we shall not rest until we have established the authority of the people of Ireland in every square mile under their jurisdiction.'[1] With these words Michael Collins took off the gloves and went to war with his former friends. Even though the new National Army was in a chaotic, disorganised condition, once he made up his mind to fight the result was practically a foregone conclusion. Many 'irregulars' joined in the shooting merely because the 'Free Staters' had fired on their comrades, or because of some friend's urgings or example. Sean Dowling, littérateur, dentist and lifelong Republican spoke for many when he said, 'against my struggling conscience, I found myself behind the barrel of a gun in Upper O'Connell St'.[2] They didn't have the people with them and they didn't have Michael Collins. They had neither the heart nor the expertise for firing on their fellow countrymen. Oscar Traynor, who like Dick McKee was a printer, had succeeded McKee as OC of the Dublin Brigade. He later became a long-serving minister under de Valera. A loyal, courageous man, Traynor lacked McKee's flair, and made the elementary mistake of seizing a number of buildings in O'Connell St on the side opposite the Four Courts so that there was no possibility of his linking up with the garrison. De Valera reported to his old unit as a private soldier. Years later Tod Andrews recalled his feelings of disgust at finding so much of the Republican leadership cooped up in the one block of buildings. After the Four Courts bombardment he made his way through the tunnelled buildings to the Gresham Hotel where he found Art O'Connor, de Valera, Robert Barton, Countess Markievicz, Austin Stack, Oscar Traynor and Brugha, 'all apparently without purpose'.[3] The anti-Treaty leaders were courageous, but woefully bad tacticians, disorganised and lacking any overall strategy.

The fighting in Dublin was over in a week, by 5 July, leaving the centre of the city in ruins for the second time in six years. Most of the group escaped the fighting, de Valera getting away in a Red Cross ambulance, but Brugha refused to flee or to surrender.[4] He was fatally wounded as he advanced on a Free State barricade manned by riflemen, revolver in hand, ignoring calls to surrender. The soldiers aimed low but a bullet severed a femoral artery. He died in hospital that night. Collins wept when he heard the news and wrote chidingly to a friend who had written to him after Brugha's death making disparaging remarks:

Many would not have forgiven – had they been in my place – Cathal Brugha's attack on me on January 7th. Yet I would forgive him anything. Because of his sincerity I would forgive him anything.

At worst he was a fanatic – though in what has been a noble cause. At best I number him among the very few who have given their all that this country – now torn by civil war – should have its freedom.

When many of us are forgotten, Cathal Brugha will be remembered.

Collins' magnanimity towards a man who had caused him so much trouble was entirely in character. What is surprising is that, not long before he died, Brugha was overheard 'saying all sorts of nice things' about Collins. Kitty Kiernan wrote to Collins telling him of a conversation, in which 'Cathal B. RIP' was reported as quoted, and then went on to say that 'he only said those things about you in the Dail to save the Republic etc, that you were one of the best men, full of energy, and that he'd like to see the man who could beat you in votes and several other things . . . it was a great surprise to them all . . .'[5] At the end of the month Collins had cause to weep again. He had written to Harry Boland in obvious distress saying:

Harry – it has come to this! Of all things it has come to this.

It is in my power to arrest you and destroy you. This I cannot do. If you will think over the influence which has dominated you it should change your mind.

You are walking under false colours. If no words of mine will change your attitude then you are beyond all hope – my hope.[6]

Boland was well aware who Collins was referring to as 'the influence which has dominated you'. Earlier that year Kitty had described how Boland had told her (in a burst of confidence) 'of Dev's dislike for you (Collins), because you are too anxious for power, that Dev likes Griffith, but Harry dislikes Griffith, and (of course) likes you, etc'.[7] Griffith had stood down for de Valera to allow him to become President of Sinn Fein. But there was no chance of Collins, a younger man, standing out of his way now and de Valera knew it. Collins seems to have taken on a new lease of life in the period following the Four Courts' shelling. Though in one part of his mind he was clearly heartbroken at the loss of personal friendships as his letter to Boland shows, in another he seemed to have clicked back into gear. The period of uncertainty and hesitancy was over. He was back doing what he could do best, soldiering. But Boland seems to have taken Collins' appeal to him as some kind of implied threat. He was certainly harbouring bitter feelings against Collins by then as a letter to Mrs Wyse Power protesting against the closing down of the Sinn Fein HQ at Harcourt St shows:

Altho' dictatorship is now the rule I hope you will not attempt to imitate 'Mick', 'Dick', and 'Owney' (O'Duffy) by arrogating to yourself the functions of the Ard Fheis as they have attempted to usurp the functions of the new National Government.[8]

He was well aware of the dark, loving, ruthless forces surrounding Collins – men who would act without hesitation or consultation to take a life if they thought it threatened 'The Big Fellow'. At any rate, during a meal with Anna Kelly at Jammet's restaurant the night after writing to Mrs Wyse Power he urged her to 'eat well, because it may be your last meal with me.'[9] The following night, 31 July, he was surprised in bed in a hotel in Skerries. Unarmed, he made a characteristic burst to get away but was shot down by an inexperienced soldier.[10] He lay wounded in Skerries for several hours before being taken to Portobello Barracks and from thence to St Vincent's Hospital. Collins immediately sought word of his condition:

Will you please send some good officer to St Vincent's Hospital and make a report on the exact condition of Mr Harry Boland. It is necessary to find out whether he has been operated on and what the doctors think of his condition.
There will not be a guard placed over him but we want to take some precaution to prevent escapes.[11]

Three nights later Boland died. As he lay dying his sister Kathleen asked him who shot him.[12] He would not tell. He asked instead that he be buried beside Cathal Brugha. Fionan Lynch was sleeping in his room in Mountjoy St when Collins burst in, weeping uncontrollably at the news.[13] Writing to Kitty he said:

Last night I passed Vincent's Hospital and saw a small crowd outside. My mind went in to him lying dead there and I thought of the times together and whatever good there is in any wish of mine he certainly had it. Although the gap of 8 or 9 months was not forgotten – of course no one can ever forget it – I only thought of him with the friendship of the days of 1918 and 1919. . . . I'd send a wreath but I suppose they'd return it torn up.[14]

That was the Soft Man, Michael Collins, the warm-hearted human being. The Hard Man, the soldier, was functioning efficiently, relentlessly. On a plane of broad strategy the story is simply told. From the signing of the Truce in July 1921 to the time of writing, the people of Ireland never again gave country-wide support and succour to the IRA at anything remotely approaching the Tan War levels. The difference between robbing banks, blowing up bridges, burning the homes and killing the sons of one's own people and those of a foreign enemy, is very great indeed. In six weeks the Provisional Government took Cahir, Cashel, Clonmel, Dundalk, Limerick, Sligo, Tipperary, Tuam and Waterford. Seaborne landings added Cork, Tralee and Westport to the total without much difficulty. The only really serious fighting occurred around Limerick City, at Kilmallock and Newcastle West. Liam Lynch, who had assumed the leadership of the anti-Treaty, or Irregular forces, after the attack on the Four Courts, was forced to take to the hills. He and Liam Deasy had been captured in Dublin during the fighting but had been released by Mulcahy, because it was thought that, having been opposed to O'Connor and the others in the Four Courts, he would neutralise his forces. In fact he became the Provisional Government's principal adversary. As one reverse followed another he became less and less inclined to surrender and after being driven from the main centres the Irregulars' campaign became one of guerrilla warfare, which generated acts of destruction and viciousness on both sides that the nation did not recover from for fifty years.

Collins became Commander-in-Chief of the Army a week after Dublin fell, in circumstances which were still generating controversy and allegations of conspiracy sixty years later. As these circumstances were wrongly held to be directly linked to his death it is important in setting the record straight to examine both the allegations and the question of the appointment itself. An allegation which one meets with in Republican circles is that Collins had been out-manoeuvred by a 'junta within the Cabinet into accepting what appears to be a military post of great importance, but one which in fact was bereft of political power'.[15] The main source of this allegation was Sean MacBride who gave two controversial interviews to me in the *Irish Press* on 16 and 18 October 1982. One reason for his theory was Collins' Northern policy which MacBride correctly surmised was unwelcome to his Cabinet colleagues and of course to the British. MacBride reasoned that British

Intelligence would have another very compelling motive for wanting Collins dead. Quite apart from the question of what Collins had already done to their agents, not inconsiderable grounds for revenge, MacBride argued that there was considerable alarm at what he might yet do to 'Thorpe', the pseudonym given to the Castle's longest-serving and probably most important informer. The Burke and Cavendish murders in the Phoenix Park of 1882 which outraged England and dashed Home Rule from Parnell's grasp were carried out by a Fenian splinter group, the Invincibles, who were thought to have been sent to the gallows by an informer called Carey who was himself subsequently murdered. But then rumours began to circulate that the real informer was 'Thorpe'.[16] Collins asked Markham to check for clues to 'Thorpe's' identity on 21 April 1922.[17] On 4 August 1922, Markham seemingly found some evidence, for on that date, an entry occurs in a Collins diary 'Markham – Thorpe – Healy'. MacBride's theory was that Collins had learned that 'Thorpe' was in fact Tim Healy, a trusted advisor of his, an uncle of Kevin O'Higgins, and destined after Collins' death to be the first Governor General of the Irish Free State. If Healy was a spy he changed Irish history, being the most active of Parnell's opponents in the disastrous split of 1890. Had Parnell succeeded, Home Rule would have been conceded and a child born that year, Michael Collins, would probably have become a prosperous businessman in an un-partitioned Ireland.

MacBride's theory was that Healy, then a member of the IRB, with a Clan na nGael emissary, returned to the Clan man's hotel unexpect-edly one evening to find the proprietor, Captain Jury, a British agent, going through the Clan man's luggage. Somehow they managed to poison Jury. The Clan man got back safely to America but the Castle made Healy an offer he could not refuse. Either he went to work for them, or he faced a murder charge. According to MacBride, Healy then became an agent and remained one throughout his long career in law and politics. Obviously this is a highly speculative tale, scarcely to be given credit were it not for (a) the stature of its teller and (b) the fact that many people think that Collins was ousted from his position as Chairman of the Provisional Government and that this ousting was in some way connected with his death.[18] Therefore a biographer is called upon to make some effort at evaluation.

The limited research I was able to conduct did turn up some odd details. Working backwards from the Parnell split I found a death certificate for a Henry James Jury, hotel proprietor, who was certified as having died from 'typhus fever 5 days uncertified' on 29 May 1882 at Donnybrook in Dublin. Poisoning could produce symptoms which to a non-medical person might appear to be those of typhus. But the interesting thing about the certificate is that it bears three different dates. The death is registered on the 22nd. It is certified as having occurred on the 20th but there is a note on the certificate saying that the typhus was certified as having existed for 'eight days four hours' on the 29th. The fact that the certification of the disease somehow took place a week after the death was registered and nine days after it occurred apparently struck someone else as strange also, because the dates 22nd and 29th are circled and linked.

One would not have thought that a prosperous hotel owner would have been left with 'typhus fever 5 days uncertified'. The Jury death is also the only one with a date in the certification column. This could merely be attributed to nineteenth-century methods of record-keeping, but it is certainly a coincidence, if nothing else, that the Invincibles carried out the Phoenix Park murders on 6 May 1882. It could also be merely a coincidence that Collins himself in his memos to Art O'Brien, at the height of the Tan War, just before Bloody Sunday, was showing a curious interest in getting O'Brien to chase up a history of the Invincibles for him. It is also true that within hours of the news of Collins' death reaching Dublin someone opened his desk in Portobello Barracks and removed documents. But it is not clear to this day whether this removal was the official one ordered by 'direction of the Provisional Government',[19] on 23 August 1922, in which all Collins' papers were collected by his secretary, Gearoid McGann, and placed 'in the ground-floor Strong Room of the President's Department in Government Buildings'.

After Collins' death Markham did find some papers which had a bearing on his Healy enquiry. They passed into the hands of Frank Gallagher, the first editor of the *Irish Press*, who in turn gave them to Dr T.P.O'Neill, de Valera's biographer, who only gave them a preliminary investigation before placing them in the National Library where, alas, up to the time of writing they have not been discovered. Markham did tell Gallagher that Collins had specifically instructed him to try to find out if Healy was 'Thorpe'.[20] So, even leaving the question of the death certificate's strange dates to one side, MacBride's theory has at least the validity that Collins himself had suspicions of Healy.

However I am bound to say that the Cabinet documents of the time, far from proving that a 'junta' ousted Collins as MacBride asserted, tend to indicate the contrary. Collins was very much in control of the Government and took over the job of Commander-in-Chief because he wanted to lick the Army into shape and win the civil war quickly, quite possibly with at least one eye on the possibility of putting himself in a position 'to walk in on top of the Northern crowd one day', as an authoritative figure of the period assured me was his intention.[21]

MacBride's theory also overlooks the Frongoch/IRB factor. Though the IRB had not been able to bridge the gap in preventing civil war, the wing, by far the largest, that remained with Collins dominated every important position in the Army.[22] Interestingly enough de Valera himself did not subscribe to the junta theory. He told T. P. O'Neill[23] that he saw it as a tactical move on Collins' part. The IRA were so mistrustful of politicians of all sorts that Collins wished to establish himself in the minds of the fighting men as one of themselves and thus establish rapport. De Valera saw Cosgrave as merely a stopgap whom Collins would replace with ease when he wanted to. The relevant Cabinet minute records that a report on the military situation was submitted and noted, 'Mr Collins announced that he had arranged to take up duty as Commander-in-Chief of the Army and would not be able to act in his Ministerial capacity until further notice.'[24] That certainly has the ring about it of the Boss making an announcement. It was also Collins himself who announced to the Cabinet the formation of the War Council of Three with Mulcahy as Chief of Staff and Minister of Defence and O'Duffy as Commander of the South-Western Division. Two days later Collins wrote to Griffith:

It would be well, I think, if the Government issued a sort of Official Instruction to me nominating the War Council of Three, and appointing me to act by special order of the Government as Commander-in-Chief during the period of hostilities. It should contain a statement which could be directed to the Army by me as an Order of the Day . . . It should be pointed out that in the present fighting the men we have lost have died for something, that the wounded are suffering for something . . . for the same principle that we fought the British for – the People's right to live and be governed in the way they themselves choose.

    This should go on to deal with the point that what the Army is fighting at present is . . . opposition to the People's will. What they are fighting for is the revival of the Nation. That this revival and restoration of order cannot in any way be regarded as a step backwards, nor a repressive, nor a reactionary step, but a clear step forward.

Griffith, in conjunction with Hugh Kennedy, duly produced the draft on the lines sought.[25] There was one big row in connection with the Cabinet decisions of 12 July, but this tends to show the power of the military wing as opposed to the political arm, rather than vice versa. Collins[26] had directed that the arrangements he had announced should be gazetted. These included four other Army postings: Fionan Lynch to be Vice Commandant of South-Western Division; Kevin O'Higgins to be Assistant Adjutant General; Joseph McGrath to be Director General of Intelligence; and Diarmuid O'Hegarty as Director of Organisation. But after the announcements appeared in the press (on the 14th) Gearoid O'Sullivan, at that stage the Adjutant General of the Army, rang up the Acting Secretary of the Provisional Government, Michael MacDunphy, to convey 'in strong terms an objection on behalf of the Army to the issue of the notices in the name of the

Provisional Government.[27] Cosgrave wrote to Collins on 25 July telling him what had happened and asking him whether he wanted the notices published in the official Government record, *Iris Oifiguil*. Collins died without replying and the result was that the appointments were never gazetted.

There was considerable feuding and jealousy over appointments and promotions at the time. And there was some very serious drinking being done also. These were young men who had lived three lifetimes of intensity in the space of a few years. The effects both of the strain they had gone, and were going, through, and of sudden access to the facilities of Officers' Messes, on young men hitherto hard-pressed to find the price of a pint, left many a noted figure of the time struggling with an alcohol problem for the rest of his life.[28] This background probably explains the reaction of O'Sullivan who had just acquired an Assistant AG he may not have been happy with, as O'Higgins was a strong critic of the Army's performance.[29]

Liam Tobin, who had been finding it difficult to adjust to his responsibilities under native Government, cannot have been greatly pleased either at being replaced by Joe MacGrath as Director of Intelligence. Collins personally directed that his appointment was not to be gazetted.[30] McGrath initially resigned but later took the job. Collins saw to it that Tobin went to Cork, with the rank of Major General, to take part in Emmet Dalton's successful campaign there. Certainly there would never be any question of O'Sullivan or Tobin opposing Collins, whom they idolised. But the failure to gazette the appointments that July day in 1922 were a contributory factor in fuelling the fires of gossip concerning Collins' death.

The 'bereft of political power' theory hardly survives a perusal of some letters that passed between Collins and Cosgrave after the Commander-in-Chief appointment was announced. Two days after Collins took over, Cosgrave, as Acting Chairman, wrote to him saying that at that day's Government meeting:

it was the general opinion that the Government should be kept in constant touch with the military situation throughout the country, and it was decided that the Army authorities should be asked to have reports forwarded regularly to me in my capacity as Acting Chairman, similar to those reports which were formerly supplied to you.[31]

Next day Collins agreed to supply reports but concluded: 'I cannot promise any definite date of starting as numerous command arrangements to receive similar reports are in hand at the present moment, and until I have these completed I cannot say precisely what my final arrangements are to be.'[32]

Cosgrave was still waiting for his reports nearly two weeks later. Writing to Collins on 27 July he says, 'I shall be glad to know whether you are yet in a position to let us have these reports, as the absence of official information at meetings of the Government is a considerable drawback.' Another letter of Cosgrave's on the same day replies to a communication in which Collins had raised the question of taking stern action against those responsible for incidents such as the ambushing of a train in County Wexford. The Government had agreed with him but before proceeding any further sought his views on the advisability of issuing a Proclamation and 'if you agree, a draft of the proposed Proclamation'. Cosgrave also wondered 'for the information of the Government' whether a Government proposal to have small undercover squads operating in Dublin 'meets with your approval'.[34] The tone and tenor of that exchange certainly does not sound as though Collins was in the grip of a 'junta'. A Government which has to plead with its Commander-in-Chief to let it know how he is conducting a civil war on their behalf sounds more as though it were controlled by the Commander-in-Chief rather than the other way around.

Certainly an important memo on propaganda which Collins wrote to Desmond Fitzgerald[35] is the work of a man who was thinking of the future, and quite confident of his standing with regard to his colleagues. It displays not only the time-honoured determination of all politicians to put their activities in the best light, but the overlay of a philosophy that, had matters turned out differently, might have helped to change the face of Ireland.

There is a constructive sense and a decency that transcends propaganda in the memo. The fact that it is addressed to Desmond Fitzgerald emphasises the fact that it is the letter of one elected representative to another. This is not simply Mick Collins sending a note to that '— stuffed shirt' Desmond Fitzgerald, whom he threw a bucket of slop water over because Dessie officiously stopped Nancy O'Brien going up to see the Great Man in Harcourt St simply because she had no appointment.[36] This is the work of a man who takes his responsibilities seriously. In the memo Collins showed a remarkable grasp of how the cinema was being used for propaganda purposes in Germany, and how Lloyd George used posters to get his message across. He proposed that all these and other methods should be used not only against the 'Irregulars' but also to rally the public behind a programme of investment and development in agriculture, fishing, forestry and industry, following the examples of countries such as Denmark, Germany and Holland.

Collins' interest in European examples extended beyond the economy to the Army. In his papers one finds references to a project for sending Ginger O'Connell and three other officers to Switzerland 'to make a report on the Swiss Army system for the Irish Government'.[37] He liked the idea of the Swiss Citizen Army model and he did not want the emerging Irish institutions to be mere slavish copies of their English counterparts. In May he had circulated his colleagues instructing them to 'outline policy to be adopted after the election, including reforms, economies, extensions and improvements'.[38] He stipulated that the new forms of Administration should be altered from the old so as to be 'thoroughly Irish . . . the use of the Irish language to be introduced wherever possible.'

Another set of military ideas he thought applicable to Ireland were those of T.E. Lawrence (Lawrence of Arabia), whom he tried unsuccessfully to attract to Ireland as a training officer.[39] Collins thought Lawrence would make a great Flying Column commander.

A combination of his Irish blood[40] and dissatisfaction with Britain's treatment of the Arabs seems to have inclined Lawrence towards the Irish cause. He is said to have met Collins first on 3 December 1921, but this is almost certainly the wrong date.[41] That they did meet during this phase of Collins' life is certain and Collins' influence may have led Churchill to intervene decisively in Lawrence's plans.

During the Treaty negotiations Lawrence was working under Churchill in the Colonial Office and growing increasingly embittered at the betrayal of British Governmental war-time promises made to the Arabs through him. He had decided to leave the Colonial Service and join the RAF as an aircraftman, under a false name, but Churchill, who regarded the idea as ludicrous, actively impeded his plans. The idea of Michael Collins and T.E. Lawrence teaming up struck Churchill as a far worse prospect than having Lawrence as an aircraftman. He withdrew his opposition and shortly afterwards 'John Hume Ross' joined the Air Force. Collins was killed five days later in circumstances which have generated even more controversy than Lawrence's own mysterious death.

One of the continuing accusations against Collins in Republican circles is that, particularly in his final phase, he drank too much. This may have been true on one tragic occasion, but overall, to paraphrase Lincoln's remark when Grant's drinking was reported to him, if Collins did drink as heavily as alleged I would seriously advocate that the cadets in the Irish Army Staff college be instructed to partake of a few glasses of his favourite John Jameson each night, because the amount of work he got through in the last days of his life was phenomenal. Apart from the overall conduct of the war he attended to a myriad details, of which the following examples of his activities form but a tiny fraction. The extracts also give some idea of the state of the country at the time:

To Director of Intelligence, 14/7/22:
It would be well to have looked up and definitely located, two brothers Greer, formerly with RIC and now residing at 86 Thomas St. Their movements are to be observed. It is thought they were with the British Secret Service.

To Lt Gen. O'Connell, Curragh Camp Operations area, 16/7/22, 7.30 pm:
Your despatch of yesterday's date, which was not timed, to hand.

You will note the following report received, check its accuracy and report the steps taken to deal with the possibility of a recurrence: BIRR: Barracks at Crinkle burned down by Irregulars Friday night, all roads blocked round locality and yesterday they occupied the three principal hotels in town. They took possession of Railway Station, and commandeered driver of train to reverse engine, and then they proceeded in direction of Roscrea. When they got about three miles out they broke up line and derailed engine and carriages. I think they are still in possession of the town.

Provisional Government Meeting, 19 July 1922:

The Minister for Agriculture reported he had instructions from the Commander-in-Chief to organise food supplies in Co. Mayo and he was making the necessary arrangements in the matter.

Collins to Government, 25 July 1922:

I wish to inform Government that in my opinion the absence of Courts will cause a very serious handicap to military action – to some extent it is causing it already, as every day cases are reported that are really not cases of the Irregulars, but cases of a criminal nature of one kind or another. What will be the procedure for bringing these men to trial before a Civil Court, and what Civil Courts are there to bring them to?

The extent to which drink was a problem for Collins in trying to instil discipline into the new army may be gauged from the following notice taken from the *Independent* of 27 July 1922:

MILITARY ORDER. It is prohibited to supply members of the National Army in uniform with intoxicating liquor. Where a member of the National Forces is found under the influence of drink in a licensed premises the licence of such will be immediately cancelled and a fine imposed.

Collins to Intelligence, 30 July 1922:

The Government say that peculiar-looking individuals were seen going in and coming out of these premises (offices in Suffolk St, Dublin). Government is good at making suggestions of this kind, but I think that constant observation would repay the trouble.

Collins to group of Northern IRA officers at Portobello Barracks, 1 August 1922:

The civil war will be over in a few weeks and then we can resume in the North. You men will get intensive training.[42]

Collins to QMG, 1 August 1922:

In going about the thing that has struck me the most is the untidiness and uncleanliness that comes from bad mattresses . . . This is of great importance from the health point of view.

Intelligence report to Collins:

Erskine Childers has been sighted in Liverpool (on 5 August) trying to get to U.S. aboard the *Carmenia*.

Cope and Kennedy proposed that he could be either kept there, charged with treason/sedition or returned to Ireland on a Dublin warrant. Collins however proposed that he be arrested merely as a 'stowaway'.[43] Unfortunately for Childers Collins' suggestion that he be held in England was not adopted and Childers escaped back to Ireland and was later executed.

A grimmer note is entering the struggle. Casualties and destruction are beginning to mount. On 4 August Collins sends Cosgrave the draft of a threatening statement he wishes to have issued 'as an official statement either now, or at some more suitable opportunity'. It contains the following:

The Government is aware of plots to murder the members of the Government who are carrying out the people's mandate to restore order to the country. They are further aware that certain Officers in the Army whose military services are well known are marked down similarly.

After stating that the reason for issuing the statement is to alert the public and enlist their assistance in scotching the plots, Collins goes on to say that 'in accordance with the precedents of all civilised countries' the prominent members of the organisation which plans and executes such outrages will, together with those personally taking part in them, be held responsible and brought to account. What part Collins himself played in the 'bringing to account' process as practised by certain members of the Squad and ASU who found themselves in a Special Branch capacity in the CID HQ in Oriel House can only be speculated on. But certainly the Squad's Tan war policy of shoot-to-kill was often indistinguishable from its activities during the civil war.

Collins to Mulcahy, 7 August 1922:

We are not in a position to repose confidence in the effectiveness of the Civic Guard as a body to maintain ordinary law . . . it is not necessary for me to illustrate this by pointing to the wretched Irish Republican Police system, and to the awful personnel that was attracted to its ranks . . . the lack of construction and the lack of control in this force have been responsible for many of the outrageous things that have occurred throughout Ireland.[44]

Collins to Kiernan, 8 August 1922 (After attending a Mass for nine soldiers who had been killed in action in Kerry):

I did not get back until very late last night, I was in Maryborough, the Curragh and so on. It was woefully cold and I was petrified when we arrived back in Barracks . . . we have had a few hard days here – the scenes at the Mass yesterday were really heartbreaking. The poor women weeping and almost shrieking (some of them) for their dead sons. Sisters and one wife were there too, and a few small children. It makes one feel I tell you.[45]

The day after the Requiem Mass[46] he wrote to the Director of Intelligence concerning the activities of a group of men engaged in robberies in County Wexford: 'Any man caught looting or destroying should be shot on sight.' The following day he is looking to the future again. In a note on the composition of a body to investigate Army pay and conditions he recommends the inclusion of 'a representative who would be in touch with rank and file – and sympathetic to the rank and file – a junior line officer of a certain type would be ideal'.[47]

He was obviously looking to the future also, though for what purpose we can only speculate, when in the midst of all the foregoing, and much else besides, he wrote to the Director of Intelligence: 'At the present moment I think we should be making every possible effort to develop the Intelligence system in the North-East.'[48]

At this period of the civil war the members of the Provisional Government were living as well as working in Government Buildings. Even to make a sortie onto the roof at night to light a cigarette was to invite a sniper's bullet. Kevin O'Higgins, who was almost shot in this way, would later describe the Government of the time as 'simply eight young men standing amidst the ruins of one administration with the foundations of another not yet laid, and with wild men screaming through the keyhole!'[49] But not all the members of Government were young men. The combined attrition from unseen foes and only too omnipresent colleagues was appalling. Early in the month it became evident that Griffith was near collapse. Although ordered to a nursing home he insisted on carrying out Cabinet business. On 12 August he suffered a brain haemorrhage and died. Oliver St John Gogarty wrote of 'his poor Arthur':

> He made the loud tyrannical foe dumb-founded
> And to relax his yoke.
> Inglorious in the gap: by many a hater
> The scoffing word was said.
> He heard from those who had betrayed him, 'Traitor!'
> The cross-grained and cross-bred
> He shook from off him with grand impatience,
> The flesh uncomforted,
> And passed among the captains in whom nations
> Live when these men are dead.[50]

Collins was making a tour of inspection through Tipperary, Limerick and Kerry when the news reached him in Tralee. He turned for Dublin to face a funeral day of double mourning. For it was on the day Griffith was buried, 16 August, that Reggie Dunne and Joseph

O'Sullivan were hanged. The strains he had caused Griffith, the fate he had brought upon Dunne and O'Sullivan, must have weighed upon him as he marched at the head of the funeral procession to Glasnevin, a fine soldierly figure of a man whose appearance at the head of the Army he had brought into being was still talked of in Dublin admiringly fifty years later. But apart from mental stress, pain was gnawing at him from what could have been either incipient appendicitis or an ulcer.[51] Seeing him gazing at the grave for an unusually long time his friend Bishop Fogarty said to him, with more solicitude than tact, 'Michael, you should be prepared – you might be next.' Collins looked at him, 'I know', he replied, and then, feeling the effects both of the long, slow, ceremonial march and his instinctive urge to attempt to joke his way out of serious moments, 'I hope nobody takes it into his head to die for another twelve months.'[52]

The one undisputed fact[53] concerning Collins' last week of life is that he was in bad physical and mental shape. Every account of those days speaks of misery to some degree or other. Frank O'Connor says:

He lived it in suffering, mental and physical. Though still full of ideas and enthusiasm, he found it hard to work. He sat at his desk, scribbled a few lines, then rose and left the room, not in the old dashing way but slowly and in dejection.

The shadow had begun to fall. To Cosgrave he said, 'Do you think I shall live through this? Not likely.' He turned to a typist and asked, 'How would you like a new boss?' It was so strange, coming from him that she repeated it to O'Reilly who worried over it. Next day, as the two of them were driving into town together, O'Reilly asked after his health. 'Rotten', replied Collins. There was a slight pause. 'How would you like a new boss?' O'Reilly's heart sank.

Collins set off on his last, ill-advised journey for a variety of reasons. He wanted to continue his tour of inspection, which was also a morale-boosting exercise, as he was the man who embodied the new State, particularly since Griffith had died. Possibly also he hoped to make some peace contacts with his native Corkonians. He certainly wanted to seize some Republican funds and he simply wanted to visit his native place. Clonakilty was calling and a glass at the Four Alls would taste better and have a more therapeutic effect than one anywhere else in Ireland.

His decision to go to Cork provoked a scene with Joe McGrath who thought he was crazy to run the risk of travelling through the area where the Irregular leadership was strongest. It is said[54] McGrath went to the extent of putting down his objections in red ink but Collins was adamant. He despatched Frank Thornton on a mission to Clonmel to ensure that the barracks there was manned only by pre-Truce Volunteers who could be trusted, if safe conducts were given,

to recognise and respect the prominent Republicans to whom they
were to be extended, probably figures of the calibre of Dan Breen.
Thornton however ran into an ambush and was so badly shot up that
he lay unconscious for days. With characteristic self-importance de
Valera deduced that he had been sent by Collins from Dublin to
murder him.[55] So whatever peace talks were intended for Clonmel
never came off. The same fate befell over-vague arrangements which
appear to have been set in train in Cork.

Mulcahy says that before he left Portobello on his last journey he
was 'writhing with pain'.[56] He roused a friend to say goodbye and
joined him in a farewell drink. Told by Joe Sweeney he was a fool to
go he replied, 'Ah, whatever happens, my own fellow countrymen
won't kill me.'[57] As he walked down the stairs to wait for his
armoured car he tripped and his gun went off, an ill-omen.[58] Roused
by the shot, Joe O'Reilly rushed to his window. He saw Collins
outside, a small green kitbag on his back, his head bent in depression.
The impression he formed of his mood caused O'Connor to say
afterwards that 'he had never seen so tragically dejected a Collins as this
man who, thinking himself unobserved, let himself fall slack in the
loneliness and silence of the summer morning'.[59] O'Reilly pulled on his
trousers and rushed downstairs. Too late; the Big Fellow was gone.

Collins first went to the Curragh Barracks where he carried out an
inspection, then to Limerick and on to Mallow. There is some
confusion over whether he paid a visit to Maryboro (now Port-
laoghaise) Jail en route to talk to Tom Malone. Malone, alias Sean
Forde, was a top East Limerick Brigade IRA officer in the Tan war
who had gone anti-Treaty and was regarded as one of the most
formidable fighting men in the country. However Tom Malone's
own account[60] states that Collins visited him on his earlier southern
tour, the one cut short by Griffith's death. Malone said: 'He asked me
would I attend a meeting of senior officers to try to put an end to this
damned thing. As he went out, he slapped one fist into a palm in
characteristic fashion: "That's fine the three Toms will fix it." The
other two Toms were Tom Barry and Tom Hales. His last words to
Jack Twomey, the Governor, were to look after me. Within a few
days however he met his death.'

Malone's version would account for sending Thornton to Clonmel
and for Collins' taking the risk of going to Cork. But Malone was old
and ill when he recorded the interview and his memory may have been
faulty. However, another prisoner[61] told me that Collins did call at the
prison on his last trip and ordered that a whitewashed stripe be painted
all around the top of the prison walls so that any would-be escapers
could be easily spotted. A timetable of Collins' journey from Dublin
jotted down at GHQ in Dublin has him arriving in Cork, via Mallow,

at 8.30 pm.[62] Another account has him arriving much later.[63] In favour of the second timing is the fact that it would also explain the report[64] that he visited an army dance in Cruises' Hotel, in Limerick, that weekend. At the bar a young priest called him a traitor. 'Immediately', says an eye-witness, 'a young officer from Dublin hit the priest who fell to the floor and rolled under some stools . . . Michael Collins never said a word. He left the dance and about midnight set out for Cork.' The second story would also explain how it was that, when he got to Cork, he found that the two young sentries on duty in the lobby of the Imperial Hotel were both fast asleep. He banged their heads together and strode on.[65]

These discrepancies and contradictions are important only inasmuch as they remind us that it was a time of extraordinary emotion, a time governed by fear, hatred, confusion, tiredness, inexperience and hard drinking that did not make for accurate record-keeping or precise recall. If there is conflict of evidence about the simple facts of how long it took Michael Collins to get from point A to point B, and what he did en route on a trip of secondary importance, it is easy to see, in a land of legend, how a journey that culminated in the death of such a mythic figure could spawn a thousand theories. The first question I was asked by almost everyone to whom I mentioned I was writing a life of Collins was, 'Did you find out who shot him?' As a writer[66] in the *Irish Times* put it: 'Who killed Michael Collins, was it friend or foe, accidental or otherwise? This question has fuelled the great Irish whodunnit industry ever since the fateful day during the Civil War in August, 1922. . .' It is a perversion of Collins' significance to Irish history that the circumstances of his death, important though they are, should have come almost to overshadow the significance of his life. In an effort to redress this imbalance somewhat I will therefore ask the reader to bear with me as I set out the facts of Collins' last hours of life, and particularly what followed, in a manner which I think should make it clear once and for all how he came to be killed. It was a very Irish ending and it appears that there was a lot less to the tragedy than met the eye of many a theorist.

Apart from his hopes for peace Collins had another important motive in making his trip to Cork. Before Emmet Dalton's seaborne landings drove the anti-Treaty men from the city their control had been so complete that it included taking over the *Cork Examiner* and entrusting its editorship to Frank Gallagher. They also took over the collection of Customs and Excise revenues – partly by sending armed men to the Cistercian Monastery at Mount Melleray where a Revenue official was 'drying out' on retreat, and forcing him to append his signature to drafts at the point of a gun.[67] This money may have been the source of the persistent rumour that one of the reasons for Collins' last journey was to recover a cache of IRB gold which he is said to have with him when he was killed.[68] There was a sizable sum involved, approximately £100,000,[69] in the revenue seizures, which in today's values would be worth well over £2 million sterling.

Even in the middle of civil war, monies of that scale alone might well have brought Collins to Cork, both to protect his struggling Government's revenues and to deny them to the State's enemies. He had already directed Joseph Brennan, the financial adviser of the Treaty negotiations, now the Auditor General, to go to London to try to trace any anti-Treaty monies in London accounts. The man who advised him on the Cork banking scene, H.A. Pelly, manager of the Hibernian Bank, Cork, warned him that 'time may be a big factor in trying to recover some of this money,'[70] and he spent a part of the Monday in consultation with Pelly, taking notes on Imperial Hotel notepaper[71] before writing to Cosgrave:

(1) The bank position is slightly obscure. It will require a full investigation and combined with that investigation there must be an examination of the Customs and Excise position . . . (2) It would be very desirable to mak‿ an examination of the destination of certain drafts on the London County, Westminster and Parrs, London. Childers (Mr and Mrs) kept and keep an account or several accounts at the Holborn (I think) Branch of this Bank . . . don't announce anything until I return.[72]

Some £38,000 was later recovered.[73]

Another interest of Collins' lay in getting normal policing restored. He also wrote to Cosgrave about this at 3.30 pm that day. 'It would be a big thing to get Civic Guards both here and in Limerick. Civil Administration urgent everywhere in the South. The people are splendid.'[74]

Contact with his own people seems to have given him a new lease of life. He met his sister, Mary Collins-Powell and sent her son Sean, his nephew, later to be Chief-of-Staff of the Irish Army, on an errand connected with the Pelly mission. It was a good example of his ability to choose unorthodox helpers. The lad was followed on his bicycle, but managed to shake off his trackers and the note got through. However, he refused to take him on his trip the next day. 'I've got my job to do and you've got yours,' he said.

He drove out later in the day as far as Macroom, inspecting military posts, visiting relatives and friends and got back to the Imperial Hotel in a far more cheerful frame of mind than he had entered it the previous evening. It is said[75] that an unidentified Frongoch friend called to urge him to make peace. Collins argued with him for some time and then made the significant reply: 'Very well, see me tomorrow night. I may have news for you.' Then the Commander-in-Chief of the new National Army challenged his friend to a 'bit of ear' and the pair ended up rolling around the floor to the alarm and perplexity of the sentries.

Top) 17 August 1921: Dail Eireann meets in public session to debate Lloyd George's proposals for talks on Dominion status

bove) The Irish Delegates during the Treaty talks: (left to right) Arthur Griffith, Eamonn Duggan, Erskine Childers, Michael Collins, Gavan Duffy, Robert Barton, John Chartres

(*Right*) Collins leaves Downing Street with relief during break from talks

(*Foot*) Collins at pro-Treaty rally, March 1922

The British team: (*Above left*) Lloyd George a Winston Churchill, *left*) Austen Chambe and (*above*) Lord Birkenhead

Commander-in-Chief Collins on day of Griffith's funeral, and (*foot*) on his fateful journey through Bandon and Skibbereen (back seat, left) on day of his death, 22 August 1922
(*Below*) Mass card of Sonny O'Neill

"All I ask of you is to remember me at Holy Communion."

Sacred Heart of Jesus,

HAVE MERCY ON THE SOUL OF

Denis O'Neill,

NENAGH,

DIED 5th JUNE, 1950.

Aged 62 years.

A light is from our household gone,
A voice we loved is stilled.
A place is vacant in our home
Which never can be filled.

(*Top*) Collins' body in Shanakiel hospital, Cork
Faces of grief: Joe O'Reilly (*above*), and Liam Tobin and Tom Cullen (*above right*) at Collins' funeral
(*Right*) Collins' brother, Johnny, the only mourner allowed at the blessing of the monument over Collins' grave, with a gravedigger in Glasnevin Cemetery, 1939

Collins set off at 6.15 pm on 22 August 1922 for a tour of West Cork. It was one of the dates he and Kitty had discussed for a wedding, along with that of 21 June, when he had planned a double wedding in Longford with Sean MacEoin. MacEoin indicates that there was something concerning peace talks in the hint Collins gave to his wrestling friend. He recalls that 'prominent Cork citizens' had communicated peace terms to Collins, via Emmet Dalton. Collins does not seem to have been overly impressed with comments made by some of the people involved. Nevertheless MacEoin's papers include the definite statement that:

General Collins agreed to a meeting on the night of 22nd of August. Republican forces supplied Dalton with details of laid mines, mined bridges etc and generally speaking assured a safe conduct for the Commander-in-Chief. As time would not allow the contacting of every outlying post, and for that reason only, an armoured escort was included to serve as it were both as deterrent to possible attack and as an identification.

This would help to explain, if not justify, the ludicrously small escort which accompanied Collins through the most strongly held Republican territory in Ireland, despite Dalton's objections and urgings that he should not go at all. All the published accounts[77] say that the escort consisted of a motor-cycle scout, followed by an open Crossley tender containing two former Squad men, Joe Dolan and Sean O'Connell, eight riflemen and, supposedly, two machine-gunners, though these last were not much heard from in the fatal ambush. Emmet Dalton sat with him in the next vehicle, an open tourer with two drivers, and bringing up the rear was the Slievenamon, a Rolls Royce armoured car. However an unpublished account which I was shown[78] says there was also another vehicle containing six unarmed members of the pro-Treaty IRA from Mayo who wanted to join the police force and were being given a lift to Dublin, on condition that they accompanied the convoy, to give a hand with removing any barricades encountered on the tour – felled trees and such-like.

The party headed first to Macroom, via Coachford, and some writers have read significance into the fact that he went back there a second time, the morning after he had visited the local army post at Macroom Castle. It is said that he went there to meet Florrie O'Donoghue. 'It seems to have been an important meeting and Collins gave O'Donoghue a safe-conduct pass. Its importance lay in the fact that it had bearing on Collins' whole outlook at this time on the civil war.'[79] Feehan's theory was that Collins was trying to make peace whereas the politicians who had ousted him wanted no truck with 'stepping stones to Republics' and were insisting on an unconditional surrender of arms by the Republicans. That is not the way O'Donoghue described the meeting[80] which seems to have occurred by sheer chance. O'Donoghue had borrowed a car to visit his mother, who was ill. Dalton, the officer commanding the area, had given him a safe-conduct pass. But he was stopped in Macroom 'by a fool' of a Free State Officer and lodged in a cell in Macroom Castle. He saw Collins through the window and managed to get a note to him via the sentry whose rifle he minded in the meantime. Collins came to his cell to let him out personally. O'Donoghue says: 'He was really talking big. I got the impression that he wanted to leave politics to take charge of the Army. He said "I've been all over this bloody county and no one has said a bloody word to me." ' He was surprised and pleased 'that no one could stop him.' It was this frame of mind, more than anything else, which caused Michael Collins' death.

The journey to Macroom was uneventful but from there on the route to Bandon was an obstacle course of blown bridges and trenched roads. Accordingly the party was provided with a guide, a local taxi driver, to direct them to Bandon. The vulnerability of the little convoy was underscored at Ballymichael Hill where the Slievenamon stalled on the hill and soldiers had to get out and push to get it to the top. Later that day the touring car also gave trouble, seemingly through overheating, and there are reports of water being required on at least two occasions, before it was finally abandoned.

The village of Kilmurry lies ahead of Ballymichael and the motor-cycle scout, Lieutenant Smith, a member of the Dublin Brigade, whether acting on orders or otherwise is not known, occupied himself during Operation Push by knocking on doors calling out, 'The Commander-in-Chief is coming.' Apart from the folly of alerting anyone who might have wanted to take a shot at Collins this was a provocative thing to do because several of the men in the area had been in the anti-Treaty party that had been beaten out of Limerick, suffering defeats also at Buttevant and Kilmallock. There was no reaction, however, and the convoy passed safely on to the cross-roads at the entrance to Bael na mBlath, an undistinguished little gap where hilly ground rises on either side of the road. Even with the guide, the maze of unsignposted little roads caused uncertainty and the party had to ask a man standing outside Long's public house for directions. Denny Long, 'Denny the Dane', as he was known locally, obligingly pointed out the road to Bandon. He was standing with one hand resting on the Wild West-style swing doors to the pub and, unknown to the Collins party, had carefully stood a rifle on its butt inside the door seconds before they appeared.

For 'Denny the Dane' was an IRA sentry. Several important IRA officers were in the pub because of a meeting of No.s 1 and 3 Cork Brigades at Murray's farmhouse up the hill behind Long's. Two days earlier, at a meeting in Ballyvourney, Liam Lynch had decreed that the war must go on, even though many of the men who were now meeting, including Tom Hales, had argued otherwise. The Ballyvourney gathering was so important that it had drawn to the area de Valera, Childers, Tom Hales, Liam Deasy and other top-ranking figures on the Republican side. One of its decisions was that the sort of conventional warfare in which the IRA had fared so disastrously in Limerick, Cork City and elsewhere should be abandoned and that the organisation would revert to its old-style 'target of opportunity', guerrilla warfare.

Denny the Dane's tip-off meant that their adversaries' prime target had just presented itself to the IRA men. Tom Hales directed that an ambush for Michael Collins and his escort be laid at Bael na mBlath on the Bandon road, a mile or so away from Long's. On a military plane the reasoning behind the ambush was that the patrol might come back the way it had gone. On an emotional level the words of Flor Begley, the man who piped through the fighting at Crossbarry, strike a more convincing note, that of the territorial imperative. Begley said:

It leaked out that Michael Collins was coming south and that some members of the Dublin Brigade were coming to protect him and that they didn't give a damn about the 3rd West Cork Brigade fellows. This 'got their goat' [that is, Kelliher, Hurley, Deasy etc], and they decided to have a go at the Dublin crowd.[81]

Deasy tends to corroborate this view in his valuable account of the civil war, *Brother Against Brother*. He regarded Collins 'as the greatest leader of our generation'. But he points to the fact that between the area around the ambush site and Bandon 'not one active Volunteer had joined the Free State Army'. He says he found it

hard to accept that the convoy was travelling merely on a social visit to West Cork. It is mere conjecture, but I rated it as the foolhardy act of a brave man who knew well the area he was driving through and the men there . . . This last expedition of his may have been the gesture of a man who felt that reconciliation was no longer possible with so many intimate friends and comrades in West Cork. Nobody knew better than Collins the area through which he would pass, and consequently he arranged to travel in full military convoy. As such there could be no question of any intention on his part, as was suggested elsewhere, of meeting us for discussions.

It seems reasonable to speculate that Collins, without the knowledge of his Cabinet colleagues, may have been attempting to bring about peace through negotiating with some Republican activists who were prepared to defy Liam Lynch. De Valera would almost certainly have been made aware of such an initiative through Frank Aiken, and would have been eager to explore the possibilities of another Collins–de Valera pact. All that is certain is that, whether because of the Thornton ambush, or for some other reason, it is obvious that no word of Collins' peace intentions had reached Bael na mBlath. However it is believed[82] that Collins was expected at the house of Canon Tracey of Crookstown during his last visit. The reason for the visit, it is said, was to make contact with some intermediaries who may have included a well-known priest Fr W.P. Hackett and figures such as Alfred O'Rahilly and Sean O'Hegarty, the officer who complained about Collins' drinking during the Treaty negotiations. During the IRA discussions which took place at Ballyvourney, Hegarty was confirmed as OC of the Cork No. 1 Brigade, even though he was recognised as being a neutral and engaged in peace moves of some sort. A stop at Crookstown would explain the seemingly inexplicably circuitous Bael na mBlath route back to Cork from Bandon which Collins took. As a glance at the map will show, it is a straight run of some twenty-one miles to Cork from Bandon via Inishannon on a main road which is said to have been open at the time.[83]

Had Collins survived the ambush and either kept his appointment at the Canon's house or with another group of peace-makers who were said to be waiting for him at the Desmond Hotel in Cork that evening,[84] it is possible that Deasy and Hales would subsequently have been contacted. Possible, but not certain, because apart from the vagueness surrounding these arrangements another ambush was apparently laid for him on the route to Crookstown from Cork. The Canon's housekeeper is said to have talked indiscreetly in Crookstown when she went in to buy extra drink and groceries for 'some important visitors' the previous Sunday.

The shop was the old-fashioned type – pub, grocery, hardware shop combined. Standing at the bar were three Irregulars[85] who heard the housekeeper tell the owner whom the extra order was for. An ambush was laid at a wooded area near Crookstown, called Farran, with a view, not to killing Collins, but to kidnapping him. Trees overhanging the route were sawn through so that they were only held upright by wires, the idea being to drop the trees so as to isolate Collins' car from the rest of the convoy. When Collins did not show up on the 21st as expected the Crookstown IRA had enquiries made in Cork. A waitress in Hoskins Hotel, Prince's St, was despatched to the Imperial to learn what she could about his movements. Some of the escort party were drinking at the bar and the girl picked up the next day's route from them. This was telephoned to Crookstown and corroborated by the garrulous housekeeper during another visit to the all-purpose shop. She said she was expected to have lunch ready at four. The Farran ambush was reactivated and remained in place all day until long after dark. It seems, therefore, that had Collins managed to get through Bael na mBlath safely he could also have been in serious danger had he visited Crookstown and left by the Farran Road.

However, blissfully ignorant of all this, Collins continued on that morning through Bael na mBlath. En route to Bandon his driver took a wrong turning – his regular driver had been injured in the Stillorgan ambush and neither of his two replacement drivers, Corry and Quinn, had any knowledge of the countryside and very little of war-time driving – and his car became detached from the rest of the convoy and drove into Newcestown. When the rest of the party caught up with him they found him in Newcestown Churchyard examining names on the tombstones. Meanwhile back at Bael na mBlath an ambush party under Tom Hales lay in wait, the road blocked by removing a wheel from a dray seized from a carter employed by the Bandon Brewery. The major part of the ambush party occupied the high ground on the left-hand side of the road, past Long's pub on the way to Bandon. On the right-hand side of the road, across a small stream behind a tall hedge overlooking the roadway, a smaller group lay hidden. Mines were placed on the roadway.

An interested observer of these preparations was Eamon de Valera, who had spent the night in a farmhouse about two miles away. He is quoted as having made a number of observations. 'What a pity I didn't meet him,' and, 'It would be bad if anything happens to Collins, his place will be taken by weaker men.' An integral part of 'the great Irish whodunnit' mystery is that de Valera had a hand in Collins' death. This is true only in the sense that he was the principal architect of the overall civil war situation. My information is that he actively tried to to prevent the actual ambush. It comes from the account,[86] given by Jimmy Flynn, the ADC assigned to him while he was in the Cork area. De Valera learned about Collins' presence in the area before Denny the Dane did. His driver saw Collins pass through Crookstown that morning and went immediately to alert de Valera, who then made for Long's where he discovered the ambush preparations in train. According to Flynn he asked that Collins be not ambushed, saying that he was in the area to meet Collins, and that arrangements had been made to bring them together.[87] Though de Valera 'virtually pleaded with them' no one accepted his arguments that surrender was a real prospect and that they would get a better deal from Collins in his native county than when he was back in Dublin amongst his Cabinet colleagues. He was told that while he was in the area his status was that of a staff officer under the Area Commander, Liam Lynch. The pub party were on active service under Lynch and intended to carry out his wishes about switching to guerrilla warfare. De Valera then 'stormed out of the meeting in a rage' and made for Kilworth where he had a meal at the home of a friend, a local doctor, who provided him with a pony and trap to get through Fermoy, a garrison town. Once through Fermoy, de Valera linked up safely with his car – cars were still rare enough in the area to draw attention to him – and drove to Fethard where he spent the night with Jimmy Flynn's parents. Later that night he heard the news of Collins' death and was 'furious and visibly upset'.

While de Valera was travelling to Fethard Collins and his party had gone into Bandon and from thence to Clonakilty, where he joined his escort in sawing through a tree across the roadway. Then on to Sam's Cross, Rosscarbery and Skibbereen, returning in the evening to Bandon, after a second visit to Rosscarbery, several hours after he was said to have been expected at Crookstown. During the course of the day his presence in the towns he passed through caused a sensation. People turned out to wave and cheer. He met several of his relatives, including his brother Sean, many old friends, like Sean Hales, the senior Free State Army officer in the area, and the mother of an old friend of his, Gerald MacDonald of Rosscarbery, whose death he had just heard of. There were crowds and handshakes, food and drink in plenty. Collins, with his usual generosity, insisted on buying drink for the escort party. One biographer allows him a pint of 'Clonakilty wrastler' at Sam's Cross [Forester], another [O'Connor], a bottle of stout at Rosscarbery, although he is said to have disliked stout. Collins himself may have had less to drink than the others, but though there is, as usual, some conflict of evidence on this point a number of accounts say that the escort was well under the influence by the time they left Bandon for the last time. Emmet Dalton, a very heavy drinker in later life, denied that the party, including Collins, was drunk. 'It's a lie', he said.[88] But with true soldierly bluntness he privately told members of the crew that made the film about his life for RTE that 'we were all arseholes!'[89] Billy Powell, Captain of Lissarda Company of the IRA, said the members of the convoy were 'in no shape for fighting. They'd been on a bit of a spree all day. Mick Collins stood them drink wherever he stopped.'[90]

Another account[91] describes a scene in Callinan's pub in Rosscarbery while Collins was away, possibly visiting Mrs MacDonald. A row broke out between Dublin members of the convoy and local troops when the machine-gunner of the Slievenamon, John McPeake, took a bottle of whiskey from a shelf in the pub. McPeake himself later admitted that there was some drinking on the trip but firmly denied[92] that it was to excess. The pub affray may have been the reason that six soldiers are said to have been disarmed and locked up, though local legend has it that they were put away by the local Commander, Captain Sean McCarthy, because they were ex-British Army personnel who were thought to be plotting against Collins. When McCarthy told Collins of his suspicions, and warned him to be careful, Collins is said to have listened to him in silence and then shaken hands saying, 'I'm going to put an end to this bloody war as soon as possible.'[93]

Both at Sam's Cross and at Bandon before he left for the journey back through Bael na mBlath Collins was warned to be careful. He may even have been specifically told, in Rosscarbery, that an ambush party was in place at Bael na mBlath. It was an open secret[94] in the district that an ambush had been laid. The postman had coined a witticism that he repeated at each farm he called at that morning: 'Collins is gone wesht, but he won't go easth.'[95] It is said that two farmers who had been drawing lime from Castlemore Quarries near Bael na mBlath became involved in a row with the ambush party when they attempted to remove the cart barricade. One of the farmers is said to have been a relation of Collins. When he got home he sent his son to Callinan's pub to warn Collins at around six o'clock that evening. The pub owner, Paddy Callinan, took the message and passed it on to Collins. A first cousin, Captain Paddy Collins, of Castle Freke, said his reaction was to shrug and say, 'Yerra, sure they'd never attack me.'[96] Captain Collins described him on that last day as being 'the same old Mick, not under any strain'. The greatest figure produced by the area, or indeed the Ireland of his day, Collins was back with his own, away from the intolerable tensions of Dublin. Forget the war, relax, take a drink, have a chat and a joke. It was human but it was not wartime behaviour. Collins would not have lasted a day had he been so unguarded during the Black and Tan period. In Bandon he said goodbye to Sean Hales, laughingly shrugging off his warnings to be careful, and set off for Bael na mBlath where Sean's brother, his close friend Tom, was waiting to kill him.

The ambush party had been in place for so long that most of them had given up, gone home, or gone to the pub, leaving six[97] members in place on the left-hand side of the road, coming from Bandon. They were: Tom Hales, Tom Kelliher, Jim Hurley, Dan Holland, Sonny O'Neill and John O'Callaghan.

Tom Hales decided that the mines should be rendered safe so that farmers could go to the creamery in the morning. He was carrying one mine and had taken the detonation leads off the other when Smith, the motor-cycle scout, appeared around the corner behind him approaching from Bandon. It was now nearly eight o'clock. Two of the men on the hill, Kelliher and Sonny O'Neill, fired warning shots and Hales[98] 'boosted' the mine over the low fence on the side of the road nearest him, that beside the stream, and tumbled over after it. It was one of the most ill-prepared ambushes of the entire period. The one Thompson sub-machine-gun available to the party had been carried back to the pub. The mines were disconnected and the handful of men on the hill were not equipped to take on a convoy which included an armoured car and men of the calibre accompanying Collins. The party's objective at that stage was to get Hales clear and make good their own escape.

The light was failing and the roadsides were overgrown and much narrower than they are now, more suited to horse-drawn traffic than to motor vehicles. In fact, beyond the barricade there was an ass and cart, temporarily abandoned by its wrathful owner because of the ambush. The ass was grazing at the side of the road and Smith skidded into a ditch avoiding it. 'Just the sort of donkey and just the sort of cart they have at home . . .'[99] Dalton realised that the convoy was in a highly dangerous situation and yelled at the driver: 'Drive like hell!' But Collins, who had tackled and disarmed gunmen who confronted him in the past, was not going to flee from an ambuscade in his own territory. Indeed, since the warning in Rosscarbery, he may have been expecting it because Dalton remembers him picking up his rifle as they neared Bael na mBlath. When the shots rang out he put a hand on the driver's shoulder and called out, 'Stop! Jump out and we'll fight them.' Dalton's account speaks of a 'heavy fusillade of machine-gun fire' sweeping the road, but the attackers had no machine-guns that I could ever find evidence of. The firepower was on the side of the convoy, the handful of attackers possessing the advantage of surprise and better positioning. The armoured car moved up and down the road, several times passing over the unremoved, but harmless, mine while McPeake kept up a heavy fire from the Vickers machine-gun. Bullets were clipping the grass all round Kelliher and he reckoned that had the gun not jammed suddenly he would have been killed. The jamming was caused by one of the inexperienced passengers in the armoured car feeding the belt awkwardly into the magazine. The gun should have been manned by two trained machine-gunners, but in the disorganisation of the time only one, McPeake, had been allocated to accompany the Commander-in-Chief. The other occupants of the Slievenamon were the drivers and two members of the escort party who had got into the armoured car because it was warmer than the Crossley tender which may also have been overcrowded through taking on extra passengers during the afternoon.[100]

The two Lewis guns in the Crossley do not appear to have greatly discommoded the ambushers. Survivors' reports speak of the Vickers only. When it ceased there was such a lull in the sound of firing that instinctively it was felt that the brief battle was nearly over.

However, both sets of riflemen continued to fire, the firing being augmented by some members of the ambush party who had re-emerged from the pub and were now firing from the top of the hill on Long's side of the road, too far away to have any bearing on the ambush. Incredibly enough it is thought that a small group of Kerry IRA men retreating back to Kerry were drawn to the scene by the sound of shooting and also loosed off a few shots at the convoy from the same side of the road as Long's party.[101] Both these firing parties were thus above and behind Collins, to his right and that of his men. For most of the fight he had remained behind the car firing in the direction of Kelliher and company, above him and to his left. But then some of the Hales-Kelliher party began to retreat. Collins saw them and called out, 'Come on boys! There they are, running up the road.'

He is then said to have left the shelter of the car and moved back in the direction of Bandon for some fifty yards to gain a better view of the men moving up the hill on his left. All this time he was out in an open roadway, with no cover, while in front and behind him some of the toughest and most experienced flying column men in the country were firing at him and his party. Accounts differ as to what happened. Some say he went down into a prone firing position, others that he remained firing standing up. Years later, Florrie O'Donoghue said that Dalton had told him, 'Mick wouldn't keep his head down. If he'd ever been in a scrap he'd have learned to stay down. For I was flat down and Mick was killed standing up.'[102] The unpublished account given by the Mayo man, who claims he and his five colleagues accompanied the convoy, also says that Collins was shot standing up, though in the back of the head, and not more than fifteen yards from the vehicles. The shooting had begun to slacken off when, Dalton says, he fancied he heard a cry of 'Emmet' and he and Sean O'Connell rushed from their shelter behind the armoured car to find Collins lying on the roadway, 'a fearful gaping wound at the base of the skull and behind the right ear'. O'Connell said an Act of Contrition and thought that he was answered by a slight pressure of the hand.

On the hillside above him Sonny O'Neill, an ex-British Army marksman, made off into the gathering dusk. He had lingered for a last, long shot and instinctively felt he might have hit the tall officer, whoever he was, but now it was a time to retreat, not to hang around checking. The whole encounter had taken not much longer than an hour, in fact some reports say only twenty minutes. What is certain is that for those on the roadside below a time of nightmare had begun.

Light and life were fading rapidly as O'Connell, under covering fire from Dalton, dragged Collins to shelter under the armoured car. Lieutenant Smith helped him to bandage the hideous wound and carry the body to the tourer, even though he had been shot through the neck and could not ride his motor-cycle which had to be abandoned.[103] Dalton cradled the body in his arms in the back seat as the convoy drove back to Cork, a distance of nineteen miles. They did not arrive there until 1.30 am. Dalton subsequently explained this by reference to the condition of the roads and bridges.[104] If the party, earlier in the day, with morale high and the services of a guide, had had to ask for directions, it is reasonable to assume that they could have been confused in darkness, on a return journey which had suffered such a cataclysm. Nevertheless the drivers had already been over the route and people in reasonable control of their faculties would have been expected to have made better progress. Certainly if word had been sent back to Bandon a few miles away, along a road which the convoy had just traversed, Sean Hales would have provided guidance. This failure to seek help from the nearest point available is one of the strangest features of that whole awful night.

The convoy is said to have left Long's at 9.30, having procured water for one of the vehicles and a cloth to wipe the blood from Collins' face. At Long's members of the party revealed who the dead man was. There were some local Irregulars in the pub, not members of the ambush party, and word was sent up the hill to Murray's where the IRA meeting had resumed.

'We had barely started,' says Deasy,

when Sean Galvin of Crookstown rushed in and excitedly told us that Michael Collins had been shot dead in the ambush and the convoy had taken his body to Cork via Crookstown, Cloughduv and Killeeny. [This would suggest that the convoy had had to again ask for directions in the pub and thus the return route became known.] The meeting was adjourned immediately and many of us left Murray's with heavy hearts. To those of us who had known Collins personally, and there were many, his death was tragic: to Tom Hales, Tadhg O'Sullivan and myself who had known him intimately, our sorrow was deep and lasting. We parted without discussion of any kind . . . each of us all too conscious of the tragedy and the loneliness that only time could heal.

The convoy stopped again at Bellmont Mills, near Crookstown, looking for the road to Cork and asking for a priest. They were told where Canon Tracey lived, outside the village, but as this would have meant a detour, and as apparently none of them knew anything about a meeting between Collins and the Canon, it was decided to drive on to Cloughduv where the curate's house was pointed out by a civilian who escorted a soldier to the door. The convoy got to Cloughduv at around eleven o'clock, an hour and a half after leaving Long's. In considering this time span it might be worth noting that at the time of writing, admittedly in daytime, under no strain and over far better roads, the same journey took me less than ten minutes. The area is so small that Canon Tracey, who was also parish priest of the Bael na mBlath district, subsequently wrote: 'It was my misfortune to be listening to the dreadful firing when Michael Collins was done to death.'[105]

Dalton's description of what happened next is as follows:

On the way back we came upon a church – with a stretch of gravel and railings in front – along the road. One of my men went in asking for a priest. A priest came out as far as the railings, looked in at the dead Collins lying on my shoulder in the back seat of the car then turned on his heel and walked back in. One of my officers raised his rifle to shoot the priest and only that I struck up the barrel the priest would have been shot. The bullet was actually discharged.

Dalton commented, 'the incident left a grim impression on the minds of the entire party.'[106] He lodged a complaint with the priest's superiors the next day. However the priest, Fr Timothy Murphy, gave a very different account.[107] He says that he went with the soldier and the civilian to the car, not merely to the railings.

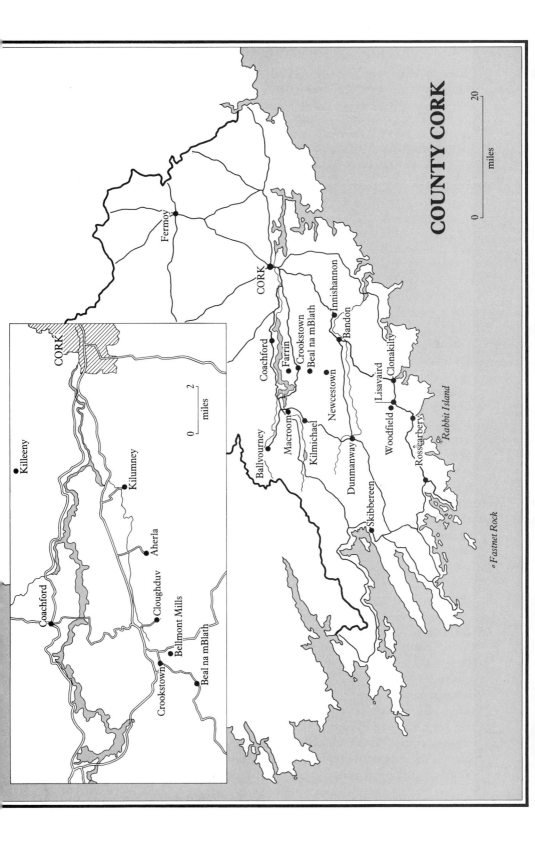

COUNTY CORK

0 — 20 miles

CORK

Fermoy

Coachford
Farrin
Crookstown
Beal na mBlath
Innishannon
Bandon
Ballvourney
Macroom
Kilmichael
Newcestown
Dunmanway
Lisavaird
Clonakilty
Woodfield
Rosscarbery
Skibbereen

Fastnet Rock

Rabbit Island

Inset map:

Killeeny
Kilumney
Aherla
Cloughduv
Belmont Mills
Crookstown
Beal na mBlath
Coachford
CORK

0 — 2 miles

It was a dark night and the soldier carried in his hand an old carbide lamp which was giving a very bad light. I walked out to the roadway where the convoy had stopped. There was a soldier lying flat with his head resting on the lap of a young officer. The young officer was sobbing and crying and did not speak. There was blood on the side of the dead man's face. I said an Act of Contrition and other prayers and made the Sign of the Cross. I told an officer to wait until I got the Holy Oils. I went to the house but when I returned the convoy had gone . . . the civilian heard an Army officer say 'that priest is not coming back' and he ordered the lorries to drive away. Some of the soldiers were hysterical.

As readers will no doubt have observed the priest does not mention any rifle shot.

Bael na mBlath, Crookstown, Cloughduv, Aherla, Killeeny, nondescript little no-places, beads on a sorrowful decade of the rosary. The traumatised convoy passed through them all on their way back to Cork, but seems to have missed coming anywhere near the ambush said to have been laid at Farran, which would probably have been lifted with the onset of darkness anyhow. At a spot on the road near the townland of Kilumney the Macroom railway bridge was blown and again there are conflicting reports as to whether a warning from a man on the road, good driving or good luck saved one or all of the vehicles from a forty-foot drop. The convoy detoured and at Kilumney, near Kilumney House, turned into a cul-de-sac and entered a farmyard by mistake. It then took to the fields across country to rejoin a road. There followed a terrible interlude of shouting and skidding and pushing as the soldiers attempted to get the vehicles across the fields, sometimes using greatcoats and petrol tins to give the wheels a purchase. Eventually the touring car was abandoned and Collins' corpse was carried to the roadway, grey matter, from what a few hours earlier had been a brilliant brain, seeping onto the shoulders of its bearers. The party finally reached Cork at 1.30 am.

Here again there are different accounts of what happened next. Almost fifty years later it was put to Dalton by an interviewer that he 'left the corpse on the Western Road with orders that it was to be taken to a hospital belonging to the British Army'.[108] Dalton's reply was: 'So far as I can remember the entire party went to the Imperial Hotel [GHQ] and that Dr Leo Aherne took the body to the Bon Secours Hospital.' In fact the body was taken to Shanakiel Hospital. About this the record is clear. The convoy appears to have encountered two members of the Cork Civic Patrol at the corner of Washington St and Grand Parade who led them there. There was a wireless link between the Imperial Hotel and Valentia Island Cable Station. According to Dalton, news of Collins'. death was transmitted by the link to the Island. In order to reach Dublin it had to be transmitted first to New York and then back across the Atlantic to London and across the Irish

Sea to Dublin. But the operator to whom he gave the telegram, Matt Quigley, was later reported[109] as saying that the message, to Mulcahy, was sent direct to Dublin, uncoded, though normally military messages were sent in code because of the presence of British warships in Cork Harbour. Possibly contacts in Dublin gave the tip-off, but both the London *Daily Express* and the *Freeman's Journal* reported the death next morning before the *Cork Examiner* had printed a word about the tragedy. The *Daily Express*, whose correspondent was particularly close to British official sources, seems to have been warned to hold its front page for the news.[110] And, during the morning, Dalton was incensed to receive a cablegram from Hearst newspapers offering £1,000 for the story.

However it was sent, Dalton's cable found its mark. Charlie Dalton, Emmet's brother, recalled his bedroom door at Portobello opening after the coded message arrived, and 'in walked the Adjutant General, Gearoid O'Sullivan. He did not greet me as customarily, but stood rather bewildered-looking for a second or two and then broke down weeping and spoke in a rather uncertain voice saying "Charlie, The Big Fella is dead."'[111] The first two they broke the news to were Joe O'Reilly and Tom Cullen. Cullen lit a candle as they entered his room and in its light looked at their faces and burst out, 'Something terrible has happened – I know what you have come to tell me – The Big Fella is dead! I've been dreaming about him.' They then went to break the news to Batt O'Connor: even sixty years later the memory of the consternation and grief caused in her home by the news made Sister Margaret Mary fall silent as she spoke to me about the telling. Messengers were sent about the city and all through the night shocked men were ushered through the sandbags and barbed wire guarding Government buildings. The shock was so palpable that Cullen and O'Reilly burst into tears when they saw the grey, taut faces. With finger raised, Cosgrave stepped forward. 'This is a nice way for soldiers to behave. . .'[112] Mulcahy slipped away to write a message to the Army directing how he thought soldiers *should* behave:

Stand calmly by your posts. Bend bravely and undaunted to your work. Let no cruel act of reprisal blemish your bright honour. Every dark hour that Michael Collins met since 1916 seemed but to steel that bright strength of his and temper his gay bravery. You are left each inheritors of that strength.

13

Honouring the Dead?

'We are losing many splendid men – many fine noble
friends. I hope someone will be left to pay due tribute to
their deeds and their memories – but only one tribute can
repay them – the freedom of this land and in God's good
time that will rest with us.'

Michael Collins

Rumours about Collins' death spread as the mourners went home to
the four corners of Ireland. His stature, the fact that he was the only
one killed in the ambush, all helped to fuel the gossip. Then, a few
months after his death, the rumours received a tremendous fillip. On
2nd December John McPeake, the machine-gunner, deserted to the
Republican side taking the Slievenamon, the armoured car, with him.
McPeake himself said the reason he left the Army was that he was
disgusted at the shooting of two prisoners by his Army comrades.[1]
Locally it is said that he was a great ladies' man who told a woman
friend that he was getting a bad time from his comrades over the
jammed gun and would have liked to get out. The girl, a Republican,
relayed this to the IRA who struck a bargain with him, promising to
look after him and get him back to Scotland, provided he would desert
with the armoured car. He was arrested in Glasgow the following
July, returned to Ireland and given six years for the theft, much of it
spent in solitary confinement. In Portlaoise Jail he joined some
Republican prisoners on hunger strike and for this and other breaches
of prison regulations had a bad time in jail. Those were harsh times
and it can be taken for granted that, had he had anything to do with
Collins' death, he would hardly have survived his arrest, never mind
his imprisonment.

On McPeake's release on 4 August 1928 a group of Dublin
Republicans took up a collection for him. It netted £60. Someone in
high places seems to have decided that he deserved more than this,
however, because after de Valera came to power, I am reliably
informed that McPeake received a Secret Service pension.[2]

The unfortunate Emmet Dalton was the target for the most
sustained allegations. He was held responsible for not ensuring a
better escort for Collins, not taking a safer route, not insisting that the
convoy 'drive like hell', accidentally shooting Collins through drink

or panic and, ugliest of all, deliberately killing him for British 'blood money'.[3] It is said that Sean Hales was shot by the British Secret Service because he was pressurising the Provisional Government into holding an inquiry 'as he did not accept Dalton's version'.[4] Sean Hales was in fact shot by the IRA and in reprisal for his death Rory O'Connor, Liam Mellowes, Joseph McKelvey and Dick Barrett were roused from their sleep in Mountjoy where they had been lodged since the fall of the Four Courts and told they would be shot at daybreak. The executions were carried out on the morning of 8 December 1922.

The facts of Hales' death are set out in a secret IRA communiqué initialled by Liam Lynch to the OC of the 1st Southern Division: 'Padraig O'Maille, Deputy Speaker, F.S. Parliament wounded, Sean Hales, F.S. T.D. and an officer of F.S. Army shot dead – unintentionally while in company with P. O'Maille. It was intended only to wound Hales, but he was mistaken for O'Maille.'[5] So far as Dalton was concerned, the disorganised and insufficient escort was a product purely of the times and, as I have indicated, of Collins' desire to go through his own county at will with a bodyguard of his own choosing. As to 'blood money', Dalton, a man of outstanding character and ability, would have shot himself sooner than have injured Collins. He found it difficult after the ambush to adjust to life, leaving both the Army through scruples about the harsh governmental measures taken against the Irregulars, and, subsequently, a comfortable post given to him by Cosgrave as Clerk of the Seanad, because of alcohol. Far from living comfortably on £10,000 blood money as alleged (the allegation is constant, only the sum changes), Dalton became so short of money that I have been told[6] that he offered Collins' Field Diary, which he had on him when he was shot, to the Government. Cosgrave is said to have phoned Johnny Collins to get him to buy it from him 'because otherwise he'll hold us up to ransom'. The diary certainly returned to the Collins family via Government sources years after Collins was killed. It is also true that Dalton was reduced to selling encyclopaedias – the set my father bought is still a treasured family possession – before pulling himself together and making a successful career in the film industry. At the outbreak of the Second World War he was approached by a racing friend, Lord FitzWilliam, to ask him to join an elite, SAS-type unit being set up by Lord Louis Mountbatten. The idea was to include men from Ireland, England, Scotland and Wales. But Dalton turned down the offer and spent the war working in the film industry, augmenting his income by travelling around to race meetings as a full-time professional punter, which, say the dedicated conspiracy theorists, was an ideal cover for intelligence work.

One of the most enduring theories is that Collins died from a Mauser pistol bullet, the implication being that the bullet came from

Dalton's gun. Commandant Frank Friel, the officer who brought Collins' body to Shanakiel Hospital, felt that a .303 rifle bullet could not have made the huge wound in the skull. I know that even some of the ambush party felt that Denis (Sonny) O'Neill must have inadvertently used a round of dum-dum. Another theory is that one of the rifles which was supposed to have been sent northwards in the undercover swap which Collins had arranged in order to arm the Northern IRA without implicating himself, was a particularly fine elephant gun. O'Neill is said to have been so taken with the weapon that he substituted another rifle for it and kept the elephant gun for himself. Thus, in a very real sense, Collins is said to have died as a result of his own Northern policy. However the Colm Connolly documentary which reconstructed the death with the aid of, amongst other experts, the Irish State Pathologist, Dr Harbinson, demonstrated that a high velocity rifle bullet, making an inconspicuous entry wound at or above the hairline could leave a gaping aperture on exiting. The bullet apparently drives not only particles of bone, but also an air pocket before it.

Obviously, had an inquest been held, such speculations might have been ended nearly seventy years ago. The fact that one was not held might be explained by a Provisional Government decision of 29 June 1922 which stated that 'Inquests should be held on all dead civilians and also on all military killed whose deaths did not occur in definite military action.'[7] Collins' death could be considered 'definite military action'. But it became known after de Valera assumed office in 1932 that the outgoing Government had issued a directive that documents relating to three classes of incident were to be destroyed, those dealing with courts martial, executions and – the death of Collins. Even though by then, in 1924, he had led what amounted to a mutiny against the Government, Liam Tobin, because of his unique Intelligence experience, was brought back from civilian life to supervise this operation and much documentation was destroyed. De Valera took a photostat of the directive (which was signed by Desmond Fitzgerald) into retirement with him, and Dr T. P. O'Neill[8] has a definite recollection of studying it during his biographical research. But there is nothing intrinsically sinister in the Collins cover-up. All three topics would have been fertile fields of propaganda in the climate of the time, and in addition, if any matters relating to a 'spree' preceding Collins' death were unearthed they would have been embarrassing for all concerned, including the Collins family.

What happened to Gogarty's post-mortem report is anybody's guess. It was said to have been placed in a safe at the Royal College of Surgeons in Dublin but, despite a diligent search, the librarian, Professor J. B. Lyons, who is also a biographer of Oliver St John Gogarty's, could find no trace of it.

And so we come to the story of the real cover-up. I am of course aware that the continuing suspicion is, and always will be, that Collins in some way fell victim to the British Secret Service. I know[9] that an account has been set down by a survivor of that day alleging that Collins was murdered and that the fatal shot was not fired by Sonny O'Neill. This account, I am informed at the time of writing, will become available on the survivor's death. Yet pending any such disclosure – and I have not been shown what proof the survivor intends to advance in support of his contention – at this stage the facts I have been able to collect and study force me to the conclusion that the cover-up was a far more benign affair than has hitherto been adverted and in fact reflects credit, not guilt, on those concerned. Initially both Free Staters and Republicans had every reason for damping down controversy. There was no glory in it for either side and much inducement to keep silent. The Government was in a weak and vulnerable position and had lost its greatest figure in circumstances which said little for its military prowess or its credibility generally. An army that could not protect Michael Collins could hardly be trusted to protect a country. The Republicans feared reprisals, and with good reason. Dalton has described how – at gun-point – he had to order some of his soldiers from the gates of Cork Jail where they were trying to get at the Republican prisoners. Joe McGrath told me that he intervened personally to prevent de Valera being shot as a reprisal and Vinnie Byrne, to give but one example, told me that for 'four or five days I'd have shot any bloody Die-hard [Irregular] I came across.' For a long time the Republican areas around the ambush site lived in dread of a Black-and-Tan-type reprisal raid by Free State troops.

But there was also, over and above all this, a 'decency factor' which accounted for a great deal of the mystery. Johnny Collins and Nancy were well aware of the details of how Michael died from within a year of the death. The ambush had been the work of men who were neighbours and friends before the civil war and they continued to be friends and neighbours after it. Tom Hales who 'cried his eyes out over the killing',[10] took the initiative in making his peace with Johnny and Nancy and then, through him, other members of the party did likewise. One of them, Jim Hurley, broke down and cried in their home when he first visited them in Dublin in 1923. 'How could we do it?', he sobbed. 'We were too young – I was only nineteen.'[11] The family was then living in Donnybrook. Many years later, when they had moved to Booterstown, and were rearing the children of the marriage, one of the children, a boy, Michael, was puzzled by the sight of a man walking up and down outside the house for a long time, glancing in and then turning away. At one stage Michael went out to him and the man asked him if that was the house Johnny Collins lived in. Michael said yes and invited him in. 'I'll go in all right, but in my own time', was the answer. Johnny then came to the door, saw who it was and exclaimed: 'Will you come in out of that.' It was Jim Hurley paying his second visit to the family. He received a warm welcome and he and Johnny became the closest of friends. But Johnny, like his brother, respected confidences, and it was many years before Michael was told the significance of Jim's visit.

Hales knew Sonny O'Neill had probably fired the fatal shot. He told Johnny what had happened, in confidence. O'Neill, a deeply religious man, had been fundamentally disturbed and upset by the killing and had confided in his Commanding Officer that he had calculated that it was probably his last shot that had killed Collins. But he lived in the area and for neighbourly reasons, as much as reasons of security, secrecy remained the order of the day, until one day, long after the civil war was but an evil memory, Sonny O'Neill was diagnosed as having a terminal heart condition. He enquired of Hales what Johnny's attitude to the shooting was and Hales assured him it was one of 'total forgiveness'. O'Neill may have been planning to visit Johnny before his illness ran its course but he collapsed and died at a railway station returning from a pilgrimage to Knock on 5 June 1950,[12] without ever having discussed 22 August 1922 with him, or anyone else for that matter. When the Colm Connolly documentary, 'The Shadow of Bael na mBlath', was screened his family was devastated. One result was that they sent me a transcript of an interview with Tom Foley, a survivor of the ambush, conducted by Fr Aidan O'Driscoll, on 2 September 1989. Foley discounted O'Neill's involvement. I believe the facts of Collins' death are as I have given them but, to make the record as fair and as complete as possible, here is a relevant extract from the transcript:

Fr O'Driscoll: . . . this statement that Sonny O'Neill fired the fatal shot . . . You were there as a seventeen-year-old . . . what were you doing exactly on the day? What was your job?

Foley: I went for the mines and I went down for the cigarettes. And any fellow wanted anything, I'd get it for him.

Fr O'Driscoll: As to the claim that Sonny O'Neill shot Michael Collins, what do you think of that?

Foley: . . . It was raining in the evening . . . Before the ambush started it got wet and that's why the lads were going away. [Sonny O'Neill] . . . had left the ambush position an hour before it.

Fr O'Driscoll: Is it possible to know who fired that shot.

Foley: Not possible! Not possible . . . you weren't going to keep your head up while they shot, were you? And McPeake cleaning the briars off the top of the ditch with the machine-gun. Not a very safe place to put your head up at all, to see or otherwise. They were firing them shots now without ever seeing where they were going to, you can be sure of that. Oh life is sweet, but an ambush like that is still sweeter.

Fifteen years after Sonny O'Neill's death Johnny Collins also died, on 30 January 1965, just when Jim Hurley, who in his lifetime had become one of Cork's legends of hurling, was diagnosed as having cancer. He went to Mount Mellary on a two-day retreat and, on his return, finding that his case was worse than had been feared, and that he had only days to live, sent for Michael Collins, who as a boy had once told him where Johnny Collins lived. Hurley wanted Michael to go to the parish priest to get him to intercede with the man who owned the plot beside the one Johnny Collins was buried in to sell it to him. 'Tell him I want to be buried beside Shafter.'[13] Hurley got his wish and today lies in Clonakilty churchyard alongside Michael Collins' brother. No shadow from Bael na mBlath falls over those graves. It appears that 'The great Irish whodunnit' mystery was largely fuelled by a decent West Cork reticence.

And by an IRB reticence. It was not to be supposed that the Brotherhood would make no effort to find out how its President died. Despite civil war and subsequent Army divisions and dissolutions the inquiry was pursued. Finally in 1966, the fiftieth anniversary of the 1916 Rising, Collins' old friend, Sean McGarry, who was also a President of the IRB, persuaded the doctor who had examined Collins' body in Shanakiel Hospital to record his account of the examination. Dr Cagney (whose willingness to talk after a lifetime's silence may have been prompted by the fact that he had just retired) bore out Dr Harbinson's description of the effects of a high velocity rifle bullet. Dr Cagney, who had served through the Great War and had 'a wide knowledge of bullet wounds' told McGarry that Collins was killed by a .303 rifle bullet. The bullet entered behind the left ear, making a small entrance wound, and exited above the left ear making 'a ragged wound' on the left side of his head. Collins' long hair hid the entrance wound. It was his fate to die, almost accidentally, in his home county, at the hands of men who admired him, in one of the most avoidable, badly organised ambushes of the period. Any one of his assailants could have fired the fatal shot. None of them would have been proud to do so.

What would have happened if Collins had lived? This again is a question asked incessantly in Ireland and though I have already dealt exhaustively with questions of speculation, and hesitate to weary the reader any further with issues which, by definition, must be totally matters of opinion, some evaluation is called for. Obviously he had a greater grasp of economics than his contemporaries and would have brought more drive, efficiency and imagination to bear upon the task of building up the country after the civil war than did anyone in any government or party that came after him. My opinion, and it has to be purely based on speculation, is that Ireland would have benefited enormously had he lived. Unlike de Valera whose talent lay in getting and holding power, Collins asked himself the question, 'All this for what?', and tried to provide the answers. However practical or impractical his recorded ideas may have been they were the thoughts of a still-young man, capable of great development; a man who, in the eye of the storm, was able to take time to try to plot a course for his people and his country. Certainly he would not have been solely dependent on Department of Finance civil servants for his economic policies as was every leader of the country who came after him except Sean Lemass. And Lemass once told[15] Collins' nephew, Michael Collins, that his economic philosophy was derived from a study of *The Path to Freedom*, a compendium of Collins' thoughts on cultural and economic matters, published as a pamplet.[16]

His philosophy was an extraordinary mixture of Gaelic revivalism, *perestroika*, the Sinn Fein 'we ourselves' approach and an idiosyncratic common sense. Collins took his starting point from the differences between British and Irish culture. 'The Romans did not come to Ireland . . . Gaelic civilisation was quite different. Their unity was not of any military solidarity. It came from sharing the same traditions . . . They never exalted a central authority . . . The land belonged to the people . . . held for the people by the Chief of the Clan.' He wanted to restore a 'democratic social polity, with the exaltation of the things of the mind and character . . . the essence of ancient Irish civilisation . . . must provide the keynote of the new.' Some would dismiss this sort of thing as mere Gaelic revivalism but Collins gave examples of what he meant:

English civilisation . . . for us . . . is a misfit. . . . the Irish . . . qualities are hidden, besmirched, by that what has been imposed upon us, just as the fine, splendid surface of Ireland is besmirched by our towns and villages – hideous medleys of contemptible dwellings and mean shops and squalid public houses. We are now free in name. The extent to which we become free in fact and secure our freedom will be the extent to which we become Gaels again . . . The biggest task will be the restoration of the language.

Collins made it clear that he did not see the language being restored for generations and then as matter of political and economic necessity as much as out of cultural desirability, to enable people to act in an innovative Irish way: 'Economically we must be democratic, as in the past . . . The people must become again the "guardians of their law and of their land".' The peculiarly Irish form of democratisation would ensure capital was not 'allowed to be an evil'. A co-operative system would mean 'our countrysides would cease to be the torpid deserts they are now, giving the means of existence and nothing more'. Agriculture was to be 'improved and developed'. Transportation, water power, harbours too. Foreign trade was to be stimulated by 'making facilities for the transport and marketing of Irish goods abroad and foreign goods in Ireland'. Investors must be encouraged to invest Irish capital in Irish concerns. 'Taxation, where it hinders must be adjusted.' He advocated land reform, breaking up the big estates, 'the ranches' and studying Denmark's, Holland's, and Germany's farming methods so as to promote agri-business, specifically, meat processing, cheese-making and dairying and a range of downstream activities, including agricultural machinery. He recommended that factories should 'as far as possible' be dispersed about the country instead of being concentrated in a few areas, both to avoid congestion, improve the earning power of the rural population and 'enlarge their horizon'.

No potential area of development was left unconsidered, be it forestry, minerals, marketing, or the expansion of Dublin port. He drew attention to the vast amount of money (£194 million in banks and £14 million post office deposits) 'lying idle in banks', the huge capital outflows and forecast 'with scope for our energies, with restoration of confidence, the inevitable tendency will be towards a return of this capital to Ireland.' He had detailed plans for developing industry, using hydro-electric power – 'the white coal of Ireland'.[17] He wanted to avoid both State socialism which he saw as merely another form of monopoly, and industrial development along 'the old commercial capitalistic lines of the huge joint stock companies':

We all realise that the industrial status quo is imperfect . . . one of the most pressing needs – if not the most pressing – is the question of labour in relation to industry, and it is consequently vitally necessary for the development of our resources that the position of employers and employees should rest on the best possible foundation.

He proposed that: 'we must not have state Departments headed by a politician whose only qualification is that he has climbed to a certain rung in the political ladder.' Government should be democratic and 'carry out for them all, and only, what is needed to be done for the people as a whole. It must not interfere with what the people can do for themselves in their own centres.'

'Our external life,' he said:

has become the expression of all we have been deprived of – something shapeless, ugly, without native life . . . Irish art and Irish customs must be revived, and must be carried out by the people themselves, helped by a central Government, not controlled and managed by it; helped by departments of music, art, national painting etc. Everybody being able to contribute we would have a skilled audience criticising and appreciating, and not only, as in England, paying for seats to hear famous performers.

His development plans were all set in a united Ireland context. The rivers Erne and Bann lie in the Six Counties but in 1922 Collins was writing about methods which would 'utilise the water-power of the

Shannon, the Erne, the Bann and the Liffey. It is probable that the Liffey and the Bann, being closely connected with urban centres can be dealt with at once.' His abiding belief was that 'a prosperous Ireland will mean a united Ireland. With equitable taxation and flourishing trade our North-East countrymen will need no persuasion to come in and share the healthy economic life of the country.'

It is easy to scoff at these ideas, or to point out the difficulties of implementing such schemes when actually running a normal peacetime Government. But Collins was a unique combination of the visionary and the practical. Throughout the difficulties of the Black and Tan war he had tried, through the underground Dail, to further constructive projects such as fishery development. But (on 11 March 1921) he recommended that all work on fisheries should cease because 'it was too big a problem in present circumstances'. The fishing schemes had all been 'disastrous to the reputation of the Dail'. Their failure, he said, 'all arose from the dishonesty on the part of the fishermen'. The man who propelled his country into the Black and Tan war, so that she might win her freedom to carry out such plans, and who also, while on the run, showed the practical ability to float a successful national loan, would have tackled fishery and allied problems with renewed force and insight when circumstances permitted. As the remarkable, lengthy memorandum on propaganda, mentioned earlier, which he wrote to Desmond Fitz-gerald[18] on 12 July 1922 (the same day that the War Council was announced), demonstrates, he had detailed, well-thought-out proposals for a campaign of films, posters and press publicity to win the people to these ideas.

Collins had political skills and powers of oratory of which the least that can be said is that he was better equipped than most men to make his dreams come true. Birkenhead was so impressed by a speech Collins gave in Cork (to the accompaniment of volleys fired over the heads of his hearers by a party of Irregulars who were trying to stampede them) that he paid him a remarkable compliment in the House of Lords (on 16 March 1922) when he told his peers that anyone who read

that speech delivered by a man without political education and, so far as I know, without very much other education will consider that it is a speech which, whether you examine the form of its literary expression, or its judgement of affairs, no member of this House need be ashamed of having delivered.

But the effect of the civil war has to be reckoned with in assessing the climate Collins would have had to work in. Estimates of the death toll vary[19] from around 1,000 to as many as 4,000 lives. The financial cost[20] was around £47 million, an appalling sum for those days. The cost in idealism, energy, and enthusiasm was probably higher.

Bitterness, cynicism, disillusionment, emigration, censorship, clericalism and stagnation became the hallmarks of Irish society until Lemass got control and age began to prise the civil war generation's fingers from the levers of power in the Sixties. And even then the spurt of prosperity was but short-lived. At the time of writing unemployment figures are nearly 100,000 higher than they were when the Labour Party made its appeal for alleviation in the days after the Treaty was first ratified.[21] For as the poets and the warriors fell by the wayside the bureaucrats took over.

The saga of poor Joe O'Reilly efforts to buy the meagre furnishings of his late Commander-in-Chief's bedroom at Portobello, is instructive. After much internal memo-writing Joe gave up in disgust. Then Collins' sister, Mrs Margaret O'Driscoll, learned of the story and made an offer. It was decided to give the furnishings to her at a reasonable figure, but someone in authority intervened. The articles had been offered to Colonel O'Reilly for a higher sum. He would have cause for complaint if they went to someone else for less. O'Reilly of course would have given them to any member of Collins' family for nothing, but more memo-writing followed before a formula was arrived at whereby Mrs O'Driscoll got the old bed, the battered wardrobe, and the washhand-basin stand at the price they were offered to Joe but 50 per cent more than she would have had to pay if the deal had not been interfered with. In all, the transaction generated a total of twenty-four letters, costing far more in civil servants' time than the furniture was worth. Just as Joe O'Reilly's face at the Collins funeral was a paradigm of Ireland's grief so does his attempt to buy some mementoes of his fallen Chief illustrate how the State that emerged from the civil war frustrated Ireland's imagination.

Collins himself might have been similarly frustrated, despite his mighty powers. The sheer strength of the forces massed against him in the North make it very hard to see how his efforts to achieve unity by force could have succeeded. He might have succeeded in destabilising the Northern statelet in the same way as the Provisional IRA have done, possibly to a greater extent, as the Catholics of all classes were more united in opposing partition then than now. But to have proceeded thus would inevitably have turned his Cabinet colleagues against him and left him dependent for support on the Army, and the more militant Republicans. This could have had harmful consequences for the development of that native Irish democracy which, despite all the problems Ireland has faced and is facing, is probably Michael Collins' most enduring testament. The evidence, however, appears to be inescapable that, the civil war won, his reaction during times of pogrom or rioting directed against Catholics would have been to turn to his Joe Dolans and Liam Tobins to deal with figures like Dawson-Bates or DI Nixon as he had with Wilson and nearly with the two hangmen. It does appear that had he lived he would certainly have made greater efforts to bring about unity than anyone who came after him. He would not have allowed an apartheid state to be erected in Northern Ireland without making serious, sustained, and perhaps violent protest. Writing about the IRB Sean O'Muirthle made what I feel is a highly significant comment: 'I think had Collins lived that he would have made further use of the Organisation towards achieving still further freedom.'[23] Collins would have had to resolve within himself the tensions of his dual role. Head of a democratic Government, head of a secret society which in fact regarded itself as a Government within a Government. Conspirator versus democrat. Destroyer versus builder. He might not have been able to resolve these conflicts and might have disintegrated in drink or disillusionment. On the other hand a period of rest and peace would have given him an opportunity to do many things himself, and to prevent others doing much that was harmful. Certainly it is reasonable to speculate on the basis of what is known of his character that he would have opposed executions such as those of Childers, Rory O'Connor and the others. It would be wrong to think he would not have prosecuted the war ruthlessly and vigorously. But merely by being there his personality and leadership would have provided a better rallying point for the forces in the country opposed to war's continuation than were his successors. Ironically it was his death and the leadership vacuum it created on the Provisional Government's side that helped to create the situation in which the Government felt it necessary to introduce a policy of reprisal executions, selecting firing squad victims from the ranks of men already in prison, either to make a point by shooting leaders, as in O'Connor's case, or to bring terror to a locality where some Irregular killings had occurred. Those who came after him had resolution but neither his charisma nor the military prowess whereby peace might have been had by other means.

With Collins gone the major political personality left in the Free State was on the other side, de Valera. His reaction to the news of Collins' death was reminiscent of his nervous attack during 1916. The leader of the eight-man escort party[24] which accompanied him across country from Fethard in County Tipperary to Callan, County Kilkenny, from whence he was smuggled to Dublin, has described how he behaved the day after Bael na mBlath. De Valera indicated that he wanted to travel alone and the party leader respected his wishes, keeping within earshot but not talking to him, while the other seven scouted well ahead:

Quite a lot of the 15 or so miles to Callan were done on foot across country and during that time de Valera seemed very distressed and he appeared to be talking or muttering to himself. Several times when he spoke out loud, not addressing me or anybody in the escort, I distinctly heard him say, 'I told them not to do it, even pleaded with them, but they wouldn't listen to me and now what will become of us all.' Dev was so distressed that when he spoke out I felt he was crying.

De Valera knew of course that news of his presence in Bael na mBlath might well seal his death warrant. In fact a local priest, Canon Cohalan of Bandon, preached a famous sermon in which he thundered: 'The day Michael Collins was killed where was de Valera? Ask the people of Bael na mBlath and they will tell you. There was a scowling face at a window looking out over that lonely valley and de Valera could tell who it was.' But he speedily recovered his composure. He had spent the night before the ambush with a family called O'Sullivan who got a letter from him a few days later asking for his binoculars to be sent on to him. Both letter and binoculars were retained.[25] But de Valera had better fortune in efforts to regain power. His pacific arguments of August had not found acceptance. A line more likely to secure extremist support was again espoused with such success that by January 1923 he had regained influence once more with the Republican military leadership to a point where he was in a position to draft a statement for Liam Lynch rejecting peace proposals. Liam Deasy, who had become increasingly disenchanted with the war, after capture had issued a statement to his fellow officers deploring the conflict which he thought had reached the stage where it might lead to British being welcomed back with more enthusiasm than was shown for their departure.[26] De Valera promptly drew up a statement rejecting Deasy's initiative with a covering letter in which he argued that peace without political advantage to his side would be 'awful'.[27] Lynch issued the statement verbatim and the civil war continued uselessly for four more months.

It ended in May 1923 leaving de Valera the undisputed leader on the Republican side. Persuaded by Sean Lemass that he should form a Constitutional Party, he did so and cut loose from his IRA following and the support of figures like Stack and Mary MacSwiney to form Fianna Fail in 1926. He then led his party into the Dail and took the Oath. Asked once[28] how he could square taking the Oath with his civil war position, he replied, 'I didn't really take an Oath. My fingers didn't touch the Bible'.

Worsening economic conditions, Kevin O'Higgins' murder in 1927 and the accidental death of Patrick Hogan, the Government's able Minister of Agriculture, combined with the hostility generated by the Government's repressive policy and the post-1929 global economic crash, all helped de Valera to oust Cosgrave at the general election of 1932, a contingency Cosgrave foresaw when he introduced legislation in 1927, after O'Higgins' murder, forcing elected representatives either to take the Oath or forfeit their seats.

Once in power, taking advantage of Britain's preoccupation with the Abdication crisis, de Valera introduced a more sectarian, but republican-sounding, Constitution which abolished the Oath and the Governor General, and stands to this day. He faced the issue of the Second Authority as ruthlessly as did his predecessors, using both internment and the death penalty to deal with the IRA. Under de Valera, Ireland continued to evolve as a sovereign, democratic state, very much as Collins had argued that it would, albeit far more inefficiently run and depending on emigration to supply de Valera's lack of an economic philosophy which Collins did have the ability to provide. The real scandal of the Treaty, partition, remained unaffected by his posturings and *volte face*. The Border was not altered by one millimetre throughout de Valera's long reign.

If one overlooks de Valera's behaviour over the Treaty and the civil war his sheer durability has to be acknowledged. His courage in controlling a nervous temperament and in fighting the blindness that affected him increasingly from the start of the Second World War, his successful struggle to maintain Irish neutrality, all speak of a man who contained within himself elements of greatness. In one area however, his attitude to Michael Collins, he consistently showed the small-mindedness of a guilty conscience.

In 1935 Joe McGrath, by then a millionaire through the operation of the Irish Hospitals Sweepstakes, mooted the idea to Johnny Collins of putting a marble cross over Collins' grave.[29] A similar proposal[30] had been put forward by Tim Healy, then Governor General, in the wake of the civil war. He said he was 'acting on behalf of an American lady who wished to remain anonymous'. Mulcahy, seeing Lady Lavery's Chicago origins looming behind the suggestion, discreetly declined the offer 'on behalf of the military Council', saying that as the grave was still in use for military casualties no plans for a memorial could be entertained at that time. McGrath had bought a quarter of a ton of Carrera marble and he offered both to donate this and defray the costs of shipping it from Italy for the memorial cross. As Collins was buried in a military grave, Johnny wrote on 13 February 1935 for the necessary permission to Frank Aiken, who was acting as Minister for Defence at the time:

The brothers and sisters of the late General Michael Collins intend to have erected, as soon as the necessary arrangements are completed, a monument over his grave in Glasnevin cemetery.

The plot in which the remains have been interred was purchased by the late Government for the State and being now I understand, vested in and maintained by the Department of Defence, I would like to know if you as the Minister responsible for the administration of that Department would have any objection to the proposal referred to above. Hoping for a reply at your earliest convenience.[31]

The reaction to this proposal may be gauged both from the tone of the reply from Aiken's secretary and its date, 3 June 1935, which indicates how the term 'earliest convenience' was interpreted:

With reference to your letter of the 13th February last and your subsequent conversation with the Minister relative to the erection of a monument on the grave of the late General Michael Collins in Glasnevin Cemetery, I am directed by the Minister for Defence to inform you that generally the erection of monuments other than those erected by the State is not permitted.

In view of the representations made on behalf of your family, however, the Minister will offer no objection to the erection of a monument if it is still your intention to do so.

However, more than three years later, we find Johnny still writing to Aiken for help in cutting through red tape. The Dublin Cemeteries Committee had objected to the fact that the base proposed for the monument would encroach three inches on the space on either side of the grave:

The Collins grave plot is 4 ft in width and 8 ft in depth and the 'Celtic Cross' intended to be erected thereon will be 11°6' in height and the sculptor has specified for a minimum base of 4°6' x 3°0' x 1°3' high. While the plot in its present layout is fully that width the committee will not allow the foundation of the monument to exceed 4° without Government authority.[32]

On 4 March 1939 Aiken's secretary was authorised to write to the Secretary of the Dublin Cemeteries Committee as follows: 'The Minister appreciates that a base 4°6' wide will encroach on the paths on each side of the grave to an extent of 3', but as it is improbable that the paths will ever be used as a burial ground, he has agreed to the proposal.'[33]

But the foregoing correspondence, indicative of delay and reluctance though it is, does not reveal anything like the full extent of de Valera's vindictiveness and pettiness in the memorial saga. Firstly the letters do not reveal the fact that at one stage the Collinses considered legal action as a method of forcing the Government to abandon the delaying tactics. Katie, then Mrs Sheridan, normally the most pacific of the girls, had become outraged at the treatment of her 'Tom Tulliver'. But Johnny Collins persuaded Katie and his other sisters to be patient while he continued the negotiations personally. In 1938 he saw de Valera twice in connection with the project. During the visit he merely listened to the proposition and said he would consider it. When he sent for Johnny the second time he agreed to the erection of the cross but with a number of stipulations. He would not agree to the use of marble, but to a limestone cross and surrounds not exceeding £300 in cost. There was to be no public subscription and no publicity. The inscription was to be totally in Irish in front. The inscription on the back had to include 'M. Collins erected by his brother and sisters'. The inscription in Irish had to be approved by him. He then went on, 'I am sorry to have to say no member of your family may be present except yourself. The Cross can be blessed by the chaplain to the cemetery and an altar boy will be necessary to carry Holy Water.'

Johnny asked, 'What about Nancy and my sisters', to which the reply was, 'Nobody but yourself can be present.'

When Nancy heard the story she at first refused to believe Johnny and then commented: 'It's not Miceal who's being belittled. He's letting himself down.' I too found the story hard to accept at first (though of course the last of the illustrations in this book speaks for itself), but through the courtesy of the cemetery staff at Glasnevin I eventually discovered a certificate of authorisation, describing the cross's dimensions and inscription. It is dated 31 July 1939 and signed by Eamon de Valera. With a final Machiavellian touch, to cover himself against a charge of pettiness at having the Prime Minister of the country interest himself in such a matter on the eve of a new world war, he describes himself as 'acting Minister for Finance'.

The wording which de Valera agreed to and which appears on the cross is (front): '*Indil-cuimne ar Miceal O'Coileain a rugad an 12ad la de mi deiread Fogmair, 1890, agus d'eag an 22ad la de mi Lugnasa, 1922.*' (In English this inscription says: 'In loving memory of Michael Collins who was born on 12 October 1890, and who died on 22nd August 1922'.) Below it, another inscription in Irish says: '*Go dtugaid Dia suaimneas Siorraide da anam* (May God give him eternal happiness).' At the bottom it says: 'Erected by his brothers and sisters'. On the back of the cross the wording is: 'Michael Collins' and then, in Irish, '*A Dia Dein Trocaire Orainn*' ('God have mercy on us').

The irony is that Johnny would never have allowed anything controversial to appear on the gravestone anyhow. Whenever memorials were erected to Michael in other parts of the country he insisted that the only wording to appear should be the name, and the dates of birth and death, nothing about the circumstances of the latter. However de Valera's stipulations were met. When the limestone cross was erected in 1939[34] the only persons present apart from Johnny, the priest and the altar boy were the foreman gravedigger, who had learned of the blessing, and a passing gravedigger. He asked, 'Where are the press?' and when he heard that none were allowed, exclaimed, 'Poor Mick, I've tended his grave since '22,' and got a passing tourist to take the picture reproduced in this book. Johnny's son, Michael, who was thirteen at the time told me: 'It was the first time my father looked old. He was terribly hurt.' However there was little Johnny could do by the way of protest. The injury to his hand meant that he had had to give up the farm at Woodfield and take a job as a civil servant in the Department of Lands where he, with a new family to rear, was in no position to fight de Valera. Later, when he had retired and returned to live with Nancy at Clonakilty, Oscar Traynor called on him. Traynor, who succeeded Aiken as Minister for Defence at the outbreak of the Second World War, was the Minister whom Johnny had approached in the first place; he had to see to it that de Valera's wishes were followed. Traynor, who had also retired at the time of his visit to Johnny and Nancy, said the cross decision had been the hardest of his life to implement. To give an idea of the scale of attendance which might have been expected at the erection of a cross over Collins' grave, it might be noted that there were tens of thousands from all over the country at the unveiling of a memorial at Sam's Cross in 1965. Masses were said in over seventy churches in West Cork alone.

The pettiness over the cross was no isolated incident. Representatives of the Army were forbidden to attend the annual commemoration service for their first Commander-in-Chief at Bael na mBlath as late as 1971. And in 1965 an official guide book, *Facts about Ireland*, produced by the Department of Foreign Affairs, had to be reprinted after controversy broke out over the exclusion of Collins' picture. Frank Aiken, then Minister for Foreign Affairs, was blamed for this but the omission occurred after consultation with de Valera.[35] There was no publicity, however, over a more significant example of de Valera's rancour which occurred a year later in 1966, the 50th anniversary of the Rising.[36] As late as 1990, there was controversy as to whether or not the President would attend the ceremony for handing over Woodfield, the Collins family home, to the nation. There was further controversy and uncertainty as to whether the Army would be allowed to attend at Woodfield or at the annual commemoration ceremony this year at Bael na mBlath. Hitherto, although under the Coalition Government an Army presence had been allowed, Fianna Fail had only permitted the Army one appearance at Bael na mBlath, on the fiftieth anniversary of Collins' death.

Joe McGrath had wanted to forge ahead with his memorial project, only on a far grander scale, at Sam's Cross. But when he consulted Johnny in 1964 Johnny made a characteristic reply. 'Joe, you've still more money than sense. Why not start a trust fund that would educate some bright boys.' In 1966 McGrath was told that he had only a few months to live and he sent for Johnny's son, Michael, by now one of Ireland's leading chartered accountants, to develop the idea. It was decided that Sean T. O'Kelly whom de Valera had succeeded as President should be approached to be a patron and then de Valera himself. O'Kelly subscribed five pounds, which was a notable gesture for him as he had a legendary tight-fistedness. But the patronage was of short standing. O'Kelly pulled out saying, 'He'd be furious if he knew I agreed', immediately on hearing de Valera's reaction to the proposal. McGrath had gone to him, telling him the state of his health, and asking him to co-operate in the Foundation project by becoming a patron, saying, 'My days are numbered and there's no differences in the grave.'

De Valera paused before replying to the suggestion. It had been his Karma to live a long and distinguished public life. Although he was then in his eighty-fifth year he was looking forward to a second seven-year term as President of Ireland. But he knew that before the bar of history his name and fame were inextricably linked and threatened by a handful of years' association with a man whose allotted span had been destined to be but a third of his own. He knew that the story of Eamon de Valera could not be told without that of Michael Collins. Already he had embarked on what he knew in his heart was a futile effort to influence the record for the benefit of posterity. His newspaper and political empires had published innumerable favourable articles, histories and recollections. And in the years ahead he planned to ensure that much more favourable comment and chronology would be collated and set down. He had fashioned a vigorous dialectic of de Valerism that would bulwark him against critical re-appraisal long into the future. But de Valera was a realist, a man whose doodlings on the back of documents took the form of mathematical symbols. He realised only too well that his party, his newspapers, his Constitution even, had grown out of his opposition to Michael Collins and the resultant civil war. He knew that eventually, in the truthful telling of history, two and two would make four. Torn between his own clarity of vision and the myths he had spun around himself, de Valera struggled painfully for words to express himself. Then he said: 'I can't see my way to becoming Patron of the Michael Collins Foundation. It's my considered opinion that in the fullness of time history will record the greatness of Collins and it will be recorded at my expense.' He could be right.

Notes

Abbreviations

pps	papers
AUTHOR	Copy in author's possession
AUTHOR'S	Original in author's possession
BMH	Irish Bureau of Military History
CAB	Cabinet Minutes
CO	Cabinet Office
NG	National Gallery of Ireland
NL	National Library of Ireland
PG	Provisional Government Minutes
PRO	Public Records Office
PRONI	Public Records Office, Belfast
SPO	State Papers Office, Dublin
SO	Stationery Office, Dublin
TCDU	Dublin University, Trinity College archives
UCD	University College Dublin archives

NOTE: where diaries are quoted, which may be available in several editions, entry dates are given rather than page numbers.

Chapter 1 (pp. 3-31)

1. Major Sirr pps, Manuscripts Division, TCDU.
2. Mary Collins-Powell was a sister of Collins who helped him in both the Anglo-Irish and the Irish civil wars. Her memoir was compiled for her grandchildren and distributed by her granddaughter, Deirdre Collins-Powell. AUTHOR.
3. Details of Collins' early life compiled from family sources and earlier biographical works, notably those written by Piaras Beaslai, Frank O'Connor, Rex Taylor and Margery Forester: see Bibliography, p. 458.
4. Memoir of Collins' sister, Sister Celestine, known to the family as 'Lena, short for Helena, written in longhand. It was subsequently photostated and circulated within the family. AUTHOR.
5. Mary Collins-Powell memoir.
6. By Rex Taylor, in *Michael Collins*, Four Square, 1961, p. 24.
7. On microfilm, National Library Dublin.
8. Mary Collins-Powell memoir.
9. Mary Collins-Powell memoir.
10. *West Cork People*, the week after her death, 14/4/07.
11. Told to author by Michael Collins, nephew.
12. Sr Celestine memoir.
13. Margery Forester, *Michael Collins: The Lost Leader*, Sphere, 1972, p. 13.
14. At the time, 9/3/22, O'Brien was a magistrate in Kenya. Letter AUTHOR'S.
15. Sr Celestine memoir.
16. This is the quotation from Wolfe Tone's writings most favoured by republicans. For a more rounded view of Tone's work, see the authoritative biography, *Wolfe Tone*, by Marianne Elliot, Yale University Press, 1989.
17. In Frongoch internment camp, writing to Kevin O'Brien, 16/10/16. Quoted by Taylor p. 25.

18. Piaras Beaslai, *Michael Collins and the Making of a New Ireland*, Phoenix, 1926, Vol. 1, p. 11.
19. Quoted by Forester, p. 12.
20. For a history of Bandon and account of life there during the period under review, *see There is a Bridge at Bandon*, by Kathleen Keyes McDonnell, Mercier Press, 1972).
21. J.B. Armour, *Against the Tide*, PRO, 1985.
22. 'Dublin', from 'The Closing Album', 1939, in *Louis MacNeice: Selected Poems*, (ed.) Michael Longley, Faber, 1988, pp. 74–5.
23. Quoted in Mary Collins-Powell memoir.
24. A fortnight before he died de Wet sent a message of congratulation to Collins, 21/1/22, in reply to Collins' letter to his boyhood hero.
25. Frank O'Connor, *The Big Fellow*, Corgi, 1969, pps. 52–3.
26. Collins family papers, quoted by Taylor, p. 27.
27. *Ibid.*
28. Quoted by Forester, p. 16.
29. Eoin MacNeill to A. MacBride, MacNeill pps, U.C.D.
30. '. . . . the printed sources were either vague, or differed in their information. We therefore opted for only recording those years for which we had some real evidence in the form, I think, of his name appearing in the voters' lists. He may very well have resided there over a longer period than that'. Letter to author, from Christopher Jeens, Borough Archivist, 24/4/89. The unveiling of the plaque was marked by a stage presentation commemorating Collins' life and death, commissioned by Hammersmith and Fulham Libraries Department. It was described as 'being very well attended.'
31. *West Cork People*, obituary and report of Marianne Collins' funeral, 16/4/07.
32. AUTHOR'S.
33. Beaslai, Vol. 1, p. 16.
34. AUTHOR: original in N.L. MS 13329.
35. Collins also became a member of the Chancery Lane Club of Sinn Fein. Further details of his life at this stage are available in the MacEoin pps, Franciscan Archives, Killiney; O'Muirthle memoir, Mulcahy pps, UCD; in P.S. O'Hegarty's *The Victory of Sinn Fein* and in biographies by Beaslai, O'Connor, Taylor and Forester.
36. P. 2 of undated letter to unnamed friend. Quoted by Taylor, p.32.
37. Quoted by Forester, p. 30.
38. O'Connor, p. 19.
39. Collins to Susan Killeen, 28/8/16, from Frongoch, AUTHOR'S.
40. Robert Mackey, Assistant Manager of the Guaranty Trust. Quoted by Brendan O'Reilly in Beal na mBlath Oration, 24/8/80. Also available in full, Collins pps, SPO.
41. O'Connor, p. 19.
42. O'Hegarty, *The Victory of Sinn Fein*, Talbot Press, 1924, p.23.
43. Collins to Susan Killeen, AUTHOR.
44. O'Hegarty, p. 139.
45. Dorothy Macardle, *The Irish Republic*, 4th edition, Irish Press, 1951, p. 50.
46. John McCoy memoir, AUTHOR'S.
47. W.S. Churchill, *Lord Randolph Churchill*, 2 vols, Odhams, 1906, vol. 11, p. 59.

48. *Ibid*, p. 65.
49. A.T.Q. Stewart, *The Ulster Crisis* Faber, 1967, p. 55.
50. Quoted by Patrick Buckland, *Ulster Unionism*, Gill & Macmillan, 1973, p. 54.
51. O'Connor, p. 57.
52. Quoted by A.T.Q. Stewart, *Edward Carson*, Gill & Macmillan, 1981, p. 39.
53. Buckland, p. 55.
54. Quoted by Stewart, *Edward Carson*, p. 27.
55. *Ibid*, p. 26.
56. Quoted by Bucknell *op. cit.*, p. 85.
57. Major the Hon. Gerald French, *The Life of Field-Marshal Sir John French, First Earl of Ypres*, Cassell, 1931, p. 193.
58. A.T.Q. Stewart's *Ulster Crisis* gives a first-class account of the entire gun-running saga.
59. Quoted by Stephen Gwynne, *Life of John Redmond*, Harrap, 1932, p. 211.
60. Quoted by Macardle, p. 92.
61. Forester, p. 29. However a note in the MacEoin pps, Franciscan Archives, Killiney, states that in 1913 Edward Lee proposed Collins for command of the company of Volunteers which Collins helped to found at 28 Princes Rd, Notting Hill – an appropriate address for a man who told William Darling (Quoted by O'Broin pp. 82–3) that one of his favourite books was Chesterton's *Napoleon of Notting Hill*.
62. Macardle, p. 92.
63. The 1916 Rising preparations are described in several works: *see* especially Leon O'Broin's *Dublin Castle and the 1916 Rising*, Helicon, 1966; Diarmuid Lynch's *The I.R.B. and the 1916 Rising*, (ed.) O'Donoghue, Mercier Press, n.d. Lynch was a senior member of the I.R.B. Max Caulfield's *The Easter Rebellion*, Four Square, 1965; Tim Pat Coogan's *Ireland Since the Rising*, Greenwood Press, Connecticut, 1976, or is *The I.R.A.* Fontana, 1970 and subsequent editions.
64. Collins pps, SPO.
65. Quoted by T. Ryle Dwyer, *Michael Collins and the Treaty*, Mercier Press, 1981, p. 5.

Chapter 2 (pp. 32–57)

1. P. S. O'Hegarty, *The Victory of Sinn Fein*, Talbot Press, 1924, pp. 24–5.
2. 'The Path of Freedom,' Talbot Press, 1922, p. 130.
3. Mulcahy pps, UCD.
4. Margery Forester, *Michael Collins: The Lost Leader*, Sphere, 1971, p. 38.
5. C. Desmond Greaves' *The Life and Times of James Connolly*, Lawrence & Wishart, 1961, or Emmet Larkin's *James Larkin*, Routledge & Kegan Paul, 1965 are both recommended for their graphic, authoritative portraits of the Dublin of the period.
6. Coogan, *Ireland Since the Rising*, Greenwood Press, 1976, p. 19.
7. Forester, p. 32.
8. See Stephen Gwynne's *Life of John Redmond*, Harrap, 1932 for the effect of the conscription crisis on Redmond's authority.
9. David Lloyd George, *War Memoirs*, new edition, 2 vols, Odhams, 1934, Vol. 1, p. 417.
10. *Ibid*, p. 453.

11. Birrell's role in the 1916 crisis is well drawn by O'Broin in *Dublin Castle and the 1916 Rising* and particularly so in *The Chief Secretary*, Sidgwick & Jackson, 1969, a biography of Birrell.
12. MacCullough to author: *see Ireland Since the Rising*, p. 10.
13. Col Pat Collins, Nancy's stepson, to author.
14. Forester, p. 48.
15. *Ibid*, p. 42.
16. Dorothy Macardle, *The Irish Republic*, 4th edition, Irish Press, 1951, p. 37.
17. Frank O'Connor, *The Big Fellow*, Corgi, 1969, p. 27.
18. Desmond Fitzgerald, Memoirs, UCD, 1969.
19. Rex Taylor, *Michael Collins*, Four Square, 1961, p. 49.
20. Eamon de Valera to Sinead, dated Easter Saturday, 1917, AUTHOR.
21. Max Caulfield's account of what happened under de Valera's command is especially vivid: *see The Easter Rebellion*, Four Square, 1965, pp. 270–77.
22. *Ibid*, p. 277.
23. Mulcahy pps, UCD.
24. Caulfield, p. 280.
25. O'Connor, pp. 31–2.
26. Desmond Ryan, *Michael Collins and the Invisible Army*, Anvil, n.d., p. 24.
27. To Sean Deasey, undated, quoted by Taylor, p. 33.
28. O'Connor, p. 32.
29. This officer's activities are well described in Ryan, p.34, and in Liam Tobin's unpublished memoir, prepared for BMH, AUTHOR.
30. Caulfield gives good descriptions of both the behaviour of the British troops in general and of Bowen Colthurst in particular.
31. Tobin memoir, AUTHOR.
32. Thornton memoir, BMH.
33. Piaras Beaslai, *Michael Collins and the Making of a New Ireland*, Phoenix, 1926, Vol.1, p. 106.
34. Taylor, p. 51.
35. O'Connor, p. 33.
36. Thornton memoir.
37. For the importance of prison in the lives of Republican prisoners and to the Republican movement generally, *see*: Tom Clarke's *Leaves from an Irish Felon's Prison Diary*, Maunsel, 1962; Tim Pat Coogan's *On the Blanket*, Ward River, 1980 and *The I.R.A.*, Pall Mall, 1970; and Sean O'Mahony's first-class *Frongoch: University of Revolution*, FDR, 1987.
38. Quoted by Forester, pp. 50–51.
39. Ryan, *Remembering Sion*, Barker, 1934, p. 215.
40. Forester, p. 51.
41. Collins to Susan Killeen, Stafford Jail, 27/5/16, AUTHOR.
42. *Ibid*, 1/6/16, AUTHOR.
43. The letter is undated, but mentions that it was written the day he arrived in Frongoch. So Susan's place in his affections obviously merited one of the first letters he wrote there.
44. Collins to Sean Deasey, n.d, quoted by Taylor, p. 55.
45. O'Mahony, pp. 100–101.
46. O'Connor, p. 108. Collins' wrestling prowess brought the IRA one of its most valuable recruits. Sean MacEoin (MacEoin pps, Franciscan Archives, Killiney) tells how he at first refused to join the Volunteers when Collins approached him, having got his name from Tom Clarke's list provided by Mrs Kathleen Clarke. He had promised his dying father that he would look after his widowed mother and her young family. After hours of argument Collins offered to settle the issue by a wrestling bout with MacEoin, a blacksmith. Collins won.
47. Roberts memoir, AUTHOR.
48. *Ibid*.
49. Collins to Susan Killeen, Frongoch, 21/9/16.
50. 3/8/16.
51. Macardle, pp. 160–1.
52. Caulfield, p. 362.
53. *Ibid*, p. 366.
54. Quoted by Freida Kelly, in *A History of Kilmainham Jail*, Mercier Press, 1988, p. 107. Also in 'The Last Words', (ed.) P.F. MacLouchlain, Kilmainham Jail Restoration Committee, 1971, p. 28.
55. Collins to Kevin O'Brien, Frongoch, 6/10/16 quoted by Taylor, p. 58.
56. O'Mahony, p. 66.
57. Coogan, *The I.R.A.*, p. 26.
58. Quoted by Forester, p. 54.
59. Collins to Hannie, 25/8/16 quoted by Forester, p, 54.
60. Collins to Susan Killeen, n.d., addressed as from Frongoch, AUTHOR.
61. Collins to Sean Deasey from Frongoch, 22/10/16, quoted by Taylor, p. 58.
62. O'Connor, p. 37.
63. Quoted by O'Mahony, p. 124.
64. O'Mahony, p. 125.
65. O'Connor, p. 37.
66. O'Connor, p. 30.

Chapter 3 (pp. 58–93)

1. Collins to Susan Killeen, 31/12/16.
2. On 20/9/13.
3. 27/5/16.
4. 30/5/16.
5. William O'Brien, *The Irish Revolution & How It Came About*, Allen & Unwin, 1923, p. 308.
6. The report by Fisher and his team, and subsequent appalled comments of Cabinet members, are recorded in the Leon O'Broin pps, NL.
7. 'The Path to Freedom' Talbot Press, 1922, p. 73.
8. In 1965, about the approaching fiftieth anniversary of the Rising.
9. 'The Path to Freedom', p. 74.
10. Brighid Lyons Thornton, quoted in Timothy O'Grady and Kenneth Griffith, *Curious Journey*, Hutchinson, 1982, p. 108. Further insights into Collins-Kiernan relationship are in MacEoin to Kevin McClory, MacEoin pps, Franciscan Archives, Killiney, and O'Connor, p. 158.
11. Lord Longford and T. P. O'Neill, *Eamon de Valera*, Gill & Macmillan, 1970, p. 57.
12. Authenticated by Mr Josh Honan, a son of de Valera's principal political worker in Clare, who was present when the incident occurred. Letter, 1/2/88, AUTHOR's.
13. Broy O'Malley, O'Malley pps, UCD.
14. What began as a series of interviews for my book

on the I.R.A. ultimately blossomed into his writing his own fascinating story, *The Spy in the Castle*, McGibbon & Kee, 1968.

15. David Neligan, *The Spy in the Castle*, p. 71.
16. *Ibid*, p. 74.
17. Piaras Beaslai, *Michael Collins and the Making of a New Ireland*, Phoenix, 1926, Vol. I, p. 212.
18. Mulcahy pps, UCD, AUTHOR.
19. Story told to author by Michael Collins, Nancy's son.
20. Beaslai article, 'Collins Memorial Supplement', *Irish Independent*, 20/8/66.
21. Details supplied to author by Liam O'Donnachadcha.
22. 15/2/21.
23. Report of meeting of Cork Commissioners, *Cork Examiner*, 11/10/66.
24. No minutes were issued for the ten meetings between 13/11/20 and 12/12/20. CAB 27, PRO, London.
25. 17/10/19, CAB 24, No. 89, PRO, London.
26. 11/11/19, CAB 24, No. 193, PRO, London.
27. Wilson's Irish anxieties are well documented in *American Opinion and the Irish Question* by Francis M. Carroll (Gill & Macmillan, 1978).
28. Wilson Diaries (Cassell, 1927), quoted by Dorothy Macardle, *The Irish Republic*, 4th edition, Irish Press, 1951, p. 253.
29. Sturgis Diaries, NL, 27/10/21.
30. CAB 27/69, PRO, London.
31. Collins to Stack, quoted by Margery Forester, *Michael Collins: The Lost Leader*, Sphere, 1972.
32. Michael Collins' election address, published by the *Southern Star*, Skibbereen, November 1918.
33. *Ibid*.
34. Shortt to PM, 4/7/18, Leon O'Broin pps, NL.

Chapter 4 (pp. 94-119)

1. In letter to Liam Tobin, 2/4/60, AUTHOR'S.
2. Murphy describes this and many other incidents involving Collins, in his unpublished autobiography, 'Murphy Beaucoup', AUTHOR.
3. Mulcahy pps, UCD, P7 D/38.
4. Michael Collins (nephew) to author.
5. Sr Margaret Mary and Liam O'Donnachadcha, a friend and relation of Nancy's, to author.
6. Barton pps, PRO, Dublin. Collins' concern for prisoners is well exemplified by correspondence with Barton's sister concerning Barton's welfare. In one letter (11/2/21) Collins asked her to 'please give him my fondest love – tell him I am constantly thinking of him and that he is no end of a loss to us', AUTHOR'S.
7. He was said to have offered a soldier £10 for a rifle. The court martial was evidently unaware that the tommies were only asking between five shillings and £2 for their weapons at the time.
8. Both Beaslai and Loughlinn McGlynn (in the authoritative *Sworn to be Free*, a compendium of IRA jail-breaks 1918–1921, Anvil, Tralee, 1971) give accounts of his imprisonment.
9. Frank O'Connor *The Big Fellow*, Corgi, 1969.
10. Piaras Beaslai, *Michael Collins and the Making of a New Ireland*, Phoenix, 1926, Vol. I, p. 241.
11. *Ibid*, Vol. I, p. 267.
12. Collins is also credited with being the chief architect of the escape in *Sworn to be Free*.

13. Beaslai, Vol. I, p. 269.
14. Lord Longford and T. P. O'Neill, *Eamon de Valera*, Gill & MacMillan, 1970, p. 87.
15. Eamon de Valera to Sinead, Lewes jail, Easter 1917, AUTHOR.
16. De Valera to Sinead, 24/8/18, AUTHOR.
17. An English reporter who asked him, 'what are Sinn Fein's objectives on reaching power?' received the immortal reply, 'Vingince, bejasus'! O'Keefe anecdote preserved in Collins family.
18. Lord Longford and T. P. O'Neill, p. 90.
19. Beaslai, Vol. I, p. 239.
20. Darrell Figgis, *Recollections of the Irish War*, quoted in *Arthur Griffith*, by Padraig Colum, Browne & Nolan, 1959, p. 193.
21. *Ibid*, p. 194.
22. Collins pps MS 1 17090, NL.
23. Minutes of Proceedings, Dail Eireann 1919–21, SO.
24. This is hardly surprising, as one of those who had a hand in its drafting was his fellow Frongoch graduate, the Labour leader, William O'Brien.
25. M. Goblet, *Irlande dans la crise universelle*, Félix Alan, Paris, 1921, pp. 356–7, quoted by Macardle, p. 276.
26. Brennan memoir, BMH.
27. Beaslai, who took part, refers to 'feeling disgusted with the atmosphere of mutual admiration' (Vol. I, p. 300).
28. Minutes of proceedings, Dail Eireann, 10/4/19, SO.
29. Dail proceedings, *op cit*.
30. *Ibid*.
31. Beaslai, Vol. I, p. 303.
32. Quoted by Margery Forester, in *Michael Collins: The Lost Leader*, Sphere, 1972, p. 101.
33. Barton letter to Margery Forester, 2/11/64, Barton pps, PRO, Dublin.
34. Quoted by Kathleen Napoli MacKenna, in Memoir, AUTHOR'S.
35. Uinseann MacEoin (ed.), *Survivors*, Argenta Press, 1980, 2nd edition 1987, p. 516.
36. Forester, p. 101.
37. Dorothy Macardle, *The Irish Republic*, 4th edition, Irish Press, 1951, p. 280.
38. AUTHOR'S.
39. CAB 27/69, PRO, London.
40. Dail Debates, 9/4/19.
41. Dail Eireann, 9/4/19, SO, p. 61, col. 2.
42. Un Uctbth, 1921, quoted by Leon O'Broin, *In Great Haste*, Gill & Macmillan, 1903, p. 23.
43. O'Connor, p. 55.
44. Eamon de Valera to Sinead, 2/6/19, AUTHOR.
45. The fact that Collins acquired this position is attested to by his fellow IRB Supreme Council member, Sean O'Muirthle, in his unpublished memoir (Mulcahy pps, UCD) and by authoritative contemporaries such as Beaslai.
46. Collins to Stack, 20/7/19, AUTHOR.
47. Daly memoir, BMH, copy in Mulcahy pps, UCD.
48. Interview with author, 14/1/88.
49. Broy to O'Malley, O'Malley notebooks, UCD.
50. CAB 24/92, PRO, London.
51. CAB 103, *ibid*.
52. Leon O'Broin pps, NL.

Chapter 5 (pp. 121–156)

1. 20/6/21 Original in O'Donoghue pps, NL, MS 31, 280 series.
2. The Flying Column idea has been variously attributed to Dick McKee, Dan Breen and Sean Treacey of Tipperary.
3. Michael Brennan memoir, BMH, AUTHOR.
4. Mulcahy pps, UCD.
5. *Ibid.*
6. Quoted by Beaslai, *Michael Collins and the Making of a New Ireland*, Phoenix, 1926, Vol. I, p. 429.
7. Collins to MacSwiney, 22/3/20, 'D/E' series, SPO.
8. O'Donoghue pps, NL, MS 31, 313.
9. Quoted by Dorothy Macardle, *The Irish Republic*, 4th edition, Irish Press, 1951, p. 432.
10. Lord Riddell in his *Intimate Diary of the Peace Conference*, Gollancz, 1933, p. 147, quotes French as saying that administration was 'as bad as can be . . . There is no proper control. It is impossible to make a satisfactory alteration under existing conditions.'
11. Quoted by Tom Jones, *Whitehall Diaries*, (ed.) K. Middlemass, Oxford University Press, 1971.
12. Cope to MacMahon, O'Broin pps. NL. After the end of hostilities and setting up of the new State, Cope wrote to MacMahon saying that without him the Free State would not have been set up, *see* Leon O'Broin's *No Man's Man*, Institute of Public Administration, 1982, p. 103.
13. Wilson Diaries, Vol. II, p. 222.
14. Frank O'Connor, *The Big Fellow*, Corgi, 1969, p. 103.
15. Kathleen Napoli MacKenna, in *Capuchin Annual*, 1970.
16. Thornton memoir, from which much of what follows is taken.
17. Collins to O'Brien, 9/12/19, Collins pps. NL.
18. *Ibid*, 20/1/20.
19. Sr Margaret Mary, daughter of Mrs O'Connor, in interview with author.
20. Thornton memoir, BMH.
21. Dave Neligan, *The Spy in the Castle*, McGibbon & Kee, 1968, p. 120.
22. Paddy Daly statement, Mulcahy pps, UCD.
23. Anna FitzSimons, subsequently Anna Kelly, the first woman editor of the *Irish Press*.
24. The relevant files in the PRONI, are closed to researchers since Michael Farrell was discovered to have gained partial access to them while researching *Arming the Protestants*, Brandon, 1983.
25. Collins to Art O'Brien, 12/5/21, Collins pps, NL.
26. 24/2/20, 'D/E' series, 2/530, SPO.
27. Thornton memoir.
28. Liam Devlin to Col Pat Collins (nephew), as told to author.
29. O'Connor, pp. 108–109.
30. Ernie O'Malley, *On Another Man's Wound*, Anvil, 1979, p.114.
31. Frank O'Connor, *My Father's Son*, 1966, pp. 122–4. O'Connor did not mention the incident in his Collins biography, saving it until O'Reilly's death, for his autobiography, completed after his own death by Maurice Sheehy. O'Reilly's daughter corroborated the incident.
32. Oscar Traynor, in O'Malley Notebooks, UCD.
33. Noyek to O'Malley, O'Malley Notebooks, UCD.
34. Related to author by his daughter, Dr C. O'Reilly.
35. Patrick Daly memoir, Mulcahy pps, UCD.
36. The story is given as O'Connor tells it, (p. 138) though Mulcahy, in his papers, adds that Collins suggested to the policeman that he mind a bicycle for them.
37. Mulcahy pps, UCD.
38. 31/3/21.
39. Uinseann MacEoin (ed.), *Survivors*, Argenta Press, 1980, p. 404.
40. In 'Sean Lemass Looks Back', a lengthy series of interviews in the *Irish Press* with political correspondent Michael Mills, between 20/1/69 and 6/2/69.
41. Montgomery's Irish Campaign is well described in 'Montgomery in Ireland', *Irish Historical Review*, Spring 1985.
42. Wilson Diaries, 29/9/20.
43. Thornton Memoir.
44. Flor Begley to Liam O'Donnachadcha, notes AUTHOR'S.
45. Tom Barry, *Guerilla Days in Ireland*, Anvil, 1962. In *On Another Man's Wound*, O'Malley also refers to reports of casualness over evidence where some IRA shootings of informers were concerned.
46. Mulcahy pps, UCD.
47. Traynor interview with O'Malley, O'Malley Notebooks, UCD.
48. Lecture by Col Joe Leonard, 9/3/48, Mulcahy pps, P7D/104, UCD.
49. I had taken him into the area on one of the few recorded visits he ever made to a cinema, to see Jane Fonda's 'China Syndrome', which interested him not as cinema, but as anti-nuclear propaganda.
50. CAB 23/21, PRO, London.
51. Charles Townshend, *The British Campaign in Ireland 1919–21*, OUP, 1975, p. 121.
52. Letter to Lloyd George's Secretariat, quoted by Townshend, p. 113.
53. Wilson Diary, quoted by Townshend. p. 116.
54. Macardle, p. 419.
55. *Ibid.*
56. Daithi O'Connell, a nephew of one of the Kerry pike victims, later became a leader of the Provisional IRA and is alleged to be the inventor of the car-bomb although no proof exists. The ensuing descriptions of shootings and atrocities were all first highlighted by the *Irish Bulletin* and later cited by both Beaslai and Macardle. Other cases may be found in Brigadier Crozier's work *Ireland for Ever* (Cape, 1932).
57. They were in the private collection of Mr W. O'Brien, former active Republican and Assistant Art Editor of the *Irish Press*.
58. *On Another Man's Wound* (pp. 247–52) details the tortures O'Malley experienced. MacEoin generally agrees with these accounts though his papers in the Franciscan Archives, Killiney, suggest that he and others were locked in their cells on the morning of the armoured-car rescue, not because of his temperature, but because the warders wanted members of a new guard to have

an opportunity of studying the prisoners. He also confirms that Collins travelled to Longford after the rescue attempt failed to assure his mother that the next time he came 'we'll have him with us.'

59. Thornton memoir.
60. This was attested to by witnesses at the time. The subsequent account of the tortures is based on a sworn affidavit by Hales, quoted by Kathleen Keyes McDonnell, *There is a Bridge at Bandon*, Mercier Press, 1972, pp. 160–61.
61. Collins to O'Brien, Collins pps, NL.
62. Kavanagh describes the incident in the winter edition of *An tOglach*, 1967, reprinted *Irish Historical Review*, summer 1987.
63. All foregoing correspondence taken from O'Donoghue pps, MS 31, 192, NL.
64. McCorley statement on Swanzy shooting. O'Donoghue pps, MS 31, 313, NL.
65. *Ibid*, MS 31, 223.
66. Report of shooting taken from Beaslai, Vol. 11, p. 33.
67. Among those who took part in agitation for their release, which Sir Henry Wilson opposed, were General Bryan Mahon, Col Morris Moore and Capt. Stephen Gwynne. Their appeal was supported by Irish officers and ex-officers of the British Army.
68. *My Fight for Irish Freedom*, Talbot Press, Dublin, 1924, p. 225.
69. 15/10/20, Mulcahy pps, UCD.
70. Beaslai, Vol. 11, p. 213.
71. Llewelyn Davies told this to Lord Longford who informed the author, 12/4/89.
72. CAB 23/23, PRO, London.
73. In a biography of *Kevin Barry* by Donal O'Donovan, Glendale Press, 1989.
74. Margery Forester, *Michael Collins: The Lost Leader*, Sphere, 1972, p. 167.
75. Beaslai, Vol. 11, p. 54–5.
76. CAB 23/22, PRO, London

Chapter 6 (pp. 157–184)

1. Two of his books at least were inspired by his Irish experiences, *Recoil* and *Never in Vain*. The quotations used here are from *Never in Vain*, Doubleday, New York, 1936.
2. Joe McGuinness and George Nolan, members of the ASU, Joe McGuinness memoir, BMH, AUTHOR.
3. Thornton memoir, BMH.
4. In his biography (*Michael Collins*, Four Square, 1961), Rex Taylor quotes a letter to Dick McKee from Collins, dated 17th, since vanished, that says 'Lt. G. is aware of things. He suggests the 21st. A most suitable date and day I think.' Dave Neligan however both told me that there was no Lt. G. and categorically said so in his book. The name may be a cover for someone else, perhaps Major Reynolds. Markham, for example, one of Collins' most important Castle informants was known as Donovan until after the war.
5. Anna FitzSimons' recollection, quoted by Taylor, p. 105. She had just got out of prison and gone to the house next door 'for a good sleep'.
6. Mattie MacDonald, O'Malley Notebooks. UCD.

7. *Ibid*.
8. O'Hanlon's son, Rory, was Minister for Health in the Irish Cabinet at time of writing.
9. Tod Andrews, *Dublin Made Me*, Mercier Press, 1979, p. 153.
10. Charles Dalton, *With the Dublin Brigade*, Peter Davies, 1929, pp. 106–8.
11. Frank O'Connor, *The Big Fellow*, Corgi, 1972, p. 124.
12. Quoted by T. Ryle Dwyer, *Michael Collins and the Treaty*, Mercier Press, 1981, p. 18.
13. *Op cit*.
14. Sr Margaret Mary to author.
15. Wilson Diaries, 25/11/20.
16. Childers Diaries, 25/11/20, TCDU.
17. Chief Secretary's report, CAB 27/108, PRO, London.
18. CAB 23/23, 29/12/20 PRO, London.
19. Rex Taylor, p. 104.
20. At Cabinet meeting, 29/12/20.
21. Quoted by Taylor, p. 106.
22. O'Donoghue pps, MS 31226, NL.
23. Collins to O'Brien, 6/6/21, Collins pps, NL.
24. David Neligan, *The Spy in the Castle*, MacGibbon &Kee, 1968, p. 83.
25. The foregoing account of the MacGrane raid and its aftermath was given to me at different times in conversations with both Broy and Neligan. A description of Collins' stratagems to save Broy can also be found in Broy's interviews with O'Malley (O'Malley Notebooks, UCD).
26. Piaras Beaslai, *Michael Collins and the Making of a New Ireland*, Phoenix, 1926, Vol. II, p. 212.
27. Collins to I.O. East Clare Brigade, quoted by Beaslai, Vol. II, p. 212.
28. Tom Jones, *Whitehall Diaries*, (ed.) K. Middlemass, OUP, 1971, Vol III, p.60.
29. Mulcahy pps, UCD.
30. J. Bowyer Bell, 'The Thompson Submachine Gun in Ireland, 1921', *The Irish Sword*, Vol VIII, no. 31, pp. 98–108.
31. Tom Barry, *Guerilla Days in Ireland*, Anvil, 1962, p. 164.
32. *Ibid*.
33. Collins to Hales, 15/12/20, AUTHOR.
34. *Ibid*, 13/8/20.
35. Collins to Art O'Brien, 21/9/20, Collins pps, NL, dispatch no. 479, no. 4.
36. Leahy memoir, O'Donoghue pps, NL *op. cit*.
37. Collins to Hales, 7/8/21, AUTHOR.
38. Hales to O'Donoghue, 11/6/53, O'Donoghue pps, NL.
39. Collins to Hales, 7/7/21, AUTHOR.
40. Michael Brennan memoir, BMH, AUTHOR's.
41. *Ibid*, published by Michael Collins Association.
42. Beaslai, Vol. II, p. 202.
43. 7/6/21.
44. Mary Collins-Powell memoir, AUTHOR's.
45. Correspondence in 'D/E' series, 2/500, SPO.
46. Childers pps, TCDU.
47. Quoted by Uinseann MacEoin, *Survivors*, 2nd edition, Argenta Press, 1987, p. 405.
48. Collins to O'Daly, 8/3/21 and 9/3/21, Mulcahy pps, UCD.
49. Mulcahy to Mellowes, 22/3/21, Mulcahy pps, UCD.
50. O'Connor, p. 141.
51. 7/D/60, F2/35, Mulcahy pps, UCD.
52. MacEoin, p. 405.

53. Mulcahy pps, UCD.
54. Collins to Sr Celestine, 5/3/21, AUTHOR.
55. Collins to Hales, 1/8/21. Genoa, AUTHOR.
56. Anecdote repeated to author by Liam O'Donna-chadcha.
57. Instruction to 16th Infantry Brigade, Fermoy, 17/6/21, O'Donoghue pps, MS 31, 2231, NL.
58. Childers pps, Ms 7808, TCDU.
59. Thornton memoir, BMH.
60. *Ibid.*

Chapter 7 (pp. 185–235)

1. CO 704/188, PRO, London.
2. *Ibid.*
3. CO 704/100, PRO, London.
4. Moylette to Rex Taylor, quoted by Taylor, in *Michael Collins*, Four Square, 1961, p. 106.
5. T. Ryle Dwyer, *Michael Collins and the Treaty*, Mercier Press, 1981, p. 18.
6. CAB 23/23, PRO, London.
7. The writer adopted the initials after his nom de plume, Aeon, was once shortened accidentally through printer's devilry.
8. Francis M. Carroll, *American Opinion and the Irish Question, 1910–1923*, Gill & Macmillan, and St Martin's Press, 1978, p. 11.
9. According to his papers in the Franciscan Archives, Killiney, de Valera made a distinction between 'big money' and 'small money'. Overall he aimed at getting funds to run an underground Irish Government from the interest of capital invested in the US. Both interest and capital were to be repaid if the Nationalists won. While the small subscribers, commented on scornfully by the *Wall Street Journal*, were plentiful, he felt that to attract the 'big money', it would be necessary to have as much capital as possible invested in the US.
10. De Valera to Cohalan, 20/2/20, quoted by Piaras Beaslai, *Michael Collins and the Making of a New Ireland*, Phoenix, 1926. Vol. I, p. 8.
11. Quoted by T. Ryle Dwyer, p.13.
12. Quoted by Beaslai, Vol. II, p. 2.
13. De Valera to Cohalan, quoted in Eamon de Valera, by Lord Longford and T.P. O'Neill, (Gill & Macmillan, 1970.)
14. Cohalan to de Valera, *op. cit.*
15. De Valera to Griffith, Beaslai, Vol. II, p. 6.
16. Collins to Griffith, 20/7/20, 'D/E' series, SPO.
17. The originals of this letter from Collins, 14/8/20, and of the correspondence alluded to between Sinead de Valera and Kathleen O'Connell are in the de Valera papers in the Franciscan Archives, Killiney. Both this collection and others (NL, SPO) contain several letters from Collins giving de Valera news of the children, their health, studies, how he played with them regularly and so on. The Franciscan Archives also hold many letters from de Valera to Sinead indicating solicitude for her welfare and that of the children.
18. Lord Longford and T.P. O'Neill, p. 113.
19. *Gaelic American*, 21/8/20 to 11/9/20.
20. Collins to Boland, 15/10/20, copy in possession of T.P. O'Neill.
21. W. Field (Collins) to J. Woods (Boland), 19/11/20.
22. Collins to Devoy, 30/9/20.
23. February 1922.
24. Quoted by Carroll, p. 161.
25. Father, later Monsignor, MacMahon, both kept a diary and wrote about the Clune initiative in 'The Cream of their Race', published as a pamphlet by the Clare *Champion*, 15/11/21.
26. *Ireland for Ever*, Cape, 1932, p. 104–5. He also detailed his charges in a letter to the press, 14/5/21, and the *Irish Press*, 13/4/36.
27. *Ibid*, 15/10/20.
28. Quoted by Leon O'Broin, *Michael Collins*, Gill & Macmillan, 1980, p. 65.
29. Collins to *Irish Independent*, 7/12/20, The full version of his statement is published in Beaslai, Vol. II, p. 116.
30. Collins to Griffith, 14/12/20, quoted by Beaslai, Vol.II, pp. 126.
31. Griffith to Collins, 13/12/20, quoted by Beaslai, Vol. II, pp. 123–5.
32. Collins to Art O'Brien, 15/11/20, 'D/E' series, 2/234, SPO.
33. CAB 23/23, 24/12/20, PRO, London.
34. CAB 23/23. PRO, London.
35. Copy also in O'Donoghue pps, 31,22391, NL.
36. Described by Dermot Keogh, *The Vatican, the Bishops and Irish Politics*, CUP, 1986, p. 64.
37. Msr Hagan, Rector, Irish College, to Archbishop Walsh, 23/1/21. Dublin Diocesan Records, Archbishop's House, Dundrum.
38. Art O'Brien to Collins, 17/2/21. Collins pps, 'D/E' series, SPO.
39. Ibid, 17/2/21.
40. Hagan to Walsh, 14/2/21, original: Archdiocesan archives, Dublin.
41. D.H. Akenson and F.P. Fallin, 'Drafting of the Irish Constitution', *Eire Ireland*, Irish American Cultural Institute, Minnesota, Spring 1970, p. 19.
42. Harding to O'Brien, 26/3/21.
43. F.M. Carroll, 'The American Committee for Relief in Ireland, 1920–1922', *Irish Historical Studies*, Vol. XXIII, No. 89, May 1982, p. 47.
44. Collins to Griffith, 21/12/20, 'D/E' series, 2/85, SPO.
45. Related to author as told to Michael Collins by his father who heard the story from Batt O'Connor, who may also have been sent by Collins to welcome de Valera home.
46. There are conflicting accounts as to who met de Valera. His official biography (Longford and O'Neill) only mentions Cullen, however Collins family sources - based on O'Connor's recollections - are adamant that O'Connor was present. There is no mention of the Big Fellow/Long Fellow exchange in the de Valera biography.
47. Quoted by T. Ryle Dwyer, p. 1.
48. T. Ryle Dwyer, p. 31.
49. *See* O'Broin and Frank O'Connor, *The Big Fellow*, Corgi, 1969.
50. Mulcahy, Mulcahy pps, UCD.
51. *Ibid.*
52. *Ibid.*
53. Minutes of Proceedings of Dail Eireann, 25/1/21, pp. 241 and 247.
54. O'Broin, p. 79, quoting Mulcahy, *Studies*, autumn 1978, and *An Cosantor*, 1980.

55. McGuinness memoir, BMH, AUTHOR.

56. Michael Brennan memoir, BMH.

57. Ernie O'Malley, *On Another Man's Wound*, Anvil Press, 1979, pp. 293–4.

58. O'Connor to Lloyd George, 16/1/21, Leon O'Broin pps, NL.

59. McCoy to O'Malley, O'Malley Notebooks, UCD.

60. Hamar Greenwood to Lloyd George, 26/1/21, quoted by O'Broin, p. 69. Greenwood's optimism was based on the fact that 20 Sinn Feiners were facing execution. With appropriate symbolism O'Connor's letter was addressed from 58 Northumberland Road, Dublin, while Greenwood's – 'the man on the spot' – notepaper was headed Irish Office, Old Queen St, London.

61. O'Hegarty to de Valera. 9/5/21, SPO, Dublin.

62. CO 904/188, PRO, London.

63. Charles Townshend, *The British Campaign in Ireland 1919–21*, OUP, 1975, p. 80.

64. Collins to O'Kelly, 28/4/22, 'D/E' series, 2/514, SPO.

65. O'Kelly to Collins, 1/5/22, 'D/E' series, SPO.

66. Collins to O'Kelly, 6/5/22, 'D/E' series, SPO.

67. O'Malley Notebooks, UCD.

68. Sturgis Diary, 12/8/22.

69. Philadelphia Public Ledger, 22/4/21.

70. Emmet Dalton in interview, Radio Telefis Eireann, 6/1/78.

71. Elections called for by Better Government of Ireland Act, which took place on 19/5/21 (in the South) and 24/5/21 (in the North).

72. Collins to de Valera, 15/1/21, 'D/E' series, SPO.

73. Wilson Diaries, Vol. II, p. 293.

74. 'D/E' series, 2/262, SPO.

75. *General Smuts* by Sarah G. Millin, London, 1936, Vol. II, pp. 319–33.

76. CAB 22/107, PRO, London.

77. Casement Diary, 23/6/20, SPO, Dublin.

78. Sturgis Diary, 26/6/21, NL.

79. The last recorded incident prior to the Truce was an attack on the RIC barracks at Kingscourt, County Cavan.

80. Report of the O.C., H Company, Cork No. 1 Brigade, 10/7/21, Mulcahy pps, UCD.

81. Liam Deasey, *Brother against Brother*, Mercier Press, 1982, p. 21.

82. Collins to Moya Llewelyn Davies, 8/7/20, quoted by Margery Forester, *Michael Collins: The Lost Leader*, Sphere, 1972, p. 201.

83. De Valera referred in the Dail to the Collins plan, without naming its author, as official policy, 26/8/21, *see* Private Sessions, Dail Eireann, 1921–22 SO, p. 77.

84. Dorothy Macardle, *The Irish Republic*, 4th edition, Irish Press, 1951, p. 460.

85. It is dated 13/7/21 and appears to have formed part of an unsent letter, quoted by Taylor, p. 112.

86. O'Connor, p. 155.

87. *Ibid.*

88. P.S. O'Hegarty, *Sunday Independent*, 3/11/46.

89. T. Ryle Dwyer, p. 31.

90. *Gaelic American*, New York, 19/2/21.

91. O'Mara pps, NL, MS 21, 549.

92. Wilson's Diary, 17/10/21, quoted by Ryle Dwyer, p. 52. Griffith used the same argument, 19/12/21, pointing out that Ireland had never sought a Republic in the correspondence with Lloyd George which had preceded the Treaty negotiations, because they knew such a request would have been refused.

93. Tom Jones, *Whitehall Diaries*, (ed.) K. Middlemass, OUP, 1971, Vol. III, p. 60.

94. Lord Riddell, *Intimate Diary of the Peace Conference*, Gollancz, 1933, p. 238.

95. CAB 23/26, PRO, London.

96. Collins in Treaty Debates, Dail reports, SO, p. 32.

97. Robert Barton 'Notes for a Lecture', PRO, Dublin, MS 1093/14.

98. Collins to Hayden Talbot, quoted by T. Ryle Dwyer, p. 46. He dates the interview as 2/8/22. De Valera may have begun to try to influence Collins into going to London earlier than 20/8/21, the date on his papers in the Franciscan Archives, Killiney, but he does not appear to have brought Boland into the argument before then.

99. Batt O'Connor, *With Michael Collins in the Fight for Irish Independence*, Peter Davies, 1929, p. 136.

100. Private Sessions, Dail Eireann, 14/9/21, p. 95.

101. De Valera to Lord Longford, 25/2/63, Childers pps, 7848/302, TCDU.

102. Private Sessions, Dail Eireann, 14/9/22, p. 95.

103. Collins to Joe O'Reilly 11/11/21, quoted by Taylor, p. 120.

104. McGarrity was the principal Irish-American leader to back de Valera during the Devoy-Cohalan row. He later split from de Valera, charging him with abandoning the Republican ideal.

105. De Valera to McGarrity, by Sean Cronin, *The McGarrity Papers*, Anvil, 1972, pp. 109–11.

106. Quoted by Macardle, p. 530.

107. P.S. O'Hegarty, *The Victory of Sinn Fein*, Talbot Press, 1924, pp. 86–7.

108. 14/10/21. 'D/E' series 2/304, SPO. Griffith of course remained unaware that some two months earlier (the document, in the de Valera papers in the Franciscan Archives, Killiney, is undated but appears to have been compiled in either late July or early August) de Valera had decided against sending the External Association proposal to the British over his own name.

109. Quoted by Mrs Tom Clarke, Private Sessions, Dail Eireann, 17/12/21, p. 262.

110. O'Muirthle memoir, Mulcahy pps, UCD.

111. Collins to Boland, quoted by Taylor, p. 113.

112. Collins to Tobin, 29/7/21, Mulcahy pps, UCD.

113. Brugha to Mulcahy, 13/9/21, Mulcahy pps, UCD.

114. At the home of Mrs Humphries, Ailesbury Rd., Dublin.

115. Mulcahy pps, UCD.

116. Beaslai, Vol. II, p. 292.

117. The letter was quoted by Taylor as addressed to John O'Kane, a London-based Irish businessman. The person alluded to did exist and was close to Collins throughout the Treaty

negotiations. However I have reason to suppose that 'O'Kane' was a pseudonym.

118. Taylor, quoted by O'Broin, p. 90.

119. He was born 31/3/1871.

120. I have relied particularly on Kathleen Napoli MacKenna's unpublished memoir and Padraig Colum's biography, *Arthur Griffith*, Browne & Nolan, 1959.

121. Collins to O'Dalaigh, 5/10/21, Mulcahy pps, UCD.

122. *Ibid*, 29/9/21.

123. It forms part of an untitled set of documents relating to the Treaty talks, memoranda, records of conferences, descriptions of disagreements, etc, compiled by Robert Barton and kindly loaned to the author by Dr T.P. O'Neill.

124. A contemporary of Collins, the authoritative Leon O'Broin, historian and former Secretary of the Department of Posts and Telegraphs, who worked with my father in local government at the time, told me he had first-hand knowledge of these meetings.

125. This is made clear in the O'Muirthle memoir, Mulcahy pps, UCD.

Chapter 8 (pp. 236–276)

1. Captured in one of the classic studies of the Anglo-Irish relationship, *Peace by Ordeal*, Sidgwick & Jackson, 1972, by Lord Longford. Birkenhead's son was at Oxford with Longford and on visits to Birkenhead's home, where a portrait of Collins hung in an honoured place, Longford was suggested by Birkenhead's daughter as the ideal person to chronicle the struggle. He subsequently co-authored de Valera's authorised biography.

2. Lord Longford, *Peace by Ordeal*, p. 106.

3. Padraig Colum, *Arthur Griffith*, Browne & Nolan, 1959, p. 282.

4. Leslie's mother and Churchill's were sisters.

5. The title of a major series of nine articles by Henry Mangan (6), Dr Nancy Wyse Power (2) and Piaras Beaslai (1), which appeared in the *Irish Independent* between 14/10/35 and 4/11/35.

6. A detailed exposition of this theory appears in *Survivors* (p. 400 *et seq*), the most important published (The O'Malley Diaries are unpublished) compendium of Republican views and reminiscences in existence: (ed.) Uinseann MacEoin, Argenta Press, 1980.

7. Collins to O'Brien, 6/8/21, Collins pps, NL.

8. Collins to Hales, 15/2/19, AUTHOR.

9. Dr Wyse Power, *Irish Independent*, 1/11/35.

10. *See* Blythe and Kennedy pps, UCD.

11. The memoir was originally conceived as a lecture, but he later expanded his notes. These, with some other relevant material, are in PRO, Dublin, nos. 1093/12 and 1093/14.

12. Compiled by Capt. C.J. O'Kelly, 12/10/21, and circulated three days later, CAB/243, PRO, London.

13. Pen portraits taken from The Earl of Birkenhead, *The Last Phase*, Thornton Butterworth, 1959, p. 150.

14. Barton memoir, PRO, Dublin.

15. Lloyd George, quoted by Longford, *Peace by Ordeal*, p. 121.

16. *Op. cit.*

17. To 'O'Kane', quoted by Rex Taylor, *Michael Collins*, Four Square, 1961, Chapter 4.

18. Erskine Childers said of Collins: 'It was he who prevented a break several times suggesting delay when it had been practically decided to break, coats on etc.' Childers Diary, Childers pps, TCDU, p. 70.

19. Barton says in his memoir that Jones arranged a meeting between Lloyd George and Chamberlain at which the Prime Minister said that better progress would be made if he could shed Greenwood and Worthington Evans and the Irish also dispense with part of their team. Longford gives much the same version of a 'ten minutes conversation' initiated by Lloyd George, though he credits Duggan with bringing back the suggestion from Cope.

20. Tom Jones, *Whitehall Diaries*, (ed.) K. Middlemas, OUP, 1971, Vol. III, p. 141.

21. 'D/E' series, 2/304:2, SPO, Dublin, quoted by Ryle Dwyer, *Michael Collins and the Treaty*, Mercier Press, 1981, p. 67. *See also* Ulick O'Connor's, *Oliver St John Gogarty*, (Cape, 1964) in which the author analyses Childers' character sympathetically, though not uncritically.

22. Churchill, in *The Aftermath*, Butterworth, 1929, and Sturgis in his Diary, are but two of the chroniclers of the period on the British side who regarded Childers as a malign influence on the Conference. His previous role as editor of the *Irish Bulletin* was also remembered.

23. de Valera to Griffith, 16/10/21, this and following letters in compilation of Barton documents on Treaty negotiations, AUTHOR.

24. de Valera to Griffith, 19/10/21. Barton Treaty compilation, AUTHOR'S.

25. de Valera to Griffith, 14/10/21, *ibid*.

26. Correspondence between de Valera and Griffith, 10–12/10/21, Barton compilation, AUTHOR'S.

27. de Valera to Griffith, 22/10/21, *ibid*.

28. The following quotations from the Sixth Plenary Session are taken from a transcript of the proceedings, AUTHOR'S.

29. Later an Irish Foreign Minister and a Nobel Peace Prize winner.

30. Note by Barton on de Valera letter and its sequel in Barton Treaty compilation, AUTHOR'S.

31. Barton compilation, AUTHOR'S.

32. Ministry of Defence Archives, NL.

33. *Ibid*.

34. The inside story of the Windsor Barracks raid was told by Brennan in his memoir, BMH.

35. Leon O'Broin, *Michael Collins*, Gill & Macmillan, 1980, pp. 100–103.

36. Recounted to author by Michael and Pat Collins (nephews).

37. Collins to Mulcahy, 23/11/21, Mulcahy pps, UCD.

38. O'Broin, p. 103.

39. British memorandum, Barton compilation, AUTHOR.

40. *ibid*.

41. Longford, *Peace by Ordeal*, p. 158.
42. According to official records of the period, such as Griffith's letters to de Valera, and informed sources such as Longford.
43. Margery Forester, *Michael Collins: The Lost Leader*, Sphere, 1972, p. 231.
44. Griffith to de Valera, 31/10/21, Barton compilation.
45. Barton, note in Treaty compilation.
46. Barton, 'Notes for a Lecture'; PRO, Dublin.
47. Barton, in Treaty compilation.
48. *Ibid.*
49. Barton, note in Treaty compilation.
50. Possibly as early as 26/10/21. After this date there is a '?' and then, in pencil, '29th'. Original in CAB 21/243, PRO.
51. As it was, Brugha created a scene which almost disrupted the final Cabinet meeting in Dublin (3/12/21) at which terms of the proposed Treaty were discussed, by suggesting that the British had opted for a sub-conference methodology in order to have Collins and Griffith selected as principal negotiators.
52. Collins to 'O'Kane', 23/11/21, quoted by Taylor, p. 125.
53. C.P. Scott, quoted by Margery Forester, p. 230.
54. The original formed part of the Collins family collection, which was loaned to a researcher, but never returned. It was undated, typed, initialled by both men, and quoted by Taylor, pp. 142 and 143.
55. Quoted by O'Broin, p. 114.
56. Birkenhead to Collins, Griffith, 3/11/21, Barton compilation.
57. Griffith to de Valera, 3/11/21, *ibid.*
58. Longford, p. 167.
59. Longford, p. 169.
60. Griffith to de Valera, 9/11/21, Barton compilation.
61. Griffith to de Valera, 9/11/21, *ibid.*
62. Craig to Lloyd-George, 11/11/21, *ibid.*
63. Griffith to de Valera, 12/11/21, *ibid.*
64. Longford, p. 177.
65. The visit and Birkenhead's forceful advocacy are described by Salvidge's son, Stanley, in *Salvidge of Liverpool*, Hodder & Stoughton, 1934.
66. CAB 23/27. PRO, London.
67. CO 904/188, PRO, London.
68. Michael Farrell, *Arming the Protestants*, Brandon, 1983, p. 76.
69. Griffith to de Valera, 16/11/22, Barton compilation.
70. Collins to 'O'Kane', 29/11/21, quoted by Taylor, p. 140.
71. Note in Barton compilation.
72. Barton compilation.
73. Earl of Birkenhead, *(F.E.) The Life of F.E. Smith: First Earl of Birkenhead*, Eyre & Spottiswoode, 1959, pp. 382-3.
74. Griffith to de Valera, 29/11/22, Barton Treaty compilation, AUTHOR.
75. Longford, p. 203.
76. O'Muirthle memoir, Mulcahy pps, UCD.
77. Childers Diary, 3/12/21, TCDU.
78. Despite de Valera's pressure, O'Hegarty had been retained in London. He came over with the delegation for these discussions and may have kept notes. But, these, along with his records of a lifetime in public service, were probably destroyed when, towards the end of his life, he burned his papers.
79. Private Session. Dail Eireann, p. 187.
80. O'Murchadha notes.
81. Childers Diary, TCDU.
82. Private session, Dail Eireann, p. 176.
83. O'Murchadha notes.
84. Anthony Gaughan, *Austin Stack*, Kingdom Books, 1971.
85. Private Session, Dail Eireann, p. 177.
86. Barton, 'Notes for a Lecture'.
87. CAB 23/27.
88. Collins, Report of Conference, 5/12/21, Barton Treaty compilation, AUTHOR.
89. Longford, p. 216.
90. Tom Jones, *Whitehall Diaries*, (ed.) K. Middlemas, OUP, 1971, p. 180.
91. *See* Longford, Ryle Dwyer.
92. Collins memorandum, written immediately after seeing Lloyd George, 5/12/21, Collins pps, AUTHOR.
93. In *Peace By Ordeal*, Lord Longford (pp. 220-21) says, 'Collins yielded at last' to repeated efforts by Jones, made through Griffith.
94. Jones, Vol III, p. 180.
95. CAB 23/27, PRO, London.
96. Barton account of Sub-conferences, Barton Treaty compilation, AUTHOR.
97. Churchill, *The Aftermath*, quoted by Longford, p. 239.
98. Austin Chamberlain, *Down the Years*, London, 1935, quoted by Longford, p. 239.
99. Barton's recollection, quoted by Longford, p. 239.
100. Churchill, *The Aftermath*, quoted by Longford, p. 241.
101. Barton, 'Notes for a Lecture.'
102. Childers' Diary, TCDU.
103. MacKenna memoir, AUTHOR.
104. Sir Geoffrey Shakespeare, *Let Candles be Brought In*, MacDonald, 1949, p. 89.

Chapter 9 (pp. 277-307)

1. Well summarised by O'Broin in *In Great Haste*, Gill & Macmillan, 1983, p. 92.
2. Treaty Debates, 3/1/22, p. 190.
3. Kiernan to Collins: 1/12/21, *In Great Haste*, p. 68.
4. Michael Collins, *The Man Who Won the War*, Mercier Press, 1990, pp. 13, 14.
5. Film screened 6/1/79, the day he died.
6. Confidential source.
7. 'In the Shadow of Bael na mBlath', produced, narrated and written by Colm Connolly.
8. Dr Arthur Schlesinger, Chair in the Humanities, City University of New York.
9. Schlesinger to author, 21/2/89, AUTHOR's.
10. Schlesinger Jr. to author, 6/12/89. Alexandra Schlesinger has an interest in Irish history, being a direct descendant of Thomas Addis Emmet, Robert Emmet's older brother. She once did some research on Collins for a file, most of it during a visit to England 'of some months'.
11. Her father, Michael Mick O'Brien of Carri-

groe, Clonakilty, was a cousin of Collins' grandfather, James O'Brien. Michael Mick married twice. His second wife was a first cousin of Collins' mother, Marianne. Nancy was the youngest daughter (of five) of this marriage.

12. Liam O'Donnachadha to author, 22/02/89.
13. To mark Collins' centenary, Liam Collins led the family in having Woodfield refurbished and given to the nation as a museum in October 1990.
14. Collins to Killeen, 02/02/20, AUTHOR.
15. Boland to Kiernan, 5/10/21, *In Great Haste*, p. 22.
16. Boland to Kiernan, 10/1/22, *ibid*, p. 99.
17. Collins to Kiernan, 30/12/21, *ibid*, p. 62.
18. Collins to Kiernan, 12/12/21, *ibid*, p. 62.
19. Kiernan to Collins, 10/2/22, *ibid*, p. 117.
20. Received 7/6/22, *ibid*, p. 176.
21. 26/6/22, *ibid*, p. 185.
22. Received 15/7/22, *ibid*, p. 196.
23. 2/8/22, *ibid*, p. 210.
24. 15/7/22. *ibid*, p. 197.
25. Told to author's parents by O'Sheil.
26. The eldest was christened Felix, after his father.
27. 17/8/22.
28. AUTHOR. Original in O'Brien pps, NL.
29. Fr P. P. Maguire, Newbliss, County Monaghan, to Collins, 4/10/21, AUTHOR'S.
30. Collins to Maguire, 15/10/21, AUTHOR.
31. Collins to Art O'Brien, 1/4/21, Collins pps, NL.
32. This was the sum Llewelyn Davies mentioned to Art O'Brien, O'Brien to Collins, 13/5/21, Collins pps, SPO.
33. Hansard, Vol. 143, 14/7/21. p. 203.
34. Collins to O'Connor, 29/5/21, Collins pps, SPO.
35. O'Connor to Collins, 3/6/21, *ibid*.
36. Collins to O'Brien, 4/5/21, *ibid*.
37. Author's note: I have found speech drafts headed 'From C.Ll.D. in Collins' papers.
38. Collins to O'Brien, 21/3/21, Collins pps, SPO.
39. Napoli MacKenna memoir, AUTHOR'S.
40. In his home at Blackrock, County Dublin, 12/1/88.
41. Hutchinson, 1958, and Four Square, 1961.
42. Lord Longford showed her a typescript of *Peace by Ordeal*, Sidgwick & Jackson, 1972, which she felt showed 'a strong bias for the viewpoint of de Valera, Barton and Childers', and she wrote to Frank Thornton, 8/8/34 (AUTHOR) asking him to 'confirm . . . that Mick never "persuaded his extremists of the I.R.B. to vote for the Treaty".'
43. Uinsean MacEoin (ed.), *Survivors*, Argenta Press, 1980, p. 507.
44. *Ibid*, p. 406.
45. Napoli MacKenna memoir.
46. O'Hegarty to Lynch, 22/11/21, Mulcahy pps, UCD.
47. Mulcahy pps, UCD.
48. 2/12/21.
49. Shane Leslie memoir of Hazel Lavery, Leslie pps, Georgetown University Library, Washington DC.

50. Methuen, 1948; Anvil 1966.
51. O'Broin reproduces the de Vere White assessment in his *Michael Collins*, Gill & Macmillan, published as late as 1980.
52. Napoli MacKenna memoir.
53. Shane Leslie to Audrey Morris, 18/6/21, Leslie pps, Georgetown University.
54. *See* last page of *Kevin O'Higgins*, by Terence de Vere White, Methuen, 1948.
55. Acrostic poem to Hazel Lavery, by Kevin O'Higgins, Kilmainham Museum, Dublin, MS 864 J.
56. Now renamed *Arus an Uachtaran* and home to the Irish President.
57. Confidential source.
58. Shane Leslie commentary on Lavery anecdote as told to Derek Patmor, Leslie pps, Georgetown University.
59. Original, Kilmainham Museum, Dublin, MS 964F.
60. Kilmainham Museum, Dublin, MS 964A.
61. *Ibid*.
62. Londonderry pps, 15/3/52, File No. D3099. PRONI.
63. H. Montgomery Hyde, *The Londonderrys*, Hamish Hamilton, 1979, p. 151.
64. *Ibid*.
65. Confidential source.
66. Quoted in *Furry Park House*, pamphlet by Seamus Cannon, Furry Park Preservation Committee, 1985.
67. Report of shooting as told by Bill MacKenna to Cannon.
68. Shaw to Hannie Collins, 24/8/22, quoted by Taylor, *Michael Collins*, Four Square, 1961, p. 209.
69. Kiernan to Collins, received 15/8/22, *In Great Haste*.
70. Confidential source.
71. One of the letters he wrote that Saturday, 19/8/22, timed 12.30 p.m., was a complaint to Desmond FitzGerald, Director of Publicity, about the fact that no publicity had been given to an attempt on his life at Stillorgan the previous day, Collins pps, SPO.
72. Dalton showed the letter to members of an RTE TV crew, who made a film of his life in 1978. After his death, it passed into the possession of his son, Mr Richard Dalton of Weybridge, Surrey, but at the time of writing, Mr Dalton said it had been mislaid. Noel Lemass was also suspected by Collins' former associates of having been responsible for shooting Sean Hales (see Chapter 13).
73. Quoted by J.B. Lyons, *Oliver St John Gogarty*, Blackwater, p. 125.
74. Ryle Dwyer, *Michael Collins and the Treaty*, Mercier Press, 1981, p. 106.
75. Lord Longford and T.P. O'Neill, *Eamon de Valera*, Gill & Macmillan, 1970, p. 168.
76. Ryle Dwyer, p. 106.
77. Childers Diary, 8/12/22, TCDU.
78. *Ibid*.
79. *Ibid*.
80. *Ibid*.
81. Piaras Beaslai, *Michael Collins and the Making of a New Ireland*, Phoenix, 1926, Vol. II, p. 312.
82. Childers Diary, 9/12/21, TCDU.
83. 23/12/21, *In Great Haste*, p. 90.

84. Batt O'Connor, *With Michael Collins in the Fight for Irish Independence*, Peter Davies, 1929, pp. 180–2.
85. Frank O'Connor, *The Big Fellow*, Corgi, 1969, p. 173, see also Margery Forester, *Michael Collins: The Lost Leader*, Sphere, 1972, p. 272.
86. Public Session Treaty Debates, Dail Eireann, 14/12/21. col. 1, p. 7.
87. Ryle Dwyer, p. 112.
88. Sean Hales, Treaty Debates, Private Session, 17/12/21, p. 263.
89. 10/12/21.
90. *Irish Times*, 20/12/21.
91. Tim Healy, *Letters and Leaders*, Thornton Butterworth, 1928, p. 645.
92. Collins to Kiernan, 20/12/21. The letter is not included in *In Great Haste*, but was quoted by Margery Forester, p. 271.
93. Desmond Ryan, *Remembering Sion*, Barker, 1934, pp. 278–9.
94. Joseph Sweeney describes such an interview in O'Malley Notebooks, UCD.
95. de Valera to McGarrity, 27/12/21, McGarrity pps, NL.
96. Childers Diary, TCDU, 28/12/21.
97. Described in *Irish Times* and *Freeman's Journal*, 4/1/22.
98. Treaty Debates, Public Session, 4/1/22, p. 217.
99. Beaslai, Vol. II, p. 332.
100. Public Session, Dail Eireann, 5/1/22, p. 277.
101. Treaty Debates, Public Session, pp. 271–5.
102. Ryle Dwyer, p. 138.
103. Treaty Debates, Public Session, p. 277.
104. Collins to Kiernan, 6/1/22. *In Great Haste*, p. 194.
105. Treaty Debates, Public Session, 6/1/22, pp. 290–2.
106. *Ibid*, p. 307.
107. *Ibid*, p. 281.
108. Beaslai, Vol. II, p. 335.
109. Treaty Debates, Public Session, pp. 324–5.
110. *Ibid*, pp. 235–44.
111. *Ibid*, p. 344.
112. *Ibid*, p. 346. De Valera's papers apparently do not contain answers to such key questions as: Exactly what policy did he intend to follow if he succeeded in destroying the Treaty; what forces did he intend to use to enforce his policy; what was his assessment of Michael Collins? It is clear from Dorothy Macardle (p. 672), whose work he regarded as the main repository of his ideas until his own official biography was published, that de Valera was aware in February and March 1922 that Collins intended to move towards a Republic if he got co-operation from his opponents. She says: 'others believed that he [Collins] was rather inviting his countrymen to co-operate with him in deceiving the British and would presently declare the Republic again. Had he received such co-operation on a large scale, [author's italics] *there is little doubt that he would have thrown all his great energies into achieving progress on those lines.*'

Chapter 10 (pp. 308–332)

1. Statistics quoted in Labour Party submission to Dail, 10/1/22, Dail Debates, SO.
2. Collins to Kiernan, 9/1/22, *In Great Haste*, (ed.) Leon O'Broin, Gill & Macmillan, 1983, p. 95.
3. T. Ryle Dwyer, *Michael Collins and the Treaty*, Mercier Press, 1981, p. 142.
4. The quotation provides the title for Florrie O'Donoghue's biography of Diarmuid Lynch, *No Other Law*, (Irish Press, 1954).
5. Traynor to O'Malley, O'Malley Notebooks, UCD.
6. Michael Hopkinson, *Green Against Green*, Gill & Macmillan, 1988, p. 16.
7. Piaras Beaslai, *Michael Collins and the Making of a New Ireland*, Phoenix, 1926, Vol. II, P.372.
8. Literally 'High Conference', usually meaning Annual General Conference.
9. The Drafting Committee met at the Shelbourne Hotel, in a large room still known today as 'The Constitution Room'.
10. Quotation from an important series, 'The Irish Civil War and the Drafting of the Free State Constitution', by D.H. Akenson and J.P. Fallon, in the quarterly, *Eire Ireland*, Irish-American Cultural Institute, Minnesota, 1970.
11. The members of the Committee were: Darrell Figgis, James Douglas, James MacNeill, C.J. France, Kevin O'Shiel, Hugh Kennedy, John O'Byrne, James Murnaghan and Alfred O'Rahilly. Douglas and France, an American lawyer, had been involved with the American Relief activities (Irish White Cross) during the Tan war. Kennedy and O'Shiel, both lawyers, were active in politico-legal affairs and O'Byrne and Murnaghan were prominent Dublin barristers; MacNeill, a brother of Eoin MacNeill, a retired Indian Civil Servant who had also worked with the White Cross. Alfred O'Rahilly, a Professor of Mathematics, was a leading Catholic intellectual. Figgis was the only paid member of the Committee.
12. Michael Hopkinson, p. 65.
13. 'Sandow' Donovan, the Irregular officer in charge of landing the *Upnor* arms, gave an account to Ernie O'Malley from which it appears that the haul was many times greater than Churchill's estimate. O'Malley Notebooks, UCD. Hopkinson, p. 74, says it took 200 lorries to carry the booty, which is nearer to the description given by Donovan, who, at that stage, in private conversation, had no reason to lie to his old comrade.
14. Collins to Churchill, 5/4/22. AUTHOR.
15. CAB 16/42, PRO, London.
16. *Ibid*.
17. Eight dead and some sixty injured.
18. Copy of original speech, AUTHOR.
19. Collins to McGarrity, 5/4/22, AUTHOR.
20. Quoted by Padraig Colum, *Arthur Griffith*, Browne & Nolan, 1959, p. 339.
21. Tom Hales to Liam O'Donnachadcha; account, AUTHOR'S.
22. *Irish Independent*, 7/3/22.
23. *Ibid*, 17/3/22.
24. *Ibid*, 18/3/22.
25. *Ibid*, 20/3/22.

26. *Ibid*, 23/3/22.
27. *Seanad Reports*, 20, 1876, quoted by Donal O'Sullivan, *The Irish Free State and its Senate*, Faber, 1940, p. 19.
28. Boland to Stack, 27/4/22, Stack pps, quoted by Ryle Dwyer, p. 145.
29. Notes taken by Archbishop Byrne, originals, Diocesan records, Archbishop's House, Dublin.
30. 1/5/22.
31. 30/4/22.
32. *Poblacht na hEireann*, 18/5/22.
33. 'In Parnell's Funeral', Gill & Macmillan, 1934.
34. Colum, p. 343.
35. Quoted in Blythe letter to Padraig Colum, Griffith's biographer.
36. Dail Debates, 27/4/22, p.303.
37. O'Broin, p. 128.
38. Sean O'Luing, *Art O'Griofa*, Sairseal agus Dill, 1953, p. 396.
39. Kennedy to Collins, 20/5/22, Kennedy pps, UCD.
40. Churchill to Collins, 15/5/22, AUTHOR.
41. O'Muirthle memoir, Mulcahy pps, UCD.
42. *Ibid*.
43. Daly to Collins, 3/4/22, Mulcahy pps, UCD.
44. Collins to Daly, 5/5/22, *ibid*.
45. Cope to Churchill, 23/5/22. CAB 43/1, PRO, London.
46. Churchill to Collins, 22/5/22, AUTHOR.
47. Lionel Curtis, who made the assessment, was at the time (6/6/22) Secretary of the British Government's Provisional Government of Ireland Committee, *see* CAB 27/154. PRO, London.
48. Churchill to Irish delegates, CAB 21/249, *ibid*.
49. Downing Street, 27/5/22. CAB 21/249, *ibid*.
50. Collins, Griffith, Duggan, Cosgrave, Hugh Kennedy and Diarmuid O'Hegarty, Secretary. The British team was Lloyd George, Chamberlain, Birkenhead, Churchill, Worthington Evans, Hamar Greenwood, Tom Jones, Lionel Curtis and Quentin Hill. The last three were Secretaries.
51. Downing Street, 1/6/22, CAB 21/257, PRO, London
52. Tom Jones, *Whitehall Diaries*, Vol III, (ed.) K. Middlemass, OUP, 1971, 1/6/22.
53. CAB 23/30, PRO, London.
54. *Ibid*.
55. *Ibid*.
56. CAB 21/249, PRO, London.
57. Kennedy to Colum, 11/6/22. Kennedy pps, UCD.
58. Lord Middleton, Andrew Jamieson, Dr J.H. Bernard and the Earl of Donoughmore.
59. *Poblacht na hEireann*, 5/6/22.
60. *Irish Independent*, 5/6/22.
61. De Valera speech, *Irish Independent*, 5/6/22.
62. *Hansard*, 26/5/22.
63. Margery Forester, *Michael Collins: The Lost Leader*, Sphere, 1972, p. 319.
64. Frank O'Connor, *The Big Fellow*, Corgi, 1969, p. 207.
65. Collins pps, quoted Forester, p. 320.
66. O'Connor, p. 207.
67. P G, 27/6/22. S. 1322, PRO, Dublin.
68. Baroon Bardon, Jonathan B. and Conlin, Stephen C., *Dublin: 1000 Years of Wood Quay*, Blackstaff, 1984, p. 26.
69. Fr Albert's Diary, Dublin Diocesan Records, Archbishop's House, Dublin.
70. O'Connor, p. 208.
71. *Ibid*.
72. Dalton, on RTE TV film, 'The Shadow of Bael na mBlath', 1989.
73. AUTHOR.
74. Churchill to Collins, 28/6/22, AUTHOR.
75. *Ibid*.
76. AUTHOR.
77. Bardon and Conlin, p. 26.
78. O'Broin, p. 137.
79. PG, 28/6/22. PG 39, SPO.

Chapter 11 (pp. 333–385)

1. Second Northern Division report, NL, MS 17143.
2. CAB 23/83, PRO, London.
3. *Cf* Cabinet meetings: 15, 19 and 22 December, CAB 23/18, PRO, London.
4. Birkenhead to Londonderry, Londonderry pps, PRO, Belfast.
5. CAB 23/23, PRO, London.
6. There was a Senate, but this, heavily representative of the land-owning lords, had little or no relevance to Catholic grievances.
7. Speaking in Stormont, 24/4/34.
8. Brookeborough to author, *see* Coogan, *The I.R.A.*, Fontana, 1987, p.58.
9. Carson to Bonar Law, Carson pps, PRONI D 1507/1/1920/16.
10. CAB 24/109/1693, PRO, London.
11. Craig to Cabinet, CAB 5/1, PRONI.
12. CAB 23/22/53, *ibid*.
13. CAB 22/107, PRO, London.
14. 1/9/20, Anderson to Bonar Law, CO/904/188, PRO, London.
15. Gen. Ricardo, Col. McClintock and Major Stevenson, D 1678/6, PRONI.
16. Intelligence Report, 3rd Northern Division, 26/10/21. Mulcahy pps, UCD, p. 7/a/26.
17. Mulcahy pps, UCD, p. 7d-1.
18. *Morning Post*, 5/9/21.
19. PG, 30/1/22, SPO.
20. 20/7/21, CAB 23/26, PRO, London.
21. The nickname derived from the frequently proposed Hales formula for dealing with Black and Tans and their allies: 'give 'em the buckshot!'
22. Aiken to O'Malley, O'Malley Notebooks, UCD, p. 17b/193.
23. Batt O'Connor, *With Michael Collins in the Fight for Irish Independence*, Peter Davies, 1929, p. 181.
24. Copy of Fawsitt's Confidential Report to Provisional Government, 3/1/22, original, SPO, AUTHOR'S.
25. PG, 20/1/22, SPO.
26. Mulcahy pps, UCD.
27. PG, No. 45, 30/1/22, SPO.
28. AUTHOR.
29. Michael Farrell, *Arming the Protestants*, Brandon, 1983, p. 91.
30. Mulcahy to Collins. 3/3/22, Mulcahy pps, UCD.
31. It exists today in the division of nationalist ranks in the Six Counties and the existence of

two separate nationalist parties, Sinn Fein, and the Social Democratic and Labour Party. (SDLP).

32. Documents allegedly proving these were found. Hopkinson, p. 79.
33. Collins to O'Duffy, 28/1/22, SPO.
34. O'Duffy to Collins, 30/1/22, SPO.
35. Craig to Lloyd George, 8/2/20, CAB 21/254, PRO, London.
36. Lloyd George to Collins, 8/2/22, CAB 21/254, PRO, London.
37. Griffith to Collins 8/2/22, CAB 21/254, PRO, London.
38. Collins to Lloyd George, 8/2/22, CAB 21/254, PRO, London.
39. Cope to Jones, 8/2/22, CAB 21/254, PRO, London.
40. Dolan memoir, BMH. Sean O'Muirthle in his memoir also mentions taking part in an attempt to call off the shooting of the hangmen, but gives different dates.
41. AUTHOR.
42. Quoted by Hopkinson, p. 81.
43. Ed. 13/1/400, PRONI.
44. Blythe pps, UCD, p. 4/386 9(15).
45. Minister for Finance, William Cosgrave, Dail Eireann, 9/11/22.
46. Ed 32/B/1/2/52, PRONI.
47. 3/4/22, At the Assembly Hall, Belfast.
48. Wilson Diaries, 15/3/22.
49. CO 906/30, PRO, London.
50. Tom Jones, Whitehall Diaries, Vol III, (ed.). K. Middlemass, OUP, 1971, p. 195.
51. Collins to Churchill, 24/3/22, CAB 6/75, PRONI.
52. In 1968, as Irish Foreign Affairs Minister, he pursuaded the United Nations General Assembly to adopt a resolution on nuclear arms limitation, which he devised. It remains the only international statutory instrument for curbing the spread of nuclear weapons.
53. Mulcahy pps, UCD, p7/1A/47 L.
54. AUTHOR.
55. AUTHOR.
56. Charles Haughey was himself dismissed from a Fianna Fail Cabinet in 1970 and unsuccessfully charged with 'illegal importation of arms into the State', after the North had again erupted in 1969.
57. Copy of formal letter of authorisation dated 22/2/22, AUTHOR'S.
58. Blythe pps, UCD, p. 24/554.
59. Statements collected by the commission's lawyers and the evidence given at the Northern Advisory Committee, which first met 11/4/22, are scattered through the several boxes of the bulky collection of Committee documentation, notably S. 10111 and S 11195, SPO.
60. Named in confidential Intelligence Report to Free State Government, 20/2/24. Blythe pps, UCD, p. 24/176.
61. Farrell, pp. 114–150.
62. PG, 30/1/22, SPO.
63. 12/4/22.
64. McCoy to O'Malley, O'Malley Notebooks, UCD, b76 and 116.

65. Macready to Jeudwine, 10/12/20, quoted by Charles Townshend, The British Campaign in Ireland, 1919–21, OUP, 1975, p. 138.
66. Collins' statements, the text of the Sinn Fein Resolution and the British invitation to talks, Freeman's Journal, 25 and 29 March, and Craig's speeches can be found both there and, in a more approving setting, in the columns of the Belfast Newsletter.
67. AUTHOR.
68. Wilson Diaries.
69. On 4/4/22 the Agreement was strongly criticised by a number of the more extreme Unionists, notably Messrs Coote, Lynn and M'Guffin.
70. The Free State Government Intelligence Document of 24/2/22, already quoted, says the killing was done at Nixon's instigation to give a pretext for what followed.
71. The information on the Arnon and Stanhope St killings is taken from 'Memos for Mr Michael Collins: Extracts from Statutory Declarations, re Arnon St and Stanhope St massacres', Collins pps, AUTHOR.
72. Complete transcript available, SPO, S. 1011.
73. Londonderry to Collins, 5/4/22, PRONI, Ed. 13/1/400.
74. PG, 21/4/21, SPO, 9.
75. PG, 25/4/22, SPO, 10.
76. Dorothy Macardle, The Irish Republic, Irish Press, 1951, p. 705.
77. See CO 739, 14, 15, 16 and CO 906/23, PRO, London.
78. CAB 739.16, PRO, London.
79. SPO, AUTHOR.
80. See D.H. Akenson, The U.S. and Ireland, Harvard UP, 1973, and by the same author, Education and Enmity: The Control of Schooling in Northern Ireland, Institute of Irish Studies, 1973.
81. Sean Moylan, Dail Debates, 28/4/22.
82. Ibid.
83. Correspondence in CO 739/16, PRO, London.
84. Available SPO, AUTHOR.
85. Ibid.
86. McCorley interview, O'Malley Notebooks on Northern campaign, UCD, Nos. 176 and 30.
87. Described to the author by an eyewitness, while researching The I.R.A.
88. Ricardo to Tallents, PRO, CO 906/27.
89. PG, 23, 24/5/22.
90. House of Commons, 26/6/22, Hansard.
91. Wilson Diaries, 10/5/22.
92. CO 739/16.
93. CAB 21/254. PRO, London.
94. Collins to Churchill, 6/6/22, telegrams nos 72, 75, AUTHOR.
95. See Jones, pp. 195, 198, 206 and 211.
96. Churchill to Cope for Collins, 7/6/22. AUTHOR.
97. Collins to Churchill, 8/6/22, ibid.
98. Minute No. 31, 9/6/22.
99. Collins to Griffith, 9/6/22, AUTHOR.
100. Morning Post, 12/6/22.
101. Churchill to House of Commons, 26/6/22.
102. These included Asquith, Londonderry, Selbourne, Salisbury, Carson, Erskine, Stanhope and Sumner, PRONI, Londonderry.

103. Wilson Diaries, 14/1/22.
104. Speech to Die-hards at Caxton Hall, 9/5/22.
105. CO 906/25, PRO, London.
106. Geoffrey Shakespeare, *Let Candles Be Brought In*, Macdonald, 1949.
107. CAB 16/42. PRO, London.
108. Michael Farrell, p. 139.
109. Churchill to Craig, CO 906/29, PRO, London.
110. Dawson Bates to Belfast Conciliation Committee, 13/4/22, CO 906/23, *ibid.*
111. Dawson Bates to Craig, 15/6/22, CO 906/29, *ibid.*
112. Tallents to Masterson Smith, 4/7/22, CO 906/30, *ibid.*
113. Tallents Report, 6/7/22, CO 906/30, *ibid.*
114. Tallents Report, p. 2.
115. Spender to Tallents, CO 906/24, PRO, London.
116. Solly-Flood to Secretary, Minister for Home Affairs, 27/6/22, CO 906/23, *ibid.*
117. Spender to Tallents, 29/6/22, *ibid.*
118. Tallents to Masterson Smith, 4/7/22, CO 906/30, *ibid.*, p. 4.
119. 18/7/22, CO 739/16, *ibid.*
120. The Cushendall affair is documented at some length in Farrell, pp, 162–3.
121. O'Malley Notebooks, UCD, pp. 171 and 31.
122. *Ibid.*
123. Tobin to O'Malley, Notebooks 17b and 94, UCD.
124. CAB 21/255, PRO, London.
125. Original in S1570, SPO.
126. CAB 21/255, PRO, London.
127. AUTHOR.
128. Gen. Sir Nevil Macready, *Annals of An Active Life*, Hutchinson, 1924, Vol. II, p. 652.
129. Quoted by Macardle, p. 740.
130. Dunne subsequently wrote accounts of the beatings meted out to himself and Sullivan, which together with other details of the Wilson shooting and its aftermath, were later collected by Florrie O'Donoghue. *See* index to the O'Donoghue Collection, NL, and in particular, MS 31, 256.
131. Tobin to O'Malley, O'Malley Notebooks 17b and 94, UCD.
132. Sweeney to O'Malley, *ibid.*
133. P.A. Murray to O'Malley, *ibid.*
134. Collins to O'Sullivan, 7/8/22, SI 570, SPO.
135. Collins to Cosgrave, 6/8/22, SI 570. PRO, Dublin.
136. Printed in Raymond P. Watson, 'Newry's Struggle', Cath Saoirse an Iuir, n.d. p. 62.
137. AUTHOR.
138. Collins to Griffith, 11/6/22, Kennedy pps, UCD, p. 237.
139. (ed.) Lyons, F. S., *Bank of Ireland Centenary Essays*, Gill & Macmillan, 1983, p. 70.
140. 6/7/22, quoted from *Bank of Ireland Centenary Essays*, p. 72.
141. O'Donoghue pps, NL, MS No. 31, 223.
142. Related to author by Michael Collins, Collins' nephew, as told to him by MacEoin.
143. Actual letter in possession of Kevin O'Sheil's daughter, Mrs Eda Segarra.
144. Collins to Churchill, CO 906/31, PRO, London.
145. Cope to Masterson Smith, *ibid.*
146. Report to CoS of situation in No.1 (Belfast) Brigade, 20/7/2, by Seamus Woods, O.C. 3rd Northern Division, Mulcahy pps, UCD.
147. Statistics quoted by Macardle p. 730.
148. Woods to Mulcahy, 2/10/22, Mulcahy pps, UCD, AUTHOR.
149. Mulcahy pps, UCD.
150. Teachers' payment references taken from Department of Finance files Nos 76/53, 118/19 and 150, PRO, Dublin.
151. O'Shiel's comments in a memo he circulated to the Cabinet on 6/10/22, Kennedy pps, UCD, p. 4/V/1.
152. PG, No. 78, 1/8/22.
153. Piaras Beaslai, *Michael Collins and the Making of a New Ireland*, Phoenix, 1926, Vol. 1, p. 211.
154. PG 94, 19/8/22.

Chapter 12 (pp. 386–415)

1. *Irish Independent*, 29/6/22.
2. Uinseann MacEoin (ed.), *Survivors*, Argenta Press, 1980, reprinted 1987, p. 406.
3. C.S. Andrews, *Dublin Made Me*, Mercier Press, 1979, p. 234.
4. Some accounts say that he had a Thompson sub-machine gun; that he pushed away a St John's Ambulance officer, Col A. J. Mac-Carthy, who was attempting to get him to surrender, threatening him with a weapon. However, all accounts agree that he advanced on a heavily armed position with the obvious intent of going down fighting.
5. Kiernan to Collins, 15/7/22, *In Great Haste* (ed.) Leon O'Broin, Gill & Macmillan, 1983, p. 198.
6. Collins to Boland, 28/7/22, quoted by Rex Taylor, *Michael Collins*, Four Square, 1961, p. 194.
7. Kiernan to Collins, 28/4/22, *In Great Haste*, p. 169.
8. Boland to Wyse Power, 29/7/22, Mulcahy pps, UCD.
9. Taylor, p. 195.
10. Like Brugha, accounts of his shooting vary. Anna Kelly, *Irish Press*, 1/8/38, said that he moved towards his bedroom door, saying 'I want to see your officer', a gun went off and he was shot in the stomach.
11. Collins to Director of Intelligence, 31/7/22, SPO.
12. Taylor, p. 195.
13. Margery Forester, *Michael Collins: The Lost Leader*, Sphere, 1972, p. 329.
14. Collins to Kiernan, quoted by Forester, p. 329.
15. John Feehan, *The Irish Press*, 18/10/82, p. 3.
16. MacEoin, p. 409.
17. *Irish Press*, 18/10/82.
18. Feehan, *The Shooting of Michael Collins*, Royal Carberry Books, 1988, p. 84.
19. MacDunphy, 2/9/36, SPO, 5.3708.
20. T.P. O'Neill quoting Gallagher to author.
21. Confidential source.
22. A list of these is given in Sean O'Mahony's *Frongoch: University of Revolution*, FDR, 1987, p. 219.
23. O'Neill to author.

24. PG Decision, 12/7/22, PG 57.
25. AUTHOR'S.
26. PG 58, No. SI. 318, SPO.
27. MacDunphy memo 1/10/22, SPO.
28. Mulcahy pps, UCD, contain an alarmed memo from Mulcahy to Collins about 'irregularities' in the mess accounts of Tobin and Cullen.
29. Mulcahy pps, UCD, contain several references to Mulcahy's difficulties with O'Higgins over the Army.
30. S. 03/09/22, SPO.
31. Cosgrave to Collins, 14/7/22 SPO.
32. Collins to Cosgrave, 15/7/22 SPO.
33. Cosgrave to Collins, S. 1336/22, SPO.
34. Ibid, S. 1376/22.
35. Collins to Fitzgerald, 12/7/22, Fitzgerald pps, UCD.
36. Pat Collins to author.
37. Collins to London contact, quoted by Piaras Beaslai, Michael Collins and the Making of a New Ireland, Phoenix, 1926, Vol. 11, p. 422.
38. Collins to each minister, Provisional Government, SPO.
39. The writer, Maurice Hennessy, vouches for the story, which was told to him by Hannan Swaffer, the journalist, a friend of Lawrence's who was present when Collins made the offer.
40. Lawrence was the illegitimate son of Sir Thomas Chapman and Sarah Turner, who took the name Lawrence when she became Chapman's housekeeper. The couple left Ireland after she became his mistress.
41. Collins was in Ireland that day for crucial discussions on the British Treaty proposals. Thomas, who contributed an important article on the Collins/Lawrence connection to the Irish Historical Review, spring 1985, published by the Michael Collins Association, says their first meeting occurred on this day. However, Collins' secret activities lend themselves to many such discrepancies, and the rest of the article is both illuminating and interesting in its own right.
42. MacPartland, Mulcahy pps, UCD.
43. Mulcahy pps, UCD.
44. Ibid, quoted Michael Hopkinson, Green Against Green, Gill & Macmillan, 1988, p. 91.
45. In Great Haste, p. 213.
46. Collins to Director of Intelligence, 9/8/22, SPO.
47. Collins' recommendation on setting up a commission on Army pay, 10/8/22, Mulcahy pps, UCD.
48. Collins to Director of Intelligence, 7/8/22, Mulcahy pps, UCD.
49. Quoted by O'Broin, In Great Haste, p. 90.
50. Quoted by J.B. Lyons, in Oliver St John Gogarty, Blackwater Press, 1980, p. 124.
51. Various writers have suggested both. Forester refers several times, as does Frank O'Connor, The Big Fellow, Corgi, 1969, to his suffering acutely from stomach pains. Eileen O'Donovan also told me he had severe stomach trouble.
52. Forester, p. 331.
53. To name but one example of conflicting reports, John Lavery has Hazel sitting in front of a window to shield Collins from the sniper in a Dun Laoghaire Hotel, rather than in Furry Park. O'Connor has him going to bed at 7.30 pm on his last night in Dublin, without going to dinner in either Clontarf or Dun Laoghaire, and John A. English gave a convincing account of meeting him at a dance in Cruise's Hotel in Limerick that night to the Limerick Weekly Echo on 26/8/72.
54. Forester, p. 333.
55. Hopkinson, p. 76.
56. Quoted by O'Connor, p. 211.
57. Ibid.
58. Col Charlie Russell, an ex-member of the Squad, told Hales about the gun incident. Hales repeated it to Liam O'Donnachadha.
59. O'Connor, p. 211.
60. MacEoin, p. 99.
61. Confidential source.
62. NL, MS 22, 77. Leon O'Broin favours this version, p.141.
63. Forester, p. 334.
64. Limerick Weekly Echo, 26/8/72.
65. Told to author by Lt Gen Collins-Powell (nephew).
66. Dick Hogan, 13/5/88, Irish Times.
67. Collins family anecdote.
68. Again, a Sean MacBride-sponsored theory.
69. Leon O'Broin, No Man's Man, Institute of Public Administration, 1982, p. 116.
70. Pelly to Collins, 21/8/22, see O'Broin, p. 115.
71. AUTHOR.
72. Brennan pps, NL, quoted by O'Broin, p. 117.
73. O'Broin, p. 119.
74. Original in possession of Michael Collins' nephew, quoted by Forester, p. 334.
75. O'Connor, p. 212.
76. Forester, p. 344.
77. These, based on statements by survivors of the ambush, were exhaustively reviewed for Colm Connolly's film, 'The Shadow of Bael na mBlath', RTE. I have also checked them against newspaper accounts of the time, biographies and discussions with Irish Army experts and works such as Feehan's re-creation of the shooting. MacEoin's hitherto unpublished insights are contained in his papers in the Franciscan Archives, Killiney.
78. On condition that I did not publish its author's name or the full details of the report.
79. John Feehan, p. 50.
80. O'Donoghue to O'Malley, O'Malley Notebooks, UCD.
81. Begley to O'Donoghue, O'Donoghue's notes, AUTHOR's.
82. Garda Hickey, a member of the newly formed Garda Siochana, or police force, was one of a three-man team which was assigned to gather whatever details there were to be had about Collins' last trip. The topic became of life-long interest to him. He was stationed for years in Crookstown and knew Canon Tracey well. When he had retired from the force, Hickey, a major proponent of the Tracey peace visit story, gave his version of the day's happenings to the Limerick Weekly Echo, in a series of articles, 26/8/72 – 16/9/72.
83. Feehan, p. 114.

84. Feehan, p. 86.
85. Hickey's account, *Limerick Weekly Echo*.
86. Flynn's account, supplied to the author by a confidential source, 26/3/90.
87. On this point, however, Dr T.P. O'Neill assures me that in later life de Valera used tc say that no such meeting was arranged. 'Collins was a realist. He'd go where the power was. He knew I had no power at that stage', was the burden of his comment.
88. *Sunday Independent*, 23/8/22.
89. Confidential source.
90. Account given to author by Liam O'Donnachadha.
91. Hickey's account, *Limerick Weekly Echo*.
92. In series of interviews with Raymond Smith and Jim Nicholl, in the *Irish Independent*, 1971.
93. Feehan, p. 56.
94. Edward O'Mahony, a native of the district, wrote an authoritative account of the day of Collins' death in *Magill* magazine, May 1989.
95. Hickey's account, *Limerick Weekly Echo*.
96. Liam O'Donnachadha to author.
97. One writer, O'Mahony, says seven. The number given by a survivor, Tom Kelliher, who accompanied Eamonn de Barra on a tour of the area, 20/9/70 says six. De Barra took down an account of the ambush from him, which he gave to Liam O'Donnachadha, who knew Kelliner well, and accepted his figure.
98. Liam Deasy in *Brother Against Brother*, Mercier Press, 1982, p. 78, says Hales accompanied him back to the pub. I am using the version given by Hales to O'Donnachadha.
99. Dalton's descriptions are taken from the official report he made to the Government, quoted by Beaslai and other biographers.
100. There are conflicting reports on this. Liam O'Donnachadha told me Collins was quoted as saying 'blasht yiz, don't you think we have enough trouble as we are,' when six would-be Garda recruits presented themselves, looking for a lift on their way to Dublin. Other accounts say they were the Mayo men already mentioned. Dalton's account of the last trip does not mention them at all. I have been reliably informed that extra passengers, from whatever county, were present on the return journey.
101. Fr Twohig, a local historian, of Mallow, County Cork, was told the identity of the man who is thought to have killed Collins from amongst that group by a penitent (*Sunday Press* 23/8/87) Robert O'Doherty, who went to live in Florida.
102. O'Malley pps. UCD. The re-creation in the Colm Connolly documentary, based in part on Dalton's information, also shows him being shot standing up.
103. Collins' cap was found the following day, washed, and buried in a biscuit tin in a local farm yard. The farmer, who was worried about the possibility of any human particles being buried in unconsecrated ground, because they might attract ghosts, mentioned its presence to a priest, who visited the house a little later on a 'station', the country custom whereby Mass is said in a house. The priest

then took the tin either to pass it on in strict confidence to the authorities or otherwise dispose of it as he saw fit. The uniform Collins was wearing was later taken to Argentina by a doctor from the hospital his body was first brought to, Shanakiel, in County Cork. The story of the cap was given to Liam O'Donnachadcha by Tom Hales. O'Donnachadcha pointed out to the author the farm where the cap was buried.
104. Dalton to MacCartaigh, *Sunday Independent*, 23/8/70.
105. Undated letter, Collins pps, AUTHOR.
106. *Sunday Independent*, 23/8/70.
107. Garda Hickey to Frank Hamilton, *Limerick Weekly Echo*, 26/8/72, and to Martin Brennan, *Evening Herald*, 12/9/70, quoted by Fr Anthony Gaughan, 'Letters to Editor', *Irish National Daily*, January and February 1990.
108. MacCartaigh, *Sunday Independent*, 23/8/70.
109. Feehan, p. 96.
110. Ibid.
111. *Sunday Independent*, 25/8/46.
112. O'Connor, p. 213.

Chapter 13 (pp. 416–432)

1. McPeake interviews, *Sunday Independent*, 1971.
2. This is not necessarily sinister; the Secret Service fund is a time-honoured method of coping with embarrassing government expenditures.
3. Micheal O'Cuinneagain, *Partition, from Michael Collins to Bobby Sands*, O'Cuinneagain, 1986.
4. John Feehan, *The Shooting of Michael Collins*, Royal Carberry Books, 1988, p. 112. An abstract of the tape-recorded discussion may be studied in Sean MacEoin's papers in the Franciscan Archives, Killiney. MacEoin tried to copy the McGarry tape, but the experiment was not a success. The whereabouts of the master tape is not known.
5. AUTHOR. Original, dated 27/1/23, held by Eamonn de Barra.
6. Confidential source.
7. PG 41, SPO.
8. Conversations with author in course of writing.
9. Confidential sources.
10. Description given by Nancy Collins to Liam O'Donnachadha, notes, made over a period of twenty years, AUTHOR.
11. Ibid.
12. Michael Collins (nephew) to author.
13. Johnny was nicknamed Shafter after making a winning throw in a weight-throwing competition at a local sports contest. Delightedly he had exclaimed, 'I'm a better weight-thrower than Shafter'. Shafter was, at the time, a world shot-putting champion.
14. Written not long before Devlin's own death from cancer on the eve of Collins' anniversary, 21/8/59.
15. Michael Collins (nephew) to author.
16. Collated after his death and published in 1922 by Talbot Press under the title of *The Path to Freedom*.
17. The phrase was first used by Lord Northcliffe in a speech in London on St Patrick's Day, 1917.
18. Fitzgerald pps, UCD.

19. In the Tan War (June 1920 – Truce, July 1921) 405 police and 150 military killed, 682 police and 345 military wounded. Official Irish civilian deaths are c. 150, but estimates vary between British and Irish sources, Overall a figure of 750, including Volunteers, is accepted by Irish historians such as Macardle, and probably between 800 and 1,000 wounded, but many Volunteer casualties were never reported.

20. Leon O'Broin, *No Man's Man*, Institute of Public Administration, n.d., p. 118.

21. Official statistics, published *Irish Times* 8/3/90, put the unemployment total at 220,000, and emigration running as high as 50,000 annually.

22. Correspondence in Department of Finance files, to inspect which I had first to sign the Official Secrets Act.

23. O'Muirthle memoir, Mulcahy pps, UCD.

24. A man called Philips, who gave the story to Col Pat Collins (nephew) towards the end of his life while a patient in the Meath Hospital, Dublin, Related to author, 21/10/89.

25. Account given by Ms A. Brennan, Rosscarbery, in letter to Mr Liam Collins, 1/5/22, AUTHOR. Ms Brennan also says that a son of the O'Sullivan family was told to leave the house and not to come back after he had burst in excitedly to announce 'we shot Mickeen'.

26. Michael Hopkinson, *Green Against Green*, Gill & Macmillan, 1988, p. 230.

27. Originals of both letters in the possession of Mr Eamonn de Barra.

28. On a visit to the Carmelite Convent in Dublin, of which Sister Margaret Mary is a member.

29. The account is given as it was told to me by Mr Michael Collins (nephew).

30. Correspondence in the Department of Finance files.

31. Johnny Collins to Frank Aiken, 13/2/35, AUTHOR's. Original in Department of Finance archives.

32. *Ibid*, 22/12,38.

33. M.J. Beary to Secretary D.C. Committee, 4/2/39. AUTHOR. Original in Department of Defence Archives.

34. Johnny and his sisters paid for the cross. Margaret and P.J. O'Driscoll, the sister and brother-in-law with whom he lived in Clonakilty are buried a few metres away.

35. Department of Foreign Affairs source.

36. Told to author by Michael Collins (nephew).

NOTE

The little boy smiling after Collins in the picture on the back cover of this book provided one of the few living links with Collins as the book was being written. Alphonsus Culliton was then fourteen. He had been brought to Collins' attention after being taken to Portobello Barracks in Dublin, having been caught up in a civil war shoot-out between Free State troops and Irregulars in New Ross, County Wexford.

When Collins discovered that Alphonsus had run away from a violent, drunken home in Liverpool, he falsified his age as sixteen so that the lad could join the Army. Collins left written instructions that in the event of anything happening to him the lad was to be brought up by Tom Keogh, a former Squad member of Collins' elite hit-team, the 'Squad'.

On the day the picture was taken, Collins was in a grim mood, striding past his protegé as he returned from a Requiem Mass for a party of his soldiers killed in a civil war engagement in Kerry. Keogh too was fighting for his life in a Limerick hospital, after being blown up by a landmine. Two weeks after the picture was taken, Alphonsus, disobeying orders, ran away again – this time to Limerick where he visited the hospital to inform Keogh that Collins himself had been killed in an ambush. Keogh died shortly afterwards and the use of landmines subsequently led some of his surviving Squad comrades to participate in some of the worst atrocities of the civil war. In Kerry captured Irregulars were tied together and forced to dismantle mined barricades.

Deprived of both his protectors, Alphonsus was brought up in the Army, and, like Collins himself, began his working career in the post office. He later emigrated to America. After his wife's death he returned to Ireland and lived in a retirement home.

Appendix

ARTICLES OF AGREEMENT AS SIGNED

on December 6th, 1921

1. Ireland shall have the same constitutional status in the Community of Nations known as the British Empire as the Dominion of Canada, the Commonwealth of Australia, the Dominion of New Zealand, and the Union of South Africa, with a Parliament having powers to make laws for the peace, order and good government of Ireland and an Executive responsible to that Parliament, and shall be styled and known as the Irish Free State.

2. Subject to the provisions hereinafter set out the position of the Irish Free State in relation to the Imperial Parliament and Government and otherwise shall be that of the Dominion of Canada, and the law, practice and constitutional usage governing the relationship of the Crown or the representative of the Crown and of the Imperial Parliament to the Dominion of Canada shall govern their relationship to the Irish Free State.

3. The representative of the Crown in Ireland shall be appointed in like manner as the Governor-General of Canada and in accordance with the practice observed in the making of such appointments.

4. The oath to be taken by Members of the Parliament of the Irish Free State shall be in the following form:

I . . . . do solemnly swear true faith and allegiance to the constitution of the Irish Free State as by law established and that I will be faithful to H.M. King George V, his heirs and successors by law, in virtue of the common citizenship of Ireland with Great Britain and her adherence to and membership of the group of nations forming the British Commonwealth of Nations.

5. The Irish Free State shall assume liability for the service of the Public Debt of the United Kingdom as existing at the date hereof and towards the payment of war pensions as existing at that date in such proportion as may be fair and equitable, having regard to any just claims on the part of Ireland by way set-off or counter-claim, the amount of such sums being determined in default of agreement by the arbitration of one or more independent persons being citizens or the British Empire.

6. Until an arrangement has been made between the British and Irish Governments whereby the Irish Free State undertakes her own coastal defence, the defence by sea of Great Britain and Ireland shall be undertaken by His Majesty's Imperial Forces. But this shall not prevent the construction or maintenance by the Government of the Irish Free State of such vessels as are necessary for the protection of the Revenue of the Fisheries.

The foregoing provisions of this Article shall be reviewed at a Conference of Representatives of the British and Irish Governments to be held at the expiration of five years from the date hereof with a view to the undertaking by Ireland of a share in her own coastal defence.

7. The Government of the Irish Free State shall afford to His Majesty's Imperial Forces:

(a)   In time of peace such harbour and other facilities as are indicated in the Annex hereto, or such other facilities as may from time to time be agreed between the British Government and the Government of the Irish Free State; and

(b)   In time of war or of strained relations with a Foreign Power such harbour and other facilities as the British Goverment may require for the purposes of such defence as aforesaid.

8. With a view to securing the observance of the principle of inter-national limitation of armaments, if the Government of the Irish Free State establishes and maintains a military defence force, the establishments thereof shall not exceed in size such proportion of the military establishments maintained in Great Britain as that which the population of Ireland bears to the population of Great Britain.

9. The ports of Great Britain and the Irish Free State shall be freely open to the ships of the other country on payment of the customary port and other dues.

10. The Government of the Irish Free State agrees to pay fair compensation on terms not less favourable than those accorded by the Act of 1920 to judges, officials, members of Police Forces and other Public Servants who are discharged by it or who retire in consequence of the change of Government effected in pursuance hereof.

Provided that this agreement shall not apply to members of the Auxiliary Police Force or to persons recruited in Great Britain for the Royal Irish Constabulary during the two years next preceding the date hereof. The British Government will assume responsibility for such compensation or pensions as may be payable to any of these excepted persons.

11. Until the expiration of one month from the passing of the Act of Parliament for the ratification of this instrument, the powers of the Parliament and the Government of the Irish Free State shall not be exercisable as respects Northern Ireland and the provisions of the Government of Ireland Act, 1920, shall so far as they relate to Northern Ireland remain of full force and effect, and no election shall be held for the return of members to serve in the Parliament of the Irish Free State for constituencies in Northern Ireland, unless a resolution is passed by both Houses of the Parliament of Northern Ireland in favour of the holding of such election before the end of the said month.

12. If before the expiration of the said month, an address is presented to His Majesty by both Houses of the Parliament of Northern Ireland to that effect, the powers of the Parliament and Government of the Irish Free State shall no longer extend to Northern Ireland, and the provisions of the Government of Ireland Act, 1920 (including those relating to the Council of Ireland) shall, so far as they relate to Northern Ireland, continue to be of full force and effect, and this instrument shall have effect subject to the necessary modifications.

Provided that if such an address is so presented a Commission consisting of three persons, one to be appointed by the Government of the Irish Free State, one to be appointed by the Government of Northern Ireland and one who shall be Chairman to be appointed by the British Government shall determine in accordance with the wishes of the inhabitants, so far as may be compatible with economic and geographic conditions, the boundaries between Northern Ireland and the rest of Ireland, and for the purposes of the Government of Ireland Act, 1920, and of this instrument, the boundary of Northern Ireland shall be such as may be determined by such Commission.

13. For the purpose of the last foregoing article, the powers of the Parliament of Southern Ireland under the Government of Ireland Act, 1920, to elect members of the Council of Ireland shall after the Parliament of the Irish Free State is constituted be exercised by that Parliament.

14. After the expiration of the said month, if no such address as is mentioned in Article 12 hereof is presented, the Parliament and Government of Northern Ireland shall continue to exercise as respects Northern Ireland the powers conferred on them by the Government of Ireland Act, 1920, but the Parliament and Government of the Irish Free State shall in Northern Ireland have in relation to matters in respect of which the Parliament of Northern Ireland has not power to make laws under that Act (including matters which under the said Act are within the jurisdiction of the Council of Ireland) the same powers as in the rest of Ireland, subject to such other provisions as may be agreed in manner hereinafter appearing.

15. At any time after the date hereof the Government of Northern Ireland and the provisional Government of Southern Ireland hereinafter constituted may meet for the purpose of discussing the provisions subject to which the last foregoing article is to operate in the event of no such address as is therein mentioned being presented and those provisions may include:

(a) Safeguards with regard to patronage in Northern Ireland:
(b) Safeguards with regard to the collection of revenue in Northern Ireland:
(c) Safeguards with regard to import and export duties affecting the trade or industry of Northern Ireland:
(d) Safeguards for minorities in Northern Ireland:
(e) The settlement of the financial relations between Northern Ireland and the Irish Free State:
(f) The establishment and powers of a local militia in Northern Ireland and the relation of the Defence Forces of the Irish Free State and of Northern Ireland respectively:

and if at any such meeting provisions are agreed to, the same shall have effect as if they were included amongst the provisions subject to which the Powers of the Parliament and Government of the Irish Free State are to be exercisable in Northern Ireland under Article 14 hereof.

16. Neither the Parliament of the Irish Free State nor the Parliament of Northern Ireland shall make any law so as either directly or indirectly to endow any religion or prohibit or restrict the free exercise thereof or give any preference or impose any disability on account of religious belief or religious status or affect prejudicially the right of any child to attend a school receiving public money without attending the religious instruction at the school or make any discrimination as respects state aid between schools under the management of different religious denominations or divert from any religious denomination or any educational institution any of its property except for public utility purposes and on payment of compensation.

17. By way of provisional arrangement for the administration of Southern Ireland during the interval which must elapse between the date hereof and the constitution of a Parliament and Government of the Irish Free State in accordance therewith, steps shall be taken forthwith for summoning a meeting of members of Parliament elected for constituencies in Southern Ireland since the passing of the Government of Ireland Act, 1920, and for constituting a provisional Government, and the British Government shall take the steps necessary to transfer to such provisional Government the powers and machinery requisite for the discharge of its duties, provided that every member of such provisional Government shall have signified in writing his or her acceptance of this instrument. But this arrangement shall not continue in force beyond the expiration of twelve months from the date hereof.

18. This instrument shall be submitted forthwith by His Majesty's Government for the approval of Parliament and by the Irish signatories to a meeting summoned for the purpose of the members elected to sit in the House of Commons of Southern Ireland, and if approved shall be ratified by the necessary legislation.

<table>
<tr><td align="center">On behalf of the British
Delegation.
Signed</td><td align="center">On behalf of the Irish
Delegation.
Signed</td></tr>
</table>

D. LLOYD GEORGE.	ART Ó GRÍOBHTHA (ARTHUR GRIFFITH).
AUSTEN CHAMBERLAIN.	MICHEÁL Ó COILEÁIN.
BIRKENHEAD.	RIOBÁRD BARTÚN.
WINSTON S. CHURCHILL.	EUDHMONN S. Ó DÚGÁIN.
L. WORTHINGTON-EVANS.	SEÓRSA GHABHÁIN UÍ DHUBHTHAIGH.
HAMAR GREENWOOD.	<i>December 6th,</i> 1921
GORDON HEWART.	

ANNEX

1. The following are the specific facilities required:

Dockyard Port at Berehaven

(a) Admiralty property and rights to be retained as at the rate hereof. Harbour defences to remain in charge of British care and maintenance parties.

Queenstown

(b) Harbour defences to remain in charge of British care and maintenance parties. Certain mooring buoys to be retained for use of His Majesty's ships.

Belfast Lough

(c) Harbour defences to remain in charge of British care and maintenance parties.

Lough Swilly

(d) Harbour defences to remain in charge of British care and maintenance parties.

Aviation

(e) Facilities in the neighbourhood of the above Ports for coastal defence by air.

Oil Fuel Storage

| (f) | Haulbowline and Rathmullen | To be offered for sale to commercial companies under guarantee that purchasers shall maintain a certain minimum stock for Admiralty purposes. |

2. A Convention shall be made between the British Government and the Government of the Irish Free State to give effect to the following conditions:

(a) That submarine cables shall not be landed or wireless stations for communications with places outside Ireland be established except by agreement with the British Government; that the existing cable landing rights and wireless concessions shall not be withdrawn except by agreement with the British Government; and that the British Government shall be entitled to land additional submarine cables or establish additional wireless stations for communication with places outside Ireland.

(b) That lighthouses, buoys, beacons, and any navigational marks or navigational aids shall be maintained by the Government of the Irish Free State as at the date hereof and shall not be removed or added to except by agreement with the British Government.

(c) That war signal stations shall be closed down and left in charge of care and maintenance parties, the Government of the Irish Free State being offered the option of taking them over and working them for commercial purposes subject to Admiralty inspection, and guaranteeing the upkeep of existing telegraphic communication therewith.

3. A Convention shall be made between the same Governments for the regulation of Civil Communication by Air.

			A. G.
D. LL. G.	B.	W. S. C.	M. O C.
A. C.		E. S. O. D.	R. B.
			S. G. D.

DOCUMENT NUMBER TWO

The Counter-proposal drafted by de Valera.

'That inasmuch as the "Articles of Agreement for a treaty between Great Britain and Ireland", signed in London on December 6th, 1921, do not reconcile Irish National aspirations and the Association of Ireland with the Community of Nations known as the British Commonwealth, and cannot be the basis of an enduring peace between the Irish and the British peoples, DAIL EIREANN, in the name of the Sovereign Irish Nation, makes to the Government of Great Britain, to the Government of the other States of the British Commonwealth, and to the peoples of Great Britain and of these several States, the following Proposal for a Treaty of Amity and Association which, DAIL EIREANN is convinced, could be entered into by the Irish people with the sincerity of goodwill':

Proposed Treaty of Association Between Ireland and the British Commonwealth

In order to bring to an end the long and ruinous conflict between Great Britain and Ireland by a sure and lasting peace honourable to both nations, it is agreed

Status of Ireland.

1. That the legislative, executive, and judicial authority of Ireland shall be derived solely from the people of Ireland.

Terms of Association

2. That, for purposes of common concern, Ireland shall be associated with the States of the British Commonwealth, viz: —The Kingdom of Great Britain, the Dominion of Canada, the Commonwealth of Australia, the Dominion of New Zealand, and the Union of South Africa.

3. That when acting as an associate the rights, status, and privileges of Ireland shall be in no respect less than those enjoyed by any of the component States of the British Commonwealth.

4. That the matters of 'common concern' shall include Defence, Peace and War, Political Treaties, and all matters now treated as of common concern, amongst the States of the British Commonwealth, and that in these matters there shall be between Ireland and the States of the British Commonwealth 'such concerted action founded on consultation as the several Governments may determine.'

5. That in virtue of this association of Ireland with the States of the British Commonwealth, citizens of Ireland in any of these States shall not be subject to any disabilities which a citizen of one of the component States of the British Commonwealth would not be subject to, and reciprocally for citizens of these States in Ireland.

6. That, for purposes of the Association, Ireland shall recognise His Britannic Majesty as head of the Association.

Defence

7. That, so far as her resources permit, Ireland shall provide for her own defence by sea, land and air, and shall repel by force any attempt by a foreign Power to violate the integrity of her soil and territorial waters, or to use them for any purpose hostile to Great Britain and the other associated States.

8. That for five years, pending the establishment of Irish coastal defence forces, or

for such other period as the Governments of the two countries may later agree upon, facilities for the coastal defence of Ireland shall be given to the British Government as follows:–

(a) In time of peace such harbour and other facilities as are indicated in the Annex hereto, or such other facilities as may from time to time be agreed upon between the British Government and the Government of Ireland;

(b) In time of war such harbour and other naval facilities as the British Government may reasonably require for the purposes of such defence as aforesaid.

9. That within five years from the date of exchange of ratifications of this Treaty a Conference between the British and Irish Governments shall be held in order to hand over the coastal defence of Ireland to the Irish Government, unless some other arrangement for naval defence be agreed by both Governments to be desirable in the common interest of Ireland, Great Britain, and the other Associated States.

10. That, in order to co-operate in furthering the principle of international limitation of armaments, the Government of Ireland shall not

(a) Build submarines unless by agreement with Great Britain and the other States of the Commonwealth;

(b) Maintain a military defence force, the establishments whereof exceed in size such proportion of the military establishments maintained in Great Britain as that which the population of Ireland bears to the population of Great Britain.

Miscellaneous

11. That the Governments of Great Britain and of Ireland shall make a convention for the regulation of civil communication by air.

12. That the ports of Great Britain and of Ireland shall be freely open to the ships of each country on payment of the customary port and other dues.

13. That Ireland shall assume liability for such share of the present public debt of Great Britain and Ireland, and of payment of war pensions as existing at this date as may be fair and equitable, having regard to any just claims on the part of Ireland by way of set-off or counter-claim, the amount of such sums being determined in default of agreement, by the arbitration of one or more independent persons, being citizens of Ireland or of the British Commonwealth.

14. That the Government of Ireland agrees to pay compensation on terms not less favourable than those proposed by the British Government of Ireland Act of 1920 to that Government's judges, officials, members of Police Forces and other Public Servants who are discharged by the Government of Ireland, or who retire in consequence of the change of government elected in pursuance hereof:

Provided that this agreement shall not apply to members of the Auxiliary Police Force, or to persons recruited in Great Britain for the Royal Irish Constabulary during the two years next preceding the date hereof. The British Government will assume responsibility for such compensation or pensions as may be payable to any of these excepted persons.

15. That neither the Parliament of Ireland nor any subordinate Legislature in Ireland shall make any law so as either directly or indirectly to endow any religion or prohibit or restrict the free exercise thereof, or give any preference or impose any disability on account of religious belief or religious status, or affect prejudicially the right of any child to attend a school receiving public money without attending a religious instruction at the school, or make any discrimination as respects State aid between schools under the management of different religious denominations, or divert from

any religious denomination or any educational institution any of its property except for public utility purposes and on payment of compensation.

Transitional

16. That by way of transitional arrangement for the Administration of Ireland during the interval which must elapse between the date hereof and the setting up of a Parliament and Government of Ireland in accordance herewith, the members elected for constituencies in Ireland since the passing of the British Government of Ireland Act in 1920 shall, at a meeting summoned for the purpose, elect a transitional Government to which the British Government and Dáil Eireann shall transfer the authority, powers, and machinery requisite for the discharge of its duties, provided that every member of such transition Government shall have signified in writing his or her acceptance of this instrument. But this arrangement shall not continue in force beyond the expiration of twelve months from the date hereof.

Ratification

17. That this instrument shall be submitted for ratification forthwith by His Britannic Majesty's Government to the Parliament at Westminster, and by the Cabinet of Dáil Eireann to a meeting of the members elected for the constituencies in Ireland set forth in the British Government of Ireland Act, 1920, and when ratifications have been exchanged shall take immediate effect.

ANNEX

1. The following are the specific facilities referred to in Article 8 (a):

Dockyard Port at Berehaven

(a)   British Admiralty property and rights to be retained as at the date hereof. Harbour defences to remain in charge of British care and maintenance parties.

Queenstown

(b)   Harbour defences to remain in charge of British care and maintenance parties. Certain mooring buoys to be retained for use of His Britannic Majesty's ships.

Belfast Lough

(c)   Harbour defences to remain in charge of British care and maintenance parties.

Lough Swilly

(d)   Harbour defences to remain in charge of British care and maintenance parties.

Aviation

(e)   Facilities in the neighbourhood of the above Ports for coastal defence by air.

Oil Fuel Storage

(f)   Haulbowline   To be offered for sale to commercial companies under
      and   guarantee that purchasers shall maintain a certain
      Rathmullen   minimum stock for British Admiralty purposes.

2. A Convention covering a period of five years shall be made between the British and Irish Governments to give effect to the following conditions:

(a) That submarine cables shall not be landed or wireless stations for communications with places outside Ireland be established except by agreement with the British Government; that the existing cable landing rights and wireless concessions shall not be withdrawn except by agreement with the British Government; and that the British Government shall be entitled to land additional submarine cables or establish additional wireless stations for communication with places outside Ireland.

(b) That lighthouses, buoys, beacons, and any navigational marks or navigational aids shall be maintained by the Government of Ireland as at the date hereof and shall not be removed or added to except by agreement with the British Government.

(c) That war signal stations shall be closed down and left in charge of care and maintenance parties, the Government of Ireland being offered the option of taking them over and working them for commercial purposes subject to British Admiralty inspection and guaranteeing the upkeep of existing telegraphic communication therewith.

(The following addendum concerning N.E. Ulster was to be proposed as a separate resolution by the President.)

ADDENDUM

NORTH-EAST ULSTER

Resolved:

That, whilst refusing to admit the right of any part of Ireland to be excluded from the supreme authority of the Parliament of Ireland, or that the relations between the Parliament of Ireland and any subordinate Legislature in Ireland can be a matter for treaty with a government outside Ireland, nevertheless, in sincere regard for internal peace, and in order to make manifest our desire not to bring force or coercion to bear upon any substantial part of the Province of Ulster, whose inhabitants may now be unwilling to accept the national authority, we are prepared to grant to that portion of Ulster which is defined as Northern Ireland in the British Government of Ireland Act of 1920, privileges and safeguards not less substantial than those provided for in the Articles of Agreement for a Treaty between Great Britain and Ireland signed in London on December 6th, 1921.

Bibliography and Sources

PRIMARY SOURCES

Collins' Diary, and information concerning Collins' career and other matters, from nephew, Mr Michael Collins.

Collins' memorabilia and material concerning Bael na mBlath ambush and aftermath, from nephew, Col Pat Collins.

Collins' papers, from nephew, Mr Liam Collins.

Collins' letters to Donal Hayes (unpublished), from Dr Dermot Keogh.

Collins' letters to Kitty Kiernan (unpublished), from her son, Mr Felix Cronin.

Collins' letters to Susan Killeen, from her daughter, Mrs Maire Mulloy.

Collins/Churchill correspondence, from Professor Edith Sagarra.

Sister Celestine, unpublished memoirs, from Collins family.

Collins-Powell, Mrs Mary, unpublished memoirs, from Collins family.

de Valera, Eamon, letters to Sinead de Valera, from anonymous source.

Foley, Thomas, transcript of interview, conducted by Fr A. O'Driscoll.

IRA and RIC documents concerning liaison activities of Sean Haughey and others in Derry around time of Derry prisoners' escape attempt (2/11/21) in author's possession.

McCoy, John, unpublished memoir; and documents relating to pension claims made under Military Service Pensions Act 1934, from Mr Harold O'Sullivan.

MacKenna Napoli, Kathleen, unpublished memoirs, from Fr P. Brennan.

Tobin, Liam, memoirs, letters and other material, from daughters, Ann Thornton and Marie Tobin.

Documents and reminiscences supplied by Mr Eamonn de Barra.

'Notes' and reminiscences concerning Collins and his associates, compiled by Mr Liam Donnachadcha.

Information and material supplied by Collins' nephew, Col Pat Collins, and by Ms Mary-Clare O'Malley.

Compilation of documents relating to Treaty signing and its aftermath; original drafts of MSS for de Valera biography dealing with de Valera's Irish-American controversies, including correspondence with Harry Boland and Collins; and memoir by Gerry Boland, from Dr T. P. O'Neill.

At some stage the author has interviewed almost all the chief actors in the Irish drama of the years circa 1916–22, and he has amassed a correspondingly large amount of documentation concerning Irish Republican activity which has been drawn on for background information in the present work. Some specific conversations which were particularly helpful include those with figures who have since passed on: Gerry Boland, Michael Brennan, Eamonn Broy, Vivion de Valera, Sean MacBride, Richard Mulcahy, David Neligan, and Peadar O'Donnell. Three survivors, still alive as this was being written, who were particularly illuminating, were Eamonn de Barra, Vinnie Byrne, Sr Margaret Mary and Ms Eileen O'Donovan.

ARCHIVES CONSULTED

ARCHDIOCESAN RECORDS
   (Dublin) Archbishop Byrne papers; Archbishop Walsh papers.
   (Perth) Archbishop Clune papers.
ARMY ARCHIVES, Cathal Brugha Barracks, Dublin
   Originals of Collins military despatches (also available on microfilm, National Gallery of Ireland, pp.911–22) and correspondence with various contacts; miscellaneous material, including Liam Lynch's despatch on Collins' death and some commemorative articles by contemporaries.
DEPARTMENT OF FINANCE, Dublin
   Collins' files containing correspondence from Gen. Richard Mulcahy, Joe O'Reilly, Tim Healy and others relating to erection of Collins Memorial and disposal of effects.
DEPARTMENT OF DEFENCE, Dublin
   Correspondence between Johnny Collins, Frank Aiken and others relating to Collins Memorial.
DUBLIN UNIVERSITY (TRINITY COLLEGE)
   Erskine Childers Diaries and papers; Frank Gallagher papers; Major Sirr papers.
GLASNEVIN CEMETERY, Dublin
   Certificate of authorisation for cross on Collins' grave, signed by Eamon de Valera.
GEORGETOWN UNIVERSITY LIBRARY, Washington D.C.
   Shane Leslie papers.
H.M. STATIONERY OFFICE, London
   Hansard, both for House of Commons and House of Lords throughout period under review, especially for developments such as those in November 1920 (Bloody Sunday and other incidents), the Irish Treaty debates (December 1921–March 1922), and the Beleek/Pettigo and Sir Henry Wilson controversies of June 1922.
IRISH BUREAU OF MILITARY HISTORY
   Memoirs of Michael Brennan, Paddy Daly; Joe Dolan; Joe McGuinness; Jim Slattery; Frank Thornton; Liam Tobin.
   Catalogue of Events 1898–1921, 3 Vols.
IRISH STATIONERY OFFICE, Dublin
   Dail Debates: First Dail 1919–21 (Private sessions); Second Dail 1921–22.
   Treaty Debates (Public sessions) 1921–22 and subsequent proceedings of the Dail until June 1922.
KILMAINHAM MUSEUM, Dublin
   Collins correspondence.
   Material on Lady Lavery and Collins, Kevin O'Higgins, Shane Leslie.
NATIONAL LIBRARY OF IRELAND
   Papers of F.S. Bourke; Michael Collins; Frank Gallagher; Thomas Johnson; Sir John and Hazel Lavery; Joe McGarrity; Kathleen Napoli MacKenna; Leon O'Broin; Art O'Brien; William O'Brien; Florrie O'Donoghue; Austin Stack.
   RIC records (microfilm).
   Mark Sturgis Diary (microfilm).

NATIONAL MUSEUM OF IRELAND
  Collins memorabilia, including 'Collins' cap', almost certainly wrongly claimed to be the cap he was wearing at the moment of his fatal wounding.
PUBLIC RECORDS OFFICE, BELFAST
  Londonderry papers.
  Col Spender material relating to Collins' Northern Ireland Education and Trades Union policy, B-Special activities and other matters.
PUBLIC RECORDS OFFICE, DUBLIN
  Robert Barton's expanded 'Notes for a Lecture' and replies to Margery Forester's questionnaire, and other miscellaneous material.
  Department of Finance material for 1922.
PUBLIC RECORDS OFFICE, LONDON
  Correspondence from figures such as Churchill, Andrew Cope, Lionel Curtis, Tom Jones, Lloyd George, Gen. Macready, Lord Middleton, Mark Sturgis.
STATE PAPER OFFICE OF IRELAND, DUBLIN
  Collins papers and correspondence (including 'D' and 'S' series dealing with Provisional Government, Dail Cabinet, and Executive Council material). Proceedings of North Eastern Advisory Committee.
  Material relating to police activities in Northern Ireland, to the Derry Prisoners' affair, the condition of nationalists in Northern Ireland, the Collins/Craig pacts. Proceedings of the Catholic Advisory Committee.
  Accounts of the Beleek/Pettigo affairs, the Boundary Commission and the Sinn Fein Funds case.
UNIVERSITY COLLEGE DUBLIN
  Earnan O'Malley Notebooks and papers.
  Papers of Ernest Blythe; Desmond Fitzgerald; Hugh Kennedy; Eoin MacNeill; Richard Mulcahy; Ginger O'Connell.

NEWSPAPERS AND PERIODICALS

Belfast Newsletter; Daily Herald; Evening Herald; Freeman's Journal; Gaelic American; Irish Bulletin; Irish Independent; Irish News; Irish Press; Irish Times; Irish World; Limerick Weekly Echo, Magill Magazine; Manchester Evening Guardian; Morning Post; Northern Whig; Poblacht na hEireann; Sunday Independent; Sunday Press; The Times.

PAMPHLETS AND ARTICLES

AKENSON, D.H. and Fallin, F.P., 'The Irish Civil War and the Drafting of the Irish Constitution', *Eire Ireland*, Irish American Cultural Institute, Minnesota, Vols. I, II, IV, 1970.
BARTON, Robert, 'The Truth about the Treaty', Republican Press, n.d.
BOYCE, D.G., 'British Conservative Opinion, the Ulster Question, and the Partition of Ireland', *Irish Historical Studies*, Vol. XVII, No. 65, 1970–1, pp. 89–112.
BUREAU OF MILITARY HISTORY, *Chronologies*, Dublin, vols I-III.
CARROLL, F.M., 'The American Committee for Relief in Ireland, 1920–1922', *Irish Historical Studies*, Vol. XXIII, No. 89, May 1982.
COLLINS, Michael, 'Arguments for the Treaty', Martin Lester, 1922; 'Free State or Chaos' (Pamphleted version of speech delivered Waterford, 24/2/22).
CURTISS, L.P., 'Anglo-Saxons and Celts', *Studies in British History and Culture*, Connecticut Conference on British Studies, 1968; 'The Anglo-Irish Predicament', *20th-Century British History and Culture*, Ireland, Vol.II, 1970, pp.37–93.
'DALTA', 'National Land Policy', Talbot Press, Dublin, 1920.
DE VALERA, Eamon, 'The Alternative to the Treaty, Document No. 2', Irish Nation Committee, Dublin, 1923.
'The Anglo-Irish Treaty and de Valera's Alternative', Irish Nation Committee, Dublin, 1924.

GALLAGHER, Frank, 'The Partition of Ireland', Gill & Macmillan, Dublin, 1947.

HAYES, Michael, 'Dail Eireann and the Irish Civil War', Studies, Dublin, Spring 1969.

MACREADY, Gen. Sir Nevil, 'Churchill and Lloyd George', Dublin, n.d. (probably 1922).

O'BEIRNE, John Ranelagh, 'The I.R.B.: Treaty to 1924', Irish Historical Studies, Vol. XX, 1976.

O'HIGGINS, Kevin, 'The New de Valera', Dublin, 1922.

O'MULLANE, Michael, 'Noel Lemass', Joe Clarke, Dublin, n.d.

O'RAHILLY, Alfred, 'The Case for the Treaty', n.d.

TELEVISION DOCUMENTARIES

CONNOLLY, Colum, (dir.), 'The Shadow of Bael na mBlath', Radio Telefis Eireann, 1989.

O'SHANNON, Cathal, (dir.), 'Emmet Dalton', Radio Telefis Eireann, 1978.

SELECT BIBLIOGRAPHY

AKENSON, D.H., Education and Enmity: the Control of Schooling in Northern Ireland, 1920–50, Newton Abbot, 1973; A Mirror to Kathleen's Face, David & Charles, 1975; The U.S. and Ireland, Harvard University Press, 1973.

ANDREWS, C.S. Dublin Made Me, Mercier Press, Cork, 1979.

ARTHUR, Sir G., General Sir George Maxwell, John Murray, 1932.

ASH, B., The Lost Dictator, Cassell, 1968.

BARRY, Tom, Guerilla Days in Ireland, Anvil, Tralee, 1962; The Reality of Anglo-Irish War, Anvil, Tralee, 1974.

BEASLAI, Piaras, Michael Collins and the Making of a New Ireland, 2 Vols, Phoenix, Dublin, 1926.

BEAVERBROOK, Lord (Max Aitken), Decline and Fall of Lloyd George, Collins, 1963.

BENNETT, Richard, The Black and Tans, New English Library, 1970.

BIRKENHEAD, Earl of, (F.E.) The life of F.E. Smith: First Earl of Birkenhead, Eyre & Spottiswoode, 1959.

BOURKE, Marcus, John O'Leary, Anvil, Tralee, 1967.

BOWMAN, John, De Valera and the Ulster Question, 1917–1973, Oxford University Press, 1982.

BOYCE, D. G., Englishmen and Irish Troubles, Cape, 1972; Nationalism in Ireland, Gill & Macmillan, Dublin, 1982; Separatism and Irish Nationalist Tradition, ed. C.H. Williams, University of Wales Press, 1982.

BOYLE, Andrew, The Riddle of Erskine Childers, Hutchinson, 1977.

BREEN, Dan, My Fight for Irish Freedom, Talbot Press, 1924, Anvil Books, Tralee, 1964.

BRENNAN, Robert, Allegiance, Irish Press, Dublin, 1950.

BROMAGE, Mary C., de Valera and the March of a Nation, Hutchinson, 1956; Churchill and Ireland, University of Notre Dame Press, Indiana, 1964.

BUCKLAND, P., Irish Unionism 1, The Anglo-Irish and the New Ireland, Gill & Macmillan, 1972; Irish Unionism 11, The Origins of Northern Ireland 1886–1922, Gill & Macmillan, Dublin, & Barnes and Noble, 1973; James Craig, Gill & Macmillan, Dublin, 1980.

CALLWELL, C.E., Field Marshal Sir Henry Wilson: His Life and Diaries, 2 Vols, Cassell, 1927.

CARROL, Francis, American Opinion and the Irish Question, Gill & Macmillan and St Martin's Press, Dublin, 1978.

CAULFIELD, Max, The Easter Rebellion, Frederick Muller, 1964, (paperback) Four Square, 1965.

CHURCHILL, Winston, *Lord Randolph*, Odhams (2 Vols), 1906, and Heinemann, 1 Vol: 1966; *The Aftermath*, Butterworth, 1929.

CLARK, Wallace, 'Guns in Ulster', *Belfast Constabulary Gazette*, 1967.

COLLINS, Michael, *The Path to Freedom*, Talbot Press, Dublin, and T. Fisher Unwin, 1922.

COLUM, Padraig, *Arthur Griffith*, Browne & Nolan, Dublin, 1959.

COOGAN, T.P., *Ireland Since the Rising*, Pall Mall, 1966; *The I.R.A.*, Pall Mall, 1970, and Fontana 1970, new editions 1980 and 1985; *On the Blanket*, Ward River, Dublin, 1980.

CORFE, Tom, *The Phoenix Park Murders*, Hodder & Stoughton, 1968.

COXHEAD, Elizabeth, *Lady Gregory*, Macmillan, 1961.

CRAWFORD, Robert, *Loyal to King Billy*, Gill & Macmillan, Dublin, 1987.

CRONIN, Sean, *Ideology of the I.R.A.*, Ann Arbor University Press, 1972; *The McGarrity Papers*, Anvil, Tralee, 1972; *Washington's Irish Policy, 1916–18*, Anvil, 1987 and Irish Books & Media, Minnesota, 1987.

CROZIER, Brig. F.P., *Impressions and Recollections*, Laurie, 1930; *Ireland for Ever*, Cape, 1932.

CURRAN, Joseph, *The Birth of the Irish Free State, 1921–23.*, Alabama University Press, 1988.

DALTON, Charles, *With the Dublin Brigades 1917–21*, Peter Davies, 1929.

DE BURCA, Padraig and Boyle, John F., *Free State or Republic?*, Talbot Press, Dublin, and T. Fisher Unwin, 1922.

DE VERE WHITE, Terence, *Kevin O'Higgins*, Methuen, 1948.

DONNELLY, J., *Landlord and Tenant in 19th-Century Ireland*, Gill & Macmillan, Dublin, 1973; *19th-Century Land and People of Cork*, Routledge & Kegan Paul, 1975; with S.Clarke, *Irish Peasants*, Manchester University Press, 1983.

DRIBERG, Tom, *Study in Power and Frustration*, Weidenfeld & Nicolson, 1956.

DUDLEY EDWARDS, Ruth, *Patrick Pearse, The Triumph of Failure*, Gill & Macmillan, Dublin, 1981.

DWANE, David T., *Early Life of Eamon de Valera*, Talbot Press, Dublin, and T.Fisher Unwin, 1922.

DWYER, T. Ryle, *Eamon de Valera*, Gill & Macmillan, Dublin, 1980; *Michael Collins and the Treaty*, Mercier Press, Cork, 1981; *de Valera's Darkest Hour, 1919–32*, Mercier Press, Cork, 1982; *Michael Collins: The Man Who Won the War*, Mercier Press Cork, 1990.

ERVINE, St John, *Craigavon, Ulsterman*, Allen & Unwin, 1949.

FANNING, Ronan, *Irish Department of Finance*, Institute of Public Administration, Dublin, 1978; *Independent Ireland*, Helicon, Dublin, 1983.

FARRELL, Michael, *Arming the Protestants*, Brandon, Kerry, and Pluto Press, 1983.

FEEHAN, Sean, *Michael Collins, Murder or Accident*, Mercier Press, Cork, 1981.

FITZPATRICK, David, *Politics and Irish Life 1913–21*, Gill & Macmillan, Dublin, 1977.

FORESTER, Margery, *Michael Collins – The Lost Leader*, Sidgwick & Jackson, 1971, Sphere, 1972.

FOSTER, Roy, *Modern Ireland, 1600–1972*, Allen Lane, 1988, Penguin Paperback, 1989.

GALLAGHER, Frank, *The Indivisible Island*, Gollancz, 1957, *The Anglo-Irish Treaty*, Hutchinson, 1965.

GAUGHAN, Anthony, *Austin Stack*, Kingdom Books, Tralee, 1971; *Constable Mee*, Anvil, Dublin, 1975; *Thomas Johnson*, Anvil, Dublin, 1980.

GEARY, Laurence, *Plan of Campaign*, Cork University Press, 1986.

GILBERT, Martin, *Winston Churchill, Vol. 111* 'The Challenge of War 1914–1916', Heinemann 1971; *Companion*, Heinemann, 1977; *World in Torment, W.S.Churchill, 1917–22*, Minerva, 1990.

GLEESON, James, *Bloody Sunday*, Peter Davies, 1962.
GOLDRING, Maurice, *Faith of Our Fathers*, Repsol, Dublin, 1982.
GREAVES, Desmond C., *The Life & Times of James Connolly*, Lawrence & Wishart, 1961; *Liam Mellowes and The Irish Revolution*, Lawrence & Wishart, 1971.
GREELEY, Andrew, *That Most Distressful Nation*, Quadrangle, Chicago, 1972.
GRIFFITH, Kenneth & O'Grady, Timothy, *Curious Journey*, Hutchinson, 1982.
GWYNN, Denis, *De Valera*, Jarrolds, 1933.
GWYNNE, Stephen, *The Life of John Redmond*, Harrap, 1932.

HAMBRO, C.J., *Newspaper Lords in British Politics*, MacDonald, 1958.
HARKNESS, D.W., *The Restless Dominion*, New York University Press, 1970.
HOLT, E., *Protest in Arms, 1916–21*, Putnam, 1960.
HOPKINSON, Michael, *Green against Green*, Gill & Macmillan, Dublin, 1988.
HYDE, Montgomery, *The Londonderrys*, Hamish Hamilton, 1979.

JENKINS, Roy, *Asquith*, Collins, 1965.
JONES, Tom, *Whitehall Diaries*, Vol. III: *Ireland 1918–25*, (ed.) K. Middlemas, Oxford University Press, 1971; *Lloyd George*, Harvard University Press, 1951.

KEE, Robert, *The Green Flag*, Weidenfeld & Nicolson, 1972.
KILFEATHER, T.P., *The Connacht Rangers*, Anvil, Tralee, 1919.
KITSON, Brig. F.E., *Low Intensity Operations*, Faber, 1971.

LAFFAN, Michael, *The Partition of Ireland*, Dundalgan Press, Dundalk, 1983.
LARKIN, Emmet, *James Larkin*, Routledge & Kegan Paul, and MIT Press, Cambridge, Mass., 1965.
LEE, Joseph and O'Tuathaig, Gearoid, 'The Age of de Valera', Ward River and RTE, Dublin, 1982; Lee, Joseph (ed.) *Towards a Sense of Place*, Cork University Press, 1985; Lee, Joseph, *Ireland 1912-1985*, Cambridge University Press, 1989.
LE ROUX, Louis N., *Tom Clarke and The Irish Freedom Movement*, Talbot Press, Dublin, 1926; *Patrick H. Pearse*, Trans: Desmond Ryan, Phoenix, Dublin, 1932.
LESLIE, Anita, *Edwardians in Love*, Hutchinson, 1976: *Clare Sheridan*, Hutchinson, 1976; *Gilt and the Gingerbread*, Hutchinson, 1981; *Cousin Randolph*, Hutchinson, 1985.
LLOYD GEORGE, David, *War Memoirs*, 2 Vols, Odhams, 1934;
LONGFORD, Lord and O'Neill, T.P., *Eamon de Valera*, Gill & Macmillan, Dublin, and Hutchinson, 1970. Lord Longford (Frank Pakenham), *Peace by Ordeal*, Sidgwick & Jackson, 1972 (First published Cape, 1935).
LUCEY, Charles, *Ireland and the Irish*, Doubleday, New York, 1970.
LYNCH, Diarmuid, (ed.) *Florence O'Donoghue*, Mercier Press, Cork, 1957; *The IRB and the 1916 Rising*, Doubleday, n.d.
LYONS, F.S.L., *Ireland Since the Famine*, Weidenfeld & Nicolson, 1971; (ed.) *The Bank of Ireland 1783–1983*, Gill & Macmillan, Dublin, 1983.
LYONS, J.B., *Oliver St John Gogarty*, Blackwater Press, Dublin, 1980; *Tom Kettle*, Glendale, Dublin, 1983.

MACARDLE, Dorothy, *The Irish Republic*, Gollancz, 1937, and Irish Press, Dublin, 1951.
MACREADY, Gen. Sir Nevil, *Annals of an Active Life*, 2 Vols, Hutchinson, 1924.
MACCARTAN, Patrick, *With de Valera in America*, Brentano, New York, 1932.
MACDONAGH, Oliver, *Ireland: The Union and its Aftermath*, Allen & Unwin, 1977.
MCDONNELL, Kathleen Keyes, *There is a Bridge at Bandon*, Mercier Press, Cork, 1972.
MACEOIN, Uinseann (ed.), *Survivors*, Argenta, Dublin, first published 1980, reprinted and enlarged 1987.

MACLOCHLAINN, Piaras F., *Last Words*, Kilmainham Jail Restoration Society, Dublin, 1971.

MACMAHON, Sean, *Rich and Rare*, Ward River, Dublin, 1984.

MACMANUS, M.J., *Eamon de Valera*, Talbot Press, Dublin, 1944.

MCCAFFREY, Lawrence J., *The Irish Diaspora in America*, Indiana Press.Bloomington, 1976.

MCCANN, John, *War by the Irish*, The Kerryman Ltd, Tralee, 1946.

MCCRACKEN, J.P., *Representative Government in Ireland*, Oxford University Press, 1958.

MARJORIBANKS, Edward, *Life of Lord Carson*, Gollancz, 1932.

MANSERGH, Nicholas, *The Irish Question 1840–1921*, Allen & Unwin, 1965.

MARTIN, F.X. (ed.), *The Irish Volunteers 1913–15*, Dublin, 1963; (ed.)*Howth Gun-Running*, Browne & Nolan, Dublin, 1964; *Leaders & Men of the Easter Rising: Dublin 1916*, Methuen, 1965.

MIDDLEMASS, Keith & Barnes, John, *Baldwin*, Weidenfeld & Nicolson, 1969.

MILLER, David, *Queen's Rebels*, Gill & Macmillan, Dublin, 1971.

MITCHELL, & O'Snodaigh, *Irish Political Documents, 1916–49*, Irish Academic Press, Dublin, 1985.

MOODY, T.W., *The Ulster Question, 1603–1973*, Mercier Press, Cork, 1974.

NEESON, Eoin, *The Civil War in Ireland 1922–1923*, Mercier Press, 1967; *The Life and Death of Michael Collins*, Mercier Press, Cork, 1968.

NELIGAN, David, *The Spy in the Castle*, McGibbon & Kee, 1968.

NI DHERIG, Isold, *The Story of Michael Collins*, Mercier Press, Cork, 1978.

O'BROIN, Leon, *Dublin Castle and the 1916 Rising*, Sidgwick and Jackson, 1966; *The Chief Secretary*, Chatto & Windus, 1969; *Fenian Fever*, Chatto & Windus, 1979; *Michael Collins*, Gill & Macmillan, Dublin, 1980; *Revolutionary Underground – The Story of the I.R.B. 1858–1924*, Gill & Macmillan, Dublin, 1976; *No Man's Man*, Institute of Public Administration, Dublin, 1982; (ed.) *In Great Haste*, Gill & Macmillan, Dublin, 1983; *Protestant Nationalism in Ireland*, Gill & Macmillan, Dublin, 1985.

O'CONNOR, Batt, *With Michael Collins in The Fight for Irish Independence*, Peter Davies, 1929.

O'CONNOR, Frank, *The Big Fellow*, first published, US, 1937. Revised and reprinted, Clonmore and Reynolds, 1965 and 1966. Corgi paperback, 1969.

O'CONNOR, Sir James, *History of Ireland, 1798–1924*, 2 Vol.s, Arnold, 1925.

O'CONNOR, Ulick, *Oliver St John Gogarty*, Cape, 1964 and NEL paperback, 1967.

O'DONOGHUE, Florence, *No Other Law: The Story of Liam Lynch and the Irish Republic, 1916–23*, Irish Press, Dublin, 1954; (ed.) *Complete Book of IRA Jailbreaks, 1918–21*, Anvil, Trailee, 1971.

O'FAOLAIN Sean, *De Valera*, Penguin, 1939.

O'FARRELL, Patrick, *Ireland's English Question*, Schocken, New York, 1971.

O'HALLORAN, Clare, *Partition and the Limits of Ideology*, Gill & Macmillan, Dublin, 1989.

O'HANLON, Thomas J., *The Irish*, Deutsch, 1976.

O'HEGARTY, P.S., *The Victory of Sinn Fein*, Talbot Press, Dublin, 1924; *The Indestructible Nation*, Maunsel, Dublin, 1918.

O'HEGARTY, P.S., and O'Hegarty, Mrs E., *A History of Ireland Under The Union, 1801–1922*, Methuen, London, 1952.

O'MAHONY, Sean, *Frongoch: University of Revolution*, FDR Teoranta, Dublin, 1987.

O'MALLEY, Earnan, *The Singing Flame*, Anvil, Dublin, 1978; *On Another Man's Wound*, Anvil, Dublin, 1979; *Raids and Rallies*, Anvil, Dublin, 1982.

O'SULLIVAN, Donal, *The Irish Free State and its Senate*, Faber, 1940.

O'SULLIVAN, Harold, with Joseph Gavin, *Dundalk, a Military History*, Dundalgan Press, Dundalk, 1987.

RIDDELL, Lord George, *Intimate Diary of the Peace Conference*, Gollancz, 1933.
RIDDLE, Patrick, *Fire over Ulster*, Hamish Hamilton, 1970.
ROSKILL, S,.W., *Hankey, Man of Secrets*, Vol. 11, Collins, 1972.
RYAN, Desmond, *Remembering Sion*, Barker, 1934; *Unique Dictator*, Barker, 1936; *Michael Collins and the Invisible Army*, 1932, reprinted Anvil, n.d.
RYAN, Meda, *The Day Michael Collins Was Shot*, Poolbeg, Dublin, 1989.

SALVIDGE, Stanley, *Salvidge of Liverpool: Behind the Political Scene, 1890–1928*, Hodder & Stoughton, 1934.
SCOTT, C.P. (ed.) T. Wilson, *Political Diaries, 1911–28*, Collins, 1970.
SENIOR, Hereward, *Orangism in Ireland and Britain*, Routledge & Kegan Paul, 1966.
SHAKESPEARE, Sir Geoffrey, *Let Candles be Brought In*, MacDonald, 1949.
SHANNON, William, *The American Irish*, Collier Macmillan, New York, 1963.
SHAW, G.B., *How to Settle the Irish Question*, Talbot Press, Dublin, 1917; *Autobiography 1898–1950*, Reinhardt Books, 1970; *Collected Letters*, Vol. 111, Reinhardt Books, 1985.
STEVENSON, Francis (ed.), *Lloyd George: A Diary*, Hutchinson, 1971.
SHERMAN, Hugh, *Not an Inch*, Faber, 1942.
STEWART, A.T.Q., *The Ulster Crisis*, Faber, 1967; *Edward Carson*, Gill & Macmillan, Dublin, 1981.
STREET, Major C.J., *The Administration of Ireland, 1920*, Philip Allen, 1921; *Ireland in 1922*, Philip Allen, 1922.

TALBOT, Hayden, *Michael Collins' Own Story*, Hutchinson, 1932.
TAYLOR, A.J.P., *War by Timetable*, MacDonald, 1969; *Churchill, Four Faces and the Man*, Allen Lane, 1969; *Beaverbrook*, Hamish Hamilton, 1972.
TAYLOR, Rex, *Michael Collins*, Hutchinson, 1958, and Four Square paperback, 1961; *Poems*, Hutchinson, 1959; *Assassination: The Death of Sir Henry Wilson*, Hutchinson, 1961.
TOWNSHEND, Charles, *The British Campaign in Ireland, 1919–21*, Oxford University Press, 1975; *Political Violence in Ireland*, Oxford University Press, 1983.

WINTER, Sir Ormonde, *Winter's Tale*, Richard's Press, 1955.

YEATS, Padraig and Wren, Jimmy, *Michael Collins*, Tomar, Dublin, 1989.
YOUNGER, Calton, *Ireland's Civil War*, Frederick Muller, 1968, and Fontana 1970; *A State of Disunion*, Frederick Muller, 1972; *Arthur Griffith*, Gill & Macmillan, Dublin, 1981.

Index

NOTE: Michael Collins is abbreviated to MC

abstentionism 65, 66, 212
Ackerman, Carl W. 192, 211, 219
Active Service Unit (ASU) 206–
7, 209, 397
Admiralty; Room 40 intelligence
section 36, 91, 150–1, 202, 379
agriculture 17, 84–5, 177, 308,
394, 422, 423
Aherne, Dr Leo 414
Aiken, Frank 339, 342–3, 350,
377, 405, 428–9
Aimes, Colonel 159
An tOglach 98, 117, 384
Anderson, Sir John 125, 199, 202,
209–10, 220, 261, 336–7
Andrews, Tod 387
Annunzio, Gabriele d' 171
'Apostles, Twelve' (Squad) 116
Argenta (prison ship) 363
Ark, the (social grouping) 291,
292
Armagh 212; South 24, 75, 377
Armistice celebrations (1918) 91
Armour, Rev J. B. 12
arms supplies: during Truce 219;
raids 85, 249, (Upnor) 314–15;
see also gun running
Army, British: budget 191;
Connaught Rangers' mutiny
151; First World War 35, 55;
and Four Courts 330, 331–2;
limited warfare 141; and
partition 335; Protestant clergy
and 202; 'separation women' 1,
45; and Truce 196, 222–3;
withdrawals halted 347; see also:
Black and Tans; Curragh
Army, Irish see: Irish Republican
Army; National Army
Articles of Agreement 299, 433–8
Ashe, Constable 148
Ashe, Thomas 66, 70, 73, 74–5,
139
Asquith, Herbert Henry 25, 27,
28, 185

Association issue see under Treaty
Auxiliary Cadets: established 125,
127, 142; and Bloody Sunday
159, 160; operations 145, 179,
195, 197; Tudor on discipline
199; Churchill supports 238

B-Specials 202, 261, 335–7, 371,
373; British arming of 327, 332,
349; operations 346–7, 363,
372; strengthened 364
Bael na mBlath 3, 404, 405, 407,
408–9
Baggelly, Captain 158, 159
Balbriggan 144–5
Balfour, Arthur 27; and Parnell
220; and Irish Committee 86,
87; visits Pope 202; and Treaty
214, 222; and The Ark 292; and
North 334, 335, 336, 368–9
Ballyvourney; IRA meeting
404–5, 406
Banbridge 149
Bandon, Lord 178
Bandon 12, 146–7, 358
Bank of Ireland 378–9
bank raids 314, 321
Bantry 145, 222
Barnard, Dr 261
Barret, Ben 116
Barrett, Dick 417
Barrie, Sir James 18, 109, 286–7
Barrington-Ward, F. T. 372
Barry, Kevin 154–5, 156
Barry, Tom 142, 164, 168–9, 315,
323, 400
Barton, Robert 98, 106, 215, 216,
387; in Treaty negotiations 230,
234, 241, 243, 244, 247–8, 253,
262, 264, (on British
advantage) 240, 255–6; in Irish
discussions of Treaty 266, 267,
268, 269; signs Treaty 271,
273–4, 275, 437; and de Valera
227, 296, 297

Bates, Dawson 349, 353, 369,
371–2
Beaslai, Piaras 45–6, 69, 98–9,
117, 134–5, 293, 297, 309; on
MC 11, 79, 114
Beatty, Admiral 243–4
Beaumont, Sean and Willie 132
Begley, Flor 141, 142, 169, 405
Belcoo 348
Belfast 24; boycott 330, 337, 340,
353, 357, 360, 361; Crumlin
Road jail riot (1918) 99;
Customs House raid 362–3;
IRA organisation 348, 349,
380–2; and Irish-Americans
111; Mater Misericordiae
Hospital 365–6; police
atrocities 351–3, 355–6, 358;
Queen's University 239; riots
(1921) 348; sectarian violence
(1922) 347, 363
Belfast Guard 351
Bell, Alan 104, 188
Belleek, Fermanagh 364–7
Belloc, Hilaire 185
Bence Jones family 4, 6
Benedict XV, Pope 202, 203–4,
245–6
Bennett, Major 159
Bernstorff, Count Von 29–30
Bethmann Holweig, Von 36
Birkenhead, F. E. Smith, 1st Earl
of: career and character 236–7;
and Casement 59; and MC 59,
236–7, 242, 424; and Treaty
236, 244, 253, 254, 260, 262;
signing of Treaty 276, 313, 437;
and Constitution 326; and
North 334, 335
Birrell, Augustine 35, 62
Black and Tans 121, 125–7, 140,
142, 199; attacks on homes 153,
233; and Customs House 207;
reprisals 144–5, 194; Sean

MacEoin and 179, 180; during truce 218
'Black Man, the' 118
Blackett, Sir Basil 378
'Bloody Sunday' 158–62, 181
Blythe, Ernest 317, 337, 340, 384
Boer War 13, 54
Boland, Gerry xi, 100
Boland, Harry 46, 79; and de Valera 71, 188, 190, 225, 231, 322, 387–8; death 114, 387–9; and Kitty Kiernan 66, 280–1, 388; leadership (1918–19) 86, 91–2; and MC 70, 113–14, 190, 231, 305, 307, 322, 331, 387–9; in run-up to civil war 320; and Treaty 227, 305, 307; and USA 109, 113, 188, 193
bomb-making 34, 94, 143, 183
Border Commission 347, 349
Bossism 189
Boundary Commission: proposed 258, 259, 260, 265, 435; Dublin views on 270, 272, 340, 342, 352; Northern views 334, 335, 340, 349, 354, 363–4
boycotts 4–5, 384–5; Belfast 330, 337, 340, 353, 357, 360, 361; Six-County 314, 330
Boyd, General 163, 199
Boyle, Richard, Earl of Cork 12
Boyne, Battle of the 23
Brady, DI 144
Braonain, Peig ni 375–6
Breen, Dan 151–2, 318, 348
Brennan, Dolly 21, 49, 50
Brennan, Joseph 402
Brennan, Lily 234
Brennan, Michael 105–6, 122, 172, 249
Bretherton (journalist) 360
Brind, Colonel 216
British Labour Commission 185
Brixton jail 155
Brooke, Sir Basil 336
Broy, Eamonn xi, recruited 64, 75–6, 77–8; escapes 96, 106, 167; work for MC 79, 81, 90–1, 107, 131, 234
Brugha, Cathal (Charles Burgess) 33, 34, 70–1; arrested (1917) 68; in Volunteers 71, 73, 85; and operations in England 153, 179, 183, (contingency plans to assassinate Cabinet) 89, 102–3, 179; in elections (1918) 102–3; and first Dail 104; proposed reward 209; and Mulcahy 232, 249; and reorganisation of Volunteers (1921) 244; and Treaty negotiations 227, 230, 231, 246, 256, 266, 268; reception of Treaty 294, 296, 304–5, 305–6, 307; and civil war 320; death 387
candle business 34, 142, 175; character 70–1, 208; and de Valera 71, 101, 104, 174, 176

191, 204, 205, 206, 227, 232, 244; and MC 34, 142, 243, 387, (accounts) 174–7, 232, 248–9, (Treaty) 229, 304–5, 305–6, (style of warfare) 70, 179, 183; military tactics 70, 141–2, 142–3; political philosophy 92–3
Burke, T. H. 390, 391
Butt, Isaac 22–3
Byrne, Charlie 346
Byrne, Dr Edward, Archbishop of Dublin 320
Byrne, Vincent 116, 117, 182, 419

C-Specials 260–1, 337
Cagney, Dr 421
Cahill, Head Constable 149
Cahill, Paddy 205–6
Cairo Café 133, 157
Cairo Gang 157–60
'Caldron' (loyalist) 162
Callinan, Paddy 409
Cambria 102
Carey (British informer) 390
Carolan, Professor 151, 152
Carson, Edward 26–7, 35, 39, 104, 237, 292, 368; retires from leadership 212; and Treaty talks 258; and North 28, 60–1, 335, 336, 342, 360, 382
Casement, Roger 29, 31, 36, 52, 59, 203
Casement, Tom 213–14, 215
Casey, Constable Paddy 148
Casey, Alderman Sean, TD 84
Catalpa 189
Catholics: American, aid from 60; civil rights 7, 29; and conscription 88–9; and IRA 12; in North 327, 334, 340, 342, 350; and peace moves 186, 199–204; and sectarianism 12, 23–4, 142
Cavendish, Lord Frederick 390, 391
Cavendish-Bentinck, Lord Henry 185
Ceannt, Eamonn 36, 39
Chamberlain, Arthur 237
Chamberlain, Austen 86, 213, 222, 369; career 237; and Treaty 236, 237, 254, 259, 264, 269–70, 273, 437
Chamberlain, Neville 292
'Charon' (RIC informant) 5
Chartres, John 108–9, 234, 238–9, 252, 262–3, 286–7
Chesterton, G. K. 33, 185
Childers, Erskine 163, 238, 239, 321, 405; Howth gun-running 30, 238; and Treaty negotiations 230, 234, 238, 242, 243–4, 253, 262, 263, 265, 274; in Dublin debate on Treaty 267, 268, 296, 297, 300; execution 397, 426
Christiansen (Norwegian sailor) 31

Churchill, Lord Randolph 23, 24–5, 333
Churchill, Randolph 25
Churchill, Winston Spencer: on Irish Committee 86; police war policy 127, 144, 145, 336; and Bloody Sunday 199; and Martial Law 213; and Treaty 94, 236, 237–8, 243–4, 246, 253, 274, 290, 313, 437; and IRA split 314, 315, 323, 368; and Constitution 325, 326, 328, 368; and Wilson's death 330, 374; and Four Courts 330, 331–2; and North 334, 336, 340, 346, 347, 358, 364, 366, 367, 368–9, 372, 374, 379; on Griffith 233; social circle 390, 392; and T. E. Lawrence 395
Citizen Army 34
civil war 315, 386–415, 417, 424–5, 427; military path to 313–18; political path to 318–29; and Northern IRA 380
civilian casualties 143, 145, 209
Clan na nGael 29, 63, 64, 168, 193; *see also* Devoy
Clancy, George 124
Clancy, Peadar 99, 152, 159, 160–1, 161–2, 182
Clare Champion, suppressed 85
Clarke, Kathleen 54, 63–4, 90, 300
Clarke, Tom 34, 36, 39, 44, 45, 54, 64
Clarke, Wallace 202
Clayton, DI, of RIC 124
Cleeves, Sir Thomas 144
Cliodhna, tales of 10–11
Clones, Co Monaghan 339, 346–7
Clonmel 313, 389, 399–400
Clonmult 173–4
Clune, Conor 159, 160, 161–2, 194
Clune, Joseph, Archbishop 187, 194–204
Cockerill, Brigadier, MP 185–7
Cohalan, Canon, of Bandon 427
Cohalan, Daniel, Bishop of Cork 201, 202
Cohalan, Judge 110, 189–90, 191
Collins, Helena (MC's sister, Sister Mary Celestine) 4, 6, 12–13
Collins, Johanna (Hannie, MC's sister) 6, 47, 48, 291, 293; and MC in London 14–15, 17–18, 19, 31
Collins, John (MC's brother): youth 6, 9, 14; and Kilmichael ambush 164; and burning of Woodfield 177, 178; imprisonment 178, 297; MC's last visit 408; and MC's memory 417, 419, 420, 428–31; death 421; marriages (first) 177, (Nancy O'Brien) 280
Collins, Katie (MC's sister, Mrs Sheridan) 6, 9, 429

Collins, Liam (MC's nephew) 178, 280

Collins, Margaret (MC's sister, Mrs O'Driscoll) 6, 14

Collins, Marianne (née O'Brien, MC's mother) 7–8, 12–13, 14, 15, 18

Collins, Mary (MC's sister, Mrs Collins-Powell) 6, 8, 9, 17, 173–4, 402; Nationalism 13, 18

Collins, Maurice (MC's uncle) 7

Collins, Michael

LIFE: family background 5–6, 33; childhood 6, 8–15, 40; in Clonakilty (1905–6) 15; in London (1906–16) 15–22, 29, 30–1; return to Ireland (1916) 31, 32, 33; and Easter Rising 37, 39–40, 43, 44, 45, 46–7, 53–4, 64; detention 2, 47–50, 49–57; release 57, 58–9; and Irish National Aid Fund 63–5; and 1917 by-elections 66–7, 70; on Sinn Fein executive 72; and Volunteers' 69, 72, 85, 86, 89–90; imprisoned (1918) 85, 89; and German plot arrests 90–1; and 1918 election 91–2; and national loan xii, 94, 106–7; Dail Minister for Finance 106–7, 108, 109, 110–11, 113; President of Supreme Council, IRB 115; forms 'Squad' 94, 116; and Black and Tans war 121, 128–9, 133–4, 137–8, 141, 142, 147, 153, 154–5; and Bloody Sunday 159, 160–2, 164; and Italian gun-running 169–72; Brugha attacks over accounts 174–7; and Cockerill peace initiative 186–7; and de Valera in USA 191–2, 193; and Clune peace initiative 195, 196, 197, 198, 200, 203; and de Valera's return 203, 204–5, 206, 208; and Customs House burning 207; and peace moves 210–11; returned in election (1921) 212; and Truce 216, 217–18, 222–3; estranged from de Valera 220, 225, 232; and Treaty negotiations xiii, 94, 226–9, 236–7, 238, 241–3, 246, 254, 256–7, (role) 231, 233, 240, 262, (problems with Dublin) 233, 247–8, (consults IRB) 234, 266, 298, (long-term strategy) 243, (and sub-conference) 243, 244, 253, (memorandum on Dominion status) 263–4, (British contacts during) 277, 278, 283–93; and Dublin discussions of draft Treaty 265–6, 268, 269; at final meeting on Treaty 270–1, 272, 276, 437; in Dublin debates on Treaty 299, 300, 301, 302, 303, 304–5, 305–6, 307, 308, 309;

Chairman of Provisional Government 309–10, 310, 315, 316; and Constitution 308, 311, 323–4, (talks in London) 312–13, 326–7, 328; and build-up to civil war 311, 313, 314–15, 316–17, 318, 320, 322, 368; electoral pact with de Valera 322–5, 328–9, 368; attack on Four Courts 330–1, 332; in civil war 387–90, 391–9, 401–2; as Army C-in-C 389–90, 391–2, 392–3, 394–5, 398, 399; in 1922 election 374; last journey 293–4, 399–406; ambushed 404–11; death 3, 114, 294, 411–21, 426–7; memorials 428–32

NORTHERN POLICY 301, 308–9, 389, 424, 425, 426; liberal attitude (pre-1922) 337–8; undercover operations (1922) 308, 333, 341, 346, 354, 362, 366–7, 391, 396, (arms supplies) 350–1, (end) 382–3, 383–4; negotiations with Craig 339–40, 341–2; and Boundary Commission 342; and Republicans in Northern jails 343–6; and kidnapping of Orangemen (Feb 1922) 343–4, 345–6; administrative obstruction 347, 358, 361; and Agreement (March 1922) 353–5; and police atrocities 352–3, 356, 358; Tallents on 370, 371, 372; and Wilson assassination 374, 376; banking controversy 378–9; and proportional representation 379–80; plans for intelligence system 352–3, 398; and end of hostilities 382–3, 383–4

PERSONAL RELATIONSHIPS: de Valera 100, 101–2, 250, (supports while in USA) 103, 104, 191–2, 193, (strain develops) 203, 204–5, 206, 208, 218, (estrangement) 220, 225, 232, (and Treaty) 227, 247–8, 299, 300, 301, 304–5, 309, (agreement) 311, (electoral pact) 322–5, 328–9, 368, (de Valera on MC's death) 407, 419, 426–7, (and memorials to MC) 428–31; friendships (1917) 69–70; O'Duffy 339; women 19–21, 48, 82, 172–3, 277–94, (see also under: Birkenhead; Boland; Brugha; Kiernan; Killeen)

PERSONALITY 8–9, 32, 47–8, 64, 205; appearance 78, 79; athlete 15–16, 32, 50–1, 52; courage 65, 138, 161–2, 164, 317; 'Big Fella' sobriquet 20, 102, 204; detail, capacity for xii, 15, 48, 55, 64–5, 95, 166–7, 395; discipline 51, 52, 136–7, 396;

drinking 19, 165, 395; emotions 13–14, 15; energy 8, 95, 395–7; health 165, 367, 399, 400; homosexuality, allegations of 278–9; horseplay xii, 79, 95, 134–5, 139, 287, 403; humour 37, 40, 51, 52, 137; impetuosity 137–8, 384; and killing 133–4, 135–6, 164, 172–3; kindness xi, 8, 64, 79, 95, 139; leadership 9, 16, 40, 86, 95; manner 77, 79, 96; and old 6, 8, 54, 56, 79; patriotism 236, 333; ruthlessness xii, 64, 91, 132, 164, 217; temper 8, 14, 15–16, 32, 47–8, 51; and young 8, 54, 56, 79, 97

PHILOSOPHY AND CULTURE 32, 33, 423; and Irish language 22, 33, 48, 395, 422; political philosophy 10, 11–14, 16, 22, 33, 65, 92, 95, 333, 341, 421–2, (and Constitution) 312; reading 9, 13–14, 17–18, 33, 47, 48, 51, 95; religion 12–13, 16, 52, 283, 338; and theatre 17–18, 159

POLITICAL CAREER: arms smuggling xii, 64, 94, 153; and economy 394, 421, 422–4; escapes 96, 113, 164, 165–8, 195; evaluation 421–6; finance, (on British) 113, (Brugha's criticism) 174–7, 232, 248–9, (in civil war) 401–2, (New Ireland Assurance Co.) 55, (national loan) xii, 94, 106–7, 424, (training) 16–17, 19; intelligence network see separate entry; and IRB 16, 54–5, 74, 115, 266, 286, 298, 340–1, 426; and jail breakouts 99, 100, 180–1; and law and order 396, 402; military tactics xii, 54, 142, 206; and propaganda 394, 424; and release of MacEoin 223, 229; and Sinn Fein 72, 115–16, 117; and Volunteers 29, 35, 69, 72, 85, 86, 89–90, 113; and USA 189, 192–3, 204, (Clan na nGael) 30, 64, 192, 193, 203, (press interviews) 211, 219; working methods 64–5, 94, 95–6, 166–7, 168, 174, 384, 395–7, (support for men) 138, 153, (use of contacts) xii, 2, 48, 51–2, 55, 147

Collins, Michael (MC's nephew) 419–20, 421, 431

Collins, Michael John (MC's father) 3, 4–5, 6–7, 8, 9, 11, 12, 14

Collins, Captain Paddy 409

Collins, Patrick (MC's uncle) 7, 8

Collins, Patrick (MC's brother) 6, 17

Collins, Tom (MC's uncle) 7

Collins-Powell, Mary see Collins, Mary

Collins-Powell, Sean 18, 402
Colthurst, Captain Bowen 44
Commonwealth *see under* Treaty
Compton Smith, Major 173
Connaught Rangers' mutiny 151
Connolly, Colum 288, 418, 420
Connolly, James 34–5, 36, 38, 39, 53, 54
Conroy, James 116
conscription 85–6, 87–9, 90, 91, 103, 106, 353
Constitution, Irish: (1922) 203, 308, 311, 312, 323–4, 325–9, 368; (1937) 428
Convention, Irish 67, 87
Cooper, Major Bryan 209
Cope, Alfred (Andy) 125, 187; and peace initiatives 196, 209–10, 215, 220; and Treaty negotiations 239, 255, 265; and Constitution 325; and North 345–6, 380; and MC 210–11, 364
Cork, County 122, 222, 316–17, 329, 358–9; *see also individual places*
Cork, city of 222; burning of 164–5, 198, 199, 208; civil war 389, 393, 401; intelligence 5, 140; jail 98, 99, 155, 173–4
Cork Examiner 401
Corrigan, Alderman 65
Corry (MC's driver) 406
Cosgrave, William Thomas: release from Lewes Jail 69; arrested (May 1918) 90; Minister of Dail 106, 110, 309; and Bloody Sunday 163; proposed reward 209; and Treaty 227, 229, 295, 296, 301–2; in Provisional Government 310, 340; and North 340, 376–7, 383; and MC's becoming Army C-in-C 393, 393–4; and MC's death 415; and Emmet Dalton 417; de Valera ousts 427–8
Council of Ireland 335, 435
courts 396; martial 73; Northern 343, 385; Sinn Fein 245; Supreme 328;
Craig, Sir James 26; first Dail and 104; talks with de Valera (1921) 211; Six Counties' Prime Minister 212, 214, 216, 222, 258; and Treaty talks 257, 258, 259, 268, 269, 270, 272, 273; and Boundary Commission 334, 335, 349, 363–4; and atrocities against Catholics 327; and Specials 336, 348; and Agreement 339–40, 341–2, 353–5, 358, 363–4; and kidnapping of Orangemen 343, 344–5, 346; and proposed Commission of Enquiry 368–9; Tallents criticises 371
Cranagh 348

Crawford, Fred 336
Creel, George 109–10
Crofts, Gerald 46
Cromwell, Oliver 23
Cromwell Clubs 337
Cronin, Captain 168
Cronin, Felix 283
Cronin, Michael Collins 283
Crookstown 405–6
Crown, status of; Constitution 312, 326, 328; *see also under* Treaty
Crozier, Brigadier General 195
Crozier, Thomas 377
Cuchullain (Irish hero) 71, 298
Culhane, Sean 149
Cullen, Captain Michael 42
Cullen, Tom: escapes 166, 278–9; horseplay 135, 287; intelligence work 83, 89, 128, 129–30, 132, 133, 134–5, 158, 232; and MC's death 415; and Sinead Mason 97; stag party 170, 172; and Treaty 234, 287, 296; and Wilson's assassins 376
cumann na mBan 375–6
Cumann na Poblachta 319
curfew 127, 138, 363
Curragh barracks 28, 39, 373, 400
Curran, Mgr M. J. 169
Curtis, Lionel 324, 327, 349, 359, 361; and Treaty 236, 239, 265
Curzon, Viscount 86, 200, 204
Cushendall 372

Dail Eireann: set up 72, 92, 302; first meeting 104–5, 106; and League of Nations 110–11; and Peace Conference 111, 113; banned 117; mourning for MacSwiney 156; de Valera and 188, 206, 224; takes over Army control 250; and Treaty 257, 267–8, 298–301, 302–7; Provisional Government 303; land-bank 98
Dalton, Charlie 160, 180, 182, 415
Dalton, Emmet xiii, 180, 181, 279, 294, 348; and Treaty 234, 244, 287; in civil war 331, 393, 401; and MC's death 403, 404, 408, 410, 411, 412, 414–15, 416–18
Daly, Charlie 350
Daly, Denis 48
Daly, Edward 54
Daly, James 151
Daly, Paddy G (Squad) 98, 116, 117–18, 129, 130, 182
Daly, Paddy (Liverpool) 233, 324–5
Davies, Alfred, MP 187
Davis, Thomas 13
de Barra, Eamonn 339
de Salis, Count 200, 202
de Valera, Eamon: and Easter Rising 40–2, 54; and 1917

elections 66–7, 68–9, 70, 71; President of Sinn Fein 71–2, 388; and Dail 72; President of Volunteers 72; and conscription 88; arrested (German plot) 90; break-out from Lincoln jail 98, 99–104; in USA 42, 100–2, 106, 113, 114–15, 187–93, 304, ('Cuba' interview) 190, 252; on return 171, 188, 203, 204–5, 206; electoral success 212; and peace initiatives 211, 213–14, 215–16, 218, 219; estranged from MC 220, 225, 232; talks with Lloyd George 221–2, 223–4; President of Republic 224–5; absence from Treaty delegation 227–9, 230, 231, 268, 299, 318–19; and Treaty 244–5, 247–8, 252, 267, 268, 271, 295, 296–7; and New Army 244, 250–1; and telegrams between Pope and George V 245–6; Document No. 2 299–300, 302–4, 305, 439–44; resignation 306, 307, 309; and build-up to civil war 311, 312, 315, 319–20, 321–2; electoral pact with MC 322–5, 328–9, 368; and Constitution 325, 328–9; on Wilson's assassination 372–3; in civil war 386–7, 392, 405; and MC's death 407, 419, 426–7; ousts Cosgrave 427–8; new Constitution 427–8; and MC's memory 428–32
character 68–9, 71–2, 428, (ego) 188, 189, 190, 191, 251, 295, 298; and Dail 72, 106, 188, 224; and economy 113, 428; establishes own primacy 71–2, 188, 189, 203, 204, 302–3, 421; and extremism 219, 228, 295, 297, 319, 321, 329, 340, 427; and Griffith 71–2, 321–2, 388; and IRB 71, 73; Irish language 298; and Machiavelli 250; manner 207, 221; marriage *see* de Valera, Sinead; military policy 73, 206, 207–8; and North 224, 353; political appeal 68–9, 71–2; procrastination 219 *see also under* Boland; Brugha; Collins
de Valera, Sinead 101, 115, 139, 192
de Valera, Vivion xi
de Vere White, Terence 288
de Wet, Christian 13, 54
Deasy, Liam 97, 138, 142, 170, 217, 323; in civil war 389, 405, 427; and MC's death 412
Declaration of Independence 104–5
Delaney brothers of Cork 164
Dempsey, Fr 287
Denzil Lane Munition Factory 143

Derby, 17th Earl of 211
Derry 24, 25, 123, 334, 343–6, 348, 362
Devlin, Joseph 104, 194, 212, 343, 356, 357
Devlin, Liam; pub 134–5, 170, 172
Devoy, John 189; and de Valera 42, 189, 190, 191, 192; and Easter Rising 29; and German arms supplies 36; and Irish Brigade 30–1; MC and 30, 64, 192, 193
Die-hards 252–60, 290, 367–8
Dillon, Colonel Hill 133
Dillon, John 5, 23, 35, 212
Dillon, Dr Thomas 34
Dilworth, Mr 347
Dineen, Major 168
Dixon, Henry 54
Dixon (ex-Connaught Ranger, sniper) 293
Dockrell, Sir Maurice 216
Document No. 2 299–300, 302–4, 305, 439–44
Dodd, Mother Patricia 175, 181
Dolan, Joe 126, 134, 152, 160, 234, 287, 346, 403
Dominion status 211, 215–16, 219, 222, 224; see also under Treaty
Donnelly, Simon 181
Donnybrook police station 158
Doran, John 99
Doran, William 133–4
Douglas, James 312
Dowling, Joseph 90–1, 130
Dowling, Sean 175, 176, 386
Doyle, Sean 116, 117
Dromore 343–4
Drumcondra 102, 117, 162
Duainaire ('Dispossessed') 6
Dublin: Castle 36, 38, 62, 81, 220, 310; Croke Park 160, 161, 163; Customs House 206–7, 218; GPO 33–4, 38, 43, 81–2; Kilmainham jail 315; Liberty Hall 1, 2, 38, 207; Loyal Orange Institute of Ireland 360; Public Records Office 332; Rotunda 29, 35, 44; University 309; see also: Easter Rising, Four Courts
Dublin Brigade 207, 209
Dublin Guards 209
Dublin Metropolitan Police 62, 78, 130, 158
Duffin brothers 351–2
Duffy, George Gavan 108, 309; and Treaty negotiations 230, 234, 240, 241, 244, 253–4, 266, 268, 269–70; and British walk-out 269–70, 271, 299; and signing of Treaty 274, 437; and Document No. 2 297
Duffy, Mrs Gavan 202–3
Duffy, Sean 79
Duggan, Eamonn J. 91, 174, 215,

216, 309, 310, 367; and Treaty 230, 234, 240–1, 255, 264, 266, 268, 274–5, 295, 437
Duke, Henry 57, 90
Dumont (US Consul, Dublin) 203
Dundalk 74, 85, 389
Dungannon Clubs 36
Dunmanway, County Cork 145, 359
Dunne, Edward F. 111–12
Dunne, Reggie 183, 373, 375, 374, 377, 398–9
Dwyer, Dr T. Ryle 219, 278, 279, 295

'Easer' (RIC informant) 5
Easter Rising (1916) 1–2, 38–44; planning 22, 29–31, 32–3, 34–5, 36–8, 53–4, 65; events 33–4, 38–44, 70; civilian casualties 44, 45; Germany and 29–30, 30–1, 52; treatment of prisoners 44–7; MC's imprisonment after 47–57; reaction to 56, 59–61; amnesty (1917) 67–8; USA and 189
economy, Irish 4, 7, 34, 58; crisis (1921–2) 143–5, 308; MC and 394, 421, 422–4; under de Valera 113, 427, 428
Edenappa, killings at 383
elections: (1917 by-) 63, 66–7, 68–9, 70, 73; (1918 by-) 75, 89, (General) 92; (1920) 122; (1921) 211–12; (1922) 311, 313, 319, 321, 322, 329, 374, 384; abstentionism 65, 66, 212; proportional representation 379–80
Ellis (executioner) 346
emigration 4, 7, 11, 150–1, 428
Emmet, Dr Thomas Addis 59
employment 142, 308, 353, 382, 425
Ennis, Tom 206
Ennistymon 145
Etchingham, Sean 300
Evening Herald 162
Evening Mail 295
evictions 11–12

Fachtna, St; shrine 13
famine 4, 6, 11, 84
Farmers' Party 322, 329
Farnan, Dr 195, 204, 215, 302
Farrin, ambush at 406, 414
Fastnet Rock lighthouse 11
Faughan, Sergeant 149
Fawsitt, Diarmuid 339
Fenians 7, 9–10, 390, 391; see also Irish Republican Brotherhood
Fermanagh, County 123, 334, 336, 344–6; triangle incidents 364–7, 368, 380
Fermoy 127, 145, 172
Fianna 39
Fianna Fáil 427

Figgis, Darrell 90, 102, 103, 245, 312, 325–6
finance: Treaty 252, 270, 434, 441; see also under Collins, Michael
Fingall, Lady 294
Fisher, Sir Warren; Report 62, 125
fishery development 10, 394, 424
FitzAlan, James Talbot, Lord 153, 211, 369
Fitzgerald, Desmond 200, 233, 293, 295, 394, 418; and Easter Rising 39–40; and North 356, 360, 384
Fitzgerald, Lord Edward 3, 4
Fitzgerald, George 183
Fitzgerald, Lt (Irish Volunteer) 41
Fitzgerald, Michael 155
Fitzgerald, Dr Seamus 84
Fitzpatrick, Commander 346
FitzSimons, Anna 131
Flanagan, Mick 159
Fleming, Pat 98–9, 376
Flood, Frank 181
Flood, Sean 183–4
Flynn, Jimmy 407
Fogarty, Michael, Bishop of Killaloe 194, 195, 196, 399
Foley, Michael 75
Foley, Tom 420–1
football, Gaelic 15, 16, 90, 343–4
Forde, Liam 313
Four Courts, Dublin: IRA seizure 315–16, 318, 381; de Valera and 320, 321; O'Donnell kidnap 329, 330–1; MC attacks 322, 330–1, 332, 368, 373, 374–5, 386–7
Fourvargue, Vincent 147
France 4, 106
Freake family of Lisavaird 8
'Free State' title 263
Freemasonry 62, 78
French, Field Marshal Lord 90, 124, 125, 137, 211
Friel, Frank 418
Friends of Irish Freedom 189
Frongoch, Merionethshire 49–57

Gaelic American 193, 218
Gaelic Athletic Association 5, 15–16, 32, 160, 161
Gaelic League 5, 32, 33, 71
Gallagher, Frank 391, 401
Gallagher, Thomas, of Illinois 110
Galvin, Sean 412
Galway County Council 196
Gaspari, Cardinal 204
Gasquet, Cardinal 200
Gay, Thomas 76, 77, 79
George III, King 26
George V, King 28, 111, 178, 214–15, 245–6
German plot 76, 86, 90–1, 99, 246
Germany: Irish Americans and 110, 188, 189; see also Irish

Brigade *and under* Easter
 Rising, gun-running
Gifford, Grace 53
Ginnell, Laurence 73
Gladstone, William Ewart 24, 25
Glandore, Co Cork; training
 camp 97
Glasnevin 162, 428–31
Gloucester jail 103
Gogarty, Oliver St John 294, 398,
 418
Gough, General H. P. 28, 124
Goulding, Sir William 209
Governor Generalship 312, 328,
 428
Granard 20, 89, 179, 280
Gray, James and John T. 377
Greene, Alice Stopford 29
Greenwood, Sir Hamar 125, 154,
 173, 208, 215; and reprisals 144,
 164, 165; and Bloody Sunday
 163, 164, 165; and Treaty 236,
 244, 437
Greer, Sir Francis 327
Gregory, Lady 293
Gretton, Colonel John 260, 367
Grey of Fallodon, 1st Viscount
 86–7
Griffin, Fr, of Galway 145
Griffith, Arthur 65–6; founds
 Sinn Fein 16; and Easter Rising
 63, 65; and Irish Convention
 67; cedes leadership of Sinn
 Fein to de Valera 72, 388;
 imprisonment after German
 plot 90, 103; Minister for
 Home Affairs 106, 112–13; plot
 to kidnap 134; and Cork
 hunger strike 155;
 imprisonment after Bloody
 Sunday 163, 199, 215; and
 peace initiatives 186, 196, 197–
 8; and Southern Unionists 216,
 261; and Treaty negotiations
 227, 230, 234, 240, 241, 246,
 254, 265, (and English) 237,
 284, (letter of assurances) 253–
 6, 257, 258, 259, 262, 271, (in
 final session) 269–70, 271, 272,
 273, 276, 437, (problems with
 Dublin) 233, 251, 268, (role)
 240, 241, 242, 251, (and
 Southern Unionists) 261, (and
 sub-conference) 243, 244, 253;
 and Document No. 2 300,
 302–3, 306; President of Dail
 Eireann 309, 311–12; and split
 in IRA 313–14, 317, 320;
 estranged from MC 322; and
 Constitution 326, 327; and
 Four Courts 331; and MC's
 becoming C-in-C of Army
 392; death 398–9
  courage 273, 317; and de
 Valera 72, 191, 321–2, 388;
 health 103, 233, 262; and North
 327, 340, 356, 359; writings 14,
 65–6

Guaranty Trust Company of
 New York 17, 19, 31
Guilfoyle, Joe 234, 287
Guinness, H. S. 378
gun-running 64, 94, 153, 169–72,
 257; German, (Howth, 1914)
 29–30, 38, 39, 238, (1916) 36,
 41, (1921) 246; Italian 169–72,
 257; to Northern IRA 350–1; to
 Ulstermen 28, 30, 125

'H' (RIC informant) 5
Hackett, Fr W. P. 406
Hagan, Mgr (of Irish College,
 Rome) 169
Hales, Donal 169, 171
Hales, Sean 51, 178, 300, 339,
 408, 409, 417
Hales, Tom 146–7, 319, 323, 359;
 and split in IRA 317, 318; in
 civil war 400, 404, 405; and
 MC's death 407, 409, 412, 419,
 420
Hall, Admiral R. C. 36, 91, 150–
 1, 202, 379
Halley, Detective Sergeant 117
Harbinson, Dr 418
Harding, Warren 203
Hardy, Captain J. L. 134, 157,
 162, 336
Harris, Eoghan 279
Harris, Tom 148
Harrison, District Insp 337, 352,
 355–6
Harte, Christy 167
Harte, Pat 146–7
'Haud Immemor' (*pseud* of
 Chartres) 238
Haughey, Sean 351
Hawtrey, R.G. 265
Hayes, Archbishop (US) 203
Hayes, Michael 384
Hayes, Thomas 21
Healy, Cahir 356
Healy, Tim 76, 379, 390–1, 428;
 and Treaty 232, 269, 301
Heaslip, James and Robert 377
Hegarty, Sean 170, 250, 367, 406
Helga (gunboat) 1, 42
Henderson, Arthur 144
Henderson, Leo 330
Hewart, Gordon, 1st Viscount
 236, 326, 328, 437
Heygate-Lambert, Col 56
Hibernians, Ancient Order of 75
Higginson, Col Commandant
 177
Hobson, Bulmer 36, 72
Hodder, Alice 359
Hoey, Daniel 46, 113, 117
Hoey, Eileen 168
Hoey, Patricia 284
Hogan, James 384
Hogan, Major General Dan 332,
 343–4
Hogan, Michael 249
Hogan, Patrick J. 310, 340, 427
Hogan (Tipperary hurling player)
 161

Holland, Dan 409
Home Rule 22–31, 60–1, 63, 78,
 86–8, 91
Horne, Sir Robert 265, 367
Horne and Co (stockbrokers) 17
Howth; gun-running 29–30, 38,
 39, 238
Hughes, Fr James 211
hunger strikes 56, 73–5, 139–40,
 150, 155
Hurley, Jim 409, 419–20, 421
Hurley, Sean (MC's cousin) 11–
 12, 14, 15, 29, 43–4, 58
Hyde, Montgomery 291

Ignatius CP (Passionate Order
 priest) 283
Igoe Gang 134, 172, 182–3, 353
Imperial Guards 363
industry 24, 237, 308, 384–5, 394,
 423
influenza epidemic (1919) 103
insurance, Irish 55
intelligence network, Collins' 45,
 75–84, 94, 140; and British
 agents 128–9, 133–4; in civil
 war 395; double agents xii, 95,
 147; in North 352–3, 398;
 organisation 148; popular
 support xii, 121–2; MC reads
 RIC files 107; merged into
 Dublin Brigade 207; *see also*
 Squad
intelligence and security, British
 12, 84, 146; Cairo gang 157–60;
 'Camerilla' 220; double agents
 95, 147; Kidd's Back 132–3,
 159, 184; and MC 132, 389–90,
 419; RIC 4, 5; strengthened
 184; *see also* Admiralty *and*
 individual agents
internment 47, 84, 363, 428; *see*
 also prisoners
Invincibles 390, 391
Iremonger, Valentine 285
Iris Oifiguil 393
Irish Brigade 30–1, 90, 131
Irish Businessmen's Conciliation
 Committee 209
Irish Citizen Army 29
Irish Committee 86, 87, 88, 119–
 20, 187, 333–4, 336, 340
Irish Home Rule League 22
Irish Labour Congress 185
Irish language 14, 90, 97, 108; *see*
 also under Collins, Michael; de
 Valera, Eamon
Irish National Aid Fund 63–5
Irish Parliamentary Party 5, 14,
 35, 61; and conscription issue
 88, 89; demise 26, 67, 73, 92
Irish Press Group 188
Irish Race Convention 110–12,
 113
Irish Republican Army 105; and
 Bloody Sunday 158; counter-
 reprisals 208; growth during
 Truce 219, 310–11; 'New

Army' 244, 249–51, 262; split over Treaty 310, 311, 313, 314–15, 321, 323 (see also Four Court); under de Valera 428; Catholics and 12; officers 33, 34; Provisional 260; schoolmasters recruit to 18–19; Women's Auxiliaries 375–6; see also Irish Volunteers and under Northern Ireland

Irish Republican Brotherhood: 1865 rising 7; Hobson revives 36; Lyons and 9–10; MC in London 16; infiltration policy 17, 29, 65; and Easter Rising 22; and Volunteers 29, 72–3; Howth gun-running 29–30; Mulcahy as C-in-C 33; cell system 54; MC revives 54–5, 64, 65, 238; Brugha and 71; de Valera and 71; and Irish Volunteers 72–3; MC becomes President of Supreme Council 115; and Treaty 234, 266, 273, 286, 296, 298; and IRA factions 317–18; and North 340–1; and Wilson 372; domination of National Army 391–2; see also Clan na nGael

Irish Self-Determination League 185

Irish Volunteers: formed 29; IRB infiltration 29, 72–3; Collins and 32, 35, 64; split from National Volunteers 35; de Valera and 41; reorganisation 64, 69, 74, 85; and Sinn Fein 65, 72, 102; Brugha and 71; arms raiding 85; recognises courts 89; new GHQ (1918) 89–90; training 97; popular support 97; becomes known as Irish Republican Army 105; and conscription 106; flying column tactics 140–2; de Valera and Brugha reorganise (1921) 244, 249–51; levies 248–9; and Treaty 308; see also Irish Republican Army

Italy; arms supplies 169–72, 257

James I, King 23
Jameson (British agent) 127–31
Jameson, Andrew 209, 216, 261
'Jennings' (RIC informant) 5
Johnston, Peig (née ni Braonain) 375–6
Jones, Tom 168, 239; and Treaty negotiations 233, 236, 239–40, 243, 244, 255, 257, 258–9, 262, 270; and Northern Ireland 335, 349
Jury, Henry James 390–1

Kavanagh, Joe 64, 76, 90–1
Kavanagh, Sean 147–8
Kelliher, Tom 409, 410
Kelly, Anna 388

Kelly, Captain 146
Kelly, Frank 137
Kelly, Thomas 350, 382–3
Kennedy, Hugh 312, 322–3, 327–8, 378, 392
Keogh, Tom 116, 118, 153, 180
Kerr, Neil xiii, 64, 89, 101, 153
Kerr, Sir Philip 200
Kerry Pike 145
Kickham, Charles Joseph 13
Kidd's Back 132–3, 159, 184
kidnappings 83–4, 183, 346–7
Kiernan, Helen 66
Kiernan, Kitty 33, 280–3; and Boland 113, 280–1, 388; and MC 66, 277–8, 281–3, 293, 294, (engagement) 20, 278, (letters) 281–2, 305, 309, 355, 387, 397–8; religion 277, 283
Kiernan, Maud 66
Kilkenny 69, 122, 208, 317
Killeen, Susan 20–1, 30, 79, 280; letters 48–50, 52, 56, 58–9, 333
Kilmainham jail 46, 181, 315
Kilmallock 127, 389, 404
Kilmichael ambush 164
Kiltartan 145
King, Major 160
King's College, London 17
Kirwan, Mrs, of Maynooth 49
Kitchener, Herbert Horatio, 1st Earl 35
Knapp and Peterson's Ltd 130
Knight, Andrew 141
Knocklong 144
Kynoch munitions factory, Arklow 237, 238

Labour movement: and conscription 88; and 1922 elections 322, 329; general strikes 89, 139; informants in 5; meetings with de Valera 320; and peace moves 185; and Specials 337; and Treaty 302
Lahinch 145, 194
land issue 4, 6, 22, 27, 98, 142, 423
Land League 6
landlordism 4–5, 6, 11–12, 22
Lane, Captain 215
Lanigan, Steve 153
Larkfield, Kimmage 32, 34
Larkin, James 34
Lavery, Hazel, Lady 20, 284, 288–91, 293, 294, 326, 428
Lavery, Sir John 238, 284, 293, 386
Law, Andrew Bonar 25, 26, 27–8, 67, 258, 335, 336
Law, Rev James 25
Lawrence, T. E. 395
League of Nations 109, 110–11
League of the Republic 319
Leahy, Mick 170–1
Lee-Wilson, Captain 44–5, 376
Lemass, Noel 282, 294
Lemass, Sean 140, 159, 422, 424, 427

Leonard, Joe 116, 117, 143, 180, 181
Leonard, Patrick 343
Leslie, Sir Shane 109, 238, 288–9, 290, 386
Lewes jail 67–8
Liddell, Sir Frederick 327
Limerick 111, 124, 127, 313–14; in civil war 389, 404; on MC's last journey 400, 401
Limerick, Treaty of 338–9
Lincoln jail 98, 99–103
Lindsay, Mrs 172
Lisavaird 8, 9–10
Lisburn 149
Lisdrumliska 377
Lismore 127, 145
List, Frederick 65
Littel, Edward and Joseph 377
Little, Mrs, of Upper Clanbrasil Street 49
'littlers' 143, 183
Liverpool 64, 153–4, 256, 259–60, 353
Llewelyn Davies, Crompton 108, 284–5, 293–4, 312
Llewelyn Davies, Moya 20, 108–9, 284, 285–6, 293
Lloyd George, David: on Volunteers 35; and Home Rule 60–1, 67; and conscription 85–6, 87, 90; and Peace Conference 93; Creel distrusts 110; and terrorism 121, 124; police war policy 141, 144; and Kevin Barry 154; and MacSwiney's cortège 155; and reprisals 124, 156; and Bloody Sunday 163; Thornton and Flood bump into 165, 183–4; and peace initiatives 184, 187, 194, 196–7, 198, 208, 211, 215, 216; on de Valera and MC 219, 220–1; meets de Valera 221–2, 223, 225; and Treaty talks 94, 235, 236, 237, 244, 246, 265, (exploits Irish divisions) 241, 242, (and Die-hards) 252–60, (offer to resign) 257, 258, 260, (and Craig) 259, (final session) 269, 270–2, (and signing of Treaty) 273–4, 275–6, 437, (and ratification) 312–13; and Constitution 312–13, 325, 326–7; and North 335, 345, 366; and Wilson's assassination 373–4; and Four Courts' men 373; use of posters 394
loan, national 94, 106–7
Lockhart, James and William 377
Lodge, Senator 112
London: arms smuggling 64; IRA in 1920 153; Irish, and Easter Rising 39–40, 43; MC in (1906–16) 15–22, 29, 30–1; Volunteers 29
Londonderry, Edith, Lady 20, 25–6, 291–3, 367–8

Londonderry, 7th Marquess of 291–3, 357, 369, 372
Long, Denny 404, 405
Long, Walter 86, 127
Longford 66–7, 70, 179
Longford, Lord (Frank Pakenham) 237, 243, 253, 255, 259, 264
Loughnane, Patrick and Henry 145–6
Lucas, General 172
Lynch, Diarmuid 69, 72, 85, 191–2
Lynch, Fionan 43, 73, 74, 89, 234, 238, 310, 388–9, 392
Lynch, John, of Kilmallock 157–8
Lynch, Liam 158, 172, 314, 323; and Treaty 310, 311; and split in IRA 317, 318, 330; supplies Northern IRA 350; in civil war 389, 404; and MC's death 405, 407, 417; and peace proposals 427
Lynch, Ned 249
Lynch, P. J. 69
Lyons, Alice 234, 338
Lyons, Denis 6, 14, 341
Lyons, Professor J. B. 418

Macardle, Dorothy 218
MacBrian of Scotland Yard 382
MacBride, Major John 54
MacBride, Sean 143, 247, 389–90, 391
MacCaba, Alasdair 67
MacCan, Pierce 103
MacCartan, Dr Patrick 68, 106, 190
McCarthy, Fr (prison chaplain) 115
MacCarthy, Dan 234
MacCarthy, Fr Dick 142
MacCarthy, John of Kanturk 148
MacCarthy, Sergeant Matt 129, 149, 353
MacCarthy, Miss, of Mountjoy Street 131
McCarthy, Captain Sean 408
MacCartney, Sergeant William 337
McClean, Captain 162
McConnell, Daniel 134
McCorley, Roger 149
McCoy, John 24, 377–8
McCrea, Pat 116, 180
McCullagh, William 377
McCullough, Dennis 36, 55, 72
MacCurtain, Tomas 122, 123–4, 148–9
MacCurtain, Mrs Tomas 173
MacDiarmada, Sean: and Easter Rising 2, 36, 37, 39, 43, 65; death 2, 39, 46, 117; MC and 34, 54
MacDonagh, Thomas 36, 39, 210
MacDonald, Gerald; mother of 408
MacDonnell, Mick 116
MacDunphy, Michael 377, 392

MacEntee, Sean 337
MacEoin, Sean 66, 179–81, 223, 225, 257, 318, 350, 370; and MC 229, 317
McGann, Gearoid 391
McGarrity, Joseph 302
MacGarry, Sean 72, 91, 100, 101, 421
McGovern, Paul 66
MacGrane, Eileen 166–7, 284
McGrath, Joseph 85, 310, 356, 392, 393; and Treaty 225, 234, 305; and MC's death 399, 419, 428, 431
McGrath, Sean 128
McGuinness, Joe 206–7
McGuinness, Joseph 66–7, 70, 303
McKee, Dick (Richard): xiii, and Bloody Sunday 159, 160–1; death 160, 161–2, 182, 386; and Squad 116, 118, 152; and Volunteers 74, 85, 97, 142
McKelvey, Joseph 350, 417
McKenna, Bill 293
MacKenna, Kathleen Napoli 108–9, 127, 131, 132, 233, 234, 275, 286–7
MacKenna, Patrick 67
McKinney, Edward 352
MacMahon, Sir James 62, 82, 115, 125, 220
McMahon, Captain John 42
MacMahon, Sean 130
MacMahon family murders 352, 353
MacNabb, Dr Russell 357
MacNamara, James 96, 129, 130, 160; recruited by MC 64, 76, 138
MacNeice, Louis 12
MacNeilis, Denis 99
MacNeill, Eoin 71, 156, 196, 212; forms Irish Volunteers 29; and Easter Rising 36–7, 53, 215; government offices 106, 304, 310, 340
MacNeill, Captain Ronald 363, 368
McPeake, John 408, 410, 416, 420
MacPherson, Ian 124, 125
McQuibban (Ministry of Education, Belfast) 347
Macready, General Sir Nevil 124–5, 152, 209–10, 336–7, 347, 353; and Four Courts 331, 332, 374–5; and Martial Law 212; and Truce 199, 216; and Wilson 349, 373
Macroom 222, 402, 403
MacRory, Joseph, Bishop of Belfast (later Cardinal) 352, 356, 357, 370
MacSwiney, Mary 228–9, 300, 307, 427
MacSwiney, Terence 69, 97, 122, 124, 142–3; hunger-strike 155–6, 157; funeral 194

Magner, Canon 145
Maguire, Sam 16, 64, 89, 147, 183, 341
Maher, Sergeant Gerry 147–8
Mahon, Sir Bryan 90
Mallow 145, 400
Malone, Captain Michael 42, 102
Malone, Tom (alias Sean Forde) 400
Manchester 57, 64, 98, 99, 153–4, 185
Mannix, Daniel, Archbishop of Melbourne 194, 196, 199, 203–4
Mannix, Sergeant 141, 158
Mao Tse Tsung xi, xii
Marchmont, Josephine 64, 83–4
Margaret Mary, Sister 97, 139, 228, 282, 285–6
Markham, Thomas 81, 382, 390, 391
Markievicz, Constance, Countess (née Gore-Booth) 90–1, 106, 191, 277, 300, 309, 387
martial law 150, 199, 208, 212–13, 217
Mary, Princess 277, 278
Mason, Sinead 97, 282, 377
Masterson Smith 371
Maynooth Seminary 88
Mellowes, Liam 176, 246, 303, 311, 417; and split in IRA 317, 318, 330
Merin, Lily 83, 133
Merry Del Val, Cardinal 200
Middleton, Co Cork 208
Midleton, Earl of 216, 261
Milltown Malbray 139
Milroy, Sean 89, 100, 101, 234
Monaghan footballers 343–4, 348
Montgomery, Bernard Law 140
Montgomery family (Griffith's friends) 317
Moore, Thomas 13
Moran, D. P. 14
Moran, Paddy 181
Moriarty, Fr, of South William Street 118
Morris, Thomas 350
Mountbatten, Louis, Lord 417
Mountjoy jail 73–5, 82, 98–9, 139, 196, 200
Moylan, Sean 361
Moylette, Patrick 186–7, 209, 239
Mulcahy, Richard 33, 122, 137–8, 142, 148, 153, 197, 200; and Volunteers 85, 89–90; and MC/Brugha rivalry 176, 179, 232, 248, 249; on Paddy Cahill 206; proposed reward for 209; and Truce 196, 216; on Sean O'Hegarty 287; Minister of Defence 309, 311; and split in IRA 313, 318; and 'New Army' 350–1; in civil war 389, 392; and North 340, 342–3, 348, 350, 356, 357, 367, 376, 382; and MC's death 415, 428

Mulloy, Fergus Brian 133
Murphy, Humphrey 318
Murphy, Joseph 155
Murphy, Pat 96
Murphy, Fr Timothy 412, 414
Murray, Fr Patrick 202

Nath, Ari xi
Nathan, Sir Matthew 38
National Aid Association 63–5
National Army 18, 209, 346
National University 212
Nationalist, The 313
Nationalist Party 212
Neligan, David xi, xii, 64, 96,
    152, 157, 165, 234; recruited
    76–7; and Bloody Sunday 159,
    160–1; and Kidd's Back 132
Neligan, Maurice 77
'Nero' (RIC informant) 5
neutrality, Irish 265
New Ireland Assurance Company
    55, 130
Newell, Sweeney 182
Nixon, Detective Inspector 352,
    355–6
North Roscommon by-election
    (1917) 63
Northern Ireland 333–85; political
    moves towards partition 28,
    60–1, 119, 212, 222, 224; gun-
    running 28, 30, 125; income tax
    proposals (1921) 265; growth
    of anarchy (1921–2) 308; Treaty
    and 241, 247, 257–61, 262, 266,
    269–70, 298, 333, 435, 436;
    Document No. 2 on 443–4;
    boundaries 333–5, 340, 342;
    Catholic rights 334, 340, 342,
    350, 353, 382, (Advisory
    Committee and) 354, 356–7;
    Parliament 335, 338, 341;
    obstruction of Government
    339, 347, 358, 361; Provisional
    Government and 339–40, 341–
    2, 385; Republican prisoners in
    340, 342, 343–6, 355, 385;
    undercover IRA operations
    308, 324, 327, 332, 333, 341,
    343–7, 349–50, 350–1, 362–3,
    366–7, 370, 371, 391, (end)
    382–3, 383–4; payment of
    Republican teachers 347, 357,
    383, 385; and Constitution 327;
    police atrocities 327, 351–3,
    356, 358; Agreement (30 March
    1922) 353–5, 356–7, 369–72;
    banning of Republican
    organisations 363; Tallents
    investigation 369–72; banking
    controversy 378–9;
    proportional representation
    333, 335, 379–80; end of
    hostilities 382–3, 383–4, 384–5;
    de Valera and 428; industry
    384–5; IRA organisation 348,
    349–50, 351, 380–2; *see also*:
    Belfast; Boundary

Commission; boycotts; MC
    (Northern policy); partition
Norway, Sir Arthur Hamilton 38
Noyek, Michael 137, 181
Nugent, Mrs Larry 210–11
Nugent, Sir Walter 209
Nunan, Sean 107, 137

'O' (Colonel Ormonde d'Epée
    Winter) 157, 183, 220
O hUidhrin, Giolla na Naomh 6
Oath of Allegiance *see under*
    Treaty
O'Brien, Art 128, 147, 171, 194,
    224
O'Brien, Constable 117
O'Brien, Kevin 53–4
O'Brien, Marianne *see under*
    Collins
O'Brien, Michael (MC's cousin)
    9, 16
O'Brien, Judge Morgan J. 203
O'Brien, Nancy (MC's cousin,
    Mrs John Collins) xii, 19, 20,
    97, 280, 394, 430; and Easter
    Rising 2, 37, 49; informs on
    GPO business 81–2
O'Brien, William Smith 5, 23, 27,
    56, 61, 375
O'Callaghan, John 409
O'Callaghan, Michael 124
O'Carroll, Fr Michael, Cssp, xi
O'Coileain Clan 5–6, 33
O'Conaire, Padraic 19, 29
O'Connell, Cardinal 91
O'Connell, Daniel 22
O'Connell, J. J. 'Ginger' 244,
    249, 251, 313; kidnap 329,
    330–1
O'Connell, Sir John 194
O'Connell, Kathleen 192
O'Connell, Mort 48
O'Connell, Sean 148, 403, 411
O'Connor, Art 387
O'Connor, Batt 98, 139, 167,
    204, 228, 285–6, 297, 415
O'Connor, Mrs Batt 129, 139
O'Connor, Frank 26, 218; on MC
    18, 46, 66, 79, 135–6, 399; on
    Joe O'Reilly 70, 135–6
O'Connor, James (Chief Justice)
    93, 120, 196, 208
O'Connor, 'Ninepence' 118
O'Connor, Rory xiii, 33, 34, 99,
    153, 166, 289, 323; and split in
    IRA 311, 317, 318; and Four
    Courts 330, 332; execution 417,
    426
O'Doherty, Dr (of Hierarchy)
    203
O'Doherty, H. C. 123
O'Donoghue, Florrie 84, 121,
    170, 317–18, 403–4
O'Donoghue, Joseph 124
O'Donoghue, Patrick 64, 84, 153
O'Donovan, Mrs xii–xiii, 138,
    161
O'Donovan Rossa, J. 5, 10, 11,
    38–9

O'Driscoll, Fr Aidan 420–1
O'Driscoll, Margaret *see under*
    Collins
O'Driscoll, Patrick 170
O'Duffy, Eoin xiii, 244, 251, 318,
    339, 392; and North 343–4,
    348, 350, 351, 356
O'Farrell, Senator J. T. 320
O'Flanagan, Fr 196–7, 208
O'Hanlon, Mick 159
O'Hanrachain family 76
O'Hegarty, Diarmuid 134–5,
    166, 361, 374, 392; MC's
    friendship 69, 137–8; and
    Brugha 70; and Treaty 234,
    238, 244, 296
O'Hegarty, P. S. 19, 20, 32, 36
O'Hegarty, Sean 287, 317, 318
O'Higgins, Kevin xiii, 200, 296,
    392, 398; and Hazel Lavery
    288–9, 290; in Cabinet 309,
    310, 340; and split in IRA 313–
    14, 331; and North 356, 357;
    death 289–90, 427
O'Higgins, Dr Tom 42
O'Keefe, Padraig 102
O'Kelly, Sean T. 106, 108, 200,
    210, 303, 304, 431
O'Lochlainn, Colm 37
O'Mahony, Sean 212
O'Maille, Padraig 417
O'Malley, Ernie 135, 181, 207–8;
    and split in IRA 313, 317, 318;
    and Four Courts 330, 332
O'Mara, James 191–2
O'Mara, Stephen 314
O'Milroy, Sean 212
O'Muirthle, Sean 266, 323
O'Murchadha, Colm 267, 268
O'Neill, Commandant 358
O'Neill, Denis (Sonny) 409, 411,
    418, 420
O'Neill, Dick 114–15
O'Neill, Sir Hugh 363
O'Neill, Laurence 88
O'Neill, T. P. 391, 418
O'Rahilly, Alfred 406
O'Rahilly, Michael Joseph 43, 53
Orange Order 24, 35, 59, 63, 334
O'Reilly, Joe 99, 130, 134–5, 137,
    160, 195; and MC 57, 69, 70,
    113, 135–6, 242, 293, 399, (and
    MC's death) 400, 415, 425
O'Reilly, M. W. 50–1, 55
O'Reilly, Mick 116
O'Reilly, 'Skinner' 331
O'Shannon, Cathal 279
O'Shiel, Kevin 94–5, 283, 312,
    353, 384
O'Silleabhin, Diarmuid 7
O'Sullivan, Gearoid xii–xiii, 33–
    4, 210; and Easter Rising 40,
    57; and MC 69, 134–5, 138,
    166; and Brugha 70; and Italian
    gun-running 170; and Treaty
    294; and split in IRA 318; and
    kidnappings of Orangemen
    346; appointment in Army 392,
    393; and MC's death 415

O'Sullivan, Joseph 373, 374, 375, 377, 398–9
O'Sullivan, Tadhg 138, 147, 412

Papacy 154, 186–7, 199–204, 245–6
Parliament, Irish see Dail
Parliament, Northern Irish 335, 354
Parliament, Westminster 4, 57, 62, 375; Defence of the Realm Act (DORA) 73, 90, 105; Government of Ireland Act (1920) 350, 435, 436; Home Rule Bills 22–3, 24–7, 28, (1886) 23, 24, (1893) 25, (1912–14) 25, 26, 28; Irish Free State (Agreement) Act (1922) 313; Military Service Act (1918) 88; Wyndham Land Act (1903) 22, 27
Parnell, Charles Stewart 23, 32, 44, 220, 390
partition: political moves towards 28, 60–1, 119, 212, 222, 224; Treaty and 241, 247, 257–61, 262, 298, 299, 333, 435, 436; under de Valera 428
Peace Conference (1919) 66, 93, 101, 102, 107–8, 110
Peace Party 220
Peace with Ireland Council 185
Pearse, Margaret 300
Pearse, Padraig 28–9, 38–9, 48, 54, 71; and Easter Rising 36, 38–9, 44, 53
Peig (Collins family maid) 97
Pelly, H. A. 402
Percival, Major (of Essex Regt) 146, 147
Peters, Dr, of Frongoch 56
Pettigo, Fermanagh 364–7
Phelan, Sean 84
Phoenix Park murders 390, 391
Pilkington, Liam 317
Plan of Campaign 4, 5, 27
plantations 23, 24
Plunkett, George 63
Plunkett, George Noble, Count 32, 63, 66, 67–8, 90, 191
Plunkett, Horace, Sir 109, 293
Plunkett, John 63
Plunkett, Joseph 33, 36, 53, 96; and Easter Rising 36, 37, 38, 39
Poblacht na hEireann 321, 322, 329
police see: Dublin Metropolitan; Royal Irish and Royal Ulster Constabulary; Scotland Yard
Pomeroy 348
Powell, Billy 408
Power, Maureen 139
Prescott Decies, Brigadier 348, 353
press, suppression of 85, 197, 314
Price, Major Ivor 38
prisoners 47, 84, 363, 428; escapes 98–103, 154, 180–1; political status 53, 55–6, 67–8, 73–5, 98,

99, 139; Republican in Northern jails 340, 342, 343–6, 355, 385; 'Republican University' 47
Privy Council 328
propaganda war 140, 394, 424
Protestants 361; and British 12, 28, 202; and Catholics 12, 23–4, 142
Provisional Government 302, 303, 309–10, 314, 339–40, 385, 437
Provisional Government of Ireland Committee 340

Quinn (MC's driver) 406
Quinn, Ellen 145
Quinlisk, H. 131–2

Rabbiatti Saloon 132
Radio Telefis Eireann 279, 288, 418, 420
railway courier system 148
recognition issue see under Treaty
rebellions: (1798) 4, 9, (1848) 9, 13, (1865) 7, 9–10
Redmond, Assistant Commissioner 117–18, 128, 129–30, 131
Redmond, John E. 23, 28, 35, 60–1, 62, 75
Redmond, Captain W. 104
Redmond, Major William 68
Register of Stocks 378
religion see Catholics; Protestants; sectarianism
reparation, concept of 113
reprisals 123–4, 156, 164–5, 194, 208; economic 143–6, 177; ended 178
Revill, Sergeant 118
Ricardo, General 363
Robbie (suspected agent) 232, 249
Roberts, Robert J. 51–2
Robinson, Lennox 293
Robinson, Seamus 305, 313
Roche, Sergeant (Irish Guards) 152, 249
Roiste, Liam de 229
Roosevelt, Franklin D. 188
Rosmuck 142
Rosscarbery 10–11, 177, 408
Rosslea 344
Royal Dublin Society 63
Royal Irish Constabulary: casualty figures 130; Catholic influence in 336; 'G' Division 45–6, 78, 107, 116, 127; intelligence system 4, 5; IRA attacks on barracks 362; MC and 59, 78, 107, 138, (recruits agents in) 75–6; nationalism in 78, 138; organisation 62, 78, 81; during Truce 22–3
Royal Ulster Constabulary 261, 348–9, 377
Russell, George (AE) 187
Russell, Sean 311

Ryan, Bernard 181
Ryan, Desmond 43, 48
Ryan, Jim 43, 48
Ryan, Michael J. 111–12
Ryan, Shankers 182

St Enda's School 28–9, 36
Salisbury, 3rd Marquess of 25
Salisbury, 4th Marquess of 367, 368
Sallins railway station 148
Salvidge, Stanley (Liverpool Unionist) 260
Sam's Cross 11, 408, 431
Santry, James 6, 9, 10, 341
Saorstat Eireann 263
Saurin, Frank 83, 132
Schlesinger, Dr Arthur Jr 279
schoolteachers, Republican 18–19; hedge 7, 8; in North 347, 357, 383, 385
Scissors and Paste 65
Scone, Stone of 77
Scotland Yard Special Intelligence 134
Scott, C. P. 256
sectarianism 12, 23–4, 62, 142, 348, 358–9; Belfast 347, 363
'separation women' 1, 45
Shamir, Yitzak xi
Shanakiel Hospital 414
Shaw, General Sir Frederick 90
Shaw, George Bernard 17, 114, 185, 293
Sheehan, Patrick 77
Sheehy-Skeffington, Francis 44
Sheerin, Phil 79
Shore (or Shaw), Major 94–5
Shortt, Edward 90, 93, 377
Sinn Fein: Griffith founds 16; reorganisation after Rising 64; Volunteers and 65, 72, 102; de Valera rises to power 71–2, 388; in elections (1917) 73, (1918) 75, 89, 91–2, 302, (1920) 122, (1921) 212; scheme to slow food exports 84–5; German plot arrests 90–1; divisions (1918–19) 102, 115–16; first Dail and 104; and Peace Conference 107–8; banned 117; British official contacts 186, 187; and peace moves 196–7, 200; excommunication 201; and Treaty 311, 313, 319, 322; united against Northern police murders 353; effect of death sentences on 208; MC and 32, 64, 115–16; not representative of all nationalists 59, 65, 72
Sirr, Henry Charles 3
Skibbereen, West Cork 11, 222, 408
Slattery, Joe 116, 152
Sligo 85, 144, 246, 317, 389
Smith, Acting Insp Gen of RIC 124
Smith, F. E. see Birkenhead

Smith, Lt 411
Smith, Major Compton 173
Smith, 'The Dog' 117
Smith (MC's driver) 409
Smith-Barry, Arthur 4, 5
Smuts, General Jan 86, 213–15
Smyth, Lt Col Bruce, VC 126, 149–51
Smyth, Major (brother Bruce) 152
Soloheadbeg 105, 151
Solly-Flood, General Sir Arthur 349, 353, 362, 364, 370, 371
Spender, Colonel Wilfred 336, 353, 370, 371
Spike Island Prison 178
Spring-Rice, Sir Cecil 60
Spring-Rice, Mary 29, 30
Squad (MC's hit unit) xii, 94, 116–18, 162, 182, 207, 209, 397
Stack, Austin 176, 210, 387; Brugha proposes as Deputy CoS 232, 249, 251; and de Valera 71, 427; imprisonment 53, 73, 89, 99, 139; as President-designate 205–6; quality 53, 97, 205; and Treaty 227, 229, 230, 231, 244–5, 267, 268, 294, 295, 296
Stafford Detention Barracks 47–50
Staines, Michael 147, 174, 196, 215, 250
Stamfordham, Lord 214
Stapleton, Bill 116
'Steam' (RIC informant) 5
Steele, John 187, 209, 321
Stephen Whitney disaster 11
Strickland, Major General Sir Peter 83, 199
strikes, general 89, 139
Sturgis, Sir Mark Beresford 91, 125, 157, 209, 211, 255
Sullivan, A. M. 13, 71
Swanzy, Det Insp 124, 149, 333
Sweeney, Joseph 179, 365, 376, 400
Sweetman, Roger 196
Swift, Jonathan 298

tactics, military 54, 70, 140, 142–3, 164
Tallents, Colonel Stephen 369–72
Tammany Hall 189, 304–5
Taylor, Rex 285
TDs (Teachtarai Dail) 183
Teeling, Frank 160, 181
Thompson, Sir Basil 127, 130
Thompson sub-machine gun 168–9
Thornton, Frank 122, 126, 138, 286; and Easter Rising 46, 68; intelligence work 45, 129, 130, 132, 133, 134–5, 158, 183; and Bloody Sunday 158, 162; bumps into Lloyd George 183–4; and MC's last journey 399–400, 405

'Thorpe' (British agent) 390–1
Thurles 127, 145, 319
Tierney, Archdeacon 357
Tierney, Eamonn 56
Tobin, Liam 77; in Easter Rising 44–5; escapes police raid 278–9; intelligence work 77, 134–5, (and British agents) 129, 130, 131, 132, 133, 134, 158, 162; and MC 70, 95, 135, 166, 286, 287, 418; replaced by McGrath 393; in Treaty negotiations 234, 287; and Wilson's assassination 376
Tone, Theobald Wolfe 4, 7, 10, 92, 116
torture 146, 159
Tory party: Die-hards 252–60, 290, 367–8; and Home Rule 23–5, 27–8, 59, 63, 86–7; and Irish Protestants 28; and partition 334, 335; and Sinn Fein 187; opposes truce 196; and Treaty 252–60
Tracey, Canon, of Crookstown 405–6, 412
trade 252, 268, 270, 273, 423
trade unions 34, 89, 139, 359
Traynor, Oscar 136, 205, 310, 311, 386, 387, 430–1
Treacy, Pat 79
Treacy, Sean 105–6, 139, 151–2
Treaty, Anglo-Irish (1922)
NEGOTIATIONS; opening of conference 241; sub-conference structure 243, 245, 247, 254, 255, 267, 271; British Memorandum (27 Oct) 251–2; Die-hards and 252–60; Griffith's letter of assurances 253–6, 257, 258, 259, 262, 271; Irish Memorandum (22 Nov) 262; draft Treaty 264–5; Dublin discussions of draft 266–8, 272; final London talks 269–75; signing of Treaty 272, 273–5, 276; terms 299, 433–8; reception in Ireland 277, 294–307, 329, 440–1; ratification 257, 267–8, 312–13; and Constitution 312, 328
IRISH DELEGATION: appointed 227–9, 236–41, 242, 299, 318–19; arrival 233–5; divisions within 230, 240, 241, 262, 265, 267, 268–9, 272–4; and Dublin government 233–4, 240, 241, 242, 244–5, 251, 254, 256, 259, 264, 267, 271; MC's British contacts 277, 278, 283–93; MC's strategy 243; powers 229–31, 233, 248, 257, 298–9
ISSUES: association with Commonwealth 230–1, 247–8, 253–6, 257, 258, 260, 262, 263, 269, 296, 433; citizenship 251; Crown 241, 247, 251, 252, 253–6, 258, 260, 262, 264, 265,

268, 433, (Oath) 234, 265, 266, 267, 268, 270, 273, 298, 312, 433; defence 246, 251–2, 253–6, 260, 262, 265, 266, 268, 270, 273, 434, 437–8; Dominion status 242, 257, 259, 260, 262–4, 267, 269, 270–1, 433; finance 252, 270, 434; recognition of Republic 225–7, 230, 235, 237, 245–6, 263; trade 252, 268, 270, 273; Ulster 241, 247, 253–6, 257–61, 262, 266, 267, 269–70, 298, 333, 335, 435, 436; see also under individual delegates' names
Truce (1921) 167, 216–18, 310–11, 348; moves towards 184, 185–7, 194–204, 208–16
'Truciers' 310–11
Tubercurry, Co Sligo 144
Tudor, General Hugh 125, 152, 153, 199
Twadell, W. J., MP 363
Twomey, Jack 400
Tyrone 123, 270, 334, 344–6, 362, 380

Ulster see Northern Ireland
Ulster Covenant 26
Ulster Ex-Servicemen's Association 353
Ulster Special Constabulary 348, 354, 362, 373, 375; Class A 344; Class C 260–1; see also B-Specials
Ulster Volunteer Force 26, 28, 39, 134, 149, 227, 336
Unionist party: and Home Rule 25, 27, 86–7; elections 75, 92, 104, 212, 309, 329; Liverpool Conference (1922) 256, 259–60, 353; Southern 216, 261, 328, 359–60; and UVF 336
United Irishman 14, 65–6
United States of America: and Easter Rising 57, 59–60; and conscription 87–8; de Valera in 106, 113, 114–15, 187–93, 304; Democratic Party 188, 189, 191; divisions, Irish-American 193; fund-raising and aid 68, 188, 190, 191, 203; and Germany 110, 188, 189; and Home Rule xii, 86–7, 91; MC thinks of emigration to 17, 30; Republican Party 188, 189, 191, 304; Smuts on 214; Wilson's policy 60, 87–8, 108, 109–10, 111, 112
unity of Ireland 253–6, 334, 423–4, 425, 426; see also partition
Upnor arms seizure 314–15
Usk jail 98, 99

Versailles, Treaty of 109
Viknor 150–1
Vivanti, Mme Annie 239
Vize, Joe 152, 170
Volunteers see Irish, London, and Ulster Volunteers

Wallace, Sam 11
Walsh, Elizabeth 355
Walsh, Frank P. 111–12
Walsh, J. J. 384
Walsh, Mrs Maud 172
War, First World 17, 22
War, Second World 265
War Council of Three 392
warders, prison 82, 95
Waterford 75, 122, 360, 389
Webb, Captain 83
West Cork People 15
Westminster Gazette 190, 252
Wexford, Co 122, 208, 315, 341, 367
Whelan, Tommy 181
White, Captain Jack 29
White, Mick 159–60
White Cross 188, 203

Whitmore, Brennan 37, 55
Wickham, Colonel 260–1
Wilde, Oscar 17, 18, 47
William III, King 23
Willis (executioner) 346
Wilson, Field Marshal Sir Henry: and Curragh incident 28; and conscription 87; and Black and Tan war 125, 141, 145; and MacSwiney's cortège 155; on Bloody Sunday 162–3; opposes truce 196, 199; and Martial Law 212; and North 341, 348–9, 355, 358, 367–8; and Specials 261, 348, 364, 375; assassination 329–30, 372–7
Wilson, President Woodrow 60, 87–8, 108, 109–10, 111, 112

Wimborne, Lord 90
Windsor Barracks arms raids 249
Winter, Colonel Ormonde d'Epée *see* 'O'
Wood, Sir R. 216
Woodfield (MC's home) 3, 4–5, 7, 10, 58–9, 146, 177–8
Woods, Seamus 350, 362, 383
Wormwood Scrubs jail 139–40, 155
Worthington Evans, Sir Lamington 220, 327, 334; and Specials 261, 348; Treaty negotiations 236, 244, 437
Wylie (Law Officer) 220

Yeats, William Butler 298, 321
Young Ireland 13

TIM PAT COOGAN is a native of Dublin. He was the editor of the *Irish Press* for twenty years and, as a leading commentator in Irish affairs, has contributed to several international newspapers. His previous books include *Ireland Since the Rising*, which was hailed as a pioneering work; and the definitive history, *The IRA*.